Managerial Reality

SECOND EDITION

Managerial Reality

Balancing Technique, Practice, and Values

SECOND EDITION

Peter J. Frost
University of British Columbia

Vance F. Mitchell
Embry-Riddle Aeronautical University

Walter R. Nord
University of South Florida

HarperCollins*CollegePublishers*

Executive Editor: Michael Roche
Developmental Editor: Pam Wilkie
Cover Illustration/Photograph: **Michael Skarsten/The New Image**
Electronic Production Manager: Eric Jorgensen
Publishing Services: Interactive Production Services
Electronic Page Makeup: R.R. Donnelley Barbados
Printer and Binder: R.R. Donnelley & Sons Company
Cover Printer: The Lehigh Press, Inc.

Managerial Reality, Second Edition

Library of Congress Cataloging-in-Publication Data

Managerial reality : balancing technique, practice, and values /
[edited by] Peter J. Frost, Vance F. Mitchell, Walter R. Nord. —
2nd ed.
    p.   cm.
    Includes bibliographical references and index.
    ISBN 0-673-99183-0
    1. Management. 2. Industrial management. I. Frost,
Peter J. II. Mitchell, Vance F. III. Nord, Walter R.
HD31.M29394 1995
658.4—dc20   94-27813
                                  CIP

94 95 96 97 98 7 6 5 4 3 2 1

Preface

The second edition of *Managerial Reality: Balancing Technique, Practice, and Values* is, like the original, directed toward students and practitioners of management. It is intended as a lively, diverse, and thought-provoking set of articles, stories, news clippings, and discussions about managing in the current turbulent era. We attempt to bridge the gap between what is taught about managing in and around organizations and what many who practice the craft describe as the practices and tensions that take place in so-called real organizations.

To create this book we repeated our process used for the first edition, which was to survey reports by keen observers of management, self-reports of practitioners, fictionalized accounts of managerial behavior in novels and short stories, professional, and on occasion, academic journals. Throughout our search, we found as before a central theme of continual tensions confronting managers between trying to do things right (by the model, by the book) and doing the right things at the point of action, while even more frequently than in the past, being forced to figure out what might be the right decisions and actions from strategies and ethical perspectives. Many of the pieces in the book deal with these tensions. Articles that highlight one or other aspect of the tensions and ways to manage the tensions include those by Bob Quinn: "The Journey from Novice to Master Energy," and Charles Burck: "The Real World of the Entrepreneur," as well as David Hurst's discussion of the bankruptcy of strategic management, Wayne Cascio's analysis of downsizing, and Dory Hollander's ideas and insights about politics in organizational life. George Tamke describes his experiences and challenges when taking control of a new job. Clinton Longenecker, Henry Sims, Jr., and Dennis Gioia describe the struggles and the power games that surround the Performance Appraisal process. Several articles, such as "Work and Family" by Michele Galen, "Beyond Success," by Rob Phillips and "To Love or To Work," by Joan Kofodimos and "Characteristics of Workaholics," by Diane Fassel each focus attention in their own way on the costs and negative consequences of managing in the "Nineties."

There is much new material in this second edition. We have changed over sixty percent of the readings from the first edition and have added sections on the topics of diversity and international management. We have continued to organize some of the material in the book around the traditionally labeled management activities. That is, we use the labels of planning, organizing, controlling, influencing, and communicating as chapter headings for several articles. In addition, we feature writings that look at the history of management as well as its future and other work that deals with managing human resources, with ethics, with diversity, with the environment and with global issues. We have featured a number of articles that make explicit some of the traps and hazards of managing in the modern organization. In particular, we present some compelling works that deal with the need to confront the dangers of workaholism, excess stress, and other debilitating aspects of managerial life. Much of this material feeds into the issues managers face when they strive for a healthy balancing of work and personal life.

While many of the managerial labels used to frame the book are traditional, the material itself is rarely so. We have found that the reports about managerial life we encountered across a diverse body of literature often challenge or shed new or different light on many of the theories that are presented in academic texts. The stories, data, arguments, and assertions in the articles provoke discussion, provide alternative ways to discuss management practice and suggest ways to build bridges between the theorists, the practitioners, the strategists, and the moral managers. Of course, these are rarely discreet components residing in particular individuals in the managerial ranks. These are issues that each manager must deal with while trying to be efficient and effective in the workplace.

Preparing this book has been a stimulating, intriguing, and educational experience. We hope that many readers likewise will find their perspectives on the practice of management revised as they make their way through the material of this book.

Our contributions are distributed equally across the book. Hence the ordering of names on the title page is alphabetical as in our previous work together. We wish to thank those who helped us with the research and preparation of this book. Thank you, Vivien Clark and Norma Walker, for your invaluable assistance in searching out and organizing the material. As in all our work, we acknowledge the debt we owe to the many professional and academic students in our courses who have asked the questions and reported the experiences that reinforced our belief in the value of the approach we have taken with this book and its predecessor. We are grateful for the support, patience, and wisdom provided us by Mellisa Rosatti and for the administrative skills of Pamela Wilke.

Peter J. Frost
Vance F. Mitchell
Walter R. Nord

Contents

Introduction:
"Doing Management"

Managers make a difference! The way they work with and through the activities of others in organizational settings influences the lives of others and the fortunes of the organizations they are entrusted to administer. Sometimes the difference is a negative one. Managers make mistakes, err in judgment, create problems for others, or behave selfishly or insensitively. As a result, people on the receiving end of the actions get hurt and organizational goals may be seriously impeded. At other times, the difference is positive. Managers anticipate errors or recover them, judge astutely, create and respond well to opportunities and behave honorably, sometimes even courageously. When this happens, people being managed blossom, organizational agendas are accomplished, and society benefits.

As Drucker observes ("The Emergence of Management" in Chapter 1, Managing: Its History, Challenge, and Nature) defining management is difficult: "It denotes a function but also the people who discharge it. It denotes a social position and a rank but also a discipline and field of study." Drucker notes further that management "is the specific organ of the modern institution."[1] Organizations are characterized by formal sets of relationships imposed on less formal relationships among humans. They involve technical systems interacting with human activities. We believe that the primary function of management is the coordination of human effort in a world characterized by tensions between formality and informality, between technology and humanity.

At its core, we think that "doing management" involves a myriad of balancing acts which are needed to facilitate and secure coordination and cooperation between and among individuals and groups in organizations. We draw on the balancing image because it captures the type of actions managers must take to coordinate people with different values, self-interests, and intentions and departments with different agendas, tasks, goals, and criteria for effectiveness. It reflects the trade-offs managers must make between using structural mechanisms for achieving coordination and cooperation (such as plans, systems of control, and of organization) and more personal techniques of leadership. The balancing image captures the dilemmas managers must face and attempt to resolve in coordinating differing perceptions and beliefs about what is right or wrong strategically and morally in the affairs and direction of the organizations they administer. It is a dynamic process, not a static function—we talk about balancing, not balance, although there clearly are points of balance.

Managers must be part artist and part scientist—drawing on intuition and logic to get the organization's work done. They are inherently drawn into political behavior, dealing as they do with the interdependencies between people and departments with differing needs, resources, and expectations. Doing management requires an ability to envision the big picture, to "see the invisible" as Jonathan Swift put it. It requires the stamina to work through the long hours and the crises that occur inevitably in organizations, as well as a willingness to persevere and to engage in the repetitive mundane activities of daily organizational life. Managers need to anticipate the future, read the patterns in the present, and comprehend the lessons of the past.

All of this is a tall order! There is a real danger that one might draw the conclusion from the above that managers need to be like "Superman" or "Wonderwoman," and this might lead one to buy the fiction of the "Superboss." This also sets up expectations of performance that cannot easily or typically be met in the real world of organizations. In fact, chasing this goal of the perfect manager creates, in the organizations (and business schools) of our modern post-industrial society, the addiction to work, and the workaholism of the professional manager that is much discussed in the media and is analyzed in the article "Characteristics of Workaholics" in Chapter 8, Managing Hazards.

Our point, made in a number of ways in the articles of *Managerial Reality*, is that doing management is complex, challenging, exacting, and exhausting but that the path to effective management is not that of the "Superboss." Clearly, to be successful, managers need to draw on their own particular skills and abilities. But they also need to work with and through the people (managers, employees, customers) *and* the systems (technical, legal, procedural) that are in and around their organizations. It is the interaction of the manager with people and systems that creates the challenge and also provides the opportunities for doing management effectively.

What is the primary focus of management? In our view it is the coordination of organizational activities and the securing of cooperation between and among organizational players (people and departments). Most textbooks deal with the functions managers engage in to establish and maintain such coordination. To help people learn about these functions, typical text headings and content deal with topics such as Planning, Organizing, Leading, Communicating, and Control. We have organized the material in *Managerial Reality* to reflect these traditional frameworks. As we have stated earlier, however, we believe that doing management is a complex balancing act and is much more dynamic than such functional categories suggest. Our choice of articles reflects this belief.

The essence of this balancing act can be understood by a simple framework that emphasizes three major organizational issues and the tensions between and among these issues. First, there is the issue of *doing things right*, that is, management that strives to use the logically correct techniques, plans, systems, and behaviors to coordinate the affairs of the organization. It involves an emphasis on managing "by the book," the book being whatever has been determined as the technically correct activity or procedure. These are the systems of selection, planning, appraisal, and of law developed in the abstract, in the laboratory, or in the "ivory tower." This is the realm of the manager as *technician*. Second, there is the

Figure 1

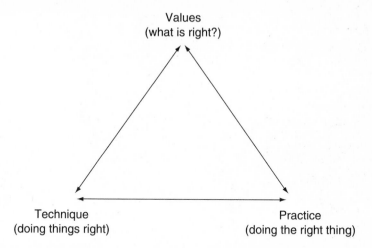

issue of *doing the right thing*, of doing what is feasible, that is, making the appropriate decisions and performing the appropriate coordinating activities, *given the circumstances in which the manager finds himself or herself*, working with the personnel and resources available at the particular time and place. The manager takes action that is feasible given the contingencies of the actual situation. This is the realm of the manager as *pragmatist*.

Finally, there is the third issue—*What is right?* strategically and ethically, given the intentions of management and others (for example, employees, customers, stockholders, governments). What *should* the organization be doing to ensure its long-term effectiveness? What *should* managers be doing to ensure that everyone's rights, themselves included, are addressed? This is the realm of the manager as *strategist*, as *moralist*.

The articles in *Managerial Reality* capture these issues and the dilemmas managers face in deciding how, in doing management, they are to incorporate logic (doing things right), pragmatic realities (doing the right things), and strategic and ethical pressures and considerations (deciding what is right).

Take, for example, the management of performance, and in particular, the appraisal of individual performance. Managers engaged in the appraisal of others must balance the technical requirements of appraisal (which are typically mandated by specialists in human resources and employment law) and the practical realities of their own objectives as managers, the circumstances surrounding the performance of their subordinates, and the particular qualities (skills, abilities, and intentions) of their subordinates.

Human resource managers typically want line managers to carry out performance appraisals that conform to the currently accepted behavioral theories and to company policy. Line managers, on the other hand, may want to bend, modify, or even ignore many of the technical and policy requirements of the performance appraisal system. They may do this to increase the performance of their subordinates, to make an example out of one subordinate so as to influence the actions of other subordinates, or even to move an unwanted employee out of their department. Managers acting in these ways act pragmatically, doing what they believe is the right thing in their efforts to meet personal and organizational goals.

Two excerpts from the article "Behind the Mask: The Politics of Employee Appraisal,"[2] (in Chapter 7, Managing Human Resources) illustrate this tension between the technical (doing it right) and practical (doing the right thing) aspects of managing performance appraisal.

Employee appraisal as a technique, as something to be done right, is illustrated by the following statement:

> At some places the PA (performance appraisal) process is a joke—just a bureaucratic thing that the manager does to keep the IR (industrial relations) people off his back... (Longenecker et al., 1987, p. 186)

The manager is expected to "do it right." "Right" in this case is seen to be rigid and narrow and of limited use to the operating manager.

On the other hand, to meet pragmatic realities (for example, to do the right things), managers sometimes choose to "adapt" techniques to suit the purposes they see as important to meet the contingencies they face. For example:

> As a manager, I will do what is best for my people and the division. . . . I've used it to get my people better raises in lean years, to kick a guy in the pants if he really needed it, to pick up a guy when he was down or even to tell him he was no longer welcome here. It is a tool the manager should use to help him do what it takes to get the job done. I believe most of us here at _____operate this way regarding appraisals. Accurately describing an employee's performance is really not as important as generating ratings that keep things cooking. (Longenecker et al., 1987, p. 185)

The clash between the technical and practical requirements facing the manager quickly conjure up the What is right? question and, thus, another balance point. What should the manager do? From a strategic point of view, the clash will likely be between those managers wanting to maintain an equitable and coherent system of evaluation (that is, the Human Resource or Personnel managers) and those who will argue that anything goes when they need to deal with what they face in the trenches. For example, line managers will likely argue that they are responsible for the bottom line, for making things happen, and should thus have the last word. The strategic aspect of employee appraisal is illustrated in the following statement by a manager:

> This thing (the appraisal process) can really turn into an interesting game when the HR (Human Resource) people come out with a blanket statement like "Money for raises is tight this year and since superior performers get 7% to 10% raises there will be no superior performers this year." Talk about making things rough for us (raters)!...They try to force you to make the ratings fit the merit allowances instead of vice versa. (Longenecker et al., 1987, p. 185)

Resolution, in such a case, will come in part from which goals in the strategic plans of the organization are given more weight in practice and in part from who has more power in the organization, the technical specialists or the practical managers. Accomplishing balance between technique, practice, and strategy in managing performance appraisal is illustrated in the following excerpt from the same article:

> *At the last couple of places I've worked, the formal review process is taken really seriously; they train you how to conduct a good interview, how to handle problems, how to coach and counsel.... You see things [appraisals] reviewed by your boss, and he's serious about reviewing your performance in a thorough manner.... I guess the biggest thing is that people are led to believe that it* is a management tool that works; it's got to start at the top! *(emphasis added) (Longenecker et al., 1987, p. 186)*

One of the issues that frustrates human resource specialists in many organizations is that they are consistently caught in the tension between technique and practice but rarely are invited to contribute to the resolution of the strategic question. Nor is their perspective on the morality of organizational action much listened to.

From an ethical point of view, what is right becomes an issue of fairness in the system, between and among individuals. Should exceptions be made to meet individual requirements and circumstances? What are the consequences for the individuals concerned, for the manager, for the organization? (Chapter 9, Managing Ethically, deals squarely with these issues of doing management.) Of course, the growing importance of the legalities of management's activities provides a direct bridge between ethics and strategy as well as between the techniques and practices of management. Increasingly, there are very real consequences for managers and organizations associated with their ignorance of, or noncompliance with, employment law.

In general, one can see that the dilemmas of "doing management" while facing these issues revolves around the following kinds of imbalance:

Overemphasis on the technical aspects of planning without taking into account the practical realities managers face in getting the job done can lead to such things as endless bureaucratic hoops, paper chases, "analysis-paralysis" and frequently a frustrated core of line managers. Some fine examples of this condition are included in "Business Fads: What's In—and Out." In that article, Donald Frey, CEO of Bell and Howell notes: "We went down to Wright Patterson Air Force Base, where they had PERT charting down to a science. They had more guys working on PERT charts than they had doing the job."

Overemphasis on the practical, day-to-day demands and contingencies of doing management, on the other hand, can lead to narrow, rigid behaviors and techniques and resistance to changes in systems and techniques that have become outmoded. This is part of the reason the automakers in Detroit got into such difficulties when the revolutionary change in oil prices hit North America in the 1970s (see "Maxwell's Warning" in Chapter 1).

Efforts to blend effectively the technical and practical requirements of work can be seen in many of the articles in the book, including those that discuss the systematic (rather than faddish) use of team building and quality circles in organizations (see, for example, "Jack Welch's Lessons for Success" and "Quality Circle Leader").

Overemphasis on strategy without attention to plans and systems can lead to empty rhetoric or hollow vision. On the other hand, too much attention to plans and systems can kill the vision and cause people to lose sight of the strategy. Furthermore, the recognition of differences (differences in values, perceptions, and self-interests) that is implicit in a strategy can be lost when the attention is all on the mechanics of plans and on their implementation. We say more about this in later sections. Resolution of these tensions can come when managers with technical biases discover the role perception plays in organizational life (see "The Journey from Novice to Master Manager") and when leaders seek to link a vision or strategy with specific plans, techniques, and systems (see Chapter 5, "More Corporate Chiefs Seek Direct Contact with Staff, Customers").

Overemphasis on technique can also blind managers to the ethical implications of their behaviors. At the same time, a concern with ethics that does not establish a system for managing ethically is likely to confuse managers or to encourage them to discount ethical stances when dealing with organizational matters (see, for example, "James Gordon, Manager").

Finally, overemphasis on strategy in the absence of attention to practical realities facing managers and the organization is likely to yield ungrounded strategic plans, ones that misguide action or are ignored by managers (see, for example, "The Creation"). Conversely, an excessive concern with the day-to-day activities or a preoccupation with the short run can prevent managers from seeing the big picture and from accurately interpreting how changes might affect their organizations in the long run (see, for example, "Why Strategic Management Is Bankrupt"). Attempts to ground strategy in reality and to make what is present resemble what might be needed in the future are required (see "Building A Learning Organization" in Chapter 12).

In the real world of organizations, doing management requires attention to all these issues and their various interactions. Not all managers are responsible for determining strategy but all are involved in its implementation. All have a role to play in acting ethically (a complex issue in itself), being technically competent and practically effective. Balancing individual and organization, technical and human systems, social and organizational contexts, and coordinating activities so that individual and organizational goals are met—is what doing management is all about.

ABOUT THIS BOOK

Managerial Reality is an anthology on management that is intended to portray through stories, anecdotes, reflections, and journalistic reports the richness, complexity, and excitement of management. We also hope to capture the diversity and challenge that managers face in their task of coordinating human effort in organizations. This book chronicles the successes and failures of managers and the ethical and strategic dilemmas they wrestle with in getting their work done. It identifies some of the ways organizations penetrate the lives of managers at work and at home, at times creating opportunities for personal growth and career advancement but often creating hazards that managers must be alert to as they strive to balance organizational and personal agendas.

The book is organized around five basic principal elements of management frequently used in textbooks. These are Planning, Organizing, Leading, Controlling, and the Management of Human Resources. Emphasis is given to the broad contexts within which management takes place from its historical roots, and its social and political environments. Attention is also given to ethical issues affecting managers.

A fundamental theme of the book is that doing management involves finding balances between and among the technical, practical, strategic, and moral issues confronting today's managers. Management action in this context is illustrated at different levels from CEO to first-line supervisor.

Examples of management are drawn from a number of settings. In addition, two industries—automotive and computers—are featured in several articles spread throughout the book. These are major arenas of managerial activity in North America and in all post-industrial countries; they are of increasing importance in developing nations as well. The reader can easily isolate the automotive and the computer examples in the book and examine the many facets of managerial reality in them, treating them as complex case studies of management practice and experience.

We include articles that deal with both women and men. The organization of today, and increasingly of tomorrow, involves women in key managerial roles. The experiences, successes, and failures of female managers in this book provide an opportunity to compare and contrast them with male managerial experiences and to explore the interaction between and among male and female managers.

We also give some attention in the choice of articles to the international management scene. We expect this topic to explode in the future and to create many new challenges and concerns for managers. What is learned from that experience will inform, in a significant way, the discussion of management, its role, functions, and activities.

We use a wide variety of sources including *Fortune, Business Week, U.S. News and World Report, The New York Times, Wall Street Journal, Harvard Business Review* as well as books and anthologies on management. The selections are durable and evocative.

We believe that this collection adds perspective to traditional books on management. In T. S. Eliot's "The Four Quartets" the statement is made that: "We had the experience but missed the meaning." We think that in trying to convey the meaning of management, textbook writers frequently miss or leave out the experience that provides the basis for the meaning they give to the activity. We believe that the articles, stories, and reports provided in *Managerial Reality*, in part, redress this imbalance by providing a sense of experience that illuminates the meanings given in management texts. We think the book also provides experiences that provide meaning to carry us beyond the current academic wisdom we have about what management is all about.

We hope *Managerial Reality* proves informative and interesting to a wide range of readers (students, academics, managers) interested in a fascinating and important topic.

Notes

1. Drucker, P. F. *Management*, New York: Harper, 1973.

2. Longenecker, C. O., Gioia, D. A., and Sims, H. P., 1987, "Behind the Mask: The Politics of Employee Appraisal," *The Academy of Management Executive* 1 [3], 183–193.

Chapter 1

Managing: Its History, Challenge, and Nature

Peter Drucker is widely recognized as the world's leading authority on management. In our first article, Drucker observes that the rise of modern management is the most important development in recent history. The nature of our society and its quality of life are vitally linked to the knowledge, abilities, visions, and values of people who manage organizations.

Few people are apt to disagree with such an assertion. At the same time, unless we are followers of media that focus on the business world, the importance of management often remains latent in our everyday awareness and we view management as a rather straightforward task.

Among other things, the selection from Drucker indicates how much has changed even in the short period in which modern organizations and their managers have existed.

Whereas Drucker directs our attention to how things have changed, the next selection by David Hurst points in a different direction in its discussion of another of modern history's great contributions to management thought: Mary Parker Follett. It reveals that if one conceptualizes things in terms of fundamental processes, there is considerable constancy. The close correspondence between observations of contemporary writers and Follett's comments made over half a century ago gives considerable support to those who would place theory and the study of basic human and social processes at the core of management education.

Concentration on history as well as contemporary issues might help overcome one of the most widespread and costly characteristics of modern management practice—rampant fads. By this we mean that managers of many organizations hear about a new system or technique in the professional literature and then try to introduce it into their organizations without analysis of the fundamental processes operating within their contexts. We suggest that one of the major benefits that a manager can gain from study of management theory and from understanding fundamental human and social processes is a wariness about such new ideas. He or she may thereby gain immunization against fads. The selection by John Byrne is intended to stimulate discussion of this issue. Although the reader will recognize that many of the specific examples Byrne treats are dated, the fundamental issue is not.

In the first paper, Drucker indicates that professional management has grown central to the operation of the organizational society our society has become. As management became professionalized, the work of managers seems to have become increasingly abstract as the size of the units managed became much larger and managers worked to run and integrate functional specialties that were several steps removed from the core operation of the business. In such cases, the focus of management came to appear out of context; that is, more like a systems engineer divorced from the particular requirements of a given business. Although consequences and accountability were still there, their nature seemed to become less dependent on the day-to-day, week-to-week operations of the core business. Indeed, to a considerable degree, much of what is written about management seems to focus on what managers of large organizations do. In such a context, ideas about how to improve performance could also be more abstract and more or less ideological as opposed to being driven by the practical need to get the daily work done. Participative management is an excellent example. Participative management has been advanced by high-ranking managers as corporate policy and by some academics (e.g., Sashkin, 1986) as a moral imperative. The selection by Charles Burck, "The Real World of the Entrepreneur," is a useful counterpoint to this general trend. Burck's conversations with managers of small businesses reveal that many of the teachings of modern students of management are applicable to smaller businesses, but not abstractly or out of ideology. Managers of these organizations involve their people in decisions primarily to meet the problems of getting the job done day to day. Similarly, the "management of diversity" is driven by pragmatic concerns rather than by the organization's effort to be a "good corporate citizen." While such organizations are unlikely to be unaffected by fads, we suggest that Burck's research indicates that they may be less affected than their larger counterparts whose managers are often dealing with less concrete tasks whose abstraction may allow style and ideology to take on relatively greater importance than substance. In any case, Burck's paper encourages us to focus on types of organizations that for some time have received little attention in the teaching of management.

In the next selection Quinn helps us realize how (because perception plays such a major role in how at least some organizations function) that style can indeed overwhelm substance. We encourage consideration of the following question: How likely would the incident described by Quinn have been to occur in the organizations described by Burck? Why? We also suggest asking another question: How susceptible are these organizations to the type of fads described in the earlier selection by Byrne? Why? We expect that answers to these questions can help us understand a great deal about the poor performance of many of today's organizations.

The next selection is from W. Edwards Deming's famous book, *Out of the Chaos.* Deming's ideas have been the foundation of the so-called total quality movement (TQM). It is of course highly debatable whether TQM is simply the most recent fad. We simply do not know whether it is or not. We include Deming's work here because of its current importance. At this point in time, any review of the history of management and efforts to meet its challenges would be incomplete without some exploration of Deming's famous 14 points. What is particularly intriguing about these points in the light of what we have said so far is that Deming is concerned that managers are too far removed from the core operations of the business to direct it. He thus criticizes one of the earlier fads—"management by walking around"— as ineffective because "someone in management, walking around, has little idea about what questions to ask, and usually does not pause long enough at any spot to get the right answer" (p. 22). We propose that one consequence of the distance between managers and core functions is that from their vantage point the systems that managers design may actually interfere with the processes required to get the work done well. Consequently, we suggest that you read Deming's 14 points with two questions in mind: What are the basic processes that Deming is attempting to introduce into organizations? How generic do you believe these are? Then, what practices or systems is he attempting to eliminate? How dysfunctional are these elements? Under what conditions?

In many ways, Deming could be viewed as warning American managers that they need to change radically what they are doing or face serious consequences in the developing global economy. The need to make radical changes is indeed one of the most difficult challenges that managers face. The problem is that organizations often become victims of their own success. The process leading to being victimized by one's own success seems to take the following general form. At some early time, call it Time I, people and organizations are faced by a set of problems. Some of them discover ways to cope with these problems and do so successfully. These solutions and the assumptions on which they are based become ingrained. When enacted by individuals, they appear as unquestioned habits. When enacted by organizations, they appear as standard operating procedures. They interfere with people and organizations that are recognizing changes that may have occurred at Time II. Moreover, when change is recognized, because the things that were done at Time I are known to have worked and are trusted, they are invoked, rather mindlessly, at Time II. This is one reason why it is important for managers to appreciate the history of management. Such an appreciation is apt to make them aware that existing modes exist, not because these methods are in any sense absolutely best, but because they worked well in relation to problems of the past. Consequently, managers must seek ways to allow themselves and their organizations to view the world in new ways and to respond accordingly.

The next two selections help us to explore the challenges of avoiding victimization by previous success. "Maxwell's Warning" by David Halberstam provides some interesting insights into the operation of the American automobile industry in the 1970s that may have contributed to its decline shortly thereafter. Halberstam's account of Charley Maxwell's journey to Detroit suggests that the major firms were so structured as to be unable even to consider the possibility that serious change was possible. One noteworthy aspect of Maxwell's encounters in Detroit is how the existing systems of power and privilege were associated with routines that pushed information about possible change to very low management ranks. The next selection, from economist Lester Thurow's important book, *Head to Head*, describes a more general problem of standard operating procedures in American industry. Basically, Thurow shows how changes in technology call for fundamentally different managerial assumptions and ways of managing. However, he too indicates that the success of previous approaches and expectations associated with power and privilege may get in the way of such necessary adjustments. In the context of Deming's discussion, what we see is that one of the most difficult challenges facing managers is to free themselves and their organizations from the very structures and systems of accountability that were so helpful in an earlier era when these systems had become virtually synonymous with professional management.

The next selection, "Quality," is a moving story told by John Galsworthy. Since the tale undoubtedly has many different messages for different people, we will not attempt to impose ours on it here. However, we do suggest reading it with the themes of the previous selections in mind. Does Mr. Gessler, the hero of the story, typify the employee that managers who follow Deming are seeking? What, if anything, would need to be done for someone such as Mr. Gessler to function in a typical modern organization? Are such things possible? Are Deming's 14 ideas pointing in the right direction? Are the entrepreneurs described by Burck apt to have a tragic end similar to that of Mr. Gessler? What would you suggest they do?

When many of us think about improving organization performance, we think about improving how we manage workers at the operating level. However, in the selection discussed earlier, Thurow observed that in modern organizations, some of the most serious blocks to performance stem from middle-level managers who are threatened by new developments. Along with other factors, this suggests to us that a major development in the evolution of organizations is the growth of the importance of managing managers. Based on their research, Clinton Longenecker and Dennis Gioia (in the final selection of this Chapter) indicate that American managers have not met this challenge very well. They suggest that some of the reasons for this failure stem from the acceptance of certain assumptions about managers that are not true. They term these assumptions *myths*. In the final selection of this chapter, these myths and some of their entailments are reprinted. Longenecker and Gioia assert that acceptance of these myths is associated with the failure of higher-level managers to manage their subordinates effectively.

When we step back and view these selections collectively, we see some important patterns. Things are changing, but the abilities of managers to recognize the changes and meet the challenges they pose are hindered by baggage that they and the organizations they have created carry from the past. On the other hand, we have noted how Follett's analysis of processes has been associated with a rather enduring set of ideas. From this we conclude that the challenge of management has substantial parallels with the task of the historian as described by E. H. Carr (1961). Knowledge of the past must be guided by a framework that helps distinguish between what is general and what is particular. One cannot ignore the past, but one cannot mindlessly generalize from the past to the present or the future. Unfortunately, this is much easier to say than to do because our current ways of understanding the present carry forth so much from the attempts of our predecessors to deal with what they faced. Of course, unlike the historian, the manager must act in the present with respect to things of major practical consequence.

The difficulties stem, in large measure, from the nature of organizations themselves. Two features are most salient. First, organizations need to achieve cooperation and coordination of a number of different individuals. Since each of these individuals is apt to have somewhat unique needs, emotions, and perceptions, achieving common direction is a very difficult challenge. Second, the context in which an organization exists (that is, its environment) is constantly changing. What is the right thing to do and the right way to do it are constantly changing. Similarly, what is right strategically and morally is not constant either.

Managers are responsible for achieving coordinated effort under these complex and changing conditions. Like other human beings who must take action but face complex and changing circumstances, managers often simplify the complexity. For example, they try to respond to today's problem using the same techniques that they used in the past. Or their search for a "quick fix"—the simple solution that will solve all the problems—leads them to become enmeshed in today's fad. To some degree, some simplification is essential. If the organization can never benefit from doing today what it learned to do yesterday, the costs would be enormous. Moreover, if every problem were approached in a way to take into account all its fine points and contingencies, action would be very slow if not impossible; by the time something were implemented, it would be obsolete. On the other hand, too much simplification or reliance on previous learning could lead the manager to navigate the organization according to a map that does not represent the terrain accurately.

Moreover, managers often lack precise instruments for directing the efforts of others. Most organizations have well-established procedures that they have used to move forward in the past. Neither they nor the people who operate them can be changed instantaneously. Even if one knows the right thing to do, what is right, and what is the right way to do it, does not mean that the organization is prepared to do any of the three.

Finally, there is the challenge of balancing the short run and the long run. Every individual, including the manager, will be part of an organization for a finite period of time. Since this period will often be shorter than the life of the organization, there are incentives for each individual to emphasize things that will produce benefits in a shorter period of time than might be good for the organization as an entity. The manager is responsible for the long-run well-being of the entity, but like any human being he or she will be tempted to work in his or her own interests.

In short, the challenge of managing is to coordinate the actions of a variety of individuals who have different and often conflicting needs and perceptions, in order to achieve a viable organization that is able to respond to complex and changing environments. This result must be achieved using imperfect information and operating under the constraints imposed by structures and learning from the past. When we understand the nature of this challenge, it is hard to be complacent about managing. We hope these articles help you appreciate the nature of this challenge more deeply. However, the enduring character of Follett's concepts leads us to expect that if we approach things at an abstract enough level we can uncover some basic processes that might be of general relevance. Thus, even though we may never discover any repeatable theme with certainty, it makes sense to observe closely what is happening and to try to see how it is the same or different from what has happened and is happening elsewhere. That is, to attempt to build and use theory based on what we observe *and* how we abstract from our observations and make predictions that may apply more generally than to just the situation or situations we actually study.

References

Carr, Edward Hallett. *What Is History.* New York: Alfred A. Knopf, 1961.

Sashkin, M. (1986). Participative Management Remains An Ethical Imperative. *Organizational Dynamics, 14,* 62–75.

◆

The Emergence of Management[*]

Peter Drucker

During the last fifty years, society in every developed country has become a society of institutions. Every major social task, whether economic performance or health care, education or the protection of the environment, the pursuit of new knowledge or defense, is today being entrusted to big organizations, designed for perpetuity and managed by their own managements. On the performance of these institutions, the performance of modern society—if not the survival of each individual—increasingly depends.

Only seventy-five years ago such a society would have been inconceivable. In the society of 1900 the family still served in every single country as the agent of, and organ for, most social tasks. Institutions were few and small. The society of 1900, even in the most highly institutionalized country (e.g., Imperial Germany), still resembled the Kansas prairie. There was one eminence, the central government. It loomed very large on the horizon—not because it was large but because there was nothing else around it. The rest of society was diffused in countless molecules: small workshops, small schools, the individual professional—whether doctor or lawyer—practicing by himself, the farmer, the craftsman, the neighborhood retail store, and so on. There were the beginnings of big business—but only the beginnings. And what was then considered a giant business would strike us today as very small indeed.

The octopus which so frightened the grandparents of today's Americans, Rockefeller's giant Standard Oil Trust, was split into fourteen parts by the U.S. Supreme Court in 1911. Thirty years later, on the eve of America's entry into World War II, every single one of these fourteen Standard Oil daughters had become at least four times as large as the octopus when the Supreme Court divided it—in employment, in capital, in sales, and in every other aspect. Yet, among these fourteen there were only three major oil companies—Jersey Standard, Mobil, and Standard of California. The other eleven were small to fair-sized, playing little or no role in the world economy and only a limited role in the U.S. economy.

While business has grown in these seventy years, other institutions have grown much faster. There was no university in the world before 1914 that had much more than 6,000 students—and only a handful that had more than 5,000. Today the university of 6,000 students is a pygmy; there are even some who doubt that it is viable. The hospital, similarly, has grown from a marginal institution to which the poor went to die into the center of health care and a giant in its own

[*]Reprinted from *Management: Tasks, Responsibilities, Practices* by Peter Drucker, pp. 3–10. Copyright © 1973, 1974 by Peter Drucker. Reprinted by permission of Harper & Row Publishers, Inc.

right—and also into one of the most complex social institutions around. Labor unions, research institutes, and many others have similarly grown to giant size and complexity.

In the early 1900s the citizens of Zurich built themselves a splendid City Hall, which they confidently believed would serve the needs of the city for all time to come. Indeed, it was bitterly attacked by conservatives as gross extravagance, if not as megalomania. Government in Switzerland has grown far less than in any other country in the world. Yet the Zurich City Hall long ago ceased to be adequate to house all the offices of the city administration. By now, these offices occupy ten times or more the space that seventy-five years ago seemed so splendid—if not extravagant.

THE EMPLOYEE SOCIETY

The citizen of today in every developed country is typically an employee. He works for one of the institutions. He looks to them for his livelihood. He looks to them for his opportunities. He looks to them for access to status and function in society, as well as for personal fulfillment and achievement.

The citizen of 1900 if employed worked for a small family-type operation; the small pop-and-mom store employing a helper or two; the family household; and so on. And of course, the great majority of people in those days, except in the most highly industrialized countries—such as Britain or Belgium—worked on the farm.

Our society has become an employee society [emphasis added]. In the early 1900s people asked, "What do you do?" Today they tend to ask, "Whom do you work for?"

We have neither political nor social theory for the society of institutions and its new pluralism. It is, indeed, incompatible with the political and social theories which still dominate our view of society and our approach to political and social issues. We still use as political and social model what the great thinkers of the late sixteenth and seventeenth centuries, Bodin, Locke, Hume, and Harrington, codified: the society which knows no power centers and no autonomous institution, save only one central government. Reality has long outgrown this model—but it is still the only one we have.

A new theory to fit the new reality will be a long time coming. For new theory, to be more than idle speculation and vague dreaming, must come after the event. It codifies what we have already learned, have already achieved, have already done. But we cannot wait till we have the theory we need. We have to act. We have to use the little we know. And there is one thing we do know: management is the specific organ of the new institution, whether business enterprise or university, hospital or armed service, research lab or government agency. If institutions are to function, managements must perform.

The word "management" is a singularly difficult one. It is, in the first place, specifically American and can hardly be translated into any other language, not even into British English. It denotes a function but also the people who discharge it. It denotes a social position and rank but also a discipline and field of study.

But even within the American usage, management is not adequate as a term, for institutions other than business do not speak of management or managers, as a rule. Universities or government agencies have administrators, as have hospitals. Armed services have commanders. Other institutions speak of executives, and so on.

Yet all these institutions have in common the management function, the management task, and the management work. All of them require management. And in all of them, management is the effective, the active organ.

The institution itself is, in effect, a fiction. It is an accounting reality but not a social reality. When this or that government agency makes this ruling or this decision, we know perfectly well that it is some people within the agency who make the ruling or the decision and who act for the agency and as the effective organ of the agency. When we speak of General Electric closing a plant, it is not, of course, General Electric that is deciding and acting, it is a group of managers within the company.

Georg Siemens, who built the Deutsche Bank into the European continent's leading financial institution in the decade between 1870 and 1880,. . . once said, "Without management, a bank is so much scrap, fit only to be liquidated." Without institution there is no management. But without management there is no institution. Management is the specific organ of the modern institution. It is the organ on the performance of which the performance and the survival of the institution depends.

MANAGEMENT IS PROFESSIONAL

We further know that *management is independent of ownership, rank, or power* [emphasis added]. It is objective function and ought to be grounded in the responsibility for performance. It is professional—management is a function, a discipline, a task to be done; and managers are the professionals who practice this discipline, carry out the functions, and discharge these tasks. It is no longer relevant whether the manager is also an owner; if he is, it is incidental to his main function, which is to be a manager. Eiichi Shibusawa's Confucian ideal of the "professional manager" in the early days of modern Japan. . . has become reality. And so has Shibusawa's basic insight that the essence of the manager is neither wealth nor rank, but responsibility.

FROM BUSINESS SOCIETY TO PLURALISM

The rhetoric of the New Left talks of our society as being a big-business society. But this is as outdated as the rhetoric of the New Left is altogether. Society in the West *was* a business society—seventy-five years ago. Then, business was, indeed, the most powerful of all institutions—more powerful even than some governments. Since the turn of the century, however, the importance of business has gone down steadily—not because business has become smaller or weaker but because the other institutions have grown so much faster. Society has become pluralist.

In the United States in the 1970s, no businessman compares in power or visibility with the tycoons of 1900, such as J. P. Morgan, John D. Rockefeller, or—a little later—Henry Ford. Few people today even know the names of the chief executive officers of America's biggest corporations; the names of the tycoons were household words. Not even the largest corporation today can compare in power and even in relative wealth with those tycoons who could hold the U.S. government for ransom.

It makes little sense to speak of the "military-industrial complex." The high level of defense spending in the United States has for many years been an economic depressant. It would make more sense to speak of the "military-university complex." No business today—in fact, no business in American history—has a fraction of the power that today's big university has. By granting or denying admission or the college degree, the university grants or denies access to jobs and livelihoods. Such power no business—and no other institution—ever had before in American history. Indeed, no earlier institution would ever have been permitted such power.

In Europe things are only slightly different. Business careers have become respectable to a degree unknown in 1900. They have gained equality with careers in government, in academic life, or in the military—all of which ranked socially much higher seventy-five years ago. But still there is no one in French business today whose influence and power can compare with that of the DeWendel family of steelmakers in the France of the Third Republic, or with the power which a few families of the Haute Banque exercised through their control of the Banque de France and of French money and credit policy. There is no businessman and no business enterprise in Germany today that can compare in power and influence with the Krupps and other steel barons of 1900, or with I. G. Farben in the 1920s. There is no business executive in today's England who can compare in power and influence with the merchant banking families who, almost down to the 1930s, ran the Bank of England and, through it, the British Treasury, as family fiefs.

Of all contemporary societies, Japan can most nearly be described as a business society. Business management has greater influence in Japan than in any other developed country. But even in Japan, there is no business manager today and no business enterprise whose power and influence stand comparison with the power and influence which the great Zaibatsu concerns of 1900 or 1920—Mitsubishi, Mitsui, Sumitomo, and Yasuda—exerted on economy and society alike.

In the United States of 1900, almost the only career opportunity open to the young and ambitious was business. Today there are untold others, each promising as much (or more) income, and advancement as rapid as a career in business.

Around the turn of the century, whatever of the gross national product did not go to the farmer went in and through the private business economy. The nonbusiness service institutions, beginning with government, accounted probably for no more than 10 percent of the nonfarm gross national product of the United States at the turn of the century and up till World War I. Today, while farming has largely become a business, more than half of the gross national product goes to or through service institutions which are not businesses and which are not held accountable for economic performance or subject to market test.

Well over a third of the gross national product in the United States today goes directly to governments, federal, state, and local. Another 3 to 5 percent goes to nongovernmental schools, that is, private and parochial, including the nongovernmental colleges and universities. Another 5 percent of GNP, that is, two-thirds of the total health-care bill, is also nongovernmental, but also nonbusiness. On top of this, there is a great variety of not-for-profit activities, accounting maybe for another 2 to 5 percent of gross national product. This adds up to 50 or perhaps as much as 60 percent of the GNP which does not go to the business sector but to, or through, public-service institutions.

Indeed, while the New Left talks of the big-business society, its actions show a keen awareness that business is not the dominant institution. Every period of public unrest since the end of the Napoleonic Wars began with uprisings against business. But the revolt against authority that swept the developed countries in the sixties centered in the institutions—especially the university—which were most esteemed by yesterday's radicals and which were, so to speak, the good guys of organization thirty or forty years ago.

The nonbusiness, public-service institutions do not need management less than business. They may need it more.

There is growing concern with management in nonbusiness institutions.

Among the best clients of the large American management consulting firms these last ten or fifteen years have been government agencies such as the Department of Defense, the City of New York, or the Bank of England. When Canada in the late sixties first created a unified military service, with army, navy, and air force all combined, the first conference of Canadian generals and admirals was not on strategy; it was on "management by objectives." The venerable orders of the Catholic Church are engaged in organization studies and in management development, with the Jesuits in the lead.

A generation or two ago, the German civil service knew that it had the answers. But now, the city of Hamburg—long known for its excellence in public administration—has created a management center for its civil service and has made management the responsibility of one of the senior members of the city's government. Even the British civil service has been reorganized with the objective of introducing "management."

An increasing number of students in advanced management courses are not business executives but executives from hospitals, from the armed services, from city and state governments, and from school administrations. The Harvard Business School even runs an increasingly popular advanced management course for university presidents.

The management of the nonbusiness institutions will indeed be a growing concern from now on. Their management may well become the central management problem—simply because the lack of management of the public-service institution is such a glaring weakness, whether municipal water department or graduate university.

And yet, *business management is the exemplar.* And any book on management, such as this one, has to put business management in the center.

WHY BUSINESS MANAGEMENT HAS TO BE THE FOCUS

One reason is history. Business enterprise was the first of the modern institutions to emerge. From the beginning, that is, from the emergence of the railroads and the "universal banks" as large businesses in the late nineteenth century, business enterprise was unmistakably a new and different institution rather than an outgrowth of older ones, as apparently were government agency, university, hospital, and armed service. There was, of course, concern about management in other institutions.° But until recently it was sporadic and undertaken usually in connection with an acute problem and confined to it. But the work on management in business and industry was from the beginning meant to be generic and continuous.

Another reason why the study of management to this day has been primarily a study of business management is that so far the economic sphere alone has measurements both for the allocation of resources and for the results of decisions. Profitability is not a perfect measurement; no one has even been able to define it, and yet it is a measurement, despite all its imperfections. None of the other institutions has measurements so far. All they have are opinions—which are hardly an adequate foundation for a discipline.

The most important reason for focusing on business management is that it is the success story of this century. It has performed within its own sphere. It has provided economic goods and services to an extent that would have been unimaginable to the generation of 1900. And it has performed despite world wars, depressions, and dictatorships.

The achievement of business management enables us today to promise—perhaps prematurely (and certainly rashly)—the abolition of the grinding poverty that has been mankind's lot through the ages. It is largely the achievement of business management that advanced societies today can afford mass higher education. Business both produces the economic means to support this expensive undertaking and offers the jobs in which knowledge can become productive and can be paid for. That we today consider it a social flaw and an imperfection of society for people to be fixed in their opportunities and jobs by class and birth—where only yesterday this was the natural and apparently inescapable condition of mankind—is a result of our economic performance, that is, of the performance of business management. In a world that is politically increasingly fragmented and obsessed by nationalism, business management is one of the very few institutions capable of transcending national boundaries.

The multinational corporation brings together in a common venture management people from a great many countries with different languages, cultures, traditions, and values, and unites them in a common purpose. It is one of the very few institutions of our world that is not nationalistic in its world view, its values, and its decisions but truly a common organ of a world economy that, so far, lacks a world polity.

It is also business management to which our society increasingly looks for leadership in respect to the quality of life. Indeed, what sounds like harsh criticism of business management tends often to be the result of high, perhaps unrealistically high, expectations based on the past performance of business management. "If you can do so well, why don't you do better?" is the underlying note. . . .

°The work of Elihu Root as Secretary of War on the organization of the General Staff of the U.S. Army is an American example; the work of Adickes and Micquel as big-city mayors and ministers of the Crown on local government in Germany is another; both were done between 1900 and 1910.

The emergence of management may be the pivotal event of our time, far more important than all the events that make the headlines. Rarely, if ever, has a new basic institution, a new leading group, a new central function, emerged as fast as has management since the turn of the century. Rarely in human history has a new institution proven indispensable so quickly. Even less often has a new institution arrived with so little opposition, so little disturbance, so little controversy. And never before has a new institution encompassed the globe as management has, sweeping across boundaries of race and creed, language and traditions, within the lifetime of many men still living and at work.

Today's developed society, sans aristocracy, sans large landowners, even sans capitalists and tycoons, depends for leadership on the managers of its major institutions. It depends on their knowledge, on their vision, and on their responsibility. In this society, management—its tasks, its responsibilities, its practices—is central: as a need, as an essential contribution, and as a subject of study and knowledge.

◆

Thoroughly Modern—Mary Parker Follett*

Over half a century ago Mary Parker Follett wrote books on management that are as relevant today as they were then

David K. Hurst

"I believe we shall soon think of the leader as one who can organize the experience of the group. . . . It is by organizing experience that we transform experience into power. . . the task of the chief executive is to articulate the purpose which guides the integrated unity which his business aims to be. . . The ablest administrators do not merely draw logical conclusions from the array of facts of the past which their expert assistants bring to them; they have a vision of the future."

The quote could be from a speech by Tom Peters or a sampling from the recent torrent of writings on charismatic leadership. But it is not from either of these sources; it is from a lecture given in 1927 by Mary Parker Follett, who lived from 1868 to 1933.

Born in Boston, Follett trained as a political scientist but became involved in education, vocational guidance, and ultimately in writing and lecturing about management. Although she came to this latter activity when she was in her fifties and her output was small, she was one of the most influential of the early writers on manage-

*Reprinted from *Business Quarterly*, Vol. 56, No. 4, pp. 55–58. Copyright © 1992.

ment. Both Chester Barnard and Peter Drucker picked up and elaborated upon her ideas, for Follett's unique blend of practical advice and theoretical sophistication made her one of the most perceptive observers of managers and their organizations.

Her own writings, however, are little read today. She had the misfortune to publish them during a time when America was preoccupied with the concepts of Scientific Management in the pursuit of efficiency. Follett's concerns with creativity, social processes and leadership attracted only a limited audience in both England and America. It is, however, her perspective on these topics that makes her writings so relevant to us today.

THEORY AND PRACTICE JOSTLE FOR SUPREMACY

During the 1980s and 1990s there has been a significant change in the sources of the advice being offered to managers by writers of books on management. In the continual struggle for supremacy between theory and practice as a guide to behavior, practice now seems to be firmly in control. This contrasts with the 30-year period after World War II when theory seemed to be dominant. During that time the frameworks of strategic planning, management by objectives, portfolio theory and a variety of management "principles" were continually being invoked to prescribe what managers ought to do. Now there is a new empiricism, a renewed examination of what successful managers actually do, the objective of which has been not to criticize their behavior but to generalize from their experiences. As a result the practices of "excellent" managers have all but driven conceptually-based prescriptions from management writings.

This preoccupation with excellent practices will undoubtedly lead to a new bout of theory building. For it seems that all systems of knowledge (theories as well as organizations) go through such oscillations, with each swing between hypothesis and experiment being required to correct the excesses of the previous cycle and to advance the process. In management literature these swings usually have the effect of rendering obsolete the majority of writings from the previous period. Those that survive are the "classics," works that capture the essence of the dialectical process and hence prove extremely durable.

When the search for new theory begins, management writers will undoubtedly turn to the works of Mary Parker Follett, for they are just such classics. Trained as an idealist philosopher, she was also an empiricist who believed that the behavior of managers was the only worthwhile object of study:

> I went. . . to a. . . meeting where a group of economists and M.P.'s talked of current affairs. . . . It all seemed a little vague to me, did not really seem to come to grips with our problem. The next evening I went to a dinner of twenty business men. . . . There I found hope for the future. These men were not theorising or dogmatising; they were thinking of what they had actually done and they were willing to try new ways the next morning. . . . Freedom & Co-ordination (F&C).

Few writers other than Mary Parker Follett have understood so well the foggy world in which managers operate, a world in which they must continually weave together the actual and the abstract, grappling with the future but forced to use conceptual instruments developed from the past:

> *Conceptual pictures are always pictures of the past; you proceed then to deduce principles, laws, rules, from the dead instead of the living. . . thought alone does not govern activity; my pictures depend on my behavior. Creative Experience (CE).*

THOUGHT AND ACTION CANNOT BE SEPARATED

[Mary Parker Follett] was totally opposed to the separation of concepts from behavior and the use of verbal logic to obtain a superficial consensus in organizations.

> *You can often get a specious consensus on the intellectual level which in virtue of the prestige of verbal agreement arrests the activity of your mind, but the only real consensus is that which arises on the motor level. The theory of consent rests on the wholly intellectualistic fallacy that thought and action can be separated. . . on the assumption that we think with our 'minds' and we don't. . . how often we see cases where we have not been able to persuade people, by our most careful reasoning, to think differently, but later, by giving them an opportunity to enter on a certain course of action, their 'minds' are thereby changed. CE.*

This is helpful advice to managers, who in the 1970s struggled so to implement strategies that had been formulated conceptually with little input from operating management. Despite their best efforts to appeal to their operators' minds by presenting the strategies as logical conclusions from a rational analysis of the situation, there was often little zest for their implementation. "There's nothing wrong with the strategy," we cried, "It was faulty implementation." But Follett's writings remind us that behavior can change our frameworks of logic and that the formulation of effective strategy may actually follow successful implementation. What we have been calling strategy may often be emergent rather than planned; implementation may precede or at least be concurrent with formulation.

Follett's practical orientation was matched by a sophisticated philosophy that yielded insights not available from the more reductionist, positivistic philosophies that have underpinned management theory in the post-World War II era. As a contemporary of both Henri Bergson (1859–1941) and Alfred North Whitehead (1861–1948) she was much influenced by their view of life and indeed of reality itself as fundamentally a creative process. For her there is no objective reality "out there," only what we construct. Experience itself is a creative integration:

> *But our true environment is psychic. . . . (E)nvironment is not a hard and rigid something external to us. . . . (B)oth self and environment are always in the making. . . . Progress implies respect for the creative process not the created thing; the created thing is forever. . . being left behind us. . . . Life is creative at every moment. The New State (TNS).*

After a lengthy love affair with behaviorism, it is only recently that mainstream American psychology has begun to be sympathetic to a more cognitive psychology that emphasizes the constructed nature of our realities. And it is only in the last few years that this perspective has started to make itself felt in management writings.

Follett paid particular attention to the social process that takes place between people in groups:

> It is an acting and reacting, a single and identical process which brings out differences and integrates them into a unity. The complex, reciprocal action, the intricate interweavings of the members of the group, is the social process. TNS.

Her message to managers (and to politicians, for she was firstly a political scientist) is "don't hug your blueprints," for the process we call experience is a creative one. Ethics, purpose, power, authority and control do not exist like blueprints, prior to and independent of action. Rather they are emergent, dynamic qualities.

ETHICS AND PURPOSE EMERGE FROM PROCESS

There is much talk today of the need for vision and values in business but little understanding of how managers go about developing them. Too often the belief seems to be that, like strategy, they can be developed rationally in the single, synoptic mind of the CEO. Follett would have rejected this view; according to her, ethics and purpose are aspects of organization that emerge from process:

> . . . morality is never static; it advances as life advances. You cannot hang your ideals up on pegs and take down no. 2 for certain emergencies and no. 4 for others. The true test of our morality is not the rigidity with which we adhere to standard, but the loyalty we show to the life which constructs standards. . . whether we are pouring our life into our visions only to receive it back with its miraculous enhancement for new uses. TNS.

Vision, then, is evolving purpose:

> The truth is that the same process which creates all else creates the very purpose. (P)urpose is involved in the process, not prior to process . . . . The whole philosophy of cause and effect must be rewritten. TNS.

She contends that loyalty develops in a similar fashion:

> Loyalty is awakened. . . by the very process which creates the group. . . . Our task is not to 'find' causes to awaken our loyalty, but to live our life fully and loyalty issues [forth]. . . . Loyalty to a collective will which we have not created. . . is slavery. TNS.

Then, in a circular response, loyalty feeds back to develop further purpose:

> We create the common will and feel the spiritual energy which flows into us from the purpose we have made, for the purpose which we seek. TNS.

POWER, AUTHORITY AND CONTROL

In a similar fashion Follett's process philosophy views power, authority and control within organizations, not as substances or entities that can be transferred, delegated or handed over, but as evolutionary products emerging from process:

> *Genuine power can only be grown, it will slip from every arbitrary hand that grasps it; for genuine power is not coercive control, but coactive control. CE.*

She explained this kind of power as follows:

> *When you and I decide on a course of action together and do that thing, you have no power over me nor I over you, but we have power over ourselves together. CE.*

True power then is "power with" another, not "power over" another. Until everyone within an organization realizes that they are bound together, each will see only their own situation. "Power with" can only come from obedience to a single, shared situation. Follett called this "the law of the situation":

> *One person should not give orders to another person, but both should agree to take their orders from the situation. Dynamic Administration (DA).*

Perhaps this is why managers in the 1970s seemed so powerless to implement "their" strategies. They had "power over"—formal power—but the strategies themselves did not generate "power with," that is, they did not emerge as the "law of the situation" whereby all could be empowered (to use the modern buzzword) to implement them.

Authority, like power, also grows from the social process:

> *. . . authority is not something from the top which filters down to those below. . . . It does not come from separating people. . . into two classes, those who command (and) those who obey. It comes from the intermingling of all, of my work fitting into yours and yours into mine, and from that intermingling of forces a power being created which will control those forces. Authority is a self-generating process. F&C.*

GROUP COORDINATION IS REQUIRED

In societies we often think of the individual as being the opposite of the group, that groups negate individuality. No doubt groups can do this, but Follett's understanding of the social process illuminates the complementary nature of individuals and groups:

> *We find the true man only through group organization. The potentialities of the individual remain potentialities until they are released by group life. Man discovers his true nature, gains his true freedom only through the group. TNS.*

The notion that groups (we would call them teams today) can evoke and release individual potential is central to Follett's view of the interweaving processes that coordinate organizations:

> . . . *you have to call out all the capacities of everyone in your organization before you can unite these capacities. Evoking, releasing, is the foundation of co-ordination. DA.*

Throughout her writings Follett emphasizes that the aim of management is to attain unity, not uniformity, and that

> *We attain unity only through variety. Differences must be integrated, not annihilated, nor absorbed. TNS.*

For her, integration always means invention, the reaching of a creative solution to the differences arising out of the social process:

> *There are three ways of settling differences: by domination, by compromise, or by integration. F&C.*

For her, the first two methods are unsatisfactory:

> *In dominating, only one way gets what it wants; in compromise neither side gets what it wants. F&C.*

The preferred method is integration:

> *Integration involves invention, the finding of the third way. . . never let yourself be bullied by an either-or-situation. . . . Find a third way. . . the third way means progress. . . integration create(s) something new. F&C.*

The ability to integrate differences is characteristic of effective managers:

> *In dissensions between executives it is never merely peace that should be our aim, but progress. We get progress when we find a way that includes the ideas of both. . . parties. . . . But this requires hard thinking, inventiveness, ingenuity. . . (it is not) a foregone conclusion; it is an achievement. DA.*

LEADERSHIP IS THE INTEGRATING PROCESS

Mary Parker Follett's writings are probably most relevant to us today in her extensive discussions of leadership as an activity, the integrating process that releases and unites the energies within organizations. Because she emphasizes the sources of leadership in knowledge and experience rather than formal position, she can articulate clearly a theory of multiple leadership within a group:

> *. . . there are different leadership qualities possessed by different men, but also different situations require different kinds of knowledge, and the man possessing the knowledge demanded by a certain situation . . . (should) become the leader at that moment. DA.*

This mobility of leadership is, of course, the essence of effective teamwork, as the lead is seized by the appropriate team members as the situations change.

There has been much written in recent times about transformational or charismatic leadership. Follett is at her best in describing this process, for she understands clearly that a leader's vision is not the expression of the lonely purpose of one individual. It is an interweaving of shared purposes, an integration of the experiences of many:

> *The leader guides the group and is at the same time himself guided by the group, is always part of the group. No one can truly lead except from within. . . the leader. . . must interpret our experience to us, must see all the different points of view which underlie our daily activities. . . He must give form to things vague, things latent, to mere tendencies. He must be able to lead us to wise decisions, not to impose his own wise decisions upon us. We need leaders, not masters or drivers. TNS.*

Perhaps none since Mary Parker Follett has better expressed this concept of leadership:

> *The skillful leader then does not rely on personal force; he controls his group not by dominating but by expressing it. He stimulates what is best in us; he unifies and concentrates what we feel only gropingly and scatteringly, but he never gets away from the current of which we and he are both an integral part. He is a leader who gives form to the inchoate energy in every man. The person who influences me most is not he who does great deeds but he who makes me feel I can do great deeds. TNS.*

Thoroughly modern, Mary Parker Follett.

MARY PARKER FOLLETT BOOKS REFERENCED

Freedom & Co-ordination: Lectures in Business Organization, Garland Publishers, N.Y., 1987.

Creative Experience, Peter Smith, N.Y., 1951.

The New State: Group Organization the Solution of Popular Government, Longmans, Green and Co., N.Y., 1918.

Dynamic Administration, Pitman, London, 1965.

◆

Business Fads: What's in—and out[*]

Executives Latch on to Any Management Idea That Looks Like a Quick Fix

John A. Byrne

Allan A. Kennedy had just delivered his $5,000, 90-minute pep talk on corporate culture to a select group of top executives of an industrial-service corporation.

The show was slick. Kennedy, a former McKinsey & Co. consultant and co-author of *Corporate Cultures,* had run through his chat on company rituals some 200 times. "By now I've got an act that could play on Broadway," he says.

Yet even Kennedy was taken aback by the audience's enthusiasm when the curtain came down. "This corporate culture stuff is great," the chairman raved at dinner following the talk. Then, turning to his president, he demanded, "I want a culture by Monday."

Astonishing as it may seem, the executive was serious. There is, of course, merit in Kennedy's belief that a corporation's culture—its shared values, beliefs and rituals—strongly influences its success or failure. But it would seem obvious to most executives that a culture must be built over years, not ordained overnight.

Or would it? Like Kennedy's client, a lot of American executives these days seem eager to latch onto almost any new concept that promises a quick fix for their problems.

Having trouble developing new products? Try "intrapreneurship," the process for getting entrepreneurial juices flowing in a big company.

Having a tough time competing against the Japanese? Try "quality circles," the managerial export from Japan that has U.S. workers and managers sitting around tables finding ways to increase productivity and ensure quality.

Having problems with employee productivity? Try "wellness," the new buzz-word for fitness programs that encourage managers to exercise, eat healthy foods, and stop smoking.

Facing the threat of a hostile takeover? Restructure your company by writing off a mature business and taking on a mountain of debt. Wall Street will almost surely respond by jacking up your stock price, and that should keep the raider at bay.

Hollow Symbols.   There's nothing inherently wrong with any of these ideas. What's wrong is that too many companies use them as gimmicks to evade the basic

---

challenges they face. Unless such solutions are well thought out and supported by a sincere commitment from top management, they are doomed to fail. They quickly become meaningless buzzwords, hollow symbols, mere fads.

Even more disturbing is how these fads change, often by 180°. In the 1960s it seemed everyone wanted to diversify, to become a conglomerate. Today, an opposite trend has emerged under the fancy rubric of "asset redeployment." It's the term for conceding that a past diversification spree was a mistake, for spinning off businesses and getting back to the basics.

Or take strategic planning. In the late 1970s it was all the rage. Following the lead of General Electric Co., many companies hired planners at corporate headquarters to chart the future plans of their businesses. Today, corporate planning staffs have been substantially reduced or eliminated because it makes more sense for line managers, closer to the business, to plot strategy.

Business fads are something of a necessary evil and have always been with us. What's different—and alarming—today is the sudden rise and fall of so many conflicting fads and how they influence the modern manager.

What's hot right now? "Touchy-feely" managers who are "demassing." Translation: Nice-guy bosses are laying off still more workers. Other companies are forming "strategic alliances"—launching a joint venture with their No. 1 competitor, perhaps, to plug a product or technology void. The thoroughly modern corporation wants to turn its managers into "leaders" and "intrapreneurs" through "pay for performance." Those same managers flock to Outward Bound expeditions to learn survival skills.

On the other hand, autocratic bosses are out. So are the corporate planners and economists who not long ago pontificated on "reindustrialization," "synergy," and "management by objectives." On the way out: the hostile takeover wave that has dominated business for the past several years, the raiders who used junkbonds, and the golden parachutes that managers devised to protect themselves from the raiders.

And so it goes, to the consternation of those whose task it is to run a business. "Last year it was quality circles," says Harvey Gittler, a Borg-Warner Corp. manager in Elyria, Ohio. "This year it is zero inventories. The truth is, one more panacea and we will all go nuts."

He is not alone in this feeling. A marketing manager with a big Midwest equipment maker feels whipsawed. "In the past 18 months, we have heard that profit is more important than revenue, that quality is more important than profit, that people are more important than profit, that customers are more important than our people, that big customers are more important than small customers, and that growth is the key to our success," he recounts. "No wonder our performance is inconsistent."

One new fad seems to be an attempt to clear up some of this confusion. Some large companies, including General Motors Corp. and Ford Motor Co., have issued managers glossy, pocket-sized cards to remind them of their companies' guiding principles—a key ingredient of their changing corporate cultures. Ford's mission statement—handed out last March—was two years in the making, involved hundreds of employees, and was O.K.'d by its board of directors. Some GM managers have been issued as many as three reminders, each adorned with a mug shot or two of the top brass. Call it Management by Card.

Why the proliferation of business fads? And why have they become more ephemeral than ever? Perhaps it's because many managers are frustrated by their inability to compete in a world marketplace. Or perhaps it's because they are under intense pressure from Wall Street to perform short-term miracles. The result is a mad, almost aimless scramble for instant solutions. "We're all looking for magic," explains Thomas R. Horton, president of the American Management Association. "If you tell me I can avoid a cold by taking half a pound of Vitamin C, I'll want to believe you even if it only gives me indigestion."

The search has fueled an industry of instant management gurus, new-idea consultants, and an endless stream of books promising the latest quick fix. Indeed, when it came time for Ralph H. Kilmann, a University of Pittsburgh business professor, to concoct a title for his new management book, he settled on *Beyond the Quick Fix,* in itself a reflection of how faddishness has come to dominate management thinking.

The book's point will probably be lost on many managers, however. A major corporation recently asked Kilmann if he could give its top 50 officers a seminar on his new book in only 15 minutes. "You mean you want me to do *Beyond the Quick Fix* quickly," he responded. The author declined the invitation.

Tangled Webs.   It is not clear how big a threat this rash of palliative trends poses. Business fads have waxed and waned through the decades, yet corporations survive. Faddish ideas began to influence U.S. executives in a major way with the emergence of the professional manager in America after World War II. Seat-of-the-pants management was becoming old hat. Instead, it became popular to follow the principles of Frederick Winslow Taylor, the inventor of time-and-motion studies 50 years earlier. He contended that running a company should be more a science than an art.

Managers rushed to try scientific methods, such as observation, experimentation, and reasoning. They immersed themselves in quantitative analysis. "Operations research" became the rallying cry. By itself, not a bad idea. But the success of operations research begat a series of unintelligible acronyms and buzzwords and an avalanche of charts, curves, and diagrams.

Remember PERT? Program Evaluation & Review Technique charts were spiderweb-like diagrams to ensure that projects would be completed on time. "We all did them," recalls Donald N. Frey, chief executive of Bell & Howell Co. "But it took so much effort to get the charts done, you might as well have spent the time getting the job done."

Frey, then a young manager at Ford, had a rude awakening about PERT's pitfalls. "We went to Wright Patterson Air Force base, where they had PERT charting down to a science. They had more guys working on PERT charts than they had doing the job. It was an enormous overhead cost just to allow the generals to show visitors their PERT charts."

Executives also found that management by objectives, another 1950s invention, often tangled them in paper. "We got so balled up in the details that we spent more time on paperwork than the whole damn thing was worth," says George W. Baur, president of Hughes Tool Co.'s tool division.

Mainframe Monkeys.   When the mainframe computer came along in the 1950s, it contributed to the mounting pile of paper. Many companies installed computers in rooms with huge display windows to show them off. "A lot of people got computers because GE got them," says Ian Wilson, a 26-year GE veteran now with the Stanford Research Institute. "It was monkey see, monkey do."

When GE decentralized its operations in 1950, scores of companies followed, thinking that this was the antidote for corporate bureaucracies. Similar moves became so fashionable that almost no executive could be heard advocating centralized management. That is, until some companies discovered that decentralizing led to more vice-presidents who built up their own cumbersome fiefdoms and gave line managers even less autonomy.

Centralized companies decentralized and then some decentralized corporations centralized. "It depended on which consultant you hired," remembers Donald P. Jacobs, dean of Northwestern's Kellogg School of Management.

In the 1960s a wave of "people-oriented" management thinkers gained prominence. Many of the fads they promoted mirrored social trends. T-Groups, group encounter sessions for executives, came into vogue as the Beatles and Bob Dylan sang to a new, less bridled generation. Their popularity heralded the start of the touchy-feely approach to business; "sensitive," participative managers started sharing the spotlight with the management-by-numbers conglomerateurs who dominated the times. The new managers espoused Theory Y, a model for participative management created by a Massachusetts Institute of Technology management professor, Douglas McGregor, in the 1950s. It was the beginning of the end for Theory X, an authoritarian form of governance that grew out of managers' World War II military experiences.

Oh, how the times had changed. John Clemens, then a young, freshly scrubbed manager for Pillsbury and now a Hartwick College professor, remembers it well. Along with 20 or so colleagues, he was summoned to a country-club meeting room to face a bearded, rather hip, psychiatrist. The T-Group trainer, Clemens recalls, instructed them to take off their ties, shoes, and name tags. Then the lights went out.

"We began crawling on the floor in the dark when I bumped into our president," he says. "It was atrocious. We would have done better figuring out how to sell more brownie mix."

Tens of thousands of managers from such companies as IBM, TRW, Union Carbide, and Weyerhaeuser trekked to T-Group sessions in search of self-awareness and sensitivity. The concept, popularized by National Training Laboratories, was simple: Mix a dozen or more people together in a room without a leader or an agenda and see what happens. Often, delegates would hurl personal insults across a room. The resulting "feedback," it was hoped, would make Theory X managers less bossy and more participative.

Plotting People.   As the decade came to an end, T-Groups gave way to Grid-Groups. And T-Grouped managers such as Clemens became G-Grouped quickly enough. Launched by Robert R. Blake and Jane S. Mouton's *The Managerial Grid* in 1964, the grid rated managers on two characteristics—concern for people vs. concern for production. "The beauty of it is that you could plot people all over the place," adds Clemens. "If you scored a high concern for people and a low concern for production, people would say, 'This guy's a wimp. He's a 1-9.' If you had a high concern for production (9-1), you were a dictator."

In the decade of the MBA, the 1970s, it was perhaps inevitable that the numbers-oriented students turned out by the B-schools would help to make strategic planning *de rigueur*. Another approach pioneered by GE, it caught the fancy of many executives. "After we put in our strategic planning system in 1970, we were deluged with people from around the world wanting to talk to us about it," recalls GE alumnus Walker.

Some of these visitors failed to distinguish between form and substance. They became engrossed in the mechanics of setting up a planning system rather than focusing on finding the answers, says Harvard business school's Michael E. Porter. "Too often it became a function of shuffling papers with no underlying value."

Dog Stars.   Porter was one of the many consultants who helped make strategic planning a buzzword. Consultants have always had a role in launching fads. They sold managers on psychological tools such as The Thematic Apperception Test in the 1950s. (Executives were told to conjure up stories based on series of pictures.) They also peddled sensitivity training in the 1960s. But consultants have been working overtime to roll out new fads since the 1970s.

One of the most rapidly spreading and widely used theories ever to emerge was the gospel according to Bruce D. Henderson's Boston Consulting Group Inc. Henderson put cows, dogs, stars, and question marks on matrix charts in hundreds of executive suites. Businesses were put into such categories as cash cows (mature companies that could be milked) and dogs (marginal performers in a market with poor prospects).

Fads multiplied in the 1980s as U.S. executives grappled for ways to contend with foreign competition—so much so that management by best-seller came into vogue. . . . William Ouchi's *Theory Z* and Richard Pascale and Anthony Athos' *The Art of Japanese Management* were the first such best-sellers when published in 1981. Both books pushed U.S. companies to adopt such Japanese management techniques as quality circles and job enrichment.

Some wags wondered if U.S. managers would soon be issued kimonos and be required to eat with chopsticks. "There wasn't an American manager who wasn't talking about it four years ago," says James J. O'Toole, a management professor at the University of Southern California. But when O'Toole's *New Management* magazine recently asked readers to name the most influential management books in recent years, not a single reader mentioned *Theory Z.*

Theory Z is still having an impact, however. Quality circles, an updated version of the employee suggestion programs and labor-management councils of the 1950s, are still in. In 1979, the International Association of Quality Circles had only 200 members. Now membership is almost 8,000.

Immortality.   Why such mass popularity? Edward E. Lawler III, director of the University of Southern California's Center for Effective Organizations, says that QCs are partly a fad. "In a number of cases we studied," says Lawler, "the CEO of the company had seen a TV program or read a magazine article on QCs and decided to give them a try. Circles were simply something the top told the middle to do to the bottom."

Quality circles may be helping some companies improve productivity, though they have received mixed reviews. Koppers Co. installed QCs in 1981 at a plant in Follansbee, W. Va. They flopped when Koppers axed half the work force. Now it's trying a program called PITCH—for People Involved in Totally Changing History. The jury is still out on PITCH, but outsiders wonder how seriously employees will take a program that seems to promise immortality for working at a plant that makes creosote roofing tar.

Taking the best-seller even further were consultants Thomas J. Peters and Robert H. Waterman Jr. Their *In Search of Excellence,* published in 1982, added Skunk Works, Management by Walking Around, and Stick to Your Knitting to the manager's vocabulary.

One *Excellence*-type slogan caught on more widely than any other: "People are our most important asset." But how seriously did executives take it? One major property and casualty insurer adopted this motto two years ago, promoting it in its annual report and in management memos. Yet as one divisional manager grouses, there was no real commitment. "Since the introduction of that campaign, our training budget has been cut in half and our employee profit-sharing plan has been eliminated," he says. "We've laid off 1,000 staff members. Our tuition reimbursement program has been dissolved, and the athletic center has been closed. A lot of those important assets are looking for new jobs."

Pies and Salads.   Some of the folks who promote new management ideas will even call a fad a fad. Take wellness, fitness programs that attempt to get employees to eat salads instead of hamburgers. "We feel it probably has a two- to three-year life cycle," figures Robert G. Cox, president of PA Executive Search Group. Cox's consulting outfit tells potential clients that managers who smoke cost them $4,000 annually in lower productivity and higher absenteeism.

On a recent engagement, PA's consultants stood duty in a corporation's cafeteria. "We noticed they picked up a lot of desserts when they went through the cafeteria line," relates Cox. "We also noticed that the lemon meringue pie was at

MANAGEMENT LINGO: HOW TO READ BETWEEN THE LINES

What's Out	What's In

Centralization Father knows best.

Conglomerates Napoleon tried it, so did Harold Geneen. Enough said.

Consultants Company doctors. At least they still make house calls.

Corporate Planners Worrying about tomorrow's problems. It's more fun than worrying about today's.

Decentralization Then again, maybe Father doesn't know best.

Experience Curve Fight for market share. What you lose on each sale, you'll make up on volume.

Factory of the Future Robot heaven. Not yet available on earth.

Golden Parachutes The executive safety net. The problem is, not everybody's a high-flier.

Management by Objectives Here an objective, there an objective, everywhere an objective.

Management by Walking Around The ultimate open-door policy. A few steps too far?

One-minute Managing Balancing reward and punishment in managing your employees. The executive equivalent of paper-training your dog.

Quantitative Management The numbers tell it all. Except what to do next.

Raiders The thrill is gone. Ask Carl Icahn.

Reindustrialization The crusade to revive Smokestack America. Back to the future?

Synergy Genetic engineering for corporations. But don't forget, when you cross a horse with a donkey, the result is a mule.

T-Groups Building team spirit. . . .

Theory Y A form of participatory management. You really do have a say in how things are run. Sure you do.

Theory Z The art of Japanese management. For those who've forgotten the ABCs of American management.

Asset Redeployment Divest losers; put your money where the growth is. Redeal. Pray for a better hand.

Back to Basics Where you go when your synergistic move into high tech flops.

Chapter 11 A new way to break labor contracts or to sidestep liability suits.

Corporate Culture Get everybody singing the same song and hope they're in key.

Demassing Slimming down at the top. The latest euphemism for firing people.

Intrapreneurship Discovering the entrepreneurs in your own ranks. That may be easier than keeping the bureaucracy at bay once you do.

Leveraged Buyouts Trading the short-term expectations of your stockholders for the short-term expectations of your bankers and bondholders.

Niches Markets your competitors haven't found. Yet.

Out-sourcing When you can't afford to make it yourself.

Pay for Performance It used to be known as piecework.

Restructuring Writing down and leveraging up.

Skunk Camp Officially, a management seminar. Unofficially, it's a boot camp with Tom Peters.

Strategic Alliances Losing market share? Sign on with the competition.

Touchy-Feely Managers The boss is a really nice guy. He's also still the boss.

Wellness Part of the health craze. You'll know it's arrived when they stop serving lemon meringue pie in the company cafeteria.

By Stuart Jackson in New York.

the beginning of the line and the salads were in the back." The consultants' solution: switching the pies and the salads.

In many cases, a fad lasts as long as the boss is interested. "Our CEO got very excited about wellness two years ago," confides a personnel manager for a major transportation company. "We all went through stress-management programs, got rewarded for stopping smoking, and had to read *Fit or Fat*. But last year wasn't profitable, and now all of that has stopped."

And today there is intense competition for the executive's attention. A slew of instant gurus have emerged to spread the differing gospels, each with a proprietary lexicon of his own. Gifford Pinchot talks of intrapreneurship. Allan Kennedy talks of corporate culture. Ichak Adizes, a self-styled "organizational therapist" based in Santa Monica, Calif., advocates consensus-building meetings and brainstorming sessions.

Dirty Hands.   Adizes has the ear of BankAmerica President Samuel H. Armacost. The banker was introduced to the Yugoslavia-born consultant by board director Charles R. Schwab in 1983 via cassette tape. Armacost, says Adizes, listened to his "Adizes Method Audio Series" until 2 A.M. one night and was so impressed that he arranged a retreat with the consulting whiz for top management at the posh Silverado Country Club in Napa County.

The upshot? The Adizes method cost BofA an estimated $3 million. Top managers, figures one BofA officer, spent much of their time trying to build consensus under the method. "Several senior guys were spending half their time in these meetings for months on end," says one insider. Adds a consultant who worked with the bank: "The real fix would have been to fire five levels of management so the top guys could get their hands dirty." A bank spokesman says Adizes helped reorganize the bank into two divisions.

The impact goes well beyond the waste of time and resources. Companies risk losing the support and confidence of their people. "The people below are often laughing at the senior management," says consultant Kilmann. "They are saying, 'How stupid can you be?'"

A little faddishness may be helpful because it makes managers think about new ways to do their jobs better. In earlier decades, fads appear to have had that effect. They tended to be in fashion for years, if not decades, and did less harm. They seemed less goofy, too.

Today, the bewildering array of fads pose far more serious diversions and distractions from the complex task of running a company. Too many modern managers are like compulsive dieters: trying the latest craze for a few days, then moving restlessly on.

◆

The Real World of the Entrepreneur*

Listen to the people who live the great adventure of starting their own companies. The lessons they are learning are useful for any business leader.

Charles Burck
Reporter Association: John Labate

To its fans, small business is the hero of the new economy—engine of growth, generator of jobs, spark of progress. Dissenters call it a swamp of lousy wages, benefits, and working conditions. But few cheerleaders or critics venture out to see firsthand what the men and women who run these companies are doing.

We did, traveling coast to coast over several months, speaking with nearly 100 small business CEOs. (Small means employing fewer than 500 people; most here have under 100.) We looked mainly for entrepreneurs who have found better ways to serve the market. The experience has put us squarely with the cheerleaders.

Most of the 18 people who tell their stories here have succeeded with innovative technologies, astute management, wit, or luck. Some of their companies are struggling. Some will likely be big tomorrow. Whether your business is big or small, you'll learn something useful from each.

You'll discover that traumas and uncertainties of the Nineties haven't sapped the fabled determination of American small business. These are pragmatic people, far more focused on what they can do than on what everyone else thinks can't be done. All the entrepreneurs here have created wealth and jobs; most expect to keep on doing so.

They have succeeded not just because of dinosaur default. The balance of power between large and small companies is shifting. The Davids have what the Goliaths so desperately want—agility and resourcefulness—and can leverage these strengths as never before. Computer and communications technologies are great levelers, giving an entrepreneur as much ability to mobilize resources as a floor full of middle managers.

Entrepreneurial business has a surprising edge over the giants in attracting and developing people. Don't be misled by those invidious comparisons with job quality at big companies—most of the statistics date to the early to mid-Eighties, and a lot has changed. Even workers who *do* feel snug in their corporate hives today face increasing workloads, stagnating pay, and eroding benefits. And when you get into the plants and offices of America's growing small businesses, you discover that working for one is apt to be a lot more rewarding.

You find a clearer sense of purpose—the company knows what it's doing and where it's trying to go. Lines of communication are short and direct, often because the boss walks out onto the factory floor several times a day. The person who dreams of making a company grow needs employees who care, people to whom he can give responsibility. He trains them and finds ways to keep competitors from stealing them.

This is life without a safety net—thrilling and dangerous. Misjudgments are punished ruthlessly. When competition gets tougher, small businesses feel it first. Financing is hard to find, sometimes impossible. Regulatory costs hurt more in companies with less fat, and many cope by hiring fewer people—one reason job growth is so slow. Owners lie awake at night worrying about what irrational government and a tort system run amok will do to them next: A bureaucratic trampling or a lawsuit can break a small company.

Yet the entrepreneurial sector thrives. "In small business there are no small mistakes"—it's a phrase that comes up time and again when you talk to the owners. Most say it proudly. The challenge excites them.

Flexibility Pays

Rick Schmidt and John Ruggeri, ITS

The plant sure doesn't look as if it houses a global competitor. It's a nondescript industrial building off a semirural road near Columbia in southwest Illinois. Inside, the stamping presses and other metal-fabricating machines are old and basic—partners Schmidt and Ruggeri bought them at auctions. The work force of 23 that bends the steel, welds the seams, and twists the screwdrivers does a lot of work by hand that you would see automated in a bigger company. The atmosphere seems informal, the pace of the work purposeful but not breakneck.

Yet ITS (In-Land Technologies Services) builds everything from simple steel cabinets housing electrical and electronic components to complete canning lines. Customers include Olin, Miller Brewing, PepsiCo, and Emerson Electric. A quarter of its $1.8 million sales last year—the company's third full year of business—were exports.

How can this little company possibly do so many things well? "Our specialty is custom manufacturing," says Schmidt. In-Land's market is a myriad of niches: one fully equipped control room here, 50 cabinets there, jobs too specialized for the customer to build himself and too small for any specialist to handle economically. ITS is a master of what's called Level 2 technology, the intermediate stage between basic assembly and full-scale integrated manufacturing, and its very simplicity is its competitive advantage.

Leanness and flexibility are not new-management mantras uttered by corporate goal setters; they're how things get done. For example, there's no wasted square footage at the plant. "That keeps our overhead lower," say Schmidt, "and it also means more productivity—there's a sense of urgency when you're short on floor space." If the company needs more for a larger project, it leases it elsewhere.

Management consists of Schmidt, who sells; Ruggeri, who runs the factory; and Herb Campbell, an electrical engineer who is the project manager. That's it. Worker supervision? "When I put a guy on a job, hopefully I won't have to talk to him again until it's done," says Ruggeri. "Each man will pass the work from one stage to another on his own." Workers have a lot of latitude in setting their hours; the only requirements are that they arrive between 6 AM and 8 AM and complete 40-hour weeks. Some work through lunch to leave early; others choose four ten-hour days.

Operating this way requires conscientious workers: "Every one has to be self-motivated, creative, and have a great interest in his job," says Ruggeri. He and Schmidt hire methodically, starting with recommendations from friends. Each new worker signs on for a trial period, typically 60 days. "The average guy has 11.5 years experience on the floor," says Schmidt. Wages in the non-union shop average $11 an hour, about the same as what union workers in the area get, and In-Land pays half their health insurance.

Schmidt, 46, and Ruggeri, 38, brought to their partnership a combined 24 years of experience at a bigger company that did the same kind of work. Neither had thought about starting a company until their employer began planning to sell the business. "We realized then that we wanted control over our own destiny," says Schmidt, "and we also figured we could do the work better on our own." They financed the business by scraping up all the cash they could and by mortgaging their houses.

They are keenly attentive to bringing in business. "We must be profitable every year, every quarter, every month, every *job*," says Schmidt. "I don't care what we did the month before. If our scheduled work won't cover our overhead this month, I get out and hustle. We cannot get complacent." But they can be choosy and are becoming so as they find more opportunities. Last year's sales were down from 1991's $2.2 million, but margins were up. "We've been more selective," says Schmidt. "We want to grow slowly. Our goal is to stabilize in the $4 million to $4.5 million range in eight years or so. We're not in this to overextend our line of credit by being too aggressive."

The Rewards of Angst

Cherrill Farnsworth TME

Her company is fit, focused, and fast growing, but when Cherrill Farnsworth describes how she manages it, you wonder if you haven't stumbled into one of those giants where people are desperately trying to change the culture. "We talk a lot about not creating institutional security," she says. "The goal, in fact, is institutional insecurity." What does that mean? "The only job security is the security you make for yourself." Farnsworth aims to make sure her managers are equal to the challenge of growth—and so charged up that they don't succumb to the complacency that comes with success.

Farnsworth, 44, founded TME nine years ago to provide magnetic resonance imaging services for hospitals that couldn't spend $1.5 million to $2 million to buy their own MRI machines. Today the company operates 20 imaging centers in nine states, serving 36 hospitals and four universities. TME employs 164 people and is adding about 18 a year. Revenues, $28 million in 1992, are growing far faster—at about a 30% annual rate.

Managing that kind of growth, says Farnsworth, means employees must be prepared for constant change. "We hire high-energy, highly intelligent people who don't look for traditional promotion situations," says Farnsworth. "All of them have to be promotable. I tell new employees it's a whole new company every six months, with a new organization chart, new reporting requirements and interactions between managers." So when TME brought its 18 marketing people to Houston headquarters recently for three days of training, they learned about a lot more than pitching. "We taught them how to understand financial statistics, margins, business plans, and the forecasts we make to investors," she says. They also studied managing time and stress, and setting goals.

"You can't look at last year to guide your future," says Farnsworth. The message is especially important for those who come from larger companies. "I tell those people to become part of the culture fast. If not, they'll be run over in the hall."

The management philosophy clearly reflects Farnsworth's restless, intensely energetic nature. TME is the fifth company she has founded. Her first, in 1974, was a bus line. After her husband was transferred from Indianapolis to Houston in 1970, she noticed that people had no way to get downtown from her northwestern suburb. "Wherever there's angst, there's an opportunity," she says. Despite heavy opposition from major bus operators, she won a franchise. But running a bus line was not nearly as much fun as starting one, and after two years she sold it for a profit. "I realized at that point what value you could get by working hard and creating something new—especially if there's no competition."

Her next three ventures leased equipment—luxury vehicles, office equipment, and oil field equipment. When MRI machines began to appear in the early Eighties, they caught her eye. "The equipment seemed to have so much merit," she says. "But more than that, when I studied the revenue streams, I could see a lot of angst." Hospitals couldn't borrow to buy the machines because Medicare had not yet approved reimbursements from insurers for the service. When she first proposed to hospital administrators that they farm the business out to her, she says, "They found the idea shocking. They giggled and rolled their eyes." When their eyes settled down long enough to scan the figures Farnsworth prepared for them, they signed up.

So did financial backers. Says she: "If I believe in a project, I can be more or less fearless when it comes to standing up in front of a crowd of investors and convincing them that the wisest thing they can do is put their money with me." Among her investors are Fayez Sarofim, Patricof & Co., Toshiba America Medical Systems, and Paine Webber.

She'll put those fund-raising skills to work again. "I'm not a 20-year player," she says. "I've got to develop an exit strategy, probably by going public. I'm very transaction oriented. I love to put something together, build stockholder value, and then raise money again for another venture. Nothing makes me happier."

How to Keep Good Employees

John C. Rennie, Pacer Systems

"Anybody working in my company could walk across the street and get 10% to 15% more," says Jack Rennie. That's been true for most of the 25 years since he founded Pacer Systems in Billerica, Massachusetts, to supply the military with design and engineering services and hardware such as testing equipment and controls. Pacer has nonetheless grown to a company with $28 million in revenues and 340 employees. Now it's about to capitalize a new environmental subsidiary by selling 20% of the unit to a group of outside investors for $6 million. Rennie, 55, clearly knows how to compete in the labor market. How does he do it?

Pacer is big enough to offer a full range of benefits. "We pay around 35 cents for every dollar of salary, including the statutory stuff," says Rennie. The perks range from health and life insurance to allowances for athletic equipment, help for career-related education, and an employee credit union. There's a stock option plan for managers, and Pacer is developing an ESOP. Most levels of employees are in annual bonus pools based on the profitability of both their unit and the company; those at the lowest levels get spot bonuses of up to $400. Employees know where their pay ranks from charts showing their places in bands that mark the upper, median, and lower ranges of people in their categories.

But it takes more still to make a company an attractive place to work, says Rennie. Such as participative decision-making. "It's kind of trendy now," he says, "but it was one of the things we latched onto intuitively right away. It was clear to me that when you're dealing with intelligent employees, whether they're engineers or secretaries, you want their input. And if they understand that they can affect what goes on—the policies we adopt, how we handle a crisis—it keeps them involved and incented."

Participation is the norm at all levels, from the executive committee to factory-floor groups. When Pacer was considering acquiring a nearby manufacturing company a few years ago, for example, groups from engineering, accounting, human resources, and other areas looked the company over before the decision was made. "Our finance group sat down with their management to see if we could merge their procedures into our control system. Then we sent over engineers to assess their products and their people, so we could get their opinions on whether we should go forward. And so on. All this took six to eight months. Finally the groups all made presentations to our executive committee." The committee recommended the acquisition to Pacer's board in a 3-to-1 vote, and, says Rennie, "it has turned out pretty good for us."

You also need to let employees know that you care about their well-being, says Rennie. "Most of the time it's just being good to the people, making them feel they have a safety net if something goes wrong." When an employee had a heart attack several years ago, for example, he was worried that his sick leave would run out, leaving him with lower short-term disability pay. "He'd been a long-term, loyal employee, and we assured him we'd cover him," says Rennie. "And though it wasn't the immediate purpose, word got around. That kind of thing pays off. It has a tremendous impact on people."

To be sure, Rennie is a lot more civic-minded than your average CEO, small business or otherwise. "We can't build up our little fiefdoms behind our walls and just let the rest outside fend for themselves," he says. Rennie spends a large part of his 90-hour workweek on outside activities. He's president of National Small Business United, which with 65,000 members is the most vigorous and grass-roots of the small-business advocacy groups. He's chairman of the Massachusetts Business Alliance for Education, the driving force behind the state's plan to fundamentally overhaul K–12 education (which awaits approval by the state Senate). He's also on the boards of several other nonprofit groups.

Treating your employees well, says Rennie, is as much a matter of necessity as of conscience. "If you try to run your company like a martinet, you're not going to last long in this environment. Business is too complex for you to handle everything yourself—the marketplace dynamics, the troubled financial community, the regulations. Unless you're as thick as two planks, it doesn't take you long to realize you can't do it all on your own."

Keep Management Down-to-Earth

Roberta Cunningham, Cunningham Field Service

With 12 offices in nine states and some 300 mostly full-time employees, 11-year-old Cunningham Field Service is a star at doing legwork for test marketers. Yet as she sits in her cramped, windowless office next to the Dillard's in Tulsa's Promenade Mall, founder Roberta Cunningham says, "I got into this by accident."

How do you accidentally become a major success story? Cunningham, 55, started out searching for a part-time job in Chattanooga, answered a newspaper ad for interviewers in market research, and discovered that she had an aptitude for the work. By the time she moved to Tulsa six years later she had started her own home-based interviewing business and acquired the urge to make it grow. Tulsa was fast becoming the test-market capital of America as researchers realized it had the most demographically representative population of any major city. But Cunningham didn't just grow with the market. She engulfed it, taking over or driving out of business most of the competition within a few years.

Cunningham's competitive edge? Energy, determination, a sharp focus on the customer's needs—and a gift for making potentially dreary work so rewarding that employees naturally strive to be productive and thorough.

The company mostly performs "mall intercepts"—its interviewers prowl the malls where it has offices, buttonholes shoppers, and brings them back to the office for a 20-minute interview about the product being researched. Sometimes a dozen or so interceptees will be assembled into a focus group. (The company also does door-to-door interviewing and store audits.) When Cunningham has enough interviews in hand—typically several hundred—it distills the findings and presents them to the client.

CFS has a reputation for rising to heroic challenges. Three years ago it got an urgent call from a desperate marketer. Three field research firms it had hired in Atlanta were unable to deliver on a project; in three weeks they had accumulated only 2,000 interviews, far short of the goal. CFS flew in 35 interviewers from Florida, Arkansas, and Tulsa. Working 12 hours daily, they pulled together 14,000 five-minute interviews in seven days. On another rush job in Dallas last year, Cunningham blitzed livestock shows, car shows, and other events to pull in 21,000 interviews in nine days.

Pounding mall pavements in search of shoppers can be draining. "Our people get rejected again and again, day after day," says Cunningham. "It can really get to them if they take it personally." But Cunningham gives her charges a lot of nurture. She coaches them about the personas they have to develop: "You've got to go out with a happy face, a strong attitude. Remember that most people love to give their opinions, and you're the only one who's listening." She helps them learn how to handle the rejections. "I've done it all; I know what they're going through. Without them we're nothing, and we tell them that."

Importantly, Cunningham's stamp is on the whole growing organization. "We don't hire administrative-type managers," she says. Indeed, there's no middle management at all. To run one of her offices, she says, "you've got to know how the butterflies in the stomach feel before you go out in the morning." Cunningham's husband, Paul, left his job as general manager of a Kmart store to be comptroller; sons Craig and Paul, who abandoned oil field jobs to join, are partners and general managers. The only other management level includes the 22 women and two men who run the mall offices, all of whom came up from the bottom. "My sons and I know all of our managers and most of the interviewers. We all have the same goals. We just assume everybody will work day and night like us. And most have."

Inventing a Niche

William Devaney and Ivan Lacina, DL Architects

Any architect in the Northeast will agree that you couldn't have picked a worse time to start a business than the late Eighties. But here's DL Architects, which Bill Devaney and Ivan Lacina opened in 1988 with tiny offices in Boston and New York. It employs 15 to 20 architects and a dozen support people, with offices also in London, Budapest, and, as of March, Prague. By year-end, says Devaney, it will be established in Asia as well. Among current projects are office buildings and bank branch offices in Miami, New York, and London, fast-food restaurants in Eastern Europe, and a waste treatment plant in Massachusetts. Last year's fee earnings came to about $4 million, from construction management more than $25 million.

Devaney, 44, and Lacina, 48, owe their success to a decision they reached after much argument in 1989. That decision made them specialists with little competition in the U.S. Devaney, who first opposed the idea, now likes to think DL "is what the whole profession will look like at the end of the Nineties."

DL's speciality is combining *two* specialties to bring in projects fast and on or under budget. In a typical commercial construction project, the owner hires an architect to produce the designs and a construction manager to oversee the work. When problems arise, they negotiate back and forth over solutions. DL's project managers are both architects and construction experts—principals, really, says Devaney, the kind who would be senior partners in a conventional firm. They solve problems—or grasp opportunities—on the spot.

"This business is about very basic stuff," says Lacina. "It always comes down to the bottom line. How can we get the right tile, the right flooring, the right lighting fixtures in Budapest fast and for the best price? What can we find that works with our design? It's total creativity and flexibility. That means the principals have to be involved in every detail; they have to be constantly thinking about how to make it work."

DL has no chains of command, file clerks, or purchasing managers. Principals in the field exchange drawings, requisitions, and purchase orders via notebook computers with architects in DL's home office, a renovated brownstone in New York City's Greenwich Village. The architects there have cost data as well as design tools at their fingertips and can respond quickly.

Whether you think having that much authority is fun depends on your idea of fun. "It takes high-energy people," says Lacina. "They'll work 18 hours a day, if necessary, or over Thanksgiving weekend. And—this is key—they can make decisions. We hire people who say, 'I love to make decisions.'"

DL's international scope reflects the partners' backgrounds and network of contacts. Devaney, a Scot, and Lacina, a Czech, met in the 1970s when both worked in New York for a Japanese architecture firm, Kajima International. They went their separate ways but got back together in 1988 doing design and construction management. After the real estate collapse, the new partners had to make a decision: Would DL specialize in construction management—which many of Devaney's clients were urging—or try to give full service, including architecture? "That's what Ivan wanted to do," says Devaney.

The argument was settled after Lacina brought in a European client that planned to renovate in New York City and didn't want to deal with separate architects and construction firms. "One-stop shopping—that's what they were looking for!" says Lacina.

How big can DL get and still retain its character? "We can only grow by figuring out ways to stay small," says Devaney. "The branch offices are four to five people each, and they can grow to maybe ten. Once bigger than that, you're no longer a small business." What they don't know, but hope to find out, is how many offices they can add around the world and still be small.

Be Prepared for Luck

Betty Handley, Diversified Drilube

It seems the kind of story a scriptwriter would dream up. Indomitable woman, down and out. She starts a business producing a rustproofing compound. The compound turns out to have wondrous lubricating properties. Today, 23 years later, her customers range from racecar builders and machine shops to Fortune 500 companies, and she is about to move operations from a cramped bungalow in Tulsa to a real plant.

Fantastic, but here's Betty Handley, owner of Diversified Drilube Inc. And here today in the bungalow are jet engine pieces and disk-drive ball bearings coated by Handley and six other women with silver-gray Ultralube, ready for shipment—tens of thousands of dollars of precision parts, arrayed neatly in rows of dime-store plastic baskets on Formica tabletops.

Is there a lesson in this story? Only that if you're plucky and lucky, you really can get by with a little help from your friends.

Ultralube is based on tungsten disulfide, a highly slippery substance. What else goes into the formula is Handley's secret, and she says she doesn't have a clue about the chemistry of it. "What I put in when I start is not what's there when I finish," she says. "The only think I know is how to make the product work. A lot is in the art of applying it. But I've had no rejects or failures in 23 years."

According to her test reports, Ultralube forms a long-lived molecular bond with metals, glass, and many other materials. Testimonial letters from customers tell of machine tools that last nine times longer after coating, Army helicopter gears that stand up to destructive testing ten times longer than untreated ones, products that release from their molds with unprecedented ease.

Extraordinary circumstances led Handley to her compound. She and her three young children ended up in Tulsa in 1961 after her husband, a helicopter pilot, was killed in a crash in Guatemala. She was en route from New Orleans, her hometown, to Los Angeles to build a new life when she ran out of money. Determined to make a decent living, she got police training, joined the force, and spent about six years as a cop before quitting and becoming a security guard at a Rockwell plant. She married again, but the marriage ended in 1969, leaving her with an infant son.

Handley wanted to find a job where she could keep an eye on her youngest. Several Rockwell engineers she knew had been developing an anticorrosion compound to be used in NASA rockets, a low-tech substance that anybody could make once the formula was nailed down, and were looking for someone to finish the job and make small batches. Says Handley: "They said to me, 'Somebody is going to do this, so why don't you try?'"

After 256 failures, she says, she produced a formula that met NASA's specifications, and became Rockwell's supplier. She began sending out samples to other companies and soon had a growing list of customers, including Texas Instruments. "One day, in walked one of their metallurgists," she says. "He had run some tests on it, and he said to me, 'I will explain your product to you.' That was the first I knew that this compound would do more than just rustproof." He wrote up a specification sheet that described its properties based on his tests, and suddenly Handley had something really special to sell. On word of mouth alone her customer list grew to include companies such as Halliburton, McDonnell Douglas, and Hewlett-Packard.

Word of mouth doesn't make for fast growth; last year Handley's revenues came to just $500,000. She was too busy with day-to-day operations to think about doing more, she says. Also, though it seems hard to believe, she says she didn't have the guts to be aggressive: "I have always been so intimidated by everybody. I had an inferiority complex." But two years ago she underwent a personal transformation. "When the recession hit, business fell off," she says. "I had the time to look at myself and restructure my outlook on life. I stopped smoking and drinking coffee and took lots of classes—in nutrition, health, business. I discovered that I could go out and talk to people. I decided I can be myself—I can be as eccentric as I want." She also decided to start promoting Ultralube and—for the first time—borrow to expand the business.

She's waiting for final approval of her financing—a joint loan from the city of Tulsa, a bank, and the Small Business Administration totaling $470,000. She'll move into a 10,000-square foot plant and expects within a year to add 20 people to her work force. Based on the work she's been offered but has turned down for lack of capacity, Handley thinks Diversified Drilube's revenues could leap to $3 million in 1993—and more if a foreign licensing agreement she's working on goes through.

Operating Beats Dealing

D. Hunt Ramsbottom Jr., Thompson Lacquer

Personable, disarming, and quick-witted, Hunt Ramsbottom left New England for California in the mid-Eighties to get rich by doing LBOs. He might now be stranded on the beach like a lot of his fellow deal-surfers if he hadn't had a smattering of hands-on business experience and a lot of persistence. "I talk once in a while to graduate students at UCLA and always come back to the will to do it," he says. "I wanted to have my own business so badly that I wasn't going to give up." Today in Los Angeles, he's running one of the country's biggest automotive paint distributors, building it by acquisitions and solid management techniques.

"Everybody and his brother was buying companies," says Ramsbottom, 35, recalling the past decade. "Everybody in the world had access to capital, with no operating experience, no people skills, no nothing—except they knew how to tap into the money. I was a small player in this league, but I got caught up, and it didn't seem so far out.

"When I think back, it was *way* out there. We would be sitting on the back porch of my brother-in-law's house—I was married at the time—just dialing up companies to buy. No broker—I didn't know a soul out here—no backing. Crazy, but just coming from Rhode Island to here, I felt like a kid in a candy store."

Ramsbottom had worked in his family's printing business in Providence but wanted to run his own show. After he arrived in California he began looking for a printing company to buy: "I figured I could flash my experience in the business to get backing." His first LBO was a $10-million-a-year printer. "I barely knew how to read a financial statement or balance sheet, so I didn't realize you couldn't leverage up a highly capital intensive business and grow it 30% a year." Nonetheless, Fleet Financial in Providence financed his venture a continent away. Ramsbottom unloaded the business at a profit after two years, selling it to Sorg Printing of New York (which went bankrupt two years later).

He left the printing company with a new partner, Mort Kline, who had joined the printer as its CFO and did know how to read a financial statement. Together they looked at some 50 companies, finally finding one that seemed just the ticket to easy prosperity.

Ramsbottom and Kline took control of Thompson Lacquer in another LBO in 1989. "It had the right profile for a buyout—good market share in the region it served, no debt, a stable market, continual growth of 10% to 12% a year with what appeared to be moderate effort on the owner's part. We said, 'We don't know this industry, but we're just going to come in here and let management do its thing and add a store a year and keep this growth going.'" They put up 10% of the money. The rest came from Heller Financial and a local investment bank, Wedbush Morgan Securities.

It worked for a year. Then recession hit just as several other trends they had overlooked took hold. Auto insurers began cracking down on padded body shop bills. Accident rates fell—partly, says Ramsbottom, because cars were getting safer and partly because of growing pressures on drunken driving.

Staring at disaster, Ramsbottom and Kline had an insight. "It turned out that this was a $1.5 billion industry nationwide and that we'd bought the leader with $25 million in sales. We said, 'If that's the case, there's gotta be one on every street corner, and this is a consolidation play.' So that's been our game plan for the past two years, merge to survive." With Heller, Wedbush Morgan, and Chemical Venture Partners behind them, they're now on their tenth acquisition. By the end of this year, he says, Thompson will generate revenues at a $60 million annual rate.

"It's been fun," says Ramsbottom. "We've transformed this sleepy little business into a move-ahead vehicle. With the industry flat and everybody cutting prices, same-store sales are going to grow very slowly. We think they'll be back in two to three years. In the meantime we depend on the acquisition program. We have the financing, and our backers like the plan."

The Employee Comes First

David Sun and John Tu, Kingston Technology

This company looks like the paradigmatic growth machine. It designs and sells to users so-called electronic enhancements—mostly components for upgrading computer memories and processors—and from 1987 to 1992 sales increased 368%

compounded annually to $251 million. Last year it headed *Inc.* magazine's list of America's fastest-growing privately held companies. So when Kingston Technology vice president of engineering David Sun, 41, tells you that growth is not his goal, you assume he's being disingenuous. Then you spend some time in Kingston's Fountain Valley, California, headquarters and conclude that he means it. Sun and his partner, President John Tu, 51, both immigrants from Taiwan, have a most unorthodox notion of corporate purpose. Put simply, their goal is just to do the right thing.

Kingston has won what it estimates is 45% of the market for upgrades of major brand-name machines by specializing in speed and service. Its upgrades are typically out in quantity before the manufacturer's own enhancements. It had a memory upgrade for Compaq's new ProLinea a week after the computer's introduction.

The company gives five-year warranties and all the technical support its customers want. The 25 customer-service people work in a huge common space along with sales and marketing people, Sun, and Tu (Dave and John to the staff). Has the customer on the phone come up against a new and baffling problem? Engineers are nearby and ready to give advice. If there's no immediate answer, they will get to the bottom of it. The engineer, in turn, may learn things he can do to improve the next iteration of design.

The underlying reason Kingston performs this well is a culture so closely knit that Sun calls it family-style management. Says he: "We feel obligated to the employee. Don't ever say the customer comes first. Your employee is your most valuable asset, and your vendor is your second most valuable asset. Take care of the first two, and the customer is taken care of."

Kingston is a highly multicultural company, where whites, blacks, Chinese, Vietnamese, and Hispanics work without divisions or barriers among them. Says Sun, pointing to Ron Seide, his marketing manager: "I come from Taiwan, so we are not brothers. The culture is different, family values different, there are a lot of differences. But I think after four years"—turning to Seide: "Four years?" Seide: "Four"—"we can communicate in the same language now. When John or I say, let's do this, he understands why and what we want. When Ron says, let's do this, I understand exactly why."

In family-style management, says Sun, "you start from the basics and let everybody understand what you're thinking. When the employees become more mature in the company they become the management, and they will carry the same philosophy. That's why we never hire managers from outside. There is no common background. You put somebody from outside in a management position, and all these people you've been working with for four or five years say, 'Who should I listen to?'"

What if the company needs somebody with a specific skill or expertise that no insider possesses? "We can always learn, as long as we are patient. We have good people." They will make mistakes as they learn, says Sun. "But as long as the people are good, if you make a mistake you can always recover, because they *care*— they care about the failure. When you cannot recover is when you have the wrong people."

Seide is doing some learning right now—Kingston is sending him to earn an MBA at Pepperdine University. Sun isn't sure how valuable the degree will be. "But there must be something the average person doesn't know that people get going through two years of study. So we're sending Ron to understand the MBA and teach us what it is all about."

Sun says it's hard for him to understand why a company would want growth as its goal. "How can you keep on saying, 'More, more, more'? I don't think that's realistic. There is nothing forever, right?" Kingston's leaders turn the growth question around: How fast can the company expand without compromising its integrity?

"When you are obligated to the employee, you are very conservative," says Sun. "You say, 'Let's make the base work first.'" What's the base? "It's whatever you do today—it's making sure that what we do today is better than what we did yesterday. Revenue is nothing. Let's make sure the base is right. So in a certain way we are very relaxed. We're patient. We say, 'Let's just do it the right way, build ethical, honest products, don't brag about our success. Just do it.'"

◆

The Journey from Novice to Master Manager*

Bob Quinn

As I listened to the man sitting in front of me, my mind ran backwards across the interviews that I had just completed. His subordinates and peers had given him glowing reviews: "Born to manage." "A great role model." "He is one person I am glad to work for."

As I tried to ask him questions that would unlock the mystery behind his success, an interesting story began to unfold. It seemed to involve both a crisis and a transformation.

After graduating from a five-year engineering program in four years, he had taken a job with his current organization. He had made a brilliant start and was promoted four times in eight years. He had the ability to take a complex technical problem and come up with a better answer than anyone else could. Initially he was seen as an innovative, action-oriented person with a bright future.

After his last promotion, however, everything started to change. He went through several very difficult years. For the first time he received serious negative feedback about his performance. His ideas and proposals were regularly rejected, and he was even passed over for a promotion. In reflecting on those days, he said:

> *It was awful. Everything was always changing and nothing ever seemed to happen. The people above me would sit around forever and talk about things. The technically right answer didn't matter. They were always making what I thought were wrong decisions, and when I insisted on doing what was right, they got pissed off and would ignore what I was saying. Everything was suddenly political. They would worry about what everyone was going to think about every issue. How you looked, attending cocktail parties—that stuff to me was unreal and unimportant. . . .*

On several occasions, the engineer's boss commented that he was very impressed with one of the engineer's subordinates. Finding the comment somewhat curious, the engineer finally asked for an explanation. The boss indicated that no matter how early he himself arrived at work, the subordinate's car was always there.

The engineer went to visit the subordinate and relayed that he had noticed that the subordinate always arrived at work before he did. The subordinate nodded his head and explained: "I have four teen-agers who wake up at dawn. The mornings at my house are chaotic. So I come in early. I read for awhile, then I write in my personal journal, read the paper, have some coffee, and then I start work at eight."

When the engineer left his subordinate's office, he was at first furious. But after a couple of minutes, he sat down and started to laugh. He later told me, "That is when I discovered perception." He went on to say that from that moment everything started to change. He became more patient. He began to experiment with participative decision making. His relationships with superiors gradually improved. Eventually he actually came to appreciate the need to think and operate in more complex ways at the higher levels of the organization. . . .

> *In the end, the frustration and pain turned out to be a positive thing because it forced me to consider some alternative perspectives. I eventually learned that there were other realities besides the technical reality.*
>
> *I discovered perception and long time lines. At higher levels what matters is how people see the world, and everyone sees it a little differently. Technical facts are not as available or as important. Things are changing more rapidly at higher levels, you are no longer buffered from the outside world. Things are more complex, and it takes longer to get people on board. I decided I had to be a lot more receptive and a lot more patient. It was an enormous adjustment, but then things started to change. I think I became a heck of a lot better manager.*

◆

Condensation of the 14 Points for Management[*]

W. Edwards Deming

Origin of the 14 points. The 14 points are the basis for transformation of American industry. It will not suffice merely to solve problems, big or little. Adoption and action on the 14 points are a signal that the management intend to stay in business and aim to protect investors and jobs. Such a system formed the basis for lessons for top management in Japan in 1950 and in subsequent years.

The 14 points apply anywhere, to small organizations as well as to large ones, to the service industry as well as to manufacturing. They apply to a division within a company.

1. Create constancy of purpose toward improvement of product and service, with the aim to become competitive and to stay in business, and to provide jobs.
2. Adopt the new philosophy. We are in a new economic age. Western management must awaken to the challenge, must learn their responsibilities, and take on leadership for change.
3. Cease dependence on inspection to achieve quality. Eliminate the need for inspection on a mass basis by building quality into the product in the first place.
4. End the practice of awarding business on the basis of price tag. Instead, minimize total cost. Move toward a single supplier for any one item, on a long-term relationship of loyalty trust.
5. Improve constantly and forever the system of production and service, to improve quality and productivity, and thus constantly decrease costs.
6. Institute training on the job.
7. Institute leadership. The aim of supervision should be to help people and machines and gadgets to do a better job. Supervision of management is in need of overhaul, as well as supervision of production workers.
8. Drive out fear, so that everyone may work effectively for the company.
9. Break down barriers between departments. People in research, design, sales, and production must work as a team, to foresee problems of production and use that may be encountered with the product or service.
10. Eliminate slogans, exhortations, and targets for the workforce asking for zero defects and new levels of productivity. Such exhortations only create

---

[*]Reprinted from *Out of the Crisis* by W. Edwards Deming by permission of MIT and W. Edwards Deming. Published by MIT, Center for Advanced Engineering Study, Cambridge, MA, 02139. Copyright 1986 by W. Edwards Deming.

adversarial relationships, as the bulk of the causes of low quality and low productivity belong to the system and thus lie beyond the power of the workforce.

11. a. Eliminate work standards (quotas) on the factory floor. Substitute leadership.

   b. Eliminate Management by Objective. Eliminate management by numbers, numerical goals. Substitute leadership.

12. a. Remove barriers that rob the hourly worker of his right to pride of workmanship. The responsibility of supervisors must be changes from sheer numbers to quality.

   b. Remove barriers that rob people in management and in engineering of their right to pride of workmanship. This means, *inter alia*, abolishment of the annual or merit rating and of management by objective.

13. Institute a vigorous program of education and self-improvement.

14. Put everybody in the company to work to accomplish the transformation. The transformation is everybody's job.

◆

Maxwell's Warning*

David Halberstam

There had been plenty of warnings. Some experts had pointed out that the sources of oil were not limitless, that consumption was rising faster than production. Some noted that certain of the oil-producing countries were politically unstable and hostile to the United States. The men of the auto industry had never heeded the warnings. They dismissed them as veiled criticisms of the cars they were making.

   In June 1973 a young man named Charley Maxwell flew from New York to Detroit to talk to the top executives of the three main auto companies. A decade later astute observers would mark that particular time, mid-1973, as the last moment of the old order in the industrialized world. It was a time when energy was still remarkably cheap and in steady supply, a time when the great business captains could still make their annual forecasts with some degree of certainty. Detroit was still Detroit in those heady days. It regularly sold eight million cars a year, and in a good year, a boomer's year, the kind loved by everyone in the business from the president of a company to the lowliest dealer, it sold ten or eleven

---

*Excerpted from *The Reckoning*, chapter 1, by David Halberstam. Copyright © 1986 by David Halberstam.

million. More, these were precisely the kind and size of cars Detroit wanted to sell—big heavy cars loaded with expensive options. In those days no one talked about energy conservation except a few scholarly types. The average American car got about thirteen miles per gallon then, a figure far below that expected of cars in most other modern countries. Detroit's cars were large, weighty, and powerful. Comfort and power, rather than economy, seemed important in the marketplace. Americans were a big people, and they liked to drive long distances. If the cars were no longer of quite the quality many of the company engineers and manufacturing men wanted, this was deemed a matter of no great consequence, for they still sold. Anyone who complained about the quality of the cars was a quibbler, more than likely an egghead who subscribed to *Consumer Reports*. After all, a car need last no more than the three years before the owner turned it in for a brand-new model, which would be equally large, or, given the American presumption of rising social status, even larger. As the new car reflected the owner's climb, so the old car now began its own journey down the social scale, ending up an owner or two later in some ghetto inhabited by members of the American underclass. There, patched and repatched, it would consume even greater quantities of gas.

The intelligentsia of America, much given to driving small, fuel-efficient, rather cramped foreign cars, often mocked Detroit for the grossness and gaudiness of its product. To many liberal intellectuals Detroit symbolized all that was excessive in the materialism of American life (just as to many small-town American conservatives, the companies' partner, the United Auto Workers, symbolized everything that was excessive about the post-New Deal liberal society). None of this carping bothered Detroit. It was a given that Americans preferred big cars—and only Detroit made big cars. There was a seldom-spoken corollary to this axiom: Big cars meant big profits, and small cars meant small profits. In early 1973 the fact that Detroit was selling what it wanted to sell was considered proof that Detroit, rather than its critics, truly understood the American customer. The future looked brighter than ever. An ugly war in Southeast Asia which had sapped the nation's strength and resources was finally ending, and Detroit was bullish about the auto economy just ahead. That bullishness seemed to be based on good reason. For if there was one benign economic certainty as far as American industrialists and American consumers were concerned, it was the low price of gas and oil, a price that seemed almost inflation-proof in the postwar era. In 1950 the price of a gallon of gas at the pump had been 27 cents, 20 cents of it for the gas itself and the rest for taxes. Twenty years later, the price of virtually every other basic consumer commodity had approximately doubled, but the price of gas had remained, tantalizingly, almost the same. At the moment that Charley Maxwell set out for Detroit in 1973, a gallon of gas cost 37 cents at the pump, 26 of it for the gas itself. The price seemed a blessing so constant that everyone had come to take it for granted.

That was the premise of the city to which Charley Maxwell was traveling. He was thirty-five years old and had spent all of his adult life in the oil business, mostly with Mobil in the Middle East and Nigeria. He was by nature scholarly, and those long years in the field had added practical experience to his theoretical expertise, a rare combination. In the late sixties, when Mobil had started replacing its American overseas employees with foreign nationals, Maxwell had been sent back to the United States. It seemed to him that his career opportunities in the oil industry had been drastically reduced, and, looking for a way to exploit his knowledge, he had become an oil analyst for a Wall Street firm called Cyrus Lawrence.

Every field has its awesome experts, but there was something about Charley Maxwell's professional authority that was almost chilling. Part of it was his appearance, the hair plastered down over his forehead and parted in the middle, the old-fashioned, almost prim wire-rimmed glasses, the slightly stooped posture, the preoccupied manner; he looked like the sort of person who as a sixth-grader had been doted upon by his teachers because he had always gotten the right answer to every question, who had been good at what his teachers wanted rather than at what mattered to his peers. . . .

In those June days of 1973, however, he was not yet well known outside his field, and his field was not yet a hot one. Americans believed that their own domestic supplies of oil were plentiful and that there were virtually limitless sources in the Persian Gulf. What Charley Maxwell intended to tell the top-level auto executives he believed he would meet in Detroit was what he had been telling his superiors for some time now—that there would soon be dramatic, indeed revolutionary, changes in the price of energy. The assumption of the past, that energy would remain cheap because it had always been cheap and its price would increase only at small, acceptable, noninflationary increments, had to be discarded. America's own resources were rapidly proving inadequate, and the nation would thus become far more dependent upon the oil-producing nations of the Middle East. But the American oil companies would no longer be able to control the prices set for Arab oil, as they had so easily in the past. The Arabs would set the prices themselves. Since oil was in those days significantly underpriced in terms of its true market value, the loss of that control would have serious consequences for American heavy industry in general and Detroit in particular.

Maxwell had seen all this coming for a number of years. As early as 1970 he had started using the phrase "energy crisis"—apparently his coinage. He used it to refer to a crucial, ominous shift in the supply and demand of oil. He calculated that worldwide oil consumption was climbing 5 to 6 percent annually, and there was no reason to believe the surge would abate. If anything, it was likely to accelerate. New nations, recently graduated from their colonial past, were fast becoming both industrialized and urbanized and demanding far greater amounts of energy. Throughout the underdeveloped world, people were leaving their tribal huts and moving into cities, and, as they did, they took new jobs in factories which required energy, they lived in apartments which required energy, and to get to work they used transportation which also required energy. It was a revolution taking place, a revolution of people who were changing their way of life and of nations that were expanding and modernizing their economies. The world, Maxwell concluded, had changed dramatically and was going to continue to change as more and more nations moved toward industrial economies. Ten and sometimes fifteen additional countries were leaving the preindustrial age each year and coming into the mechanical age. But there had not as yet been any reflection of this trend in the price of the ingredient most precious to the modern industrialized state, oil. There was going to be one terrible moment, Maxwell was sure, when the price would simply shoot up, out of anyone's control, the oil seeking its true market value. . . .

Maxwell knew that he was not alone in his pessimism, that a number of other energy experts, using much the same research, had come to similar conclusions. But most of these experts worked for the large oil companies, where the darker view had not yet been accepted. Maxwell's own superiors at the Wall Street investment firm of Cyrus Lawrence, however, had been greatly impressed by his estimates and the dispassionate way in which he presented his evidence. Both as a courtesy and also out of their own self-interest, for it would not hurt to lend out so brilliant a man with such original and important perceptions, they decided to send him to Detroit. There, the Cyrus Lawrence people proposed, he would talk to executives at the highest level, who surely would be more than anxious to hear these findings that had such fateful implications for their companies.

Maxwell himself was not so sure. He knew Detroit and he knew it well. He had grown up there, his stepfather had been employed at a middle level by Ford, he himself had even gone to Cranbrook, the city's elite prep school, where many of his classmates were sons of auto titans. Maxwell knew how stratified the city was, how isolated and insular. It was, he believed, a place of bedrock beliefs, a place where new truths did not seep easily from the bottom to the top. In Detroit, truth moved from the top to the bottom.

Maxwell had been promised meetings with the high auto executives, people who operated at the ultimate level of power. He was dubious about that. He might be well known in the world of oil, but he was young, and Detroit did not readily listen to junior people. Detroit believed in hierarchy and seniority rather than in individual brilliance. One advanced in Detroit not necessarily by being brilliant— brilliance meant that someone might be *different* and implied a threat—but by accommodating oneself with attitudes of those above one. Maxwell, because of his age and the nature of his message, would almost surely be looked upon as impertinent. These men would have their own sources of information, among them the men who headed the great oil companies, the men still resistant to the pessimistic vision of Maxwell and his kind. Powerful, successful, and conventional, typical of the corporate class, they believed that tomorrow would be like today because it had always been like today and because they wanted it to be like today. In their view, if the price of oil went up, it would go up slowly over many decades. They had controlled the oil world—and thus the price of energy—in the past. They would control that world and the price of energy in the future. So Charley Maxwell had been skeptical from the start that he would get the very top people as promised. If his supporters thought so, he knew better, and he had automatically translated his prospects downward. He would be lucky, he decided, to meet people at the 65 percent level of power. That, he soon learned, was too sanguine an expectation.

He did not do badly at the start. He went first to Chrysler, where Tom Killefer, the senior financial officer, had assembled a group of upper-middle-level executives. They listened quietly as Maxwell made his solemn little speech, saying in effect that all their estimates about what kind of cars Americans could and would drive were about to fly out the window. Killefer himself had been pleasant; he was a Rhodes scholar, different from the average Detroit executive, less narrow, in better touch with the outside world. When Maxwell finished, Killefer thanked him and said, "Well, what you say is very, very impressive, very impressive indeed, and of course if it's true, then we're going to have to give it a hard, hard look." There were questions, and bright young men in the group, perhaps less complacent because Chrysler was already a shaky company, were clearly interested. But even as he was finishing his presentation, Maxwell had a sense that it was all to no end, that these men would leave the meeting and shake their heads and say how interesting it had been, what a bright fellow Maxwell was, maybe a bit rash, something of an alarmist, didn't they think, but bright and interesting nonetheless. Worth thinking about. That would be it, Maxwell thought, possibly a letter or two thanking him, but no real penetration of the process.

Chrysler, unfortunately, turned out to be by far the best of the three meetings. He had been taken seriously there, and Killefer was, whatever else, a representative of top management. Ford was a good deal worse. At Ford he met two people at the lower planning level. They were junior executives, making, he suspected, about $25,000 a year, which was a very small salary in executive Detroit. They were, he knew instantly, completely without power, and they had been sent there because a steadily descending series of Ford executives had told their immediate subordinates that someone had to go and cover the meeting, until finally, far down the line, there had been two men so unimportant that they had no subordinates to send. These two were there precisely because they were powerless. Maxwell felt a bit odd, standing in that room saying that Detroit was going to have to change its whole line of cars and that an entire era had ended, and saying this to men who could not change the design of an ashtray. Somehow that thought made his presentation more impassioned than ever.

General Motors, of course, was the worst. There were no high-level meetings scheduled. In fact, there were no meetings scheduled at all. Someone very junior asked Maxwell if he would like to drive out to the testing grounds and meet with some GM people there. He did, encountering no one in any position of responsibility, though for his troubles he was able to see some of GM's new models. They looked rather large to him, cars that would surely use a great deal of gas.

Such was Charley Maxwell's trip to Detroit. He had not even gotten across the moat. Detroit was Detroit, and more than most business centers it was a city that listened only to its own voice. But he left town worried about what he was sure was going to happen to a vital American industry. Maxwell did not think that the coming change in price would necessarily be so great that even a Detroit that was prepared for change would be severely damaged. Rather, he was worried because Detroit was unprepared—because no one in America seemed willing to practice even the most nominal kind of conservation, which suggested that the country was physically unready for major increases. A big jump in price might trigger a panic, which would compound the difficulty of entering a new economic order. Those who were set up for change could deal with it, he suspected; those who were not were likely to come apart. Detroit, he feared, was going to have to learn its new truths the hard way.

A few months later, on October 6, 1973, on the eve of Yom Kippur, the holiest of Jewish holy days, Egypt tried a military strike on Israel. Eventually Israel struck back and once again, for the third time since World War II, defeated the Egyptians. To the Arab world this humiliation was one more demonstration of its powerlessness. The Arabs blamed Israel's existence on its American sponsorship. Thwarted both militarily and politically, the Arabs now turned at last to their real strength, their economic leverage. They began an oil embargo on the West. Before it was over, the price of oil had rocketed from $3 a barrel to $12 a barrel. The United States, long accustomed to cheap energy, was completely unprepared to respond to the Arab move. Unwilling to increase the taxes on gasoline and oil and thus at least partially stabilize the price of energy, it had in effect permitted the Arabs to place a tax not just on the American oil consumer but on the entire country. The effects on the American economy at every level were dramatic. The era of the cheap energy upon which so much of America's dynamism and its broad middle-class prosperity was premised was beginning to end. A new era with profound implications for the industrial core of America, the great Middle Atlantic and Midwestern foundry of the nation, had arrived. Occasionally in later years Charley Maxwell would run into Tom Killefer, who by then had left Chrysler to become the chairman of the United States Trust Company, and when he did, Killefer would shake his head and say, "You—you're the one man I hate to see. God, I still remember that warning. . . ."

Head to Head[*]

Lester Thurow

Consider the conventional "do-no-harm" rule for deciding when medical treatment should be stopped. If every treatment is carried to the point where its negative side effects become worse than the original effects of the disease, doctors prescribe treatments far beyond the rational economic stopping rule (marginal costs should equal marginal benefits) and run up huge costs in situations where few benefits are to be expected—more than one third of all U.S. medical costs are incurred in the last year of life.

In the past employing every available procedure to the point where it actively began to harm the patient did not cost very much, since there weren't very many expensive technologies to be employed in most illnesses. But when such technologies arise and give doctors and their patients a lot of expensive technological options with submarginal payoffs, the old stopping rule can become a very expensive decision rule that can no longer be afforded. Yet thus far Americans have not been able to change their standard operating procedures in medicine.

What is true in medicine is also true in business. In business the equivalent of "do no harm" is the proposition that the boss should "know everything." In principle he should be knowledgeable enough to make every decision. As long as the technology did not exist to implement that decision rule, it wasn't very harmful. But when a technology (the computer) came along that makes it possible to attempt to know everything, that rule became a very expensive stopping rule.

Role models for what one "ought to do" are important in determining behavior in every walk of life. Take the proposition that the best boss is the boss that has the most knowledge and can intelligently make the most decisions per day. In the late 1960s and early 1970s, the business press set up bosses such as Harold Geneen of ITT as role models for others to emulate. He was, in the words of the business press of the day, the "world's greatest business manager." He had a "managerial system of tight control" with "elements of a spy system." He "worked extraordinarily long hours and absorbed thousands of details about ITT's business." "Tales of Geneen's incredible stamina at these marathon affairs (affairs where he demonstrated that he knew more about their numbers than middle level bosses knew about their numbers) and of his brutality to any manager who dared to dissemble before him are retold today like epic poems." "Everything the company does is totally number orientated." "His unique form of management allows him

---

[*]Reprinted from: *Head to Head: The Coming Economic Battle Among Japan, Europe, and America* by Lester Thurow. Copyright © 1992 by Lester Thurow. Reprinted by permission of William Morrow Co., Inc. For footnotes to quoted material, please see the original.

finger tip control over his vast empire." Was he "an ogre in a business suit? The greatest corporate manager of his time? An unimaginative numbers grubber? A great leader of Men?"

Geneen, and managers like him, supposedly knew more about middle-level management's job than the middle-level managers themselves knew. He was famous for making thousands of rapid decisions. He was the prototypical boss who bossed. He was the macho manager whom lesser managers attempted to emulate. In lists of America's toughest bosses, he was regularly at the head of the list. He knew the numbers. Management by the numbers became the American way—it was how management was supposed to manage.

Such beliefs about the ideal boss may have long existed, but most managers could not implement them without the technological office revolution of the 1970s and the 1980s. Previously, firms had to decentralize and bosses had to delegate decisions to those on the scene since there was no feasible way for them to know what they had to know to make good decisions. But with the onset of the new information technologies, ordinary bosses could implement what extraordinary bosses had always preached. Bosses could do a lot more bossing, just as doctors could do a lot more doctoring.

To do so, however, one had to build up enormous information bureaucracies. Information could be gotten, but only at the cost of adding a lot of white-collar workers to the system. The problem is graphically seen in accounting. During the period when accounting was being computerized, from 1978 to 1985, the number of accountants on American payrolls rose 30 percent from 1 million to 1.3 million, while output was rising only 16 percent. Accounting productivity fell 14 percent, despite the computerization of accounting.

Computers made accounting faster, but that speed was used not to reduce the employment of accountants but to increase the frequency and types of accounting. Old accounts that in the past had been calculated every three months were now ordered up every day. Whole systems of new accounts (management-information systems, cost accounting, inventory control, financial accounting, etc.) that had been previously impossible to calculate were put on-line. Yet there was no evidence that all of these new accounts improved decision making enough to justify their cost. In fact, given the huge increases in white-collar employment required to generate all of this new information, there was evidence to the contrary. But power and style called for ordering up all of those new accounts, and so it was done.

To the boss, more information seems like a free good. He orders it from subordinates, and the cost of acquiring it appears on the budgets of his subordinates. Subordinates in turn can neither refuse to provide the requested information nor know if the information is valuable enough to justify the costs of its acquisition. To the subordinate, costs are irrelevant. They are not even calculated. One does what one's boss orders. Essentially, both bosses and subordinates are imprisoned in standard operating procedures that create an institutional set of blinders. While efficient firms that do not operate in this way will eventually drive inefficient firms out of business, nothing guarantees that the efficient firms won't all be Japanese, while the inefficient ones will all be American.

Beliefs about the *right* management styles change very slowly and only under great duress. To do away with those white-collar workers and the information system they support is to delegate one's decision-making power to those on the spot who have the necessary information without the benefits of an information system. To do so is to become a boss who does less bossing. But this is contrary to one's conception of one's own role. No American becomes a boss to do less bossing.

Participatory management is a case in point. It may be an efficient way to cut white-collar overheads and raise productivity, but it requires a reduction in the boss's power. In experiment after experiment in participatory management, the problems have not been found among workers but among middle-level managers who feel threatened. They block experiments with new, more efficient forms of production because they fear the loss of their job or their authority. The personal dangers in the American system are not imaginary. They are real. Personal rationality intervenes to prevent system rationality from being achieved.

As stated in a *Fortune* magazine article on "The Revolt Against Working Smarter," ". . . the participative process doesn't always fit easily with traditional management methods and measurements. . . . Fearing a loss of power, many middle managers torpedoed early participative programs. . . . It is tempting for some of our managers to say, 'It's our turn; we've got the club.'. . . The higher up the corporate ladder, the tougher seems the shift to participative mode. . . . Information is power and it remains a clear badge of rank with managers. . . . The skills required for would-be participative managers—communicating, motivating, championing ideas—are sandy intrusions in the gearbox of many traditional executives."

Quality*

John Galsworthy [1867–1933]

I knew him from the days of my extreme youth because he made my father's boots; inhabiting with his elderly brother two little shops let into one, in a small by-street—now no more, but then most fashionably placed in the West End.

That tenement had a certain quiet distinction; there was no sign upon its face that he made for any of the Royal Family—merely his own German name of Gessler Brothers; and in the window a few pair of boots. I remember that it always troubled me to account for those unvarying boots in the window, for he made only what was ordered, reaching nothing down, and it seemed so inconceivable that what he made could ever have failed to fit. Had he bought them to put there? That, too, seemed inconceivable. He would never have tolerated in his house leather on which he had not worked himself. Besides, they were too beautiful— the pair of pumps, so inexpressibly slim, the patent leathers with cloth tops, making water come into one's mouth, the tall brown riding boots with marvelous sooty glow, as if, though new, they had been worn a hundred years. Those pairs could only have been made by one who saw before him the Soul of Boot—so truly were they prototypes incarnating the very spirit of all foot-gear. These thoughts, of course, came to me later, though even when I was promoted to him, at the age of perhaps fourteen, some inkling haunted me of the dignity of himself and brother. For to make boots—such boots as he made—seemed to me then, and still seems to me, mysterious and wonderful.

I remember well my shy remark, one day, while stretching out to him my youthful foot:

"Isn't it awfully hard to do, Mr. Gessler?"

And his answer, given with a sudden smile from out of the sardonic redness of his beard: "Id is an Ardt!"

Himself, he was a little as if made from leather, with his yellow crinkly face, and crinkly reddish hair and beard, and neat folds slanting down his cheeks to the corner of his mouth, and his guttural and one-toned voice; for leather is a sardonic substance, and stiff and slow of purpose. And that was the character of his face, save that his eyes, which were gray-blue, had in them the simple gravity of one secretly possessed by the Ideal. His elder brother was so very like him—though watery, paler in every way, with a great industry—that sometimes in early days I was not quite sure of him until the interview was over. Then I knew that it was he, if the words, "I will ask my brudder," had not been spoken; and, that, if they had, it was his elder brother.

When one grew old and wild and ran up bills, one somehow never ran them up with Gessler Brothers. It would not have seemed becoming to go in there and stretch out one's foot to that blue iron-spectacled glance, owing him for more than—say—two pairs, just the comfortable reassurance that one was still his client.

For it was not possible to go to him very often—his boots lasted terribly, having something beyond the temporary—some, as it were, essence of boot stitched into them.

One went in, not as into most shops, in the mood of: "Please serve me, and let me go!" but restfully, as one enters a church; and, sitting on the single wooden chair, waited—for there was never anybody there. Soon, over the top edge of that sort of well—rather dark, and smelling soothingly of leather—which formed the shop, there would be seen his face, or that of his elder brother, peering down. A guttural sound, and tip-tap of bast slippers beating the narrow wooden stairs, and he would stand before one without coat, a little bent, in leather apron, with sleeves turned back, blinking—as if awakened from some dream of boots, or like an owl surprised in daylight and annoyed at this interruption.

And I would say: "How do you do, Mr. Gessler? Could you make me a pair of Russia leather boots?"

Without a word he would leave me, retiring whence he came, or into the other portion of the shop, and I could continue to rest in the wooden chair, inhaling the incense of his trade. Soon he would come back, holding in his thin, veined hand a piece of gold-brown leather. With eyes fixed on it, he would remark: "What a beautiful biece!" When I, too, had admired it, he would speak again. "When do you wand them?" And I would answer: "Oh! As soon as you conveniently can." And he would say: "To-morrow fordnighd?" Or if he were his elder brother: "I will ask my brudder!"

Then I would murmur: "Thank you! Good-morning, Mr. Gessler." "Goot-morning!" he would reply, still looking at the leather in his hand. And as I moved to the door, I would hear the tip-tap of his bast slippers restoring him, up the stairs, to his dream of boots. But if it were some new kind of foot-gear that he had not yet made me, then indeed he would observe ceremony—divesting me of my boot and holding it long in his hand, looking at it with eyes at once critical and loving, as if recalling the glow with which he had created it, and rebuking the way in which one had disorganized this masterpiece. Then, placing my foot on a piece of paper, he would two or three times tickle the outer edges with a pencil and pass his nervous fingers over my toes, feeling himself into the heart of my requirements.

I cannot forget that day on which I had occasion to say to him: "Mr. Gessler, that last pair of town walking-boots creaked, you know."

He looked at me for a time without replying, as if expecting me to withdraw or qualify the statement, then said:

"Id shouldn'd 'ave greaked."

"It did, I'm afraid."

"You goddem wed before dey found demselves?"

"I don't think so."

At that he lowered his eyes, as if hunting for memory of those boots, and I felt sorry I had mentioned this grave thing.

"Zend dem back!" he said. "I will look at dem."

A feeling of compassion for my creaking boots surged up in me, so well could I imagine the sorrowful long curiosity of regard which he would bend on them.

"Zome boods," he said slowly, "are bad from birdt. I can do noding wid dem, I dake them off your bill."

Once (once only) I went absent-mindedly into his shop in a pair of boots bought in a emergency at some large firm's. He took my order without showing me any leather, and I could feel his eyes penetrating the inferior integument of my foot. At last he said:

"Dose are nod by boods."

The tone was not one of anger, nor of sorrow, not even of contempt, but there was in it something quiet that froze the blood. He put his hand down and pressed a finger on the place where the left boot, endeavoring to be fashionable, was not quite comfortable.

"Id 'urds you dere," he said. "Dose big virms 'ave no self-respect. Drash!' And then, as if something had given way within him, he spoke long and bitterly. It was the only time I ever heard him discuss the conditions and hardships of his trade.

"Dey get id all," he said, "dey get id by adverdisement, nod by work. Dey dake it away from us, who lofe our boods. Id gomes to this—bresently I haf no work. Every year id gets less—you will see." And looking at his lined face I saw things I had never noticed before, bitter things and bitter struggle—and what a lot of gray hairs there seemed suddenly in his red beard!

As best I could, I explained the circumstances of the purchase of those ill-omened boots. But his face and voice made so deep impression that during the next few minutes I ordered many pairs. Nemesis fell! They lasted more terribly than ever. And I was not able conscientiously to go to him for nearly two years.

When at last I went I was surprised to find that outside one of the two little windows of his shop another name was painted, also that of a bootmaker—making, of course, for the Royal Family. The old familiar boots, no longer in dignified isolation, were huddled in the single window. Inside, the now contracted well of the one little shop was more scented and darker than ever. And it was longer than usual, too, before a face peered down, and the tip-tap of the bast slippers began. At last he stood before me, and, gazing through those rusty iron spectacles, said:

"Mr. _____, isn'd it?"

"Ah! Mr. Gessler," I stammered, "but your boots are really *too* good, you know! See, these are quite decent still!" And I stretched out to him my foot. He looked at it.

"Yes," he said, "beople do nod wand good boods, id seems."

To get away from his reproachful eyes and voice I hastily remarked: "What have you done to your shop?"

He answered quietly: "Id was too exbensif. Do you wand some boods?"

I ordered three pairs, though I had only wanted two, and quickly left. I had, I do not know quite what feeling of being part, in his mind, of a conspiracy against him; or not perhaps so much against him as against his idea of boot. One does not, I suppose, care to feel like that; for it was again many months before my next visit to his shop, paid, I remember, with the feeling: "Oh! well, I can't leave the old boy—so here goes! Perhaps it'll be his elder brother!"

For his elder brother, I knew, had not character enough to reproach me, even dumbly.

And, to my relief, in the shop there did appear to be his elder brother, handling a piece of leather.

"Well, Mr. Gessler," I said, "how are you?"

"I am breddy well," he said slowly; "but my elder brudder is dead."

And I saw that it was indeed himself—but how aged and wan! And never before had I heard him mention his brother. Much shocked, I murmured: "Oh! I am sorry!"

"Yes," he answered, "he was a good man, he made a good bood; but he is dead." And he touched the top of his head, where the hair had suddenly gone as thin as it had been on that of his poor brother, to indicate, I suppose, the cause of death. "He could nod ged over losing de oder shop. Do you wand any boods?" And he held up the leather in his hand: "Id's a beaudiful biece."

I ordered several pairs. It was very long before they came—but they were better than ever. One simply could not wear them out. And soon after that I went abroad.

It was over a year before I was again in London. And the first shop I went to was my old friend's. I had left a man of sixty, I came back to one of seventy-five, pinched and worn and tremulous, who genuinely, this time, did not at first know me.

"Oh! Mr. Gessler," I said, sick at heart; "how splendid your boots are! See, I've been wearing this pair nearly all the time I've been abroad; and they're not half worn out, are they?"

He looked long at my boots—a pair of Russia leather, and his face seemed to regain steadiness. Putting his hand on my instep, he said:

"Do dey vid you here? I 'ad drouble wid dat bair, I remember."

I assured him that they had fitted beautifully.

"Do you wand any boods?" he said. "I can make dem quickly; id is a slack dime."

I answered: "Please, please! I want boots all round—every kind!"

"I will make a vresh model. Your food must be bigger." And with utter slowness, he traced round my foot, and felt my toes, only once looking up to say:

"Did I dell you my brudder was dead?"

To watch him was painful, so feeble had he grown; I was glad to get away. I had given those boots up, when one evening they came. Opening the parcel, I set the four pairs in a row. Then one by one I tried them on. There was no doubt about it. In shape and fit, in finish and quality of leather, they were the best he had ever made me. And in the mouth of one of the Town walking-boots I found his bill. The amount was the same as usual, but it gave me quite a shock. He had never before sent it in till quarter day. I flew downstairs, and wrote a cheque, and posted it at once with my own hand.

A week later, passing the little street, I thought I would go in and tell him how splendidly the new boots fitted. But when I came to where his shop had been, his name was gone. Still there, in the window, were the slim pumps, the patent leathers with cloth tops, the sooty riding boots.

I went in, very much disturbed. In the two little shops—again made into one—was a young man with an English face.

"Mr. Gessler in?" I said.

He gave me a strange, ingratiating look.

"No, sir," he said, "no. But we can attend to anything with pleasure. We've taken the shop over. You've seen our name, no doubt, next door. We make for some very good people."

"Yes, yes," I said; "but Mr. Gessler?"

"Oh!" he answered; "dead."

"Dead! But I only received these boots from him last Wednesday week."

"Ah!" he said; "a shockin' go. Poor old man starved 'imself."

"Good God!"

"Slow starvation, the doctor called it! You see he went to work in such a way! Would keep the shop on; wouldn't have a soul touch his boots except himself. When he got an order, it took him such a time. People won't wait. He lost everybody. And there he'd sit, goin' on and on—I will say that for him—not a man in London made a better boot! But look at the competition! He never advertised! Would 'ave the best leather, too, and do it all 'imself. Well, there it is. What could you expect with his ideas?"

"But starvation—!"

"That may be a bit flowery, as the sayin' is—but I know myself he was sittin' over his boots day and night, to the very last. You see I used to watch him. Never gave 'imself time to eat; never had a penny in the house. All went in rent and leather. How he lived so long I don't know. He regular let his fire go out. He was a character. But he made good boots."

"Yes," I said, "he made good boots."

And I turned and went out quickly, for I did not want that youth to know that I could hardly see.

◆

Ten Myths of Managing Managers[*]

Clinton O. Longenecker and Dennis A. Gioia

Myth 1   Managers are self-starting, self-directing, and autonomous, or they would not be managers.

- **The myth revisited**   Good managers *are* self-managing, often to an extraordinary degree. They want, appreciate, and accept autonomy, but they also want input, attention, and guidance that only their superiors can provide.

Myth 2   Managers worth their salt know what their jobs really entail.

- **The myth recast**   Even savvy managers need an unambiguous picture of what they are responsible for in their jobs and, just as important, what they are not responsible for. Without leadership from the boss, the subordinate manager has less clarity of purpose and is less effective.

Myth 3   Good managers know how well they are performing.

---

[*]Reprinted from *Sloan Management Review*, Vol. 33, No. 1, pp 81–90. Copyright © 1991.

- **The myth reconsidered**   Managers want and need regular feedback on their performance. Managers performing ambiguous work want unambiguous feedback, and they want it on a regular basis.

Myth 4   Good managers seek out the information they need.

- **The myth refurbished**   Good managers *are* proactive information-seekers. Yet they often do not have access to the information that their bosses have. Their proactiveness is thus wasted on unnecessary work that their superiors could eliminate with better information flow.

Myth 5   Goals are adequate guides for effective managerial action.

- **The myth reframed**   Goals must be carefully established, provide for mutual input, and include some discussion of means and process. To use goal setting in a cavalier manner breeds poor communication, Monday-morning quarterbacking, and, ultimately, a stymied manager.

Myth 6   Competition among managers is good for the soul and for business.

- **The myth reconstructed**   Competition is effective *among* businesses, but not necessarily *within* a business. Collaboration and cooperation within the organization are demonstrably better strategies for improving competitiveness in the business arena. Upper-level managers must be careful to manage the resources that their subordinates need and to take proactive steps to reduce internal conflict.

Myth 7   Meetings and documentation are a central part of a manager's job.

- **The myth revamped**   Meetings and paperwork should be designed to facilitate work and not to reduce time for performance-enhancing activities. A key question should be: Does the meeting or the paperwork increase the manager's ability to do the job?

Myth 8   Management style cannot be changed so there is no point in discussing it with managers.

- **The myth reformulated**   Managerial style should not be a taboo subject. Managers realize that their management styles might include ineffective traits and types of behavior. Thus they want systematic discussion of their styles with their superiors *before* a problem or crisis.

Myth 9   Formal training and development programs can best accomplish management development.

- **The myth revitalized**   Managers want their superiors to take a more active role in their development. They need formal development, but it is the informal attention of their immediate superior that makes the real difference.

Myth 10   The formal performance appraisal adequately monitors and guides managerial performance.

- **The myth reassessed** If evaluation is to be effective, the appraisal process must be ongoing and must have structure and substance. To give less than professional appraisals to professional managers creates the impression that performance and its evaluation are not well linked. It also fosters the impression that the evaluation process is not necessarily accurate and is fraught with politics.

Chapter 2

Planning

Many words we use to discuss work and management have moralistic connotations. For example, in our society, to describe a person as not motivated to work often implies a basic character or moral flaw. Consequently, many of us feel guilty when we shirk or even think of shirking.

In our view, the idea of planning has similar moral connotations. We are taught very early how important it is that we plan our time. A little later in life we are urged to plan our careers. In college, we are admonished—often as freshmen—to make a plan of what courses we will take. In fact, if we showed evidence of not taking planning seriously, we may have been screened out of certain colleges because we appeared to lack direction or did not seem to know what we wanted to do. In the workplace we are taught to plan ahead, whether that be for the day, the week, the year, or longer. To be criticized as failing to plan is a telling criticism.

This stress on planning has spawned many techniques to help motivate us to plan and to plan effectively. Clearly these efforts have been of great benefit to many people. Given limited time and resources and many competing demands, planning helps individuals to focus on what they judge to be important and to know what things to say no to. Moreover, planning can increase the likelihood that needed resources will be available when needed. (The advantages that Japanese manufacturers obtain from their "just-in-time" system, where parts arrive at exactly the time they are needed, are a prime example of the benefits of systematic and careful planning.) There is no doubt that planning deserves much of the homage we pay it.

On the other hand, like most virtues, piety can replace substance. Mechanistic rituals (filling out forms; sorting tasks into piles by priority; holding daily, weekly, or annual planning meetings) demonstrate to oneself and to others that planning has been done. With this mind set we often think that once the plan has been created and agreed to, planning has been done. When approached in this way, planning is often suboptimal. For one thing, in a rapidly changing world we recognize that what we assume today may be very different tomorrow. Consequently, it is difficult to motivate ourselves to plan—"What's the use?" we ask ourselves. Moreover, the plan sometimes takes on a life of its own. Having forced ourselves to do all the work of developing a detailed plan, people often resist changing it. Later, when we see how far off our previous plan was, we find it difficult to motivate ourselves to plan again. Our mistake has been to substitute the thought or the idea for the action by equating the development of a plan with planning.

Because plans developed with this mind set have often yielded disappointing results, planning has gotten a bad name. (See the first selection in this chapter—"The Creation.") In fact, C. Northcote Parkinson, a most astute observer of organizations, has concluded that "perfection of planning is a symptom of decay."[1] Focusing on the planning of buildings, Parkinson found that perfection of planned layout by organizations "is achieved only by institutions on the point of collapse."[2] Why should this be so? Parkinson explained that an organization engaged in discovery and progress has no time to plan its corporate headquarters. More recently, another astute observer, Karl Weick, wrote that "plans have been overrated as a crucial component for accomplishment of effective actions."[3]

Weick, however, argued that plans are still important, but for reasons other than what people normally think. He suggested, for instance, that plans function as advertisements that can attract potential investors. In this sense, plans help people who read them (that is, managers, customers, or shareholders) to see ways that their needs can be met. Moreover, plans can serve as symbols that signal new directions to members or outsiders. Plans also serve as screens to evaluate the strength of commitments of people. In this sense, Weick views them as games—if people in the system want something badly enough they demonstrate this by embedding their energies in a plan. Finally, Weick notes that plans are excuses for interaction; creating plans requires that actors from various parts of the system (often those who would need to work together to implement the plan) talk with each other. This interaction helps people get to know each other and learn from each other. As a result, the organization becomes better prepared to implement the plan as well as respond to other problems. In Weick's words, "Plans are a pretext under which several valuable activities take place in organizations."[4]

Weick's ideas lead directly to the view of planning we advanced in this chapter. Planning is not an end in itself; rather, it is a process that facilitates making things happen in an organization. For example, planning influences the knowledge and motivation people have about the organization and a particular project or task. Moreover, the planning process is intricately related to other processes within the organization. For example, the communication process in an organization influences how much and what kind of information people have available for deciding what is the right thing to do. (Many of these ideas are effectively illustrated in David Hurst's paper in this chapter entitled "Why Strategic Management Is Bankrupt.")

When we view planning as a process perspective, we can appreciate why the ritualistic approach that focuses on creating "the plan" is so inadequate. In some sense, that approach leads to the activity of planning and the plan itself becoming an end in itself. People become more concerned with technique—doing planning right rather than with doing the right thing. A plan can also become detached from the strategic questions that underpin it in the first place. People lose sight of what issues the plan was designed to address. In short, the planning becomes separate from the real activity of the organization.

In the articles that follow, we see many of the outcomes of this divorce. We see top-level managers and corporate staffs becoming so far removed from the concrete needs of the organization that they misunderstand what is happening. Somehow the sophisticated planning techniques of the specialists must be harmonized with the realities of implementation. In other instances, we see how the very techniques that people use to communicate successfully in some ways make it difficult for them to develop an effective strategic plan. They become wedded to past techniques and processes. On the other hand, we see many instances where planning is an integral part of other activities, and that the *way* planning is done can communicate the mission of an organization. Moreover, it should become clear that planning never stops and, since plans will often fail, organizations need to be prepared to respond to these failures. It is our view that such responses will be most apt to be effective when the plans themselves have been developed organically—that is, as a process that is fully integrated with the ongoing activities of the organization.

Finally, plans do not automatically become reality. As Drucker put it so well, "The best plan is *only* a plan, that is, good intentions, unless it *degenerates into work.*"[5] To make a plan more than a hope—to implement it—often requires considerable skill and effort. There are always conflicting objectives and preferences within an organization, and plans can become the stimulus for forcing these conflicts to be recognized and addressed. Throughout these selections, we see various ways—force, commitment to mission, skill in framing decisions—that are used to make plans become reality.

To reiterate, planning is a process that is integrally related to other organizational processes. To fail to recognize this organic relationship is to misunderstand an important part of how effective managers manage. To accept the more mechanistic view is to increase one's vulnerability either to not planning and feeling guilty, or to planning and being frustrated by not seeing one's hopes become real. We hope the following articles help cement the more organic view.

Notes

1. C. N. Parkinson, *Parkinson's Law.* Boston: Houghton Mifflin, 1957, p. 61.

2. Ibid., p. 60.

3. K. E. Weick, *The Social Psychology of Organizing,* 2d ed. Reading, MA: Addison-Wesley, 1979, p. 10.

4. Ibid., p. 11.

5. P. R. Drucker, *Management.* New York: Harper & Row, 1974, p. 128.

◆

The Creation

Anonymous

In the beginning was the plan
and then came the assumptions
and the assumptions were without form
and the plan was completely without substance
and darkness was upon the faces of the workers.
And they spake unto their group heads, saying:
"It is a crock of shit, and it stinketh."
And the group heads went unto their section heads, and sayeth:
"It is a pail of dung, and none may abide the odour thereof."
And the section heads went unto their managers, and sayeth unto them:
"It is a container of excrement, and it is very strong,
such that none here may abide by it."
And the managers went unto their Director, and sayeth unto him:
"It is a vessel of fertilizer, and none may abide its strength."
And the Directors went unto their Director-General, and sayeth:
"It contains that which aids plant growth, and it is very strong."
And the Director-General went unto the assistant Deputy Minister, and sayeth
unto him:
"It promoteth growth, and it is very powerful."
And the ADM went unto the Deputy Minister, and sayeth unto him:
"This powerful new plan will actively promote the growth and
efficiency of the department, and this area in particular."
and the Deputy Minister looked upon the plan,
and saw that it was good,
and the plan became policy.

◆

Why Strategic Management Is Bankrupt*

David K. Hurst

The strategic management paradigm, the dominant management paradigm in North America, fails when it comes to helping a company move
successfully into new ventures. The author proposes placing strategic
management within the larger "creative management" paradigm. . . .

*Abridged, by permission of the publisher, from "Why Strategic Management Is Bankrupt,"
by David D. Hurst, from *Organization Dynamics*, Autumn 1986. Copyright © David K. Hurst
1986. Published by American Management Association, New York. All rights reserved.

ONE COMPANY'S EXPERIENCES

Our experiences over the past 25 years with the strategic management model are instructive and, as the reader will see, appear to parallel those of many North American corporations. When our company first went public in 1962, it was a tiny steel distribution business with five branches and $14 million in sales. The management group consisted of the president, the only member of the founding family working in the company, and his manager, a seasoned steel operator who had spent 20 years in the business. Both men were intimately involved with the day-to-day activities of the steel distribution operation, and their objectives and strategy reflected a determination to stick to that business.

The early 1960s was a good time to be in the steel service-center industry in Canada. Driven by the demands of the baby boom, the country was developing an infrastructure with the necessary manufacturing industries, and steel users were poorly serviced by distributors. The general economy appeared in excellent shape, and there was much talk of economists' newly found ability to fine tune the important variables. Government at last seemed to have solved the perennial problems of cyclical recessions and unemployment. In the private sector the talk was all of growth and planning.

Sometime between 1962 and 1964 our company president caught that growth bug and resolved to make the company grow. His operating manager, a tough, hard-nosed taskmaster from the old school, was clearly not the man to make this happen. But the president found an individual who fitted the requirements perfectly. An engineer with a Harvard M.B.A., this man had spent 15 years at Procter and Gamble. He was organized, understood strategic planning, and was determined to make businesses grow. He joined the company in 1965 as executive vice-president.

The organization changed in several ways after he joined. First, it became a good deal more formal, with written policies and plans. Second, a split was created between operating units and the holding entity—a split between managers and investors, between divisions and the head office.

At this time, comprehensive planning was introduced into the corporation. Divisions were asked to submit five-year forecasts to the corporate office which, faced with competing demands for scarce funds, would then allocate capital using various financial tests and minimum requirements for return on investments.

Two groups with distinctly different perspectives and interests began to emerge in the company: the operating managers who ran the profit centers and the "investors," the corporate office heads who ran the holding company on behalf of the public shareholders. This second group acted as a kind of mediating investment group, investing on behalf of the shareholders in a portfolio of divisions.

To give themselves the perspective and space needed to plan for growth, the president and executive vice-president moved their offices away from the steel operations. They saw themselves as "informed directors," supplying advice and counsel to the divisions as required. They recognized that they could not be operators and could not provide general management support. Their management function was limited to the assessment, reward, and replacement, if necessary, of the operating management.

This form of organization, dubbed *federal decentralization* by Peter Drucker, is undoubtedly good for operating managers. In our company it gave them the necessary space to operate without interference, even though at times their autonomy bordered on complete independence. But federal decentralization creates a head office of powerful, driven managers who have no businesses to run, only a group of autonomous divisions to oversee. The head office makes decisions in the areas of portfolio structure, capital allocation, and senior personnel, but these activities are not enough to engage the full attention of top executives. The temptation for the corporate office to buy something is nearly irresistible. Thus, when the president and executive vice-president moved to a corporate office, the stage was set for the company to grow by acquisition.

LESSONS FROM ACQUISITIONS

Between 1964 and 1980, when we were acquired by another firm, our corporation made 27 separate acquisitions, which involved more than 40 distinct businesses. This program expanded the company's size tremendously through the 1970s; but in the process, the investment function and its needs totally overpowered the management function and its concerns. The situation made the company vulnerable to a takeover and was a major factor in the subsequent collapse of the organization.

Specifically, the initial four acquisitions were failures. The first company bought was a small manufacturer of precision equipment, primarily for the auto industry. Since the owner/manager wanted to retire, our vice-president of administration was put in charge "to introduce the necessary organization and control" and to work with the acquired company's existing management. However, the acquired company's management was in turmoil for the next 18 months: All managers were replaced, and many skilled workers were lost.

Fortunately, a surge in the marketplace brought the business back into the black. At that time, our corporation decided to acquire a similar business and merge the two. This led to the second disaster.

On paper the numbers looked impressive. It seemed that a combination of cost savings and margin improvements would result in a significant profit. Instead, the combination of the two businesses became almost instantly unprofitable. Sales sagged and margins shrank as the business cycle turned down. It became clear that the businesses were not nearly as similar as they had appeared. Each one served slightly different markets and had different ways of operating. The complete merging of the two businesses led to a predictable loss of good people. The combined business never did make an operating profit. In 1972 we were relieved to sell it to ITT Canada.

Early in the game we also acquired a steel distribution operation very similar to those in our core business. We planned at the outset that this business would be run by our own operating managers. In fact the returns were predicated upon their ability to turn the business around. The first year was expected to be tough, but the medium- and longer-range views called for the acquisition to be an important source of new income. The purchase appeared to involve little financial risk because the major asset being acquired was steel inventory. The deal proceeded.

A year later only one member of the acquired company's original management team was left. It would take five years and a good deal of help from the 1973–1974 economic boom before the business again became profitable. During that time the operating management was so preoccupied with problems that it missed out on most of the considerable growth in the markets served by the acquisition. The employees who had left in the first year formed their own business, and with new equipment and financing they became very successful. They outstripped the business we had acquired in both size and profitability—a very perverse outcome.

Our fourth acquisition in this "program of planned corporate growth" was in high technology. The business was "in applications engineering in the field of process control and instrumentation," as the acquisition recommendation put it. Reasons for the acquisition of the business included:

- The high growth rate of the industry.
- The presence of an undeveloped niche in the marketplace.
- Large potential markets, of which a small share would generate significant sales volumes.
- Diffuse and scattered competition.
- Technical synergies available to other businesses.
- The parent company's ability to provide financial management and policy direction.

The investment was made by way of a debenture in March 1968. We were forced to call the loan and put in a receiver to wind up the company's affairs. The problem was that this high-tech company had never really been an organization; rather, it had been a group of technical experts, all doing whatever interested them. There had been no core of competence.

A Reevaluation

Following these inauspicious beginnings senior managers in the corporate office took stock. They again asked themselves what business they were in and concluded that it was "industrial distribution." This new definition coincided (unfortunately, as it turned out) with their first successful acquisition.

This time a family-owned distributor of ballbearings and power transmission equipment was acquired. The family, keen to sell but concerned that the employees and the business be well looked after, approached us through a mutual friend. The business had always been profitable, and several other buyers were willing to pay the asking price. However, we were selected as the buyer because of the closer personal rapport the family felt it had with our company's senior management.

The existing management team stayed with the business after we acquired it. The business continued to be profitable, growing steadily by branch network expansion, and it became a major contributor to our results. Unfortunately, this success was attributed to the "industrial distribution" strategy. After making two more steel-related acquisitions, we set off on what was to become a disastrous course, a series of acquisitions in the building supplies industry.

The Grand Design

By 1972 we were still earning less than $100 million in revenue. Outside of the steel business, our only successful acquisition was the bearings distribution operation. This industry continued to be extremely attractive to us, but in both Canada and the United States few of the distributors were for sale. Those that were for sale were quickly snapped up by Bearings Inc. and Genuine Parts, the two largest operators in the industry.

In its search for new growth opportunities, senior management came upon a hardware supply business in eastern Canada. Run by a self-made man, a political figure in the region, the business had an astonishing growth record. This man had parlayed a bank loan and his political contacts into a small group of assorted trading companies. With the sale of his business he became financially independent. In addition, he was given a mandate to make the new division grow—and grow it did. Between 1972 and 1976 we invested more than $50 million (much of it borrowed) in the Building Supplies Group, as it came to be called. Twelve business units, located between Nova Scotia and British Columbia, were acquired.

Acquisition was piled on acquisition without any attempt on our corporation's part to digest what were essentially small family businesses. Unfortunately, the businesses were not particularly profitable; rampant inflation and FIFO accounting (which allows increases in inventory costs to be reflected in profits) made them appear much more profitable than they really were. The profit picture for each acquisition developed into a pattern. The business would generate profits for the first one or two years after acquisition and then slump badly. Economic forecasts for each unit began to show the "hockey stick" effect—losses for the short term followed by a steady recovery to handsome profits in the long term.

Even though senior management accepted this outlook, the stock market did not. Our share price, after many years of trading at around book value, began to fall below that range.

Why did corporate management allow this acquisition activity to continue? One of the chief opponents of this course, a steel operator, argued that cash was being siphoned off from his steel operations to finance a reckless acquisition spree. Nevertheless, dedication to growth undoubtedly made the corporate office amenable to strategies that promised growth. Perhaps even more important, at the root of corporate management's inability to see reality was a grand strategic design developed by the management of the Building Supplies Group.

The grand design culminated in a national chain of supplies stores linked by a sophisticated on-line computer system and operating at several levels of distribution—retail, wholesale, commercial. Numerous examples of this kind of organization were cited, including Lowes and Hechinger (two successful U.S. regional building supplies distributors) and (one trembles to remember it) Wickes (which went into Chapter 11 in 1981, the second largest U.S. company ever to do so). Because of the emphasis on formal, written communications and the investor-manager distinction, these strategies, which looked good on paper, were never tested in practice. Corporate management never went into the field to talk to employees without the filter of senior management.

Much later, while walking around a particularly dilapidated Building Supplies Group operation in 1979, I was reminded of Liddel Hart's report of the World War I general visiting the battlefield: "This highly placed officer from general headquarters was on his first visit to the battlefront—at the end of the four months' battle. Growing increasingly uneasy as the car approached the swamp-like edges of the battle area, he eventually burst into tears, crying, 'Good God, did we really send men to fight in that?' To which his companion replied that the ground was far worse ahead."

For us, the further we proceeded with the acquisition(s) program, the harder it became to get out of it. In theory the investor role of the corporate office allowed it to divest itself of a business, but in practice this did not work. There were always objections from the various group managements, the inevitable "hockey stick" forecasts, and the arguments that one more acquisition would complete the puzzle and fulfill the grand design. The company had become trapped in its own conceptual framework.

The pace of acquisitions continued, with profits coming primarily from the steel operations and the bearing distribution companies. The inflationary growth of the late 1970s, together with the Canadian government's reckless investment incentives designed to encourage energy self-sufficiency, helped sustain the trend. The steel cycle peaked in 1979: The company produced a net income of $14 million on revenues of $535 million, with the Building Supplies Group producing 7% of the profit on 30% of the revenue. The steel cycle faltered in 1980 and recovered briefly in 1981 before plunging into its steepest decline since the Great Depression.

After the Fall

The downward plunge in the business cycle caused problems in all of our businesses, but the failure of our strategic framework was brought home to us most forcibly in the collapse of the Building Supplies Group. This group of operations, which had been acquired at such great cost over the previous ten years, collapsed in two senses: financially and conceptually. The severe recession battered the entire economy, and many marginal businesses failed. On the conceptual level, the entire grand design, the coast-to-coast network of distribution operations, was suddenly revealed to be a management delusion, a paper plan without substance. In hindsight, every strategic view taken by the management team of the Building Supplies Group seemed to have been a wishful pattern imposed upon the future by a small number of managers at the top.

Now the reader may well feel that these corporate disasters are indicative of management incompetence, faulty analysis, and misdirected strategy. Indeed, the proponents of strategic planning usually make this argument. "There is nothing wrong with the model," they say. "All you have to do is apply it properly." Well, there *is* something wrong with the model.

The problem with the strategic paradigm is the assumptions underlying it. The paradigm assumes that businesses are like complex, mechanical clockworks operating in an environment that can be objectively determined by senior managers of the business. It is supposed that this knowledge, together with the managers' assessment of their organizations' strengths and weaknesses, can be used to devise a strategy of objectives, plans, and so forth. These strategies are meant to allow managers to structure their organizations and adapt to and/or take control of the environment.

But these strategic structures are built on retrospective foundations. They work for the future only so long as the pattern of the future mimics that of the past. Such stability is unusual and does not last for long. The last such period was the 30 or 35 years after World War II. This largely benign economic environment caused the strategic view of business to become extremely popular. Like the economists' ability to "fine tune" the economy, the strategic method appeared to work—at least for a while.

A deeper problem with the strategic model is the economic framework upon which it is based. This framework assumes that capital is the scarce resource to be rationed among many competing investment opportunities. In fact, the current situation in North America is quite the opposite: Opportunities are scarce, while capital is plentiful. I shall argue that the inability of the strategic model to create such opportunities lies at the heart of its problems.

TOWARD AN ALTERNATIVE MODEL

Alfred North Whitehead once wrote that "understanding has two modes of advance, the gathering of detail within assigned pattern, and the discovery of novel pattern with its emphasis on novel detail." This is also the case with the progress of business organizations. On the one hand is the strategic mode, with its gathering of data within an existing conceptual framework. On the other hand is a more naive mode, by which data are gathered apparently without pattern, and in that process new patterns are formed. In contrast to the strategic mode, this might be called the mission mode—a search for mission, purpose, and meaning for both the organization and its employees.

Exhibit 1 shows clearly the contrast between the two modes, although the reader is cautioned that the conceptual problem lies less with the nouns and the verbs than it does with the conjunctions used to connect them. Western thought is biased toward "either. . . or" rather than toward "both. . . and." This bias is largely the result of our failure to reconnect the conceptual categories to which we have reduced reality by our exclusive use of rational thought structures. It reflects our penchant for linear thought and notions of cause and effect, as opposed to cyclical, interactive concepts. The key to understanding strategy and mission rests primarily on our ability to grasp the complex dynamic relationship that exists between the two.

The Task of Strategy

The lists in Exhibit 1 can be read both horizontally and vertically. The strategic management mode is a conscious, deliberate activity that focuses on a particular organization in a particular environment. The strategic manager stands outside of these "objects" and analyzes them, reducing them to some fundamental

EXHIBIT 1 **TWO ORGANIZATIONAL PROCESSES**

Strategy	Mission
Planned	Spontaneous
Analysis	Synthesis
External	Internal
Things	Phenomena
States	Relationships
Strengths/weaknesses	Competencies/preferences
Reduction	Emergence
Fundamentals	Purpose
Designed	Evolves
Objectives	Values
Precise	Vague
Targets	Directions
Set	Appear
Focus	Awareness
Search	Recognition
Means	Ends
How	Why
Make it happen	Let it happen
Today's business	Tomorrow's business

categories. This analysis is achieved, of course, by the use of complex conceptual frameworks that allow managers to generalize and manipulate aspects of reality. Targets are set to measure the corporation's progress toward objectives. The focus is on programs—how to "make it happen."

Now this is a very valuable process, but not for the purposes for which many managers use it. The strategic mode is helpful for looking *backward* rather than *forward,* for what it *excludes* rather than what it *contains.* The strategic mode cannot tell managers where they are going, only where they have been. It is useful for managing today's business, the business that already exists. The strategic mode requires some content that can be analyzed. An organization has to exist *before* the strategic mode can be applied. Otherwise, there is nothing on which to focus and from which to generalize.

This requirement of the strategic mode interferes with the strategic manager's ability to discover new business opportunities. Discovery is only partially a problem of search; it is mainly a problem of recognition. The history of product innovation in business abounds with examples of this. After a comprehensive study carried out in the early 1950s, Arthur D. Little assured IBM that there would never be a market for more than 5,000 copiers of the kind then being developed by Haloid (which later became Xerox), and IBM rejected the license to the new process. In the 1980s both Parker Brothers and Milton Bradley turned down the opportunity to market Trivial Pursuit.

Thus exclusive use of the strategic mode leads to discovery of only what is recognized. A historical pattern is imposed on reality and, unless the world stays very stable, this pattern may not be appropriate in the future. This was what our company discovered during our acquisition years. Our view of the future was continually determined by our interpretation of past events.

Even though the strategic mode may not be very useful for creating new businesses, it is invaluable for getting rid of old ones, for "sloughing off yesterday's business," as Peter Drucker has put it. Any manager who has been through a turnaround can testify to the power of formal, strategic analysis applied to existing businesses. Without its use, organizations become complacent and overweight. To use a farming analogy, strategic management is a weeding device that allows healthy, productive crops to grow unharmed by weeds. But in the process it ensures that a different crop will never be grown.

The task of strategy is to "make it happen," but too often all the emphasis is put on the *make* and none on the *it*. To make anything happen, a person must first know what *it* is. When dealing with an existing business, managers may know what *it* is; but when they try to bring about change and develop new businesses, they usually don't know. The question "What is *it*?" is crucial. The role of the mission mode is to answer that question.

The Role of Mission

The mission mode consists of a process that is spontaneous rather than planned. It involves the gradual synthesis of phenomena internal to the organization, a growing awareness on many levels of relationships, competencies (things a person does well), and preferences (things a person likes to do). As the process proceeds, ideas begin aggregating in clusters around particular people and groups. Visions of what *could* be and a sense of purpose become clearer to the members of the organization. Values are discussed openly; as they are spread, refined, and shared, they begin to allow a *recognition* of what directions to take. The external environment of opportunity begins to crystallize, and these directions appear.

The role of the mission process, then, is to open up the organization to new opportunities by relaxing the tight downward focus of the existing strategy. The process releases to the surface deeply, perhaps unconsciously, held convictions and beliefs about what the organization means to its members. These values form a soft framework in which new opportunities at the periphery of vision may be netted. In other words, the role of the mission process is the "let it happen," when "it" is the process leading to the "it" of strategy.

The Interaction Between Mission and Strategy

The interaction between the mission and strategy modes is extraordinarily difficult for members within an organization to see, for the processes are "nested" inside one another. The processes of the mission mode precipitate strategic actions which, in turn, trigger mission processes, and the two modes are present simultaneously. A somewhat simplified model of the organization, Exhibit 2, shows the two processes connected by spirals. The power for the spin is provided by the twin processes of mission and strategy: Mission pulls while strategy pushes.

EXHIBIT 2 **A MODEL OF ORGANIZATION PROCESSES**

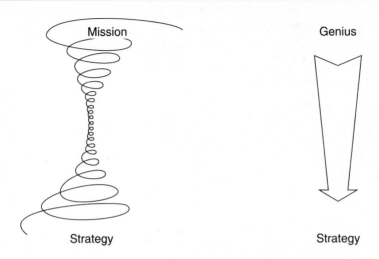

Of course strategy can also be generated by the lone genius who knows just what to do. This method is a more direct process.

The mission process can be thought of as a way to pull the organization into the future. It brings opportunities (by ensuring that they are recognized) into the vortex of the organization, where they are transformed from ideas into innovations and from innovations into new products, services, or whatever. This transformation is accomplished by the strategy process, which cuts out old, unprofitable products and services and reduces innovations to practical programs. Mission supplies the form to which strategy can give substance.

This part of the process can be compared to the precipitation of crystals from a supersaturated solution. A liquid (people in the organization) is heated and stirred so that an amorphous powder (potential opportunities) can be dissolved (assimilated). As the liquid stops moving (changes mode) and cools (becomes rational), large crystals (good ideas) will appear out of the solution, solidify, and grow.

The analogy is fine as far as it goes, but it does not reflect the reverse process in which the decisions made affect the opportunity-recognition process. The organization's understanding of what has happened in the past will have an important influence over the way it sees the future.

This aspect of the process is best illustrated by Exhibit 3, which shows a returning outer set of spirals connecting strategy to mission. The inner and outer spirals combine to create a swirling toroidal, or doughnut, shape (the layers of the doughnut will be explained shortly). Thus, an organization can be conceived of as being dynamic. Like the vortex that forms in bath water when one pulls out the plug, the structure of the organization is sustained only so long as energy is poured through the system. In this model the doughnut shape of the organization is sustained by mission (supplied either by process or genius) and strategy. Like Janus, the Roman god of the threshold, the organization looks forward to the future and

EXHIBIT 3 **A DYNAMIC MODEL OF ORGANIZATION PROCESSES**

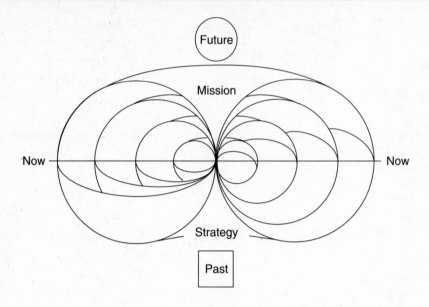

back to the past. Mission prospects while strategy retrospects. The two meet in the present. The potentially perceivable environment is all around, but the environment actually perceived is represented by the "skin" of the doughnut. Thus the organization grows (learns) by expanding its perceived environment—by recognizing and processing opportunities. . . .

WHY STRATEGIC MANAGEMENT IS BANKRUPT

The test of business solvency is not the size of assets but the relative balance of assets and liabilities. Strategic management has enormous assets, but often the claims against it exceed those assets. Instead of recognizing it as a rational tool for managing stability—for elaborating on success and culling failure—too many advocates view strategic management as a way to create innovation and lead change. Our experience suggests that this is not the case. The strategic management model is essential for managing today's business, but it cannot create tomorrow's because the strategic paradigm is sterile.

The strategic model also runs into trouble when it is used as an instrument to manage managers by objectives. By starting with the concept of objectives, the paradigm ignores the critical roles of imaginative vision and shared values. As a result, instead of growing from within the organization, vision and values turn into extensions of the personality of senior managers. The prevalence of the "tool" or "instrument" metaphor in strategic management is illustrative of this tendency. The manager is seen as a rational tool user who stands outside the situation. Objects are changed by the tool user but do not affect either the tool or its user. Thus the strategic management of people can easily become manipulative and elitist. In the absence of genius, purpose and meaning will be lost. So will the organization's ability to innovate—that is, to evolve.

Strategic management is a fine methodology with which to pursue given ends. But it functions poorly as a philosophy for reaching an agreement within an organization as to what those ends should be.

LEADERSHIP

In the past many writers on management have described leadership in terms of the qualities a single individual may possess. These qualities bear a striking resemblance to the various stages of the creative management process. Leaders, they say, have vision and values, conceptualize rapidly, and act decisively. We can now see that leadership is really a process, an ongoing dynamic relationship among a number of individuals in search of meaning. If leadership is effective, then these individuals will develop a shared vision, a sense of common purpose, and the ability to make their own unique contributions. Their work will satisfy their need for both identity and community, their striving both to become what they are and, at the same time, to belong to something larger than themselves.

Leadership is the process by which each individual is allowed to play his or her best role at the appropriate stage. We call the effective mingling of strengths a team. The achievement of teams within an organization is the result of true leadership. "When the great leader has done his work, the people will say 'We did it ourselves,'" wrote Lao Tzu in the fifth century B.C.

Too few business leaders today are innovators and developers of new industries. Most of our heroes are either paper entrepreneurs, assisted mightily by our tax laws, or technicians. (Keep in mind Maslow's definition: "A technician is a man who understands everything about his job except its ultimate purpose and its place in the order of the universe.") The result has been a profound loss of meaning for both the managers and the managed.

This loss of meaning is not restricted to business organizations. It pervades our social institutions, churches, governments, universities, and families. We have the answers but we have forgotten the important questions. This "freedom" from the important has made us slaves to the urgent. Too many managers have lost the vision of what they can become, of their sense of purpose.

The search for and the recognition of purpose and meaning are the mainsprings of all motivation. In this way, the processes discussed here are at the heart of both the most glorious and the most infamous periods in human history. When great leaders released these processes within their people, philosophy and art flourished and societies had their golden age. When great tyrants used the same processes for their own purposes, they led their people into darkness and disaster.

In business, the point at which everything starts to go wrong is also the point at which management believes that it can stand outside the system and manipulate the processes for its own benefit. Such actions generate perverse reactions because management is not outside the system looking in; it is inside the system looking at itself. The perverse outcomes of many acquisitions and mergers have been documented repeatedly. Following acquisitions, hundreds of major corporations have attempted to restructure their operations, usually by shedding the acquired businesses and returning to their core operations. Many acquisitions, especially those carried out by the large integrated oil companies, were based on the most rational and logical of reasons. Yet the results have often been the opposite of those intended.

Perverse outcomes are also endemic to government at all levels. Government housing programs have usually achieved results opposite those intended. Energy self-sufficiency programs lead to line-ups and shortages. Efforts to prop up foreign governments often succeed in alienating them from the people that they govern.

We persist with our efforts to achieve unilateral control and domination over complex systems. But we are part of these systems, and the systems are alive. They react *and* respond to our efforts to change them. In the short term we may get the logical results of our actions. In the longer run these results may be overwhelmed by natural consequences.

To change complex systems we need to start by changing ourselves. We do not have to change to anything *different*. We need only to stop trying to be things that we are not.

The change begins with the recognition that reality is not a given that is accessible to clear-eyed, rational perception. To be sure, parts of the world are accessible in this way, but reality is mostly multidimensional, and we as individuals are intimately involved in its construction. The business environments that strategists scan are as much an *output* of our culture as they are an *input* from reality. The recognition of this must have profound effects on our understanding of the meaning of objectivity. C. West Churchman has put it well: "Instead of the silly and empty claim that an observation is objective if it resides in the brain of an unbiased observer, one should say that an observation is objective if it is the creation of many inquirers with many different points of view."

These different points of view correspond to the different stages of the creative process. We need to abandon our notions of the lone manager as hero, who rationally solves the problems of the world. We must assemble teams to handle the total process. We need to combine the two great human gifts, reason and passion, the head and the heart, and we need to stand at the threshold of the present, looking at both the past and the future. Now is the only time. In that process our organizations may realize their potential. We may become what we are.

The Wall Street Journal, October 4, 1991

Straight Shooter*

Douglas Lavin

Robert J. Eaton has a theory about vision: Keep it short.

In late July, Mr. Eaton, the recently appointed chairman of Chrysler Corp., gathered scores of senior managers for an announcement of Chrysler's second-quarter earnings—the best since 1984. After patting them on the back, Mr. Eaton rattled off snippets of press accounts hailing Chrysler's turnaround.

Then came the kicker: The accolades had been written in 1956, 1965, 1976 and 1983. At least once a decade. Chrysler had sprung from its deathbed to a miraculous recovery. "I've got a better idea," Mr. Eaton told his managers. "Let's stop getting sick. . . . My personal ambition is to be the first chairman never to lead a Chrysler comeback."

Staying healthy is hardly a grand vision of Chrysler's future, or a daring career strategy for Bob Eaton. But welcome to the 1990s. Vision may not exactly be dead in corporate America, but a surprising number of chief executive officers are casting aside their crystal balls to concentrate on the nuts-and-bolts of running their businesses in these leaner times. Consider just a partial roster of other concerns that have recently appointed CEOs whose notion of vision is a sharp eye on the short-term bottom line: Apple Computer Inc., International Business Machines Corp., Aetna Life & Casualty Co., and General Motors Corp.

"Internally, we don't use the word vision," says Mr. Eaton, whose low-key, no-nonsense style couldn't be more different from that of his predecessor, Lee A. Iacocca.

"I believe in quantifiable short-term results—things we can all relate to—as opposed to some esoteric thing no one can quantify."

Good Company

If that sounds familiar, recall what IBM's new chairman, Louis V. Gerstner, recently said when asked about his recipe for an IBM comeback: "The last thing IBM needs right now is a vision."

And even some honest-to-goodness visionaries think the premise of visionary leadership is overrated if the fundamentals of running a business are overlooked. "Being a visionary is trivial," William Gates, chairman of Microsoft Corp., said not long ago.

What's going on here? "The valves of growth are shut off and the competitive pressure is rolling in," explains George B. Bennett, chief executive officer of Symmetrix Inc., a Boston-area consulting firm. In the double-digit growth days of the 1980s, he notes, even inefficiently run companies could make money while the CEO mused about long-term strategy. Now, with growth rates stalled "and new competition coming through the keyhole, you are forced to change the fundamentals," Mr. Bennett says.

Case by Case

There are caveats to this, of course. While personal computers have shaken out into a commodities business, there is still room, and need, for visionaries plotting the next leap in technology. And cable-television

---

and telephone-company CEOs without a sense of the future probably have little future themselves. "You have to look industry by industry. There are times when you need a radically new idea to win in the marketplace," says Noel Tischy, a University of Michigan professor who directed management training at the General Electric Company.

The car industry, by contrast, is among a number of mature industries where current market conditions argue strongly for the kind of "mundane blocking and tackling" that Mr. Eaton is bringing to Chrysler, Mr. Tischy adds. "Eaton has a deep understanding of what it takes to build that kind of corporate culture."

Chrysler's tapping of Mr. Eaton for its top post couldn't send a clearer signal that it is steering a back-to-basics course, both in style and philosophy. Mr. Iacocca, who won acclaim for bringing Chrysler back from the brink and restoring its health, nevertheless comported himself as something of a corporate prince while in office. His ghostwritten autobiography was a best-seller. He was the very visible patron of an effort to restore the Statue of Liberty. He played statesman by publicly pushing for protectionist trade policies.

He also tried to thrust the company in new directions. At one point Chrysler was trying to become an aerospace and technology conglomerate through diversification; at another it was toying with becoming a global auto maker through merger. The company bought—and subsequently was forced to shed—Gulfstream Aerospace Corp. and E. F. Hutton Credit Corp.

Far from being a good listener, Mr. Iacocca often couldn't stop talking. A candidate for a high post at Chrysler tells of being interviewed by Mr. Iacocca. The Chrysler boss, he says, asked and answered his own questions so quickly that the candidate was able to utter a single word— "Well. . . "—the entire time.

The 53-year-old Mr. Eaton, on the other hand, is largely viewed by Chrysler insiders as a coach and a listener who eschews the trappings of power in favor of teamwork and consensus-building. When asked to sum up his business strategy, Mr. Eaton says he has no miracles up his sleeve. "This is a business of fundamentals. There isn't any magic. I don't believe in things like leapfrogging." His goal for Chrysler, he adds, is "getting a little bit better every single day."

"He has no ego," marvels Howard Kehri, a former vice chairman at GM who supervised Mr. Eaton for years before he jumped from GM Europe to Chrysler last year.

Man in the Middle

Some might argue that the one thing Chrysler had a surplus of was ego. Mr. Eaton's promotion to chairman and chief executive officer came at the expense of Robert A. Lutz, Chrysler's president and the architect of the company's successful new line of automobiles. No shrinking violet, the cigar-smoking Mr. Lutz often knocked heads with Mr. Iacocca while making no secret of his desire to succeed him.

That Mr. Eaton, during his nine-month-long transition to power, was able to maintain amicable relations with both men—and keep Mr. Lutz at Chrysler—is a testament to the success of his low-key approach. Says Maryann Keller, an analyst with Furman Selz in New York, "For him to be accepted speaks well of him."

For many, in fact, the change from Mr. Iacocca's big-stick style to Mr. Eaton's more informal, collegial approach is a shock. Mr. Iacocca liked summoning underlings to his office and reminding them that he took his management style from his mentor, Henry Ford II, an old-style corporate autocrat who delighted in the arbitrary use of power. Few people ever got to talk to Mr. Iacocca without going through a secretary.

Many, of course, think Mr. Iacocca's imperial style was just right for guiding Chrysler out of the fix it found itself in during the '80s. "It was the force of his personality that saved Chrysler," says Wendy Beale Needham, an analyst at Smith Barney Shearson.

Mr. Eaton's style makes it clear that the '90s will be different. He is fond of dropping in, sans jacket, for informal chats with Chrysler subordinates. He often picks up the telephone himself.

It is such a switch that the auto maker has created a kind of post-Iacocca therapy for senior executives. Called the "Senior Management Behavior Team," it is designed to teach officers to be approachable, to encourage subordinates to speak up, to listen when they do, and to be, well, nice to their co-workers. Executives are reluctant to explain exactly how the team works, but one vice president describes it as a kind of trickle-down behavior modification.

The theory is, "if you don't have eye contact with your people, they're not going to have eye contact with their people," the executive adds.

Encouraging Initiative

Declaring eye contact beneficial is hardly visionary, but it is a small part of a serious effort to change the culture at a company where the former chairman exercised veto power over everything from ad copy to hub-cap design. Mr. Eaton, by contrast, doesn't even review advertisements and product designs.

Instead, he has created two new vice president positions, one charged with customer satisfaction, another with continuous improvement. He also has launched a production-systems team in which a small group of middle managers has trotted the globe studying ways to improve manufacturing.

Throughout the ranks he wins points for encouraging independence and initiative. "Eaton lets you run your business," says Theodor R. Cunningham, executive vice president of sales and marketing.

Some Chrysler executives, in fact, seem almost relieved that they aren't forced to act on their leader's hunches. "This is a guy who gets up every morning and puts both feet on the ground," says E. Thomas Pappert, Chrysler's vice president of sales. "You will see us get our balance sheet in order. You won't see us buying Italian car

companies or jet companies. You will see us get rid of our nickname: 'Financially Beleaguered.'"

Mr. Eaton's folksy, pragmatic approach stems from his roots in the small town of Arkansas City, Kan., near the Oklahoma border, where he returned recently to speak at the high-school graduation. The son of a railroad worker and a beautician, Mr. Eaton delivered newspapers, worked at Montgomery Ward, and spent his spare time hanging out at Bay's Junkyard and Moody's Machine Shop, two Arkansas City mainstays. At age 11, he bought his first car, a Chevrolet, for $10 and spent another $15 to make it run. He studied engineering at the University of Kansas because he loved cars, and he landed a job at GM—it was the only company he chose to interview with.

At GM, he worked his way up, largely through the engineering staffs, to a position of vice president in charge of advanced engineering, reporting to Mr. Kehri. At the time, Mr. Eaton, in his 40s, was an executive who rode dirt bikes as a hobby and didn't see his career rising much higher than it had.

"I asked him, 'Do you want to be on the executive committee some day?'" remembers Mr. Kehri. "He stepped back, a little surprised and said, 'Yeah, I guess so.'" Mr. Kehri chuckles at the memory of shocking Mr. Eaton with the possibility of career advancement. "He's a very straightforward guy."

Mr. Kehri credits Mr. Eaton with playing a significant role in the creation of GM's Saturn, its hot-selling budget car, by forcing the advanced-engineering and manufacturing staffs to work together. The effort went so far as to enlist union workers to help design the Saturn in a way that would make it easier to assemble than standard GM cars.

But while Saturn was in the gestation stage, Mr. Eaton argued against the radical decision to make Saturn a separate GM division on the ground that Saturn's cooperative approach to car building should be spread GM-wide. With hindsight—and GM struggling to make itself more efficient—Mr. Eaton's approach looks insightful.

Pragmatism won another round in Mr. Eaton's career when he headed GM Europe from 1988 to 1992. He inherited from John F. Smith Jr., now GM's chief executive, a division that had turned around and was solidly in the black. During Mr. Eaton's tenure, he watched his chief competitor, Carl W. Hahn, chairman of Volkswagen AG, launch a "visionary" effort to make VW into Europe's first global auto maker.

VW, though it was hardly an efficient producer of cars at home, spent heavily to invest in Czechoslovakia, China and Mexico while acquiring SEAT SA, the Spanish car maker. Then came global recession. VW's $30 billion global gambit has largely been a bust, and VW is awash in red ink.

Mr. Eaton, by contrast, eased GM into new East European markets while concentrating on improving productivity at existing European plants. The result: Despite a sudden downturn in European sales—about 17% this year—GM Europe is expected to finish the year with a profit.

"I used to sit back and think, man I didn't understand something," Mr. Eaton says of VW's expansion. "Well, the fact is they were doing all that as opposed to working on their costs and getting better."

Despite his rise at GM, Mr. Eaton never had a chance to take the top spot there, in part because he is only a year younger than GM's CEO, Mr. Smith. When Chrysler came calling, Robert C. Stempel, then GM's chairman, made little effort to persuade Mr. Eaton to stay, infuriating the company's outside directors.

Mr. Eaton seems determined to bring his low-key style to other Chrysler endeavors. Only a year ago, Chrysler's annual dealer convention was held in Las Vegas and became a lavish tribute to Mr. Iacocca and his leadership. Actors, comedians and Tip O'Neill paid their respects. Frank Sinatra performed the finale, singing "My Way" while a giant video screen recapped the high points of Mr. Iacocca's career.

This year, Mr. Eaton invited dealers to Detroit "to meet the family." They got a tour of a Chrysler laboratory, then a chance to discuss their concerns with Mr. Lutz and other vice presidents in a sort of Phil Donahue-style chat session. All the while, Mr. Eaton stayed mainly in the background.

The finale: Hundreds of Chrysler "team members" rushed on stage clapping and waving white baseball caps as a gospel choir sang exuberantly: "It's a brand new day. It's a brand new day. Oh, yeah, it's a brand new day."

———————◆———————

The Performance Measurement Manifesto[*]

Robert G. Eccles

Revolutions begin long before they are officially declared. For several years, senior executives in a broad range of industries have been rethinking how to measure the performance of their businesses. They have recognized that new strategies and competitive realities demand new measurement systems for their companies.

[*]Reprinted from the *Harvard Business Review,* Jan/Feb 1991, Vol 69, no. 1. Reprinted by permission of the President and Fellows of Harvard College.

At the heart of this revolution lies a radical decision: to shift from treating financial figures as the foundation for performance measurement to treating them as one among a broader set of measures. Put like this, it hardly sounds revolutionary. Many managers can honestly claim that they—and their companies—have tracked quality, market share, and other nonfinancial measures for years. Tracking these measures is one thing. But giving them equal (or even greater) status in determining strategy, promotions, bonuses, and other rewards is another. Until that happens, to quote Ray Stata, the CEO of Analog Devices, "When conflicts arise, financial considerations win out."[1]

The ranks of companies enlisting in this revolution are rising daily. Senior managers at one large, high-tech manufacturer recently took direct responsibility for adding customer satisfaction, quality, market share, and human resources to their formal measurement system. The impetus was their realization that the company's existing system, which was largely financial, undercut its strategy, which focused on customer service. At a smaller manufacturer, the catalyst was a leveraged recapitalization that gave the CEO the opportunity formally to reorder the company's priorities. On the new list, earnings per share dropped to last place, preceded by customer satisfaction, cash flow, manufacturing effectiveness, and innovation (in that order). On the old list, earnings per share stood first and almost alone.

In both companies, the CEOs believe they have initiated a sea change in how their managers think about business performance and in the decisions they make. Executives at other companies engaged in comparable efforts feel the same— rightly. What gets measured gets attention, particularly when rewards are tied to the measures. Grafting new measures onto an old accounting-driven performance system or making slight adjustments in existing incentives accomplishes little. Enhanced competitiveness depends on starting from scratch and asking: "Given our strategy, what are the most important measures of performance?" "How do these measures predict long-term financial success in our business?"

Dissatisfaction with using financial measures to evaluate business performance is nothing new. As far back as 1951, Ralph Cordiner, the CEO of General Electric, commissioned a high-level task force to identify key corporate performance measures. (The categories the task force singled out were timeless and comprehensive: in addition to profitability, the list included market share, productivity, employee attitudes, public responsibility, and the balance between short- and long-term goals.) But the current wave of discontent is not just more of the same.

One important difference is the intensity and nature of the criticism directed at traditional accounting systems. During the past few years, academics and practitioners have begun to demonstrate that accrual-based performance measures are at best obsolete—and more often harmful.[2] Diversity in products, markets, and business units puts a big strain on rules and theories developed for smaller, less complex organizations. More dangerously, the numbers these systems generate often fail to support the investments in new technologies and markets that are essential for successful performance in global markets.

Such criticisms reinforce concern about the pernicious effects of short-term thinking on the competitiveness of U.S. companies. Opinions on the causes of this mind-set differ. Some blame the investment community, which presses relentless-ly for rising quarter earnings. Others cite senior managers themselves, charging that their typically short tenure fosters shortsightedness. The important point is that the mind-set exists. Ask almost any senior manager and you will hear about some company's failure to make capital investments or pursue long-term strategic objectives that would imperil quarterly earnings targets.

Moreover, to the extent that managers do focus on reported quarterly earn-ings—and thereby reinforce the investment community's short-term perspective and expectations—they have a strong incentive to manipulate the figures they report. The extent and severity of such gaming is hard to document. But few in management deny that it goes on or that managers' willingness to play the earn-ings game calls into question the very measures the market focuses on to deter-mine stock prices. For this reason, many managers, analysts, and financial econo-mists have begun to focus on cash flow in the belief that it reflects a company's economic condition more accurately than its reported earnings do.[3]

Finally, many managers worry that income-based financial figures are better at measuring the consequences of yesterday's decisions than they are at indicating tomorrow's performance. Events of the past decade substantiate this concern. During the 1980s, many executives saw their companies' strong financial records deteriorate because of unnoticed declines in quality or customer satisfaction or because global competitors ate into their market share. Even managers who have not been hurt feel the need for preventive action. A senior executive at one of the large money-center banks, for example, grew increasingly uneasy about the Euro-pean part of his business, its strong financials notwithstanding. To address that concern, he has nominated several new measures (including customer satisfac-tion, customers' perceptions of the bank's stature and professionalism, and market share) to serve as leading indicators of the business's performance.

Discontent turns into rebellion when people see an alternative worth fighting for. During the 1980s, many managers found such an alternative in the quality movement. Leading manufacturers and service providers alike have come to see quality as a strategic weapon in their competitive battles. As a result, they have committed substantial resources to developing measures such as defect rates, response time, delivery commitments, and the like to evaluate the performance of their products, services, and operations.

In addition to pressure from global competitors, a major impetus for these efforts has been the growth of the Total Quality Movement and related programs such as the Malcolm Baldrige National Quality Award. (Before a company can even apply for a Baldrige Award, it must devise criteria to measure the perfor-mance of its entire operation—not just its products—in minute detail.) Another impetus, getting stronger by the day, comes from large manufacturers who are more and more likely to impose rigid quality requirements on their suppliers. Whatever the stimulus, the result is the same: quality measures represent the most positive step taken to date in broadening the basis of business performance measurement.

Another step in the same direction comes from embryonic efforts to generate measures of customer satisfaction. What quality was for the 1980s, customer satisfaction will be for the 1990s. Work on this class of measures is the highest priority at the two manufacturing companies discussed earlier. It is equally critical at another high-tech company that recently created a customer satisfaction department reporting directly to the CEO. In each case, management's interest in developing new performance measures was triggered by strategies emphasizing customer service.

As competition continues to stiffen, strategies that focus on quality will evolve naturally into strategies based on customer service. Indeed, this is already happening at many leading companies. Attention to customer satisfaction, which measures the quality of customer service, is a logical next step in the development of quality measures. Companies will continue to measure quality on the basis of internally generated indexes (such as defect rates) that are presumed to relate to customer satisfaction. But they will also begin to evaluate their performance by collecting data directly from customers for more direct measures like customer retention rates, market share, and perceived value of goods and services.

Just as quality-related metrics have made the performance measurement revolution more real, so has the development of competitive benchmarking.[4] First, benchmarking gives managers a methodology that can be applied to any measure, financial or nonfinancial, but that emphasizes nonfinancial metrics. Second (and less obvious), it has a transforming effect on managerial mind-sets and perspectives.

Benchmarking involves identifying competitors and/or companies in other industries that exemplify best practice in some activity, function, or process and then comparing one's own performance to theirs. This externally oriented approach makes people aware of improvements that are orders of magnitude beyond what they would have thought possible. In contrast, internal yardsticks that measure current performance in relation to prior period results, current budget, or the results of other units within the company rarely have such an eye-opening effect. Moreover, these internally focused comparisons have the disadvantage of breeding complacency through a false sense of security and of stirring up more energy for intramural rivalry than for competition in the marketplace.

Finally, information technology has played a critical role in making a performance measurement revolution possible. Thanks to dramatically improved price-performance ratios in hardware and to breakthroughs in software and database technology, organizations can generate, disseminate, analyze, and store more information from more sources, for more people, more quickly and cheaply than was conceivable even a few years back. The potential of new technologies, such as hand-held computers for employees in the field and executive information systems for senior managers, is only beginning to be explored. Overall, the range of measurement options that are economically feasible has radically increased.

Veterans know it is easier to preach revolution than to practice it. Even the most favorable climate can create only the potential for revolutionary change.

Making it happen requires conviction, careful preparation, perseverance, and a decided taste for ambiguity. As yet, there are no clear-cut answers or predetermined processes for managers who wish to change their measurement systems. Based on the experience of companies engaged in this revolution, I can identify five areas of activity that sooner or later need to be addressed: developing an information architecture; putting the technology in place to support this architecture; aligning incentives with the new system; drawing on outside resources; and designing a process to ensure that the other four activities occur.

(1) Developing a new information architecture must be the first activity on any revolutionary agenda. Information architecture is an umbrella term for the categories of information needed to manage a company's businesses, the methods the company uses to generate this information, and the rules regulating its flow. In most companies, the accounting system implicitly defines the information architecture. Other performance measures are likely to be informal—records that operating managers keep for themselves, for instance—and they are rarely integrated into the corporate-driven financial system.

The design for a new corporate information architecture begins with the data that management needs to pursue the company's strategy. This may sound like a truism, but a surprising number of companies describe their strategies in terms of customer service, innovation, or the quality and capabilities of their people, yet do little to measure these variables. Even time—the newest strategic variable—remains largely underdeveloped in terms of which time-based metrics are most important and how best to measure them.

As part of this identification process, management needs to articulate a new corporate grammar and define its own special vocabulary—the basic terms that will need to be common and relatively invariant across all the company's businesses. Some of these terms (like sales and costs) will be familiar. Others, however, will reflect new strategic priorities and ways to think about measuring performance. For example, both a large money-center bank and a multidivisional, high-technology manufacturer introduced the use of cross-company customer identification numbers so they could readily track such simple and useful information as the total amount of business the company did with any one customer. It sounds elementary and it is—as soon as you start to look at the entire measurement system from scratch.

Uniformity can be carried too far. Different businesses with different strategies require different information for decision making and performance measurement. But this should not obscure the equally obvious fact that every company needs to have at least a few critical terms in common. Today few large companies do. Years of acquisitions and divestitures, technological limitations, and at times, a lack of management discipline have all left most big organizations with a complicated hodgepodge of definitions and variables—and with the bottom line their only common denominator.

Developing a coherent, companywide grammar is particularly important in light of an ever-more stringent competitive environment. For many companies, ongoing structural reorganizations are a fact of life. The high-technology company described above has reorganized itself 24 times in the past 4 years (in addition to a number of divisional and functional restructurings) to keep pace with changes in its markets and technologies. Rather than bewail the situation, managers relish it and see their capacity for fast adaptation as an important competitive advantage.

A common grammar also enhances management's ability to break apart and recombine product lines and market segments to form new business units. At a major merchant bank, for example, the organization is so fluid that one senior executive likens it to a collection of hunting packs that form to pursue business opportunities and then disband as the market windows on those opportunities close. The faster the company can assemble information for newly formed groups, the greater the odds of success. So this executive who calls himself the czar of information has been made responsible for developing standard definitions for key information categories.

How a company generates the performance data it needs is the second piece of its information architecture. Not surprisingly, methods for measuring financial performance are the most sophisticated and the most deeply entrenched. Accountants have been refining these methods ever since double-entry bookkeeping was invented in the fifteenth century. Today their codifications are enforced by a vast institutional infrastructure made up of professional educators, public accounting firms, and regulatory bodies.

In contrast, efforts to measure market share, quality, innovation, human resources, and customer satisfaction have been much more modest. Data for tracking these measures are generated less often: quarterly, annual, or even biannual bases are common. Responsibility for them typically rests with a specific function. (Strategic planning measures market share, for example, while engineering measures innovation, and so on.) They rarely become part of the periodic reports general managers receive.

Placing these new measures on an equal footing with financial data takes significant resources. One approach is to assign a senior executive to each of the measures and hold him or her responsible for developing its methodologies. Typically, these executives come from the function that is most experienced in dealing with the particular measure. But they work with a multifunctional task force to ensure that managers throughout the company will understand the resulting measures and find them useful. Another, less common, approach is to create a new function focused on one measure and then to expand its mandate over time. A unit responsible for customer satisfaction might subsequently take on market share, for example, or the company's performance in human resources.

Unlike a company's grammar, which should be fairly stable, methods for taking new performance measures should evolve as the company's expertise increases. Historical comparability may suffer in the process, but this is a minor loss. What matters is how a company is doing compared with its current competitors, not with its own past.

The last component of a corporate information architecture is the set of rules that governs the flow of information. Who is responsible for how measures are taken? Who actually generates the data? Who receives and analyzes them? Who is responsible for changing the rules? Because information is an important source of power, the way a company answers these questions matters deeply. How open or closed a company is affects how individuals and groups work together as well as the relative influence people and parts of the company have on its strategic direction and management. Some companies make information available on a very limited basis. At others, any individual can request information from another unit as long as he or she can show why it is needed. Similarly, in some companies the CEO still determines who gets what information—not a very practical alternative in today's world. More often what happens is that those who possess information decide with whom they will share it.

Advances in information technology such as powerful workstations, open architectures, and relational databases vastly increase the options for how information can flow. It may be centralized at the top so that senior executives can make even more decisions than they have in the past. Or it may be distributed to increase the decision-making responsibilities of people at every level. The advantages of making information widely available are obvious, though this also raises important questions that need to be addressed about the data's integrity and security. In principle, however, this portion of the information architecture ought to be the most flexible of the three, so that the company's information flows continue to change as the conditions it faces do.

(2) Determining the hardware, software, and telecommunications technology a company needs to generate its new measurement information is the second activity in the performance revolution. This task is hard enough in its own right, given the many choices available. But too often managers make it even harder by going directly to a technology architecture without stopping first to think through their information needs. This was the case at a high-tech manufacturing company that was growing more and more frustrated with its information systems planning committee. Then the CEO realized that he and the other senior managers had not determined the measures they wanted before setting up the committee. Equipped with that information, the committee found it relatively easy to choose the right technology.

(3) Once the information architecture and supporting technology are in place, the next step is to align the new system with the company's incentives—to reward people in proportion to their performance on the measures that management has said truly matter. This is easier said than done. In many companies, the compensation system limits the amount and range of the salary increases, bonuses, and stock options that management can award.

In companies that practice pay-for-performance, compensation and other rewards are often tied fairly mechanically to a few key financial measures such as profitability and return on investment. Convincing managers that a newly implemented system is really going to be followed can be a hard sell. The president of one service company let each of his division general managers design the performance measures that were most appropriate for his or her particular business. Even so, the managers still felt the bottom line was all that would matter when it came to promotions and pay.

The difficulty of aligning incentives to performance is heightened by the fact that formulas for tying the two together are rarely effective. Formulas have the advantage of looking objective, and they spare managers the unpleasantness of having to conduct truly frank performance appraisals. But if the formula is simple and focuses on a few key variables, it inevitably leaves some important measures out. Conversely, if the formula is complex and factors in all the variables that require attention, people are likely to find it confusing and may start to play games with the numbers. Moreover, the relative importance of the variables is certain to change more often—and faster—than the whole incentive system can change.

For these reasons, I favor linking incentives strongly to performance but leaving managers free to determine their subordinates' rewards on the basis of all the relevant information, qualitative as well as quantitative. Then it is up to the manager to explain candidly to subordinates why they received what they did. For most managers, this will also entail learning to conduct effective performance appraisals, an indirect—and invaluable—benefit of overhauling the measurement system.

(4) Outside parties such as industry and trade associations, third-party data vendors, information technology companies, consulting firms, and public accounting firms must also become part of the performance measurement revolution. Their incentive: important business opportunities.

Industry and trade associations can play a very helpful role in identifying key performance measures, researching methodologies for taking these measures, and supplying comparative statistics to their members—so can third-party data vendors. Competitors are more likely to supply information to a neutral party (which can disguise it and make it available to all its members or customers) than to one another. And customers are more likely to provide information to a single data vendor than to each of their suppliers separately.

Consulting firms and information technology vendors also have important roles to play in forwarding the revolution. Firms that specialize in strategy formulation, for example, often have well-developed methods for assessing market share and other performance metrics that clients could be trained to use. Similarly, firms that focus on strategy implementation have a wealth of experience designing systems of various kinds for particular functions such as manufacturing and human resources. While many of these firms are likely to remain specialized, and thus require coordination by their clients, others will surely expand their capabilities to address all the pieces of the revolution within a client company.

Much the same thing is apt to happen among vendors of information technology. In addition to helping companies develop the technological architecture they need, some companies will see opportunities to move into a full range of services that use the hardware as a technology platform. IBM and DEC are already moving in this direction, impelled in part by the fact that dramatic gains in price-performance ratios make it harder and harder to make money selling "boxes."

Finally, public accounting firms have what may be the single most critical role in this revolution. On the one hand, they could inhibit its progress in the belief that their vested interest in the existing system is too great to risk. On the other hand, all the large firms have substantial consulting practices, and the revolution represents a tremendous business opportunity for them. Companies will need a great deal of help developing new measures, validating them, and certifying them for external use.

Accounting firms also have an opportunity to develop measurement methods that will be common to an industry or across industries. While this should not be overdone, one reason financial measures carry such weight is that they are assumed to be a uniform metric, comparable across divisions and companies, and thus a valid basis for resource allocation decisions. In practice, of course, these measures are not comparable (despite the millions of hours invested in efforts to make them so) because companies use different accounting conventions. Given that fact, it is easy to see why developing additional measures that senior managers—and the investment community—can use will be a massive undertaking.

Indeed, the power of research analysts and investors generally is one of the reasons accounting firms have such a crucial role to play. Although evidence exists that investors are showing more interest in metrics such as market share and cash flow, many managers and analysts identify the investment community as the chief impediment to revolution.[5] Until investors treat other measures as seriously as financial data, they argue, limits will always exist on how seriously those measures are taken inside companies.

GE's experience with its measurement task force supports their argument. According to a knowledgeable senior executive, the 1951 effort had only a modest effect because the measures believed to determine the company's stock price, to which incentives were tied, were all financial: earnings per share, return on equity, return on investment, return on sales, and earnings growth rate. He believed that once the financial markets valued other measures, progress within companies would accelerate.

Investors, of course, see the problem from a different perspective. They question whether managers would be willing to publish anything more than the financial information required by the SEC lest they reveal too much to their competitors. Ultimately, a regulatory body like the SEC could untie this Gordian knot by recommending (and eventually requiring) public companies to provide nonfinancial measures in their reports. (This is, after all, how financial standards became so omnipotent and why so many millions of hours have been invested in their development.) But I suspect competitive pressure will prove a more immediate force for change. As soon as one leading company can demonstrate the long-term advantage of its superior performance on quality or innovation or any other nonfinancial measure, it will change the rules for all its rivals forever. And with so many serious competitors tracking—and enhancing—these measures, that is only a matter of time.

Designing a process to ensure that all these things happen is the last aspect of the revolution. To overcome conservative forces outside the company and from within (including line and staff managers at every level, in every function), someone has to take the lead. Ultimately, this means the CEO. If the CEO is not committed, the revolution will flounder, no matter how much enthusiasm exists throughout the organization.

But the CEO cannot make it happen. Developing an information architecture and its accompanying technology, aligning incentives, working with outside parties—all this requires many people and a lot of work, much of it far less interesting than plotting strategy. Moreover, the design of the process must take account of the integrative nature of the task: people in different businesses and functions including strategic planning, engineering, manufacturing, marketing and sales, human resources, and finance will all have something to contribute. The work of external players will have to be integrated with the company's own efforts.

Organizationally, two critical choices exist. One is who the point person will be. Assigning this role to the CEO or president ensures its proper symbolic visibility. Delegating it to a high-level line or staff executive and making it a big piece of his or her assignment may be a more effective way to guarantee that enough senior management time will be devoted to the project.

The other choice is which function or group will do most of the work and coordinate the company's efforts. The CEO of one high-tech company gave this responsibility to the finance function because he felt they should have the opportunity to broaden their perspective and measurement skills. He also thought it would be easier to use an existing group experienced in performance measurement. The president of an apparel company made a different choice. To avoid the financial bias embedded in the company's existing management information systems, he wanted someone to start from scratch and design a system with customer service at its core. As a result, he is planning to combine the information systems department with customer service to create a new function to be headed by a new person, recruited from the outside.

What is most effective for a given company will depend on its history, culture, and management style. But every company should make the effort to attack the problem with new principles. Some past practices may still be useful, but everything should be strenuously challenged. Otherwise, the effort will yield incremental changes at best.

Open-mindedness about the structures and processes that will be most effective, now and in the future, is equally important. I know of a few companies that are experimenting with combining the information systems and human resource departments. These experiments have entailed a certain amount of culture shock for professionals from both functions, but such radical rethinking is what revolution is all about.

Finally, recognize that once begun, this is a revolution that never ends. We are not simply talking about changing the basis of performance measurement from financial statistics to something else. We are talking about a new philosophy of performance measurement that regards it as an ongoing, evolving process. And just as igniting the revolution will take special effort, so will maintaining its momentum and reaping the rewards in the years ahead.

Notes

1. Ray Stata, "Organizational Learning—The Key to Management Innovation," *Sloan Management Review,* Spring 1989, pp. 63–74.

2. Donald A. Curtis, "The Modern Accounting System," *Financial Executive*, January–February 1985, pp. 81–93; and H. Thomas Johnson and Robert S. Kaplan, *Relevance Lost* (Boston: Harvard Business School Press, 1987).

3. Yuji Ijiri, "Cash Flow Accounting and Its Structure," *Journal of Accounting, Auditing, and Finance.* Summer 1978, pp. 331–348.

4. Robert C. Camp, *Benchmarking* (Milwaukee, Wisconsin: ASQS Quality Press, 1989).

5. "Investors Look at Firms' Market Share," *Wall Street Journal,* February 26, 1990, pp. C1–2.

Chapter 3

Organizing

Organizations have been so prevalent in the lives of most of us that we simply take their existence for granted. As a result, we fail to appreciate their relationship to other dimensions of human activity and their newness in human history. To be sure, organizations have played a significant role in many religious, military, and governmental activities for centuries. The dominant role in economic activities played by formal organizations—social systems that have been deliberately designed to achieve stated objectives—has been a relatively recent phenomenon. In the United States, for example, even late in the nineteenth century, most work was done in very small and personally run structures, such as the family- and owner-run and managed enterprises. Today, even though small businesses are a major source of employment, when people think and talk about managing, they are usually envisioning some large, complex organization—the modern corporation being the prototype.

What people know about these organizations is often gathered through "snapshots." An organization's mammoth physical plant or its palatial headquarters is very visible. Certain key events such as the introduction of a new product or service are also easily seen as a result of media coverage. The processes, however, behind these observables are obscure to outsiders. Only rarely are we cognizant of the previous facilities that the existing ones replaced or of the history associated with the organization's growth that a movie or even a series of snapshots would reveal. Even though we hear of mergers and bankruptcies, the number and size of the buildings, and of the organizations that own them, often lead us to assume that the organizations are permanent fixtures on the earth's surface. We see them as stable objects that have existed and probably will continue to exist for a long time. From this perspective, we tend to see organizations *only* as "things"—as concrete entities. We suggest that such a viewpoint leads us to overlook how the constantly changing nature of organizations and the numerous events that threaten an organization's survival complicate the balancing act managers must perform (see, for instance, "Jack Welch's Lessons for Success").

We suggest the importance of an alternative perspective that emphasizes two elements. First, when thinking about management, it is better to view organizations as being processes rather than as things. While for some purposes it may be useful to think of organizations as "things" (such as considering them as legal entities when writing or enforcing laws), for managing them it is often far more useful to think of them as processes. In other words, any given organization is constantly evolving as it interacts with its environment. As information and resources move in and out of an organization, the fabric of the organization changes. Moreover, organizations get older; they grow and contract; they appear to go through cycles of one type or another. They may add new parts (for example, departments, personnel, technologies) and/or rearrange the relationship among their parts as shown in "The Horizontal Corporation." A snapshot simply cannot capture such developments.

Secondly, we believe it is important to view modern organizations in the context of economic and social history. Successful economic activity requires that individual human beings coordinate their actions. At a very basic level, organizations function to help humans attain effective coordination. In some sense, this assertion simply states the obvious. On the other hand, it calls attention to the fact that organizations are but *one* of a number of ways of coordinating. Human actions are also coordinated through the institution we call markets that rely on people influencing each other's actions through prices they are willing to pay and demand for their goods and services. Likewise, they are coordinated through negotiation and by contracts enforced by governments and other third parties. Also, as in the case of the smaller economic enterprises, actions are coordinated through individual leadership and/or face-to-face communication. As the size of the enterprise gets very large, however, such approaches become less effective. Moreover, organizations based on personal relationships are extremely vulnerable to all types of individual failings such as greed, corruption, sickness, and death. While organizations never completely rid themselves of such dependencies, they attempt to reduce their significance by *adding* other forces to make coordination more predictable—that is, less dependent on any particular individual(s).

For successful coordination, a number of things must take place. For example, information needs to be exchanged among people. Likewise, people need to pay attention to the "right" elements at the "right" time; if they do not, their collective performance will be disjointed and ineffective. Moreover, people need to know what they are supposed to do, have the competence to do it, and be motivated to behave accordingly. Some tasks, such as a tug of war, require everyone to do pretty much the same thing. Successful performance of other tasks, such as in football, depends upon different individuals doing complementary tasks. Despite these contrasts, the managerial tasks are similar—disseminating knowledge of requirements, assuring proper timing and competence, or motivating.

The managerial work can be accomplished in a variety of ways. In some cases, one person whom we might call a leader can see that all these things are done by giving directions and announcing rewards and punishments. In other cases, we might need an extensive system of contracts or simply provide a market place where individuals can transact their business. At other times, it seems that developing rules and procedures, hiring people to supervise others, establishing formal communication and authority relationships among employees, training people and monitoring performance of assigned tasks, and so forth, are needed to achieve coordination. It is this latter set of approaches that we call organizing and that, when used, produce the type of systems we call organizations. Generally, a combination of these approaches is found.

So far, our discussion of organizing has centered on formalizing interactions that previously were less formal or did not exist at all. Today, however, the problems managers face are not simply adding these types of formal mechanisms to informal relationships. Instead, they are attempting to change the formal relationships that already exist. In essence, they are trying to *re*focus attention or change established communication patterns among people. These changes are better seen as reorganizing rather than organizing. Most of the articles included in this chapter suggest that many of the problems modern managers face require reorganization rather than simply organization.

In some ways, reorganizing may be more difficult than organizing. (See "Bitter Survivors," for instance). Reorganizing requires that old established ways be discarded. Some people, however, may have a vested interest in the old ways. For example, a professor whose status (and perhaps even whose job) depends upon being a skilled lecturer is apt to resist a new curriculum and teaching assignments that emphasizing coaching and experiential learning. Reorganizing requires redirecting the efforts of professors who may have strong and very rational (as well as less rational) commitments to the previous approach. If organizations are to grow and are to respond effectively to changing environmental conditions, reorganizing is essential.

The articles in this section reveal why organizing is so important to today's managers. These reasons include the following: changes brought about by new technologies, changes induced by competition, and changes in the nature of customer desires which alter the nature of products and services a firm produces. These articles also show additional problems that reorganizing introduces: learning and unlearning, battles over turf, and responding to new demands without sacrificing the organization's traditional strengths. It should be clear that efforts to organize are closely interrelated with other ways that coordination is achieved in an organization. Moreover, they demonstrate the even greater challenges that confront contemporary managers whose task in reorganizing is balancing the old and the new.

The Horizontal Corporation*

John A. Byrne

WANTED: Bureaucracy basher, willing to challenge convention, assume big risks, and rewrite the accepted rules of industrial order.

It's a job description that says nothing about your skills in manufacturing, finance, or any other business discipline. And as seismic changes continue to rumble across the corporate landscape, it's the kind of want ad the 21st century corporation might write.

Skeptical? No matter where you work, it's likely that your company has been, in today's vernacular, "downsized" and "delayered." It has chopped out layers of management and supposedly empowered employees with greater responsibility. But you're still bumping up against the same entrenched bureaucracy that has held you back before. The engineers still battle manufacturing. Marketing continues to slug it out with sales. And the financial naysayers fight everyone.

That's because, despite the cutbacks, you probably still work in the typical vertical organization, a company in which staffers look up to bosses instead of out to customers. You and your colleagues feel loyalty and commitment to the functional fiefdoms in which you work, not to the overall corporation and its goals. And even after all the cutting, too many layers of management still slow decision-making and lead to high coordination costs.

Mere downsizing, in other words, does little to change the fundamental way that work gets done in a corporation. To do that takes a different organizational model, the horizontal corporation. Already, some of Corporate America's biggest names, from American Telephone & Telegraph and DuPont to General Electric and Motorola, are moving toward the idea. In the quest for greater efficiency and productivity, they're beginning to redraw the hierarchical organization charts that have defined corporate life since the Industrial Revolution.

"Wave of The Future."   Some of these changes have been under way for several years under the guise of "total quality management" efforts, reengineering, or business-process redesign. But no matter which buzzword or phrase you choose, the trend is toward flatter organizations in which managing across has become more critical than managing up and down in a top-heavy hierarchy.

The horizontal corporation, though, goes much further than these previous efforts: It largely eliminates both hierarchy and functional or departmental boundaries. In its purest state, the horizontal corporation might boast a skeleton group of senior executives at the top in such traditional support functions as finance and human resources. But virtually everyone else in the organization would work together in multidisciplinary teams that perform core processes, such as product development or sales generation. The upshot: the organization might have only three or four layers of management between the chairman and the staffers in a given process.

If the concept takes hold, almost every aspect of corporate life will be profoundly altered. Companies would organize around process—developing new products, for example—instead of around narrow tasks, such as forecasting market demand for a given new product. Self-managing teams would become the building blocks of the new organization. Performance objectives would be linked to customer satisfaction rather than profitability or shareholder value. And staffers would be rewarded not just for individual performance but for the development of their skills and for team performance.

For most companies, the idea amounts to a major cultural transformation—but one whose time may be at hand. "It's a wave of the future," declares M. Anthony Burns, chairman of Ryder System Inc., the truck-leasing concern. "You just can't summarily lay off people. You've got to change the processes and drive out the unnecessary work, or it will be back tomorrow." Such radical changes hold the promise for dramatic gains in productivity, according to Lawrence A. Bossidy, chairman of AlliedSignal Inc. "There's an awful lot more productivity you're going to see in the next few years as we move to horizontally organized structures with a focus on the customer," says Bossidy.

How so? Just as a light bulb wastes electricity to produce unwanted heat, a traditional corporation expends a tremendous amount of energy running its own internal machinery—managing relations among departments or providing information up and down the hierarchy, for example.

A horizontal structure eliminates most of those tasks and focuses almost all of a company's resources on its customers. That's why proponents of the idea say it can deliver dramatic improvements in efficiency and speed. "It can get you from 100 horsepower to 500 horsepower," says Frank Ostroff, a McKinsey & Co. consultant. With colleague Douglas Smith, he coined the term "the horizontal organization" and developed a series of principles to define the new corporate model.

The idea is drawing attention in corporate and academic circles. In the past year, Ostroff has given talks on the horizontal organization before sizable gatherings of corporate strategic planners, quality experts, and entrepreneurs. He has also carried the message to MBAs and faculty at the University of Pennsylvania and Yale University, and he boasts invitations from Harvard University and several leading European business schools.

Process and Pain.   But this is much more than just another abstract theory making the B-school lecture rounds. Examples of horizontal management abound, though much of the movement is occurring at lower levels in the organizations. Some AT&T units are now doing annual budgets based not on functions or departments but on processes such as the maintenance of a worldwide telecommunications network. They're even dishing out bonuses to employees based on customer evaluations of the teams performing those processes. DuPont Co. has set up a centralized group this year to nudge the chemical giant's business units into organizing along horizontal lines. Chrysler Corp. used a process approach to turn out its new Neon subcompact quickly for a fraction of the typical development costs. Xerox Corp. is employing what it calls "microenterprise units" of employees that have beginning-to-end responsibility for the company's products.

In early December, nearly two dozen companies—including such international giants as Boeing, British Telecommunications, Stockholm-based L. M. Ericsson, and Volvo Europe—convened in Boston under the auspices of Mercer Management Consulting, another consulting shop peddling the idea, to swap stories on their efforts to adopt horizontal management techniques. Indeed, nearly all of the most prominent consulting firms are now raking in tens of millions of dollars in revenues by advising companies to organize their operations horizontally.

What those consultants' clients are quickly discovering, however, is that eliminating the neatly arranged boxes on an organization chart in favor of a more horizontal structure can often be a complex and painful ordeal. Indeed, simply defining the processes of a given corporation may prove to be a mind-boggling and time-consuming exercise. Consider AT&T. Initially, the company's Network Services Division, which has 16,000 employees, tallied up some 130 processes before it narrowed them down to 13 core ones.

After that comes the challenge of persuading people to cast off their old marketing, finance, or manufacturing hats and think more broadly. "This is the hardest damn thing to do," says Terry M. Ennis, who heads up a group to help DuPont's businesses organize along horizontal lines. "It's very unsettling and threatening for people. You find line and function managers who have been honored and rewarded for what they've done for decades. You're in a white-water zone when you change."

Some management gurus, noting the fervor with which corporate chieftains embrace fads, express caution. "The idea draws together a number of fashionable trends and packages them in an interesting way," says Henry Mintzberg, a management professor at McGill University. "But the danger is that an idea like this can generate too much enthusiasm. It's not for everyone." Mintzberg notes that there is no one solution to every organization's problems. Indeed, streamlined vertical structures may suit some mass-production industries better than horizontal ones.

Already, consultants say, some companies are rushing to organize around processes without linking them to the corporation's key goals. Before tinkering with its organization chart, Ostroff says, a company must understand the markets and the customers it wants to reach and complete an analysis of what it will take to win them. Only then should the company begin to identify the most critical core processes to achieve its objectives—whether they're lowering costs by 30% or developing new products in half the time it normally required.

Different Climate.   In the days when business was more predictable and stable, companies organized themselves in vertical structures to take advantage of specialized experts. The benefits are obvious: Everyone has a place, and everyone understands his or her task. The critical decision-making power resides at the top.

But while gaining clarity and stability, such organizations make it difficult for anyone to understand the task of the company as a whole and how to relate his or her work to it. The result: Collaboration among different departments was often a triumph over formal organization charts.

To solve such problems, some companies turned to so-called matrix organizations in the 1960s and 1970s. The model was built around specific projects that cut across departmental lines. But it still kept the hierarchy intact and left most of the power and responsibility in the upper reaches of the organization.

Heightened global competition and the ever increasing speed of technological change have since altered the rules of the game and have forced corporate planners to seek new solutions. "We were reluctant to leave the command-and-control structure because it had worked so well," says Philip Engel, president of CNA Corp., the Chicago-based insurance company that is refashioning its organization. "But it no longer fit the realities."

Indeed, many companies are moving to this new form of corporate organization after failing to achieve needed productivity gains by simple streamlining and consolidation. "We didn't have another horse to ride," says Kenneth L. Garrett, a senior vice-president at AT&T's Network Systems Division. "We weren't performing as well as we could, and we had already streamlined our operations."

In all cases, the objective of the horizontal corporation is to change the narrow mind-sets of armies of corporate specialists who have spent their careers climbing a vertical hierarchy to the top of a given function. As DuPont's Terry Ennis puts it: "Our goal is to get everyone focused on the business as a system in which the functions are seamless." DuPont executives are trying to do away with what Ennis calls the "disconnects" and "handoffs" that are so common between functions and departments. "Every time you have an organizational boundary, you get the potential for a disconnect," Ennis says. "The bigger the organization, the bigger the functions, and the more disconnects you get."

Speedier Cycles.   The early proponents of the horizontal corporation are claiming significant gains. At General Electric, where Chairman John F. Welch Jr. speaks of building a "boundaryless" company, the concept has reduced costs, shortened cycle times, and increased the company's responsiveness to its customers. GE's $3 billion lighting business scrambled a more traditional structure for its global technology organization in favor of one in which a senior team of 9-to-12 people oversees nearly 100 processes or programs worldwide, from new-product design to improving the yield on production machinery. In virtually all the cases, a multidisciplinary team works together to achieve the goals of the process.

The senior leadership group—composed of managers with "multiple competencies" rather than narrow specialists—exists to allocate resources and ensure coordination of the processes and programs. "They stay away from the day-to-day activities, which are managed by the teams themselves," explains Harold Giles, manager of human resources in GE's lighting business.

The change forced major upheavals in GE's training, appraisal, and compensation systems. To create greater allegiance to a process rather than a boss, the company has begun to put in place so-called "360-degree appraisal routines" in which peers and others above and below the employee evaluate the performance of an individual in a process. In some cases, as many as 20 people are now involved in reviewing a single employee. Employees are paid on the basis of the skills they develop rather than merely the individual work they perform.

Ryder System is another convert. The company had been organized by division—each with its own functions—based on product. But it wanted an organization that would reduce overhead while being more responsive to customers. "We were reaching the end of the runway looking for cost efficiencies, as most companies have," says J. Ernie Riddle, senior vice-president for marketing. "So we're looking at processes from front to back."

To purchase a vehicle for leasing, for instance, required some 14 to 17 hand-offs as the documents wended their way from one functional department to another at a local, and then a national, level. "We passed the baton so many times that the chances of dropping it were great," says Riddle. By viewing this paper-work flow as a single process from purchasing the vehicle to providing it to a customer, Ryder has reduced the handoffs to two from five. By redesigning the work, weeding out unnecessary approvals, and pushing more authority down the organization, the company cut its purchasing cycle by a third, to four months.

"Clean Sheet." Some startups have opted to structure themselves as horizontal companies from the get-go. One such company is Astra/Merck Group, a new stand-alone company formed to market anti-ulcer and high-blood-pressure drugs licensed from Sweden's Astra. Instead of organizing around functional areas, Astra/Merck is structured around a half-dozen "market-driven business processes," from drug development to product sourcing and distribution. "We literally had a clean sheet of paper to build the new model company," says Robert C. Holmes, director of strategic planning. "A functional organization wasn't likely to support our strategic goals to be lean, fast, and focused on the customer."

Some fairly small companies are also finding the model appealing. Consider Modicon Inc., a North Andover (Mass.) maker of automation-control equipment with annual revenues of $300 million. Instead of viewing product development as a task of the engineering function, President Paul White defined it more broadly as a process that would involve a team of 15 managers from engineering, manufacturing, marketing, sales, and finance.

By working together, Modicon's team avoided costly delays from disagreements and misunderstandings. "In the past," says White, "an engineering team would have worked on this alone with some dialogue from marketing. Manufacturing wouldn't get involved until the design was brought into the factory. Now, all the business issues are right on the table from the beginning."

Team Hats. The change allowed Modicon to bring six software products to market in one-third the time it would normally take. The company, a subsidiary of Germany's Daimler Benz, still has a management structure organized by function. But many of the company's 900 employees are involved in up to 30 teams that span several functions and departments. Predicts White: "In five years, we'll still have some formal functional structure, but people will probably feel free enough to spend the majority of their time outside their functions."

So far, the vast majority of horizontal experimentation has been at the lower levels of organizations. Increasingly, however, corporations are overhauling their entire structures to bear a closer resemblance to the horizontal model defined by consultants Ostroff and others. Eastman Chemical Co., the $3.5 billion unit of Eastman Kodak Co. to be spun off as a stand-alone company on Jan. 1, [1994], replaced several of its senior vice-presidents in charge of the key functions with "self-directed work teams." Instead of having a head of manufacturing, for example, the company uses a team consisting of all its plant managers. "It was the most dramatic change in the company's 70-year history," maintains Ernest W. Deavenport Jr., president of Eastman Chemical. "It makes people take off their organizational hats and put on their team hats. It gives people a much broader perspective and forces decision-making down at least another level."

In creating the new organization, the 500 senior managers agreed that the primary role of the functions was to support Eastman's business in chemicals, plastics, fibers, and polymers. "A function does not and should not have a mission of its own," insists Deavenport. Common sense? Of course. But over the years the functional departments had grown strong and powerful, as they have in many organizations, often at the expense of the overall company as they fought to protect and build turf. Now, virtually all of the company's managers work on at least one cross-functional team, and most work on two or more on a daily basis. For example, Tom O. Nethery, a group vice-president, runs an industrial-business group. But he also serves on three other teams that deal with such diverse issues as human resources, cellulose technology, and product-support services.

These changes in the workplace are certain to dramatically alter titles, career paths, and the goals of individuals, too. At AT&T's Network Systems Division, each of 13 core processes boasts an "owner" and a "champion." While the owners focus on the day-to-day operations of a process, the champions ensure that the process remains linked with overall business strategies and goals. Through it all, collaboration is key. "An overriding challenge is how you get marketing people to talk to finance people when they've thrown rocks at each other for decades," says Gerald Ross, co-founder of ChangeLab International, a consulting firm that specializes in cultural transformation. "Your career will be dependent on your ability to work across boundaries with others very different from you."

Don't rush to write the obituary for functional management, however. No companies have completely eliminated functional specialization. And even advocates of the new model don't envision the end of managers who are experts in manufacturing, finance, and the like. "It's only the rarest of organizations that would choose to be purely vertical or horizontal," says consultant Douglas Smith. "Most organizations will be hybrids."

Still, the horizontal corporation is an idea that's gaining currency and one that will increasingly demand people who think more broadly and thrive on change, who manage process instead of people, and who cherish teamwork as never before.

◆

Jack Welch's Lessons for Success[*]

Noel M. Tichy and Stratford Sherman

More than any other executive, Jack Welch is known for breakthrough management ideas and the will to apply them. As General Electric's chief executive since 1981, Welch, 57, has led the revolution that is transforming GE from a stodgy industrial giant into one of the world's most valuable and competitive companies. His remarks here are from the new book about his tenure at GE: *Control Your Destiny or Someone Else Will* by Noel M. Tichy and Stratford Sherman.

The authors spent over 100 hours interviewing Welch, and spoke with scores of other GEers, from heads of businesses to young management trainees. Tichy, a professor of organization at the University of Michigan, was a key participant in the GE revolution. A consultant there since 1982, he ran GE's Crotonville management-development school for two years. Sherman, a member of *Fortune's* board of editors, has been writing about GE for over a decade. Their book explains how companies and individuals can face accelerating change and intensifying competition, and win.

Welch's managerial focus has shifted over the years from cost cutting and restructuring to the murky realm of human values. But the man *Fortune* once named America's toughest boss insists he has not gone soft after 12 years on the job. He also discusses the lessons he has learned, sharing personal reflections on his own mistakes and offering new insights into the art of management.

The Value Decade has already begun, with global price competition like you've never seen. It's going to be brutal. When I said the 1980s was going to be a white-knuckle decade and the 1990s would be even tougher, I may have understated how hard it's going to get.

Everywhere you go, people are saying, "Don't tell me about your technology, tell me your price." To get a lower price, customers are willing to sacrifice the extras they used to demand. The fact is, many governments are broke, and people are hurting, so there's an enormous drive to get value, value, value.

During the global expansion of the 1980s, companies responded to rising demand by building new factories and facilities in computers, airplanes, medical equipment—almost every industry you can think of. Then, when the world economy stopped growing, everybody ended up with too much capacity.

Globalization compounds the problem: It doesn't matter where you are anymore because distribution systems now give everybody access to everything.

Capacity can come from anywhere on the planet, and there's too much in just about every industry in every developed country. No matter where you go, it's the same story.

This worldwide capacity overhang, coming at a time when everybody feels poor, is forcing ferocious price competition. As it intensifies, the margin pressure on all corporations is going to be enormous. Only the most productive companies are going to win. If you can't sell a top-quality product at the world's lowest price, you're going to be out of the game. In that environment, 6% annual improvement in productivity may not be good enough anymore; you may need 8% or 9%. And while that bar keeps getting raised higher, higher, we're all going to be experiencing slow revenue growth. It's brutal!

In our aircraft engines business our customers aren't asking about the latest advances, the last 2% of fuel burn. They want to know, "How much will it cost? Can you provide financing? Can we walk away from the lease? Boeing and ourselves lost a billion-dollar plus bid at United Airlines to Airbus. Simply put, we couldn't afford to sell them the planes.

Technology is still absolutely critical, but in industry after industry it will be value driven. Who can make the most energy efficient light bulb or refrigerator? Whose medical imaging system is the most cost-effective? The medical diagnostic imaging business is a perfect example of what's happening everywhere. The market is shifting away from the technology leader in the high-end niche to the guy with the basic, proven, low-priced systems that produce acceptable images. Governments have decided they don't want to pay more for health care, so if you're trying to pitch some new hot technology the customer's going to say, "See you later."

Environmental soundness is another form of value. We won an order from Swissair for jet engines because ours produced the lowest emissions. Multinational companies have to maintain worldclass environmental standards wherever they go—even where local laws are lax—in their plants as well as their products. In the end, there's going to be a global standard for the environment, and anyone who cuts corners today will wind up with enormous liabilities down the road. If we're going to be global citizens, we can't have one set of standards in some countries and different standards in others.

Some of the biggest dangers I see ahead come from governments. You can do everything right as a manager, and then government deficits, or interest rates, or whatever, can cause a currency to change value by 30% or 40% and knock your business completely out of whack. About 65% of GE's manufacturing base is still located in the U.S. I have to worry about whether government policies here will allow us to deliver the productivity we need to win on a global basis.

But it's not just the U.S.: Wherever you travel these days, you encounter increasing fear of government. Constituents want more. And to get more, they seem willing to accept enormous increases in government power. I worry about a return to overregulation and protectionism. I don't want to see governments meddling in industrial policy—bureaucrats picking winners and losers. Governments set out to create Silicon Valley and wind up building the Motor Vehicle Department.

In terms of jobs, government may become the world's main growth industry. When the European Community was formed, it created thousands of jobs for bureaucrats. Now they are telling the French which cheese is good and which isn't. It's frightening!

I think the U.S. is in a great position competitively. We're looking better compared with Germany and Japan than we did five or ten years ago, and many of our companies are in a position to win. We've restructured our industries. Our businesses have better leaders than ever before. Our people have learned the value of their jobs and the principle that job security comes from winning. Some of the most passionate pleas for worker productivity I've ever read have been made by tough union leaders. They lecture our managers on the subject at Crotonville. That change in attitude is one of the most positive developments I've seen.

The U.S. did have a gap in product quality before, but during the 1980s we made great strides in closing it. Our cars are better, and so are our computers and semiconductors. We thought they'd all be Japanese by now, but they're not. And if you look at the J. D. Power surveys of customer satisfaction—U.S. vs. foreign auto companies—we're pretty close. A few years ago few would have believed that could happen.

What we have to do now is educate our people. Companies have to get involved in the school systems, with dollars and volunteers. Within GE, we've got to upgrade workers' skills through intense and continuous training. Companies can't promise lifetime employment, but by constant training and education we may be able to guarantee lifetime employability. We've got to invest totally in our people.

For U.S. companies, at least, globalization is getting increasingly difficult. The expansion into Europe was comparatively easy from a cultural standpoint. As Japan developed, the cultural differences were larger, and U.S. business has had more difficulties there. As we look ahead, the cultural challenges will be larger still in the rest of Asia—from China to Indonesia to Thailand to India—where more than half the world lives. U.S. companies will have to adapt to those cultures if they are to succeed in the 21st century.

Trying to define what will happen three to five years out, in specific, quantitative terms, is a futile exercise. The world is moving too fast for that. What should a company do instead? First of all, define its vision and its destiny in broad but clear terms. Second, maximize its own productivity. Finally, be organizationally and culturally flexible enough to meet massive change.

The way to control your destiny in a global environment of change and uncertainty is simple: Be the highest-value supplier in your marketplace.

When I try to summarize what I've learned since 1981, one of the big lessons is that change has no constituency. People like the status quo. They like the way it was. When you start changing things, the good old days look better and better.

You've got to be prepared for massive resistance.

Incremental change doesn't work very well in the type of transformation GE has gone through. If your change isn't big enough, revolutionary enough, the bureaucracy can beat you. When you get leaders who confuse popularity with leadership, who just nibble away at things, nothing changes. I think that's true in countries and in companies.

Another big lesson: You've got to be hard to be soft. You have to demonstrate the ability to make hard, tough decisions—closing plants, divesting, delayering—if you want to have any credibility when you try to promote soft values. We reduced employment and cut the bureaucracy and picked up some unpleasant nicknames, but when we spoke of soft values—things like candor, fairness, facing reality—people listened.

If you've got a fat organization, soft values won't get you very far. Pushing speed and simplicity, or a program like Work-Out [in which GEers of all levels team up to find better ways of working], is just plain not do-able in a big bureaucracy. Before you can get into stuff like that, you've first got to do the hard structural work. Take out the layers. Pull up the weeds. Scrape off the rust.

Every organization needs values, but a lean organization needs them even more. When you strip away the support systems of staffs and layers, people need to change their habits and expectations or else the stress will just overwhelm them. We're working harder and faster. But unless we're also having more fun, the transformation doesn't work. Values are what enable people to guide themselves through that kind of change.

To create change, direct, personal two-way communication is what seems to make the difference: exposing people—without the protection of title or position—to ideas from everywhere, judging ideas on their merits. You've got to be out in front of crowds, repeating yourself over and over again, never changing your message no matter how much it bores you. You need an overarching message, something big but simple and understandable. Whatever it is every idea you present must be something you could get across easily at a cocktail party with strangers. If only aficionados of your industry can understand what you're saying, you've blown it.

Another take-away for me: Simplicity applies to measurements also. Too often we measure everything and understand nothing. The three most important things you need to measure in a business are customer satisfaction, employee satisfaction, and cash flow. If you're growing customer satisfaction, your global market share is sure to grow too. Employee satisfaction gets you productivity, quality, pride, and creativity. And cash flow is the pulse—the key vital sign of a company.

Another thing I've learned is the value of stretching the organization by setting the bar higher than people think they can go. The standard of performance we use is: Be as good as the best in the world. Invariably people find the way to get there, or most of the way. They dream and reach and search. The trick is not to punish those who fall short. If they improve, you reward them—even if they haven't reached the goal. But unless you set the bar high enough, you'll never find out what people can do.

I've made my share of mistakes—plenty of them—but my biggest mistake by far was not moving faster. Pulling off a Band-Aid one hair at a time hurts a lot more than a sudden yank. Of course you want to avoid breaking things or stretching the organization too far—but generally human nature holds you back. You want to be liked, to be thought of as reasonable. So you don't move as fast as you should. Besides hurting more, it costs you competitiveness.

Everything should have been done in half the time. When you're running an institution like this, you're always scared at first. You're afraid you'll break it. People don't think about leaders this way, but it's true. Everyone who's running something goes home at night and wrestles with the same fear: Am I going to be the one who blows this place up? In retrospect, I was too cautious and too timid. I wanted too many constituencies on board.

Timidity causes mistakes. We didn't buy a food company in the early 1980s because I didn't have the courage of my conviction. We thought about it, we discussed it at Crotonville, and it was the right idea. I was afraid GE wasn't ready for a move like that. Another thing we should have done is eliminate the sectors right away. [GE eliminated the sectors—a layer of top management between the CEO and the operating businesses—in 1985.] Then we could have given the sector heads—who were our best people—big jobs running businesses. We should have invented Work-Out five years earlier. I wish we'd understood boundarylessness better, sooner. [Boundarylessness is Welch's term for the breaking down of barriers that divide employees—such as hierarchy, job function, and geography—and that distance companies from suppliers and customers.] I wish we'd understood all along how much leverage you can get from the flow of ideas among all the business units.

Now that we've got that leverage, I wonder how we ever lived without it. The enormous advantage we have today is that we can run GE as a laboratory for ideas. We've found mechanisms to share best practices in a way that's trusting and open. When our people go to Xerox, say, or their people come here, the exchange is good—but in these "flybys" the takeaways are largely conceptual, and we both have difficulty getting too far below the surface. But when every GE business sends two people to Louisville for a year to study the Quick Response program in our own appliance business, the ideas take on intensity and depth. [The Quick Response streamlining program enabled GE Appliances to cut the 80-day cycle time from receipt of an order to delivery of a finished product by over 75%. The business reduced inventory by $200 million and increased return on investment by 8.5 percentage points.] The people who go to Louisville aren't tourists. When they go back to their businesses to talk about Quick Response they're zealots, because they're owners of that idea. They've been on the team that made it work.

All those opportunities were out there, but we didn't see them until we got rid of the staffs, the layers, and the hierarchies. Then they became obvious. If I'd moved more quickly in the beginning, we'd have noticed those opportunities sooner, and we'd be further ahead than we are today.

The only way I see to get more productivity is by getting people involved and excited about their jobs. You can't afford to have anyone walk through a gate of a factory, or into an office, who's not giving 120%. I don't mean running and sweating, but working smarter. It's a matter of understanding the customer's needs instead of just making something and putting it into a box. It's a matter of seeing the importance of your role in the total process.

The point of Work-Out is to give people better jobs. When people see that their ideas count, their dignity is raised. Instead of feeling numb, like robots, they feel important. They are important.

I would argue that a satisfied work force is a productive work force. Back when jobs were plentiful and there was no foreign competition, people were satisfied just to hang around. Now people come to work with a different agenda: They want to win against the competition because they know that the competition is the enemy and that customers are their only source of job security. They don't like weak managers because they know that the weak managers of the 1970s and 1980s cost millions of people their jobs.

With Work-Out and boundarylessness, we're trying to differentiate GE competitively by raising as much intellectual and creative capital from our work force as we possibly can. That's a lot tougher than raising financial capital, which a strong company can find in any market in the world.

Trust is enormously powerful in a corporation. People won't do their best unless they believe they'll be treated fairly—that there's no cronyism and everybody has a real shot. The only way I know to create that kind of trust is by laying out your values and then walking the talk. You've got to do what you say you'll do, consistently, over time.

It doesn't mean everybody has to agree. I have a great relationship with Bill Bywater, president of the International Union of Electronic Workers. I would trust him with my wallet, but he knows I'll fight him to the death in certain areas, and vice versa. He wants to recruit more members for the union. I'll say, "No way! We can give people everything you can and more!" He knows where I stand. I know where he stands. We don't always agree—but we trust each other.

That's what boundarylessness is: an open, trusting sharing of ideas. A willingness to listen, debate, and then take the best ideas and get on with it.

If this company is to achieve its goals, we've all got to become boundaryless. Boundaries are crazy. The union is just another boundary, and you have to reach across, the same way you want to reach across the boundaries separating you from your customers and your suppliers and your colleagues overseas.

We're not that far along with boundarylessness. It's a big, big idea, but I don't think it has enough fur on it yet. We've got to keep repeating it, reinforcing it, rewarding it, living it, letting everybody know all the time that when they're doing things right, it's because their behavior is boundaryless. It's going to take a couple more years to get people to the point where the ideas of boundarylessness just becomes natural.

Who knows exactly when I'll retire? You go when it's the right time to go. You pray to God you don't stay too long.

I keep asking myself, "Are you regenerating? Are you dealing with new things? When you find yourself in a new environment, do you come up with a fundamentally different approach?" That's the test. When you flunk, you leave.

Three or four times a year, I hop on a plane and visit something like seven countries in 15 days. People say to me. "Are you nutty?" No, I'm not nutty. I'm trying to regenerate.

The CEO succession here is still a long way off, but I think about it every day. Obviously, anybody who gets this job must have a vision for the company and be capable of rallying people behind it. He or she has got to be very comfortable in a global environment, dealing with world leaders. Be comfortable dealing with people at all levels of the company. Have a boundaryless attitude toward every constituency—race, gender, everything. Have the very highest standards of integrity. Believe in the gut that people are the key to everything, and that change is not something you fear—it's something you relish. Anyone who is too inwardly-focused, who doesn't relish customers, who isn't open to change, isn't going to make it.

Finally, whoever gets the job will have to have what I call an edge—an insatiable passion for winning and growing. In the end, I think it will be a combination of that edge and those values that will determine who gets this job.

I think any company that's trying to play in the 1990s has got to find a way to engage the mind of every single employee. Whether we make our way successfully down this road is something only time will tell—but I'm as sure as I've ever been about anything that this is the right road.

If you're not thinking all the time about making every person more valuable, you don't have a chance. What's the alternative? Wasted minds? Uninvolved people? A labor force that's angry or bored? That doesn't make sense!

If you've got a better way, show me. I'd love to know what it is.

◆

The Termination of Eric Clark[*]

Clive Gilson

Yes, I had several summer jobs during my time as a student, but the real world always seemed to be somewhere over the horizon. My world was one which flowed between papers, exams and results. And back again. In fact the completion of my Ph.D signalled almost ten years in higher education. It was now September of 1979 and I was about to begin another year at University, this time as an educator.

While sitting in my office preparing for the coming semester, I pondered the reality of my position. A simple problem. It did not seem real at all. Taking stock I decided with uncharacteristic clarity that I should leave at once—escape if you will, perhaps I might even learn how to be human. So I left. Within 48 hours and with Ph.D in hand, I took a job as a medium haul truck driver at a large local bakery, which employed close to 1,000 workers.

---

[*]This case was prepared by Clive Gilson, St. Francis Xavier University, Antigonish, Nova Scotia, Canada. Reprinted with permission of the author.

I will never forget my first morning. It started at 4.00 AM. My lasting memory will always be the smell of sweet fresh cream amid the acrid aroma of diesel fuel and exhaust fumes. The assault upon my senses also included the earthy didactic commentary of a grizzled supervisor named Johnny Poole, who frequently called into question the status of my parentage and also implied for good measure that relations between myself and my mother were at best unconventional. No place for dignity here. I was shocked. However, I was lucky enough to be sent out on the road with driver Eric Clark who was to show me the ropes and without conscious knowledge, transmit to me some of the values and behaviors of those who "really" worked for a living. Eric was the educator; I had come to school.

I could barely keep up. Eric was 55 years old yet seemed able to cope with the constant grinding strain of the road and the loading and unloading of bakery goods (which incidentally are much heavier than you could ever imagine). Several times I would verbalize my admiration, commenting that his fortitude in the face of hard work, low pay and a perniciously cruel supervisor, was hard to understand. His response was always the same—"Press on regardless." Much later I was to learn that such phrases were important mechanisms which enabled workers at the bakery to find solace and meaning in their labours. Like his co-workers Eric rarely, if ever, questioned his subjugation to managerial authority and only occasionally, its terms. Anyway, that's pretty much how Eric coped, actually more than coped. He retained a wonderfully optimistic approach towards all people. His infectious zest for life even under what I considered to be considerable adversity, was remarkable. He was an honest man whose essential nature was to do a good day's work. And taking his example, I tried to do the same. Finally, I was actually *working* for a living.

My three weeks spent with Eric Clark made a brutalizing experience manageable. Not only was I able to master the art of handling a 40-ton trailer, more importantly, I had obtained a valuable lesson in how workers see the world—and the distance between them and those who controlled our destiny. I had no idea that 5 years later our paths would cross again and I would learn another lesson which would alter my world forever.

Christmas of 1979 brought unbelievable exhaustion. I had not realised that eating was a seasonal habit. Our work load doubled and then tripled. Days seemed to merge together. In the week before Christmas "piggy-back" shifts started at 3.00 AM and finished at 9.00 PM. For once my pay-check appeared reasonable, although my initial pleasure was fettered somewhat by the knowledge that January would almost certainly bring at best short-time working and at worst, extended lay-off until the Spring months. Through all this I had grown very cynical towards the management. I was astonished at their ineptitude and apparent distance from the workers. This compelled me to join the local union and seek representative office as Shop Steward. In the Summer of the following year I was elected to the position of plant Convener in charge of negotiations for just under 1,000 workers. I was both proud and filled with trepidation. My fellow workers expected and demanded miracles. From management I got hostility.

For the next two years I struggled mightily to improve the working conditions which my fellow workers endured. Many times I would come off the road from an eight-hour shift and have to represent one of my members who, unable to deal with the daily pressures, had engaged in verbal acts of insubordination—and sometimes worse behaviour still. This was not the rational world which I had frankly expected. My emotional and physical investment also conspired to rob me of many of the critical and analytical faculties which I had nurtured during my "academic" years. Reading and cultural activities were reduced to tabloid newspapers and watching sitcom re-runs. Bed at 8.30 PM or 9.00 PM

In the Autumn of 1981 I was called into the office of the owner and Managing Director and given an ultimatum. Join management or face dismissal. My role as an articulate workers' advocate apparently caused considerable disquiet among some managers, who felt threatened by my persistent questioning of their decisions—they simply wanted me out. The Managing Director saw the situation differently and reasoned that in the right place I could be an asset rather than an irritant. Driven by naivety and selective optimism I assumed the role of Transport and Distribution Manager. In the first few months of the job, my new power enabled me to introduce many of the changes which I had long sought as a union official. The workers greatly appreciated my progressive style. So did the owner of the company. Within six months I had been promoted to the position of Assistant Director in charge of all company operations.

For the next two years I was immersed in the world of executive decision making. Work began at 7.30 AM or 8.00 AM (although I still woke up at 3.45–4 AM–a legacy which continues to this day) and was full of creativity and responsibility. Power and influence became seductive aphrodisiacs. I had finally found the real world.

Unfortunately, the real world also included the storm clouds of economic recession. By late 1983 it seemed as if people had stopped eating. The company had a very poor Christmas period and the Winter months looked bleak. For the first time I instituted strict performance and appraisal programs with the intention of reducing our labour costs. I had no choice, the books spoke the unequivocal truth. In February of 1984 my General Manager made a sombre yet excellent presentation which concluded that the appraisals had revealed that we should release 150 workers—permanently. Each decision was based on a combination of seniority and performance. Since I was the one who carried the responsibility for this critical initiative, I announced that I would personally inform each worker that he was going to be released. I asked the general manager to prepare the list and to leave it on my desk so I could begin this unenviable task the following morning.

After sleeping well I arrived at work a little earlier than usual and sat down at my desk. I opened the envelope and found six pages of names—those who were to be terminated. At the top of the list was Eric Clark. I was stunned. In haste I retrieved his personal file. It made devastating reading. Twelve months earlier his wife, June (whom I had also met) had died of cancer of the brain—I knew that Eric worshipped her. I had not known that his work had deteriorated since then. Apparently, he had slowed down considerably, become forgetful and incurred a number of minor traffic violations. I had not known of June's death either.

Eric was summoned to see me early in the afternoon. By now the word had spread and Eric knew what our meeting was about. He entered my office walking tall with his shoulders square. He shook my hand and said, "Good afternoon, Sir." Despite the difficult circumstances, Eric's dignity enabled him to maintain his natural deference to authority. I asked him to be seated and began my long explanation concerning the rationale behind his release. After I had finished there was a long and uneasy silence. At this point I remember that I found it difficult to look Eric in the face.

Eventually, in a quiet voice Eric started to speak. I cannot remember his precise words so I will try to summarise them for you. He told me that in the Second World War he was a marine commando and was part of the allied forces which liberated Italy. He had fought for his own and future generations and he could not understand that within his own lifetime, he was being discarded. Why? More directly he expressed his disbelief that he was being rejected by the very generation which he had fought for. Eric, of course, was the same age as my own parents, which made my task doubly awkward. Indeed, not a few years earlier, I had heard similar incantations from my father whenever I had acted selfishly or had been disrespectful to my elders. I had also heard many stories about the bravery and heroism of the marine commandos—at school we were taught that they were the ones who won the war. Eric also told me that his last operation was on the beaches at Anzio, where he was seriously wounded. I also remember my father telling me that the carnage at Anzio was so appalling that those who fought, lived and died on those beaches were legends who were accorded a special status. They stood next to God.

Eric had never mentioned or talked about his life to me in those few weeks we had spent together in the fall of 1979. In fact I suspect that he had never related his story to anyone. I do not think for one moment that he deliberately tried to make me feel uncomfortable (although this was clearly the result). I sensed that he truly could not comprehend the world, its values and its short memory.

Downsizing: What do we know? What have we learned?*

Wayne F. Cascio
UNIVERSITY OF COLORADO

Downsizing, the planned elimination of positions or jobs, is a phenomenon that has affected hundreds of companies and millions of workers since the late 1980s. While there is no shortage of articles on "How To" or "How Not To" downsize, the current article attempts to synthesize what is known in terms of the economic and organizational

---

*Reprinted from Academy of Management Executive, Vol. 7, No. 1, pp. 95–104. Copyright © 1993 Academy of Management.

consequences of downsizing. We argue that in many firms anticipated economic benefits fail to materialize, for example, lower expense ratios, higher profits, increased return-on-investment, and boosted stock prices. Likewise, many anticipated organizational benefits do not develop, such as lower overhead, smoother communications, greater entrepreneurship, and increases in productivity.

To a large extent, this is a result of a failure to break out of the traditional approach to organization design and management—an approach founded on the principles of command, control, and compartmentalization. For long-term, sustained improvements in efficiency, reductions in headcount need to be viewed as part of a process of continuous improvement that includes organization redesign, along with broad, systemic changes designed to eliminate redundancies, waste, and inefficiency.

American Telephone & Telegraph, Eastman Kodak, Citicorp, Goodyear, Digital Equipment, Amoco, Chevron, Exxon, Black & Decker, CBS, ABC. The list reads like a "who's who" of American business. Is there no end to it? It seems to be endemic to the 1990s. In fact, it's hard to pick up a newspaper on any given day and not read about another well-known organization that is announcing a corporate restructuring (a.k.a., cutting workers, and, in some cases, selling off other assets). By the end of 1992, just to cite a few well-known examples, International Business Machines will pare down by another 40,000 workers, and Xerox will cut 2,500 workers from its document-processing division. By mid-1993 the Postal Service will eliminate 30,000 of 130,000 management jobs, and TRW, Inc. will cut its work force by 10,000 people, or fourteen percent. By 1995, General Motors will cut 75,000 workers. More than eighty-five percent of the *Fortune* 1000 firms downsized their white-collar work forces between 1987 and 1991, affecting more than five million jobs. More than fifty percent downsized in 1990 alone. Across the total economy, counting *only* jobs held for at least three years, 5.6 million people lost permanent jobs from 1987 through 1991.[1] In short, companies large and small are slashing jobs at a pace never before seen in American economic history.

WHAT'S DIFFERENT ABOUT THE CURRENT CUTS?

In previous business downturns, manufacturing has tended to take the big hits. Since 1980, U.S. manufacturing firms have cut more than two million workers. However, the most recent recession has had a decidedly white-collar pattern to it, with more middle managers eliminated during the downturn. For example, while middle managers make up only five to eight percent of the work force, they accounted for seventeen percent of all dismissals from 1989 to 1991. Further evidence comes from the fact that in 1992 white-collar employees constituted thirty-six percent of the unemployed workers in the U.S., compared with twenty-two percent during the 1982 slump. Nearly a million U.S. managers earning more than $40,000 a year lost their jobs in 1991, and, in fact, each year for the past three years, between one and two million middle managers were laid off.[2]

The major reason for this, according to a Boston University survey of manufacturers, is that overhead (which includes staff and white-collar salaries) comprises

26.6% of manufacturing costs in the U.S., compared to 21.6% in Germany, and just 17.9% in Japan. Indeed, after benchmarking its performance against other international chemical companies, Du Pont decided to slash $1 billion from its costs. How? Largely by cutting, 1,900 white-collar jobs from its fibers business, plus 550, or twenty percent of the total, from in-house engineering.

ORIENTATION

Although the subject of downsizing has been addressed from a number of perspectives, this article focuses on just two major issues: (1) What are the economic and human consequences of such massive restructuring? and (2) What have we learned? To provide answers to these questions, I did two things. First, I reviewed more than 500 published articles on the subject of downsizing. Then I conducted semi-structured interviews with twenty-five senior executives—ten who had authorized downsizing actions at their companies, and fifteen who had been laid off as a result of downsizing activities. Let us begin by considering some basic questions: What is downsizing? Who is most likely to downsize, and what do they expect to get out of it?

Definition   Downsizing refers to the planned elimination of positions or jobs. Let us be clear about these terms. While there are as many positions as there are employees, jobs are groups of positions that are similar in their significant duties—such as computer programmers or financial analysts. Downsizing may occur by reducing work (not just employees) as well as by eliminating functions, hierarchical levels, or units. It may also occur by implementing cost containment strategies that streamline activities such as transaction processing, information systems, or sign-off policies.

Downsizing does not include the discharge of individuals for cause, or individual departures via normal retirement or resignations. The word "normal" is important. Voluntary severance and early retirement packages are commonly used to reduce the size of the work force, especially among firms with traditional "no-layoff" policies. Even if targeted workers are called "redundant," "excessed," or "transitioned," the result is the same—employees are shown the door. It's just called something else.

WHO IS MOST LIKELY TO DOWNSIZE?

The most likely candidates (though by no means the only candidates) are firms that are struggling to get through hard times, saddled with more debt than ever. Over twenty-six percent of corporate cash flow currently goes to meet debt payments, compared with only nine percent at the start of the 1974 recession, and eighteen percent going into the 1982 slump.[3] As an example, consider Marriott Corporation. Marriott eliminated 2,500 jobs at headquarters and also by closing down its hotel construction and development unit. Yet such savings pale against the cost of servicing more than $1 billion in debt taken on in an overly aggressive hotel construction program. Debt can be a cruel master, forcing firms to take drastic steps to ensure sufficient cash flow to service it. In the meantime, companies that didn't take on debt, including foreign competitors, can gain significant market share. Loss of market share, along with a concomitant loss of profitability, stimulates more downsizing.

Anticipated Results   Downsizing is expected to yield economic as well as organizational benefits. Let us consider each of these in turn. In terms of economic benefits, downsizing firms expect to increase value for their shareholders. Executives conclude that future costs are more predictable than future revenues. Thus, cutting costs by cutting people is a safe bet to increase earnings, and, by extension, the price of the company's stock. Judging by the 1,000 companies that the American Management Association follows, downsizing is a popular strategy. From 1989 to 1991 those companies eliminated 212,598 jobs— saving $8 billion per year.[4] Here are some specific company examples.

E.I. du Pont de Nemours took a $125 million, one-time charge against earnings to gain a $230 million recurring, annual, aftertax savings. Union Carbide spent $70 million in up-front charges to obtain $250 million in annual savings subsequently. Consider a third example. An IBM analyst estimated that if 8,000 employees accepted one of IBM's early retirement offers, the company would realize an extra 40 cents per share in earnings the following year, plus a 50-cents-per-share increase in the years afterward. An additional attraction that encourages businesses to consider this retirement cost strategy is the almost $100 billion surplus in overfunded U.S. corporate pension accounts.

In terms of organizational benefits, proponents of downsizing cite six expected outcomes:

- Lower overhead
- Less bureaucracy
- Faster decision making
- Smoother communications
- Greater entrepreneurship
- Increases in productivity

People costs comprise roughly thirty to eighty percent of general and administrative costs in most companies. In capital-intensive industries, such as commercial airlines or oil refining, the cost is about thirty to forty percent. Among savings institutions, that figure is roughly fifty percent, and in highly labor-intensive operations, such as the postal service, the figure may exceed eighty percent.[6] Hence, cutting costs by cutting people appears to be a natural strategy, especially for companies struggling to stay alive in an unprecedented, globally competitive market. Carving out entire echelons of middle-level managers certainly does reduce overhead and trims the number of layers in the organizational hierarchy. In theory this should lead to less bureaucracy and faster decision making. At Sears, for example, there are only four levels of management from the top to the bottom of the corporation. With fewer layers of middle managers to "filter" information, communications should be smoother and more accurate, entrepreneurship should flourish, and productivity should climb. It all seems so logical.

To be sure, the gains expected to result from downsizing are tantalizing. When coupled with advice from popular business books and journals to "cut out the fat," to get "lean and mean," senior executives might well find the lure of downsizing to be irresistible. Are the proponents of downsizing right? To what extent have the economic and organizational benefits actually followed? We will try to provide some answers in the following sections.

ANTICIPATED VERSUS ACTUAL ECONOMIC RESULTS OF DOWNSIZING

A 1991 survey by the Wyatt Company of 1,005 firms suggested that most restructuring efforts fall far short of the objectives originally established for them:[7]

- Only forty-six percent of the companies said their cuts reduced expenses enough over time, in part because four times out of five, managers ended up replacing some of the very people they had dismissed;
- Fewer than one in three said profits increased as much as expected; and
- Only twenty-one percent reported satisfactory improvements in shareholders' return on investment.

What happens to the stock prices of companies that downsize? The answer to that question only makes sense by examining stock prices at different time intervals prior to and subsequent to the initial announcement of downsizing. To provide at least a partial answer to that question, Mitchell & Company, a consulting firm in Weston, Mass., examined what happened to the stock prices of sixteen companies in the Value Line data base that wrote off ten percent or more of their net worth between 1982 and 1988.[8]

In most cases, the stock in question already had lost some ground in the few months before the company announced its decision to downsize. Typically, it will have lagged behind the market by twelve percentage points or so. ("The market" in this study was defined as Standard & Poor's 500-stock index for large stocks, and the Nasdaq composite index for small stocks.) On the day that the announcement is made, stock prices generally increase, but then there usually begins a long, slow slide. Two years later, in the Mitchell & Co. study, ten of the sixteen stocks were trading below the market by seventeen to forty-eight percent and, worse, twelve were below comparable firms in their industries by five to forty-five percent. To understand some of the reasons why this is so, we need to examine the impact of downsizing on the day-to-day functioning of organizations.

IMPACT OF DOWNSIZING ON ORGANIZATIONAL FUNCTIONING

One poll of 1,142 companies that recently downsized, conducted by the American Management Association, revealed that nearly half were "badly" or "not well" prepared for the dismantling and had not anticipated the kinds of problems that developed subsequently. More than half reported that they had begun downsizing with no policies or programs—such as employee retraining or job redeployment—to minimize the negative effects of cutting back. Succumbing to the pressure to produce short-term results, many ignored the massive changes in organizational relationships that result from reorganization. As one observer noted, "In the process, they misused and alienated many middle managers and lower-level employees, sold off solid businesses, shortchanged research and development, and muddled the modernization of their manufacturing floors.[9]

Apparently, a number of top managements have put the concerns of their employees and subordinate managers at the very bottom of their priority lists—and they pay a price for doing so. David Heenan, chief executive officer of Honolulu-based Theo H. Davis and Co. noted, "Corporate America has neglected the downside of downsizing." For just one example of this, consider the impact of extensive reductions of headquarters staffers whose jobs focus on corporate planning.

Once these specialists are gone, operating managers may be expected to fill the void. To do so, however, they need to develop the kinds of skills that will allow them to make groupwide contributions. Yet many line managers have neither the training nor the perspective to see beyond the segment of the business they are assigned to run. Moreover, organizations that employ cut-and-slash tactics are also those least likely to make long-term investments in training and management development. Remaining staff experts who could help subsidiary managers develop a policy-making perspective refuse to plant the seeds of their own destruction.[10] Moreover, they are likely to be demoralized, less productive, and unable to monitor, control, and support business units effectively. The result? Strategic planning suffers.

Furthermore, it's unrealistic to ask department or division heads to make long-term decisions about research and development expenditures, capital investments, or work force training when they are paid to attend to short-term profit or production. Last, the loss of staff support means that vital information may not be available to help the chief executive and other top managers make decisions that only they can make. Computer networks and video conferences cannot completely replace the human interaction that is so essential to achieving honest communication.

In summary, managers who remain after a downsizing often find themselves working in new, and not necessarily friendly, environments. These survivors are often stretched thin, they manage more people and jobs, and they work longer hours. Many are not willing or able to work under these conditions.[11] More on this shortly, but first let us examine why anticipated cost savings often don't materialize.

WHY ANTICIPATED COST SAVINGS OFTEN DON'T MATERIALIZE

Consider three such reasons: (1) newly lean companies replace staff functions with expensive consultants (as a result of conditions described previously); (2) subsidiary business units recreate the kinds of expertise that headquarters staffers formerly supplied by hiring their own trainers and planners; (3) companies discover that it's expensive to train line managers to handle tasks formerly performed by staff specialists.

The net result of all of this reshuffling is that some severed employees will be hired back permanently, and others will return on a part-time basis as consultants. One executive recruiter estimated that downsizing companies wind up replacing ten to twenty percent of those they dismissed previously.

During an interview, one senior manager of a *Fortune* 500 company described a situation where a bookkeeper making $9 an hour was let go in a downsizing effort. However, the company later discovered that it lost valuable institutional memory in the process, for the bookkeeper knew "where's, why's, and how-to's" that no one else apparently did. The result? The former bookkeeper was hired back as a consultant for $42 per hour! Another senior manager for a *Fortune* 500 firm noted that after a downsizing, "Head count went down, but overall human resources expenses went up." How can that be? Because payroll records reflected only the number of full-time employees. Victims of downsizing who were later rehired as part-timers or consultants were paid from subsidiary accounts. Thus, they were not officially listed as part of overall headcount. In other words, an accounting gimmick masked the actual impact of downsizing on labor costs. Now let's consider the impact of downsizing, as usually practiced, on productivity.

IMPACT OF DOWNSIZING ON PRODUCTIVITY

Unfortunately in many companies, downsizing is limited to reductions in head-count (rather than being integrated with organization redesign or broad, systemic changes designed to root out redundancies, waste, and inefficiency).[12] Firms take a one-time charge to earnings, their operating margins improve, and the financial markets cheer. In many companies, however, the gains are short-lived, for despite all of the layoffs, automation, and just-in-time inventory management, U.S. non-farm productivity rose a scant 1.2% a year during the 1980s. That's almost no improvement from the 1970s. In fact, in terms of average productivity growth—a key to future prosperity—the U.S. ranks fifth, behind Japan, Great Britain, France, and Italy.

From a historical perspective, consider what this implies. Beginning in the late nineteenth century the yearly rise in productivity of England, then the world's foremost industrial nation, was just slightly less (one percent) than that of its industrial rivals, mainly the United States and Germany. By the mid-twentieth century that seemingly small difference proved to be enough to tumble England from its previously undisputed industrial prominence.

Now back to the present. More than half the 1,468 restructured companies surveyed by the Society for Human Resource Management reported that employee productivity either stayed the same or deteriorated after the layoffs. Moreover, a four-year study of thirty organizations in the automobile industry revealed that very few of the organizations implemented downsizing in a way that improved their effectiveness. Most deteriorated relative to their "pre-downsizing" levels of quality, productivity, effectiveness, and human relations indicators.[13]

The term productivity is an abstract concept, but the nervousness and gloom that pervaded Bell & Howell during and subsequent to a three-way takeover battle and reports of impending layoffs during a six-month period took a toll on productivity that was very real. Senior executives at the company figured that the drop in productivity may have dragged down the company's profits for the half by as much as eleven percent or $2.1 million.

Among firms that execute downsizing well (for example, almost fifty percent of the firms surveyed by the Society for Human Resource Management where productivity went up as a result of downsizing), certain characteristics, each an apparent contradiction, seem to be common. Consider six such characteristics:[14]

- Downsizing is implemented by command from the top, with recommendations from lower-level employees, based on job and task analyses of how work is currently organized.
- Both short-term (workforce reduction) and long-term (organization redesign and systemic change in the organization's culture) strategies are used, together with across-the-board and targeted downsizing.
- Special attention is paid both to those employees who lost their jobs (e.g., through outplacement, generous severance pay, retraining, family counseling), and to those who did not (by increasing information exchange among top managers and employees).
- Through internal data gathering and data monitoring, firms identify precisely where redundancy, excess cost, and inefficiency exist. They then attack those areas specifically. They treat outside agents (suppliers, distributors) as involved partners as well as potential targets of their downsizing efforts.
- Reorganizations often produce small, semi-autonomous organizations within large, integrated ones. However, geographic or product reorganizations often produced larger, more centralized units (e.g., information processing) within decentralized parent companies.
- Downsizing is viewed as a means to an end (that is, as an aggressive strategy designed to enhance competitiveness), as well as the targeted end.

In summary, it seems that the best explanation for the difference between firms that downsized effectively and those that did so ineffectively was the existence of apparent contradictions. Effective downsizing often involves contradictions—that is, processes that are thought to be opposite or incompatible. Organizations that downsized ineffectively generally tried to maintain consistency, harmony, and fit in their downsizing approach. The key seems to be to adapt a "both/and" approach to downsizing, even though this is not consistent with traditional approaches to change.

IMPACT OF DOWNSIZING ON EMPLOYEE MORALE AND MOTIVATION

Study after study shows that following a downsizing, surviving employees become narrow-minded, self-absorbed, and risk averse. Morale sinks, productivity drops, and survivors distrust management. In fact, this constellation of symptoms is so common that it has taken on a name of its own: *survivors' syndrome.*[15]

A survey by Right Associates, a Philadelphia outplacement firm, illustrates these findings. Among senior managers at recently-downsized companies, seventy-four percent said their workers had low morale, feared future cutbacks, and distrusted management. This has a long-term impact that extends far beyond the short-term benefits of reducing headcount. Thus, in a survey of about 1,000 readers by *Industry Week* magazine, sixty percent of middle managers said they were less loyal to their employers than they were five years ago. Consider just one indicator of lack of employee involvement. According to Consolidated Edison Co. of New York, the rate of suggestions for improvement per employee is only one per 25 in the electric utility industry, compared to one per seven for U.S. industry as a whole.

To a large extent, this may be due to lack of communication. Only forty-four percent of companies that downsized in the last five years shared details of their plans with employees, and even fewer (thirty-four percent) told survivors how they would fit into the company's new strategy, according to a 1992 survey of 1,020 directors of human resources.[16] This has a predictable effect on morale. Two-thirds of those polled said that since the restructuring, workers have lost trust in their companies; eighty percent said survivors can't manage their work without stress. The remedy? Plan downsizing *with* employees instead of springing it on them unannounced.

Diminishing expectations   Another survey by the Hay Group reported that in 1979, almost seventy-five percent of middle managers were optimistic about their chances for advancement. Now less than a third still think their futures look sunny. What this implies is a lack of commitment to a given employer and makes career transitions more frequent. How much more frequent? Twenty years ago a manager worked for only one or two companies in his or her entire career. Even as late as 1981, average job tenure was twelve years. By 1988, that figure had fallen to nine, and by late 1992 it was under seven years. Indeed, workers under age 35 stay on a job a median of only 2.5 years. Soon managers will hold seven to ten jobs in a lifetime. As one observer noted: "People used to be able to count on the organization and its stability. But the myth that institutions will take care of us has been shattered."[17]

From the perspective of the individual, the implications of all of this can be summarized succinctly: our views of organizational life, managing as a career, hard work, rewards, and loyalty will never be the same. Unfortunately, far too many senior managers in the United States seem to regard employees as "units of pro-duction," costs to be cut rather than as assets to be developed. This is a "plug-in" mentality—that is, like a machine, plug it in when you need it, unplug it when it is no longer needed. Unlike machines, however, employees have values, aspirations, beliefs—and memories.

From the perspective of organizations, the long-term implications of reduced morale and employee commitment are not pleasant. Consider just one area that is likely to be affected: *efforts to enhance the quality of goods and services.* A key ingredient that is necessary to sustain programs of total quality management is high morale. This is so because employees must "buy in" to the management strat-egy of improving quality, they must align their interests with those of manage-ment, and they must become involved and committed to bring about genuine, lasting improvements in this area.[18] When was the last time you saw an organiza-tion try to improve morale and commitment by cutting workers?

Again and again, executives interviewed for this article echoed the same theme: far too often, downsizing is done indiscriminately. The resulting low morale and lack of trust have ripple effects on virtually every people-related aspect of business activity. For firms intent on downsizing or restructuring, is there a better way? In our next section we present one possible alternative.

REDEFINING THE WAY WORK IS ORGANIZED AND EXECUTED

We have already seen the economic and human consequences of simple reductions in headcount without concomitant changes in the reorganization of work. Why do so many organizations seem to be "stuck" in this mode? Perhaps because they operate on the basis of a traditional 3-C system of organization: *command, control,* and *compartmentalization.*[19] In the typical pyramidal hierarchy, senior managers are in command and exercise control through personal supervision, policies, and procedures. Job descriptions compartmentalize specific responsibilities and activities, and, all too often, the larger the organization the more rigid the job descriptions. Organizations that function on 3-C logic are most effective in stable environments. However, they tend to be unresponsive to customers, slow to adapt, and limited in creativity.

Not all large U.S. organizations continue to operate under the 3-C system. General Electric, under the leadership of chief executive officer John F. Welch, exemplifies a different approach. Since 1986 GE's "Work-Out" program has tried to achieve the following objectives: (1) to identify and eliminate sources of frustration, bureaucratic inefficiency, and unproductive work to energize employees; (2) to encourage feelings of ownership and self-worth at all levels of the organization; and (3) to overhaul how managers are evaluated and rewarded.

The basic features of the Work-Out system are similar to those that characterize Japanese manufacturing systems: teamwork, communication, efficient use of resources, elimination of waste, and continuous improvement. This is a deceptively simple, yet profound way to view the organization of work. It is based on the assumption that managers are creators of contexts that facilitate the execution of work by other people. One of the important mechanisms that managers can use to do this is to act in ways that add value to others' work.[20]

Perhaps the major advantage of this system is its recognition that continuous improvement eliminates the need for radical "restructurings" whose only outcome is a reduction in headcount. How has GE done? Under Welch's leadership, it has achieved world market-share leadership in nearly all of its fourteen businesses. While GE's approach may someday serve as a model for other firms, for the present and for the immediate future, certain trends seem clear.

Trends
- Downsizing begets more downsizing. Kodak restructured four times between 1982 and 1992. Honeywell is shrinking for the second time in four years. Xerox, Digital Equipment, IBM, and TRW, just to name a few major companies, have announced multiple cutbacks through the 1990s.
- Ongoing staff reductions have become etched into the corporate culture. This is true even among firms with record profits, such as GE Appliance

Division, Nordstrom, Saks Fifth Avenue, and Compaq Computer. In late 1992, Compaq announced it would shrink its work force by about 1,000 people, or ten percent of its world-wide total, over several months, despite record revenue and unit shipments. Why? In *anticipation* of a continuing intensely competitive market environment for personal computers.

Conventional wisdom holds that recessions are good opportunities to improve productivity, often by dropping people and putting in automated equipment. However, almost fifty percent of respondents to an American Management Association survey reported that downsizing had nothing to do with the recession. Mergers and acquisitions, plant obsolescence or newly automated processes, and transfers of operations elsewhere have turned work force reductions into an ongoing activity that continues without regard to current financial performance.

- "Companies are managing their workers as they manage their inventories of unsold goods. They are trying to keep both sets of inventories—employees and merchandise—as low as possible," according to Leslie McNulty, research director of the United Food and Commercial Workers Union. This approach, which may well characterize the 1990s, has been termed "Kanban employment," using the Japanese term for just-in-time delivery and no stockpiling or inventorying of resources.[21]
- Downsize first, ask questions later. Companies often say they turn to layoffs as a last resort. But Right Associates, in polls of 1,204 and 909 companies that had reduced staffing levels, found that only six percent of the employers had tried cutting pay, nine percent had shortened work weeks, nine percent used vacation without pay, and fourteen percent had developed job-sharing plans. Clearly they are not listening to employees, for when a Time/CNN poll asked 1,250 adult Americans, "If your company needed to cut expenses in order to stay in business, would you prefer they cut everyone's pay by ten percent or lay off ten percent of the work force?" Eighty percent preferred the pay cut.[22]
- Many unionized blue-collar workers are trading off wage freezes or concessions for job security. White-collar workers in manufacturing and service jobs don't have that security in the lower echelons—and they are being hit hard. Consider the agreement between Uniroyal Goodrich Tire Co. and the United Rubber Workers at the company's 71-year-old Eau Claire, Wisconsin plant. The union agreed to a 63-cent-an-hour reduction in pay, one less vacation week, three fewer annual holidays, no cost-of-living increases, and extensive work-rule changes. In return, Uniroyal guaranteed the jobs of the workers during the life of the contract.

IMPLICATIONS FOR MANAGERS

The experience of hundreds of downsizings during the late 1980s and early 1990s has spawned a vast literature. Some answers to the questions, "What do we know?" and "What have we learned?" can be summarized in terms of ten key lessons for managers.

1. Downsizing will continue as long as overhead costs remain noncompetitive with domestic and international rivals.
2. Firms with high debt are most likely to downsize by aggressively cutting people.
3. Far too many companies are not well prepared for downsizing, they begin with no retraining or redeployment policies in place, and they fail to anticipate the kinds of human resource problems that develop subsequently.
4. Six months to a year after a downsizing, key indicators often do *not* improve: expense ratios, profits, return-on-investment to shareholders, and stock prices.
5. Survivors' syndrome is a common aftermath. Be prepared to manage it. Better yet, try to avoid it by actively involving employees in the planning phase of any downsizing effort.
6. Recognize that downsizing has exploded the myth of job security and has accelerated employee mobility, especially among white-collar workers. It has fundamentally altered the terms of the psychological contract that binds workers to organizations.
7. Productivity and quality often suffer because there is no change in the way work is done. The same amount of work as before a downsizing is simply loaded onto the backs of fewer workers.
8. To downsize effectively, be prepared to manage apparent contradictions— for example, between the use of top-down authority and bottom-up empowerment, between short-term strategies (headcount reduction) and long-term strategies (organization redesign and systemic changes in culture).
9. To bring about sustained improvements in productivity, quality, and effectiveness, integrate reductions in headcount with planned changes in the way that work is designed. Systematically question the continued appropriateness of 3-C logic.
10. Downsizing is not a one-time, quick-fix solution to enhance competitiveness. Rather, it should be viewed as part of a process of continuous improvement.

Notes

1. There have been many accounts of such cuts in the business press. Two examples are: "How Job Losers Have Been Faring," *Business Week*, September 28, 1992, 16; and A. Murray and D. Wessel, "Swept Away: Torrent of Job Cuts Shows Human Toll of Recession Goes On," *The Wall Street Journal*, December 12, 1991, A1:A9.

2. A. B. Fisher, "Moral Crisis," *Fortune*, November 28, 1991, 70–72; 76; 80. See also J. Greenwald, "The Great American Layoffs," *Time*, July 20, 1992, 64–65; and S. Overman, "The Layoff Legacy," *HR Magazine*, August 1991, 29–32.

3. B. Dumaine. "How To Manage in a Recession," *Fortune*, November 5, 1990, 58–60; 64, 68, 72. See also "All That Lean Isn't Turning Into Green," *Business Week*, November 18, 1991, 39–40.

4. F. Laili, "Learn From My Mistake." *Money*, February 1992, 5.

5. D. A. Heenan, "The Downside of Downsizing," *The Journal of Business Strategy*, November–December 1989, 18-23.

6. There are various sources for these figures. For example, see W.F. Cascio, *Costing Human Resources: The Financial Impact of Behavior in Organizations,* 3rd ed. (Boston: PWS-Kent, 1991). See also A.R. Karr. "Letter Bomb: Postal Service Again Asks for Rate Increase as Automation Lags," *The Wall Street Journal,* March 7, 1990. A1; A2; and K. Severinsen, "Cost-Cutting Measures Boost the Bottom Line," *Savings Institutions,* February 1989, 50–53.

7. Laili, 1992, op. cit.

8. J. R. Dorfman, "Stocks of Companies Announcing Layoffs Fire Up Investors, But Prices Often Wilt," *The Wall Street Journal,* December 10, 1991, C1; C2.

9. The source of the quotation is T. J. Murray, "For Downsizers, the Real Misery Is Yet to Come," *Business Month,* February 1989, 71–72; but see also E. R. Greenberg, "The Latest AMA Survey on Downsizing," *Compensation and Benefits Review,* 22, 1990, 66-71.

10. Heenan, op. cit.

11. R. Zemke. "The Ups and Downs of Downsizing," *Training,* November 1990, 27–34.

12. The first large-scale research study to demonstrate this was conducted by K. S. Cameron, S. J. Freeman, and A. K. Mishra, "Best Practices in White-Collar Downsizing: Managing Contradictions," *Academy of Management Executive,* 5(3), 1991, 57–73.

13. Converging evidence on this point comes from Cameron et al., 1991, op. cit.; A. B. Fisher, "The Downside of Downsizing," *Fortune,* May 23, 1988, 42–52; and R. Henkoff, "Cost Cutting: How To Do It Right," *Fortune,* April 99, 1990, 40–49.

14. Cameron et al., 1991, op. cit. identified these characteristics.

15. A considerable amount of research has been done on the issue. For a summary of it see J. Brockner, "The Effects of Work Layoffs on Survivors: Research, Theory, and Practice." In B. M. Staw and L.L. Cummings (eds.) *Research in Organizational Behavior,* Greenwich, CT; JAI Press, 1988. See also D. Rice and C. Dreilinger, "After the Downsizing," *Training and Development,* May 1991, 41–44.

16. J.E. Rigdon, "Lack of Communication Burdens Restructurings," *The Wall Street Journal,* November 2, 1992, B1.

17. The source of the quotation is T.F. O'Boyle, "Loyalty Ebbs at Many Companies as Employees Grow Disillusioned," *The Wall Street Journal,* July 11, 1985, 29; but see also E. M. Fowler, "A Good Side to Unwanted Job Changes," *The New York Times,* February 21, 1989, 1H.; also "Labor Letter," *The Wall Street Journal,* October 20, 1992, A1.

18. See United States General Accounting Office, *Management Practices: U.S. Companies Improve Performance Through Quality Efforts,* Washington, D.C.; USGPO, May 1991.

19. The 3-C system was pointed out to me by V. Nilakant, "Total-Quality Management: What Is It Really All About?" *Management Bulletin,* August 1992, No. 1. University of Canterbury, Christchurch, New Zealand, 3.

20. Nilikant, 1992, op. cit.; see also J. P. Womack, D. T. Jones, and D. Roos, *The Machine That Changed the World,* NY: Rawson Associates, 1990.

21. E.R. Greenberg, "Downsizing: AMA Survey Results," *Compensations and Benefits Review,* 23(4), 1991, 33–38.

22. The term "Kanban employment" comes from A. Freedman, "How the 1980s Have Changed Industrial Relations," *Monthly Labor Review,* May 1988, 35–38. The source of the quotation is L. Uchitelle, "Layoffs Are Rising Even at Companies in Good Condition," *The New York Times,* October 29, 1990, A1; B7.

◆

Bitter Survivors

Thomas J. Murray

On the face of it, William Jeffries (not his real name) was a lucky guy—the only one of seven loan officers at a Los Angeles area branch of Crocker National Bank who wasn't fired after Crocker was taken over by Wells Fargo & Co. last year [1986]. Jeffries, a 35-year-old MBA, had made his reputation as a crack salesman, and that was why Wells Fargo kept him on. But he was so grateful to survive the company's massive layoffs, he willingly took on the daunting task of converting all of Crocker's commercial accounts to Wells Fargo's accounting and operating systems. With no guidelines or support staff to help him, he toiled away seven days a week for six months to complete the job.

It was a mistake. While Jeffries was slaving over the conversion, his fellow loan officers were out drumming up new business. In January, his job performance was rated unsatisfactory, and since then he has been given only the smallest and most troublesome accounts to manage—"the junk work," as he puts it. "All they are interested in is developing new accounts, which I had no time for during those hectic months," he says bitterly.

Becoming increasingly agitated as he discusses his plight, Jeffries exclaims heatedly, "I've been watched closely for the past several months, I have to account for every trip out of the office while my peers don't, and I'm being tested all the time for every move I make."

Unfortunately, variations of Bill Jeffries' tale are being heard in companies across the industrial spectrum. For middle managers who have survived the corporate takeovers and restructuring of the last few years, elation has turned to frustration, anger and a sense of helplessness. As survivors, they had figured they were among the elite, with unique opportunities to catch top management's eye and advance their careers. Now their hopes have crumbled, and many fear their careers have come to a dead stop. "I get depressed just walking into the office every morning," says one. "My only hope is that I have enough self-esteem and drive left to convince some other company to hire me."

Of course, no one faults industry for its massive drive to reorganize and downsize. Faced with intense competition from abroad, the profound effects of deregulation and technological change, hundreds of major corporations had no choice but to slash fat payrolls. In their zeal to streamline management ranks, however, few companies gave any thought to how drastically the relationships between managers and the organization would change as responsibilities were shifted and subordinates were swept out. "Old bonds have been shattered and new ways of operating introduced," says Myron Roomkin, professor of human resources management at Northwestern's Kellogg School of Management. "But all that many companies tell their managers is, "You're a professional. Get the job done!'"

The "survivor" problem has hardly been recognized by corporate America, let alone tackled. But management experts believe it will haunt industry over the next decade and cause untold long-term damage to many companies. By undermining the competitive spirit of their middle managers now, they say, companies are sacrificing the development of top-notch senior managers for the future. In the process, they are undermining their long-term growth and productivity.

A case in point: AT&T. Some observers think it will take the communications giant years to recover from the management disruptions caused by its reorganization and wholesale layoffs (some 60,000 employees in all). Internally, staff psychologist Joseph Moses recently issued a hard-hitting report charging that top management's neglect of "people issues" has led to a middle-management morale crisis that threatens "irreparable damage" to the company. According to Moses' evaluation, "Survivors are often disillusioned, frustrated, bitter and most of all, lacking in hope." He concluded: "The amount of suppressed, covert hostility lurking just below the surface is truly frightening."

It's ironic to think that the survivors may actually be the biggest losers in this era of restructuring. Certainly, many companies have treated the middle managers they let go better than those who remain. As President William Bridges of California management consulting firm Pontes Associates points out, "Those who left often received handsome severance packages and outplacement assistance, while those still on the job have been overworked and given little or no guidance during a difficult transition period."

Getting the survivors to talk about their travails is difficult. Convinced there will be another bloodletting, they are extremely anxious about their job security. As a result, all of the dozen or so managers who were willing to be interviewed by *Business Month* agreed to tell their stories only after being assured of anonymity.

What becomes clear in talking to these managers is that they are being forced to take on a huge work load. Most claim they are doing the job of two or three managers, with sharply reduced staff and clerical support. And to a man, they say, they are getting no help from top management.

A typical example is Randolph Smith (not his real name), manager of new-product development at a unit of Atlantic Richfield Co. Following a company-wide reorganization and deep personnel cutbacks, Smith says, he lost four of his six subordinates virtually overnight and had to put in an additional twenty-to-thirty hours a week to keep pace with a growing number of new assignments. "Upper-level management wouldn't acknowledge that so many people had left, yet it kept on wanting more results every time we increased our work load," he says. "I wanted to be aggressive and crank out the best products possible, but without the people to back you up and support your efforts, you just can't do the job right. I'm getting more and more frustrated every day."

Some managers have so much additional work and responsibility thrown at them that their positions are, in effect, completely changed. And with no guidance from above, many quickly find themselves in over their heads. The branch manager at one AT&T California unit explains that his job has changed dramatically over the past few years to accommodate not only management cutbacks but the introduction of new technology in the office and the consolidation of the company's communications and information organizations. "In my heart I know it makes sense to present our new markets with a solid front," he says, "but I've gotten so little direction from upstairs that it's endless confusion for me. And all the time I'm sweating out the chance I'm on the hit list for the next layoff."

Perhaps most disheartening, reorganization has meant actual demotion for many of the survivors. Scores of managers at Exxon, E.I. du Pont and Telex Corp., among others, have been dropped several grades, with little or no chance for advancement.

Ward Bell (not his real name), for one, saw his position as a national operations manager at a Raytheon Co. division vanish the day after Telex acquired the unit in 1985. While two security guards stood by and a locksmith changed desk and door locks, four managers were fired on the spot. This eliminated two whole levels of management, and Bell was reduced to running a Los Angeles area branch. "After working my way up from technician to national ops manager, Black Friday comes along and I'm pushed back two layers," he sighs. "The company keeps putting on these PR campaigns telling us what great career opportunities we have, but that's a laugh. There's very little upward mobility around this company anymore, and I'm out of here as soon as I can land something decent."

Those are brave words, but most of the managers interviewed show little confidence in their ability to find new, meaningful jobs. For most, it is evident, their biggest fear is joining their former co-workers on the unemployment line. Many have lost their mentors as well as their industry contacts. "I feel lost since my main man took early retirement," says the AT&T branch manager. "He was always there when I needed a pep talk or wanted guidance on my career moves."

Most damaging, insecurity is affecting middle managers' job performance. Consultants warn of early "burnouts," and many survivors admit they are increasingly afraid to make decisions. "I see lots of dispirited managers who are no longer contributing 100% to the job," says Telex' Bell. "They're scared their jobs will go up in smoke if they pop their heads out of their foxholes, and I'm afraid a lot of us will need therapy to get our careers going again."

Eastman Kodak Co., which has let more than 10,000 employees go over the past few years, is already paying the price for middle-management insecurity, according to one insider. To help regain its dominance in the camera market against severe new competition, in 1984 Kodak started up several small business units to speed up new-product development. However, according to one technology director, some of the managers heading up the units have been so apprehensive about making decisions that the businesses are floundering, and many key personnel have quit. "They know they have only so much time to produce a winner or they will be shut down," he explains. "But they're also scared they will make a wrong decision too soon and be terminated overnight."

Job pressures, needless to say, are shaking up the survivors' personal lives. Many worry about how little time they get to spend with their families and complain of fatigue and various physical ailments. Robert McCarthy, who heads his own outplacement firm in Los Angeles, has seen many of these "walking wounded" come through his door. "They're losing the balance in their lives," he says. "I'm afraid many of them will become victims of alcoholism, drugs and divorce."

These experiences seem to confirm what a number of critics are saying: that industry could be defeating the whole purpose of downsizing. To begin with, it is no secret that a number of companies have let some of their best managers slip through the net; du Pont and Atlantic Richfield are just two that unexpectedly lost many top performers when they offered attractive financial packages for voluntary resignations and retirements.

As for those unhappy managers who tough it out and stay, the cumulative effects of overwork, fear and top management indifference could be devastating over the long term. Joseph Moses' speculations about AT&T's survivors says it all: "One can't help wondering what kind of managers they will be like in the future when they populate senior levels at AT&T."

Despite the army of executives on the street, some large corporations are already finding it more difficult to get top talent. Many job-hunting managers are deliberately avoiding the giants with tarnished reputations, recruiters report.

Equally ominous, big business is less attractive these days to promising young university graduates and MBAs. College placement officers at UCLA, Stanford and Duke University's Fuqua School of Business all say that more and more of their graduates are rejecting careers with large corporations in favor of smaller companies, where they perceive greater stability, entrepreneurial spirit and opportunities for rapid advancement.

In fairness, it must be allowed that the survivor problem is so new that many top managements have yet to realize that they could have a full-blown crisis on their hands. But there's no doubt that most companies are simply closing their eyes to the situation. "Too many companies think business will just go back to normal without any positive action on their part," says Lucia Cappachione, a Los Angeles consultant who has been helping Walt Disney Co. solve transition problems since its big layoffs in 1984.

Amid the general neglect, two companies that stand out for their early recognition of the survivor problem are Ford Motor Co. and Apple Computer, Inc. Ford CEO Donald Peterson and Apple CEO John Sculley were quick to introduce new training programs to help managers cope with added responsibilities and staff cutbacks in the aftermath of massive layoffs and corporate restructuring.

A few other companies have begun to tackle the problem. At du Pont, where 35,000 employees have been let go since 1982, H. Gordon Smyth, senior vice president of employee relations, claims that managers have reacted well for the most part to increased authority and responsibility. They were helped substantially, he says, by the company's adoption of a new team concept that calls for every department to set its own goals. Du Pont is also holding seminars to teach marketing skills to all managers.

At AT&T, John C. Petrillo, director of human resources, says that top management is responding to the Moses report and earlier internal studies. It is providing counseling for managers with psychological problems. And it is offering one- and two-week education and training programs to all personnel, including managers, to indoctrinate them in the new corporate environment and strategy and help them rethink their jobs. "It's not easy to accomplish because we're deal-ing with deep-set ways of thinking and behaving at this company," he says. "But we realize the frustrations our people are feeling and believe we can help them through this turbulent time."

There are other signs of movement. The Conference Board, in tandem with Northwestern's Myron Roomkin, is launching the first major study on the sur-vivors. Several concerned CEOs on the Board's Research Council urged the group to look into the issue and try to come up with some answers, according to a spokesman. Du Pont's Smyth also is urging senior executives to use industry meet-ings as a forum for swapping ideas. Besides that, a number of outplacement firms say they plan to expand their assistance programs for disgruntled survivors.

Too little, too late? Roomkin blames "stupid top management" for failing to predict the current "debacle" ten years ago and plan for it. He argues that the demographics available at that time, mainly the flood of baby-boomers into mid-dle-management jobs, clearly indicated that a crunch was coming with the first major recession. Even now, after all the layoffs of recent years, he says disgustedly, "No one has figured out how to run a company well with fewer managers."

According to the experts' prognosis, the problem of middle-management stagnation could fade away on its own by the mid-1990s. By then, a new and much smaller generation of young people will be entering the managerial work force, and opportunities for advancement will speed up again. But for now, it seems, shortsighted companies are creating a generation of alienated middle managers, with all the implications that holds for corporate growth and stability.

Chapter 4

Influencing

Often, when a person attempts to influence others the attempt is toward some end. The end can be the creation of something or the destruction of something. While conventional wisdom tends to place a higher value on the former than on the latter, both are often necessary for human achievement. For people and organizations to learn to do something new, old habits often need to be replaced. This process might be called "unlearning." However, since people who are to "unlearn" often have considerable investments in their previous ways of doing things, special efforts may be needed to reduce the influence of the past. As Weick (1979) observed: "We sometimes need to treat memory as an enemy." Alternative ways of reducing the influence of the past include demolition and some degree of alteration combined with building on the past—such as making only minor changes in the previous ways and incorporating them into new ways. In modern organizations, managers often must do some of each method. The unknown author of the first selection in this chapter, a short poem entitled "Wreckers," clearly places little value upon the tearing-down process; the writer dismisses those who tear down by calling them unskilled. We question such easy dismissal because we believe that some demolition is required and that some of it is highly skilled. Consider modern demolition experts, who, using dynamite, are able to make room for a new building in a matter of seconds, turning a tall building located in the middle of a busy city into a pile of debris without damaging structures only a few feet away. Such work is highly skilled. While we, too, value the skills needed for building (see, for example, the selection by George Tamke called "Taking Control in a New Job" in Chapter 6), we wish to call attention to the other side of the process in which managers and other "agents of progress" must exercise influence to achieve.

As we have suggested in earlier chapters, the development of modern management has entailed the replacement of the seemingly highly personal, informal influence processes of earlier times with more formal and bureaucratic means of influence. Of course, both means themselves have been evolving. Among the major elements in the recent evolution of the formal processes has been recognition that often the processes work best when supplemented by less formal approaches. In fact, since the 1960s, pressure to substitute less formal for more bureaucratic methods has grown as some influential writers have predicted the death of bureaucracy. These predictions fall on the fertile soil provided by an ideology of individualism carried forth from earlier times that glorifies the heroic individual fighting against evil, large organizations.

The debate among those favoring hierarchical designs and those advocating less formal processes may be most fruitful if framed in the following terms. A major, important function of managers is to influence. Organizational hierarchies are, under many conditions, tools for exercising necessary influence. They are not, however, the only means for doing so and under many conditions they face important counterforces, among those being their inconsistency with the high value conventional American ideology places on individual autonomy. The problem, as with much else about managerial reality, is one of achieving balance.

As we have asserted, organizations are one of several ways that human beings use to coordinate their efforts. Organizing formally can replace, but seldom replaces fully, other means of integrating human action. Over the last century or so, however, as the more traditional personal means of influencing people to cooperate proved to be insufficient, the importance of formally organized procedures increased dramatically.

Despite this increase, even within highly formalized organizations, the traditional and more personal modes of influence continue to play a major role. They grease the wheels of the organization's machinery and give life to its internal processes. Furthermore, the abilities of managers to employ these modes has much to do with the success of a group or an organization as well as with the personal advancement of the individual.

Many aspects of personal influence are probably similar to what they were centuries ago, before formal organizations became so important (although perhaps brute physical force plays a less central role than it did in earlier times). As before, in almost all social systems individuals attempt to alter the behavior of others to the advantage of one or more individuals or to the group as a whole. What is radically different, however, is that these traditional and less formal actions take place in organizations—in social systems that are formally structured. This context creates new elements that managers must balance.

While there can be enormous differences in how such balance is achieved or not achieved, one constant is that most are grounded in a complex network of values and thought patterns of people. Undoubtedly, some of these values and thought patterns help to explain why, for so long, students of organizations failed to address the role of politics in organizations. In the second selection, "Politics: The Don't Go Anywhere Without It Skill," Dory Hollander observes this silence about the role of power and politics in organizations and argues persuasively that managers and other organization members are greatly handicapped by such inattention. Hollander points out that even in modern, formally designed organizations, a much less formal process, "politics" is a major avenue for exercising influence. She proposes that politics be viewed not only as a skill but as an *essential* one. Please note: In this selection, Hollander uses terminology from her insightful book, *The Doom Loop System*. This terminology (e.g., Quadrant I of the doom loop) may be confusing to one not familiar with the book. If you find the terms a problem, we suggest getting a copy of the book and/or skipping ahead to the selection entitled "The Doom Loop," which is reprinted in Chapter 8, Managing Hazards.

Values, and the role they play in shaping attitudes toward management, are also the focus of our last selection, "Dangerous Liaisons: The 'Feminine-in-Management' meets 'Globalization.'" Marta Calás and Linda Smircich question whether recent discussion about the need for a more "feminine" approach to management reflects a genuine commitment to fundamental change. They suggest that feminizing national organizations, while at the same time creating powerful hierarchies at the global level, merely shifts the traditional balance of power to the international arena.

In this context, the third selection, "Ways Women Lead," by Judy Rosener, is especially interesting. In addition to raising the often-discussed matter of whether women do and/or should employ different styles of leadership than men, many of the features of the ways Rosener describes the women she studied lead (e.g., enhancing the self-worth of others, sharing power and information with others) are some of the very things that Calás and Smircich argue could effect radical change in the way we think about management.

The fourth selection in this chapter, from Robert Jackall's thought-provoking *Moral Mazes*, portrays a far less harmonious view of present organizational life and organization–environment relations. In fact, Jackall finds that much of what happened in the organizations he studied was less directed toward developing harmonious relationships with the environment than toward finding ways that kept managers' options open to enable them to avoid unwanted interference from the environment. In addition, Jackall returns us to the idea of Chapter 1 by reminding us of how important the process of control has been in the history of management and how social science has come to play a growing role in this process. In addition, his discussion of the influence of top management's whims in determining the amount of attention given to the ideas of various consultants provides additional insight into some of the dynamics that might be at the root of the ebb and flow of various fads discussed by Byrne in Chapter 1. Importantly, throughout this selection, Jackall calls our attention to how language and symbols (including consultants and their rhetoric) are used to paper over contradictions in organizations and to legitimize what the organization's more influential managers want to have happen. As astute political scientists such as Murray Edelman (1977) have pointed out, language and symbols are vital tools for the exercise of influence in our society.

References

Edelman, M. *Political Language: Words That Succeed and Policies That Fail.* New York: Academic Press, 1977.

Weick, K. E. *The Social Psychology of Organizing*, 2nd ed. McGraw-Hill, 1979.

◆

Wreckers

Anonymous

I watched them tearing a building down,
A gang of men in a busy town,
With a hi-heave-ho and a lusty yell,
They swing a beam and the side walls fell.
I asked the foreman, "Are those men skilled
As the men you hire if you had to build?"
He gave me a laugh and said, "No indeed!
Just common labor is all I need.
I can easily wreck in a day or two
what builders have taken years to do."
I thought to myself as I went my way,
Which of these roles have I tried to play?
Am I a builder who works with care,
Measuring life by the rule or square?
Am I shaping my deeds to a well made plan,
Patiently doing the best I can?
Or am I wrecking like he who walks the town
Content with the labor of tearing down?

◆

Politics: The Don't Go Anywhere Without It Skill*

Dory Hollander

Politics. I'm not good at them, I don't like them, and I'm not going to play.

—New MBA, marketing

I hate the massive egos, the backbiting, wondering who's trying to get my job.

—Burned-out senior editor, publishing

It's a constant battle of one-upmanship. You worry all day about doing something wrong. I've learned you're either in control or you're the victim.

—Executive director, trade association

After the CEO who hired me left, they poisoned the well! They blocked my projects, reassigned my staff, even had me report to a manager I had trained.

—Demoted director, corporate fund-raising

ORGANIZATIONAL POLITICS: A WELL-KEPT SECRET

Organizational politics upset a lot of people. Rightly so. Caught off guard by factors they deem wholly peripheral to their work, they feel demeaned, devalued, and traumatized. What, they wonder, does any of this gratuitous backbiting have to do with work? When politics rob you of recognition and status you believe you deserve, it's normal to feel resentful and angry. But most people know little about political self-defense. They don't know how to decipher the intricate unwritten rules that govern success and failure in most organizations. Most don't even know what hit them until well after they've emptied their desks and are visiting their outplacement counselors.

This gives politics a bad reputation. Politics are so distasteful to many hardworking types that they despair of ever getting past them. When you're politically vulnerable it's easy to think politics are dirty business—dishonest scheming to give undeserving characters advantages they couldn't otherwise achieve. This leads many people to feel they're above "playing" organizational politics. But as much as people malign politics, they're still an unavoidable fact of daily life in any workplace with more than one worker.

Yet when it comes to getting help in understanding them, they're one of the best-kept secrets of modern organizational life.

Finding out how to handle politics is a lot like finding out how to use birth control was for a teenager in the 1950s. You know there is something you ought to be doing, but you can't find anyone who will tell you what or how.

You thought it was hard to get good coaching in managing your career? Well, try your luck at getting someone to coach you in politics. If you're like most people, nobody ever coached you in political one-upmanship when you got your first job or any time thereafter. You're on your own. Looking back at my own career, it seems to me that my mentors knew less about organizational politics than I did—and that certainly wasn't much. Nor can you rely on business school or graduate school professors to give you basic survival training in organizational politics; most business and graduate school courses quickly gloss over politics, if they mention them at all. Even the library colludes in keeping politics a secret; look up politics in popular management books and you'll find the gurus strangely silent.

All this silence makes it easy for you to plunge into your career with built-in vulnerability to dangerous political undertows. Compounding the problem is a set of time-honored cultural assumptions—like the one that says hard work pays off or the one about openness promoting trust—that leave you unprepared for managing the informal, often invisible, power structures that govern your success.

But stick around. Power politics are indigenous to the dynamics of any group. Before long, you'll confront the P-word face to face, bigger than life—infiltrating your meetings, projects, and relationships, and influencing outcome after outcome. Even though your sights are set on your capstone, politics creep up to wreak havoc with your plans. Unless you enjoy watching your pet projects, staff, and job security buffeted by subtle but cataclysmic forces that have nothing to do with the tasks at hand, you have to be prepared in advance. You can't afford to ignore the political crosswinds for long if you want to hold onto what you've got.

When the impact of politics first dawns on you, it can take the wind out of your sails. This unsettling feeling of being blindsided often marks the beginning of your induction into a lifelong high-stakes on-the-job training course. Some people take this instruction well; some people fight it.

Although this has probably always been true, in today's lean-and-mean corporate environments, rife with justifiable insecurity and radically shifting power bases, you will need every bit of political moxie you can muster. The newly restructured organizations of the 1990s are competitive playing fields without referees, cluttered with confusing ambiguities and competing factions. The resulting double messages about teamwork, loyalty, and security place more responsibility on you for managing your own career. Although the responsibility is greater, you'll find fewer guidelines for decoding what it actually takes to succeed. And the increasingly diverse work force of the past few years has made the few remaining rules obsolete. It's hard for most of us to know what's expected anymore. All this calls for greater ability to read between the lines. Survivors can expect to negotiate treacherous hidden agendas and mixed messages throughout their careers.

If you don't activate your political horse sense, you might as well park your career plan in a time capsule.

Political skills channel your attention to the murky gray areas of corporate cultures where alliances are forged, where information is exchanged, where stakeholders in various outcomes fight to preserve their own interests. You must become an expert at interpreting innuendo in social situations, at figuring out who has what at stake where and when, and at distinguishing who actually controls resources versus who merely appears to. It's these competing patterns of personal and professional self-interest that make organizational power politics hum. And as they play out against the stark backdrop of what your organization rewards and punishes, you will be well advised to protect your own turf.

Sure it sounds overwhelming. But the only thing that will truly overwhelm you is putting your head in the sand. It's too late to argue that you don't like politics or that you're not going to play. That's a rookie's mentality that will push you right out the door.

THE DANGERS OF IGNORING ORGANIZATIONAL POLITICS

My advice here is simple and succinct: don't. Lots of people have hoped that if they ignored them, politics would go away. Mostly the people went away. There's the marketing director who was passed over for promotion after ten years of productive work in her company, the corporate vice president who lost a mentor and the right to be heard by key decision-makers, the bank officer who was fired after righteous whistle-blowing on a colleague, and the widely published professor who lost his second battle for tenure.

Each of these bright, hardworking people ignored, misread, or was caught unaware by organizational politics. As a result, each faced painful career derailment and gut-wrenching angst. They addressed the wrong issues—and not so surprisingly came up with the wrong solutions.

The marketing director addressed a political problem, her boss's patently unfair positioning of two junior coworkers for a promotion she knew she deserved, by working even harder to prove how good she was. But all she did was wear herself out and speed her fall from grace.

The whistle-blowing bank officer fought for what he believed was right in the face of strong, unified opposition. Although he did the right thing, it failed to solve the problem, win him kudos, or pay his children's private school tuition. It did, however, give him an opportunity to learn, the old-fashioned way, that martyrdom is a career-stopping liability.

Sometimes people try to ignore politics by leaving a volatile work setting for altogether new vistas. Although this sometimes works, a change of scenery can plunge you into an unknown setting with an even less friendly bunch of dragons where history is likely to repeat itself. The professor who was twice denied tenure lost to two different, but equally outrageous, clutches of political dragons.

When politics halt you in your tracks or keep you from being effective, it's natural to feel discouraged and paranoid, or to construe politics as evil. After all, you're just trying to do your job, whereas someone else is purposely trying to make you look bad. You just want to slink off to lick your wounds and recover.

But whether you see politics as the use or abuse of power usually depends on which side you're on. The problem is that when you ignore politics altogether, you may not even realize there are sides. And you emerge from difficult situations sadder, but no wiser.

Organizational politics, like mountains, cannot be ignored. They command your attention just because they're there, and because there are few easy ways to get around them. No matter which quadrant of your Doom Loop you're in or where you are in your career, you're never too old, too rich, or too smart to get a better handle on organizational politics.

THE DOOM LOOP AND POLITICS

This is where the rubber meets the road. If you intend to get the mileage you need from your Doom Loop strategy, plan on topping off your personal career mosaic with high-octane political savvy. Don't misunderstand. I'm not suggesting that you trade your capstone, your target mosaic, or your commitment to professional excellence for Machiavellian tactics. But it helps to be on a first-name basis with the positive side of power politics.

Let's look at how the Doom Loop strategy interacts with political awareness to yield four strategic career positions that affect your work life.

FOUR STRATEGIC CAREER POSITIONS

	Politically Naive	Politically Savvy
Non-Doom Looper (Unintentional)	Rudderless	Machiavellian
Doom Looper (Intentional)	Blindsided	Concordant

This is an altogether different matrix from the Doom Loop matrix, so don't confuse them. All I have done is combine the question of whether or not you are using an intentional career management system with whether you are politically naive or savvy. The matrix shows four different strategic career positions:

- **Blindsided**—Although you're an intentional career manager, politically you're a novice. You don't even realize you're a sitting duck.
- **Rudderless**—You're neither an intentional career manager nor a political ball of fire. You're unprepared to do anything but drift.
- **Machiavellian**—Without a career management plan, but with plenty of political horse sense, you're like an opportunistic virus seeking a host.
- **Concordant**—You're an intentional career manager who is tuned in to the power dynamics of your workplace. All bets are on you.

Which combination best describes you? Each one leads to different approaches that affect your career success. Let's look at each strategic career position and how it plays out.

Blindsided

Doom Loopers who ignore all but the most blatant organizational politics are at high risk for being hit broadside. If blindsided describes your approach, you may be paying too much attention to the tasks at hand and not enough attention to people, contexts, and politics. Unfortunately, this will land you in Quadrant III's organizational backwaters.

That's what happened to Hal Franchetti. Hal was a high-achieving, no-nonsense sales manager who carefully constructed an A+ target mosaic for his capstone of district manager, only to be dismissed before he arrived there. Despite his high performance, Hal was blindsided because he ignored a few too many obvious political realities—an inbred clique of old college buddies, a high premium on off-the-job socializing, and a tacit "don't rock the boat" rule.

Hal was a typical high achiever—impatient, brimming with ideas, hooked on challenge and unswervingly goal-oriented. His autonomous, workaholic style set him apart from the rest of the sales force. Eventually all his innovative ideas were implemented by his company—without Hal at the helm. He just didn't fit. And he made matters worse by not looking up from what he was doing long enough to realize it. When Hal was fired he belatedly got the picture, and it hurt.

Like Hal, many nonpolitical, highly driven professionals are blindsided. From their perspective, they're doing a great job; it's their coworkers and supervisors who create chaos. And maybe they're right. Too bad that being right doesn't get them what they want.

Who is most likely to be blindsided? High achievers, task-oriented worka-holics, productivity addicts who hate to schmooze, lone rangers who opperate out-side the "buddy" news network, independent creative types, and goal-driven career managers who can't see the forest for the trees. New entries to the work force and people who work in independent areas like research and development are also likely candidates. Even old-timers who fail to keep up with new organiza-tional dictates like self-managing work groups and team decision making can be blindsided by the changing order. When you are blindsided, you have your eyes on the twin balls of competence and career progression, but you miss the fact that there are three balls up there. When the third one lands it can knock you off your feet. You need to know how to juggle all three.

The lesson to be learned here is that if you are a serious Doom Looper you can't afford to ignore or misread organizational power bases, changes in the orga-nizational climate, or the personality mix of the key players. If you do, expect to be blindsided, sandbagged, or worse. It's important to see political skills for what they are—basic survival skills. Without a crash course in them, you'll be the one to crash.

Rudderless

This position is one to shun. For all practical purposes it is a Quadrant IV look-alike. With neither political nor career management know-how, the rudderless person is reduced to following other people's agendas—taking orders and moving through a series of jobs that get him or her nowhere. Such people are career flot-sam, aimlessly bobbing wherever the tide pulls them. Shirley Dubin could write a book about being adrift in a career. She got her nursing degree right after high school and became a night nurse to support her husband's medical school educa-tion. She hated the work, but the money was steady, so she stayed. Twenty-five years and two husbands later, Shirley is appalled that she's still in nursing. She says, "Every single day I'm reminded I don't want to be there—ninety percent of my job consists of what I don't like." What's worse is her steady stream of com-plaints about the power politics of her hospital: the doctors have to be treated like gods. The orderlies sleep on the job, so she has more to do. She is given all the bad shifts and the toughest floors. The head nurse makes her a scapegoat. Et cetera.

All this is a given for Shirley. She accepts it and feels beaten down because she has no defenses against either career doom or political mistreatment. By relin-quishing her control to others, she has embraced the victim's role. She is rudder-less on all counts. No one is taking care of Shirley's career, least of all Shirley, and she has acquired no organizational savvy or clout. Like many people with no career plan and no political horse sense, Shirley drifted into her career—then helplessly watched the scenario play out. Like other rudderless souls, she has been in Quadrant IV so long she's not sure she's capable of managing anything else. She doesn't realize she should be scanning the organizational horizon, taking a self-protective stance, taking care of herself. Instead she feels trapped, a pawn who exercises little control over her life.

Who is likely to be rudderless? You'll discover some unlikely bedfellows in this group. The usual occupants are people in their first jobs who haven't yet learned the ropes and lifers who are stuck in low-control, high-stress pink- and blue-collar ghettos without easy exit. But in pared-down organizational structures, many traditional managers have been cut adrift and suddenly find themselves rudderless. In restructured and decentralized organizations you'll find many managers who haven't yet recovered their bearings. They've lost the traditional vertical pecking order they know and trust as well as their mentors and power bases. For the time being they lack their old career direction and political know-how.

If rudderless describes your career management position, realize this is a common problem. Your first task is to see that you still have many choices and that you deserve much better than this in your career. Exercise your personal power by taking one step at a time to extricate yourself and regain a sense of direction; there's a lot to learn.

The primary lesson to be learned here is that no one will take care of you in your career but you. When you abdicate responsibility for your own direction and ignore organizational power plays and operating systems, you're doomed to drift.

Machiavellian

When people think about workplace politics at their worst, it's the Machiavellian types that come to mind. These are the highly self-interested, politically glib glad-handers whose main career strategy rests on being in the right place at the right time or hitching their own wagons to someone else's rising star. Like roulette, when this strategy works, the payoff is high. But since the wheel is fickle, their career success depends on external forces they don't control.

Lenny Terrill was a classic Machiavellian type. He had a simple "it's not what you do, it's who you know" formula for getting ahead in advertising. He lunched in the right places, hobnobbed with the right people, appeared in the right gossip columns. Networking is a euphemism for Lenny's entrenchment in the grapevine. "They can't fire me," he laughed, "I've got too much on everyone." He exploited his contacts and successfully positioned himself for opportunities before they became public. For a long time, this approach worked well for Lenny. Then Lenny's mentor became involved in his own legal and ethical morass and was deposed. Considerably tarnished by association, and without his mentor to protect him, Lenny rapidly fell from grace and became the agency pariah. Although Lenny was no slouch, he hadn't built a skill-based, qualified career profile, either. This limited his options. His career progress, for all its stylish bravado, was largely dependent on serendipity. Lenny was on his way out.

Who is likely to use the Machiavellian approach? All kinds of people looking for quick career fixes and shortcuts. Some are convinced it's the way the world turns. At some point, power brokering becomes highly addictive. Bright, ambitious types in cutthroat industries may bet on politics to give them the needed edge. Sometimes Machiavellis lack credentials, confidence, or both. Power politics help them camouflage their deficiencies. But personality can also be a factor. If you are motivated by the need to control people and resources, influence events and outcomes, and cut back-room deals, organizational politics offer you quite a nice bailiwick for your natural preferences!

The worst of the Machiavellian types are pathological game players who have little empathy for other people's positions. These relentlessly self-centered parasites take what is yours and what is theirs. They make little distinction. They are the ones who run roughshod over others and give politics their nightmare reputation.

Just remember, this is different in kind and degree from ordinary self-interest. There is nothing wrong with self-interest in and of itself; self-interest motivates. In fact, it is essential for anyone who wants to achieve career success.

Issues of self-interest aside, there are still serious problems in using a Machiavellian strategy. Pragmatically speaking, success rests too heavily on unpredictable factors and too little on your own skills and abilities. Ironically, in fast-changing organizational environments, this approach gives all but the very talented political strategist far too little control.

The lesson to be learned here is that Machiavellis often risk their career success with every unforeseen shift in organizational leadership and structure. As competitive pressures destabilize and downsize organizations, Machiavellis are hard-pressed to figure out just where to hitch their wagons. This may lead them to take larger risks and make serious errors. It could be time for the Machiavellis to switch their strategy to the concordant style discussed next. This is the best tactic for regaining control during changing times.

Concordant

This is the ideal style—that of the intentional career manager who has acquired considerable aplomb in heeding and reading organizational environments. Jenny Davis is a good example. She is the highest-ranking female executive in a large financial institution. After college she worked her way up from a clerical position in the pension division. She formulated her capstone—a bank CEO—about five years ago, and most of the pension division's power brokers concur that she is on her way. She has developed relevant skills and credentials with the single-minded focus of a kid playing a video game. Whenever Jenny approaches the top of the Loop and moves toward Quadrant III, she deploys her favorite work credo: "If the job doesn't change, change the job." But Jenny never does it alone. Jenny is a master networker who has the support of mentors, allies, and plenty of fans, inside and outside the company. Her political skills are impressive. She holds standard pre-meeting meetings before raising new issues. She carefully positions her accomplishments inside the company with key people, avid supporters, and witty memos that command attention. She maintains high visibility in the community by serving on prestigious voluntary boards.

People like Jenny have learned to read the organizational norms and align them with their own professional needs. They have decoded what the organization really rewards. They understand the informal power structure. This enables them to unobtrusively position their daily achievements with decision-makers, gaining the visibility they need for success.

When your career and political goals are concordant, there's a good fit between your personal career strategies and the context of the particular position. Jenny is an excellent example of this. She has aligned her personal career strategies with the particular context of her position, making her career and political goals concordant.

The lesson to be learned here is that mastering political survival skills like reading norms, networking, quiet diplomacy, marketing, empowerment tactics, positioning projects, and resolving conflict, along with your Doom Loop strategy and tactics, will enable you to reach your capstone—intact.

WHAT ARE ORGANIZATIONAL POLITICS, ANYWAY?

What do politics mean to you? Your answer depends largely on your experience. Politics mean many things to many people—mostly negative things, I might add. Everyone complains about them; nearly everyone recognizes them (even if it's too late), but few can say exactly what they are. But even when they can't say what politics are, most people will say they don't like them.

This creates a double-edged problem. If you're going to add a set of skills to your target mosaic to help you maneuver through troubled political waters, you ought to know just what you're dealing with. And if you're going to stay motivated to learn this set of skills, you'd better not be repulsed.

Try asking a group of people to describe organizational politics, and you'll get as many answers as people. There's no common definition, but the trend line is unmistakable. For different people politics are:

- empire building
- the use and abuse of power
- hidden agendas and alliances
- playing people off against each other
- infighting over power and control
- selling your soul to people you don't like
- one-upmanship, putdowns, and sabotage
- being rewarded and punished for things other than performance
- personality clashes and bad will

What links these descriptions is a pervasive sense of disenchantment, distrust, and disempowerment. Politics are seen as nasty business. No wonder people avoid them.

Let's agree to deviate from the path. Let's take a more upbeat approach that lets you use politics to your own advantage in your career. Politics have three components that affect your career progress:

- clashing needs and interests
- hidden alliances among stakeholders
- insider-outsider people sorting

Understanding these components will help you recast politics in a more positive light. As a Quadrant I student of politics, you'll find that keeping an open mind will serve you well.

Clashing Needs and Interests

Everyone has self-interest, including you. But because no two people are alike, neither are any two sets of self-interest. This translates into a real-life drama of power plays and continuing clashes over control of resources. Conflict in organizations is not dirty; it's simply evidence that everyone is still breathing.

Once you see politics as motivations and behaviors that serve basic self-interest, it's easy to see how power and control crawl out of the woodwork wherever people relate to each other. That's why you can't duck politics. They're everywhere—at work, in the PTA, at neighborhood association meetings, and in the family. Once you begin to think like this, politics get less irritating. If politics are simply normal friction caused by competing self-interest among people and groups, then why should politics be distasteful? Why not see them as just another skill to be mastered?

People who make a holy war out of avoiding organizational politics see politics as a repulsive Quadrant IV skill set. This keeps them from investing the time and energy they need to become politically literate. They couldn't play politics if they wanted to! As a result, no one is minding their interests.

Hidden Alliances Among Stakeholders

Webster's New World Dictionary (Second College Edition, 1984) defines politics, in part, as "factional scheming for power." Although you may find scheming for power objectionable, it's actually quite normal for people who have something at stake to get together to protect their interests. If the state tried to take your property through eminent domain, you bet you and your neighbors would meet to discuss how to act together to protect your homes. There is nothing inherently evil about wanting to protect your own interests. The problem is that different groups of stakeholders have different sets of interests. And the interests of each group are not always obvious. So you had better ferret out what various stakeholders are up to. But don't count on anyone giving you a play-by-play account.

Contrary to popular opinion, most people's scheming and collusion are strictly kid stuff. Even seasoned political pros rarely orchestrate their plans in majestic detail. Much of what happens takes place in the heat of the moment. There's no master blueprint. Because political scheming is dicey, you'll need to protect yourself, well before all the facts are in. Techniques won't help you as much as general principles. Since your adversaries will probably be shooting from the hip, you'll have to make sense of events by understanding the nature of political alliances. These alliances usually:

- concentrate power in a few trusted hands
- help some stakeholders meet their needs at the expense of others
- allow entrenched power brokers to maintain the status quo

- get things done quickly through nonstandard channels
- speed critical information to key decision-makers
- stop threats to the old order through rituals, policies, and so on
- slow down the overall rate of change and cut losses
- determine how newcomers are hazed and otherwise persuaded to accept established ways of doing things
- keep out people who are too different or who will escalate change

So when you look at some political action, ask yourself how it serves these purposes. Which stakeholders get what payoffs? Your job is to figure out what's going on and to get the situation to work for you rather than against you.

For better or worse, politics are a tool with many uses that serves many masters. By learning to read a group's power dynamics, you gain an edge. You don't have to hurt anyone or do anything unethical. Understanding is power. The goal is to manage yourself with less vulnerability and more control. This improves your chances of reaching your capstone intact.

Insider-Outsider People Sorting

Go anywhere in the world, and you'll see that people constantly sort each other into two basic camps—"us" and "them." It's simple. If you're "one of us," you're a trusted insider. If you're "one of them," forget it. No matter how good your work is, if you're an outsider you'll have a harder time getting recognized. This puts you at a big disadvantage. It takes much more effort for you to be effective. You get more criticism and less support for your accomplishments. As one outsider put it, "When I do good work I get no feedback. That's how I know I'm doing well."

As an outsider you feel far less appreciated because you *are* less appreciated. You're locked out of lunch meetings where insiders swap information. You're not invited to the tribal pre-meeting meetings where insiders set each other up for success. When you're an outsider, you're all dressed up with nowhere to go. You're taken for granted until you do something wrong; then you may be vilified. No wonder you're so astounded and angry when someone who does mediocre work wins accolades from the group in power.

Despite this widespread "us" versus "them" trend, most people cling to the idea that they should be judged solely on the quality of their work. But quality of work is just one blip on the large screen when insiders judge you. For many hard-working types this whole approach is an outrage. They react with anguish and upset. They say things like, "I'm so angry I'd like to take a month off to go beat some rugs somewhere," or, "I don't get any support around here," or, "I've gotten to the point where I don't enjoy going to work anymore." They don't need a big push to blame office politics.

In fact, it will help make you a better career manager if you mentally separate your job performance from the context of your job. Then you can think of politics as anything besides job performance that involves other people at work and that adversely affects your ability to be effective and get rewards. Note the word "adversely." It's interesting that people rarely complain about cliques, alliances, and social banter that they enjoy or that work in their favor. When you're "one of us," rather than "one of them," it's odd how politics lose much of their sting.

THE BIG CHALLENGE: ACHIEVING POLITICAL LITERACY

It's never too late to wage a full-scale war on your own political illiteracy. You may be a Ph.D. who can't read the unwritten codes for behavior, can't decipher the hidden agendas that create havoc in meetings, and can't understand the power alliances that govern decisions. You may be a top manager who is so task-oriented that you forget all about maintaining good relations with your people. In either case, your political illiteracy sets you up for predictable failure. The more you see politics as personally repugnant, the less likely you are to invest in learning them. So it's in your best interest to change this perception and see politics as an essential skill to master. The challenge is to become politically literate without damaging your integrity.

Actually this is easier than most political illiterates believe. Political skills are like any other skills, with a few exceptions. First, you won't see these skills listed in most job descriptions. Second, they are mandatory protective gear for nearly any job. Political skills are group survival skills. They require you to focus on the human side—the relational and motivational side of the workplace. They help you avoid the predictable pitfalls that keep you from reaching your capstone. They reduce the restraints that hold you back from success. It's tough to attain your capstone without them. Achieving political literacy helps you reach concordance and avoid being blindsided.

Look over the political skills literacy checklist on the next page and identify the skills you still need to master. Then decide in which quadrant of your Doom Loop the ones you have checked fall. Add any other political skills you believe are important but not included in this list.

Take out some paper and list the Quadrant I political skills you have checked; then list the Quadrant IV political skills you still need to acquire. These two subsets outline the skills that belong on your master target mosaic list. They require your immediate attention. Your task will be to learn each one without requiring damage control. Start with your Quadrant I skills to get you moving, since these skills are ones you like but are not yet good at.

But first a word of caution. Whenever you're learning Quadrant I and IV skills, by definition you're a novice. You can expect to make mistakes. That's the evidence that you're learning something. But when you're learning political skills, you're dealing with volatile, sometimes hidden issues that could affect many stakeholders in your organization and determine your future.

So your safest bet as a novice is learning your new political skills outside the workplace. Try voluntary professional and local groups. They are usually rich fiefdoms of power dynamics where you'll learn everything you ever needed to know about politics and more. Or hire a consultant. Look for an experienced career coach or an old salt in your field who has spent a lifetime observing political infighting. Another good choice is someone who has recently retired from your line of work. Ask to buy his or her services as a personal consultant on a short-term basis.

POLITICAL SKILLS LITERACY CHECKLIST

Mastery Status (Yes or No)	Doom Loop Quadrant Status (I, II, III, or IV)	
1. _____	_____	You recognize which family, professional, and cultural myths (e.g., hard work will be rewarded) you have been using to guide you.
2. _____	_____	You know what your own personal and professional needs are.
3. _____	_____	You can "read" an organizational culture's unwritten rules.
4. _____	_____	You know what makes a person an "us" versus a "them" in your organization.
5. _____	_____	You look and dress the part of someone successful in this group.
6. _____	_____	You play the part of someone who fits your organization's culture.
7. _____	_____	You pace your style and tempo to the group's (in terms of work rate and quality, social amenities, and so on).
8. _____	_____	You know how to identify and attract a mentor in new situations.
9. _____	_____	You routinely get help from key people on your projects and problems—whether you need it or not.
10. _____	_____	You periodically analyze the organization's informal information network to learn how information gets around—where channels are open, blocked, and dead-ended and by whom.
11. _____	_____	You know how to use information channels to promote yourself and your projects.
12. _____	_____	You can identify the stakeholders in any project and note their special interests and alliances.
13. _____	_____	You know who the gatekeepers in the organization are and how to get past them.
14. _____	_____	You like people without confusing this with trust.
15. _____	_____	Your emphasis is on being effective rather than on being right.
16. _____	_____	You pay close attention to what people do, as opposed to what they say.
17. _____	_____	You learn who has which hidden agendas and why.
18. _____	_____	You observe what's really rewarded in this place, not what they say is rewarded.
19. _____	_____	You observe what leaders and key players are doing—including alliances, shifts, and detours.
20. _____	_____	You align your own needs with what the organization actually rewards.

21. _____ _____   You develop relationships with key stakeholders, gate-keepers, and power brokers that foster common interests.

22. _____ _____   You form working alliances with stakeholders and power brokers that protect your interests.

23. _____ _____   You deliberately promote your accomplishments with top stakeholders and decision-makers.

24. _____ _____   You cultivate an extensive network, including some unlikely allies.

25. _____ _____   You consistently take good care of coworkers and support staff.

26. _____ _____   You earn your stripes in both the task and relational aspects of your job.

27. _____ _____   You use a small-wins strategy to keep yourself and your successes visible in ways that don't threaten anyone.

28. _____ _____   You use conflict resolution skills to acknowledge others' viewpoints, listen to their stories, and learn their interests.

29. _____ _____   You adopt protective camouflage, moving with the flow of group thinking, not against it, blending with norms to get breathing space.

30. _____ _____   You have sufficient people skills to manage the difficult people who work with you and still gain their support.

31. _____ _____   You deliberately network and form alliances outside the organization.

32. _____ _____   You know when to cut your losses and move on.

Keep in mind that political skills are sophisticated ones that spiral and build on themselves and on experience. So wherever you are in your career, you'll always be able to find new levels of political challenge requiring new levels of political skill mastery.

◆

Ways Women Lead*

Judy B. Rosener

Women managers who have broken the glass ceiling in medium-sized, nontraditional organizations have proven that effective leaders don't come from one mold. They have demonstrated that using the command-and-control style of managing others, a style generally associated with men in large, traditional organizations, is not the only way to succeed.

The first female executives, because they were breaking new ground, adhered to many of the "rules of conduct" that spelled success for men. Now a second wave of women is making its way into top management, not by adopting the style and habits that have proved successful for men but by drawing on the skills and attitudes they developed from their shared experience as women. These second generation managerial women are drawing on what is unique to their socialization as women and creating a different path to the top. They are seeking and finding opportunities in fast-changing and growing organizations to show that they can achieve results—in a different way. They are succeeding because of—not in spite of—certain characteristics generally considered to be "feminine" and inappropriate in leaders.

The women's success shows that a nontraditional leadership style is well suited to the conditions of some work environments and can increase an organization's chances of surviving in an uncertain world. It supports the belief that there is strength in a diversity of leadership styles.

In a recent survey sponsored by the International Women's Forum, I found a number of unexpected similarities between men and women leaders along with some important differences. (For more on the study and its findings, see The IWF Survey of Men and Women Leaders on p. 144.) Among these similarities are characteristics related to money and children. I found that the men and women respondents earned the same amount of money (and the household income of the women is twice that of the men). This finding is contrary to most studies, which find a considerable wage gap between men and women, even at the executive level. I also found that just as many men as women experience work-family conflict (although when there are children at home, the women experience slightly more conflict than men).

But the similarities end when men and women describe their leadership performance and how they usually influence those with whom they work. The men are more likely than the women to describe themselves in ways that characterize what some management experts call "transactional" leadership.[1] That is, they view job performance as a series of transactions with subordinates—exchanging rewards for services rendered or punishment for inadequate performance. The men are also more likely to use power that comes from their organizational position and formal authority.

The women respondents, on the other hand, described themselves in ways that characterize "transformational" leadership—getting subordinates to transform their own self-interest into the interest of the group through concern for a broader goal. Moreover, they ascribe their power to personal characteristics like

---

[1] Transactional and transformational leadership were first conceptualized by James McGregor Burns in *Leadership* (New York: Harper & Row, 1978) and later developed by Bernard Bass in *Leadership and Performance Beyond Expectations* (New York: Free Press, 1985).

charisma, interpersonal skills, hard work, or personal contacts rather than to organizational stature.

Intrigued by these differences, I interviewed some of the women respondents who described themselves as transformational. These discussions gave me a better picture of how these women view themselves as leaders and a greater understanding of the important ways in which their leadership style differs from the traditional command-and-control style. I call their leadership style "interactive leadership" because these women actively work to make their interactions with subordinates positive for everyone involved. More specifically, the women encourage participation, share power and information, enhance other people's self-worth, and get others excited about their work. All these things reflect their belief that allowing employees to contribute and to feel powerful and important is a win-win situation—good for the employees and the organization.

INTERACTIVE LEADERSHIP

From my discussions with the women interviewees, several patterns emerged. The women leaders made frequent reference to their efforts to encourage participation and share power and information—two things that are often associated with participative management. But their self-description went beyond the usual definitions of participation. Much of what they described were attempts to enhance other people's sense of self-worth and to energize followers in general, these leaders believe that people perform best when they feel good about themselves and their work, and they try to create situations that contribute to that feeling.

Encourage participation   Inclusion is at the core of interactive leadership. In describing nearly every aspect of management, the women interviewees made reference to trying to make people feel part of the organization. They try to instill this group identity in a variety of ways, including encouraging others to have a say in almost every aspect of work, from setting performance goals to determining strategy. To facilitate inclusion, they create mechanisms that get people to participate and they use a conversational style that sends signals inviting people to get involved.

One example of the kinds of mechanisms that encourage participation is the "bridge club" that one interviewee, a group executive in charge of mergers and acquisitions at a large East Coast financial firm, created. The club is an informal gathering of people who have information she needs but over whom she has no direct control. The word *bridge* describes the effort to bring together these "members" from different functions. The word *club* captures the relaxed atmosphere.

Despite the fact that attendance at club meetings is voluntary and over and above the usual work demands, the interviewee said that those whose help she needs make the time to come. "They know their contributions are valued, and they appreciate the chance to exchange information across functional boundaries in an informal setting that's fun." She finds participation in the club more effective than memos.

Whether or not the women create special forums for people to interact, they try to make people feel included as a matter of course, often by trying to draw them into the conversation or soliciting their opinions. Frieda Caplan, founder and CEO of Frieda's Finest, a California-based marketer and distributor of unusual fruits and vegetables, described an approach she uses that is typical of the other women interviewed: "When I face a tough decision, I always ask my employees, 'What would you do if you were me?' This approach generates good ideas and introduces my employees to the complexity of management decisions."

THE IWF SURVEY OF MEN AND WOMEN LEADERS

The International Women's Forum was founded in 1982 to give prominent women leaders in diverse professions around the world a way to share their knowledge with each other and with their communities and countries. The organization now has some 37 forums in North America, Europe, Asia, Latin America, and the Middle East. To help other women advance and to educate the public about the contributions women can and are making in government, business, and other fields, the IWF created the Leadership Foundation. The Foundation commissioned me to perform the study of men and women leaders on which this article is based. I conducted the study with the help of Daniel McAllister and Gregory Stephens (Ph.D. students at the Graduate School of Management at the University of California, Irvine) in the spring of 1989.

The survey consisted of an eight-page questionnaire sent to all the IWF members. Each respondent was asked to supply the name of a man in a similar organization with similar responsibilities. The men received the same questionnaire as the IWF members. The respondents were similar in age, occupation, and educational level, which suggests that the matching effort was successful. The response rate was 31%.

The respondents were asked questions about their leadership styles, their organizations, work-family issues, and personal characteristics. The following are among the more intriguing findings, some of which contradict data reported in academic journals and the popular press:

- The women earn the same amount of money as their male counterparts. The average yearly income for men is $136,510; for women it is $140,573. (Most other studies have shown a wage gap between men and women.)
- The men's household income (their own and their spouse's) is much lower than that of the women—$166,454 versus $300,892. (Only 39% of the men have full-time employed spouses, as opposed to 71% of the women.)
- Both men and women leaders pay their female subordinates roughly $12,000 less than their male subordinates with similar positions and titles.
- Women are more likely than men to use transformational leadership—motivating others by transforming their self-interest into the goals of the organization.
- Women are much more likely than men to use power based on charisma, work record, and contacts (personal power) as opposed to power based on organizational position, title, and the ability to reward and punish (structural power).

- Most men and women describe themselves as having an equal mix of traits that are considered "feminine" (being excitable, gentle, emotional, submissive, sentimental, understanding, compassionate, sensitive, dependent), "masculine" (dominant, aggressive, tough, assertive, autocratic, analytical, competitive, independent), and "gender-neutral" (adaptive, tactful, sincere, conscientious, conventional, reliable, predictable, systematic, efficient).
- Women who do describe themselves as predominately "feminine" or "gender-neutral" report a higher level of followership among their female subordinates than women who describe themselves as "masculine."
- Approximately 67% of the women respondents are married. (Other studies report that only 40% to 50% of women executives are married.)
- Both married men and married women experience moderate levels of conflict between work and family domains. When there are children at home, women experience only slightly higher levels of conflict than men, even though they shoulder a much greater proportion of the child care—61% of the care versus 25% for the men.

Of course, saying that you include others doesn't mean others necessarily feel included. The women acknowledge the possibility that their efforts to draw people in may be seen as symbolic, so they try to avoid that perception by acting on the input they receive. They ask for suggestions before they reach their own conclusions, and they test—and sometimes change—particular decisions before they implement them. These women use participation to clarify their own views by thinking things through out loud and to ensure that they haven't overlooked an important consideration.

The fact that many of the interviewees described their participatory style as coming "naturally" suggests that these leaders do not consciously adopt it for its business value. Yet they realize that encouraging participation has benefits. For one thing, making it easy for people to express their ideas helps ensure that decisions reflect as much information as possible. To some of the women, this point is just common sense. Susan S. Elliott, president and founder of Systems Service Enterprises, a St. Louis computer consulting company, expressed this view: "I can't come up with a plan and then ask those who manage the accounts to give me their reactions. They're the ones who really know the accounts. They have information I don't have. Without their input I'd be operating in an ivory tower."

Participation also increases support for decisions ultimately reached and reduces the risk that ideas will be undermined by unexpected opposition. Claire Rothman, general manager of the Great Western Forum, a large sports and entertainment arena in Los Angeles, spoke about the value of open disagreement: "When I know ahead of time that someone disagrees with a decision, I can work especially closely with that person to try to get his or her support."

Getting people involved also reduces the risk associated with having only one person handle a client, project, or investment. For Patricia M. Cloherty, senior vice president and general partner of Al Patricof Associates, a New York venture capital firm, including people in decision making and planning gives investments longevity. If something happens to one person, others will be familiar enough with the situation to "adopt" the investment. That way, there are no orphans in the portfolio, and a knowledgeable second opinion is always available.

Like most who are familiar with participatory management, these women are aware that being inclusive also has its disadvantages. Soliciting ideas and information from others takes time, often requires giving up some control, opens the door to criticism, and exposes personal and turf conflicts. In addition, asking for ideas and information can be interpreted as not having answers.

Further, it cannot be assumed that everyone wants to participate. Some people prefer being told what to do. When Mary Jane Rynd was a partner in a Big Five accounting firm in Arizona (she recently left to start her own company—Rynd, Carmeal & Associates), she encountered such a person: "We hired this person from an out-*of-s*tate CPA firm because he was experienced and smart—and because it's always fun to hire someone away from another firm. But he was just too cynical to participate. He was suspicious of everybody. I tried everything to get him involved—including him in discussions and giving him pep-talks about how we all work together. Nothing worked. He just didn't want to participate."

Like all those who responded to the survey, these women are comfortable using a variety of leadership styles. So when participation doesn't work, they act unilaterally. "I prefer participation," said Elliott, "but there are situations where time is short and I have to take the bull by the horns."

Share power and information Soliciting input from other people suggests a flow of information from employees to the "boss." But part of making people feel included is knowing that open communication flows in two directions. These women say they willingly share power and information rather than guard it and they make apparent their reasoning behind decisions. While many leaders see information as power and power as a limited commodity to be coveted, the interviewees seem to be comfortable letting power and information change hands. As Adrienne Hall, vice chairman of Eissman, Johns & Laws, a large West Coast advertising firm, said: "I know territories shift, so I'm not preoccupied with turf."

One example of power and information sharing is the open strategy sessions held by Debi Coleman, vice president of information systems and technology at Apple Computer. Rather than closeting a small group of key executives in her office to develop strategy based on her own agenda, she holds a series of meetings over several days and allows a larger group to develop and help choose alternatives.

The interviewees believe that sharing power and information accomplishes several things. It creates unity by signaling to coworkers and subordinates that they are trusted and their ideas respected. It also sets an example for other people and therefore will enhance the general communication flow. And it increases the odds that leaders will hear about problems before they explode. Sharing power and information also gives employees and coworkers the wherewithal to reach conclusions, solve problems, and see the justification for decisions.

On a more pragmatic level, many employees have come to expect their bosses to be open and frank. They no longer accept being dictated to but want to be treated as individuals with minds of their own. As Elliott said, "I work with lots of people who are bright and intelligent, so I have to deal with them at an intellectual level. They're very logical, and they want to know the reasons for things. They'll buy in only if it makes sense."

In some cases, sharing information means simply being candid about work-related issues. In early 1990, when Elliott hired as employees many of the people she had been using as independent contractors, she knew the transition would be difficult for everyone. The number of employees nearly doubled overnight, and the nature of working relationships changed. "I warned everyone that we were in for some rough times and reminded them that we would be experiencing them together. I admitted that it would also be hard for me, and I made it clear that I wanted them to feel free to talk to me. I was completely candid and encouraged them to be honest with me. I lost some employees who didn't like the new relationships, but I'm convinced that being open helped me understand my employees better, and it gave them a feeling of support."

Like encouraging participation, sharing power and information has its risks. It allows for the possibility that people will reject, criticize, or otherwise challenge what the leader has to say or, more broadly, her authority. Also, employees get frustrated when leaders listen to—but ultimately reject—their ideas. Because information is a source of power, leaders who share it can be seen as naive or needing to be liked. The interviewees have experienced some of these downsides but find the positives overwhelming.

Enhance the self-worth of others One of the byproducts of sharing information and encouraging participation is that employees feel important. During the interviews, the women leaders discussed other ways they build a feeling of self-worth in coworkers and subordinates. They talked about giving others credit and praise and sending small signals of recognition. Most important, they expressed how they refrain from asserting their own superiority, which asserts the inferiority of others. All those I interviewed expressed clear aversion to behavior that sets them apart from others in the company— reserved parking places, separate dining facilities, pulling rank.

Examples of sharing and giving credit to others abound. Caplan, who has been the subject of scores of media reports hailing her innovation of labeling vegetables so consumers know what they are and how to cook them, originally got the idea from a farmer. She said that whenever someone raises the subject, she credits the farmer and downplays her role. Rothman is among the many note-writers: when someone does something out of the ordinary, she writes them a personal note to tell them she noticed. Like many of the women I interviewed, she said she also makes a point of acknowledging good work by talking about it in front of others.

Bolstering coworkers and subordinates is especially important in businesses and jobs that tend to be hard on a person's ego. Investment banking is one example because of the long hours, high pressures, intense competition, and inevitability that some deals will fail. One interviewee in investment banking hosts dinners for her division, gives out gag gifts as party favors, passes out M&Ms at meetings, and throws parties "to celebrate ourselves." These things, she said, balance the anxiety that permeates the environment.

Rynd compensates for the negativity inherent in preparing tax returns: "In my business we have something called a query sheet, where the person who reviews the tax return writes down everything that needs to be corrected. Criticism is built into the system. But at the end of every review, I always include a positive comment—your work paper technique looked good, I appreciate the fact that you got this done on time, or something like that. It seems trivial, but it's one way to remind people that I recognize their good work and not just their shortcomings."

Energize others   The women leaders spoke of their enthusiasm for work and how they spread their enthusiasm around to make work a challenge that is exhilarating and fun. The women leaders talked about it in those terms and claimed to use their enthusiasm to get others excited. As Rothman said, "There is rarely a person I can't motivate."

Enthusiasm was a dominant theme throughout the interviews. In computer consulting: "Because this business is on the forefront of technology, I'm sort of evangelistic about it, and I want other people to be as excited as I am." In venture capital: "You have to have a head of steam." In executive search: "Getting people excited is an important way to influence those you have no control over." Or in managing sports arenas: "My enthusiasm gets others excited. I infuse them with energy and make them see that even boring jobs contribute to the fun of working in a celebrity business."

Enthusiasm can sometimes be misunderstood. In conservative professions like investment banking, such an upbeat leadership style can be interpreted as cheerleading and can undermine credibility. In many cases, the women said they won and preserved their credibility by achieving results that could be measured easily. One of the women acknowledged that her colleagues don't understand or like her leadership style and have called it cheerleading. "But," she added, "in this business you get credibility from what you produce, and they love the profits I generate." While energy and enthusiasm can inspire some, it doesn't work for everyone. Even Rothman conceded, "Not everyone has a flame that can be lit."

PATHS OF LEAST RESISTANCE

Many of the women I interviewed said the behaviors and beliefs that underlie their leadership style come naturally to them. I attribute this to two things: their socialization and the career paths they have chosen. Although socialization patterns and career paths are changing, the average age of the men and women who responded to the survey is 51—old enough to have had experiences that differed *because* of gender.

Until the 1960s, men and women received different signals about what was expected of them. To summarize a subject that many experts have explored in depth, women have been expected to be wives, mothers, community volunteers, teachers, and nurses. In all these roles, they are supposed to be cooperative, supportive, understanding, gentle, and to provide service to others. They are to derive satisfaction and a sense of self-esteem from helping others, including their spouses. While men have had to appear to be competitive, strong, tough, decisive, and in control, women have been allowed to be cooperative, emotional, supportive, and vulnerable. That may explain why women today are more likely than men to be interactive leaders.

Men and women have also had different career opportunities. Women were not expected to have careers, or at least not the same kinds of careers as men, so they either pursued different jobs or were simply denied opportunities men had. Women's career tracks have usually not included long series of organizational positions with formal authority and control of resources. Many women had their first world experiences outside the home as volunteers. While some of the challenges they faced as managers for volunteer organizations are the same as those in any business, in many ways, leading volunteers is different because of the absence of concrete rewards like pay and promotion.

As women entered the business world, they tended to find themselves in positions consistent with the roles they played at home: in staff positions rather than in line positions, supporting the work of others and in functions like communications or human resources, where they had relatively small budgets and few people reporting directly to them.

The fact that most women have lacked formal authority over others and control over resources means that by default they have had to find other ways to accomplish their work. As it turns out, the behaviors that were natural and/or socially acceptable for them have been highly successful in at least some managerial settings.

What came easily to women turned out to be a survival tactic. Although leaders often begin their careers doing what comes naturally and what fits within the constraints of the job, they also develop their skills and styles over time. The women's use of interactive leadership has its roots in socialization, and the women interviewees firmly believe that it benefits their organizations. Through the course of their careers, they have gained conviction that their style is effective. In fact, for some, it was their own success that caused them to formulate their philosophies about what motivates people, how to make good decisions, and what it takes to maximize business performance.

They now have formal authority and control over vast resources, but still they see sharing power and information as an asset rather than a liability. They believe that although pay and promotion are necessary tools of management, what people really want is to feel that they are contributing to a higher purpose and that they have the opportunity as individuals to learn and grow. The women believe that employees and peers perform better when they feel they are part of an organization and can share in its success. Allowing them to get involved and to work to their potential is a way of maximizing their contributions and using human resources most efficiently.

ANOTHER KIND OF DIVERSITY

The IWF survey shows that a nontraditional leadership style can be effective in organizations that accept it. This lesson comes especially hard to those who think of the corporate world as a game of survival of the fittest, where the fittest is always the strongest, toughest, most decisive, and powerful. Such a workplace seems to favor leaders who control people by controlling resources, and by controlling people, gain control of more resources. Asking for information and sharing decision-making power can be seen as serious disadvantages, but what is a disadvantage under one set of circumstances is an advantage under another. The "best" leadership style depends on the organizational context.

Only one of the women interviewees is in a traditional, large-scale company. More typically, the women's organizations are medium-sized and tend to have experienced fast growth and fast change. They demand performance and/or have a high proportion of professional workers. These organizations seem to create opportunities for women and are hospitable to those who use a nontraditional management style.

The degree of growth or change in an organization is an important factor in creating opportunities for women. When change is rampant, everything is up for grabs, and crises are frequent. Crises are generally not desirable, but they do create opportunities for people to prove themselves. Many of the women interviewees said they got their first break because their organizations were in turmoil.

Fast-changing environments also play havoc with tradition. Coming up through the ranks and being part of an established network is no longer important. What is important is how you perform. Also, managers in such environments are open to new solutions, new structures, and new ways of leading.

The fact that many of the women respondents are in organizations that have clear performance standards suggests that they have gained credibility and legitimacy by achieving results. In investment banking, venture capital, accounting, and executive placement, for instance, individual performance is easy to measure.

A high proportion of young professional workers—increasingly typical of organizations—is also a factor in some women's success. Young, educated professionals impose special requirements on their organizations. They demand to participate and contribute. In some cases, they have knowledge or talents their bosses don't have. If they are good performers, they have many employment options. It is easy to imagine that these professionals will respond to leaders who are inclusive and open, who enhance the self-worth of others, and who create a fun work environment. Interactive leaders are likely to win the cooperation needed to achieve their goals.

Interactive leadership has proved to be effective, perhaps even advantageous, in organizations in which the women I interviewed have succeeded. As the work force increasingly demands participation and the economic environment increasingly requires rapid change, interactive leadership may emerge as the management style of choice for many organizations. For interactive leadership to take root more broadly, however, organizations must be willing to question the notion that the traditional command-and-control leadership style that has brought success in earlier decades is the only way to get results. This may be hard in some organizations, especially those with long histories of male-oriented, command-and-control leadership. Changing these organizations will not be easy. The fact that women are more likely than men to be interactive leaders raises the risk that these companies will perceive interactive leadership as "feminine" and automatically resist it.

Linking interactive leadership directly to being female is a mistake. We know that women are capable of making their way through corporations by adhering to the traditional corporate model and that some women may prefer that style. We also know from the survey findings that some men use the transformational leadership style.

Large, established organizations should expand their definition of effective leadership. If they were to do that, several things might happen, including the disappearance of the glass ceiling and the creation of a wider path for all sorts of executives—men and women—to attain positions of leadership. Widening the path will free potential leaders to lead in ways that play to their individual strengths. Then the newly recognized interactive leadership style can be valued and rewarded as highly as the command-and-control style has been for decades. By valuing a diversity of leadership styles, organizations will find the strength and flexibility to survive in a highly competitive, increasingly diverse economic environment.

◆

Dexterity with Symbols[*]

Robert Jackall[†]

The density of the social structure of the corporation is matched by an intricate ideological complexity. At any given moment in most major corporations, one can find a vast array of vocabularies of motive and accounts to explain, or excuse and justify, expedient action; ideas and schemes of every sort peddled to managers by

[*]Reprinted from *Moral Mazes: The World of Corporate Managers,* Chapter 6, pp. 134–166. New York, Oxford: Oxford University Press, 1988.

various outside consultants that purport to solve organizational problems or simply provide further rationales for what has to be done; and the ideological constructions of managers grappling with the whirlwinds of discontent and controversy endemic to our society that, it seems, inevitably envelop the corporation. Managers have to be able to manipulate with some finesse these sophisticated, often contradictory, symbolic forms that mask, reflect, and sometimes merely sweep through their world.

The indirect and ambiguous linguistic frameworks that managers employ in public situations typify the symbolic complexity of the corporation. Generally speaking, managers' public language is best characterized as a kind of provisional discourse, a tentative way of communicating that reflects the peculiarly chancy and fluid character of their world.

Managers' public language is, more than anything else, euphemistic. For instance, managers do not generally criticize or disagree with one another or with company policy openly and in public except at blame-time and sometimes not even then, since innuendo is often more executive than direct statements. The sanction against such criticism is so strong that it constitutes, in the view of many managers, a suppression of professional debate. This seems to be rooted in a number of the social conditions of managerial work already discussed. Most important, although some top managers consider abusiveness toward subordinates a prerogative of corporate success, managers' acute sense of organizational contingency makes them speak gingerly to one another since the person one criticizes or argues with today could be one's boss tomorrow. Even if such dramatic reversals of fortune were not at issue, managers know that the remembrance of offenses received, whether real or imagined, occupies a special nook in people's cognitive maps and can undercut effective work, let alone potential alliances. Moreover, the crucial premium in the corporation on style includes an expectation of a certain finesse in handling people, a "sensitivity to others," as it is called. As one manager says: "You just can't push people around anymore." Discreet suggestions, hints, and coded messages take the place of command; this, of course, places a premium on subordinates' abilities to read correctly their bosses' vaguely articulated or completely unstated wishes. One cannot even criticize one's subordinates to one's own superior without risking a negative evaluation of one's own managerial judgment. Still further, the sheer difficulty of penetrating managerial circles other than one's own and finding out what actually happened on a given issue, let alone being able to assess its organizational significance, makes the use of oblique language imperative, at least until one gets the lay of the land.

This leads to the use of an elaborate linguistic code marked by emotional neutrality, especially in group settings. The code communicates the meaning one might wish to convey to other managers, but since it is devoid of any significant emotional sentiment—one might also say here strong conviction or forceful judgment—it can be reinterpreted should social relationships or attitudes change.

Here, for example, are some typical phrases describing performance appraisals, always treacherous terrain, followed by their probable intended meaning.[1]

Stock Phrase Probable	Intended Meaning
°Exceptionally well qualified	Has committed no major blunders to date
°Tactful in dealing with superiors	Knows when to keep his mouth shut
°Quick thinking	Offers plausible excuses
°Meticulous attention to detail	A nitpicker
°Slightly below average	Stupid
°Unusually loyal	Wanted by no one else
°Indifferent to instruction	Knows more than one's superior
°Strong adherence to principles	Stubborn
°Requires work-value attitudinal readjustment	Lazy and hardheaded

Or, to take an example of a different kind of euphemism, one "talks in circles," that is, one masters the art of juxtaposing several sentences that contain implicit contradictions but that one makes seem related by one's forcefulness or style of presentation. One can thus stake out a position on every side of an issue. Or one buries what one wants done in a string of vaguely related descriptive sentences that demand textual exegesis.

For the most part, euphemistic language is not used with the intent to deceive. Managers past a certain point, as suggested earlier, are assumed to be "maze-bright" and able to "read between the lines" of a conversation or a memorandum and to distinguish accurately suggestions from directives, inquiries from investigations, and bluffs from threats. Managers who are "maze-dense," like the manager at Weft Corporation who, though told somewhat indirectly that he was fired, did not realize his fate until the following day, might consider the oblique, elliptical quality of managerial language to skirt deceit. However, most often when managers use euphemistic language with each other (and it is important to remember that in private among trusted others their language can be very direct, colorful, and indeed earthy), its principal purpose is to communicate certain meanings within specific contexts with the implicit understanding that should the context change, a new, more appropriate meaning can be attached to the language already used. In this sense, the corporation is a place where people are not held to what they say because it is generally understood that their word is always provisional.

Euphemistic language also plays other important roles. Within the corporation, subordinates often have to protect their bosses' "deniability" by concealing the specific dimensions of a problem in abstract, empty terms, thus maximizing the number of possible subsequent interpretations. The rule of thumb here seems to be that the more troublesome a problem, the more desiccated and vague the public language describing it should be. Of course, when a troublesome problem bursts into public controversy, euphemism becomes a crucial tool of those managers who have to face the public in some forum. The task here is to defuse public criticism and sometimes outrage with abstract unemotional characterizations of issues. Thus, to take only a few examples, in the textile industry, cotton dust becomes an "air-borne particulate" and byssinosis or brown lung a "symptom complex." In the chemical industry, spewing highly toxic hydrogen fluoride into a neighboring community's air is characterized as a "release beyond the fence line." The nuclear power industry, precisely because of its publicly perceived danger, is, of course, a wonderland of euphemisms. For example, the "incident" at Three Mile Island in March 1979 was variously call an "abnormal evolution" or, perhaps better, a "plant transient."[2] A firm that speculates in radioactive and chemical waste disposal renamed itself U.S. Ecology Inc., hoping that the new appellation "would make people feel comfortable."[3] The same kinds of rules apply for industrial managers' opposite numbers in the regulatory agencies. For instance, at the request of the food industry, the Department of Agriculture renamed the "powdered bone" increasingly used in processed meats as "calcium";[4] for a time, the Environmental Protection Agency called acid rain "poorly buffered precipitation";[5] and the National Transportation Safety Board in the Federal Aviation Accident Investigation Records names an airplane crash as a "controlled flight into terrain."[6] Such abstractions help obfuscate issues and thus reduce the likelihood of unwanted interference in one's work from some public, but it also allows managers themselves to grapple dispassionately with problems that can generate high emotions.

II

The higher one goes in the corporate world, the more essential is the mastery of provisional language. In fact, advancement beyond the upper-middle levels depends greatly on one's ability to manipulate a whole variety of symbols without becoming tied to or identified with any of them. Managers' use of certain kinds of expertise, namely that generated by management consultants of various sorts, themselves virtuosos in symbolic manipulation, aptly illustrates their peculiar symbolic skills.

In order to explore this issue properly, I want to discuss the ethos of management consulting itself in some detail. Except for the most narrowly defined technical areas, management consultants are perfect examples of what might be called ambiguous expertise—that is, their clients possess at least experientially the basic knowledge that management consultants claim. Moreover, because their expertise is therefore subject to continual negotiation, management consultants get drawn into the world of their clients and become subject to the political context and rules of that world.

Historically, management consulting grew and flourished with the ascendancy of the status group of corporate managers. The thrust of the consulting profession from its inception has been to help managers get control of the workplace, first in industrial settings, and then later in the burgeoning white-collar sector. The ethos of the contemporary consulting profession is rooted in three main historical developments that continue to shape it today.

The first of these, of course, was the scientific management movement founded by Frederick Taylor, which emphasized the application of engineering principles to measuring and accelerating efficiency at work.[7] Scientific management developed the assembly line, time-and-motion studies, the speedup, and, more generally, the systematic segmentation and routinization of complex work tasks, all to a fine degree. In manufacturing industries today, in particular, this kind of industrial engineering is pervasive and taken for granted. Weft Corporation, for example, electronically monitors each block of looms of every weaver. A supervisor roaming the shop floor can gauge with a glance at a television screen how many times in an hour each loom in a block is stopping and how many yards of cloth each is producing. The monitor also provides an overall index of weaving efficiency either for an individual loom or for a weaver's entire block as a whole. Such information is crucial for plant management in adjudicating the inevitable competition between workers on a piece system, itself a product of scientific management. It was precisely through such rationalization, on the supposedly neutral ground of scientific and technical rationality, that the scientific management movement aimed to bring capital and labor together. Scientific observation and experimentation could and, it was argued, should be applied to the work process in order to achieve greater efficiency, productivity, and consequently a bigger economic pie. The functionally rational perspective of the movement, of course, meshed completely with the thoroughgoing pragmatism of managers. Almost all management consulting programs today at least purport to help managers systematically calculate the best means to reach prescribed goals, usually under the aegis of an appeal to scientifically derived knowledge.

The theory and practice of scientific management came under assault not only from workers but even from some managers. The logic of Taylor's system extends, of course, to management, and of course, managerial work, especially at the lower levels, is as thoroughly rationalized as that of workers. Elton Mayo and his associates at Harvard[8] began a series of studies aimed at the same general problem that concerned the Taylorites—how to create industrial peace. Specifically, they wanted to establish cooperation between management and labor, the principal warring factions of the chaotic industrial workplace. At the base of Mayo's vision was a notion of "Garden America," a romantic image of an idyllic past that could, he thought, be reestablished with careful study of the informal as well as the formal dimensions of the modern workplace and by institutionalizing ways of making people happy at work. This amelioristic concern in particular became and remains today the hallmark of the human relations approach in industry and is the second important root of the ethos of management consulting. Few major firms today are without sports teams that compete in industrial leagues, in-house newsletters and magazines to keep employees abreast of official versions of reality, counseling programs designed to help employees accept their organizational fates, and, at the white-collar level, various committees to arrange the picnics, dances, danish and coffees, the aesthetic decor of the office, and, of course, the cocktail parties, all thought essential to improve the *esprit de corps* of employees. High morale is variously thought to improve productivity[9] or, at the least, to "make for a family spirit." Only a few managers are willing to voice what a top official of Weft Corporation thinks is actually a widespread managerial sentiment about workers' happiness: "Let them be happy on their own time."

Management consulting is also rooted in the application of social science to help managers establish control of the workplace. This process has included, to name only a few examples, the extensive and haphazard use of psychological tests to ascertain worker characteristics in both blue-and white-collar workplaces,[10] procedures continued today despite their extremely dubious efficacy; the transformation of the sociology of bureaucracy into a branch of administrative science; and the extensive use of pretested survey instruments to gauge employee sentiment on a whole range of issues. The strictly pragmatic character of such applications may be gauged from an incident at Images Inc., which prides itself on the surveys it performs for its clients. Alarmed at the markedly low morale among their own employees in the aftermath of some economic reversals and subsequent organizational shake-ups, the firm's top management decided, amidst great fanfare, to conduct an extensive employee survey to locate and address the sources of discontent. When the responses came back, according to insiders, top management itself received severe criticism for, among other things, what employees saw as favoritism, nepotism, mismanagement, and stinginess. The results were buried and no one ever heard about them again. Similarly, the results of a survey on the "corporate cultures" of each of the several operating companies at Covenant Corporation became the closely guarded property of one small segment of the corporate staff, that is, a weapon of sorts in the ongoing battles in that corporation. Important social science knowledge can emerge serendipitously from such pragmatic research, sometimes even years later. But, more typically, the knowledge gained is narrowly focused and yields only crude empirical generalizations.

Whatever contributions to the accumulation of knowledge such pragmatic research may make, there is little doubt that both specific techniques and broader theoretical perspectives of social science are the basic stock in trade of management consultants. Regarding the latter, in fact, management consultants probably play a signal role in the systematic condensation, simplification, and popularization of important thought in all the social sciences. At one private conference of management consultants that I recently attended, one speaker gave a virtuoso performance of such syncretic ability. Among those theorists whose ideas were clearly recognizable, though unacknowledged, were not only Marx, Weber, and Freud, but also Ferdinand Tönnies, Emile Durkheim, Robert Merton, Daniel Bell, and C. Wright Mills. The performance concluded with dire prophecies of corporate disaster unless the consultant's warnings were heeded.

The professionalization of the managerial class itself spurred the real growth of managerial consulting. As corporate managers developed the requisite apparatus and distinctions of professionalism, they turned increasingly toward specialized counseling to service special needs. Reliable estimates on the rate or extent of the growth of consulting firms are difficult to obtain. A publication of the leading newsletter for management consultants says that there were ten consulting firms established before 1900 in the United States.[11]One researcher tracked down 305 management consulting firms in the classified telephone directories of eight major cities in 1938, but this figure includes equipment vendors, trade associations, advertising agencies, and auditing firms, none of which are, properly speaking, considered management consulting today.[12] A more recent estimate (1981) suggests that there are currently more than 2,500 firms plying a $2–$3 billion a year market with as many as 50,000 consultants working full or part-time advising management in a host of areas.[13] By 1983, management consultants had become such a permanent and important part of the corporate scene that they were attacked in *Forbes* magazine as one of the causes of the nation's economic malaise. One of the symbols of social arrival in our society is, of course, to be blamed publicly for social ills.[14]

One must keep in mind both the roots of the ethos of the management consulting profession and the ambiguous expertise consultants offer in order to grasp the meaning of consultants' ideas and programs to managers.[15] The further the consultant moves away from strictly technical issues—that is, from being an expert in the ideal sense, a virtuoso of some institutionalized and valued skills—the more anomalous his status becomes. He becomes an expert who trades in others' troubles. In managerial hierarchies, of course, troubles, like everything else, are socially defined. Consultants have to depend on some authority's definition of what is troublesome in an organization and, in most cases, have to work on the problem as defined. As it happens, it is extremely rare that an executive declares himself or his own circle to be a problem; rather, other groups in the corporation are targeted to be "worked on."

The relationship between the consultant and the group to be worked on may be described as a polite, arms-length embrace. The target group knows that whatever is revealed to the consultant will be passed back to a higher authority; the target group knows too that this information may be used in ways that the consultant never intended and further that the consultant is powerless to prevent such use. At the same time, one cannot refuse to cooperate with consultants when they are mandated by higher authority without running the risk of validating the original definition of being troublesome. The task, then, for the target group is to persuade the consultant that whatever problem might exist exists elsewhere in the organization or, failing that, to negotiate with the consultant in an oblique way some amelioristic program that will disrupt a given bailiwick as little as possible.

From the consultant's perspective, maintaining the stance of rational expert in such a situation becomes very difficult and the more contact the consultant has with the target group, the truer this becomes. No one likes to deal with people in trouble, at least on a regular sustained basis, but at the same time, consultants have to make a living too and this involves putting on programs to solve problems defined by others. The temptation to accept the target group's redefinition of the trouble at issue is, therefore, always great if that redefinition is plausible and salable to the authority who hired the consultant. Of course, the "real trouble" in any organization may lie completely apart from the authority's definition of the situation or the target group's redefinition. I shall comment further on this shortly.

Sometimes the issues that consultants are retained to address are so benign on their face that no group is likely to be threatened by their presence. However, even benign programs—like special training sessions for executives or promising young managers—may be seen to have hidden organizational functions, usually in the area of prestige allocation. In any event, whatever the nature of the consultant's work, it cannot become institutionalized without a continuing commitment from top management. When top management ceases to pay attention to a program, no matter how much time, effort, and money has been poured into it, the program withers and dies. There is scarcely much mystery to this. The whole bureaucratic structure of big corporations fosters and demands attentiveness to top management's whims. Both managers and their consultants must keep up with changing whims. One might ask, of course, why top managers are unable or unwilling to sustain long-term interest in programs that they themselves initiate. Once again, the clue lies in the social structure of corporations.

There is a premium in the higher circles of management on seeming fresh, dynamic, innovative, and up-to-date. In their social minglings and shoptalk with one another, particularly with their opposite numbers in other large companies, say, at the Business Roundtable, at high-level conferences at prestigious business schools, at summer galas in the Hamptons, or at the Super Bowl, the biggest business extravaganza of all, executives need to seem abreast of the latest trends in managerial know-how. No one wants to appear stodgy before one's peers nor to have one's firm defined in managerial networks, and perhaps thence to Wall Street, as "slow on the uptake." Executives trade ideas and schemes and judge the efficacy of consultant programs not by any detached critical standards but by what is socially acceptable, desirable, and, perhaps most important, current in their circles.

There is a dialectical process at work here. The need of executives for fresh approaches fuels the large and growing industry of consultants and other managerial sages who write books and articles and develop new programs to "aid management," that is, get the business of well-placed managers. This burgeoning industry in turn fuels executive anxiety with a never-ending barrage of newly packaged schemes, all highly rational, most amelioristic, and the great majority making operational some social science insight. Despite their fresh appearances, certain themes recur constantly in the programs offered by consultants. Perhaps the most common are how to sharpen decision making, how to restructure organizations for greater efficiency, how to improve productivity, how to recognize trouble spots in an organization, how to communicate effectively, how to humanize the workplace, and how to raise morale.

The language that consultants use to describe their programs has its own interest, marked as it is by the peculiar combination of appeals to a solid scientific basis, promises of organizational betterment, vague, abstract lingo, and upbeat exhortation. For instance, a leading management consultant firm offers a "unique series of workshops designed for leaders in organizations experiencing significant challenge and change." The basis for these is "extensive research into the management styles and management structures required to increase organizational competitiveness." In addition to helping participating managers "develop a *dynamic* concept of management leadership," the workshop will "identify the difference between being a problem solver and managing or leading others in opportunity-seeking and problem-solving." It will as well "utilize personal, useful feedback on their style" to "develop action plans that allow them to have a greater positive impact on others and their organization."

A higher level version of the same workshop for an "executive management team" promises a "research-based orientation" to "getting competitive." This orientation "can be tailored to the organization's unique situation" through a series of pre-interviews with participants that form "the basis for a 'real time' case which the executive team works on." Pre-interviews are, of course, a crucial strategy in helping the consultant ascertain just what the defined troubles of an organization are and who does the defining. The contentless quality of the language used here is, of course, related to this strategy; the lack of specificity precludes hasty judgments by prospective clients about the range or limits of a consultant's expertise and implicitly promises nearly infinite adaptability.

Recently, other consultants have promoted the importance of "corporate cultures," that is, the idea that specific values, beliefs, rites, and rituals at the core of particular organizations determine social behavior in them. Through a mastery of stagecraft and an understanding of the "hidden hierarchy"—the real "cultural network" of "spies, storytellers, priests, whisperers, [and] cabals"—gained through a kind of instant ethnography, "symbolic managers" can dominate their situation and provide effective leadership.[16] Another recent approach recycles ideologies and slogans from segments of the 1960s New Left, all tailored for the executive suite. The concerns here are with "empowerment," "energizing the grass roots," learning "power skills," and becoming "corporate entrepreneurs."[17]

In reading such materials, one can discern some basic rules that seem to undergird most of the genre of business consultant writing and program presentation. These rules also tell us something about the managerial audience for such writing. The rules seem to be: (1) suppress all irony, ambiguity, and complexity and assert only the most obvious and literal meanings of any phenomenon; (2) ignore all theoretical issues unless they can be encapsulated into a neat schematic form easily remembered, "operationalized," and preferably diagrammed; (3) always stress the bright side of things, inflating, say, all efforts for change, whether major or minor, into "revolutionary" action; downplay the gloomy, troublesome, crass, or seamy aspects of big organizational life or, better, show managers how to exploit them to their own advantage; (4) provide a step-by-step program tied, of course, to one's own pathbreaking research, that promises to unlock the secrets of organizations; and (5) end with a vision of the future that makes one's book, program, or consulting services indispensable.

The result of the untiring efforts of consultants and the reciprocal anxiety of executives is the circulation at or near the top of organizations of ever changing rhetorics of innovation and exhortation. These rhetorics get disseminated throughout a corporation and become rallying cries for a time, and sometimes are instituted, until new rhetorics overtake them. For some time in Weft Corporation, the magic words were "modernization" and "retraining," as managers developed sets of rationales to quell workers' anxieties about new labor-displacing machinery. For a while, the watchword at Covenant Corporation was "productivity" and, since this was a pet project of the CEO himself, it was said that no one ever went into his presence without wearing a blue *Productivity!* button and talking about "quality circles" and "feedback sessions," organizational devices that had in fact been instituted right down to the plant level. But then managers at the upper-middle levels noticed that there had not been a single mention of productivity at executive meetings, and the program fell into disuse just as managers in charge further down the line felt that the quality circles at least were beginning to bear fruit. Managers kept their ears to the ground to anticipate the newest rumblings from the executive suites. This turned out to be an emphasis on creating "entrepreneurial cultures" in all the operating companies of the conglomerate. The president of one company pushes a series of managerial seminars that endlessly repeat the basic functions of management—planning, organizing, motivating, and controlling. So set are the scripts for these sessions that managers who have already completed the seminars are able to cue friends about to take them to key words to be used in key places. Of course, younger managers come already armed for such situations with the well-honed responsiveness to social expectations that marks their profession. As one comments about these seminars, "Whenever I find myself in a situation like this, I always ask: 'What is it they want from me here? What am I expected to do?'" So they attend the sessions and with a seemingly dutiful eagerness learn literally to repeat the requisite formulas under the watchful eyes of senior managers. Of course, senior managers do not themselves necessarily believe in such programs. In one seminar that I attended, the senior manager in charge startled a room of juniors by saying:

> *Fellows, why aren't any of you asking about the total lack of correspondence between what we're preaching here and the way we run our company?*

But such outspokenness is rare. Managers privately characterize such programs as the "CEO's incantations over the assembled multitude," as "elaborate rituals with no practical effect," or as "waving a magic wand to make things wonderful again." They refer to consultants as "whores in pin-stripe suits." They admit, however, that the marvelously high fees that consultants command (currently as high as $2,000 a day in New York City) enhance their legitimacy and encourage managers to lend credence to their schemes. Publicly, of course, managers on the way up adopt with great enthusiasm those programs that have caught their bosses' fancy, participate in or run them very effectively, and then quietly drop them when the time is right.[18]

The short-term ethos is crucial in determining managers' stances toward consultants and their programs. A choice between securing one's own success by jumping on and off the bandwagon of the moment, or sacrificing oneself for the long-run good of a corporation by diverting resources and really seeing a program through is, for most managers, no choice at all. Ambitious managers see self-sacrificing loyalty to a company as foolhardy. Moreover, middle and upper-middle level managers upon whom requests for self-sacrifice for the good of the organization are most likely to fall do not see top executives sacrificing themselves for the common good. For example, just after the CEO of Covenant Corporation announced one of his many purges, legitimated by a "comprehensive assessment of the hard choices facing us" by a major consulting firm, he purchased a new Sabre jet for executives and a new 31-foot company limousine for his own use at $1,000 a foot. He then flew the entire board of directors to Europe on the Concorde for a regular meeting to review, it was said, his most recent cost-cutting strategies. As other managers see it, bureaucratic hierarchy gives top bosses the license to act in their own interests and to pursue with impunity the arts of contradiction.

A few other dimensions of the relationships between consultants and managers are worth mentioning. The consultant encounters particular difficulties when he becomes aware that the "real issues" facing him are the political and social structures of a corporation rather than the problem defined for him. Of course, in such cases one may assume that executives are fully aware of the real issues. Most likely, executives are using the consultant to: legitimate already desired unpleasant changes, such as reorganizations; throw rival networks of executives off the track of one's real strategy by diverting resources to marginal programs; undercut consultants employed by other executive groups by establishing what might be called counterplausibility; or advance, as already suggested, a personal or organizational image of being up-to-date, with-it, and avant-garde. The consultant who perceives such discrepancies has to devise his own strategies for handling them. Some of these include: rejecting the assignment altogether; accepting the problem as defined and confining oneself to it for the sake of future contracts even though one knows that any action will be inefficacious; or accepting the assignment but trying to persuade the client to address the underlying social and political issues, that is, redefining the problem. The consultant's own strategy is limited by the constraint that he present his findings according to a certain etiquette, one that has deep roots in the history of the profession—that is, as a rational, objective, scientific judgment that will improve the organization. The consultant's claim to expertise and legitimacy rests on this. As it happens, even if the consultant sees that the real issues are political and social ones and is willing to address them, this emphasis on a pragmatic rational objectivity often produces a somewhat stultifying reification of abstract concepts rather than a detailed explanation of the intricacies of political networks that might lay bare the actual troubles of an organization. But then, managers need and desire the mask of objectivity to cover the capriciousness and arbitrariness of corporate life; consultants want to maintain their occupational self-image as experts. Each group fuels the other's needs and self-images in an occupational drama where the needs of organizations get subordinated to the maintenance of professional identities.

Notes

1. These terms were culled from a much longer list that was posted on a prominent bulletin board in Alchemy Inc. with no source given. I showed the list to a dozen of my interviewees at Alchemy to gauge how accurately the terms present the incongruities between words and contextual meaning in the corporate world. There was strong general agreement that the list was uncannily accurate, although tinged with bitter humor. I published part of the list in 1983 (see Robert Jackall, "Moral Mazes: Bureaucracy and Managerial Work," *Harvard Business Review,* Vol. 61, No. 5 (September-October 1983, pp. 118–130). The following summer, while doing secondary research in preparation for this book, I came across a similar, though shorter, list of euphemisms that seems to have been the basis for the list posted at Alchemy. See Jack Mabley, "'Personnel Code' Not a Laughing Matter," *Chicago Tribune,* October 29, 1981, Section 1, p. 21, col. 2. Since Mabley's article was based on an interview with the president of a personnel consulting firm, it is likely that similar lists have appeared in a myriad of other publications read by businesspeople. Stories and jokes that accurately reflect behavioral and emotional truths make the rounds repeatedly in the business world, altered to suit particular contexts. In the list presented here, I have starred those phrases that appeared only on the Alchemy list.

For an excellent sociological analysis of the subtle uses of language, see Hans Speier, "The Communication of Hidden Meaning," *Social Research,* Vol. 44, No. 3 (Autumn 1977), pp. 471–501.

2. Stephen Hilgartner, Richard C. Bell, and Rory O'Connor, *Nukespeak: The Selling of Nuclear Technology in America* (San Francisco, Calif.: Sierra Club Books, 1982), p. xiii.

3. National Council of Teachers of English, Committee on Public Doublespeak, *Quarterly Review of Doublespeak* (Urbana, Ill.: National Council of Teachers of English, 1111 Kenyon Road, Urbana, Ill.), Vol. VII, No. 4 (July 1981), p. 1.

4. *Quarterly Review of Doublespeak,* Vol. X, No. 2 (January 1984), p. 1.

5. *Quarterly Review of Doublespeak,* Vol. IX, No. 2 (January 1983), p. 1.

6. *Quarterly Review of Doublespeak,* Vol. XI, No. 2 (January 1985), p. 1. Issue misnumbered as Vol. IX.

7. See Frederick Winslow Taylor, *The Principles of Scientific Management* (New York and London: Harper & Brothers Publishers, 1929 [Copyright © 1911]). See also the interesting recent treatment of Taylor and Taylorism by Judith A. Merkle, *Management and Ideology: The Legacy of the International Scientific Management Movement* (Berkeley, Los Angeles, and London: University of California Press, 1980).

8. The classic statement of the human relations school is Elton Mayo, *The Human Problems of an Industrial Civilization* (Boston, Mass.: Division of Research, Graduate School of Business Administration, Harvard University, 1946).

9. As it happens, morale and productivity are probably unassociated. See Victor H. Vroom, "Industrial Social Psychology," in *The Handbook of Social Psychology,* edited by Gardner Lindzey and Eliot Aronson (Reading, Mass.: Addison-Wesley Publishing Company, 1969), Vol. V, p. 199.

10. See Loren Baritz's analysis of the origins and practice of psychological testing in industry in *The Servants of Power* (Westport, Conn.: Greenwood Press, Publishers, 1974).

11. Consultants News, *A Cross-Section of the Management Consulting Business* (Fitzwilliam, N. H.: Consultants News, 1979).

12. Joel Dean, "The Place of Management Counsel in Business," *Harvard Business Review*, Vol. 16 (1937-1938), pp. 451–465, especially pp. 451–453. See also his more extended monograph, *The Management Counsel Profession* (Bloomington, Ind.: Indiana University Publications Social Science Series, No. 2, 1940).

13. James H. Kennedy, "An Overview of Management Consulting in the United States Today" (Fitzwilliam, N. H.: Consultants News, 1981), p. 5.

14. John A. Byrne, "Are All These Consultants Really Necessary?" *Forbes*, October 10, 1983, pp. 136–144.

15. I am indebted to Gerald L. Moore, "The Politics of Management Counsulting," Ph.D. Diss., Department of Sociology, Graduate Center, City University of New York, 1982, and especially to several conversations with Joseph Bensman for alerting me to many of the issues in the analysis that follows. I am indebted too to Elizabeth S. Tice and Frank J. Navran for providing me with the occasion to draw together my field data on management consultants and managers' experiences with consultants in a paper entitled "The Vicissitudes of Organizational Tinkering," Sixth Organizational Effectiveness Professional Development Clinic, BellSouth Corporation, Atlanta, Georgia, December 7, 1983.

16. See Terrence E. Deal and Allen A. Kennedy, *Corporate Cultures: The Rites and Rituals of Corporate Life* (Reading, Mass.: Addison-Wesley Publishing Company, 1982), *passim*, but see especially pp. 85–103.

17. See, for example, Rosebeth Moss Kanter, *The Change Masters* (New York: Simon and Schuster, 1983), *passim*.

18. A note with methodological implications may be apposite here. Precisely because managers have such a sharply defined responsiveness to authoritatively established criteria evident to them in a given situation, they are often unconcerned with facts as facts are normally conceptualized. In one company, in which nonconfidential surveys of all sorts relating to business matters are regularly circulated, managers say that they often "pull numbers out of the air" to satisfy the perceived demands of higher-ups. This makes data from, say, surveys administered through hierarchies somewhat problematic. Unless complete confidentiality is promised, one may not be measuring an individual's perception of reality but rather his perception of what reality is expected to be or what he wishes others to think his perception is.

◆

Dangerous Liaisons: The "Feminine-in-Management" Meets "Globalization"*

Marta B. Calás and Linda Smircich

HELP WANTED

Seeking transforming manager. Impatient with rituals and symbols of hierarchy. Favors strengthening networks and interrelationships, connecting with coworkers, customers, suppliers. Not afraid to draw on personal, private experience when dealing in the public realm. Not hung up by a "What's in it for me?" attitude. Focuses on the whole, not only the bottom line; shows concern for the wider needs of the community. If "managing by caring and nurturing" is your credo, you may be exactly what we need. Excellent salary and benefits, including child care and parental leaves.

Contact CORPORATE AMERICA
FAX: 1-800-INTRUBL

An Equal Opportunity Employer
We do not discriminate on the basis of sex, race, age, disabilities, or sexual orientation.

How soon can we expect to see such a want ad? Soon, no doubt, if recent literature is to be believed. Since the mid-1980s, books and articles have appeared that, like our fictitious advertisement, support approaches to management based on traits and orientations traditionally associated with women, the female, and the feminine. A common story runs through these examples: Currently, business firms in the U.S. are suffering countless setbacks. Changes are needed. Therefore, if women *and* women-oriented qualities are brought into organizations and allowed to exert influence, it is likely that changes in the right direction will occur. Tom Peters (1990) best articulated this sentiment:

> *It's perfectly obvious that women should be better managers than men in today's topsy-turvy business environment. As we rush into the 90s, there is little disagreement about what business must become: less hierarchical, more flexible and team-oriented, faster and more fluid. In my opinion, one group of people has an enormous advantage in realizing this necessary new vision: women.*

---

*Reprinted from "Dangerous Liaisons: The `Feminine-in-Management' Meets `Globalization'" by Marta B. Calás and Linda Smircich. (*Business Horizons*, Vol. 36, No. 2). Copyright © 1993 by the Foundation for the School of Business at Indiana University. By permission of JAI Press, Inc.

In principle, we cannot do other than share the sentiment, as Peters' statement seems to argue for more managerial opportunities for women. But it is important to approach this discussion by cautiously asking the following questions: What is the historical significance of recent discussions about "women's ways of leading" and the "female advantage"? Do they really help create new opportunities for women? Do they mark a new era of openness to difference, signaling the arrival of real receptivity to qualities that were once undervalued? Or do they signal only more of the same, or worse?

Recent research has argued that there are dangers associated with such "feminine-in-management" positions. We have pointed out (Calás et al. 1991) that although these positions are presented as a call for change in organizational thinking, they in fact do little more than restate existing management approaches under a different name. The dangers, we argued, are very real insofar as their apparent valuing of some "essential women's" qualities maintains an illusion of opportunity and equality for women in the managerial world while obstructing critical examination of the pervasive theoretical assumptions sustaining that world.

In this article we further analyze the problems and dangers associated with the feminine-in-management positions. As we point out below, the current appearance of these positions is not arbitrary, nor do they represent a natural progression toward more advanced organizational knowledge. Rather, we see a repetition of a cycle common in both academic and managerial circles when a need for change appears. On those occasions there is a tendency to obscure the need for fundamental change—which would alter the established balance of power—with a surface change that maintains that same balance while creating the appearance of a radical rethinking of what if. Women have been used for this purpose on more than one occasion. Therefore, if such is the case with the feminine-in-management, what is the "essential female" obscuring? What else is happening that propels managers and management theorists to "cherchez la femme"?

Other writings that call attention to the contemporary economic scene faced by American corporations have been appearing concurrently (Reich 1991; Kuttner 1991; Porter 1990; Ohmae 1990; Thurow 1992). In these writings the corporate actor is discussed within the wider environmental context of a "global reality." Different from earlier times, the arguments go, American corporations are no longer competing on familiar grounds. Contemporary managers face a more complicated competitive field where not all actors play by the same rules. Like the feminine-in-management literature, these writings announce changes, both behaviorally and structurally, for America's corporate ways.

But why these parallel discourses now? We argue that there is, in fact, a close relationship between feminine-in-management and "globalization." If approached separately, each of these managerial discourses *appears* to bring about fundamental changes in corporate America. However, when taken together, one—the feminine-in-management—maintains the *domestic* balance of power that allows for the other—globalization—to fight for continuing that same balance in the *international* arena. Together they keep in place America's traditional social, cultural, and economic values, not effecting any transformational changes.

We propose that the lines of thought portrayed by these two parallel discourses might hurt both women and organizations insofar as their "solutions" to managerial troubles repeat an old quick-fix way of thinking prevalent in the U.S. Therefore, we will also analyze the more long-term dangers associated with such positions. As we will show in our conclusions, "thinking feminine" may be the necessary thing to do at this point, but not as it has been so far presented by the feminine-in-management.

A BRIEF HISTORY OF THE FEMININE-IN-MANAGEMENT RHETORIC

For about 20 years, literature on women and management stressed women's abilities as managers as equivalent to those of men. But in the mid-1980s, general discussions about the place of women in management took a turn. Besides talk about how women could perform managerial roles as well as men (the equality discussion), a case was now being made that women's unique "feminine skills" could make important contributions to organizational management (the difference discussion), on which the feminine-in-management rhetoric is based.

The "women's difference" talk finds its support in recent research literature on the psychology of women (Gilligan 1982; Chodorow 1978; Miller 1976). These works show that traditional views of gender differences have not been culturally neutral; rather, qualities associated with males have been prized and those associated with females have been devalued. Yet, because value systems are social and cultural constructions, it is possible to reconceptualize female characteristics as positive—even though different—rather than as inferior to male characteristics.

Clearly, the appeal of these ideas stems from their implications for revaluing women and feminine qualities in various kinds of activities, including approaches to management. For instance, Marilyn Loden (1985) was one of the first to argue, under the women's difference umbrella, that women's managerial styles could be what was needed for solving American productivity problems. Similar arguments followed in other periodicals (*Cosmopolitan, Organization Dynamics, Harvard Business Review, Academy of Management Executive*) and books (*Reinventing the Corporation, Megatrends 2000, The Female Advantage*). In these writings, what was once disparaged as female patterns in need of overcoming for success in management were now positioned as special and useful for organizations.

For example, Jan Grant (1988) proposed that "women may indeed be the most radical force available in bringing about organizational change," thanks to qualities gained in experiences with their families and communities. In Grant's view, women's skills at communication and cooperation, their interests in affiliation and attachment, and their orientation toward power as a transforming and liberating force to be used for public purposes rather than for personal ambition and power over others are critically needed human resource skills in contemporary organizations.

More recently, Judy Rosener (1990) described "interactive leadership" as characteristic of some of the executive women she studied. Patterns unique to women's socialization made them comfortable with encouraging participation and facilitating inclusion, sharing power and information, enhancing the self-worth of others, and energizing and exciting others about their work.

Perhaps the best representative of these ideas in the popular business literature has been posited by Sally Helgesen (1990) in her close-up study of four female executives, whose images of organizational structure were more similar to a web or circle than a hierarchy or pyramid. From this, Helgesen articulates a notion of authority not at the head of an organization, but at its heart, as "authority comes from connection *to* the people around rather than distance *from* those below." Helgesen, like others, argues that the "integration of the feminine principles into the public realm offers hope for healing" the conditions of modern life, pervaded by "feelings of pointlessness, sterility and the separation from nature."

The writings about the feminine-in-management have been challenged on scientific grounds. Serious concerns have been raised about the adequacy of their research methods and the empirical base of their claims. Our concerns about them here are more cultural and historical. As these writings are gaining an important status as new representations of *good* management, they deserve analysis that goes beyond the question of their scientific adequacy—are they true?—in favor of asking, "Why are they being spoken?" and "Why are they being spoken now?"

Our argument is this: The appropriation of the "women's difference" discourse by management writers is merely another episode in a long history of economic reasoning that ends up valuing women out of instrumental necessity. From the girls of the Lowell mills in the 1800s to Rosie the Riveter in World War II, we have seen the ebb and flow of cultural discourses that support the movement of women from the domestic to the public sphere and back again.

From a historical perspective, the current female advantage rhetoric is part of another repetition of this cycle—in this case because there are instrumental advantages to feminizing the national economy under conditions of globalization. We consider that this recent turn toward "women's ways of leadership" is nothing other than a 1990s version of the "conquest" by women of the American business office in the 1930s. As analyzed in *Fortune* ("Women in Business. . . " 1935), the business office was the "new land lying in the wilderness at the frontiers of industrial advance" that women came to dominate—not because female labor was cheaper, as the "crass economist" might argue, or because they were "physically better adapted" to the office, as "the solemn findings of [psychometric] science" might contend. Instead, *Fortune* asserted:

> The whole point of the whole problem is merely that the modern office necessitates a daily, intimate, and continuing relation which is much more possible between a man and a number of women than between a man and a number of men. . . . It is, if you will, a relation based upon sex. . . The whole point of the whole problem, in other words, is that women occupy the office because the male employer wants them there.

At a time when sexism did not need to be covered up with a veneer of civility, the *Fortune* writer candidly observed that women make the office "a more pleasant, peaceful, and homelike place." In a very perceptive analysis, the writer further stated:

> In the field of the office it was not the work of the home which was carried over into the industrial setting, but the setting of the home which was carried over to the industrial work. The work was new work but it was done by women not because it was new but because they were women. And more importantly, it was the employing male, not the eager female applicant, who was responsible for the result. . . . Indeed, and at the risk of further roiling the feminist pride, it must be said that woman's greatest industrial conquest has been made not only through the male but through the institution of marriage. It is marriage—or rather its imitation—which, as we have seen, explains and justifies the existence of the lady at the secretary's desk.

This writer's commentary is particularly interesting because in its bluntness (or, as some might say today, his incisive structural analysis), it uncovers the powerlessness embodied in the feminine-in-management, which now as then merely contributes to supporting the industrial activities of a patriarchal society.[1] This is clearly seen when the author refers to the achievements of two particular women:

> . . . in spite of their success, in spite of the importance of their positions and the satisfaction of their work, it still remains true that the women of the office have won their places not by competition with men but by the exercise of qualities with which no competition was possible. . . . Both of them are there as women. It is a great triumph. But it is a triumph for their womanhood and not for their ambition. [emphasis added]

The current feminine-in-management discourse parallels this earlier discourse. They both incorporate a partiarchally defined "female" into traditional managerial activities and their instrumental orientation. The feminine-in-management rhetoric maintains intact—even strengthens—traditional managerial ideologies, because it is the "female" constructed under patriarchy who is given voice and presence, *extending* the patriarchal family's female role from the private to the public domain. As we shall see, this is the primary role that the feminine-in-management performs in the discourses of globalization—as suggested by the saying, "Behind every successful man there is a woman."

EXTENDING THE HOUSEHOLD UP TO THE NATIONAL BORDER

Consider the following scenario: Some years have passed and most organizations are "globalized." Decisions are no longer made at the national level under national premises. Globalization means a trans- or supranationally coordinated decision-making system that feeds from a network of national organizations, both large and small. Who are the players in this situation, and how are they positioned?

The rhetoric enabled by the feminine "wed-and-connection" metaphors plays very well here. Web-and-connection brings to mind dual images: those of good, caring interpersonal communications and, at the same time, closer interorganizational relations. The first image supports changes toward "flatter" national organizations, where team-based groups would reduce hierarchy and reduce the "bossing" systems; the second image supports strong network structures and new, more powerful hierarchies at the global level.

In this order of things, non-hierarchical ("feminized") national organizations would be the equivalent of the feminized 1930s offices, because the feminine-in-management would bring the traditional values of the American household up to the national border. That is, the private/public divide (women in the household, men out in the world) will not have disappeared. It will have been displaced and recreated on a larger scale as the hierarchy and authority system are reenacted beyond the "national household" in the global arena. Said differently, the national organization—as feminine as it might become—would be a powerless pawn in a globalized organizational world.

More than international imperatives drive this turn of events. If we observe the feminine-in-management within the context of current American society, some other very important facts are uncovered that further promote the structural feminization of national organizations. Demographically, it is evident that America's labor force is becoming increasingly diverse. Many have praised these demographic changes as a guarantee that the "diverse," including women, will occupy better organizational positions denied them in the past. It is seldom acknowledged that the trends toward flatter organizations (that is, more team-based and with less middle management layers) may eliminate many of these opportunities.

At the same time, close scrutiny of the discourses of globalization reveals that the issue of diversity is treated by speaking simultaneously from "both sides of the mouth." America's "diversity" is often presented as a complicating factor in its competitive situation. It is easy to find very open claims about Japan's—or even Sweden's—advantages because, as this rhetoric goes, those countries have a homogeneous population. Others consider that Japanese plants in the U.S. have an unfair advantage because they are able to choose "prime" locations where the population is young, non-diverse, and non-unionized. Ironically, these comments are often made by the same people who criticize Japan for not offering equal opportunities to women, for engaging in sexual harassment, or for having hinted that the U.S. is in trouble because of racial problems.

In this situation, the "web-and-connection" metaphor plays a fundamental role. At the domestic level, reducing the organizational hierarchy reduces the number of the "diverse" who will be appointed to managerial positions. Meanwhile, the feminine-in-management would help in converting "diversity" into homogeneous "team-players" under a caring, motherly gaze. Yet whose idea of a "good mother" is portrayed by the feminine-in-management? One cannot fail to observe that the values represented by the feminine-in-management literature are those of white, formally educated, middle- to upper-middle-class American women, and that it is their mothering styles, family values, and relationship to children that are represented in the "authority through connection" metaphors.

We should not be too quick to praise the feminine-in-management arguments insofar as they distract us from observing their dire consequences: the feminine-in-management simply extends the established power structure by moving the values of those who are "second best" into the vacated domestic (national) managerial spaces. By focusing only at the micro-organizational level, the feminine-in-management creates an illusion of opportunity and change. But when placed at the larger macro-societal level, it becomes a major support for the discourses of globalization, which benefit only a selected few. The organizations created by the meeting of these two discourses locate a certain class of feminine values in the "middle manager" position (the home office) while the rank-and-file—embodied in the values of the "diverse"—keep the national (home) fires burning. In the meantime, the strategists (not a feminine or diverse image, to be certain) move to a higher, more valuable international playing field where decisions are made.

Therefore, the second "conquest of the office" by women represents little more than a simple displacement of power from the national to the global economy. This displacement further legitimizes the traditional power-holders as certain "family values" become reenacted in the public domain, and a whole army of "organizational wives" (Huff 1990) play their patriotic roles in sustaining the heroic "boys" who serve abroad.

TO SERVE WITH PRIDE AND DISTINCTION

The discourses of globalization create awareness of another national reality: America is not a high-wage manufacturing economy anymore, and manufacturing's replacement, the service economy, will not bring about high-wage jobs ("The Global Economy. . . " 1992). One of the marks of globalization is the move of labor-intensive operations toward low-wage world regions coupled with the concomitant displacement of national workers from manufacturing jobs. Yet even manufacturing firms maintaining national operations often restructure into workplaces with lower wages (or fewer jobs). In the meantime, most new jobs in the service sector are in lower-paying occupations. Is it accidental that the rank-and-file jobs for "the new labor force"—comprising a higher proportion of women and minorities—are not the same high-paid, "making-things" jobs of a past American economy?

Beyond the rank-and-file level, global competitiveness has also brought about the age of the lean-and-mean organization. Regardless of the causes (takeover events and associated reorganizations, added control capabilities "at a distance"

with sophisticated management information systems), the very material consequence of these organizational activities is the elimination of middle management
layers, resulting in a large number of mostly white males being "outplaced" by
their organizations. Under these conditions, cheaper managers are needed and,
from our viewpoint, the feminine-in-management rhetoric provides precisely the
low-cost answer for national restructuring toward global competitiveness.

Both Tom Peters and Lester Thurow give us glimpses of the positive economic consequences of "feminizing" national organizations. For Peters (1990), in an
abnormal world (topsy-turvy) the "abnormal" (women) must have the advantage
by being able to do what no man seems capable of doing: work in a less hierarchical organization. How much are these less hierarchical jobs worth? Obviously not
too much, if "outplaced" executives are not rushing to take them. This becomes
even more explicit in Thurow's words, which, though not referring to women,
clearly articulate a "feminized" workplace (Thurow 1992):

> *To use office automation efficiently requires major changes in office
> sociology. The efficient way to use word processors is to eliminate secre-
> taries or clerks and to require managers to type their own memos and
> call up their own files. But a personal secretary is a badge of prestige
> and power. No one wants to give up that badge.*

These changes, as Thurow reminds us, would require "a boss to do less bossing," something that he believes American executives are incapable of doing
because they covet power too much. His prescribed ideological changes for solving this problem are perfectly matched by Grant's (1988) version of the feminine-
in-management, in which women's transforming and liberating force works
toward public purposes rather than for personal ambition and power over others.
But what Grant does not say and Thurow does is that to obtain more efficient and
less hierarchical organizations, bosses should not only boss less and reduce organizational layers, but also "reduce their own salaries and employment opportunities"
(Thurow 1992).

Under conditions of globalization, the feminine-in-management rhetoric can
contribute several images that eventually naturalize the further exploitation of
labor rather than improving managerial opportunities for women. Think, for
example, of the following clichés associated with women: "a woman's work is never done," which is equivalent to extended hours for the same pay; "she did it as a
labor of love," which is equivalent to unpaid work.

As has been well documented, occupations that become "feminized"—
including managerial and professional positions—experience declines in salaries
and wages. Whereas explanations for this fact vary, the condition remains. Such a
situation, however, provides the ideal context for the globalized firm, which would
encounter equally ready and willing "affordable labor" on any side of the border.

Moreover, because the feminine-in-management rhetoric is based on the possibility of abstracting some "essential human traits" that can be observed in many
people (and that may even be sex-neutral), "feminized" jobs may end up mostly

occupied by men as unemployment, provoked by globalization, soars. For example, Jelinek and Adler (1988) note that women can be role models and coaches for men: "Increasingly, the best of our male managers too will be working to acquire and hone important skills formerly seen as 'female'—those centering on relationships, communication, and social sensitivity."

Uncritical support for the feminine-in-management ignores the way it contributes unintentionally to the formation of a "feminized" work culture (in a patriarchal sense), where all work available, regardless of the job holder's sex, would be "women's work" and women's salaries (Ferguson 1984). The feminine-in-management, as it extends the values of the household to the workplace, would provide the ideal metaphor for carefully done, high-quality, cheap work, performed by docile workers: "housework" (Folbre 1991). Globalization, meanwhile, as it extends the rhetoric of national emergency to the international marketplace, would provide the ideal motto: "To serve with pride and distinction."

TRAINING THE DOER FOR FEELINGS, NOT THINKING

Another aspect of the globalization rhetoric that has acquired prominent coverage refers to education. The typical storyline in this respect emphasizes American students' lack of general education and the cost of such a lack because of competition with better-educated workers from other nations (mostly Japan and Germany). The problem is frequently stated as one in which the U.S. is falling behind in technological innovation; the solution is usually stated in terms of more general training in science and mathematics. Behind this story also lies a promise: more and better (high-paying) jobs for better-educated people.

Various elements are problematic in this story. For example, there is no acknowledgment that very well-educated people (people with college degrees) have trouble finding jobs, or that there is a difference between training and education, between being a doer and being a thinker, between technological competence and knowledge. Further, it is seldom acknowledged that the secondary education of Japanese and European students not only contains more math and science, but also spans other socio-humanistic subjects and critical thinking skills.

Unfortunately, in the American context, education for globalization translates into higher education for a few elite thinkers—the "smartest" 25 percent of the population, according to Thurow—while the rest would require no more than a basic "doer" training. In Thurow's view, what is needed is

> . . . to set a quality standard for the non-college bound. Here the high-wage business community in each state should write an achievement test that would cover what they think high-school graduates need to know to work at America's best firms. . . [T]hose that had passed this "business achievement test" would have their diplomas so stamped. . . [L]eading high-wage business firms would commit themselves to hiring

only those with stamped diplomas. . . [T]he achievement test. . . would be written by employers to insure that Americans clearly understood that this is what their children must learn if they want to have high-wage jobs. It wouldn't be a test written by ivory-tower professors or education bureaucrats.

The turn toward "vocational training" for the majority of the population under the guise of "better education" may be supported by various aspects of the feminine-in-management rhetoric. The imagery of women as "concrete-feelers" in contrast to men as "abstract-thinkers" has been with us for several centuries. Rarely, we observe, has the feminine-in-management rhetoric argued for women's superior intellectual capabilities. Rather, it emphasizes the traditional oppositions of "thinking/feeling" and "abstract/concrete" by focusing on women's better interpersonal relations and trustworthiness, their care-and-connection practices that would humanize the workplace, the healing processes they could contribute for the wellness of an alienated work force, and their concrete, no-nonsense attitude and practical orientation toward everyday problems.

These abilities, we agree, are probably going to be very much in demand for managing the large percentage of "educated" American workers who will not find high-wage jobs, regardless of their stamped diplomas. They would be particularly useful as ways to pacify emotionally the vast majority of these workers (euphemistically, "human capital") who will have to adjust downward their expectations of better pay under globalization. In the meantime, the truly educated few—the abstract thinkers, or "symbolic analysts" as Robert Teich would call them—will reap the fruits of this situation from the distance of their own very well-paid, cosmopolitan global spaces.

HEART-TO-HEART OR HEAD-TO-HEAD?

In the rhetoric of globalization, there is little that is not written in the language of warfare. For example, Thurow's book's subtitle is *The Coming Economic Battle Among Japan, Europe, and America;* Ohmae's is *Power and Strategy in the Interlinked Economy.* References are constantly made to "winners and losers" in the global economy, where the world is a battleground, and where the U.S. should be able to outsmart everyone else. Predictably, the imagery also refers to intellectual prowess in which one would strategize a better game than one's opponent ("war games").

It would appear that this discourse offers little space for Helgesen's "female advantage" to reduce—as she urges us to do—the Warrior values of our dominant culture. Yet for all her talk about women's more holistic view of the world and greater social consciousness, at the end the "female advantage" offers no more than the ability to "master the Warrior skills of discipline, will and struggle necessary to achieve success in the public realm" (Helgesen 1990). Furthermore, she suggests incorporating these values with those of another Jungian archetype, the Martyr, to produce an androgynous Magician who—irrespective of Helgesen's praise—is little more than a shrewd trickster and manipulator.

Another way to understand the feminine-in-management rhetoric is as a cover-up for the usual way managerial activities have been portrayed from time immemorial in the U.S.: as a fight and struggle among enemies (labor and management, business and government, local and international competitors). The words "competitive advantage" and "female advantage" seem to be used unselfconsciously in the same paragraphs that claim some kind of unique "all heart, all peace" managerial goodness assumed to come from women's qualities. Yet aside from the oxymoronic quality of these juxtapositions, their more problematic material consequence is the way they objectify women managers into convenient weapons for the international fight, as when women are a "powerful resource for sustainable competitive advantage" (Jelinek and Adler 1988), or when "treating women as a business imperative is the equivalent of a unique R&D product for which there is a huge demand" (Schwartz 1992).

Perhaps the feminine-in-management rhetoric simply fuels the current version of the Trojan wars under the guise of globalization. How many rescues of how many Helens of Troy might be used as the occasion for another "war"? Will it be the rescue of "sexually harassed" Japanese women who lack the "real opportunities" given to American women, as *Business Week* claims ("Revenge of the 'Office Ladies'" 1992)? Will the "new-and-improved," restructured, and globalized American corporation serve as the Trojan Horse?

IMPLICATIONS: OTHER IMAGES OF WOMEN FOR RETHINKING GLOBALIZATION

We want to call attention to the relationships that may exist between two currently popular managerial discourses—the feminine-in-management and globalization—both of which claim to be bringing much needed changes to the managerial field. Our primary intention is to argue that, despite their claims, the assumed changes are only a surface rhetoric. Analyzed together, they cancel each other as they maintain existing power relations that benefit only a few. For example, these discourses speak of better opportunities for all but hold onto the established order when facing the reality of an increasingly diverse work force. They speak of growing productivity and wealth while making acceptable the lowered expectations brought about by a service economy. They speak of the importance of education and human capital while fostering little more than technical competencies for narrow thinkers. They bring in an emblematic sign of peace to soften the rough edges of a rhetoric that bespeaks of war.

Though our analysis may appear as merely an exercise in criticism, our intention is to unmask the impossible promises resulting from the contradictions in these discourses once they are placed in their broader institutional and social contexts. We believe analyses that cut through the rhetoric of the latest managerial quick-fix have important implications for management. They help us understand the connections that exist between the activities of any particular organization—when following these popularized prescriptions—and the perhaps unintended consequences those same activities may bring to the greater society to which we all belong.

For example, uncritical support of a "care-and-connection" managerial style could be a very naive way to try to manipulate a labor force that is neither naive nor reacting to any prior managerial style but is rather concerned about layoffs or poor pay. Uncritical support of what is little more than vocational training in secondary education—as a way of reducing short-term organizational training costs—would merely contribute to reducing underemployment, since in the long run few would be educated enough to merit high wage jobs. Who would be the critical thinkers? Who would innovate and create new and better employment opportunities for a whole society? The feminine-in-management and their counterpart discourses of globalization are short-sighted, elitist palliatives for the realities of the contemporary world. Thus, it may be possible that in a few years we will look back and view our business organizations—those "feminine" and "globalized" American corporations—as the main perpetrators of a situation from which there is no return: bringing the capabilities of our nation to its lowest common denominator in the name of doing just the opposite.

In these last paragraphs we offer a different way of thinking "feminine": a way that would bring a different set of images of "women" into a globalized economy. Yet this time, they are images that call for effecting a radical change in the way we think about management and the way we would design our organizations for a better society. These images, which are already around us, are the more critical aspects of "the feminine" discussed in feminist theory and appearing in some management writing. Unfortunately, the more critical inspirations from feminist theories have been absent in the feminine-in-management literature because the latter, as it stands now, is just another form of women pleasing men—of making sure it says what is acceptable to say in management *now*, by maintaining privileges for a few even if the rest of society is worse off.

For example, conventional managerial wisdom considers that, in a global economy, good management creates opportunities to produce and sell an abundance of goods in foreign markets, keep jobs at home, and keep the home population's ability to consume ("the good standard of living") alive and well. This ideal situation is supported by exporting both the goods and the values of a consumer society so the rest of the world will live (consume) as we do while supporting our "democratic values." Yet shouldn't we be wary of managerial strategies that promote consumerism both at home and abroad while pretending this is what we should call "a good standard of living" for the whole world?

The imagery that sustains these strategies is actually a feminine one of "the consumer as impulse shopper" (Fischer 1993) of the "buy now and pay later" variety, scrambling for scarce bargain basement merchandise. It is the imagery of short-term gratification in spite of the impoverishing consequences of these consumption activities in the long run, as we are experiencing now in our own country. This is an imagery that the feminine-in-management promotes as much as any other managerial approach (Helgesen's descriptions of her women's cocktail parties, meeting places, and Hérmès scarves), because what it promotes, regardless of method, are the same old goals: more sales, better market share, and to take away from competitors, particularly those from other nations.[2]

In contrast, we want to offer the imagery of "the frugal housewife," who can do with consuming less and [instead] saving for "a rainy day"; who is able to improve what she already has by conserving and preserving; who shares scarce resources with her neighbors (baby clothes) to be able to produce a "common wealth." Such imagery may be able to bring about a form of management that not only avoids exploitation of both people and resources but that is more likely to effect a true cooperation among nations—a better life for all, yet a better life that doesn't hinge on incremental consumption of disposable "goods."

Perhaps the "world-class standards" we export to other nations could be a concept of the good life in which people would better appreciate their own abilities and endowments; where good health and good education—not training—are the primary goods to be had for everybody in every society: where decent food and living conditions would be basic human rights and the basis for a pact among nations—a pact under the premises of "sustainable growth"; where growth is meaningful insofar as it contributes to sustaining "the global family."

We could play with many more images. What about redefining "innovation" through imagery of "female ingenuity" (being able to do anything with a hairpin)? Such imagery would help us appreciate the talents of many different peoples—particularly those who, because of scarcity, have been able to make do with much less—while helping us learn from them, instead of killing those talents with instrumental education of the "What is it good for?" variety. (Remember that old phrase about necessity being the mother of invention?)

What about using "women's gossiping" as imagery to construct an extended network of real worldwide information for the "global village"? That is certainly not what we have right now, in spite of all our claims about the information age and communication satellites. For example, Headline News's "Around the World in 30 Minutes" repeats the same very selective "news" for 24 hours with a minimum of information about the realities of other nations—especially nations that do not agree with our point of view. Or what about fully embracing "mother nature" as a female who hasn't yet been offered "equal opportunity," or who hasn't been covered by "affirmative action," or who has been blatantly "sexually harassed?" Would it help in giving the environment a better chance?

What about the image of the "hysterical woman"? The hysterical woman releases her emotions to cry and scream in moral indignation for the crimes against humanity that are constantly committed in the name of economic rationality. She would denounce, time and again, the illogic and the irrationality of a world in which millions of people die of hunger while productive lands are kept barren to maintain a reasonable price for food in the market.

Perhaps the day that we, who are in business professions in capitalist societies, allow this image of the "hysterical woman" to overcome us as an inspiration for a management theory will be the day that, paradoxically, we will come back to our senses. That will be the day when we will define "the good economy" as the positive results of having complied with worldwide social imperatives rather than the other way around. Otherwise, we will have to confess that the logic of democracy and capitalism, of our organizations, and of our governments, would all have failed miserably.

So, perhaps we need to place another advertisement:

HELP WANTED

Seeking hysterical person. Willing to become enraged when observing world-wide exploitation, esp. when done in the name of free market economy. Ready to act in world forums to denounce such conditions. Ready to help others develop their critical voices to create a global network of well-informed peoples, who won't accept being called "less developed" or be undervalued for their own local talents and capabilities. Not afraid to call attention to the travesty of conspicuous consumption in the name of progress and demonstrate the negative long-term consequences of a "First World standard of living." If you are willing to create new forms of business organizations ready to promote sane globalization for a sustainable planet,

Contact THE WORLD
FAX: 1-800-IS-READY

We are the best in the business of
Thinking and Acting Globally and Locally.

Notes

1. While the notion of "patriarchy" varies somewhat in different feminist theories, here we mean sex-gender relations that naturalize and universalize social practices wherein men/masculine values dominate over women/feminine values. This form of domination is particularly pervasive when women uncritically assume stereotypical feminine patterns within traditional structural arrangements.

2. Popularized "managerial wisdom" explains the global economy as one that produces opportunities to sell an abundance of goods in foreign markets, keeping jobs and a high standard of living at home. Seldom is it explained that such is only one side of the story. The true ideal of a globalized free market economy means that no country will import more than it is able to export, and that the end value of such transactions should equal zero at both the individual country and aggregate global level. Otherwise, globalization translates into exploitation of other nations through consumerism.

References

"America Isn't Creating Enough Jobs, and No One Seems to Know Why," *The New York Times,* September 6, 1992, Section 4, pp. 1, 3.

W. Bruce, review of *The Female Advantage,* by S. Helgesen, *Public Productivity and Mangement Review,* 15, 3 (1992); 382–387.

M. B. Calás. "An/Other Silent Voice? Representing 'Hispanic Woman' in Organizational Texts," in A.J. Mills and P. Tancred, eds., *Gendering Organizational Analysis* (Newbury Park, Calif.: Sage, 1992), pp. 201–221.

M. B. Calás, S. Jacobson, R. Jacques, and L. Smircich, "Is a Woman Centered Theory of Management Dangerous?" Paper presented at the National Meetings of the Academy of Management, Miami, August 1991.

M. B. Calás and R. Jacques, "Diversity or Conformity? Research by Women on Women in Organizations." Paper presented at the Annual Conference on Women and Organizations, Long Beach, Calif., August 1988.

M. B. Calás and L. Smircich, "Using the 'F' Word: Femininist Theories and the Social Consequences of Organizationl Research," in A.J. Mills and P. Tancred, eds., *Gendering Organizational Analysis* (Newbury Park, Calif.: Sage, 1992), pp. 222–234.

L. M. Calvert and V. J. Ramsey, "Bringing Women's Voice to Research on Women in Management: A Feminist Perspective," *Journal of Management Inquiry, 1,1* (1992): 79–88.

S. S. Case, "The Collaborative Advantage: The Usefulness of Women's Language to Contemporary Business Problems," forthcoming in *Business in a Contemporary World.*

N. Chodorow, *The Reproduction of Mothering* (Berkeley: University of California Press, 1978).

"Corporate Women: How Much Progress?" *Business Week,* June 8, 1992, pp. 74–83.

R. Eisler, "Women, Men and Management: Redesigning Our Future," *Futures,* January-February 1991, pp. 3–18.

K. E. Ferguson, *The Feminist Case Against Bureaucracy* (Philadelphia: Temple University Press, 1984).

E. Fischer, "A Poststructural Feminist Analysis of the Rhetoric of Marketing Relationships," *International Journal of Research in Marketing,* January 1993.

J. Fletcher, "Feminist Standpoint Research and Management Science: Castrating the Female Advantage." Unpublished manuscript, Northeastern University, June 1992.

N. Folbre, "The Unproductive Housewife: Her Evolution in Nineteenth-Century Economic Thought," *Signs, 16,* 3 (1991): 463–484.

C. Gilligan, *In a Different Voice: Psychological Theory and Women's Development* (Cambridge, Mass.: Harvard University Press, 1982).

"The Global Economy: Who Gets Hurt?" *Business Week,* August 10, 1992, pp. 48–53.

J. Grant, "Women as Manager: What They Can Offer to Organizations," *Organizational Dynamics,* Spring 1988, pp. 56–63.

S. Helgesen, *The Female Advantage: Women's Ways of Leadership* (New York: Double-day/Currency, 1990).

A. S. Huff, "Wives—Of the Organization." Paper presented at the Women and Work Conference, Arlington, Texas, May 11, 1990.

"If Women Ran America," *Life,* June 1992, pp. 36–46.

J. A. Jacobs, "Women's Entry into Management: Trends in Earnings, Authority, and Values among Salaried Managers," *Administrative Science Quarterly,* June 1992, pp. 282–301.

M. Jelinek and N. J. Adler, "Women: World Class Managers for Global Competition," *Academy of Management Executive,* February 1988, pp. 7–19.

A. Kingston, "A Woman's New Place Is in the Latest Management Theory," *Women in Management,* 2, 2, (no year), p. 2; London, Ontario: The National Centre for Management Research and Development, The University of Western Ontario.

R. Kuttner, *The End of Laissez-Faire: National Purpose and the Global Economy After the Cold War* (New York: Alfred A. Knopf, 1991).

G. Lloyd, *The Man of Reason: 'Male' and 'Female' in Western Philosophy* (Minneapolis: University of Minnesota Press, 1984).

M. Loden, *Feminine Leadership—or—How to Succeed Without Being One of the Boys* (New York: Times Books, 1985).

J. Marshall, *Women Managers: Travelers in a Male World* (Chichester, England: Wiley, 1984).

R. Marshall and M. Tucker, *Thinking for a Living: Education and the Wealth of Nations* (New York: Basic Books, 1992).

J. Martin, "Deconstructing Organizational Taboos: The Suppression of Gender Conflict in Organizations," *Organization Science,* 1 (1990): pp. 334–359.

J. B. Miller, *New Psychology of Women* (Berkeley, Calif.: University of California Press, 1976).

J. Naisbitt and P. Aburdene, *Megatrends 2000* (New York: Avon, 1990).

J. Naisbitt and P. Aburdene, *Re-inventing the Corporation* (New York: Warner, 1985).

S. Nelton, "Men, Women and Leadership," *Nation's Business,* May 1991, pp. 16–22.

K. Ohmae, *The Borderless World: Power and Strategy in the Interlinked Economy* (New York: Harper, 1990).

T. Peters, "The Best New Managers Will Listen, Motivate, Support: Isn't That Just Like a Woman?" *Working Woman,* September 1990, pp. 216–217.

J. Pfeffer and A. Davis-Blake, "The Effect of the Proportion of Women on Salaries: The Case of College Administrators," *Administrative Science Quarterly,* 32, 1 (1987): 1–24.

M. E. Porter, *The Competitive Advantage of Nations* (New York: Free Press, 1990).

R. B. Reich, *The Work of Nations* (New York: Knopf, 1991).

B. F. Reskin and P. Roos, eds., *Job Queues, Gender Queues: Explaining Women's Inroads Into Male Occupations* (Philadelphia: Temple University Press, 1990).

"Revenge of the 'Office Ladies,'" *Business Week,* July 13, 1992, pp. 42–43.

J. F. Rosener, "Ways Women Lead," *Harvard Business Review,* November-December 1990, pp. 119–125. (See also page 142 of this book).

F. N. Schwartz, "Women as a Business Imperative," *Harvard Business Review,* March-April 1992, pp. 105–113.

J. F. Siler, "The Corporate Woman: Is She Really Different?" *Business Week,* June 25, 1990, p. 14.

L. Smircich, "Toward a Woman-Centered Organization Theory." Paper presented at the Annual Meetings of the Academy of Management, San Diego, Calif., August 1985.

L. Thurow, *Head to Head: The Coming Economic Battle Among Japan, Europe and America* (New York: Morrow, 1992).

C. Weedon, *Feminist Practice and Poststructuralist Theory* (London: Basil Blackwell, 1987).

"Why Smart Companies Are Crazy About Women Executives," *Cosmopolitan,* 4, April 1990, pp. 184–187.

"Women in Business: II . . . being a commentary upon the great American office and the distinction between the girl who works to marry and the girl who marries to work," *Fortune,* August 1935, pp. 50–86.

Chapter 5

Communicating

We have been viewing managing as a difficult balancing act required for coordinating human effort toward achieving the purposes of an organization. Information, perhaps more than anything else, affects coordination. In performing their balancing acts, managers depend upon the flow of information. They need to obtain valid information about what things are important, and they depend upon other people receiving information that directs their attention and effort appropriately. Communication is the word used to refer to the activities of sending and receiving information.

Early in the study of management, communication was seen primarily as flowing up and down the organization's formal hierarchy as diagrammed on the organizational chart. It did not take long before people realized that other communication channels existed and were essential. For the actions of people to be coordinated effectively, the people doing the work needed to interact with each other. If only the formal hierarchy was used, the flow of information was too slow.

Perhaps even more important, the hierarchical channel introduced considerable distortion. People at higher levels in the hierarchy often lack the technical expertise to act as effective communication links. The channel has insufficient capacity to process the rich information adequately. Consequently, a great deal of attention has been given to developing new channels to link organizational units— laterally and across the hierarchy. Management textbooks frequently discuss these steps under the headings of liaison mechanisms and matrix structures.

It was also apparent that there were other problems in the upward and downward flow of information. At first, considerable attention was given to how managers could send information more effectively. Clarity, redundancy, and persuasiveness were stressed as ways to be sure that information was transferred from the people who made the decisions to those who would be charged with implementing them. As we see in the poem by Simon Roman on MBAs, such matters are still of great importance in vertical communication.

Communicating effectively is a challenge to managers worldwide even when the workforce is culturally homogeneous. However, when different languages and cultural backgrounds are involved, effective two-way communication becomes even more difficult.

Also, techniques affect the process. For example, telecommuting has introduced further difficulties for those managers who elect to use this communication pathway. Customer and vendor relationships cannot always be monitored effectively from afar.

There are numerous impediments to the flow of valid and timely information. The readings in this section highlight but a few. Intimidation is one of the most important. People who have power intimidate those with less power. The intimidation may flow from a defensive effort of the superior to turn off unwanted information and/or from inhibitions (from real or imagined sources) in the minds of subordinates. Regardless, valid and important information does not flow. Moreover, upper-level managers often deal with the problems of lower-level members through numbers and other symbols that reflect the performance and the problems of the lower-level participants in highly abstracted form. As a result, the managers do not have an accurate picture of what is happening—they lack the context to make appropriate interpretations. Consequently, some (see, for example, "More Corporate Chiefs Seek Direct Contact with Staff, Customers") special efforts are required.

In sum, the flow of valid, timely information is an essential ingredient for an effective organization. Achieving it is not easy under the best of circumstances, and organizations are far from the best of circumstances. The articles that follow provide insight into the problems and suggest some remedies.

◆

Communicating Across Cultural Barriers*

Nancy J. Adler

All international business activity involves communication. Within the international and global business environment, activities such as exchanging information and ideas, decision making, negotiating, motivating, and leading are all based on the ability of managers from one culture to communicate successfully with managers and employees from other cultures. Achieving effective communication is a challenge to managers worldwide even when the workforce is culturally homogeneous, but when one company includes a variety of languages and cultural backgrounds, effective two-way communication becomes even more difficult.

Lack of Cultural Self-Awareness.   Although we think that the major obstacle in international business is in understanding the foreigner, the greater difficulty involves becoming aware of our own cultural conditioning. As anthropologist Edward Hall has explained, "What is known least well, and is therefore in the poorest position to be studied, is what is closest to oneself." We are generally least aware of our own cultural characteristics and are quite surprised when we hear foreigners' descriptions of us. For example, many Americans are surprised to discover that they are seen by foreigners as hurried, overly law-abiding, very hard working, extremely explicit, and overly inquisitive (see the example that follows). Many American businesspeople were equally surprised by a *Newsweek* survey reporting the characteristics most and least frequently associated with Americans. Asking a foreign national to describe businesspeople from your country is a powerful way to see yourself as others see you.

To the extent that we can begin to see ourselves clearly through the eyes of foreigners, we can begin to modify our behavior, emphasizing our most appropriate and effective characteristics and minimizing those least helpful. To the extent that we are culturally self-aware, we can begin to predict the effect our behavior will have on others.

Projected Similarity.   Projected similarity refers to the assumption that people are more similar to you than they actually are, or that a situation is similar to yours when in fact it is not. Projecting similarity reflects both a natural and a common process. American researchers Burger and Bass worked with groups of managers from fourteen different countries. They asked each manager to describe the work and life goals of the colleague from another country. As shown in Figure 5.3, in every case the managers assumed that their foreign colleagues were more like themselves than they actually were. Projected similarity involves assuming,

---

*Excerpted and copied with permission from *International Dimensions of Organizational Behavior,* 2nd. ed., by Nancy J. Adler. Wadsworth Publishing Company, Belmont, California, 1991.

CROSS-CULTURAL AWARENESS

Americans as Others See Them

People from other countries are often puzzled and intrigued by the intricacies and enigmas of American culture. Below is a selection of actual observations by foreigners visiting the United States. As you read them, ask yourself in each case if the observer is accurate, and how you would explain the trait in question.

India "Americans seem to be in a perpetual hurry. Just watch the way they walk down the street. They never allow themselves the leisure to enjoy life; there are too many things to do."

Kenya "Americans appear to us rather distant. They are not really as close to other people—even fellow Americans—as Americans overseas tend to portray. It's almost as if an American says, 'I won't let you get too close to me.' It's like building a wall."

Turkey "Once we were out in a rural area in the middle of nowhere and saw an American come to a stop sign. Though he could see in both directions for miles and no traffic was coming, he still stopped!"

Colombia "The tendency in the United States to think that life is only work hits you in the face. Work seems to be the one type of motivation."

Indonesia "In the United States everything has to be talked about and analyzed. Even the littlest thing has to be 'Why, Why, Why?' I get a headache from such persistent questions."

Ethiopia "The American is very explicit; he want a 'yes' or 'no.' If someone tries to speak figuratively, the American is confused."

Iran "The first time. . . my [American] professor told me, 'I don't know the answer, I will have to look it up,' I was shocked. I asked myself, 'Why is he teaching me?' In my country a professor would give the wrong answer rather than admit ignorance."[1]

imagining, and actually perceiving similarity when differences exist. Projected similarity particularly handicaps people in cross-cultural situations. As a South African, I assume that my Greek colleague is more South African than he actually is. As an Egyptian, I assume that my Chilean colleague is more similar to me than

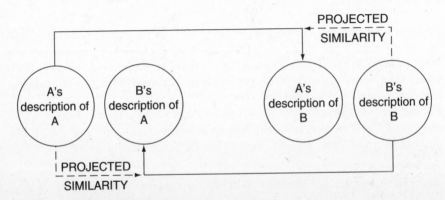

Figure 5.3 **Projected Similarity**

she actually is. When I act based on this assumed similarity, I often find that I have acted inappropriately and thus ineffectively.

At the base of projected similarity is a subconscious parochialism. I assume that there is only one way to be: my way. I assume that there is only one way to see the world: my way. I therefore view other people in reference to me and to my way of viewing the world. People may fall into an

> . . . illusion of understanding while being unaware of . . . [their] misunderstandings. "I understand you perfectly but you don't understand me" is an expression typical of such a situation. Or all communicating parties may fall into a collective illusion of mutual understanding. In such a situation, each party may wonder later why other parties do not live up to the "agreement" they had reached.

Most international managers do not see themselves as parochial. They believe that as world travelers they are able to see the foreigner's point of view. This is not always true.

Example

> When a Danish manager works with a Saudi and the Saudi states that the plant will be completed on time, "En shah allah" ("If God is willing"), the Dane rarely believes that God's will is really going to influence the construction progress. He continues to see the world from his parochial Danish perspective and assumes that "En shah allah" is just an excuse for not getting the work done, or is meaningless altogether.
>
> Similarly, when Balinese workers' families refuse to use birth control methods, explaining that it will break the cycle of reincarnation, few Western managers really consider that there is a possibility that they too will be reborn a number of times. Instead, they assume that the Balinese do not understand or are afraid of Western medicine.

While it is important to understand and respect the foreigner's point of view, it is not necessary to accept or adopt it. A rigid adherence to our own belief system is a form of parochialism, and parochialism underlies projected similarity.

One of the best exercises for developing empathy and reducing parochialism and projected similarity is *role reversal*. Imagine that you are a foreign businessperson. Imagine the type of family you come from, the number of brothers and sisters you have, the social and economic conditions you grew up with, the type of education you received, the ways in which you chose your profession and position, the ways in which you were introduced to your spouse, your goals in working for your organization, and your life goals. Asking these questions forces you to see the other person as he or she really is, and not as a mere reflection of yourself. It forces you to see both the similarities and the differences, and not to imagine similarities when differences actually exist. Moreover, role reversal encourages highly task-oriented businesspeople, such as Americans, to see the foreigner as a whole person rather than someone with a position and a set of skills needed to accomplish a particular task.

CROSS-CULTURAL MISEVALUATION

Even more than perception and interpretation, cultural conditioning strongly affects evaluation. Evaluation involves judging whether someone or something is good or bad. Cross-culturally, we use our own culture as a standard of measurement, judging that which is like our own culture as normal and good and that which is different as abnormal and bad. Our own culture becomes a *self-reference criterion:* since no other culture is identical to our own, we judge all other cultures as inferior. Evaluation rarely helps in trying to understand or communicate with people from another culture. The consequences of misevaluation are exemplified in the following:

> *A Swiss executive waits more than an hour past the appointed time for his Latin colleague to arrive and sign a supply contract. In his impatience, he concludes that Latins must be lazy and totally unconcerned about business. He has misevaluated his colleague by negatively comparing him to his own cultural standards. Implicitly, he has labeled his own group's behavior as good (Swiss arrive on time and that is good) and the other group's behavior as bad (Latins do not arrive on time and that is bad).*

COMMUNICATION: GETTING THEIR MEANING, NOT JUST THEIR WORDS

Effective cross-cultural communication is possible, but international managers cannot approach it in the same way as do domestic managers. First, effective international managers "know that they don't know." They assume difference until similarity is proven rather than assuming similarity until difference is proven.

Second, in attempting to understand their foreign colleagues, effective international managers emphasize description, by observing what is actually said and done, rather than interpreting or evaluating it. Describing a situation is the most accurate way to gather information about it. Interpretation and evaluation, unlike description, are based more on the observer's culture and background than on the observed situation. To that extent, my interpretations and evaluations tell me more about myself than about the situation. Although managers, as decision makers, must evaluate people (e.g., performance appraisals) and situations (e.g., project assessments) in terms of organizational standards and objectives, effective international managers delay judgment until they have had sufficient time to observe and interpret the situation from the perspective of all cultures involved.

Third, when attempting to understand or interpret a foreign situation, effective international managers try to see it through the eyes of their foreign colleagues. This role reversal limits the myopia of viewing situations strictly from one's own perspective.

Fourth, once effective international managers develop an explanation for a situation, they treat the explanation as a guess (as a hypothesis to be tested) and

WHAT DO I DO IF THEY DO NOT SPEAK MY LANGUAGE?

Verbal Behavior
- *Clear, slow speech.* Enunciate each word. Do not use colloquial expressions.
- *Repetition.* Repeat each important idea using different words to explain the same concept.
- *Simple sentences.* Avoid compound, long sentences.
- *Active verbs.* Avoid passive verbs.

Non-Verbal Behavior
- *Visual restatements.* Use as many visual restatements as possible, such as pictures, graphs, tables, and slides.
- *Gestures.* Use more facial and hand gestures to emphasize the meaning of words.
- *Demonstration.* Act out as many themes as possible.
- *Pauses.* Pause more frequently.
- *Summaries.* Hand out written summaries of your verbal presentation.

Attribution
- *Silence.* When there is a silence, wait. Do not jump in to fill the silence. The other person is probably just thinking more slowly in the non-native language or translating.
- *Intelligence.* Do not equate poor grammar and mispronunciation with lack of intelligence; it is usually a sign of second language use.
- *Differences.* If unsure, assume difference, not similarity.

Comprehension
- *Understanding.* Do not just assume that they understand; assume that they do not understand.
- *Checking comprehension.* Have colleagues repeat their understanding of the material back to you. Do not simply ask if they understand or not. Let them explain what they understand to you.

Design
- *Breaks.* Take more frequent breaks. Second language comprehension is exhausting.
- *Small modules.* Divide the material into smaller modules.
- *Longer time frame.* Allocate more time for each module than usual in a monolingual program.

Motivation
- *Encouragement.* Verbally and nonverbally encourage and reinforce speaking by non-native language participants.
- *Drawing out.* Explicitly draw out marginal and passive participants.
- *Reinforcement.* Do not embarrass novice speakers.[2]

not as a certainty. They systematically check with other foreign and home country colleagues to make sure that their guesses—their interpretations—are plausible. This checking process allows them to converge meanings—to delay accepting their interpretations of the situation until they have confirmed them with others.

Understanding: Converging Meanings

There are many ways to increase the chances for accurately understanding foreigners. The excerpt on p. 187 suggests what to do when business colleagues are not native speakers of your language. Each technique is based on presenting the message through multiple channels (for example, stating your position and showing a graph to summarize the same position), paraphrasing to check if the foreigner has understood your meaning (and not just your words), and converging meanings (always double-checking with a second person that you communicated what you intended).

Standing Back from Yourself

Perhaps the most difficult skill in cross-cultural communication involves standing back from yourself, or being aware that you do not know everything, that a situation may not make sense, that your guesses may be wrong, and that the ambiguity in the situation may continue. In this sense the ancient Roman dictum "knowledge is power" becomes true. In knowing yourself, you gain power over your perceptions and reactions; you can control your own behavior and your reactions to others' behavior. Cross-cultural awareness complements in-depth self-awareness. A lack of self-awareness negates the usefulness of cross-cultural awareness.

One of the most poignant examples of the powerful interplay between description, interpretation, evaluation, and empathy involves a Scottish businessman's relationship with a Japanese colleague. The following story recounts the Scottish businessman's experience.

CROSS-CULTURAL COMMUNICATION

Japanese Pickles and Mattresses, Incorporated

It was my first visit to Japan. As a gastronomic adventurer, and because I believe cuisine is one route which is freely available and highly effective as a first step towards a closer understanding of another country, I was disappointed on my first evening when the Japanese offered me a Western meal.

As tactfully as possible I suggested that some time during my stay I would like to try a Japanese menu, if that could be arranged without inconvenience. There was some small reluctance evident on the part of my hosts (due of course to their thought that I was being very polite asking for Japanese food which I didn't really like, so to be good hosts they had to politely find a way of not having me eat it!). But eventually, by an elegantly progressive route starting with Western food with a slightly Japanese bias through to genuine Japanese food, my hosts were convinced that I really wanted to eat Japanese style and was not "posing."

From then on they became progressively more enthusiastic in suggesting the more exotic Japanese dishes, and I guess I graduated when, after an excellent meal one night (apart from the Japanese pickles) on which I had lavished praise, they said, "Do you like Japanese pickles?" To this, without preamble, I said, "No!" to which reply, with great laughter all round, they responded, "Nor do we!"

During this gastronomic getting-together week, I had also been trying to persuade them than I really did wish to stay in traditional Japanese hotels rather than the very Westernized ones my hosts had selected because they thought I would prefer my "normal" lifestyle. (I should add that at this time traditional Japanese hotels were still available and often cheaper than, say, the Osaka Hilton.)

Anyway, after the pickles joke it was suddenly announced that Japanese hotels could be arranged. For the remaining two weeks of my stay, as I toured the major cities, on most occasions a traditional Japanese hotel was substituted for the Western one on my original schedule.

Many of you will know that a traditional Japanese room has no furniture except a low table and a flower arrangement. The "bed" is a mattress produced just before you retire from a concealed cupboard, accompanied by a cereal-packed pillow.

One memorable evening my host and I had finished our meal together in "my" room. I was expecting him to shortly make his "good-night" and retire, as he had been doing all week, to his own room.

However, he stayed unusually long and was, to me, obviously in some sort of emotional crisis. Finally, he blurted out, with great embarrassment, "Can I sleep with you?!"

As they say in the novels, at this point I went very still! My mind was racing through all the sexual taboos and prejudices my own upbringing had instilled, and I can still very clearly recall how I analyzed: "I'm bigger than he is so I can fight him off, but then he's probably an expert in the martial arts, but on the other hand he's shown no signs of being gay up until now and he is my host and there is a lot of business at risk and there's no such thing as rape, et cetera. . . !

It seemed a hundred years, though it was only a few seconds, before I said, feeling as if I was pulling the trigger in Russian roulette, "Yes, sure."

Who said that the Orientals are inscrutable? The look of relief that followed my reply was obvious. Then he looked worried and concerned again, and said, "Are you sure?"

I reassured him and he called in the maid, who fetched his mattress from his room and laid it on the floor alongside mine. We both went to bed and slept all night without any physical interaction.

Later I learned that for the traditional Japanese one of the greatest compliments you can be paid is for the host to ask, "Can I sleep with you?" This goes back to the ancient feudal times, when life was cheap, and what the invitation really said was, "I trust you with my life. I do not think that you will kill me while I sleep. You are my true friend."

To have said "No" to the invitation would have been an insult—"I don't trust you not to kill me while I sleep"—or, at the very least, my host would have been acutely embarrassed because he had taken the initiative. If I refused because I had failed to perceive the invitation as a compliment, he would have been out of countenance on two grounds: the insult to him in the traditional context and the embarrassment he would have caused me by "forcing" a negative, uncomprehending response from me.

As it turned out, the outcome was superb. He and I were now "blood brothers," as it were. His assessment of me as being "ready for Japanization" had been correct and his obligations under ancient Japanese custom had been fulfilled. I had totally misinterpreted his intentions through my own cultural conditioning. It was sheer luck, or luck plus a gut feeling that I'd gotten it wrong, that caused me to make the correct response to his extremely complimentary and committed invitation.[3]

Notes

1. John P. Feig and G. Blair, *There Is a Difference*, 2d ed. (Washington, D.C.: Meridian House International, 1980).

2. Based on Nancy J. Adler and Moses N. Kiggundu, "Awareness at the Crossroad: Designing Translator-Based Training Programs," in D. Landis and R. Brislin, eds. *Handbook of Intercultural Training: Issues in Training methodology*, vol. II (New York: Pergamon Press, 1983). pp. 124–150.

3. A Scottish executive participating in the 1979 Managerial Skills for International Business Program at INSEAD, in Fontainebleau, France.

References

Burger, P., and Bass, B. M. *Assessment of Managers: An International Comparison* (New York: Free Press, 1979).

Hall, E. T. *Beyond Culture*. (Garden City, N.Y.: Anchor Press/Doubleday and Company, 1976). Also see E. T. Hall's *The Silent Language* (Doubleday, 1959, and Anchor Books, 1973) and *The Hidden Dimension* (Doubleday, 1966, and Anchor Books, 1969).

Kanungo, R. N. *Biculturalism and Management* (Ontario: Butterworth, 1980).

Maruyama, M. "Paradigms and Communication," *Technological Forecasting and Social Change*, vol. 6 (1974), pp. 3-32.

Prekel, T. "Multi-Cultural Communication: A Challenge to Managers." Paper delivered at the International Convention of the American Business Communication Association, New York, November 21, 1983.

The New York Times, September 20, 1992

The Mixed Blessings of Telecommuting*

Leah Beth Ward

Last February, Nabil Kabbani swapped his Armani suits for jeans from The Gap and moved his family across country from Augusta, Ga., to a spacious home there with a view. The change was not just sartorial or geographic. Mr. Kabbani, 44, attests that he's a new person, too. "I have smelled the roses," he says.

Telecommuting is the key to Mr. Kabbani's happiness these days. From Santa Fe, he runs Eye Group Inc., an optometry company based in Augusta that has operations in a number of Lenscrafters stores in three Southern states under a lease arrangement. Having given up the proverbial rat race that kept him on the treadmill seven days a week, Mr. Kabbani now relies on a fax machine and computer to deliver sales figures and other statistics that keep him abreast of the operation.

At first, Mr. Kabbani was skeptical about long-distance management. But he installed a trusted team and convinced himself to let go. "I don't have to be there. I can make a lot of decisions through the computer," he said. "If I notice things are slow at one location, I talk to management and say we need to beef up advertising."

Telecommuting, narrowly defined as working off-site, typically at home, for a company based in an urban area, was hailed a few years ago as the great liberator of executives, managers and employees. Armed with phones, faxes, computers, software and modems—the relatively inexpensive agents of this so-called work revolution— businesspeople could operate in such idyllic spots at Telluride, Colo., and Vermont.

Though there can be painful pitfalls to managing from afar, and the recession has put the plans of some would-be telecommuters on hold, the phenomenon appears to have taken hold nationally. What was once a fad is now an official trend that has attracted the inevitable cottage industry of associations and consultants. A recent telecommuting conference in Denver attracted more than 200 people.

Environmentalists are tapping the idea as a way to reduce air pollution in cities like Denver and Phoenix. Large corporations like AT&T are testing the concept, too, looking for happier, more productive employees—who take up less office space. And telecommunications gurus envision attacking unemployment in poor rural areas by wiring up entire communities to distant corporate headquarters.

But the telecommuting trailblazers for the most part have been independent businesspeople who seize the chance to shed the armor of a road warrior for the relative informality and calm of small-town life. "It used to be people could only afford to live in Vermont if they sacrificed their pocketbooks for quality of life," said Linda Dierks, director of the Brattleboro Area Chamber of Commerce. "But now, we're finding this fast-growing modem society."

Modems and faxes, as the long-armed tools of the trade, are obviously indispensable. But they need not be fancy, said Brent Bonwelli, manager of a Computerland store in Santa Fe. "Whether you're a poet or a business type, all you really need is the basic stuff," he said. For example, Randall Spinney, a management training consultant in Gilford, Vt., says he spent just a little more than $5,000 to set up his home office.

But if faxes and phone lines are the engines of the trend, they can also take telecommuters for a ride. Consider the experience of Joshua Freilich, who found out the hard way that an office with a view is sometimes no substitute for hands-on management.

Mr. Freilich, who owns an optical supply company in North Hollywood, Calif., started telecommuting from Santa Fe five years ago. He spent his time thinking about new products, long-range planning and advertising. He left customer relations and operating decisions to the team that remained behind. The result, as he describes it, was not good.

"When you're getting data from afar, you're not in touch with the soul of the business anymore," said Mr. Freilich, a burly 40-year-old fond of baseball shirts. "You don't know how customers are being treated over the phone because you're not there to hear it. You can see vendors are being paid on time by running reports here in Santa Fe, but you don't know how they are really being treated. That's what happened to me."

Mr. Freilich became aware of the problem at a trade show last fall where once-loyal customers complained about deficient shipments and inattentive service. "I was stunned," he recalled, adding that the problem had apparently been going on for a year. Rebuilding customer and vendor relations meant more involvement on his part, and Mr. Freilich now catches a 5 A.M. shuttle to the Albuquerque airport on Tuesdays so he can be in North Hollywood by 10 A.M. He's back in Santa Fe Thursday night in time to spend the weekend with his family.

"All the electronic communications are simply back-up," Mr. Freilich advises. "I just hadn't factored the importance of personal loyalty and contact into the equation, and I was very, very wrong."

Mr. Freilich's experience is probably not unique. Indeed, there aren't any statistics yet that show if telecommuting is good or bad for business or simply irrelevant, according to Richard Lowenberg, an expert on the subject who lives in Telluride. "Are workers more efficient or less efficient with the lack of management oversight? We don't know," he said.

Still, to converts like Mr. Kabbani, the risk is worth taking. Gesturing toward the mountains from his sun-splashed office, Mr. Kabbani has a simple piece of advice for those contemplating telecommuting. "Do it."

Poem on MBAs*

Simon Roman

Sir—There may be many American MBA's but their education is seldom impressive. They are often poor communicators, even if their secondary education has been of the literary European variety.

Far beyond Bermuda, beyond the Tempest's isle,
The Business Schools all chatter and, Oh, their speech is vile
They seek to turn out leaders, to make a business go,
Administrative experts, the civil GSO,
But yet this type of training full many a mind has blown
And left it almost speechless, no words to call its own.
Untaught in public speaking, mark how man's wit is slow,
Unversed in forceful writing, they wreak industrial woe,
Mewed up in penthouse office, the real world cramps their style.
They read accountants' fiction, from plant they run a mile.
For they have not the diction t'inspire the rank and file.
For all their thoughts are figures, as bottom line they toe,
But math don't cheer the workers, who find such men their foe!

---

*Reprinted by permission of *The Economist*.

The Wall Street Journal
Criticizing Your Boss*

Hendrie Weisinger and Norman M. Lobsenz

"Criticize my boss?" "I don't have the right to." "I'd get fired." "It's his company, not mine."

Many executives recognize that it's important to encourage criticism from their subordinates. Walking about United Airlines, Ed Carlson solicited criticism, both as a source of information and as a way of conveying respect to middle managers. At ITT, Harold Geneen was well-known for the way he bawled out subordinates, but he also structured the organization to encourage criticism of superiors, including himself. Mr. Geneen felt that criticism of superiors would enable problems to surface more quickly, so they could be nipped in the bud. Konosuke Matsushita built his namesake company with a philosophy stressing criticism as a form of self-discipline necessary to the growth of the individual and the company.

Unfortunately, not everyone has the good fortune to work in such companies. George Steinbrenner, owner of the New York Yankees, is said to have given manager Billy Martin a contract specifically prohibiting him from criticizing his superiors. And the business sections of newspapers and magazines are filled with examples of criticism of top executives with the source consciously being kept anonymous.

If you think things could be improved in your company, but aren't quite sure how your boss will respond to criticism, the following guidelines may be helpful:

1. Make sure it is appropriate to criticize your boss. You must have a direct line of communication to him, and his work must affect your job or the job of your subordinates. It is inappropriate to criticize your superior if his decisions or actions have nothing to do with you.

2. Acknowledge that the boss is the boss, that you are not claiming to be right while he or she is wrong. Any criticism that sets up a power struggle will make your superior more intent on defending his position. Phrase your remarks in a *two-sided solution*. Summarize the situation you believe should be changed; present your criticism as a productive alternative. By offering both sides of the situation you are, in effect, acknowledging your superior's view and defusing his need to defend it. The decision—to make a change or not—is left with the boss.

3. Build the validity of your criticism. By offering it as information you want to share for the common good, you maximize its importance. Cite authoritative sources, submit supporting data from objective and reliable sources. While Mr. Geneen welcomed criticism, he did not suffer fools. He demanded that his people have what he called "unshakable facts." Thus, instead of having to accept or reject a "criticism," your superior is in a position of evaluating material you supplied.

4. Ask for your superior's help in resolving the problem you are calling to his attention. By doing so you will not be "criticizing" your superior but seeming to criticize yourself by tak-

ing responsibility for the "problem." You are making your superior your ally. For example, if your boss is chronically late in providing you with data you need to function effectively, you can say, "I'm having trouble running my department when I don't have the necessary data on time. Can you give me some suggestions for improving this situation?" If your criticism is valid, chances are your superior will "solve the problem"—and resolve the criticism—by meeting his or her deadlines more promptly.

There also may be ways to determine how receptive your superior is to criticism. If he interacts with you outside of structured meetings, and if he is flexible enough to make changes in organizational policy from time to time, he probably tends to see criticism as a source of information rather than as an emotional attack. If your boss keeps to himself and seldom encourages change, criticism will probably not be acceptable despite its constructive intent, and you will likely be seen as a complainer.

What about those impossible bosses—the ones with short tempers, the ones who "never listen"? Can or should you attempt to offer criticism to them? Only if you can be clever and creative. Gear your strategy to this fundamental question: "How can I communicate this information so that my superior perceives it as being useful?"

The Wall Street Journal

More Corporate Chiefs Seek Direct Contact with Staff, Customers*

One Executive Interviews Employees at Breakfast; Others Try Spot-Checks Handpicking Boss's Potatoes

Thomas F. O'Boyle and Carol Hymowitz

WASHINGTON—J. Willard Marriott Jr., the chief executive officer of Marriott Corp., is wandering around the basement of his flagship hotel here. Randomly yanking a dinner plate out of a storage cabinet, he spots a splotch of dried food. "You really ought to soak some of these dishes," he reminds the hotel manager.

In Cupertino, Calif., James G. Treybig (pronounced try-big), the chief executive of Tandem Computers Inc., is peering into a computer terminal scanning the complaints and suggestions that he has solicited from managers and production workers.

And halfway across the world in Taiwan, Joseph A. Baute, the chief executive of Markem Corp., listens to a customer's complaint that orders of Markem's labeling machines aren't arriving on time. Within minutes, Mr. Baute is telephoning company headquarters in New Hampshire rearranging deliveries.

Firsthand Knowledge

These executives are among a small but growing number of corporate chiefs who are determined to know firsthand exactly what is happening to their companies and

---

who are willing to go out of their way to find out. As a result, they are breaking with management practices in vogue since the 1950s that emphasized an aloof, rigid financial analysis rather than direct contact.

Many chief executives are content to remain in headquarters suites, insulated from the day-to-day workings of their corporate kingdoms. Their information is gleaned from committee reports and financial statements, or it is passed on by layers of lower managers, who often filter out the bad news.

"The No. 1 managerial productivity problem in American is, quite simply, managers who are out of touch with their people and customers," asserts Thomas J. Peters, a management consultant and co-author of "In Search of Excellence." "The alternative doesn't come from computer printouts," he says. "It comes from wandering around, directly sampling employees' environments."

Many executives say they do that. But all too often, their visits to company facilities are mere formalities that yield little insight or new information. "It's easy for them to delude themselves into thinking they know what's going on, but it's a tremendous misconception," says Ralph Kilmann, a University of Pittsburgh business-school professor. Mr. Kilmann recalls an executive who described visits to several plants in which he waved to employees but never got out of his limousine.

Promotes Loyalty

The chief executives who reject this isolation often head new high-technology and service companies, rather than more mature—and more traditional—manufacturing concerns. Some have built their companies from scratch. They see management informed by firsthand knowledge as critical to forging a corporate environment that promotes employee and customer loyalty.

The executives have distinct styles of intelligence gathering. John Sculley, the president and chief executive of Apple Computer Inc., listens to customer com-

plaints on Apple's toll-free 800 number, and insists that other top executives do the same. John B. McCoy, the president of Bank One Corp. in Columbus, Ohio, reads "exit" interviews with employees who leave the company.

Richard G. Rogers, the president of Syntex Corp., a pharmaceutical maker, eats breakfast each morning at 7:30 in the employee cafeteria in Palo Alto, Calif. Over coffee and toast, he queries employees, and in exchange he is often asked to give career counseling and advice.

Of course, this direct approach can't replace financial analysis and other standard management tools. There is also a risk that executives who spend too much time gathering minute details may miss the broader picture. Then, too, actually obtaining reliable information can be difficult because employees, fearing retaliation, may withhold or distort facts.

False Data

Sometimes information gathering can border on spying. A chief executive at a publishing company used to read the messages that employees had left in the company's computer system. A chief executive at a large Midwestern manufacturing concern acknowledges that during a strike he got information from certain managers who were friendly to the union and used those managers to transmit false information he knew would frighten the strikers. The false information involved the suggestion that the company planned to contract out work to nonunion employees.

Nevertheless, experts say, management based on direct knowledge offers benefits that outweigh being aloof and out of touch. The advantages were apparent at Marriott Corp., where the practice is a family tradition begun by J. Willard Sr., Mr. Marriott's father. With his wife, Alice, the senior Mr. Marriott visited his Hot Shoppes restaurants constantly, ordering meals, talking to customers and employees, even rummaging through garbage cans to check for waste.

Now the Marriott empire is a lot bigger.

The younger Mr. Marriott, now 52 years old, estimates he logged 200,000 miles last year visiting more than 100 of the chain's 141 hotels and resorts.

Often he checks out his hotels at odd hours: midnight in the kitchen, for instance, or 5 A.M. in the laundry room. "When you start trying to anticipate what he'll find, you get better as a manager," says John Dixon, the general manager of the new JW Marriott hotel here.

On a recent visit, Mr. Marriott found plenty. Seconds after entering the atrium-style lobby, his eyes darted left to a pink marble pillar. On a visit to the hotel a few weeks before, Mr. Marriott had noticed an unwaxed strip about half an inch wide circling the pillar's base. "I see you cleared up that problem. Looks good," he said approvingly, shaking Mr. Dixon's hand.

A few minutes later, Mr. Marriott was in the kitchen. Looking like a man running for office, he greeted about a dozen employees with firm pumps of the hand, a broad smile, and a "Hi, how ya doin'?" He addressed a few of the old-timers by their first names and embraced one.

Then he grimaced as he discovered a batch of hash browns left over from breakfast two hours earlier, a violation of one of the strict written rules that dictate food portions and preparations. "This is a penny business," says Wes Merhige, the general manager of the Santa Clara, Calif., Marriott, "and Bill knows how to keep track of the pennies."

Before his two-hour tour ended, Mr. Marriott peeked in on the front desk, the laundry ("good, no wrinkles"), the loading dock, the exercise spa, storage lockers ("what's hidden in here?"), and about half a dozen rooms and suites. At the employee cafeteria, he swept through the room shaking hands with at least 50 startled workers.

In fact, Mr. Marriott is so involved in every detail of his business that he selects the color of the carpeting for hotel lobbies. Some managers argue that this style can usurp decision making from lower levels and cause resentment. But Marriott Hotels' occupancy rate is 10% above the industry average, and Mr. Marriott believes his involvement has given the company an advantage. "The edge in this business is people," he says. "I'm trying to communicate that I care and that the role they play in the organization is an extremely vital one."

While Mr. Marriott queries employees, Mr. Baute, the plain-spoken 57-year-old chief executive of Markem Corp., calls on customers, especially those with complaints. "I don't like to make honey-and-roses calls," he says. "I like to go where I can make a difference." Besides, he adds, "if you only want to hear the good news, you miss most of what's happening."

During a recent trip to the Far East, Mr. Baute visited a customer in Tokyo who was having difficulty using one of Markem's printing machines. After a quick call to a company engineer, Mr. Baute was able to show the customer how to adjust the machine.

Sometimes a customer's complaints aren't justified. "I've had people tell me that we didn't send them what they wanted only to find out later that they didn't order correctly," he says, noting that "you have to be careful to check out the information you collect."

Nevertheless, Mr. Baute, who spends 25% of his time visiting customers, believes his emphasis on service has helped Markem enlarge its market and win back a few disgruntled buyers since he took over as chief executive four years ago. Revenue at the closely held company last year approached $100 million.

Customer Complaints

At Markem's Keene, N.H., headquarters, Mr. Baute answers his own office phone. He also insists that the company's 1,200 managers and workers listen to tapes of customers from more than a dozen industries, describing their diverse needs. "It's not Joe the chairman talking, it's the person paying the bills," he says. "There's a lot more credibility when employees hear complaints directly from the customer."

Not all direct contact yields reliable

information. As chief executive of Frito-Lay Inc., Michael H. Jordan used to marvel at the quality of the potato chips he sampled at the company's Dallas plant. Then he discovered that plant supervisors hand-picked potatoes in preparation for his visits and made sure he sampled only perfectly shaped chips. From then on, Mr. Jordan sampled potato chips that he purchased off supermarket shelves.

Embarrassing Questions

In another attempt to get the facts, Mr. Jordan, who is now the executive vice president of parent PepsiCo Inc., installed a computer terminal at his desk to monitor business. The computer provided him with data on everything from inventories and sales to marketing. "I wanted some raw facts that hadn't been scrubbed by layers of management," he explains.

To uncover the truth, executives also have to overcome human obstacles. Workers may feel intimidated and awkward talking openly to the top boss. "When I first started visiting plants, managers were apprehensive," says Markem's Mr. Baute. "They thought workers might ask embarrassing questions, like why didn't they get raises." But, as it turned out, "employees were afraid. We had to work like the dickens to convince them there would be no retribution" if they spoke honestly.

Quentin C. McKenna, the chief executive of Kennametal Inc., a Latrobe, Pa., cutting-tool maker, always travels alone when visiting one of the company's 43 manufacturing and sales sites. It's an approach he adopted three years ago in a effort to raise employee productivity and involvement. His visits are announced—a surprise call once caused "panic" among workers, he says. But by traveling without an entourage of public-relations staff and other corporate lieutenants, he believes he can communicate more easily.

One of his techniques: randomly inviting half a dozen employees to lunch or dinner when he visits their plant. Some employees think the invitation is a prank, and a few even decline. But those who do

accept usually provide Mr. McKenna with valuable information. He learned of a union organizing drive at one plant, and at another he discovered that an expensive piece of new equipment wasn't operating.

Rapid Growth

Maintaining contact with employees requires an enormous commitment, executives at many high-growth companies have discovered. At People Express Airlines, for example, Donald C. Burr, the chief executive and founder, acknowledges that "people can get lost quickly when you have very rapid growth." In just four years, the airline, now the nation's 12th-largest carrier, has expanded to 4,000 employees from 250.

Mr. Burr, who requires all employees to do a variety of jobs, used to share tasks, too, from taking reservations to checking baggage. "We'd all put in 12-hour days and share pizza at the end," recalls Gail Taylor-May, a customer-service manager at People's Pittsburgh terminal and one of its first employees. Today, she says, there are newer employees who wouldn't know top executives if they saw them.

Mr. Burr still lectures at orientation sessions for new employees, and, to create more of a community feeling, he is reorganizing the company into smaller operating units. But, he laments, "I can't afford to spend all my time traveling around the system. I have to rely on other people's eyes and ears."

Checks Facts

Other companies, such as Tandem Computers, use technology to link the chief executive with employees. Every morning Mr. Treybig of Tandem switches on his computer terminal and reads at least two dozen new messages from virtually every department and rank in the company. One recent message came from an employee in Austin, Texas, who complained that co-workers who had worked for his supervisor at another company were being favored for promotions. When Mr. Treybig checked out the complaint, he found that it was false—and wrote the employee directly to quell his concerns.

Another communications technique is the "beer busts" Tandem holds every Friday afternoon at each of the computer maker's 132 offices world-wide. The intention, says Mr. Treybig, who founded the company in 1974, is to create an informal environment where employees, including himself, can exchange ideas. "People feel intimidated to walk into your office," he says. But over beer and popcorn, "employees are more willing to talk openly."

Mr. Treybig believes that the "beer busts" and electronic mail have helped give Tandem a turnover rate that is half that of competing high-technology companies in Silicon Valley; three-quarters of the 32 original employees are still with Tandem today.

One employee, recalling how he has seen a sweating Mr. Treybig in shorts walking through the company lobby after his daily jog, says, "It makes me comfortable to know that the president is one of the guys. This is a human company."

◆

The Manager: Master and Servant of Power[*]

Fernando Bartolomé and André Laurent

Most managers are action oriented. As a result, many are not inclined to be introspective about how they relate to others on the job. They don't fully realize, for example, how power differences can disturb interpersonal relations at work and, consequently, undermine organizational effectiveness.

Let's look at three typical problems:

Brian Dolan and John Miller, both senior engineers in an electronics company, had worked well as colleagues in their company's R&D department. Their relationship was friendly and informal. Each felt free to drop in unannounced on the other to discuss technical problems or swap company gossip.

Then Brian was promoted to director of R&D, and shortly thereafter he called John and asked him to come to his office to discuss installation plans for the company's new computer-aided design system. The call puzzled and angered John. Brian was only two doors away. Why didn't he just drop by? After all, they were good friends. Why did he have to play the boss? When John went to Brian's office, it was all he could do to hide his irritation. Brian greeted him warmly, but John was reserved during their discussion.

Why, Brian wondered on the trip home that evening, had John acted so oddly? Was it because he had been promoted and not John? That had to be it. John was jealous. John, on the other hand, didn't understand how Brian's new position could make him insensitive to how John might react.

Mary Scarpa, divisional director for a specialty steel fabricator, asked Roger Harrison, a middle manager, for his opinion on a major capital investment decision she was about to make. Roger had serious reservations about the assumptions underlying her cash flow projections. He wanted to level with her, but he also worried that honest criticism would upset her. He knew Mary could be very touchy. Although she had asked for candid feedback, Roger wasn't sure she really meant it; he sensed she really wanted reinforcement. Feeling caught in a bind, Roger conveniently "forgot" her request.

Annoyed by Roger's behavior, Mary complained to a colleague at another company about problems with her subordinates, saying they just wouldn't stick their necks out. They were afraid to give honest opinions because they were insecure, she said. On his part, Roger was insensitive to the reasons why bosses may find it risky to have subordinates challenge their judgment, even when they ask for it.

Dick Rapp, vice president of production for a household appliance manufacturer, told his subordinates that his priority was quality control and cost containment. He wanted defect and scrap rates brought down. He wanted the division to be results driven, not rule driven. "If you have to bend a rule to get the job done, do it," Rapp would say.

His employees took him at his word at first and assumed that any improvement in efficiency would be welcome. But they quickly learned otherwise. Dick Rapp cared as much about style and form as he did about substance. How memos were worded and typed, for example, seemed to concern him as much as what they said. He also chewed out several plant supervisors for approving ad hoc scheduling and other changes and not going through the chain of command.

Understandably, this behavior frustrated Dick's subordinates. They faced conflicting expectations, and they had to take time away from important tasks to meet what they considered frivolous demands. No one tried to understand, though, why bosses prefer to have things done their way and how this may be their means of heightening their feelings of being in control and reducing uncertainty. And nobody dared to explore these issues with Dick, nor could he see that he was sending mixed messages and burying people in the very red tape he wanted them to cut through.

How did these situations develop? Did Brian Dolan subconsciously need to pull rank on subordinates? Did Mary Scarpa relish putting her employees in a double bind? Did Dick Rapp enjoy tripping up his people? Were the subordinates rebellious people, unwilling to accept authority and take direction?

Such problems occur with surprising frequency in work situations. Usually they arise not because superiors are inherently insensitive or power hungry or because subordinates are naturally rebellious but because people don't understand how strongly hierarchical position affects behavior in organizations. Workplace conflicts are often attributed to personality differences, but the root of the problem is usually structural. The organization's power hierarchy can distort mutual expectations.

POWER IN THE ORGANIZATION

Unevenness of power in the organization subtly influences how managers and subordinates relate to each other. Mary couldn't understand Roger's reticence. But if she had reflected on her own experiences as a subordinate, she might have realized that she too had been cautious at times about giving honest feedback to superiors. Had Brian been able to put himself in John's shoes and think of a new

R&D director officiously summoning *him,* he might have better understood John's behavior.

Dick was a results-driven manager who said he cared about quality, not style. Today he works for superiors whose preference for ritualistic, by-the-book action frustrates him. Yet he can't see that he's doing the same thing. He doesn't relate to his own experience as a subordinate to the feelings and behavior of the people working for him.

Brian, Mary, and Dick all had trouble putting themselves in their subordinates' shoes. In subordinate roles, on the other hand, John and Roger couldn't see how it might feel to be a boss. This lack of sensitivity on both sides can have ripple effects throughout the organization. Managers who believe they are on the receiving end of unreasonable or unfair actions from their bosses, for example, may act similarly toward those below them in the organizational pyramid. And the pattern may repeat itself down the chain of command. Or relations with peers may suffer. A troubled relationship at one level can affect many other relationships.

When superiors can't see how their behavior affects their subordinates, their authority may also deteriorate. Most bosses know instinctively that their power depends more on employees' compliance than on threats or sanctions. When managers create no-win situations for people, as Mary did, or make confusing demands on workers, as did Dick, subordinates may respond by losing enthusiasm or withdrawing commitment. If workers think they've been put in impossible situations or if a superior's exaggerated need for power makes them feel inferior, they may give the company their worst rather than their best. The response could mean just going through the motions of the job or even sabotaging organizational goals.

True, managers have power. They can call on official sanctions for punishing uncooperative subordinates. But such blatant use of their clout is rarely able to restore effective working relationships. It is a weak rather than a strong pillar of authority.

There are other consequences arising from this asymmetry in power relations and role perceptions, as we can see when we look at managers as subordinates. If the danger for superiors is being insufficiently sensitive about their subordinates' potential reactions, the danger for subordinates tends to be excessive concern about superiors' potential reactions. Managers who worry excessively about offending their bosses are much less likely to defend subordinates when higher-ups deal unfairly with them.

But if a manager doesn't defend subordinates, he or she will lose their respect. When subordinates sense that the boss won't defend them against unfairness, their morale will plummet and they will withdraw commitment to the job. A vicious circle results. As their performance deteriorates, their superior's position weakens further. The boss will receive fewer rewards and resources to dispense to subordinates, thus further undermining his or her effectiveness as distinct from merely titular authority.

It's ironic that so many managers are insensitive to this problem because almost all managers occupy a dual position in the organization. They have subordinates who report to them, and they report to superiors. Being both masters and servants of power, they should be able to understand the perspectives of the two groups of people who play the most important roles in their professional lives—namely, their superiors and subordinates.

To probe this duality of the manager's role and the sharp differences in expectations that power differences create, we recently collected questionnaires from 105 executives of major companies. We divided the people into two similar groups, matched according to age, management position, and other characteristics. We asked one group of managers to describe the expectations they had for their superiors, the second, to describe expectations for subordinates. In addition, we had conversations with a number of the executives we surveyed.

. . . The expectations of the two groups differed sharply. Of the managers we asked to take the superior role, 78% said they are primarily concerned about subordinates' performance. A majority also said they expect subordinates to be loyal and honest. A typical comment was "I expect effective performance and loyalty even when difficult or unpleasant duties have to be performed."

The superiors we talked to view loyalty, honesty, and performance as linked. They also see honest communication and a willingness to follow orders as necessary to get the job done. But at the same time, they don't see the potential conflict that lies in demanding loyalty and desiring honesty and frankness from subordinates. Many seem unaware of the extent to which they confuse loyalty with agreement and obedience. They also seem to underestimate the difficulty subordinates have in being honest about their own problems or weaknesses with people who have so much influence on their careers.

What happens when the shoe is on the other foot?

When managers take the subordinate position, they expect leadership and good communication from their superiors. A director of finance we talked to said, "I expect my superior to give me clear messages about what he expects from me." A vice president of engineering commented, "The boss should establish his requirements absolutely clearly."

Why do subordinates want clear communication and decisive leadership from their superiors? One reason is that they need reassurance that their bosses are competent. Clear communication is a good measure of competence. Subordinates also want to minimize uncertainty in their environment. Clear communication reduces guesswork. But decisiveness and clarity of communication alone aren't enough. Our interviews revealed that subordinates also want consistency.

Managers in both interview groups gave initiative and autonomy much lower ratings than we had expected. Fewer than a third of the people who took the superior role said they expect initiative from subordinates. Only 37% of those in the subordinate position said it is important for their superiors to grant them autonomy. This is odd when one considers how strongly management experts today endorse job autonomy and broad participation in decision making.

Subordinates don't want superiors to be constantly peering over their shoulders. Instead, they want enough leeway to do the jobs as they see fit. "The boss shouldn't interfere in details," a sales manager said, and "My manager should give me enough space to do my job," said an administrative officer.

Subordinates also want fair performance appraisals, support, and encouragement. Another sales manager said, "My superior should show fairness, objectivity, honesty, and a willingness to give feedback without my having to ask for it." A division manager answered, "I expect help, encouragement, and coaching, and the opportunity to learn from my mistakes." And an R&D director reported, "I expect support in conflict situations."

Managers as Superiors

As bosses, managers are not only often unaware of how they misuse their power in relation to subordinates, but they are also frequently unaware of the contradictory messages they send and their motives for doing so. For example, they may tell subordinates that they expect them to be candid and to feel free to offer criticism. Yet at the same time, they communicate disapproval of candid feedback through subtle and sometimes not so subtle cues.

Managers may even confuse excessive deference (pleasing behavior) with the normal level of compliance that they feel they have a legitimate right to expect. They may not see the ways in which they signal to subordinates demands for excessively deferential behavior—and they are also often unaware of the deep resentment that these demands produce.

In the superior role, most managers say that they are more concerned about their subordinates' performance than with obedience for its own sake or with workers doing things the boss's way. Despite the overt message they send, however—"good performance is what really counts in my department"—many managers communicate subtly to subordinates that obedience and deference are just as important, if not more so. This is usually subconscious on the managers' part.

Most executives have trouble learning about the expectations their subordinates have of them simply because they are rarely forthright about how they'd like *their* bosses to behave. Actually, most subordinates work hard to adapt their behavior to what they think the boss expects. Although the chief's actions may be very frustrating to them, few will express openly their dislike of the behavior or try to persuade the boss to change—even when invited to criticize.

This reticence can lead to surprising angry outbursts when smoldering resentment suddenly surfaces. The superior ends up wondering, "Why didn't you come to me earlier with this problem?" Bosses will often deny blame and claim they've always had an open-door policy. Many apparently assume that such a policy alone is sufficient to guarantee a fully open relationship and to minimize the effects of power.

Managers as Subordinates

As subordinates, managers develop an exaggerated concern over pleasing their bosses because they believe they have very little power to change the superior's behavior. Whatever the boss's rhetoric may be, they are convinced they know the real score. As a result, they spend much time scrutinizing the boss's behavior for cues that indicate approval or disapproval.

As one manager put it, "I suppose it's true: I study [my manager's] likes, dislikes, and other personal tastes; his objectives and motivations and the time pressure he may be under." One division head said of his superior, "I take into account how his thinking differs from mine, what things he is likely to view in a different way."

Managers as superiors know how much they depend on their subordinates' performance and, therefore, how much real power, as opposed to formal power, their subordinates have over them. But when bosses are subordinates, they often forget this reality of organizational life. They forget that the boss's performance depends heavily on how committed the subordinates are to their jobs and on the quality of their work. Consequently, the subordinates often seem to focus too much on accommodating their superiors' stylistic preferences and not enough on performance per se. They don't always recognize that they possess real power that they can use with their bosses to negotiate and obtain satisfaction for their legitimate needs and demands. They seem unable to transfer their experiences as bosses to their behavior as subordinates.

Because subordinates perceive themselves as being too weak to alter their superiors' behavior, managers in the subordinate role are extremely concerned with whether they have a natural match ("good chemistry") with their bosses. When relating to subordinates, on the other hand, managers don't seem concerned about compatibility. They assume that their subordinates can easily learn to conform to their expectations and that this reshaping of behavior will not harm the organization. In reality, however, having to adapt like this is likely to keep subordinates from making a full contribution. In most cases, inhibiting people this way creates resentment.

CONSEQUENCES OF POWER

When managers fail to understand how deeply the unequal distribution of power can hurt interpersonal relations and productivity, serious problems can arise from the organization. The most important and pervasive negative effect of the hierarchical structure can be summarized in the saying, "Trust flees authority." Good ideas often remain unexpressed because subordinates believe they will be punished for disagreeing with their superiors or showing too much competence. Honest feedback about the superior's managerial style is withheld because subordinates are afraid they'll be blackballed when decisions on promotions are made.

Reducing the upward flow of ideas and feedback can have many adverse consequences. Take, for example, the many MBO programs that run into difficulty. An honest contract between superiors and subordinates, based on a fair exchange of contributions and rewards between the individuals and the organization, should be at the core of an MBO program. This is only possible, however, if subordinates feel that they will not be punished for defending their interests or balking at unreasonable demands from the top. Unfair MBO agreements may work in the short term, but they will usually fail in the long haul.

When managers are dissatisfied with the contracts they have with their bosses, unfair contracts may follow at each level down the ladder. Such a pattern can damage management's credibility as well as the whole organization's authority.

What Can Managers Do?

Nobody is to blame for these distortions of hierarchical power. The problem is inherent in organizational life because authority differences are both inevitable and also functional to a degree. The problem cannot be avoided, but it can be controlled if managers strive to link their two roles as masters and servants of power.

When they are in the superior role, they should ask themselves, "How would I feel if my boss behaved this way or demanded this of me?" For example, Brian in our first case might have stopped to think, "I need to talk to John, but if I summon him, he may think I'm trying to remind him that I got the promotion and he didn't. And why, after all, am I doing this? Can't I get the information just as well by phone? Come to think of it, I remember the time I got angry when *my* boss asked me to come running on a moment's notice."

Managers can also ask whether the tasks they assign to subordinates are truly critical to the job—as distinct from ritualistic demands motivated by an unconscious desire to show people that "rank has its privileges" or to reassure themselves that they can make people do what they want them to do. "Power: use it or lose it," as another saying goes.

The burden for getting relationships back on a healthy basis falls mainly to bosses because they have more power and because it would be unrealistic to expect subordinates to take the initiative and complain about their bosses' unreasonable or unfair conduct. Even if superiors encourage honest feedback, people rarely believe that they mean it. So, generally they won't risk testing the boss's sincerity.

When they are the superior, managers need to ask themselves, "What can I do to increase my employees' trust, or at least decrease their mistrust? What signals may indicate problems?" Managers need to learn to monitor subordinates' subtle cues. It helps to understand that it's easier for subordinates to learn about bosses' reactions and desires because superiors are more likely to express their feelings openly. By the same token, it's more difficult for bosses to find out their subordinates' real feelings; they're likely to express them indirectly and with caution.

Directly questioning subordinates rarely works when you're trying to find out what's wrong. Managers must look for subtle cues. Eventually, they can create the necessary atmosphere of trust for solving problems, but they can't do it instantly. It will come only from consistently demonstrating fairness and honesty toward the people working for them.

In the subordinate role, on the other hand, managers may find that they can more easily manage their relationships with superiors by just asking them what they want. This approach should work with competent and insightful superiors. But for some people, asking questions may not be enough; observing behavior is often equally important. Once again, the managerial subordinate should take advantage of his or her own experience as a boss and ask, "What do I care most about when I'm in the superior role?" Managers who can answer this question insightfully and realistically should be able to move ahead in the important process of understanding and managing their own superiors.

Chapter 6

Controlling

I t should come as no surprise that some of the themes treated in Chapter 4—"Influence"—will reappear in the current chapter on controlling. "Controlling" is concerned with how managers get diverse individuals to move in some common direction and how organizations interact with their environments.

In fact, most of the previous chapters have shared a number of specific themes. One such theme is that organizations are composed of individuals who have needs and interests that are, at least in part, unique to themselves. A second is that organizations superimpose formal systems on informal relationships among the people within the organization, creating new patterns of relationships and new sets of interests. Third, a major function of managing is achieving coordination among individuals and groups with these diverse interests.

The sections on organizing, influencing, and telecommuting illustrate a number of ways that managers work to achieve such coordination. A fundamental question is: How does controlling differ from these other activities? In an important way, it does not—controlling entails a set of activities designed to achieve coordination. On the other hand, "controlling" has a quite different connotation than do "influencing" and "communicating." "Controlling" implies greater inequalities of power and less mutuality than do the others. For instance, Webster's dictionary defines the verb "control" as "To have under command; to regulate; to check; to restrain; to direct."[1] In contrast, "to influence" is defined as "To act on the mind, to sway, to bias, to induce."[2] These differences in definition and connotation are important. Guided by the word "control" and the connotations it evokes, managers' efforts to coordinate may often lead them to mechanistic approaches that are detached from the organic system they are attempting to improve. The reality of the matter is that they need to balance individual interests with the interests of the organization as a whole.

On the other hand, control can be quite flexible. (See, for example, "Mrs. Fields' Secret Ingredient" in this chapter). The key to successful control is fit. Regardless of the type of control device, it must be suited to the requirements of the organization and not become an end in itself. Also, people in the system must understand the method of control, and this method must be perceived as consistent with the current system. If it is not, the results can be disastrous. All of us can cite examples where a control system itself interferes with the organization achieving its ends. When employees become concerned with looking good as judged by standards that are only partially related to the goals of the organization, something is wrong with the control system.

One of the most intriguing features of the control system's fit at Mrs. Fields is the ability it gives top-level managers to exercise a general control while *helping* the local store owners to do their work and allowing sufficient flexibility to adapt to the daily weather conditions of each local franchise.

Whereas the control problem for a franchise operation such as Mrs. Fields is to exercise a necessary amount of central control while allowing the local units to operate independently enough to adapt to their particular conditions, the problems presented during a merger are quite different. These problems stem from the need to make previously high autonomous units into one unit. It is increasingly recognized that many seemingly very logical mergers fail because of problems in integrating two social systems. Claudia Deutsch's account of the merger of CNBC and FNN, two previously antagonistic news broadcast organizations, highlights some of these problems. Deutsch refers to largely symbolic gestures by CNBC, such as taking group photos and combining labels, as "bordering on the hokey." Since this selection is brief, it only highlights some of the concerns and actions. Nevertheless, it captures many of the salient topics that research has found interfere with the success of mergers. Establishing control without crushing an acquired unit and allowing the acquired managers to maintain their status and esteem are every bit as sensitive problems as the one faced by a franchise operation such as Mrs. Fields in exercising general direction while allowing the autonomy necessary to adapt to conditions at local levels. Taken together, the themes of these two selections highlight the general problems of exercising control in modern organizations.

In the next selection, "Increasingly, A Prison Term is the Price Paid by Polluters," Allan Gold raises a number of issues involved in controlling large organizations. Among these are the question of how a society can induce large organizations to behave so as not to harm the physical environment. The possibility that high-level executives may go to jail for violating fairly technically based laws raises a special question of control for these executives: "How can I control such aspects of this large system—where a very low-level employee may dump a barrel of waste—without engaging in excessive micromanagement?" Gold's article raises another question of control: How can society control the actions of the people to whom it assigns governmental roles so that they exercise their power fairly and responsibly? Gold's piece makes it clear that the problems of control in managerial reality surpass the bounds of individual organizations.

The next selection deals with another control issue that exceeds boundaries. A problem of control that has received a great deal of attention in the news recently as well as in academic discussions, is the so-called agency problem concerning the ability of shareholders to exercise control over the executives and other managers who are hired as agents to run the company in their interest. Recent research has indicated that the compensation of high-level executives is not closely related to the performance of the corporations they lead. In their study of executive compensation in 1,400 publicly-held companies from 1974 to 1988, Jensen and Murphy (1990) found that for the median CEO of the 250 largest companies, a $1,000 change in corporate value corresponded to a change in salary and bonus of only 6.7 cents over two years. In "Executives, Take Your Risks," Claudia Deutsch describes several attempts of companies to try to align the incentives of their executives more closely with the interests of stockholders. Deutsch views the problem in terms of inducing appropriate levels of risk and points to the concern that executives might leave in bad times. In contrast, Jensen and Murphy's research lead them to be concerned with the other edge of the matter—the possibility that the absence of performance-related pay reduces the incentives of the "best and brightest" to pursue careers in top management. Despite these differing concerns, they would seem to support, for quite different reasons, the desirability of linking the pay of executives more directly to the financial performance of their companies. Such linkages would enhance the ability of stockholders to control the actions of their executives largely through traditional market forces. We encourage you to consider two questions. What would be the likely consequence of movement in this direction? Why does executive pay appear to be as lowly correlated with a company's financial performance as both Deutsch and Jensen and Murphy suggest?

In the final selection in this chapter, George Tamke describes his approach for taking control of an organization he is put in charge of. We have found that many people come away from Tamke's article believing that he has provided a useful guide for managers in a wide variety of situations. While we see some merit in such a conclusion, it is important to note that much of his experience involved entering organizations that were experiencing "visible problems." Nevertheless, if we understand why some of Tamke's methods work, we probably have learned a great deal about leadership and the exercise of effective control in organizations.

Notes

1. *Webster's Dictionary* (Larchmont, NY: Book Essentials Publications, 1981), p. 86.
2. Ibid.

References

M. C. Jensen and Kevin Murphy (1990). CEO Incentives—It's Not How Much You Pay, But How.

Harvard Business Review. May/June 1990, 138–153.

---◆---

Mrs. Fields' Secret Ingredient[*]

The real recipe behind the phenomenal growth of Mrs. Fields Cookies cannot be found in the dough

Tom Richman

Part of the late Buckminster Fuller's genius was his capacity to transform a technology from the merely new to the truly useful by creating a new form to take advantage of its characteristics. Fuller's geodesic designs, for instance, endowed plastic with practical value as a building material. His structures, if not always eye-appealing, still achieved elegance—as mathematicians use the word to connote simplicity—of function. Once, reacting to someone's suggestion that a new technology be applied to an old process in a particularly awkward way, Fuller said dismissively, "That would be like putting an outboard motor on a skyscraper."

Introducing microcomputers with spreadsheet and word-processing software to a company originally designed around paper technology amounts to the same thing. If the form of the company doesn't change, the computer, like the outboard, is just a doodad. Faster long division and speedier typing don't move a company into the information age.

But Randy Fields has created something entirely new—*a* shape if not *the* shape, of business organizations to come. It gives top management a dimension of personal control over dispersed operations that small companies otherwise find impossible to achieve. It projects a founder's vision into parts of a company that have long ago outgrown his or her ability to reach in person.

In the structure that Fields is building, computers don't just speed up old administrative management processes. They alter the process. Management, in the Fields organizational paradigm, becomes less administration and more inspiration. The management hierarchy of the company *feels* almost flat.

What's the successful computer-age business going to look like in the not-very-distant future? Something like Randy Fields' concept—which is, in a word, neat.

What makes it neat, right out of the oven, is where he's doing it. Randy Fields, age 40, is married to Debbi Fields, who turns 31 this month, and together they run Mrs. Fields Cookies, of Park City, Utah (see "A Tale of Two Companies," *Inc.*, July 1984). They project that by year end, their business will comprise nearly 500 company-owned stores in 37 states selling what Debbi calls a "feel-good feeling." That sounds a little hokey. A lot of her cookie talk does. "Good enough never is," she likes to remind the people around her.

But there's nothing hokey about the 18.5% that Mrs. Fields Inc. earned on cookie sales of $87 million last year, up from $72.6 million a year earlier.

Won't the cookie craze pass? people often ask Debbi. "I think that's very doubtful. . . I mean," she says, "if (they are) fresh, warm, and wonderful and make you feel good, are you going to stop buying cookies?"

Maybe not, but the trick for her and her husband is to see that people keep buying them from Mrs. Fields, not David's Cookies, Blue Chip Cookies, The Original Great Chocolate Chip Cookie, or the dozens of regional and local competitors. Keeping the cookies consistently fresh, warm, and wonderful at nearly 500 retail cookie stores spread over the United States and five other countries can't be simple or easy. Worse, keeping smiles on the faces of the nearly 4,500, mostly young, store employees—not to mention keeping them productive and honest—is a bigger chore than most companies would dare to take on alone.

Most don't; they franchise, which is one way to bring responsibility and accountability down to the store level in a far-flung, multi-store organization. For this, the franchisor trades off revenues and profits that would otherwise be his and a large measure of flexibility. Because its terms are defined by contract, the relationship between franchisor and franchisee is more static than dynamic, difficult to alter as the market and the business change.

Mrs. Fields Cookies, despite its size, has not franchised—persuasive evidence in itself that the Fieldses have built something unusual. Randy Fields believes that no other U.S. food retailer with so many outlets has dared to retain this degree of direct, day-to-day control of its stores. And Mrs. Fields Cookies does it with a headquarters staff of just 115 people. That's approximately one staffer to every five stores—piddling compared with other companies with far fewer stores to manage. When the company bought La Petite Boulangerie from PepsiCo earlier this year, for instance, the soft-drink giant had 53 headquarters staff people to administer the French bakery/sandwich shop chain's 119 stores. Randy needed just four weeks to cut the number to 3 people.

On paper, Mrs. Fields Cookies *looks* almost conventional. In action, however, because of the way information flows between levels, it *feels* almost flat.

On paper, between Richard Lui running the Pier 39 Mrs. Fields in San Francisco and Debbi herself in Park City, there are several apparently traditional layers of hierarchy: an area sales manager, a district sales manager, a regional director of operations, a vice-president of operations. In practice, though, Debbi is as handy to Lui—and to every other store manager—as the telephone and personal computer in the back room of his store.

On a typical morning at Pier 39, Lui unlocks the store, calls up the Day Planner program on his Tandy computer, plugs in today's sales projection (based on year-earlier sales adjusted for growth), and answers a couple of questions the program puts to him. What day of the week is it? What type of day: normal day, sale day, school day, holiday, other?

Say, for instance, it's Tuesday, a school day. The computer goes back to the Pier 39 store's hour-by-hour, product-by-product performance on the last three school-day Tuesdays. Based on what you did then, the Day Planner tells him, here's what you'll have to do today, hour by hour, product by product, to meet your sales projection. It tells him how many customers he'll need each hour and how much he'll have to sell them. It tells him how many batches of cookie dough he'll have to mix and when to mix them to meet the demand and to minimize leftovers. He could make these estimates himself if he wanted to take the time. The computer makes them for him.

Each hour, as the day progresses, Lui keeps the computer informed of his progress. Currently he enters the numbers manually, but new cash registers that automatically feed hourly data to the computer, eliminating the manual update, are already in some stores. The computer in turn revises the hourly projections and makes suggestions. The customer count is OK, it might observe, but your average check is down. Are your crew members doing enough suggestive selling? If, on the other hand, the computer indicates that the customer count is down, that may suggest the manager will want to do some sampling—chum for customers up and down the pier with a tray of free cookie pieces or try something else, whatever he likes, to lure people into the store. Sometimes, if sales are just slightly down, the machine's revised projections will actually exceed the original on the assumption that greater selling effort will more than compensate for the small deficit. On the other hand, the program isn't blind to reality. It recognizes a bad day and diminishes its hourly sales projections and baking estimates accordingly.

Hourly sales goals?

Well, when Debbi was running *her* store, *she* set hourly sales goals. Her managers should, too, she thinks. Rather than enforce the practice through dicta, Randy has embedded the notion in the software that each store manager relies on. Do managers find the machine's suggestions intrusive? Not Lui. "It's a tool for me," he says.

Several times a week, Lui talks with Debbi. Well, he doesn't exactly talk *with* her, but he hears from her. He makes a daily phone call to Park City to check his computerized PhoneMail messages, and as often as not there's something from Mrs. Fields herself. If she's upset about some problem, Lui hears her sounding upset. If it's something she's breathlessly exuberant about, which is more often the case, he gets an earful of that, too. Whether the news is good or bad, how much better to hear it from the boss herself than to get a memo in the mail next week.

By the same token, if Lui has something to say to Debbi, he uses the computer. It's right there, handy. He calls up the FormMail program, types his message, and the next morning, it's on Debbi's desk. She promises an answer, from her or her staff, within 48 hours. On the morning I spent with her, among the dozen or so messages she got was one from the crew at a Berkeley, Calif., store making their case for higher wages there and another from the manager of a store in Brookline, Mass., which has been struggling recently. We've finally gotten ourselves squared away, was the gist of the note, so please come visit. (Last year Debbi logged around 350,000 commercial air miles visiting stores.)

Here are some other things Lui's computer can do for him.

Help him schedule crew. He plugs his daily sales projection for two weeks hence into a scheduling program that incorporates as its standards the times Debbi herself takes to perform the mixing, dropping, and baking chores. The program gives him back its best guess of how many people with which skill levels he'll need during which hours. A process that done manually consumed almost an hour now takes just a fraction of that time.

Help him interview crew applicants. He calls up his interview program, seats the applicant at the keyboard, and has him or her answer a series of questions. Based on the answers given by past hirees, the machine suggests to Lui which candidates will succeed or fail. It's still his choice. And any applicant, before a hire, will still get an audition—something to see how he or she performs in public. Maybe Lui will send the hopeful out on a sampling mission.

Help with personnel administration. Say he hires the applicant. He informs the machine, which generates a personnel folder and a payroll entry in Park City, and a few months later comes back to remind Lui that he hasn't submitted the initial evaluation (also by computer), which is now slightly past due. It administers the written part of the skills test and updates the records with the results. The entire Mrs. Fields personnel manual will soon be on the computer so that 500 store managers won't forget to delete old pages and insert revised ones every time a change is made.

Help with maintenance. A mixer isn't working, so the manager punches up the repair program on the computer. It asks him some questions, such as: is the plug in the wall? If the questions don't prompt a fix, the computer sends a repair request to Park City telling the staff there which machine is broken, its maintenance history, and which vendor to call. It sends a copy of the work order back to the store. When the work gets done, the store signs off by computer, and the vendor's bill gets paid.

That's a lot of technology applied to something as basic as a cookie store, but Randy had two objectives in mind.

He wanted to keep his wife in frequent, personal, two-way contact with hundreds of managers whose stores she couldn't possibly visit often enough. "The people who work in the stores," says Debbi, "are my customers. Staying in touch with them is the most important thing I can do."

It's no accident, even if Lui isn't consciously aware of why he does what he does, that he runs his store just about the same way that Debbi ran her first one 10 years ago. Even when she isn't there, she's there—in the standards built into his scheduling program, in the hourly goals, in the sampling and suggestive selling, on the phone. The technology has "leveraged," to use Randy's term, Debbi's ability to project her influence into more stores than she could ever reach effectively without it.

Second, Randy wanted to keep store managers managing, not sweating the paperwork. "In retailing," he says, "the goal is to keep people close to people. Whatever gets in the way of that—administration, telephones, ordering, and so on—is the enemy." If an administrative chore can be automated, it should be.

Store managers benefit from a continuing exchange of information. Of course, Park City learns what every store is doing daily—from sales to staffing to training to hires to repairs—and how it uses that information we'll get to in a minute. From the store manager's perspective, however, the important thing is that the information they provide keeps coming back to them, reorganized to make it useful. The hour-by-hour sales projections and projected customer counts that managers use to pace their days reflect their own experiences. Soon, for instance, the computer will take their weekly inventory reports and sales projections and generate supply orders that managers will only have to confirm or correct—more administrative time saved. With their little computers in the back room, store managers give, but they also receive.

What technology can do for operations it can also do for administration.

"We're all driven by Randy's philosophy that he wants the organization to be as flat as possible," says Paul Quinn, the company's director of management information systems (MIS).

"There are a few things, " says controller Lynn Quilter, "that Randy dislikes about growth. . . . He hates the thought of drowning in people so that he can't walk in and know exactly what each person does. . . . The second thing that drives him nuts is paper."

"The objective," says Randy, "is to leverage people—to get them to act when we have 1,000 stores the same way they acted when we had 30."

He has this theory that large organizations, organizations with lots of people, are, per se, inferior to small ones. Good people join a growing business because it offers them an opportunity to be creative. As the company grows, these people find they're tied up managing the latest hires. Creativity suffers. Entropy sets in. Randy uses technology to keep entropy at bay.

He began by automating rote clerical chores and by minimizing data-entry effort. Machines can sort and file faster than people, and sorting and filing is deadly dull work, anyway. Lately he's pushed the organization toward automated exception reporting for the same reason. Machines can compare actual results with expected results and flag the anomalies, which are all management really cares about anyway. And within a few years, Randy expects to go much further in his battle against bureaucracy by developing artificial-intelligence aids to the running of the business.

Understand that it's not equipment advances—state-of-the-art hardware—that's pushing Mrs. Fields Cookies toward management frontiers. The machines the company uses are strictly off the shelf: an IBM minicomputer connected to inexpensive personal computers. It is, instead, Randy's ability to create an elegant, functional software architecture. He has, of course, had an advantage that the leader of an older, more established company would not have. Because Mrs. Fields is still a young enough company, he doesn't have to shape his automated management system to a preexisting structure. Every new idea doesn't confront the opposition of some bureaucratic fiefdom's survival instinct. Rather, the people part and the technology part of the Fields organization are developing simultaneously, each shaped by the same philosophy.

You see this congruence at corporate headquarters and in the company's operational management organization.

Between Debbi as chief executive officer and the individual store managers is what seems on paper to be a conventional reporting structure with several layers of management. But there's an additional box on the organization chart. It's not another management layer. It transcends layers, changing the way information flows between them and even changing the functions of the layers.

The box consists of a group of seven so-called store controllers, working in Park City from the daily store reports and weekly inventory reports. They ride herd on the numbers. If a store's sales are dramatically off, the store controller covering that geographical region will be the first to know it. If there's a discrepancy between the inventory report, the daily report of batches of cookies baked, and the sales report, the controller will be the first to find it. (It is possible for a smart thief to steal judiciously for about a week from a Mrs. Fields store.) "We're a check on operations," says store controller Wendy Phelps, but she's far more than just a check. She's the other half of a manager's head.

Since she's on top of the numbers, the area, district, and regional managers don't have to be—not to the same degree, at any rate. "We want managers to be with people, not with problems," says Debbi. It's hard, Randy says, to find managers who are good with both people and numbers. People people, he thinks, should be in the field, with numbers people backing them up—but not second-guessing them. Here's where the company takes a meaningful twist.

Problems aren't reported up the organization just so solutions can flow back down. Instead, store controllers work at levels as low as they can. They go to the store manager if he's the one to fix a discrepancy, a missing report, for instance. Forget chain of command. "I'm very efficiency minded," says Randy.

So the technology gives the company an almost real-time look at the minutiae of its operations, and the organizational structure—putting function ahead of conventional protocol—keeps it from choking on this abundance of data.

Some managers would have problems with a system that operates without their daily intervention. They wouldn't be comfortable, and they wouldn't stay at Mrs. Fields. Those who do stay can manage people instead of paper.

If administrative bureaucracies can grow out of control, so can technology bureaucracies. A couple of principles, ruthlessly adhered to, keep both simple at Mrs. Fields.

The first is that if a machine can do it, a machine *should* do it. "People," says Randy, "should do only that which people can do. It's demeaning for people to do what machines can do. . . . Can machines manage people? No. Machines have no feelie-touchies, none of that chemistry that flows between two people."

The other rule, the one that keeps the technological monster itself in check, is that the company will have but one data base. Everything—cookie sales, payroll records, suppliers' invoices, inventory reports, utility charges—goes into the same data base. And whatever anybody needs to know has to come out of it.

Don't enforce this rule, and, says Randy, "the next thing you know you have 48 different programs that can't talk to each other." Technology grown rampant.

Having a single data base means, first, that nobody has to waste time filing triplicate forms or answering the same questions twice. "We capture the data just once," says controller Quilter.

Second, it means that the system itself can do most of the rote work that people used to do. Take orders for chocolate, for instance. The computer gets the weekly inventory report. It already knows the sales projection. So let the comput-er order the chocolate chips. Give the store manager a copy of the order on his screen so he can correct any errors, but why take his time to generate the order when he's got better things to do—like teaching someone to sell. Or, take it fur-ther. The machine generates the order. The supplier delivers the chips to the store and bills the corporate office. A clerk in the office now has to compare the order, the invoice, and what the store says it got. Do they all match? Yes. She tells the computer to write a check. The more stores you have, the more clerks it takes. Why not let the computer do the matching? In fact, if everything fits, why get peo-ple involved at all? Let people handle the exceptions. Now, the clerk, says MIS director Quinn, instead of a processor becomes a mini-controller, someone who uses his brain.

The ordering process doesn't happen that way yet at Mrs. Fields, although it probably will soon as Randy continues to press for more exception reporting. You can see where he's going with this concept.

"Eventually," he says, "even the anomalies become normal." The exceptions themselves, and a person's response to them, assume a pattern. Why not, says Randy, have the computer watch the person for a while? "Then the machine can say, 'I have found an anomaly. I've been watching you, and I think this is what you would do. Shall I do it for you, yes or no. If yes, I'll do it, follow up, and so on. If no, what do you want me to do?'" It would work for the low-level function—administering accounts payable, for instance. And it would work at higher levels as well. "If," Randy says, "I can ask the computer now where are we making the most money and where are we making the least and then make a decision about where not to build new stores, why shouldn't that sort of thing be on automatic pilot too? 'Based on performance,' it will say, 'we shouldn't be building any more stores in East Jibip. Want me to tell (real-estate manager) Mike (Murphy)?' We're six months away from being able to do that."

The ability to look at the company, which is what the data base really is, at a level of abstraction appropriate to the looker, is the third advantage of a single data base—even if it never moves into artificial-intelligence functions. It means that Debbi Fields and Richard Lui are both looking at the same world, but in ways that are meaningful to each of them.

The hurdle to be overcome before you can use technology to its best advan-tage—and that isn't equivalent to just hanging an outboard motor on a skyscraper, as Buckminster Fuller said—isn't technical in the hardware sense. Randy buys only what he calls plain vanilla hardware. And it isn't financial. For all its relative sophistication in computer systems, Mrs. Fields spends just 0.49% of sales on data processing, much of which is returned in higher productivity.

Much more important, Randy says, is having a consistent vision of what you want to *accomplish* with the technology. Which functions do you want to control? What do you want your organization chart to look like? In what ways do you want to leverage the CEO's vision? "Imagination. We imagine what it is we want," says Randy. "We aren't constrained by the limits of what technology can do. We just say, 'What does your day look like? What would you *like* it to look like?'" He adds, "If you don't have your paradigm in mind, you have no way of knowing whether each little step is taking you closer to or further from your goal."

For instance, he inaugurated the daily store report with the opening of store number two in 1978. The important thing was the creation of the report—which is the fundamental data-gathering activity in the company—not its transmission mode. That can change, and has. First transmission was by Fax, then by telephone touch tone, and only recently by computer modem.

Having a consistent vision means, Randy says, that he could have described as far back as 1978, when he first began to create it, the system that exists today. But he doesn't mean the machines or how they're wired together. "MIS in this company," he says, "has always had to serve two masters. First, control. Rapid growth without control equals disaster. We needed to keep improving control over our stores. And second, information that leads to control also leads to better decision making. To the extent that the information is then provided to the store and field-management level, the decisions that are made there are better, and they are more easily made.

"That has been our consistent vision."

The New York Times, September 29, 1991

Making a Merger of Rivals Work[*]

Claudia H. Deutsch

Turning competitors into colleagues requires honesty and a lot of hand-holding.

Merging two companies is never easy. Merging two competing companies can be a recipe for disaster. Salespeople must tout the rival they once sold against. Researchers and marketers must share trade secrets with people they were conditioned to distrust. And everyone, even people who fear for their jobs, must make their former rivals feel welcome.

It takes heavy-duty ego stroking, attention to emotional detail and a policy of honesty even when it hurts to make that kind of a merger work. As Elena S. Ferretti, a television news producer, put it, "Rivals are not people you're geared to think of as nice."

She speaks from experience. On May 21, her former employer, the bankrupt Financial News Network, became part of NBC's Consumer News and Business Channel.

It was a potentially explosive situation. Although CNBC had interviewed 236 members of FNN's staff and made offers to 76 of them, it wound up hiring only 61—and seven of those as freelancers. CNBC had left jobs that were vacated through normal attrition unfilled in anticipation of the merger, but half of those 61 people still wound up in jobs that impinged on CNBC staffers' territory.

"We definitely feared they'd set up a victor/vanquished situation," said Ron Insana, one of eight FNN anchors who joined CNBC.

The explosion never happened. Sure, there were integration pains. One FNN salesperson, for example, had to move to a new territory because her former contacts had grown used to hearing her trash CNBC.

But such dislocations were the exception. "We started off thinking, 'Oh, my God, we have to hire these people,'" said Caroline L. Vanderlip, a CNBC vice president. "We've ended up glad to have them."

Here is how CNBC and FNN made the merger work.

As soon as the Fort Lee-based CNBC and the Los Angeles-based FNN agreed to merge in February (a subsequent attempt by Dow-Jones Inc. to outbid CNBC kept the merger from actually happening until May), Albert F. Barber, CNBC's president and Michael C. Wheeler, FNN's president, visited FNN locations together, in good part to underline a sense of equality between the two networks.

Often, they answered questions they would have preferred to duck. For example, Mr. Barber conceded that CNBC planned to close FNN's Los Angeles operation. "It makes no sense to try to deceive smart people," Mr. Barber said. Mr. Barber even appeared as a guest on the FNN anchor Bob Griffeth's show to discuss the merger—and offered him a job on air. (He took it.)

Back in Fort Lee, Peter M. Sturtevant, CNBC's vice president of news was spending 85 percent of his time "laying hands on backs" in the newsroom. "There wasn't a person whose on-air role wasn't altered, so of course there was anxiety," he said.

Actually, CNBC's lean newsroom staff had mixed reactions to the influx from FNN. They welcomed relief from grueling hours and the chance to upgrade the shows. But some were loath to share the limelight.

Mr. Barber had to scuttle a plan to have John Murphy and John Bollinger, respectively the technical stock market analysts for CNBC and FNN, debate on the air. The men refused to appear together.

Still, most CNBC managers say the staff has responded well to simple welcoming techniques that some might say bordered on the hokey. Management took a picture of the on-air anchors as a group, and gave each a print. It held parties, distributed CNBC mugs and bottles of wine sporting a CNBC/FNN label, had CNBC veterans call the newcomers to welcome them.

Mark H. Rosenzweig, director of nighttime programs, placed thumbnail biographies of his new FNN hires on his staff's desk so they would not treat newcomers as unknowns. Elizabeth A. Tilson, CNBC's supervising producer of daytime programming, prepared a comprehensive kit of welcome letters, style rules, phone extensions and the like. FNN people found the kit in their hotel rooms when they flew in the day of the merger.

There were more substantive cultural signals, too. Mr. Wheeler, although not part of CNBC's management, goes to all staff meetings. And, he is under contract to CNBC to develop business-to-business services, like special shows for brokerage houses.

"We annointed Mike as critical to CNBC's future, and that makes an important statement about how we feel about FNN's people," said Thomas S. Rogers, president of NBC Cable and Business Development.

Mr. Rogers put that feeling in writing. On May 23 he sent an all-points memo crediting the FNN people for the smoothness of the first post-merger day. "They know a lot about this business," he wrote, "and we can learn a lot from them."

The New York Times, February 15, 1991

Increasingly, a Prison Term Is the Price Paid by Polluters[*]

Allan R. Gold

Law enforcement officials are using criminal statutes more and more instead of civil or administrative proceedings to prosecute polluters. The shift in policy has sent shivers down the spines of company executives and prompted a sharp debate about the appropriate way to punish those who damage the environment.

Federal and state prosecutors say they have set their sights beyond the "midnight dumpers," who unload hazardous waste when no one is looking, to the likes of corporate vice presidents who decide a company's environmental policies. To maximize the deterrent effect, the prosecutors are more often pressing for jail sentences rather than fines alone.

Now, "people realize there is a real risk" of a prison term when environmental damage can be traced specifically to a company's acts, said Richard B. Stewart, an Assistant Attorney General in the Justice Department, who is responsible for prosecuting violators of Federal environmental laws.

"The word has really gotten out because of the increased level of enforcement," he said.

So far, the number of people jailed for Federal environmental crimes remains low, 90 in the last 5 years, the Justice Department reports. But the number of indictments has risen from 40 in 1983 to 134 last year. And many more cases are expected to end in jailings as more criminal prosecutions begin to fall under 1987 Federal sentencing guidelines, which toughened penalties for various crimes.

A Booming Law Business

The tougher penalties and stepped-up enforcement are "very scary," said J. Michael Nolan Jr., a partner at Pitney, Hardin, Kipp & Szuch, in Morristown, N.J., one of dozens of law firms with a booming environmental practice. "You don't have much flexibility. If you make a mistake, the guy's going to jail."

Further, the recently revised Clean Air Act sharply expanded the number of crimes that can be treated as felonies. Under the old law, for example, violating air emission standards could subject a company to civil penalties of $25,000 for each day of violation, said John Quaries, an environmental lawyer with the firm of Morgan, Lewis & Bockius in Washington. Under current law, the same violation could be treated as a criminal case with corporate or individual fines of up to $250,000 for each day of violation and imprisonment.

Federal resources dedicated to investigations of environmental crimes are increasing. Several states, including New York, New Jersey, Pennsylvania, Ohio and Arizona, have active criminal enforcement programs, and many other states are establishing them.

Jail as a Deterrent

E. Dennis Muchniki, chief of the environmental enforcement section of the Ohio Attorney General's Office, said, "Only the criminal process, with its threat of jail time for managers and its stamp of disapproval on the good name of a company that violates a permit, can assure the public that businesses will really be held accountable for their health and safety."

In 1982, the environmental crimes section of the Justice Department had 3 lawyers; now there are 25. The Environmental Protection Agency's criminal enforcement program has grown from 23 investigators in 1982 to more than 60, and a new law directs it to hire 500 eventually.

After the E.P.A. investigates crimes, they are referred to the Justice Department for possible prosecution. The Federal Bureau of Investigation has also added agents devoted to environmental crimes. The agents gather evidence of crimes, and the cases are referred to the environmental crimes section of the Justice Department.

The Government's efforts are pleasing neither corporate officials, who say they are being made scapegoats, nor environmentalists, who say the prosecutions are too few and are aimed only at smaller companies.

Company officials and defense lawyers assert that overzealous, publicity-seeking prosecutors may portray bad business judgments or negligence as criminal intent.

"There are some circumstances where people break the law and deserve to go to jail," said Kathy Bailey, assistant general counsel for the Chemical Manufacturers Association, a Washington-based trade group. But, she added, "people make mistakes" for which prison is not appropriate.

In one strongly contested case, a self-employed businessman, John Pozsgai, was found guilty by a Federal jury of filling in wetlands in Pennsylvania without a permit. Mr. Pozsgai was sentenced in 1989 to three years in prison and fined $202,000. His defense lawyers asserted that no environmental damage occurred when he used topsoil to fill in five acres of his own property. But the prosecutor argued that Mr. Pozsgai had no right to fill the property, a mostly dry lot designated a wetland by the Government because of its vegetation, without a proper permit.

Some environmental advocates say, however, that they are still not convinced that Washington means business.

"The Government has an interest in showing it is doing a better job, and in some cases it is," said Robert W. Adler, a senior lawyer with the Natural Resources Defense Council in Washington. But the number of people going to prison is still quite small, Mr. Adler asserted. In addition, he said, few of the nation's biggest companies have been criminally prosecuted, raising the question of whether the Government is picking on easier targets.

Few Major Corporations

Mr. Adler could not cite a specific example of a large company that he believed should be charged. But he said a study by his organization had found that of corporations prosecuted by the Federal Government for environmental violations since 1984, only 6 percent were on the *Fortune* 500 list of the biggest industrial concerns.

In the 1980s, Congress added tougher criminal penalties to Federal environmental statutes like the Clean Water Act and the Resource Conservation and Recovery Act, the major law regulating disposal of hazardous and solid waste. The Clean Air Act, as amended last year, contains provisions that make nearly all "knowing violations," meaning when a person has knowledge of a criminal act, subject to criminal prosecution.

Last November, Federal prosecutors obtained a 26-month prison term for a company president under the Clean Water Act, the longest sentence ever handed down in a Federal environmental case in Massachusetts. The sentence, in U.S. v. Borjohn Optical Technology, is under appeal. Another Federal prosecution brought a two-year sentence, the longest in Missouri history, for a company research director accused of altering disposal records of polychlorinated biphenyls, a regulated toxic substance.

Defense lawyers contend that high-ranking executives are increasingly, and unfairly, accountable for finding and preventing violations. "Failure by senior management to take steps to curb the actions of subordinates, even when those actions are not fully known to senior officials, may result in criminal indictment and conviction," warned Judson W. Starr, a partner at Venable, Baetjer, Howard & Civiletti, a Washington law firm. Mr. Starr, who represents individuals and companies accused of polluting, was head of the environmental crimes unit at the Justice Department from 1982 to 1988.

One prosecutorial tactic involves following the chain of command after a plant manager, for example, conducts an environmental audit, finds violations and recommends remedies. If a company's finance committee reviewed the recommendations and decided not to allocate money to correct the violations, the committee members could be held criminally liable, Ms. Bailey said.

Seeking Fairness In Sentencing

Environmental prosecutors disagree with the assertion that their primary motive is publicity. "I'm not a headhunter," said Steven J. Madonna, New Jersey's special environmental prosecutor. "What we're looking for are responsible corporations. There's no place for irresponsibility in the operation of a corporation."

In general, the Federal sentencing guidelines that took effect in November 1987 were an attempt to make sentencing more uniform, so, for example, cases in California would end with the same result as those in Maine. But the development of guidelines for environmental crimes differed from others because there was not much sentencing history upon which to draw.

The United States Sentencing Comission based its recommendation on society's view of crimes against the environment, and, as a result, put them on a par with other major criminal offenses, comparable to a drug-related felony, Mr. Starr said. As a result, jail has become much more likely for defendants in environmental cases, even for first-time offenders.

Criminal defense lawyers and others assert that the sentences required by the guidelines are often too harsh. There has been discussion by the Justice Department and Environmental Protection Agency about revising the environmental sentencing guidelines downward, lawyers familiar with the situation say.

"It is somewhat haphazard," Mr. Starr said, "and runs the risk, without checks and balances, of overreaching in a very serious way: someone can lose their freedom.

The New York Times, January 27, 1991
Executives, Take Your Risks*

Claudia H. Deutsch

In these hard times, forget the cash—your money goes where the shareholders' does.

Anthony Luiso, the International Multifoods Corporation's chief executive, was due for a $100,000 raise last year. He not only turned it down but also told the board to hold back $100,000 of his bonus. In their place, he took $200,000 in stock options, exercisable in 10 years at $32.625 each, the price on the day the deal was signed.

"Executives should have enough at risk so that they spend a couple of sleepless nights over their decisions," Mr. Luiso said.

So far, he has reason to toss. As he figures it, the stock, which was trading in the mid-30's last week, must hit $40 a share before he will have access to something worth the money he gave up. And it would have to go much higher than that for him to make anywhere near what he might have by investing the money. Nonetheless, the 46-year-old Mr. Luiso is committed to the same trade-off for four more years—and has asked four other executives to do the same. "We should be in the same shoes as the shareholders," he said.

The idea of aligning management's interest with that of shareholders is nothing new. But traditionally, companies have offered stock or stock-related incentives in addition to—not in lieu of—salary or cash bonuses.

In these hard times, that is slowly changing. On Wall Street, where salaries once paled in comparison to hefty bonuses, Merrill Lynch, Morgan Stanley, Lehman Brothers and others are asking their top people to take part of their already decimated bonuses in stock—or, in the case of privately held companies, "phantom stock," whose value is tied to profits or other performance measures. Compensation consultants report that manufacturing companies, whose executives have come to expect income stability, are adding risk to their compensation systems.

"They finally realize that stock programs that are all upside and no downside do not assure that executives will act in the interest of all shareholders," said Ira T. Kay, managing director of the Hay Group's executive compensation practice in New York. The result, said Alan M. Johnson, managing director of Handy Associates' executive compensation consulting practice in New York, is that "companies are finally getting serious about requiring executives to own stock."

The Chrysler Corporation certainly is. In April, Chrysler issued guidelines for how much stock it expected each of its 100 top executives to hold, based on that executive's salary and position. According to Thomas F. Houston, manager of media relations, the company offered neither loans nor price breaks—just a strong suggestion that careers might depend on it.

"They were told—firmly, I think is the fair description—that they were expected to reach a certain level of ownership by the end of 1990," Mr. Houston said. He added that he did not know how many complied—but doubted whether any did not.

Companies willing to use blatant coercion remain rare, however.

One wants its executives to forgo the blocks of stock they had been promised and accept instead options for three times as many shares at a price 50 percent higher than the stock is now selling for, according to Louis J. Brindisi Jr., a senior partner at Strategic Compensation Associates in New York. There is, however, a problem. "They're pretty sure the stock will rise and the executives could triple their money," said Mr. Brindisi, an adviser to the company. "But they can't bring themselves to ask yet."

Similarly, another company had 11th-hour jitters about a program meant to force officers to take part of their compensation in stock, said Pearl Meyer, a New York compensation consultant who designed the program. They feared losing executives in bad times. "If executives make $50,000 instead of a couple hundred thousand in a year that they worked like heck, they're going to be open to offers," said Ms. Meyer.

F. Kenneth Iverson, the Nucor Corporation's chief executive, would probably laugh at such wimpishness. For close to 20 years, Nucor, a steel company in Charlotte, N.C., has paid its top 15 people about 75 percent of what they could have made elsewhere. And it pegs their bonuses to the company's return on equity. If the return is below 8 percent, they get just salary. But if it hits 20 percent, they get salary—plus 91 percent of salary in cash and another 41 percent in stock. At 14 percent, which has been Nucor's typical return on equity, the officers make about 66 percent on top of base salary, or about what they would get elsewhere.

Around Nucor, the compensation system is called the "Share the Pain" program, even though for the most part the officers have done quite well. "People in the plants should know that, if they are put on four-day weeks, the officers are not making great money either," Mr. Iverson said.

Taking Control in a New Job*

George Tamke

I want to describe, in some detail, what I do when entering a new job. Throughout my career, when changing jobs, I have always moved into an organization that had very visible problems (cost, quality, schedule and/or people-related difficulties). As a consequence, whether pressured directly or not, I have always felt under a time crunch to get the ball moving in the right direction. For this reason, I have invariably jumped in with both feet to try to understand what is going on around me.

------

*This case was prepared by George Tamke under the supervision of David Bradford, Lecturer in Organizational Behavior, Stanford Graduate School of Business. This case was prepared as a basis for class discussion and not to indicate either correct or incorrect handling of administrative problems.

In my last two jobs I was responsible for a functional entity: manufacturing and production control. In each job, I was at the fourth level of management, with three layers of management reporting to me. The two organizations were comprised of lower-level employees, compared with those in areas like engineering, marketing, new products, etc. It is also important to note that in each of those jobs, I was new to the location and as a consequence did not know any of the employees personally. From a size standpoint, the organizations consisted of 300 to 500 people, with approximately 50 managers (36 first level, 10 second level, and 4 third level).

OBTAINING TECHNICAL CONTROL OF THE ORGANIZATION

One of the very first things that I do, after my arrival has been announced to the organization, is to hold a staff meeting with all of the people who will report directly to me. Working from an agenda prepared prior to the meeting, I discuss the following points:

1. My background, specifically covering the organizations and the locations that I have worked in.
2. My administrative style. For example,

   a. Weekly status report due to me by 9:00 a.m. Monday, covering the following items:
   —accomplishments
   —problems/concerns
   —planned activity for the coming week

   b. As reports, letters, etc., get distributed from my office, a number of them will have questions/comments addressed to specific individuals. Unless otherwise noted, I would expect a response within two days, recognizing that a valid response may require more time.

   c. I expect all appraisals to be completed on time and objectives to be in place for all employees.

   d. I want to review all management appraisals before they are given.

3. Please get on my calendar within the next five days and be prepared to discuss with me the following topics:
   —workload versus people on board versus approved budget plan
   —product cost posture by product by operation (actual versus targets)
   —quality performance by product
   —expense budget posture (actual versus target)
   —major project commitments with status
   —latest opinion survey results with action plan highlights
   —planned promotion activity
   —appraisal distribution
   —absenteeism and overtime trends
   —major objectives for the next 12 months
   —personnel problems

4. My view of my job.

Basically it is one of helping my managers get their job done. If they feel that I am being overbearing on a particular issue or with my specific requests, I would hope that they would bring it up so we could discuss it. Also if they don't understand why I'm asking for a certain work product or don't agree with my appraisal on a problem, I would also hope that they would mention it.

My main intent, from a technical standpoint, is to get the information needed to understand the decisions that will be made in my organization. Unless I am aware of the numbers, the plans, and the problems that my organization is living with, I feel very uncomfortable in the leadership role. I think this is caused by my almost complete dependence on the people working for me, when I do not yet know the producers from the parasites. Also, the fact that the only reason I am there is because the organization is in trouble does not make me feel comfortable in this position. Therefore, I always attempt to get myself up to speed as quickly as possible. Apart from the selfish reason of trying to become less dependent (initially, until I know whom I can trust) another gain from this meeting is that an hour after the staff meeting is over, the grapevine will have heard about all of the "demands that new guy has made" and as a result, all of the managers will be on their toes—not really knowing what to expect, but recognizing that "he is serious."

As the individual review meetings take place, I usually find that there is a general attempt to satisfy my requests, but not sufficient thought given to the issues. The managers quickly find themselves with many more questions than answers, and more work to do. Word gets out, and the quality of the presentations improves, as does the level of anticipation within the management ranks.

OBTAINING PEOPLE CONTROL OF THE ORGANIZATION

The key point that I try to stress from day one is "tough but fair" and I attempt to do that by my actions, rather than by what I say. There are some tools/techniques that I use:

1. **Past Opinion Survey Review**

One of the areas that I probe into very deeply, very quickly, is the temperature of the water among the workers. I use the results from an annual company-wide survey to measure employee attitudes about work conditions and their supervision. Each supervisor receives a summary of responses from his/her subordinates and from this develops an Opinion Survey Action plan aimed at correcting any problems. By examining the supervisor's action plan I begin to get a feel as to the level of thought that was put into the plan. By asking how frequently the managers review the status of their plan with their people, I get a feeling for the level of commitment that is felt on the manager's part. The purpose of this review is really twofold; I quickly become familiar with how the people feel about their jobs, their manager, etc., and—as important, if not more important—it sends out another signal to the managers that I am really serious about this area.

The reason I feel very strongly about this is that, in my view, if people are basically happy with what they are doing and how they are being treated, a lot of the other problems (cost, quality, schedule) tend to go away. In addition, I also feel that an individual's morale basically revolves around his/her view of the immediate manager and what kind of a job that person is doing. This is an area that my management team will be spending a lot of time working on, and I like to get the seed planted in their minds early that I think this is an important area.

2. Shadow Program

Beginning with my first week on the job, I have each third-line manager spend a full week with me. This activity entails going to the meetings I go to, reading the mail I read, discussing issues as they come up, etc. This allows me to get to know each manager and also allows them to get to know me personally—to see how I react, how I think, and hopefully to relieve some of the anxieties/tensions that may have built up since my arrival.

3. Meeting with Each First-Line and Second-Line Manager Individually

Over the course of the first few weeks, I schedule a one-hour meeting with each manager, to give me an overview of their departments or project covering their mission, their department morale, and what they consider to be their biggest accomplishment and/or biggest problem. With the first-line managers, this meeting ends with a tour of departments where I meet the employees. More times than not, questions come up which are not answered to my satisfaction and which require follow-up on the part of the manager. Again the results are twofold; I get to know each manager and his/her views of their department, and they get to tell me about something which should be very familiar to them. They recognize that this is a very time-consuming process on my part, and I think they appreciate the fact that I am willing to take the time.

4. Employee Breakfast Meetings

Once I have been around to all of the departments and have met all of the people, I schedule a breakfast meeting a few times a week with 15 non-management people at a time. The purpose of the meeting is to discuss whatever issues they may have on their minds, to give them my views of what we are, and where we are headed, etc. The only topics which I cut off are those which deal with specific individuals. Those types of problems I cover with the individuals who brought them up outside of the group meeting.

I think as a result of these and similar techniques, I begin to get people control of the organization. I meet all of the people, and they meet me. I stress to my management team the importance of good people management and try to show it with the resource that is most valuable to me—my time. Early on, I consciously try to find ways to show how I feel about certain things, by doing and saying rather than by just saying.

MY RELATIONSHIP WITH MY PEERS

In addition to working downward in my organization, I also sit down and discuss with my peers their views of my organization, and the problems that they or their people have in dealing with it. I like to do this near the start of the sequence of things so that I am not clouded by my own views. Later on, this also helps me determine in my own mind whose views I agree with and/or respect, and whose views leave me cold. This data becomes very useful to me.

Depending upon the way the meetings evolve, I also think it gets our relationship off on the right foot. I am asking for their opinion on something, and this tends to make them feel good. I also take copious notes during these meetings, which further supports their good feelings. From my perspective, I form impressions of them on the basis of how prepared they are, and who feels basically secure or insecure in their own job. This allows me also to determine my peer power structure.

MY RELATIONSHIPS WITH MY SUPERIORS

This is an area that I don't spend a lot of time thinking about because I have made sure, before accepting the job, that my new boss understands my level of aspirations and the type of relationship that I hope we will have. I emphasize the fact that I would like to know at any time if he isn't pleased with my work or the way that I do my job; I don't like surprises in this area. Once this has been established, I do not remember having to bring it up again. I find that there is a degree of mutual respect that exists and tends to carry over as the relationship develops.

Once I have taken the job, I find that my other activities (interactions with subordinates and peers) dovetail nicely with meetings with my boss. I quickly appear to understand the numbers and to have drawn some conclusions about past problems. In addition, as a result of having walked through the significant problems with my subordinates I either understand and agree with the action being taken, or I have initiated additional work. I am able to discuss what we plan to do and report any status to date. The peer conversations also have a way of getting back to the boss, and when coupled with the other things going on, appear to choke off the normal additional requests that tend to come from the boss to the new organization member. I think these requests are in part the boss's attempt to make sure the right things are being looked at. If his curiosity can be satisfied early in the process, I believe the probability of significant future requests is also greatly diminished. For this to work effectively, another requirement is to keep him properly informed on the major things that are going on and what is being done about them, so that he is able to field any questions that his boss may have about your operation.

I think that this is a necessary ingredient to getting effective control of your organization. Without it, the priorities you have set will be continuously jockeyed around to satisfy your boss's requests. The result on your managers would be catastrophic, leading them to wonder (rightly so) who is running your organization.

I have tried to explain and characterize the management style that I use when I enter a new job. I work hard and long trying to get a quick, effective grasp on my new area of responsibility. I get to know the people as quickly as possible and continually emphasize to my management team the importance of being an effective people manager.

In the early stages, I would say my decision-making style is predominantly participatory in that I actively solicit comments and input from my managers and tend to ride with their decisions. As I become more knowledgeable, although I still solicit comments and inputs to the same degree, I tend to play the devil's advocate much more, push harder and, depending upon the situation, it would not be above me to be downright autocratic.

I emphasize to my managers and my people that I consider helping them to get their job done one of my main responsibilities. If they have a problem, and they think I might be able to help, I urge them to come in and see me. I try to be open and honest with my managers and share with them any information I have that is work related. I also emphasize the importance of good two-way communication and how I really use the data they provide me. This point becomes crucial because I can very easily lose my credibility if they provide me with "bum data." To the degree that it is practicable, I try to establish the same openness and honesty in my dealings with my peers and my boss. I find it much easier to tell everybody the truth, than to selectively "curb the truth" and try to remember what I have told to whom.

Chapter 7

Managing Human Resources

I f, as we have been suggesting, organizations are formally designed systems superimposed on less formal relationships among humans, and the primary function of managing is the coordination of human effort, it goes without saying that managing human resources is a central concern of managers. Clearly this expectation is confirmed. (Managers often see the human resources issues as the ones they feel are most important and the ones that they wish they had given more attention to learning about when they were students.) Managers want to find ways to help people perform what the organization is attempting to accomplish in a cost effective manner.

Most management textbooks devote a great deal of attention to summarizing knowledge that managers can use towards this end. We will make no attempt to repeat these efforts here. Instead, we want to complement them by exploring a few matters that illustrate some of the tensions that often exist in meshing the needs of the organization and the characteristics of human beings, but are seldom given much attention in conventional textbooks on human resources. The topics we chose are only a small sample of these tensions.

Although until now we have been most concerned with the fact that organizations are superimposed on human beings, it is also true that human beings instill their interests in the organization. Whereas earlier, particularly in our discussions of influencing and communicating, we tended to see the impact that personal inclinations make as positive for coordinating human effort, here the articles treat a number of ways in which this impact might have dysfunctional consequences for the operation of the formal systems of the organization. We also see additional examples of how the demands of the organization can be dysfunctional for the individual.

As we see it, human society is currently evolving ways of organizing cooperative relationships that will reduce the impact of these tensions. It seems likely that progress along this path will mean that organizations as well as individuals will change. For example, compare a typical factory today with one of the late nineteenth or early twentieth century. Things we take for granted today such as toilets, drinking fountains, ventilation, and numerous safety measures were simply absent then. Similarly, working hours and even the design of jobs themselves have been altered (to some degree) to be more consistent with a number of human needs and preferences. On the other hand, most people have become much more prepared to work in organizations as we know them. Many people have the basic educational skills that organizations require and the personal and social discipline that suits them far better for bureaucratic organizations than was true a century ago. However, failure of the public schools to equip so many students with the literacy and mathematical skills required by today's technology has generated a serious problem for both human resource managers and for the individuals concerned. Whether these developments are evaluated positively or negatively depends on the set of values one selects for building criteria. Our only point is that both individuals and organizations appear to have accommodated to each other and we expect more of this in the future. There are still many sources of tension—many of which are manifested around topics associated with managing the human resource.

Central concerns of human resource management often include the following: selection, training and development, appraisal, compensation, and termination. While these functions often seem relatively simple to perform, the articles in this section reveal that they are not. "Behind the Mask. . ." demonstrates the political dimensions of employee appraisal. The final article introduces other consequences performing these functions have for both the people who do them and for those who are affected by them. In exploring them we see new elements of the human drama that organizations spawn for managers, as they try to balance their organizational missions with that they and others judge as right.

◆

Behind the Mask: The Politics of Employee Appraisal[*]

Clinton O. Longenecker
THE UNIVERSITY OF TOLEDO

Henry P. Sims, Jr.
GEORGE MASON UNIVERSITY AND THE PENNSYLVANIA STATE UNIVERSITY

Dennis A. Gioia
THE PENNSYLVANIA STATE UNIVERSITY

There is really no getting around the fact that whenever I evaluate one of my people, I stop and think about the impact—the ramifications of my decisions on my relationship with the guy and his future here. I'd be stupid not to. Call it being politically minded, or using managerial discretion, or fine tuning the guy's ratings, but in the end I've got to live with him, and I'm not going to rate a guy without thinking about the fallout. There are a lot of games played in the rating process and whether we [managers] admit it or not we are all guilty of playing them at our discretion.

According to management books and manuals, employee appraisal is an objective, rational and, we hope, accurate process. The idea that executives might deliberately distort and manipulate appraisals for political purposes seems unspeakable. Yet we found extensive evidence to indicate that, behind a mask of objectivity and rationality, executives engage in such manipulation in an intentional and systematic manner. In performance appraisal, it appears that some of the Machiavellian spirit still lives.

Our original goal was to conduct a scholarly investigation of the cognitive processes executives typically use in appraising subordinates. We held in-depth interviews with 60 upper-level executives who had extensive experience in formally evaluating their subordinates on a periodic basis. During these interviews, we heard many frank admissions of deliberate manipulation of formal appraisals for political purposes. In this article we'll discuss the "why and the how" of such politically motivated manipulation.

ON THE APPRAISAL PROCESS

Almost every executive has dreaded performance appraisals at some time or other. They hate to give them and they hate to receive them. Yet, like them or not, every executive recognizes that appraisals are a fact of organizational life. In terms of time, a formal appraisal of a subordinate takes perhaps three or four hours out of

[*]Reprinted from the Academy of Management *Executive,* 1987, Vol 1, No. 3, pp. 183–193.
Reprinted by permission of the publisher and the authors.

the working year; in terms of impact on the lives of executives and their employees, appraisals have significance that reaches far beyond the few hours it takes to conduct them.

Because of the important role appraisals play in individual careers and corporate performance, a great deal of attention has been given to trying to understand the process. Special attention has been directed toward the issue of accuracy in appraisals.[1] Academicians in particular have expended (some might say wasted) substantial energy trying to design the perfect instrument that would yield an accurate appraisal. That effort now appears to be a hopeless, even impossible, task.

More recently, a flurry of activity has centered on the arcane mental processes of the manager who gives the appraisal. It is an intriguing approach because it involves a kind of vicarious attempt to climb inside an executive's head to see how he or she works. Predictably, however, this approach has confirmed the elusiveness of deciphering managerial thought processes. Moreover, it has not yet resulted in appraisals that are any more accurate than existing appraisals.[2]

Even more recently, some effort has been directed toward demonstrating that appraisal is, in addition to everything else, a highly emotional process as well. When emotional variability gets dragged into the process, any hope of obtaining objectivity and accuracy in appraisal waltzes right out the office door.[3]

Taken together, all these approaches apparently lead to the depressing conclusion that accuracy in appraisals might be an unattainable objective.[4] More realistically, perhaps accuracy is simply a wrong goal to pursue. Even if we have a perfect understanding of instruments and mental and emotional processes, would that result in accurate appraisals? Our research indicates that it would not. All of these avenues to understanding appraisal tend to ignore an important point: Appraisals take place in an organizational environment that is anything but completely rational, straightforward, or dispassionate. In this environment, accuracy does not seem to matter to managers quite so much as discretion, effectiveness or, more importantly, survival. Earlier research has either missed or glossed over the fact that executives giving appraisals have ulterior motives and purposes that supercede the mundane concern with rating accuracy.

ON POLITICS IN PERFORMANCE APPRAISAL

Any realistic discussion of performance appraisal must recognize that organizations are political entities and that few, if any, important decisions are made without key parties acting to protect their own interests.[5] As such, executives are political actors in an organization, and they often attempt to control their destinies and gain influence through internal political actions.

Thus, it is likely that political considerations influence executives when they appraise subordinates.[6] *Politics* in this sense refers to deliberate attempts by individuals to enhance or protect their self-interests when conflicting courses of action are possible. Political action therefore represents a source of bias or inaccuracy in employee appraisal. To understand the appraisal process thoroughly, thus, we must recognize and account for the political aspects of the process.

POLITICS IN APPRAISAL: FINDINGS FROM THE STUDY

The political perspective emerged as a surprisingly important and pervasive issue affecting the way executives appraise their employees. Conclusions derived from our interviews are summarized in Exhibits 1 through 4. Because a strong attempt was made to allow executives to speak for themselves in describing the politics of performance appraisals, direct quotations from the interviews have been included in our analysis, where appropriate. Our findings are discussed below.

Politics as a Reality of Organizational Life

The most fundamental survey finding was an open recognition and admission that politics were a reality in the appraisal process. In fact, executives admitted that political considerations *nearly always* were part of their evaluation process. One vice-president summarized the view these executives shared regarding the politics of appraisal:

> As a manager, I will use the review process to do what is best for my people and the division. . . . I've got a lot of leeway—call it discretion— to use this process in that manner. . . . I've used it to get my people better raises in lean years, to kick a guy in the pants if he really needed it, to pick up a guy when he was down or even to tell him that he was no longer welcome here. It is a tool that the manager should use to help him do what it takes to get the job done. I believe most of us here at—operate this way regarding appraisals. . . . Accurately describing an employee's performance is really not as important as generating ratings that keep things cooking.

Executives suggested several reasons why politics were so pervasive and why accuracy was not their primary concern. First, executives realized that they must live with subordinates in a day-to-day relationship. Second, they were also very cognizant of the permanence of the written document:

> The mere fact that you have to write out your assessment and create a permanent record will cause people not to be as honest or as accurate as they should be. . . . We soften the language because our ratings go in the guy's file downstairs [the Personnel Department] and it will follow him around his whole career.

Perhaps the most widespread reason why executives considered political action in the appraisal process was that the formal appraisal was linked to compensation, career, and advancement in the organization. The issue of money was continually cited as a major cause of intentional distortions in ratings.

> I know that it sounds funny, but the fact that the process is ultimately tied to money influences the ratings a person receives. . . . Whenever a decision involves money things can get very emotional and ticklish.

Although the logic of tying pay to the outcome of performance ratings is sound, pay linkages increase the likelihood that ratings will be manipulated. Both managers and the organization as a whole are guilty of using the rating process as an opportunity to reach salary objectives regarding employee compensation that have little, if any, relationship to pay for performance. A director of research and development very candidly described the predicament from the rater's perspective:

> Since the pay raise my people get is tied to the ratings I give them, there is a strong incentive to inflate ratings at times to maximize their pay increases to help keep them happy and motivated, especially in lean years when the merit ceiling is low. . . . Conversely, you can also send a very strong message to a nonperformer that low ratings will hit him in the wallet. . . . There is no doubt that a lot of us manipulate ratings at times to deal with the money issue.

At times, an organization uses the appraisal process as an instrument to control merit increase expenditures. The manipulative process can be summarized as follows:

> This thing [the appraisal process] can really turn into an interesting game when the HR [Human Resources] people come out with a blanket statement like, "Money for raises is tight this year and since superior performers get 7% to 10% raises there will be no superior performers this year." Talk about making things rough for us [raters]!. . . They try and force you to make the ratings fit the merit allowances instead of vice versa.

EXHIBIT 1   POLITICS AS A REALITY OF ORGANIZATIONAL LIFE

- Political considerations were nearly always part of executive evaluative processes.
- Politics played a role in the evaluation process because:
  —executives took into consideration the daily interpersonal dynamics between them and their subordinates.
  —the formal appraisal process results in a permanent written document.
  —the formal appraisal can have considerable impact on the subordinate's career and advancement.

Influences on Political Culture

Executives made it clear that if an organization was political, the appraisal process would reflect these politics:

> Some organizations are more aggressive and political than others, so it just makes sense that those things carry over into the rating process as well. . . . The organization's climate will determine, to a great extent, how successful any rating system will be, and it follows that if any organization is very political, the rating system will be political. . . .

Several factors were identified by the executives as having a strong influence on the political culture in which the performance appraisal process operates. Perhaps the strongest was the extent to which the formal appraisal process was "taken seriously" by the organization. A plant manager in this study describes what it means for an organization to "take the process seriously":

> *At some places the PA [performance appraisal] process is a joke—*
> *just a bureaucratic thing that the manager does to keep the IR [indus-*
> *trial relations] people off his back. At the last couple of places I've*
> *worked, the formal review process is taken really seriously; they train*
> *you how to conduct a good interview, how to handle problems, how to*
> *coach and counsel. . . . You see the things [appraisals] reviewed by your*
> *boss, and he's serious about reviewing your performance in a thorough*
> *manner. . . . I guess the biggest thing is that people are led to believe that*
> *it is a management tool that works; it's got to start at the top!*

This quote suggests another important factor that turns the appraisal process into
a political process: the extent to which higher level executives in the same company use political factors in rating subordinates. A "modeling" effect seems to take
place, with managers telling themselves, "If it's okay for the guys upstairs to do it,
then we can do it, too."

According to one executive we interviewed,

> *I've learned how not to conduct the review from the bosses. . . but*
> *you do learn from your boss how much slack or what you can get away*
> *with in rating your people. . . . It seems that if the manager's boss takes*
> *it [the appraisal] seriously, the subordinate [manager] is more likely to*
> *follow. If the boss plays games with the review, it seems like the subordi-*
> *nate [manager] is more likely to do so.*

The economic health and growth potential of the organization appeared as important factors influencing the organization's culture and, consequently, the appraisal
event. Similarly, the executive's own personal belief system—his or her perception
of the value of the appraisal process—also seemed to have an impact. Generally,
executives who honestly believed the process contributed to the motivation of
their subordinates were less likely to allow political factors to affect the appraisal.
Conversely, executives who saw the appraisal as a useless bureaucratic exercise
were more likely to manipulate the appraisal.

Moreover, if executives believed the appraisals would be seriously scrutinized, reviewed, and evaluated by their superiors, then the influence of political
factors was likely to be reduced.

> *If somebody is carefully reviewing the marks you give your people,*
> *then the game playing is reduced. . . [but] as you rise in the organiza-*
> *tion, your boss has less direct knowledge of your people and is less likely*
> *to question your judgment, so the door is open for more discretion.*

The degree of open communication and trust between executives and subordinates seemed to have some influence on the impact of political factors. The more
open the communication, the less likely that politics would play a role:

> *If the manager and employee have a trusting and open relationship*
> *and shoot straight with each other, then the manager is less likely to*
> *play games with ratings.*

Last, but not least, the appraiser's level in the organization's hierarchy also seemed
to have an influence. Executives generally believed the appraisal process became
more political and subjective as one moved up the organizational ladder:

The higher you rise in this organization the more weird things get with regard to how they evaluate you. . . . The process becomes more political and less objective and it seems like the rating process focuses on who you are as opposed to what you've actually accomplished. . . . As the stakes get higher, things get more and more political.

EXHIBIT 2 FACTORS INFLUENCING THE POLITICAL CULTURE OF THE ORGANIZATION

- The economic health and growth potential of the organization.
- The extent to which top management supported and, more important, did or did not practice political tactics when appraising their own subordinates.
- The extent to which executives sincerely believed that appraisal was a necessary and worthwhile management practice or just a bureaucratic exercise.
- The extent to which executives believed that their written assessment of their subordinates would be evaluated and scrutinized by their superiors.
- The extent to which an organization was willing to train and coach its managers to use and maintain the performance appraisal system.
- The degree to which the appraisal process was openly discussed among both executives and subordinates.
- The extent to which executives believed the appraisal process became more political at higher levels of the organizational hierarchy.

Inflating the Appraisal

Although academicians have been preoccupied with the goal of accuracy in appraisal, executives reported that accuracy was not their primary concern. Rather, they were much more interested in whether their ratings would be effective in maintaining or increasing the subordinate's future level of performance. In fact, many reported they would deliberately misstate the reported performance level if they felt performance could be improved as a result:

When I rate my people it doesn't take place in a vacuum. . . so you have to ask yourself what the purpose of the process is. . . . I use this thing to my advantage and I know my people and what it takes to keep them going and that is what this is all about.

Overall, executives reported that deliberate distortions of the appraisal tended to be biased in the subordinate's favor:

Let's just say that there are a lot of factors that tug at you and play on your mind that cause you to tend to soften the ratings you give. It may not have a great impact all the time but when you know a "5" will piss a man off and "6" will make him happy. . . . You tell me which one you'd choose. . . . Plus, you don't want to be the bad guy, the bearer of gloom. It seems like ratings are almost always a little inflated at a minimum because of people aspects in the evaluation process.

Typically, executives tended to inflate the overall rating rather than the individual appraisal items. Interestingly, although the overall rating was generally the last item on the appraisal form, this overall rating was determined first; then the executive went back and completed the individual items.

> *Most of us try to be fairly accurate in assessing the individual's performance in different categories. . . . If you are going to pump up a person's ratings, for whatever reason, it's done on the subordinate's overall evaluation category. That's all they really care about, anyway. . . . The problem is these things have to match up, so if you know what the guy's overall rating is in the first place it will probably color the rest of the appraisal.*

Of course, this backward procedure is usually contrary to the recommended procedure and is also inconsistent with the typical assumptions about how decisions are supposed to be made "objectively." Executives articulated several reasons as justification for consciously inflating subordinate ratings. The most frequently given reason was to maximize the merit increases that a subordinate would be eligible to receive. This reason was more likely to be given by executives in organizations that closely linked the numerical score on the formal appraisal and the subsequent merit raise.

Sometimes executives wanted to protect or encourage a subordinate whose performance was temporarily suffering because of personal problems. In a similar vein, executives would sometimes inflate a rating simply because they felt sorry for a subordinate. They wanted to avoid short-term "punishment" in the hope that the subordinate would recover and perform once again at an acceptable level.

> *It may sound kind of funny to say this, but sometimes there is a tendency to give subordinates ratings a little higher than they deserve because you feel sorry for them. . . . I just had a guy go through a divorce and I'm not going to kick him when he's down, even if his performance drops off. . . . If anything, you might use the review to help pick him up and get him back on his feet.*

If the appraisal was reviewed by people outside the department, executives sometimes inflated ratings to avoid "hanging dirty laundry out in public." Clearly, many executives preferred to keep knowledge of problems contained within the department.

> *There are two reviews at times, the written one and the spoken one. The spoken review is the real one, especially if there are things of a sensitive nature. . . . I generally don't put those things down on paper in the review for the whole world to read because it is generally none of their damn business. . . . I could make all of us look bad or worse than we really are.*

Executives also admitted to inflating a rating to avoid a confrontation with a subordinate with whom the executive had recently had difficulties. They took this action mainly to avert an unpleasant incident or sometimes to avoid a confrontation that they believed would not lead to an effective outcome.

On occasion, an executive might inflate the rating because the subordinate's performance had improved during the latter part of the performance period, even though the overall performance did not merit such a rating. Again, the motivation for this higher-than-deserved rating was a desire to encourage the subordinate toward better performance in the next period:

> *Many of us have trouble rating for the entire year. If one of my peo-*
> *ple has a stellar three months prior to the review. . . . you don't want to*
> *do anything that impedes that person's momentum and progress.*

Executives also recognized effort, even though the effort might not pay off in actual performance:

> *If a man broke his back trying to do the best job humanly possible,*
> *his ratings will generally reflect this if his boss understands people. Take*
> *two people with the same performance, but one tried much harder—*
> *their ratings will show it in my department. Low ratings might trample*
> *that person's desire to put forth effort in the future.*

Last, although not frequently reported, a few executives admitted to giving a higher rating to a problem employee to get the employee promoted "up and out" of the department. Although executives only occasionally admitted to this, the "up and out" rating process was almost universally discussed as something *other* managers actually do. One plant manager candidly remarked:

> *I've seen it happen, especially when you get a young guy in here*
> *who thinks he's only going to be here a short while before he gets pro-*
> *moted. People like that become a real pain in the ass. . . . If you want to*
> *get rid of them quick, a year and a half of good ratings should do it. . . .*
> *A lot of people inflate ratings of people they can't stand, or who think*
> *they are God's gift to the department, just to get rid of them. Amen.*

Of course, this practice helps an executive avoid dealing with performance problems and passes the problem along to someone else. Mainly, this tactic was employed when an executive felt unable or unwilling to deal with a performance problem or, especially, when the source of the problem seemed to be based on "personality" or "style" conflicts.

EXHIBIT 3   INFLATING THE APPRAISAL

- Executives inflated the appraisal to provide ratings that would effectively maintain or increase the subordinate's level of performance (the primary concern was not the accuracy of the ratings).
- Inflated ratings occur primarily on the overall performance rating as opposed to the individual appraisal items.
- Executive justification for inflating the appraisal:
  —to maximize the merit increases a subordinate would be eligible to receive, especially when the merit ceiling was considered low.
  —to protect or encourage a subordinate whose performance was suffering because of personal problems (feeling sorry for a subordinate also resulted in an inflated appraisal).
  —to avoid hanging dirty laundry out in public if the performance appraisal would be reviewed by people outside the organization.
  —to avoid creating a written record of poor performance that would become a permanent part of a subordinate's personnel file.
  —to avoid a confrontation with a subordinate with whom the manager had recently had difficulties.
  —to give a break to a subordinate who had improved during the latter part of the performance period.
  —to promote a subordinate "up and out" when the subordinate was performing poorly or did not fit in the department.

Deflating the Appraisal

For the most part, executives indicated that they were very hesitant to deflate a subordinate's rating because such a tactic would lead to subsequent problems:

> *I won't say I've never given a subordinate lower rates than he or she deserves because there's time and place for that type of thing, but let's just say I hesitate to do that sort of thing unless I'm very sure of what the outcome will be and that it won't backfire.*

Nevertheless, negative distortions did occur. Executives gave several reasons for using this tactic. First, an overly negative rating was sometimes used to jolt a subordinate to rise to his or her expected performance level:

> *I've used the appraisal to shock an employee. . . . If you've tried to coach a guy to get him back on track and it doesn't work, a low rating will more often than not slap him in the face and tell him you mean business. . . . I've dropped a few ratings way down to accomplish this because the alternative outcome could be termination down the road, which isn't pretty.*

Also, a deliberately deflated rating was sometimes used to teach a rebellious subordinate a lesson:

> *Occasionally an employee comes along who needs to be reminded who the boss is, and the appraisal is a real tangible and appropriate place for such a reminder. . . .*

Deflated ratings were also used as part of a termination procedure. First, a strongly negative rating could be used to send an indirect message to a subordinate that he or she should consider quitting:

> *If a person has had a questionable period of performance, a strong written appraisal can really send the message that they aren't welcome any longer and should think about leaving. . . . The written review sends a clear message if the person has any doubt.*

Second, once the decision has been made that the situation was unsalvageable, negative ratings could then be used to build a strongly documented case against the marginal or poor performer:

> *You'll find that once a manager has made up his or her mind that an employee isn't going to make it, the review [the written document] will take on an overly negative tone. . . . Managers are attempting to protect themselves. . . . The appraisal process becomes downwardly biased because they [the managers] fear that discussing and documenting any positives of the employee's performance might be used against them at a later point in time.*

Of course, this tactic has recently become more common because of lawsuits challenging the traditional "employment at will" concept. The courts have clearly stated that terminations must not be frivolous; they must be justified by economic constraints or documentation of poor performance. In these cases managers will use the process to protect themselves from litigation associated with an unlawful termination lawsuit.[7]

EXHIBIT 4   DEFLATING THE APPRAISAL

- Executives indicated that they were very hesitant consciously to deflate a subordinate's ratings because of potential problems associated with such a tactic.
- Nevertheless, they sometimes deflated appraisals:
  —to shock a subordinate back on to a higher performance track.
  —to teach a rebellious subordinate a lesson about who is in charge.
  —to send a message to a subordinate that he or she should consider leaving the organization.
  —to build a strongly documented record of poor performance that could speed up the termination process.

SUMMARY

Our research clearly showed that executives believed there was usually a justifiable reason for generating appraisal ratings that were less than accurate. Overall, they felt it was within their managerial discretion to do so. Thus our findings strongly suggest that the formal appraisal process is indeed a political process, and that few ratings are determined without some political consideration. Although research on rater "error" has traditionally suggested that raters can and do inflate ratings (leniency errors) and deflate ratings (stringency errors), researchers have typically not accounted for the realities of the appraisal context to explain why these errors occur.

In the minds of the managers we interviewed, these thoughts and behaviors are not errors but, rather, discretionary actions that help them manage people more effectively. Executives considered many factors beyond the subordinate's actual performance in their ratings. Thus, organizational politics was a major factor in the intentional manipulation of subordinate ratings.

Our findings provide support for the following political realities of organizational life: (1) executives in large organizations are political actors who attempt to avoid unnecessary conflict; (2) they attempt to use the organization's bureaucratic processes to their own advantage; and (3) they try to minimize the extent to which administrative responsibilities create barriers between them and their subordinates.

We also conclude that the organizational culture in which the appraisal event occurs significantly influenced the extent to which political activity would both develop and operate. Of course, organizationwide patterns are also strongly influenced by the support and practice of top management. Indeed, we know that lower-level managers tend to emulate high-status executives, and the way they use the appraisal process is no exception. Thus, if top managers prepare ratings poorly or deliberately distort them, this behavior will tend to cascade down the organization.

Given these findings, what informative observations or constructive recommendations might we make to minimize, or at least manage, the detrimental effects of politics in employee appraisal? In fact, we have several for both the individual manager and the organization as a whole.

THE INDIVIDUAL MANAGER

1. Quite frankly, our data suggest there are times in organizational life when political necessity supercedes the usually desirable goals of accuracy and honesty in appraisal. The executives interviewed suggested several compelling reasons for exercising managerial discretion contrary to traditional appraisal research recommendations. Clearly, there are times when individual employees and the organization as a whole can benefit as a consequence. The caveat, of course, is that the occasions when politics and discretion necessarily intrude on the appraisals process should be chosen judiciously. The overall effect on the organization should be given due consideration.

2. Performance appraisal is perhaps most usefully viewed as a high-potential vehicle for motivating and rewarding employees, rather than as a mandatory, bureaucratic exercise used only for judgmental or manipulative purposes. Ideally, it should be treated as an opportunity to communicate formally with employees about their performance, their strengths and weaknesses, and their developmental possibilities.

3. Executives should bear in mind that appraisal-related actions, like many other organizational activities, serve as guides for subordinates. Employees who must conduct appraisals often learn appraisal attitudes and behaviors from their bosses. Thus, if appraisals are to be effective, high-ranking executives must treat the process as significant so that political manipulation is discouraged.

4. In addition, openness and trust between managers and subordinates seems to be associated with a lower level of detrimental political activity. Cultivating understanding seems to reduce the perceived need for resorting to interpersonal politics.

5. Finally, inflating or deflating appraisal ratings for political ends might serve temporarily to help executives avoid a problem with certain employees or to accomplish some specific purpose. However, such intentional manipulation may eventually come back to haunt the perpetrating executive and, ultimately, the organization as a whole. This is especially likely if the company comes to accept political manipulation of appraisals as part of the norm.

THE ORGANIZATION AS A WHOLE

1. The appraisal process should operate in a supportive organizational culture. Effective appraisal systems are characterized by the support of top managers (who conduct appraisals themselves), training, open discussions of the appraisal process on an annual basis (perhaps a quality circle approach to appraisals), and rewarding the efforts of managers who do top-notch appraisals.

2. Systematic, regular, and formal appraisals should start at the top of the organization. We found that top executives want formal appraisals and rarely get them. If appraisals are not done at the top, the message sent to the rest of the organization is, "They aren't very important and thus

shouldn't be taken seriously." As a result, the door to more political activity is opened wider.

3. Further, although training on *how* to do effective appraisals is important, managers also need to be trained on *why* they need to be done. Understanding the rationale for appraisals is important in building the perception that the appraisal process is an effective managerial tool and not merely a required bureaucratic procedure.

4. Open discussion of the political aspects of the appraisal process (and their legal ramifications) should be included in appraisal training programs. Although managers made it clear that political manipulation of rating is commonplace, political issues were *never* openly discussed in either training programs or in management development efforts.

5. When money is tied to the rating process, politically oriented ratings tend to increase. This creates a dilemma: A "pay for performance" management philosophy depends on the "objective" measurement of performance. Yet the realities of politics in the measurement process often mean that measurement will not be objective. Should we therefore divorce appraisal ratings from salary decisions? We think not. Pay for performance is still a good concept in our view, even in light of our findings. Attention to the recommendations we present in this section should minimize the impact of manipulative politics in appraisal ratings.

6. In addition, the number of people who have access to the written appraisal should be minimized. The more people who have access to the appraisal, the greater the temptation for the rater to "impression manage" it. Remember, the fact that the appraisal is written down often means that it is less than completely accurate, simply because it is publicly available.

7. The findings of this study have legal implications as well. Organizations are more susceptible to litigation involving charges of unlawful discharge or discrimination than ever before. Accurate, valid appraisals can help an organization defend itself; inaccurate, invalid appraisals can put the organization at risk. Of course, the relatively recent practice of extensive documentation of poor performance has been in part a response to the modern legal climate. Paradoxically, that climate has arguably *increased* the role of politics in formal appraisal, as organizations try to maintain legal grounds for termination decisions. Still, the often politically motivated practice of building a case for dismissal via documentation of poor performance has come under closer scrutiny as trends in employee appraisal are given closer examination. The best advice here is to stress honesty in appraisal as a "default option" policy. Credible and consistent appraisal practices are the best defense against litigation. Thus some counseling in the legal ramifications of appraisal should become part of executive training.

CONCLUSION

Perhaps the most interesting finding from our study (because it debunks a popular mythology) is that accuracy is *not* the primary concern of the practicing executive in appraising subordinates. The main concern is how best to use the appraisal process to motivate and reward subordinates. Hence, managerial discretion and effectiveness, not accuracy, are the real watchwords. Managers made it clear that they would not allow excessively accurate ratings to cause problems for themselves, and that they attempted to use the appraisal process to their own advantage.

The astute manager recognizes that politics in employee appraisal will never be entirely squelched. More candidly, most of us also recognize that there is some place for politics in the appraisal process to facilitate necessary executive discretion. The goal, then, is not to arbitrarily and ruthlessly try to eliminate politics but, instead, to effectively manage the role politics plays in employee appraisal.

Notes

1. For an extensive discussion of this point, see F.J.Landy and J.L. Farr's "Performance Rating," *Psychological Bulletin,* 1980 87, 72–107. This issue is further developed in Landy and Farr's book. *The Measurement of Work Performance.* New York: Academic Press, 1983. It is clear that the psychometric aspects of the appraisal process are only one part of understanding and improving appraisals.

2. DeNisi, Cafferty, and Meglino have recently discussed the key issues and complications associated with understanding the psychology of managerial decision making in the appraisal process in their recent article. "A Cognitive View of the Performance Appraisal Process: A Model and Research Prospective, "*Organizational Behavior and Human Performance,* 1984. 33. 360–396. For a discussion of further cognitive complications in the appraisal process as a result of unconscious information processing, refer to D. A. Gioia and P. P. Poole, Scripts in Organizational Behavior," *Academy of Management Review,* 1984, 9, 449–459.

3. For an exploration of some of the emotional and affective factors that might bear on appraisal processes, see O. S. Park, H, Sims, Jr., and S. J. Motowidlo's "Affect in Organizations: How Feelings and Emotions Influence Managerial Judgment," in H. P. Sims and D. A. Gioia and Associates (Eds.) *The Thinking Organization.*

4.Jack Feldman suggests in his article, "Beyond Attribution Theory: Cognitive Processes in Performance Evaluation," *Journal of Applied Psychology,* 1981, 66. 127–148, that raters have certain cognitive flaws in information processing that make complete objectivity and validity in rating unobtainable, Also see W. C. Borman's "Explaining the Upper Limits of Reliability and Validity in Performance Ratings," *Journal of Applied Psychology,* 1987, 63. 135–144.

5. Jeffrey Pfeffer, in his book *Power in Organizations,* Marshfield, MA: Pittman Publishing Co., 1981, makes a strong case that political gamesmanship and the use of power in organizations surround almost every important decision in organizational life. The implications of the appraisal process (e.g., pay raises, promotions, terminations) make the appraisal of performance an important decision-making enterprise.

6. Bernardin and Beatty in their book *Performance Appraisal: Assessing Human Behavior at Work,* Boston, MA: Kent, 1984, suggest that extraneous variables that are not performance related have an effect on the rater's decision processes and that this influence is in fact a primary source of bias and inaccuracy in performance ratings.

7. For an in-depth treatment of the legal issues concerning performance appraisal, see P. S. Greenlaw and J. P. Kohl's *Personnel Management,* New York: Harper & Row, 1986, 171–173. See also W. F. Cascio and H. J. Bernardin's "Implications of Performance Litigation for Personnel Decisions," *Personnel Psychology,* Summer 1981, 217.

◆

Civility Rediscovered*

M. Scott Peck

After completing my psychiatry residency training in mid-1967 I owed the army three years of "payback" time. To fulfill this obligation I was assigned, at the age of thirty-one, to be the director of psychiatry at the U.S. Army Medical Center in Okinawa. In this position I was to manage a department of approximately forty. One senior sergeant was considerably older than I. The three other psychiatrists were approximately my age. Two junior officers were in the late twenties. The remaining thirty-five personnel were enlisted men and women in their late teens or early twenties.

Until that time I had never managed anybody. Through college, medical school, internship, and residency I had always been at the very bottom of the hierarchy. Nor, typical of such schooling, had I ever received anything faintly resembling management training. Yet from the moment I took over the department I was perfectly clear in my own mind about what my management style would be: I was going to be just as different from every authoritarian boss who had ever been in charge of me as I could possibly be.

I had no idea how to define consensus, but I was going to strive for it. Certainly my model was a highly consultative one. Not only did I never make an administrative decision without consulting everyone involved; I did my very best to see that, within the constraints of professional competence, the people under me made their own decisions wherever possible about the matters that affected their own lives. Because ours was a medical, "professional" department, I felt we could ignore the matter of rank. I discouraged them from addressing me as "Major Peck." Soon everyone was calling me Scotty. I was "Mr. Nice Guy." And it worked. The mood was euphoric. Everybody spoke glowingly of what a good leader I was and how relieved they were to be free of that stupid old lieutenant colonel, their previous commander. The work ran smoothly. The department morale was superb.

After just about six months, however, things began to go sour. It was almost imperceptible at first. The euphoria was gone. The men stopped talking about what a great place it was to work. "All right," I told myself, "the honeymoon's over. What else could you expect? Now it's work as usual, but nothing's wrong." But by the nine-month mark it began to get worse. While the work went on, petty bickering started. I wondered whether there might be a problem, but I could see nothing to account for it. Certainly it had nothing to do with me, for hadn't I shown myself to be a born leader? By the year mark, however, it was clear there was a problem. The bickering had escalated and the work was beginning to suffer. Little things were being left undone. At this point fate seemed to come to my rescue. A

---

*Reprinted from *A World Waiting to be Born: Civility Rediscovered* by M. Scott Peck M.D. New York; Bantam, 1993.

major new outpatient medical complex was in the final stages of construction, and the hospital commander told me that the clinic, the largest part of our department, would move there. Our current offices were cramped, cold, and gloomy. The new ones would be modern and airy, with views out over the Pacific and wall-to-wall carpeting. Surely the morale would improve at the prospect of such a pleasant move.

Only it didn't. It got worse. As moving day approached the entire staff grew ever more irritable. They began to squabble with each other over who would get which office in the new building. The packing of the files fell way behind schedule. It was now finally obvious it was my responsibility to do something. But what? I announced to the staff that we were going to meet over in the new conference room for the entirety of the next morning. And that we would continue to meet in that way every successive morning—even though it meant working in the evenings—until we got to the bottom of the problem.

The two four-hour meetings we had were two of the stormiest I have ever attended. Everyone took potshots at me and at each other. Everyone was angry. Everyone had something to complain about. Yet all the complaints were picky, superficial, and seemingly unreasonable. It was unrelieved chaos. But toward the end of the second morning one of the enlisted men said, "I feel I don't know where I stand." I asked him if he would elaborate. He couldn't. He became inarticulate and the group continued with its random conflict. But the young man's words reverberated through my mind. Earlier that morning someone else had said, "Everything's vague around here." And the day before another young man had voiced the complaint: "It's like we're at sea." I told the group that I needed time to think, that they should get back to work, and that we would not have any more of these meetings for the foreseeable future.

We returned to the old building, and I sat in my office staring at the ceiling, my lunch on the desk beside me, uneaten. Was it possible the department needed more structure than I had provided it? What kind of structure? A clearer sense of rank? What did they want me to do—boss them around like a bunch of children? That was totally against my nature. But then most of them were rather young, after all. Could it be that they wanted me to be some kind of father figure? Yet if I started ordering them around like an autocrat, wouldn't they hate me? I wanted to be Mr. Nice Guy. But, come to think of it, it was not my job to be popular; it was my job to run the best possible department I could. Maybe they did need a stronger kind of leadership from me.

I called the noncommissioned officer in charge (NCOIC) of the department, asked him to find the plans for the new building, and bring them to me as soon as possible. When he arrived, we unrolled the floor plan for the psychiatry outpatient clinic onto my desk. I pointed to the larger corner office. "That will be mine," I announced. Then, intermittently pausing just long enough for him to write each assignment, I proceeded along the blueprint through the smaller offices: "We'll put Captain Ames here, you here, Sergeant Ryan there, Lieutenant Hobson here, Private Coopermen there, Captain Marshall here, Sergeant Mosely here, Private Enowitch there," and so on down the map. "Now please go inform each of them of the office I've assigned him to."

You could practically hear the howls of dismay across the island. But by evening the morale had begun to improve. The next day I watched it escalate. By the end of the week it was back to where it had been at its best. They still called me Scotty and my overall style of leadership continued to be relatively—although no longer rigidly—nonauthoritarian. Yet the morale stayed high for the remaining year of my tour of duty.

You could think of this as a success story. I did eventually acknowledge that there was a problem and that it was my responsibility. I finally took the correct steps to diagnose it. I was able to readjust my behavior to meet the needs of the organization. Indeed, the story is used in part precisely because it is such a dramatic example of how a system can be successfully changed by a single simple intervention.

I prefer, however, to regard it as a story of failure. For the fact of the matter is that the department—the organization and the individuals within it—*suffered* for over six months on account of my poor leadership. It was indelibly clear that we had a significant morale problem at least six months before I took corrective action. Why did I take so long?

One reason was my self-esteem. I simply did not want to believe that there was anything wrong with Scott Peck or that his leadership was anything other than perfect.

Fueling that conceit, however, were my needs: my need to offer the department a simplistically compassionate, nonauthoritarian style of supervision, and my need to receive back the constant affection and gratitude of my subordinates. Until that final day I never even stopped to ask whether my needs were in consonance with those of the organization. It almost required a veritable revelation for me to realize that it was not necessarily my job—my role in the organization—to be popular.

It also never occurred to me that there was anything other than one best way to run any organization. I had never heard of contingency theory. My group consciousness was so limited I gave no thought to how remarkably young the members of the department were, and hence no thought to the possibility that the department might require a different style of leadership than an organization whose personnel were more mature. So it was that we suffered needlessly for months.

Would it have been different had I received some management training before being assigned to Okinawa? Would Lily and I have suffered substantially less, I wonder, had we had the benefit of some instruction on marriage before the fact? These questions are too hypothetical to answer with certainty, but at the very least, the response should be a guarded yes.

It must be a guarded response since, being different, individuals have different styles of learning. Some children learn better in open classrooms while others do best in more structured situations. Some young adults benefit far more from formal instruction than from experience, while others do far better with experiential learning. Moreover, certain types of instruction are more or less suitable depending on the type of material being presented. Contingency theory again! I cannot be sure how much I could have benefited from management training until I actually became a manager. Or how much a course in marriage would have meant before I had an actual marriage to deal with.

The New York Times, January 9, 1993

Shock in a Land of Lifetime Jobs: 35 Managers Dismissed in Japan[*]

Andrew Pollack

Tokyo, Jan. 8—The unthinkable has happened in Japan, and it has touched a nerve in the ranks of the nation's middle managers.

A well-known maker of audio and video equipment, Pioneer Electronic, conceded today that it was essentially firing 35 middle managers, a candid admission that Japanese companies have begun to violate their long-cherished policies of lifetime employment.

Such a move would barely attract notice in the United States, where thousands of employees are sometimes given pink slips in a day. But in Japan, the commitment to keeping people employed through good times and bad is a pillar of a management system in which Japanese workers remain highly dedicated to their companies. And the move, in the midst of a severe economic slump, portends significant changes in the Japanese corporate culture.

'It Has Come to This'

"My first reaction, honestly, was, 'My God, it has come to this,'" an automobile executive said. But he quickly added, "If the current slump continues for another year or two, a lot of companies will be doing the same thing."

Pioneer, a Tokyo-based maker of car stereos, laser-disk players and other electronics gear, did not actually fire the employees outright, a spokesman said. Rather, it told the managers in late December that they would have until the end of January to retire.

If the managers, all in their 50's, did retire, they would receive a hefty bonus. If they didn't, they would eventually be dismissed. "This is actually, practically, a dismissal," the spokesman, Yojiro Orita, said.

Takeo Naruse, deputy general manager of the Japan Federation of Employers' Associations, a lobbying group, called the Pioneer move "shock therapy." He said most other companies would not resort to such drastic actions, which could hurt company morale. Still, he said, "Gradually, Japanese employment practices are changing."

To be sure, lifetime employment has never been universal. Small and medium-sized companies, which often supply components to large companies, frequently lay off workers and act as a buffer to help the big companies maintain full employment. And even at large corporations, the job guarantee does not apply to legions of part-time or temporary workers. But in the case of Pioneer, a leading electronics company, the affected managers are full-time employees.

Some experts said Pioneer's approach was a slightly stricter version of what was now happening quietly in many businesses, with managers being asked to retire for the good of the companies. The procedure is called "kata tataki," or a tap on the shoulder. Most employees accept the offer, although they usually have the option of declining if they are willing to accept lower pay or a lesser job.

Many employers insist that they are not dismissing workers, but the boundary between forced resignations and voluntary departures is becoming very narrow. "Most companies have been terminating middle managers already for a long time," said

---

Kazunori Morishita, president of Bright Career, a firm that helps workers find new jobs. "But they don't say, 'If you don't agree, you will be fired.' "

Many economists have questioned how much longer Japanese companies can continue their practice of lifetime employment in the face of the severe economic slump. During the speculative "bubble economy" of the late 1980s, companies actively hired, believing the economy would keep expanding. Now that the economy has slowed, many employees are no longer necessary.

Redundant Workers

Some economic research organizations estimate that about 1 million employees in Japanese companies, out of the nation's total employment of about 65 million, are redundant. This underemployment, which drags down corporate earnings, is in some sense a bigger problem than unemployment, which is still a low 2.3 percent.

So far, many companies have announced plans to cut thousands of employees in the next few years. But they insist they will do that by reducing hiring, offering voluntary retirements or transferring employees to other divisions or to subsidiaries.

Many companies bend over backward to avoid layoffs—by paying people to stay home, for example. Or a steel company with excess employees might lend them to an auto company with a shortage of workers.

Fears of Worker Shortage

Part of the resolve to hang on to employees stems from fear that because of Japan's low birth rates, the severe worker shortage that plagued the nation until recently will reoccur when the economy recovers.

Another aspect of Japanese management that is changing is the seniority system, in which promotions and salaries tend to rise with the length of service. That has weighed down companies with many middle-aged managers with high salaries but little opportunity to advance. Now, some

leading companies like Honda and Fujitsu are moving toward a system in which pay is based on merit, at least for top managers.

"In the old, traditional system, you work long and are eventually promoted to manager," said Mr. Orita, the Pioneer spokesman. "That system can no longer work because we're moving into a severe economic situation. So we're forced to look at each manager's achievements."

Mr. Orita said the 35 employees, whose identities were being kept secret even in the company, were chosen because they were not performing up to par. Because of their seniority, many have the rank and salary of a section chief but have no one reporting to them.

Morale May Suffer

Some outsiders questioned the move, saying that eliminating 35 employees out of more than 1,000 managers saves Pioneer barely any money and will hurt morale. While its profits are dropping, Pioneer is still making money, unlike many other consumer electronics companies.

A few months ago, the president of TDK, a manufacturer of magnetic tapes, proposed paying about 50 older managers 90 percent of their salaries if they would stay home until they reached retirement age. But the employees revolted, forcing the president to rescind the plan.

Mr. Orita said that when Pioneer employees learned about the forced retirements from newspapers or television—the company did not announce them internally—some managers were shocked and feared they would be the next to get the tap on the shoulder. But, he said, the move could raise the morale of younger executives who resent having promotions blocked by older managers who do not work as hard.

As he emerged from work today at the company's headquarters, one manager in his 30s said the action was "drastic" and would hurt morale. Another merely shrugged, "It's strict," he said, "but it's unavoidable."

The New York Times, September 20, 1992

It's Lit, Not Just Lite, at Coors*

Barbara Presley Noble

The Colorado brewer offers literacy programs to its workers.

For 27 years, Mayers T. Caldwell worked on the shop floor for the ceramics subsidiary of the Adolph Coors Company in Golden, Colo. He showed his supervisors how to do the work often enough that he knew he could probably have been a supervisor himself. But Mr. Caldwell, who turned 61 yesterday, had a problem that precluded mobility. The eighth-grade education he received in his native Kentucky left him barely able to read.

Mr. Caldwell retired three years ago without making the leap off the line. He encouraged his son to go to college, and the son repaid the favor. "He said, 'You told me to go to school, now you go,'" Mr. Caldwell said. He enrolled at Red Rock, the local community college, to learn basic math and got straight A's. By the time he was ready to tackle his reading, Coors made it very easy for him: earlier this year, it established a literacy program for employees—current and retired—in Golden.

Mr. Caldwell's experience may sound like something out of another era, but employers and government alike are worried about the lack of basic skills among potential workers. The Labor Department recently reported that 35 to 45 percent of young people with a high-school diploma or equivalent who participate in Federal job training and employment programs have low literacy skills. Among nongraduates, the figure rises to 90 percent.

Even worse, a survey by the National Alliance of Business, a Washington education advocacy group, indicates that even educators are dubious about the skills of recent graduates. Of the high-school principals surveyed, fewer than 40 percent think their students know enough math to hold an entry-level job; only 42 percent think they read well enough and just over a quarter think they write adequately.

Even if schools are the source of the problem, employers pay the piper. Yet Coors is relatively rare in the extent of its support for literacy: of some 400 employers surveyed recently by the Olsten Corporation, only about 25 percent have formal workplace literacy programs.

And Coors's commitment may seem surprising. The Coors family has been known as opposers of unions, embracers of conservative causes, but hardly as coddlers of employees. The Coors Brewing Company was bruised when a 1977 strike evolved into an A.F.L.-C.I.O.-led consumer boycott that took a decade to resolve and seriously undermined the beer's image as a brew for partying Zen hipsters.

If the literacy lab is part of a grand plan to rehabilitate the Coors name, it is nevertheless also part of a national Coors scheme to consolidate its charitable giving—and to encourage people to read. "We were taking a shotgun approach to making contributions and providing resources," said Celia Sheneman, who directs Coors's national literacy program. "We wanted to focus on one cause where we could really make a difference." At the beginning of 1990, Coors pledged $40 million to a five-year effort, called "Literacy: Pass It On," to raise the awareness of literacy problems and to provide money for the programs that actually teach reading.

The external literacy campaign was the proximate raison d'être of the learning center where Mr. Caldwell is improving his skills. It is run with help from Red Rock, where Mr. Caldwell had gone for help with his math. Coors pays for a reading specialist from Red Rock, who trains employee-volunteers—25 of them—to tutor reading one-on-one. Because employees arrive with different needs, instruction is tailored to the individual using phonics, computer-aided learning, writing exercises and other strategies. Since it opened at the beginning of this year, more than 180 of Coors's 6,000 Colorado employees have used the center.

Employees get to the program variously. Some come face to face with the march of progress. As their jobs increase in complexity, they can no longer disguise and work around their inability to read. Suddenly, for example, a forklift operator may need to be able to read a computer screen. "Some come in because they can't help their kids anymore, and that's a motivation," said Michael Aden, who runs the learning center for Coors. "Some have lived with the challenge and hidden it long enough."

Mr. Caldwell's job didn't require a lot of reading, and he was able to cope, though, he said, "It held me back." He appreciates the program at Coors, he said, and if he wishes he had learned to read better a little earlier, he doesn't waste much time on regrets. He has been poring over phonics exercises and working at a keyboard for several months now, steadily improving. "I look one way, straight ahead," he said. "You got to fight when you want to do something. It takes initiative."

The New York Times, December 26, 1992

Boss Knows Best? Well, Here's a Way to Find Out[*]

Associated Press

Workers and bosses switch jobs for a day at a Ford plant. Each side learns something from the other. And bosses find that not all their ideas are good ones.

White collars were traded with blue ones recently at a Ford Motor Co. assembly plant, where managers spent the morning at the conveyor belt and laborers spent the afternoon in the front offices.

The switch seemed to be going well until an office-type pressed the wrong button and sent the hook of a hoist ripping into a steel guardrail. The assembly line stopped while a maintenance worker welded it back together.

"I was a little embarrassed," said Phil Brand, a supervisor of manufacturing and engineering on any other day. "It would have to happen to me."

Then there was area manager, Pete Corbett, who kept dropping parts and forgetting to install bearing caps. Production supervisor Gene Gyle was slowing down the line as he nursed his sore thumbs.

"I know what I'm supposed to be doing but am having a hard time keeping up,"

Gyle said. "These girls do it with long fingernails that never break on them. I don't know how they do it."

Blue-collar workers were at the sides of managers, making sure quality was not sacrificed at the hands of their bosses.

"He's done pretty good—for management," Leatha Harmon said as she watched Gyle do her job.

The "job sharing" day at the Sterling Heights plant, where all Ford axles, drive shafts and I-beams are made, began two years ago after a manager told laborers a new idea would work easily on the assembly line.

"The other guy says, 'You should walk in my shoes before saying that,'" said Vince LeVigne, employee resource coordinator with the United Auto Workers.

"It used to be dog-eat-dog out here. Now, we work together," said UAW plant president Frank Savalle. He traded jobs with the plant manager for the day. "We still have grievances and problems, but we get more accomplished sitting and talking about problems than when we were at war."

LeVigne said the team approach has resulted in better auto parts. All six final drive-line components made by the plant were awarded "best in class" among makers this year.

After last year's switch, a manager who ran a forklift that broke down twice in a day got the worker a new one.

Corbett, who scraped his arm on the axle's sharp edge, said the assembly line was awkward. The laborer who spends his day there had scars on his arm from machinery.

"We have to ergonomically redesign the job to make it more efficient but with less wear and tear on the body," Corbett said.

The Wall Street Journal, November 2, 1991

Finding Motivation in the Little Things[*]

Joan E. Rigdon

Some companies use creative gimmicks to motivate workers.

Each year, John Brady Design Consultants, Pittsburgh, gives a jar of 12 marbles to its 18 employees, a different color for each person. Over the year, employees give the marbles as rewards to co-workers who help them out or achieve great feats. At year's end, the firm can see who recognizes others and who doesn't. The program is better than bonuses, profit sharing and other approaches that "cost me a lot of money," says John Brady, president.

Berlin Packaging, Chicago, used a contest to spur employees to handle increased work during a computer conversion earlier this year. Workers who exceeded production goals got to take three shots at a basketball hoop in the president's office. The prizes: $25 for making one basket, $50 for two and $75 for three.

Critics say pay-for-performance plans are best, because gimmicks can be demeaning. But on a small scale, offbeat programs are fun, Mr. Brady says: "Workers love showing off their marbles."

◆

The Case of the Mismanaged Ms.*

Sally Seymour

It started out as one of those rare quiet mornings when I could count on having the office to myself. The Mets had won the World Series the night before, and most of the people in the office had celebrated late into the night at a bar across the street. I'm a fan too, but they all like to go to one of those bars where the waitresses dress like slave girls and the few women customers have to run a mine field of leers when they go to a ladies' room labeled "Heifers." Instead, I watched the game at home with my husband and escaped a hangover.

So I was feeling pretty good, if a little smug, when Ruth Linsky, a sales manager here at Triton, stormed past my secretary and burst into my office. Before I could say good morning, she demanded to know what business it was of the company who she slept with and why. I didn't know what she was talking about, but I could tell it was serious. In fact, she was practically on the verge of tears, but I knew she wasn't the type to fly off the handle.

Ruth had been with the company for three years, and we all respected her as a sensible and intelligent woman. She had been top in her class at business school and we recruited her hard when she graduated, but she didn't join us for a couple of years. She's since proved to be one of our best people in sales, and I didn't want to lose her. She fumed around the room for a while, not making much sense, until I talked her into sitting down.

"I've had it with this place and the way it treats women!" she shouted.

I allowed her to let off some more steam for a minute or two, and then I tried to calm her down. "Look, Ruth," I said, "I can see you're upset, but I need to know exactly what's going on before I can help you."

"I'm not just upset, Barbara," she said, "I'm damned mad. I came over to Triton because I thought I'd get more chances to advance here, and I just found out that I was passed over for director of the marketing division and Dick Simon got it instead. You know that I've had three outstanding years at the company, and my performance reviews have been excellent. Besides, I was led to believe that I had a pretty good shot at the job."

"What do you mean, 'led to believe'?"

"Steve heard through the grapevine that they were looking for a new marketing director, and he suggested I put in my name," she said. "He knows my work from when we worked together over at Forge Techtronics, and he said he'd write a letter in support. I wouldn't have even known they were looking for someone if Steve hadn't tipped me off."

Steve Baines is vice president of manufacturing. He's certainly a respected senior person in the company and he pulls some weight, but he doesn't have sole control of the marketing position. The hierarchy doesn't work that way, and I tried

---

to get Ruth to see that. "Okay, so Steve wrote a letter for you, but he's only one of five or six VPs who have input in executive hiring decisions. Of course it helps to have his support, but lots of other factors need to be considered as well."

"Come off it, Barbara," Ruth snapped. "You know as well as I do there's only one thing that really matters around here and that's whether you're one of the boys. I've got a meeting this afternoon with my lawyer, and I'm going to file a sexual discrimination suit, a sexual harassment suit, and whatever other kind of suit she can come up with. I've had it with this old-boy crap. The only reason I'm here is that, as human resources director, you should know what's going on around here."

So the stakes were even higher than I had thought; not only did it look like we might lose Ruth, but we also might have a lawsuit on our hands. And to top it off, with the discrimination issue Ruth might be trying to get back at us for promoting Dick. I felt strongly about the importance of this legal remedy, but I also knew that using it frivolously would only undermine women's credibility in legitimate cases.

"Ruth," I said, "I don't doubt your perceptions, but you're going to need some awfully strong evidence to back them up."

"You want evidence? Here's your evidence. Number one: 20% of the employees in this company are women. Not one is on the board of directors, and not one holds an executive-level position. You and I are the only two in mid-level positions because they never know when they're available. When a vacancy comes up, the VPs—all men, of course—decide among themselves who should fill it. And then, over and over again I hear that some guy who hasn't worked half as hard as most of the women at his level has been given the plum. Number three: there are plenty of subtle and sometimes not-so-subtle messages around here that women are less than equal."

"Ruth, those are still pretty vague accusations," I interrupted. "You're going to have to come up with something more specific than feelings and suppositions."

"Don't worry, Barbara. Just keep listening and maybe you'll learn something about how this company you think so highly of operates. From the day Ed Coulter took over as vice president of marketing and became my boss, he's treated me differently from the male sales managers. Instead of saying good morning, he always has some comment about my looks—my dress is nice, or my hair looks pretty, or the color of my blouse brings out my eyes. I don't want to hear that stuff. Besides, he never comments on a guy's eyes. And then there's that calendar the sales reps have in their back office. Every time I go in there for a sales meeting, I feel like I've walked into a locker room."

So far, this all seemed pretty harmless to me, but I didn't want Ruth to feel I wasn't sympathetic. "To tell the truth, Ruth, I'm not so sure all women here find compliments like that insulting, but maybe you can give me other examples of discriminatory treatment."

"You bet I can. It's not just in the office that these things happen. It's even worse in the field. Last month Ed and I and Bill, Tom, and Jack went out to Dryden Industries for a big project meeting. I'll admit I was a little nervous because there were some heavy hitters in the room, so I kept my mouth shut most of the morning. But I was a team member and I wanted to contribute.

"So when Ed stumbled at one point, I spoke up. Well, it was like I had committed a sacrilege in church. The Dryden guys just stared at me in surprise, and then they seemed actually angry. They ignored me completely. Later that afternoon, when I asked Ed why I had gotten that reaction, he chuckled a little and explained that since we hadn't been introduced by our specific titles, the Dryden guys had assumed I was a research assistant or a secretary. They thought I was being presumptuous. But when Ed explained who I was, they admitted that I had made an important point.

"But that wasn't all," she went on. "The next day, when we explained to them that I would be interviewing some of the factory foremen for a needs assessment, one of the executives requested that someone else do it because apparently there's a superstition about women on the factory floor bringing bad luck. Have you ever heard of anything so stupid? But that's not the worst of it. Ed actually went along with it. After I'd pulled his bacon out of the fire the day before. And when I nailed him for it, he had the gall to say, 'Honey, whatever the client wants, the client gets.'

"Well, we got the contract, and that night we all went out to dinner and everything was hurray for our team. But then, when I figured we'd all go back to the hotel for a nightcap, Ed and the guys just kind of drifted off."

"Drifted off?" I asked.

"Yeah. To a bar. They wanted to watch some basketball game."

"And you weren't invited?"

"I wasn't invited and I wasn't disinvited," she said. "They acted like they didn't know what to say."

By this point Ruth had cooled down quite a bit, and although she still seemed angry, she was forthright in presenting her case. But now her manner changed. She became so agitated that she got up from her chair to stare out the window. After a few minutes, she sort of nodded her head, as if she had come to some private, difficult decision, and then crossed the room to sit down again. Looking at her lap and twisting a paper clip around in her hands, she spoke so softly that I had to lean forward to hear her.

"Barbara," she began, "what I'm going to tell you is, I hope, in confidence. It's not easy for me to talk about this because it's very personal and private, but I trust you and I want you to understand my position. So here goes. When Steve Baines and I were both at Forge, we had a brief affair. I was discreet about it; it never interfered with business, and we ended it shortly after we both came to work here. But we're still very close friends, and occasionally we have dinner or a drink together. But it's always as friends. I think Ed found out about it somehow. The day after I notified the head office that I wanted to be considered for the director position, Ed called me into his office and gave me a rambling lecture about how we have to behave like ladies and gentlemen these days because of lawsuits on sexual harassment.

"At the time, I assumed he was referring somehow to one of our junior sales reps who had gotten drunk at the Christmas party and made a fool of himself with a couple of secretaries; but later I began to think that the cryptic comment was meant for me. What's more, I think Ed used that rumor about my relationship with Steve to block my promotion. And that, Barbara, is pure, sexist, double-standard hypocrisy because I can name you at least five guys at various levels in this company who have had affairs with colleagues and clients, and Ed is at the top of the list."

I couldn't deny the truth of Ruth's last statement, but that wasn't the point, or not yet. First I had to find out which, if any, of her accusations were true. I told her I needed some time and asked if she could give me a week before calling in a lawyer. She said no way. Having taken the first step, she was anxious to take the next, especially since she didn't believe things would change at Triton anyway. We dickered back and forth, but all I could get from her was a promise to hold off for 24 hours. Not much of a concession, but it was better than nothing.

Needless to say, I had a lot to think about and not very much time to do it in. It was curious that this complaint should come shortly after our organization had taken steps to comply with affirmative action policies by issuing a companywide memo stating that we would continue to recruit, employ, train, and promote individuals without regard to race, color, religion, sex, age, national origin, physical or mental handicap, or status as a disabled veteran or veteran of the Vietnam era. And we did this to prevent any problems in the future, not because we'd had trouble in the past. In fact, in my five years as HRM director, I'd never had a sexual discrimination or harassment complaint.

But now I was beginning to wonder whether there had never been grounds for complaint or whether the women here felt it was useless or even dangerous to complain. If it was the latter, how had I contributed to allowing that feeling to exist? And this thought led me to an even more uncomfortable one. Had I been coopted into ignoring injustices in a system that, after all, did pretty well by me? Was I afraid to slap the hand that buttered my bread?

Questioning one's own motives may be enlightening, but it's also time consuming, and I had more pressing matters to deal with before I could indulge in what would likely be a painful self-analysis. I asked my secretary to find George Drake, CEO of Triton, and get him on the phone. In the meantime, I wrote down as much as I could remember of what Ruth had just told me. When George finally called, I told him I knew his schedule was full but we had an emergency of sorts on our hands and I needed an hour of his time this morning. I also asked that Ed Coulter be called into the meeting. George told me I had the hour.

When I got to George's office, Ed and George were already waiting. They were undoubtedly curious about why I had called this meeting, but as I've seen people do in similar situations, they covered their anxiety with chitchat about ball games and hangovers. I was too impatient for these rituals, so I cut the conversation short and told them that we were going to have a serious lawsuit on our hands in a matter of days if we didn't act very quickly. That got their attention, so I proceeded to tell Ruth's story. When I began, George and Ed seemed more surprised than anything else, but as I built up Ruth's case their surprise turned to concern. When I finished, we all sat in silence for I don't know how long and then George asked Ed for comments.

"Well, George," Ed said, "I don't know what to say. Ruth certainly was a strong contender for the position, and her qualifications nearly equaled Dick's, but it finally came down to the fact that Dick had the seniority and a little more experience in the industrial sector. When you've got two almost equally qualified candidates, you've got to distinguish them somehow. The decision came down to the wire, which in this case was six months seniority and a few more visits to factory sites."

"Were those the only criteria that made a difference in the decision?" George wanted to know.

"Well, not exactly. You know as well as I do that we base hiring decisions on a lot of things. On one hand, we look at what's on paper: years at the company, education, experience, recommendations. But we also rely on intuition, our feel for the situation. Sometimes, you don't know exactly why, but you just feel better about some people than others, and I've learned that those gut reactions are pretty reliable. The other VPs and I all felt good about Dick. There's something about him—he's got the feel of a winner. You know? He's confident—not arrogant—but solid and really sharp. Bruce had him out to the club a couple of times, and I played squash with him all last winter. We got to know him and we liked what we saw; he's a family man, kids in school here, could use the extra money, and is looking to stick around for a while. None of these things mean a lot by themselves, of course, but together they add up.

"Don't get me wrong. I like Ruth too. She's very ambitious and one of our best. On the other hand, I can't say that I or any of the VPs know her as well as we know Dick. Of course, that's not exactly Ruth's fault, but there it is."

I had to be careful with the question I wanted Ed to respond to next because Ruth had asked for my confidence about the affair. I worded it this way: "Ed, did any part of your decision take into account Ruth's relationship with anyone else at the company?"

The question visibly disturbed Ed. He walked across the room and bummed a cigarette from me—he had quit last week—before answering: "Okay, I didn't want to go into this, but since you brought it up. . . . There's a rumor—well it's stronger than a rumor—that Ruth is more than professionally involved with Steve Baines— I mean she's having an, ah, sexual affair with him. Now before you tell me that's none of my business, let me tell you about some homework I did on this stuff. Of course it's real tricky. It turns out there are at least two court cases that found sexual discrimination where an employer involved in a sexual relationship with an employee promoted that person over more qualified candidates.

"So here's what that leaves us with: we've got Steve pushing his girlfriend for the job. You saw the letter he wrote. And we've got Dick with seniority. So if we go with Ruth, what's to keep Dick from charging Steve and the company on two counts of sexual discrimination: sexual favoritism because Ruth is Steve's honey and reverse discrimination because we pass over a better qualified man just to get a woman into an executive position. So we're damned if we do and damned if we don't. We've got lawsuits if we don't advance Dick, and, so you tell me, lawsuits if we don't advance Ruth!"

We let that sink in for a few seconds. Then George spoke up: "What evidence do you have, Ed, that Steve and Ruth are having an affair?" he asked.

"Look, I didn't hire some guy to follow them around with a camera, if that's what you mean," Ed said. "But come on, I wasn't born yesterday; you can't keep that kind of hanky-panky a secret forever. Look at the way she dresses; she obviously enjoys men looking at her, especially Steve. In fact, I saw them having drinks together at Dino's the other night and believe me, they didn't look like they were talking business. All that on top of the rumors, you put two and two together."

Well, that did it for me. I'd been trying to play the objective observer and led Ed and George do all the talking, but Ed's last comment, along with some budding guilt about my own blindness to certain things at Triton that Ruth had pointed out, drove me out in the open. "Come off it, Ed," I said. "That's not evidence, that's gossip."

Now Ed turned on me: "Look," he shouted, "I didn't want to talk about this, but now that you've brought it up, I'll tell you something else. Even if we didn't have to worry about this sexual discrimination business, I still wouldn't back Ruth for the director's job." He calmed down a bit. "No offense, Barbara, but I just don't think women work out as well as men in certain positions. Human resources is one thing. It's real soft, person-to-person stuff. But factories are still a man's world. And I'm not talking about what I want it to be like. I'm talking facts of life.

"You see what happens when we send a woman out on some jobs, especially in the factories. To be any good in marketing you have to know how to relate to your client; that means getting to know him, going out drinking with him, talking sports, hunting, whatever he's interested in. A lot of our clients feel uncomfortable around a woman in business. They know how to relate to their wives, mothers, and girlfriends, but when a woman comes to the office and wants to talk a deal on industrial drills—well, they don't know what to do.

"And then there's the plain fact that you can't depend on a woman the way you can on a guy. She'll get married and her husband will get transferred, or she'll have a baby and want time off and not be able to go on the road as much. I know, Barbara, you probably think I'm a pig, or whatever women's libbers call guys like me these days. But from where I'm sitting, it just made good business sense to choose Dick over Ruth."

"Ed, I don't believe it," I said. "The next thing you'll tell me is that women ought to stay at home, barefoot and pregnant." There was a long silence after that—my guess was that I had hit on exactly what Ed thought. At least he didn't deny it. Ed stared at the rug, and George frowned at his coffee cup. I tried to steer the conversation back to the subject at hand, but it dwindled into another silence. George took a few notes and then told Ed he could go back to work. I assumed I was excused too, but as I started to leave, George called me back.

"Barbara, I'm going to need your help thinking through this mess," he said. "Of course we've got to figure out how we can avoid a lawsuit before the day is out, but I also want to talk about what we can do to avoid more lawsuits in the future. While Ed was talking I took some notes, and I've got maybe four or five points I think we ought to hash out. I'm not saying we're going to come up with all the answers today, but it'll be a start. You ready?"

"Shoot."

"Okay, let's do the big one first," he began. "What should I have done or not done to avoid this situation? I mean, I was just patting myself on the back for being so proactive when I sent out that memo letting everyone know the company policy on discrimination. I wrote it not thinking we had any problem at Triton. But just in case we did, I figured that memo would take care of it."

"Well, it looks like it's not enough just to have a corporate policy if the people in the ranks aren't on board. Obviously it didn't have much of an effect on Ed."

"So what am I supposed to do? Fire Ed?"

Being asked for my honest opinion by my CEO was a new experience for me and I appreciated it, but I wasn't going to touch that last question with a ten-foot pole. Instead I went on to another aspect: "And even if you get your managers behind you, your policy won't work if the people it's supposed to help don't buy it. Ruth was the first woman to complain around here. Are the others afraid to speak up? Or do they feel like Ed about a woman's place, or have husbands who do? Maybe they lack confidence even to try for better jobs, that is, if they knew about them."

"Okay," he said, "I'll admit that our system of having the VPs make recommendations, our 'old-boy network,' as Ruth called it, does seem to end up excluding women, even though the exclusion isn't intentional. And it's not obvious discrimination, like Ed's claim that Ruth is unqualified for a position because she is a woman. But wouldn't open job posting take away our right to manage as we see fit? Maybe we should concentrate instead on getting more women into the social network, make it an old boys' and old girls' club?"

"To tell you the truth, George, I don't much want to play squash with you," I replied, "but maybe we're getting off the subject. The immediate question seems to be how we're going to get more women into executive positions here, or, more specifically, do we give Ruth the director of marketing position that we just gave Dick?"

"On that score, at least, it seems to me that Ed has a strong argument," George said. "Dick is more qualified. You can't get around that."

I had wanted to challenge Ed on this point when he brought it up earlier, but I wasn't quite sure of myself then. Now that George was asking me for advice and seemed to be taking what I had to say seriously, I began to think that I might have something valuable to offer. So I charged right in. "George, maybe we're cutting too fine a line with this qualifications business. I know a lot of people think affirmative action means promoting the unqualified over the qualified to achieve balance. I think that argument is hogwash at best and a wily diversion tactic at worst. To my mind, Ruth and Dick are equally qualified, or equal enough. And wouldn't it make good business sense to get a diverse set of perspectives—women's, men's, blacks', whites'—in our executive group?"

"But isn't that reverse discrimination—not promoting Dick because he's a man? How would a judge respond to that? That's a question for a lawyer."

George leaned forward. "Let's talk about my last point, the one I think we've both been avoiding. What about this affair between Ruth and Steve? Boy, this is one reason why women in the work force are such trouble—no, just joking, Barbara, sorry about that. Look, I don't like lawsuits any more than anyone else, but I'd do anything to avoid this one. We'd be a laughing stock if it got out that Triton promoted unqualified people because they slept with the boss. I don't know how I'd explain that one to my wife."

"Look, George," I said, "in the first place, Dick's superior qualifications are debatable; in the second place, we have no proof that Ruth and Steve are involved in that way; and in the third place, what if they were once involved but no longer are? Does a past relationship condemn them for life? Isn't there a statute of limitations on that kind of thing, or are we going to make her put a scarlet letter on her briefcase? I thought these discrimination laws were supposed to protect women, but now it looks like a woman can be denied a promotion because someone thinks she's a floozy."

"Wait a second, Barbara. Don't make me look like such a prig," George said. "I realize that when men and women work together sexual issues are bound to crop up. I just don't know what I'm supposed to do about it, if anything. In some cases a woman may welcome a guy coming on to her, but what if it's her boss? And then there's that subtle stuff Ruth brought up—the calendar, dirty jokes, the male employees excluding women by going to bars to watch TV—and other women. And Ruth's treatment at that factory—how can we control our clients? I'm not sure these are things you can set policy on, but I am sure that I can't ignore them any longer."

And there we were. All the issues were on the table, and we had about 21 hours to make our decisions and act on them. . . .

◆

Getting Serious About Sexual Harassment[*]

Troy Segal with Kevin Kelly and Alisa Solomon

More companies are addressing it, but there's still a long way to go.

Co-pilot Kathy Gillies had endured plenty from her male colleagues in the three years she had worked for United Airlines Inc.: propositions, pornographic pictures in the cockpit, discussions of masturbation. But this summer, after she charged that she was attacked by her flight captain in a hotel room, she filed a sexual harassment claim with the airline, requesting not to be assigned with him again. United investigated, but concluded ". . . we have been unable to establish that what you alleged to have occurred between you and Captain X actually took place." So United refused to guarantee the two would not be scheduled together.

That was the final straw for Gillies, one of 436 female pilots out of 8,400 at United. On Oct. 13, she filed suit in Los Angeles Superior Court against the airline and several employees. UAL Inc. hasn't responded to the charges of sexual harassment and discrimination, saying only: "We treat any such claims as serious."

LAME STEPS

Kathy Gillies is a pilot in Los Angeles, but she could be an attorney in Miami, a bus mechanic in Louisville, or a former city council aide in New York City, to name a few instigators of sexual-harassment suits or charges that have surfaced with increasing regularity. A year after the Anita Hill–Clarence Thomas hearings, the Equal Employment Opportunity Commission reports a 50% jump in harassment claims. Management consultants, labor lawyers, and private advocacy groups, such as 9 to 5 and the NOW Legal Defense & Education Fund, report that calls for information from companies and individuals have tripled. A recent survey of 607 women conducted by the National Association for Female Executives (NAFE) finds that 60% say they have experienced sexual harassment—up 7 percentage points from a poll taken right after the hearings.

More than half the pollees said their companies still haven't addressed the problem. When they do, they all too often try a token approach—posting a policy or handing out a list of dos and don'ts. "It's encouraging that there's lots of talk about harassment still," says Helen Neuborne, executive director of the NOW Legal Defense & Education Fund. "But has there been real change in corporate behavior? No."

Still, the hearings did induce some employers to take sexual harassment seriously. In particular, it introduced many to "hostile workplace" harassment—a corporate atmosphere or behavior that would offend a reasonable woman—which is far more common than the explicit-threat type. Companies now have a financial incentive as well: The passage of the Civil Rights Act of 1991 means victims of sexual harassment can receive punitive and compensatory damages. Says Susan M. Benton-Powers, a partner at Chicago law firm Sonnenschein, Nath & Rosenthal: "The hearings made them concerned about the issue. The act raised the concern of the bottom line."

Figuring it costs less to invest in prevention than in litigation, many companies have established training programs or revised their current ones. Seattle management consultant Susan L. Webb, author of *Step Forward: Sexual Harassment in the Workplace,* notes that at one time, companies routinely ordered 20 to 50 copies of a training video or manual on dealing with sexual harassment. Now, it's more like 2,000 to 3,000—indicating a desire to educate the entire work force, not just senior managers. Miami-based Knight-Rider Inc. now requires all employees to take a two-hour workshop on sexual harassment issues. In the past 10 months, 6,000 out of 20,700 staffers have attended. Responding to requests from front-line managers, Conoco Inc. in Houston has also intensified its training, augmenting a two-year-old program with a workshop specifically devoted to hostile-work place harassment.

Other companies, in reaching for a broader audience, have customized their policies, tailoring language and examples of offensive behavior for the warehouse and executive office. Instead of a lecture, training sessions are now more interactive, involving role-playing. And some companies have employees do the teaching. Mining company FMC Wyoming Corp. in Green River, Wyo., hired a consultant to teach staffers to train its work force of 1,200. "This way, it's not a commandment coming down from management but something you can relate to with your peers," says Judy Boyce, FMC training coordinator. With consultants charging up to $2,000 a day, internal trainers can also save the company a bundle.

Unfortunately, the organizations that have responded the most in the past year tend to be the ones that are already enlightened. The hearings did send many first-timers to consultants, but only to request unrealistically short programs—gender awareness in an hour. Wider Opportunities for Women, a national employment group, has received five times the number of calls it got in 1991. But when companies hear about WOW's hours-long, systemic training program, about 70% of them back off.

Sometimes, the training just doesn't take. Ellen Bravo, national director of 9 to 5, recounts a company where, after leaving a training seminar, men reported to female co-workers: "From now on, we'll call you 'stupid jerk' instead of 'stupid bitch.'" And at a Colorado oil company, several male employees played porn videos in the company cafeteria just weeks after finishing a training program. "When training doesn't work," says Susan Webb, "the problems are usually not around the training but about management's stance and its handling of complaints."

NEW CHANNELS

Many companies are reevaluating their complaint systems. In the NAFE survey, 46% of the women whose companies had taken steps since the hearings said their employers had established a grievance procedure. Where once they advised a victim to go to her boss, many corporate policies now call for an independent person within the company (usually female) to investigate complaints. Other companies establish both formal and informal channels. Palmer & Dodge, a 360-employee law firm in Boston, believes it's the first in the country to establish an ombudsperson to counsel victims privately. It also lets employees file a complaint through an impartial mediator.

Northern States Power Co. in Minneapolis has strong carrot-and-stick approaches. Even before the hearings, it was developing a thorough investigation policy. Alleged victims could file complaints through their supervisors, the human resources department, or a panel of peers. Results of investigations—with names deleted—are available to any employee and published annually. This past year, after a 15% jump in requests, sexual harassment workshops were offered. One plant manager credited the training with helping him deal quietly but effectively with a pornographic cartoon found on the property. All 7,000 employees, 27% of whom are women, received a brochure and a letter from CEO James J. Howard reiterating the company's "zero tolerance for sexual harassment." Says Hazel R. O'Leary, executive vice-president for corporate affairs: "This is a business issue. It doesn't have to do with law or morality but about having a productive work force."

In other cases, management's efforts have sparked tension. In the wake of diligent anti-harassment efforts, UNUM Life Insurance Co. in Portland, Me., has had an increase in complaints and subtle changes in the work atmosphere. "With even so much as a simple compliment, you have to be careful in telling people they look nice," says Administrative Assistant Deborah J. Winters. Freada Klein, a management consultant in Cambridge, Mass., has seen a more substantial backlash: companies forbidding office romances, or male executives declaring they won't put a woman on a team that travels out of town or ask a female subordinate to join them for a business dinner.

Chapter 8

Managing Hazards

Throughout the book we have encountered numerous examples of the tensions generated by the imperfect meshing of the characteristics of formal organizations and the characteristics of individuals. When students of management first confronted these tensions, their inclination was often to try to separate the two. Specifically, they sought to eliminate the impact of the personal factors from the organization. As Joseph Massie observed, the early writers encouraged managers to ignore personal problems and characteristics.[1] Management was viewed primarily as planning and formalizing relationships. Supervisors were urged to model rationality and objectivity and avoid feelings and emotions. Adequate planning and the development of rules and procedures could make the organization into an efficient machine, buffered from the idiosyncrasies of human beings.

It soon became apparent that human beings—both the workers and the managers—brought their human emotions, needs, and individual differences with them into the organization. Separation was impossible—the *mutual* influence of human beings and organizations are simply too deep. The initial tendency, however, to separate the two lives on, albeit to a lesser degree.

Even though it is widely recognized that the influence is mutual, the study of management has centered mainly on the influence of individuals on the organization. Managers are taught how to recruit, select, train, supervise, motivate, and communicate with individuals so that their efforts become coordinated to achieve the organization's goals. Although the approaches are much more informed by knowledge of human behavior than were the approaches described earlier, they are still concerned with protecting the organization from the problems that humans can introduce. In this section, we are concerned with both directions, but we are more concerned with the consequences that organizations have for individuals both in and outside of the workplace. These articles center on the effects that organizations can have on individuals. Since we deal here mainly with what we judge to be the negative consequences, we use the word hazards.

Many hazards stem from inabilities to manage the demands, challenges, and opportunities of one's job, to find a healthy balance between work and play, or to create a meaningful alignment within one's career. This sense of loss, of the hazards associated with living a life, perhaps uncritically and without sufficient reflection, is captured in the short poem: "If I Had My Life to Live Over." An analysis of productive versus unproductive career experiences is presented in "The Doom Loop." In this excerpt from the book *The Doom Loop System,* author Dory Hollander argues that people who stay in the same job repeating skills are doomed to travel through a predictable loop: from a job they like and are still learning, to one they like and are good at, to one they are good at but bored by and, eventually, to a job they dislike and at which they are no longer good. Hollander provides suggestions for ways out of the loop.

Several articles in this chapter deal with choices and trade-offs between careers and other non-work values. Work and the workplace can be very hazardous to the lives of people who find themselves torn between the demands and adrenalin-induced "highs" of work and the opportunities and responsibilities they face away from the job. Trying to find the right or at least an appropriate balance in this domain is a source of constant stress for many people in the workforce. It is seldom clear quite how one strikes and maintains such a balance. ("Weighing the Fast Track Against Family Values" and "To Love or to Work: Must We Choose?" deal with this issue.)

Dealing effectively with "success" and coping with failure are perhaps opposite sides of the same coin. Each condition places demands on the individuals affected. Each condition is in part organizationally induced. Each experience can induce dramatic changes in the way people see and feel about themselves. Each experience requires an adjustment of expectations and a willingness to respond to challenges in ways that enable individuals to read their situations more sensitively. There are important coaching and mentoring roles to be played by managers and their organizations to help individuals come to terms with either success or failure. Individuals cannot regain their balance and their effectiveness alone. ("Beyond Success"; "Middle Aged Managers Find Willingness to Adapt Aids Rebound from Layoffs"; and "Unmasking Incompetent Managers" provide insights on the hazards of succeeding and of failing.)

One of the most toxic of all aspects of working environments is the "clean" addiction of workaholism. It is an admired and encouraged set of responses to work. Organizations provide many systematic reinforcers that feed the addiction. Workaholism engenders attitudes and behaviors in those afflicted that seem to lead to a loss of creativity, of self-control and of effective performance. It may be a factor in the development of life-threatening diseases such as heart attacks. In "Characteristics of Workaholics," Diane Fassel provides some of the ways in which the addiction to work manifests itself and leads to unmanageable lives.

It is not yet clear whether a healthy balance is achievable for people in the modern corporation. The articles in this chapter may help in the search for useful answers to the question of how to manage hazards in and around work successfully.

Notes

1. J. L. Massie, Management Theory. In J. G. March, ed., *Handbook of Organizations* (Chicago: Rand McNally, 1965.), pp. 387–422.

◆

If I Had My life to Live Over[*]

Nadine Stair, 85-years-old
LOUISVILLE, KENTUCKY

I'd dare to make more mistakes next time. I'd relax. I would limber up. I would be sillier than I have been this trip. I would take fewer things seriously. I would take more chances. I would take more trips. I would climb more mountains and swim more rivers. I would eat more ice cream and less beans. I would perhaps have more actual troubles, but I'd have fewer imaginary ones.

You see, I'm one of those people who live sensibly and sanely hour after hour, day after day. Oh, I've had my moments and if I had it to do over again, I'd have more of them. In fact, I'd try to have nothing else. Just moments, one after another, instead of living so many years ahead of each day. I've been one of those persons who never goes anywhere without a thermometer, a hot water bottle, a raincoat, and a parachute. If I had to do it again, I would travel lighter than I have.

If I had my life to live over, I would start barefoot earlier in the Spring and stay that way later in the Fall. I would go to more dances. I would ride more merry-go-rounds. I would pick more daisies.

◆

The Doom Loop[†]

Dory Hollander

When I first came across the Doom Loop in the summer of 1985, I was intrigued. Here in a disarmingly simple form—a half-loop plotted on a two-by-two matrix—was a powerful career management tool that resembled nothing I had seen before. Somehow this matrix created an instant mirror and self-assessment tool that encouraged people to view their past, present, and future jobs with new, sometimes startling insight.

I am an organizational psychologist and career coach. My clients tend to be bright, motivated people who are discontented with their careers. The seemingly elusive goal they seek is a more fulfilling work life. In the Doom Loop I sensed the

---

potential for a remarkable shortcut to that end—one that also promised to be fun to use. Part of the Doom Loop's appeal was that it could be tailored to benefit nearly anyone—whether that person was just beginning a career, was suffering from a bad case of midcareer blahs, or had recently been spewed into the swelling ranks of the unemployed; whether he or she was a banker, a secretary, or a rocket scientist.

Helping people effect positive career change is my business. And the Doom Loop, despite its ominous name, had possibilities.

In the coming years I would witness similar "aha" reactions from all kinds of people—students, professionals, small-business owners, executives, entertainers, military personnel, office workers, and technicians. What these people had in common was a keen desire to find happiness in their work. Merely grasping the Doom Loop's simple concept seemed to help many of them get a better grip on what they had to do to avoid or resolve career crises, and to steer themselves toward more satisfying career paths.

What is the Doom Loop and where did it come from? To answer that question, let's go back to 1978 and the Harvard Business School.

THE GENESIS

Charles Jett is a leading career management consultant. In the spring of 1978 he was in Cambridge, conducting interviews with the latest batch of hopeful, eager Harvard MBAs, many casting longing eyes in the direction of management consulting jobs. As Charlie tells the story, after a long day of interviewing, the last candidate appeared. After a few minutes of talking to him, Charlie could see that this young man was not cut out for a consulting career, despite his aspirations. Charlie decided it would be an act of mercy to convince him that a consulting career was a disaster waiting to happen.

When the young man started talking about a matrix approach to strategic planning—an approach that was then very much in vogue—Charlie decided to fight fire with fire. He would use this same matrix approach to convince the young MBA that consulting just wasn't in the cards for him.

He began by asking the young man to list ten basic consulting skills that a consultant would need to acquire during the first few years on the job. The young man thought about what he had learned in his basic business courses that might apply to consulting, and about the consulting jobs that two of his professors had described to him. He realized he would have to interview a variety of consultants in some depth to figure out what the basic ten skills might be, but being bright and eager to please, he still took a stab at it. And his impromptu list of consulting skills turned out to be reasonably accurate. It included proposal writing, fact-finding, problem identification, interviewing, analysis, drawing conclusions, writing reports, making recommendations, and a few other skills.

Charlie then requested that the young MBA rate himself along the following lines: whether he liked or disliked those skills and whether or not he was any good at them.

After going through the list, the young MBA decided he wasn't really very good at any of the skills, primarily because he had never had any job experience that required them. Still, that didn't seem to faze him. After all, as an ambitious

new MBA in search of the right fast track, he certainly wasn't afraid of hard work
and learning. It did, however, make him wonder out loud at the sheer magnitude
of work and learning a consulting job would entail.

When he rated the skills he "liked" and "didn't like," the new graduate said he
didn't like two critical areas: writing and analysis. There were a few others he
wasn't over-enthusiastic about, either. What he did like was the people contact:
interviewing and making recommendations.

He and Charlie plotted his ratings of all the skills he had listed on the following matrix. They then used the following matrix to plot the ratings of all the identified skills.

	Like	Don't Like
Good At	QUADRANT II	QUADRANT III
Not Good At	QUADRANT I	QUADRANT IV

Then Charlie asked the aspiring consultant to analyze each of the four quadrants in the matrix by answering a simple question: "How would you feel if most of
the skills of your job clustered here?" They started with Quadrant I.

	Like	Don't Like
Good At	Happy Satisfied QUADRANT II	Frustrated Bored QUADRANT III
Not Good At	Anxious Challenged Uptight QUADRANT I	Unhappy Miserable QUADRANT IV

Here is an approximate reconstruction of what the graduate said:

- Quadrant I—If he were doing something he liked that he was not yet good at, he would feel challenged, but it could be a mixed bag. He might feel pretty insecure about his performance and about hanging on to his job. On the other hand, even though he might be uptight and anxious, he decided that these feelings might not be all bad. In fact, they might motivate him to learn more quickly.
- Quadrant II—If he were doing something that required skills he was good at and liked, he would probably feel happy and satisfied. Why not? Wouldn't anyone?
- Quadrant III—If he had the skills to do the job well, but didn't like most of them, he would feel frustrated and bored. He'd had enough classes like that. A job in this quadrant was totally unappealing to him.
- Quadrant IV—If he found himself working at a job that he neither liked nor was good at, then he would probably be extremely unhappy and would look for an immediate change of scenery. He certainly wouldn't choose a job in this quadrant.

It was a simple and obvious exercise, permitting straight forward conclusions. But, in fact, when the MBA plotted his ratings for the ten consulting skills he had listed, he saw that most of them clustered in Quadrant IV. He thought a minute: then his eyes lit up. It was a revelation. "Okay," he said. "I get it! If I go into consulting, the odds are that I won't be particularly good at them, either. So I've been interviewing for the nightmare job without knowing it. I guess I'd better rethink my career choice, and find something that capitalizes on what I like. Something like working in the sales and marketing end of a business using people skills—right?"

Without any browbeating, the matrix had helped him see for the first time that consulting might not be the right career for him. But instead of feeling bad about it, he walked away feeling relieved, ready to try something more promising, more satisfying, that fit his own particular pattern of likes.

After the young man left, Charlie studied the matrix. He was stunned. In his many years as a consultant, he'd often tried to convince people to change careers they obviously weren't cut out for. It was no easy task. Yet the matrix had achieved that objective almost instantly. It was enough to deter a determined and strong-willed MBA from blindly making a poor choice.

How else could the matrix be used? Charlie found out when he met the president of a large Midwestern university who faced an altogether different career crisis.

DOOMED

Richard Keefer had served successfully as a university president for ten years. Though he had been enthusiastic about his job early on, he gradually found himself becoming bored and distracted. A robust man in his mid-fifties, he figured he still had enough good years left to try another career. But what would he do? Where could he go? To another school? To a different type of institution? Back to a professorial or departmental chairperson's slot? To something altogether new? His crystal ball was cloudy. Nothing really excited him.

Charlie trotted out the matrix. He wasn't sure it would work. After all, Keefer was a seasoned professional who was set in his ways. Any way you viewed it, his situation was substantially different from the young MBA's.

Richard Keefer had been elevated to the rank of full professor at thirty-five. Three years later he was appointed college dean. He become a university president in his early forties. In his first years as president, he was understandably anxious about proving himself on the job. He was challenged, sometimes even overwhelmed, by the job's ever-expanding demands. Though being a university president was his capstone—the long-range goal that represents personal career success—he didn't possess enough of the skills that were necessary to succeed in his capstone—skills like jousting with the state legislature for funds and dealing with the escalating demands of departmental fiefdoms.

But he loved the challenges and possibilities the position offered. And the prestige and the trappings that came with the job sweetened the pot. So he pushed hard and eventually acquired the skills necessary to perform effectively. He established a track record for himself by helping the school successfully weather a few serious financial storms and a particularly rending tenure dispute.

In time, Richard Keefer settled into his role. And why not? He was happy, successful, and skilled. After a number of years in the job, however, Richard began to stagnate. He began to feel inexplicably bored with the daily tasks of running a university. Little things began to irritate him, and he found himself oscillating between frustration and apathy. He was tired of grappling with cigar-smoking politicians for tax dollars and weary of going to the same old parties and fund-raisers year after year. The campus press labeled him the "old man," and on his fifty-third birthday, after ten years on the job, he felt like one.

At the annual faculty meeting a particularly outspoken critic suggested that Richard had exceeded the life cycle of his job. Things were taking a downturn. Richard complained to Charlie, "I'm doomed if I keep doing what I've been doing."

Doomed. The word would stick in Charlie's mind.

Charlie helped Richard examine his career progression through the matrix's perspective. Looking at the quadrants, there was no denying that his career as a university president had slowly progressed from Quadrant I to II to III. He had taken on the presidency in Quadrant I, liking the skills involved but still having to acquire the whole array of proficiencies required to be an expert administrator. Over time he mastered the skills demanded of a university president. Then, to his amazement and eventual chagrin, he found that performing these skills well in a stable and prestigious job often as not bored and irritated him. Though Richard intuitively knew that something was wrong, he couldn't get a handle on it. He wondered if perhaps the problem was in him.

When he saw his career progression through the matrix's windows, the light poured in. He was bored and frustrated because he had mastered nearly all the skills his job required. What he needed was the challenge of new learning: it was time for a change. The "aha" experience for Richard Keefer was that he was ensconced in Quadrant III of the matrix.

To help Richard make the right change, Charlie asked him about the skills he used in his job that he liked—skills that could return him to Quadrant I or II of the matrix. Richard was thoughtful. He considered the various skills required in a typical week's work. A pattern emerged. His Quadrant I and II skills involved dealing with academics, mingling with important people, working toward culturally significant goals, and providing an educational experience. His Quadrant IV skills involved dealing with faculty grievances, university politics, and classroom teaching.

Given his likes and dislikes and the skills he possessed, Charlie suggested that Richard might search for a job as head of a cultural institution. Such a job would recycle the university president into Quadrant I, providing him with renewed energy and fresh challenges.

The following fall, Richard Keefer accepted an offer to head a prestigious historical society. He called Charlie after a year on the job and exulted, "I'm back in Quadrant I and I love it!"

THE LOOP

Charlie was impressed. Thinking about Richard Keefer's progression through the matrix's quadrants, it occurred to him that a pattern actually showed up over time—a pattern that might apply not only to Keefer's career, but to anyone's.

	Like	Don't Like
Good At	Satisfied t_2 QUADRANT II	QUADRANT III
Not Good At	t_1 Anxious QUADRANT I	QUADRANT IV

For example, suppose an individual starts working at time "t-1." This person is in a position she likes, but she still has a lot to learn. At "t-1" the concentration of required job skills (plotted as points on the matrix) is primarily in Quadrant I. Now suppose that several months or even a year later, this person takes a second measurement. She rates the skills of her job according to whether or not she likes them and whether or not she is good at them. She finds that some things have changed. Now, at time "t-2," the concentration of points has moved upward and slightly to the right, into Quadrant II.

This movement takes place because the person has the ability and motivation to learn (upward matrix movement) and has gained greater mastery. But other movement takes place because daily repetition of the same skill knocks some of the fun and challenge out of the job (movement to the right). Still, the bottom line is that this person has become more competent over time and feels genuinely happy and satisfied with her work.

Now, suppose more time passes, and this person takes another measurement at time "t-3." Now the concentration of her job skills (plotted as points) has moved farther to the right and has ceased moving upward. What's happened? In Quadrant III this person has reached the top of her learning curve, mastering all the requisite skills. Yet this is the very same job that once caused excitement and satisfaction. Boredom and frustration have set in, not because the skills are inherently dull, but because they've been repeated ad nauseam. Unchanging job content, paired with decreased challenge, will guarantee nearly anyone's eventual arrival in Quadrant III.

	Like	Don't Like
Good At	Satisfied t_2 QUADRANT II	Frustrated/Bored t_3 QUADRANT III
Not Good At	t_1 Anxious QUADRANT I	 QUADRANT IV

Unfortunately, the process doesn't stop there. Staying in any job too long can ensure downward movement into Quadrant IV. Here an individual loses interest in the job, failing to keep up with changes in the field, new technologies, and competitors' advances. Motivation flags; performance plateaus. At the "t-4" measurement, the person not only doesn't like what she is doing, but her skills have actually diminished through neglect and lassitude. She has unwittingly tumbled into Quadrant IV.

As you can see, this progression through the quadrants forms a half-loop. Anyone who stays in the same job long enough, repeating the same old skills day in and day out, is *doomed* to ride the loop. If you're not learning new skills, the excitement and challenge will eventually vanish along with your enthusiasm. If you have the capacity to learn—and the learning stops between "t-2" and "t-3"—you'll ride the downside of the Doom Loop into Quadrants III and IV.

	Like	Don't Like
Good At	Satisfied t_2 QUADRANT II	Frustrated/Bored t_3 QUADRANT III
Not Good At	t_1 Anxious QUADRANT I	t_4 Miserable QUADRANT IV

Almost everyone experiences the Doom Loop in one job or another at some time in his or her career. It's not that people intentionally choose this outcome or want to be doomed in their work. Quite the contrary. Most of us long to be happy and satisfied in our livelihoods. But it's been drummed into our heads that career advances depend on our experience, longevity, and staying power. When economic conditions tighten, fear and job insecurity worsen this tendency. We develop a recession mentality. We think security rather than challenge and growth. We fear that changing jobs, even hated ones, will leave us stranded on the curb, put us in serious career jeopardy, or label us "job hoppers." So instead we keep our noses to the grindstone, failing to look up and see what else is out there after we've mastered a job's skills. We feel secure but bored. We wish we enjoyed our work more but have made an uneasy peace with what we have chosen to call reality. The learning stops, career crises develop, and we make poor career decisions.

Perhaps we need a new framework for thinking about our careers that works in every economic climate and that puts us in greater charge of our own career outcomes.

LEARNING HOW TO USE THE LOOP

In 1986, Charlie Jett asked me to help develop and expand the concept of the Doom Loop. The result was the creation of a series of career management strategies and tactics that revolved around the Loop. These strategies and tactics applied in one aspect or another to virtually every career situation we had encountered—from identifying the ideal first job to planning the ideal career capstone position, from managing a traumatic life crisis like being fired to evaluating an enticing midcareer opportunity.

The uninterrupted progression of the Doom Loop shows one all too common career outcome among many possible ones. We tackled the problem of how people could halt or reverse this process and avoid plateauing in Quadrant III and bottoming out in Quadrant IV. We found that the first step was simply being aware that Doom Loops happen. Once people saw the matrix and plotted their own career course through the quadrants, many of their long-held myths and assumptions about careers began to fade. Seeing their own career progression through the perspective of the matrix allowed them to stop blaming themselves for feeling unhappy in their lackluster jobs and to take a fresh, upbeat approach in their next round of career decision-making.

The New York Times, June 24, 1990

Weighing the Fast Track Against Family Values*

Deirdre Fanning

Susan Lawley seemed to have it all. As a vice president at Goldman, Sachs & Company, Mrs. Lawley earned $250,000 a year in 1988 supervising the administration of the firm's mortgage securities department. She and her husband, Robert, then a vice president at Bankers Trust Company, owned a four-bedroom house in New Jersey, drove to work in a Mercedes-Benz and a Lincoln Continental, tooled around the waters off their Long Island beach house in a sleek new motorboat and even wore matching Rolex watches. At least once a year, they whisked their son, Greg, now 11 years old, away on a European vacation.

So why give up this world of power, prestige and wealth? "I was driving home from work around 10 o' clock one night and as I crossed into New Jersey I suddenly burst into tears," recalled Mrs. Lawley. "I couldn't see the road I was crying so hard. I realized that tonight, like almost every night, I would miss seeing my son because he was already in bed. I realized that life is too short to live like that."

A few weeks later, in early 1989, Mrs. Lawley quit her job to set up her own human resources consulting firm closer to home. She adjusted her work schedule to jibe with Greg's school hours and set out to find the things she felt she had missed while struggling up the corporate ladder.

The professional world is littered with executives who complain about the personal sacrifices required by their fast-track careers. But Mrs. Lawley is among the few who have actually made a dramatic change.

Along the way, she hoped she could instill in her son the same middle-class values that were the source of her own drive and ambition. "My parents were Depression people and I saw how hard they worked, for how little," said Mrs. Lawley. "One day my dad was visiting and my son Greg had his wallet out. Greg counted his money and had more in his wallet than my dad did. My father was appalled. I realized that all my son had ever seen was a life where everyone made a lot of money. As far as he was concerned, there was nothing he couldn't have."

Her own childhood was very different. Mrs. Lawley grew up in Greenwich Village in New York City. Her mother ran the household while her father operated a profitable but small manufacturing business.

Mrs. Lawley went to a Catholic girls high school and quickly established herself as a straight-A student. She won a scholarship to the City University of New York, finished college in three years and took an entry-level management position with the American Telephone and Telegraph Company. By 1980, she was in charge of all non-management staffing and was earning $38,000 a year.

She left for Bankers Trust, ultimately to become vice president in charge of administration for the company's burgeoning investment banking department. "I loved my job," she said. "I had power, responsibility and influence. I was surrounded by smart people." And money. Her first bonus at the bank was $25,000. "It was more than my dad earned in his best year," she said.

Those bonuses increased as the division grew until by 1987 she was earning a total of about $225,000 a year. She negotiated an even sweeter deal from Goldman Sachs, at $250,000 in salary and various bonuses.

Her husband, meanwhile, whom she had married in 1978, was now vice president in charge of Bankers Trust's telecommunications. Between the two of them, they had annual income of more than half a million dollars.

Yet the more she earned, the more competitive she became. She says she was sometimes jealous of the bigger bonuses some investment bankers in her department earned. "There was a feeling of entitlement there that was contagious," she said.

Worse, her son Greg "was turning into a demanding brat." As she recalled it, "He got every toy and went to every movie he wanted because I wanted to make him happy. His teachers called me from school to say he was disruptive and doing badly in class. How could he know any better? We didn't give him a value system—no one was there to teach him at home. He really believed all of this money happened automatically."

That is when Mrs. Lawley started her own firm, Cameron Consulting Group Inc., giving up a private secretary to share one with eight others in her office, once the building's coffee room. At about the same time, her husband decided to leave Bankers Trust and start his own telecommunications firm, Gain Communication. The two companies now share office space in Parsippany, N.J.

For the Lawleys, it has been an eye-opening transition. As with new ventures in general, business did not take off instantly; the Lawleys now make do with an annual income of less than $100,000.

"Sometimes I still worry," said Robert, the son of a British coal miner. "I think, 'Gee, I walked away from all that money.' But we think now before going out and blowing $1,000 and that's the way it should be."

Greg also seems positively contented, according to his mother. He is making A's at school instead of C's. Now, when he can't choose between toys at the store, he picks one or gets none. He says he even plays with the old, but little-used toys in his toy box. For the first time, his spending money is limited—to a weekly allowance of $5, for which he does chores.

Mrs. Lawley feels proud of the way she and her family now live. "I wanted Greg to see me struggle, like my parents did," she said. "I wanted him to see me worrying about writing bills, so he could appreciate the real, hard work that goes into making money."

The Wall Street Journal, February 8, 1991
Middle-Aged Managers Find Willingness To Adapt Aids Rebound From Layoffs [*]

Amanda Bennett

A bank marketer starts a business of his own. A program manager for a non-profit group takes a big pay cut. A telecommunications specialist becomes a subcontractor.

These people are all victims of corporate cutbacks. They're all 50 or older. And they all have found ways to start over.

It's never been easy being over 50 and out of work. These days, it's tougher than ever. New waves of recession-induced cutbacks flood the market with younger job hunters. Meanwhile, penny-pinching companies balk at matching the high salaries older executives once commanded.

But even in this climate, many middle-aged executives are finding jobs. For some, the winning strategy is: be prepared to compromise, to think of new ways to use old skills, and to flaunt—not hide—the benefits of age and experience.

After losing her job at the American Lung Association, 50-year-old Joyce Waite didn't shrink from acknowledging her age. Her resume, directed at nonprofit associations, reflected only her 15 years' experience in that field. When interviewers suggested she was older than that experience would indicate, she "turned it into a positive," she says, by immediately discussing her 10 years of prior corporate experience, what she had learned and how it was valuable to nonprofit work.

Within six months, she became vice president for development of a Ronald McDonald House in New York, a nonprofit affiliate of McDonald's Corp.

Many other middle-aged executives are focusing on packaging their age and experience effectively. Forty Plus, a network of self-help organizations for older job seekers, counsels its members to augment their traditional resume with one that identifies business problems the job seeker has successfully handled. "We teach our executives to market themselves," says John Pugh, executive vice president of Forty Plus of Greater Washington.

Sometimes that involves taking steps to minimize disadvantages of age. Mr. Pugh cites one former Forty Plus member in his mid-50s who had had quadruple-bypass heart surgery. He landed a corporate job by agreeing to work on contract and letting the company know at the outset that he wouldn't demand insurance coverage.

Because some out-of-work executives see the recession as only temporarily hurting their job prospects, they are following a stopgap strategy by pursuing work closely related to their old businesses. "I'm trying to run on parallel tracks," says William Wood, who lost his job late last year as a sales manager for a bank in the Washington, D.C., area.

The 53-year-old Mr. Wood recently started a business representing clients who offer products and services—such as check printers and computer software—used in the cash-management business, his old specialty. He expects his business to generate some income while keeping him in touch with companies and contacts that may eventually generate job leads.

"For me to say I will only accept employment in a cash-management department of another bank is so limiting that it is ludicrous," Mr. Wood says. "I have to be prepared to switch careers, switch locations and be very flexible."

Being ready to weather a long search may also be prudent. Statistics collected by Drake Beam Morin Inc., an outplacement firm, show that last year executives over 50 took an average of 8.3 months to find a job, 22% longer than their younger colleagues. Moreover, the data show that older executives' average job searches have begun to outlast their severance pay.

Some find that being willing to move helps. A 47-year-old bank marketer in New York who lost his job last year quickly decided that slowdowns in several big industries had made New York a "desert" for job hunters. But in three months, he found a position similar to his old one in Philadelphia. He is making the four-hour daily commute while looking to relocate.

Outplacement firms and other counselors are putting new emphasis on encouraging jobless older executives to rethink their careers. Murro & Associates, an outplacement firm in Phoenix, Ariz., last year started a three-hour seminar for what it calls "age-advantaged" job hunters. "We ask them to look at alternatives—consulting, entrepreneurship, public and community service, academia—that they may not have focused on," says Frank Goushas, who helps run the program. He cites himself as an example: At age 61, he moved to Phoenix last year from Dallas to start an outplacement career, after 23 years in corporate human resources and a stint at running his own business.

Though age isn't always a problem, some older executives find their pay is. No one mentioned age to 50-year-old Hinton Thomas, who was a director of telecommunications at a television network until three years ago. But prospective employers balked at his network job's salary of over $100,000 a year. When he offered to work for less, they still balked.

"I told them I was prepared to work for less if the job was challenging and interesting and had a future, and they came up with the idea that I wouldn't be loyal because they weren't paying me what I was used to," Mr. Thomas says. "There was no way I could win this argument."

Employment specialists are divided about offering to take a pay cut. "I try to discourage price cutting unless it is a career change" into an industry with a lower salary structure, such as nonprofit work, says Gayle Hinchman, managing principal at Right Associates, an outplacement firm in Denver.

But many people don't have that luxury. William Morin, chairman of Drake Beam Morin, says many longtime unemployed executives now believe "any money is better than no money." Thus, he says, "we aren't as diligent" anymore in counseling people to hold out for higher pay.

After a year of job searching, Nancy Nicalo took nearly a 50% pay cut—to $22,000 a year—when she became program director of the Institute of International Education, a New York group that arranges educational exchanges. Ms. Nicalo, 62, had spent 26 years in a nonprofit disaster-aid organization before losing her job. She says she doesn't regret her choice, because she finds the new job interesting and challenging. "You have to figure out what's the bottom line for you," she says.

For many older executives, their most valuable resource is the network of contacts they have built up over their careers. According to the Drake Beam figures, nearly two-thirds of new jobs are found through such contacts. Ms. Waite found her job when a friend alerted her that the incumbent was leaving. The New York bank marketer now working in Philadelphia says a friend introduced him to the recruiter handling the search that landed him his new job.

Some have to overcome reluctance to use that network. "I've always been a provider of help," says Mr. Thomas. "Now, for the first time in my life, I am learning how to ask people for help, and I'm finding out that there's nothing wrong with that." He found his new job, subcontracting on some telecommunications work for a big record company, through friends who have the main contract.

Others simply find emotional support in peers and colleagues. During her year of joblessness, Ms. Nicalo occasionally gathered a group of friends to help her plot strategy and keep her morale up.

Indeed, Mr. Pugh of Forty Plus in Washington finds a network of colleagues so essential that he offers this tongue-in-cheek advice to employees who fear they might lose their jobs: "Keep your Rolodex at home."

◆

Unmasking Incompetent Managers[*]

Daniel Kagan

According to some psychologists, the biggest threat facing U.S. business today is the incompetent manager, most notably the one who displays narcissistic tendencies. For these executives, their self-interests are far more important than the welfare of the organization. As a result, experts are working on ways to help recruiters spot potential incompetents—before they become problems in the office.

What is the biggest threat facing American business? Forget rising interest rates and Japanese imports. Corporate America's worst problem, says psychologist Robert Hogan, may be managerial incompetence: the failure of executives to advance the interests of their companies because they can't motivate their staffs, change their approach when they are in error, plan strategically or forge alliances with each other.

Incompetent executives are not simply failing because their jobs are too tough, says Hogan, director of the Tulsa Institute of Behavioral Sciences. Managers are usually assumed to be basically competent because most have been chosen for their confidence, assertiveness, charm, ambition and charisma—qualities known to correlate highly with good performance.

But Hogan says that just those qualities often accompany executive incompetence rooted in serious personality disorders, and he warns that the usual means by which managers are hired and promoted—assessment testing, personality profiles, supervisor evaluations, interviews and so on—actually select a significant number of people in whom seemingly positive traits are really symptoms of psychological abnormalities.

With strong apparent leadership traits, such people move steadily up the promotion ladder because they do well in assessments and interviews and are good at ingratiating themselves with their superiors and at making themselves look good.

[*]Reprinted from Insight, May 21, 1990, pp. 42–44.

All the while, they are detrimental or even dangerous to their organization. They may actually destroy a company.

"Superior self-presentation skills drive careers, not competence," Hogan says ruefully. Someone with a narcissistic personality disorder, for instance, is motivated to succeed because of an unhealthy craving for attention and recognition, not out of a desire to do a good job.

In these disorders, traits that are normal and necessary in a manager become twisted or intensified while appearing as a mask of normal behavior. In narcissistic managers, for example, self-confidence is distorted to the point that they believe no one else has anything of value to say. They will not listen to criticism and devalue anyone who offers it and so cannot learn from experience or change behavior that leads to wrong decisions.

A resentful or revengeful manager with a passive-aggressive or paranoid personality disorder might use persuasiveness and charm to lull subordinates or peers into a false sense of trust, while at the same time quietly gathering damaging information on them and feeding it to others who will use it against them or the company.

Someone with an avoidant or dependent personality disorder may become the often-promoted but unproductive manager who "falls upward"—what Hogan calls a "high likability floater." Self-confident on the surface and charming, poised and congenial, such a manager quells deep insecurity by carefully conforming to the demands of the social environment. Loyal to a fault, these managers never argue or complain and are well-liked. But they accomplish almost nothing because they have no goals, no point of view and will not take a stand on issues. Such people are nearly impossible to fire because they have no enemies and lots of friends. Says Hogan: "The arteries of large organizations are clogged by such congenial, cautious, conforming mid-level managers."

In studying 25 years of survey research in industrial and organizational psychology, Hogan found high levels of employee dissatisfaction with superiors, a huge number of people who reported considerable time working for an intolerable boss and polls showing the primary source of stress in the workplace is the tyrannical boss. "I think a substantial part of American productivity is damaged by this," he says.

The potentially most damaging disorder among managers is narcissism because narcissistic traits such as self-confidence, extroversion, ambition, persuasiveness, energy, achievement-orientation and dominance rate so high in the executive selection process. In healthy amounts, these traits are assets: Chrysler Chairman Lee A. Iacocca is named by experts as a good example of a manager with a high but healthy level of narcissism, which has helped him become a genuine success and an effective leader.

But assessment procedures cannot determine whether those traits exist at a pathological level, where self-confidence is a mask for egotism, or dominance and leadership are really expressions of exhibitionism. The positive trait of persuasiveness may actually reflect manipulativeness, so that subordinates and peers are pawns to be exploited in order to glorify the narcissistic manager, who is indifferent to the feelings of others but will feign interest to get what he wants. Apparent ambition can mask a drive toward self-glorification, which is the only goal, with the needs of the company coming last. Narcissists will not accept responsibility for their failures but project them onto others. Inside they are emotionally empty and riddled with insecurity.

Yet such a type does not always stand out. "This kind of dealing often fits in with a company's corporate culture," says Larry Hirschhorn, who heads the Wharton Center for Applied Research. "Companies are often based on the systematic distortion of truth. So much of corporate culture is about what can't be said, how appearances must be managed, how things are supposed to be imaged. The narcissist is good with this kind of fakery, [so he] is not just a problem individual different from the milieu around him." Often camouflaged by their surroundings, the more they rise, the worse things can get.

"The higher up we go in an organization, the more the milieu tells us the world revolves around us," says Howard Schwartz, an organizational behavior expert at the Oakland University School of Business in Rochester, Mich. "This creates a kind of narcissistic separation from reality."

To complicate matters, some narcissists possess high levels of valuable abilities. They may rise to become CEOs or corporate raiders whose real goal is to glorify themselves by wielding power over those who work for the companies they acquire. "Put these characteristics together with real talent and you can have a real success. But they leave behind them scorched earth," says Hogan.

Larry Gould, a psychologist who treats many narcissistic managers, believes such executives are exceptions. "Severely disordered people rarely rise to the heights. If they do, they don't last long. They seem to thrive only in organizations where narcissism is the coin of the realm, where everyone supports everyone else's glory-seeking."

Most narcissists derail or hit a plateau at the middle or upper-middle management level. Typically, they do not manifest poisonous traits strongly until they win some authority. "They get a chance to manage people, their traits blossom and their ineffectiveness becomes obvious. They get fired, they get blocked in their careers," says Gould, who thinks these types are less of a threat than do other experts. "They tend to stick out and be destructive and take up too much room. If they can be politically bumped off, they are."

Michael Lombardo, director of the leadership development research group at the Center for Creative Leadership, unearthed the concordance between narcissism and executive failure while researching why promising careers go off the track. "We found that the common reasons for derailment were also traits common to narcissistic personalities," he says. The failed managers were insensitive to others, cold, aloof, arrogant, destructively competitive and overly self-focused in order to please top management; they also showed a lack of composure under stress and betrayed trust.

Narcissists may terrorize subordinates by manipulating them, playing favorites and cultivating sycophants. They create a tense atmosphere in which the staff is afraid to speak truthfully and must show inordinate loyalty. They denigrate people because they feel superior to them and fail to give subordinates credit. Morale and productivity falter, absenteeism rises.

Alternatively, a narcissist may initially charm and dazzle staff into following him. "When they enter an organization, they often cause a sensation. . . . Initially they infuse a lot of energy," says Hogan. Their influence can be seductive.

"People in the orbit of a narcissistic superior feel a pull to want to satisfy them. It is like being sucked into being a codependent with an alcoholic," says Hirschhorn. "He will use your normal tendencies against you. He manipulates. He plays to weak spots in your self-esteem, sucks you in with compliments and stroking. In the beginning, he may idealize his subordinates, feed their egos. They tell him what he wants to hear because he strokes them. This can create a kind of groupthink among his staff. He projects failures outside the unit. It is the fault of the guy down the hall, of the marketplace. This cements the groupthink."

"Their high outward self-confidence convinces us. We all subconsciously admire that. It makes us feel good about them," says Harry Levinson, a psychologist who runs the Levinson Institute in Belmont, Mass. And the narcissist has an uncanny knack, he says, "to make you believe that if you don't go along with what they want, there is something wrong with you."

Meanwhile, such managers are carefully cultivating a winning image, manipulating superiors into thinking they are doing a fabulous job as subordinates languish under their thumb or in their shadow. "They fawn upward and dump downward," Levinson says. Subordinates will not speak up, figuring that upper management knows what this person is and likes it that way. In some cases, upper management recognizes the narcissism but tolerates it as a trade-off for valued traits, such as the ability to sweet-talk and con difficult clients, government regulatory officials or hostile consumers.

So the damage mounts. The narcissist is very good at creating the illusion of success over the short haul. To attempt to look good by appearing to cut costs, for example, such a manager may take over a troubled unit and show on-paper savings by destroying its resources—firing key personnel or jettisoning critical strategic strengths. The damage will not surface until after the manager has moved on to avoid responsibility for the collapse of the unit, been promoted again or been fired.

Or the narcissist will create chronic problems. James Krantz, assistant professor at the Yale School of Organization and Management, gives the example of a manufacturing plant that has four sections, one of which is managed by a narcissist whose staff is demoralized and unproductive. "The whole plant has problems, but the cost accounting system can't pinpoint the problem," he says. Or the narcissist can become bitter and resentful, influencing subordinates against management, complaining to customers about upper management in the role of a sort of heroic ombudsman, or actively colluding against management with suppliers or customers. "This can go on for years."

Eventually, the narcissistic manager is brought down in several ways. Often, says Levinson, a key subordinate valued by upper management quits in exasperation, telling senior staff the reason for the departure. Management may confront the narcissist, who may flee rather than take responsibility. In other cases "a union starts, work productivity drops. . . or [the narcissist] gets caught sexually harassing a female employee. Sooner or later it all catches up with them," says Hogan.

Unfortunately, they usually find similar jobs elsewhere. The firing company will often write glowing recommendations to keep them speaking well of the company and to avoid a lawsuit. They often bounce from job to job, using their formidable interview skills to talk their way into new positions. Headhunters and search firms also favor such types by overemphasizing self-presentation qualities and turning executive recruitment into a beauty contest, as Hogan calls it, that favors a manipulative, glamorous narcissist.

Consequently, experts are trying to develop ways to spot narcissists or sift them out during hiring. Levinson, who estimates that narcissistic managers are the cause of about 15 percent of the problems he is hired to solve as a corporate consultant, uses a specialized interviewing technique to unmask them.

"I don't ask him to tell me what he does. I ask him how he does it. What kinds of trouble he has had with peers, subordinates, others," he says. "And there is a consistency of response. They will talk about other people's inadequacy and how they are not very good. Or they will say they are the target of the rivalry or jealousy of their peers because they get along so well with others. Or they will talk about their victories, how they won because they were so bright."

Levinson has a prescription for spotting narcissists during hiring. "I tell people to beware the person you like too well too quickly. I say, 'Ask yourself: What do they do that I like them so much after 10 minutes?' Are they too cordial? This should be a red flag."

Hogan and his colleagues have been developing a written personality inventory that can spot abnormally high levels of narcissistic traits—and of traits of other personality disorders as well. They are doing this because the standard inventories used in executive assessment "have no real predictive power in the real world. The scores. . . have nothing to do with the person's actual performance," says Hogan.

His inventory has so far been tested on 5,000 employees and managers and has shown a high correlation between job performance and strong trends in personality disorders. Those who score high in disorder traits tend not to do well in job areas that would be damaged by those traits. Several large companies have begun using the inventory experimentally in internal evaluations.

Hogan thinks the central issue is that executive evaluation methods focus almost exclusively on analyzing the elements that add up to competence, while ignoring the equally influential flaws, ingrained in individuals, that may cause incompetence no matter what positive attributes exist. More effort should be made, he thinks, to study the personal dynamics of failure rather than the requirements for success.

"There is a general lack of concentration by organizations on the dark side of management and human nature," says Lombardo. "Organizations are afraid to look at it. It is a nasty topic." He decries the tradition of assessing only the positive aspects of leadership. "It creates the idea of leadership as some kind of mechanical engineering or as an asset sheet. But the problem is, you get all the assets but none of the liabilities [in the personality]. This takes an unbalanced, naive, mechanical view of the role of human nature."

◆

Beyond Success[*]

Rob Phillips

It typically shows up at thirty- or forty-something—a feeling that past accomplishments won't be repeated, trepidation about maintaining current achievements. But "encore anxiety" can be conquered.

So you made the "club." You brought a million dollars' worth of business to the company and were named Sales Associate of the Year. Pretty heady stuff. So how come the glow doesn't last?

Or you got promoted. Your new boss says she's looking forward to building on your success, but you're nagged by doubts about how you attained it in the first place.

Or maybe you sold your first novel. Nobody succeeds with a first novel, but the signs are this one just might make it. And already you're starting to fret about your second one.

Time to smell the roses? No way. Prune the ones you've got and plant some more. Your friends say you've got it made. Somehow you don't feel that way, mostly because nobody told them or you on the way up that there's a downside to success.

It even qualifies as a syndrome and has one of those boutique-y names. Called "encore anxiety," it applies to people who fear their own success the way most of us fear failure. The name was coined by Boston-area psychologist Dr. Steven Berglas, author of *The Success Syndrome: Hitting Bottom When You Reach the Top*.

Typically, it shows up at thirty- or forty-something, when people get the feeling they won't be able to repeat a past triumph or when they think they won't be able to maintain the success they've already attained.

Dr. Kathleen Shea, a Chicago-based psychologist, says a person's success may actually diminish his or her sense of self-esteem. Of the clients she deals with in her practice, most in marketing and sales, she says many feel successful only if they manage to meet constantly rising sales quotas. When they burn out, they're in trouble, "especially if they feel they *are* what they *do*," meaning they define their value as human beings strictly in terms of their sales accomplishments.

Other successful people battle secret guilt over what Berglas calls "noncontingent success"—achievement that is not strictly the result of one's own efforts. Like Robert, the boss' son, for example. He may appear competent as he takes over the company, but he may also harbor feelings that he's a fraud for having

[*]Reprinted from, SKY, November 1992. pp. 18–22.

risen to the top because of his family connection. Sooner or later, he thinks, he's going to be revealed for the impostor he really is.

Freudian psychologists, who have a thing about Oedipus, might interpret Robert's success as a symbolic victory over his father for the affection of his mother. Having succeeded, Roger then treats his accomplishment as a fluke to avoid retribution from his father.

A less elegant theory explains Kathy's problem with success. She is promoted from district manager to regional supervisor, but keeps herself from savoring her achievement because of the image she carries of her parents. They taught her all through school that straight As in the tough subjects was the standard. Anything less wasn't good enough. Regional supervisor? That's nice, dear. What's next?

There are nearly 500 books in print in the English language that have some form of the word *success* in the title. Only a handful of them run contrary to the chronic optimism that attends the conventional version of success. Yet you see evidence every day in the newspaper and on TV, in your office, in your home, maybe in your own shoes, of people who are struggling with this newly defined distress.

Sometimes successful people become wary about who wants to talk to them and why.

One newly appointed university administrator was astonished when the Rotarians asked him to join the club—25 years after he had come to town, but just one day after he was named vice president.

A reporter for a daily newspaper was pleased (and a little cynical) to discover that important people returned his telephone calls once he was made editor of the newspaper's editorial page.

A staff engineer began to notice that his jokes got funnier when he was named supervising engineer.

Other successful people complain about their loss of privacy. A newspaper writer, winner of two Pulitzer prizes, is swamped by requests to critique other people's stories.

Members of the U.S. Olympic basketball "Dream Team" become testy when the media hype and number of fans far exceed those attending other professional athletes.

A company president delights in talking with strangers when out of town "because they don't bring an agenda with them."

Washington, D.C. psychologist Dr. Douglas LaBier, author of *Modern Madness: The Emotional Fallout of Success*, says that more than half the successful people he interviewed for a research project told him they "like the perks [of success], but they say their life is too thin, too boring, and that they don't know what to do about it."

According to LaBier, sometimes such achievement-based angst leads to stomach trouble, high blood pressure, fatigue, headaches, and sleep disturbances.

But revisionists like Berglas and LaBier don't leave us twisting in the wind. The solution, they say, is to redefine success. "There is no more direct route to self-esteem than climbing the ladder and reaching for the top—when pursued from a balanced perspective," says Berglas.

A young doctor cuts back his highly successful practice to spend more time with his wife and two children.

An upward-bound executive declines a transfer from the community where she's put down roots.

A business owner wears a beeper on his belt so his wife and children can reach him at any time.

A senior lawyer derives satisfaction from helping disadvantaged families through his church, and adjusts his calendar accordingly.

Billionaire Malcolm Forbes, who was born rich and died richer, acted out his life as if the purpose of doing business was not to pile up a fortune but to produce happiness.

"The entire materialism of the '80s has become politically incorrect," says Berglas. "The rewards of success are less clear than in the yuppie era. They are more ambiguous now."

The decline of the American economy has forced people to reassess what it means to be successful, says LaBier. "Now there is a window of opportunity to integrate meaning into the short-term self-interest that was characteristic of the last decade."

The real issue of midlife—from age 35 on—he adds, "is the developmental issue. It has to do with redefining success, rethinking the basis of pleasure and fulfillment and practicing a life that builds that."

The principle of diversification is not foreign to businesspeople. Dr. Gene Ondrusek of the Scripps Center for Executive Health in La Jolla, California, tells of a California auto-sales executive who saw two-thirds of his network of dealerships collapse. "While his partner never recovered from the blow," Ondrusek says, "the executive found a whole new career selling a different car. It's an example of learned optimism, a way of explaining events to oneself, a way of dealing with bad things that happen."

In the same way, psychologists use the term "differentiation" to describe the egos of people who are able to balance love and work, a notion that dates back past Sigmund Freud to Aristotle.

Harvard psychologist Dr. Jeffrey Speller, author of *Executives in Crisis*, suggests that a person copes with the stresses of success as well as failure through individual adjustment of his or her perception of the world by developing a sense of humor, by balancing play and work, and by getting involved socially.

As Berglas told a *Time* magazine interviewer last year: "Be a part of the community. It's the only antidote for narcissism. Be an Indian, not a chief. Lose your identity in a group. The healthiest people have that commitment."

◆

To Love or to Work: Must We Choose?*

Joan R. Kofodimos

Larry Grant was a model of competence and effectiveness, a manager whose work life at Chemco consisted of success after success. But is there enough time for him to be a husband and father as well? Is time really the issue?

[The events of the story presented here, though taken from a variety of sources, are not fiction; they exemplify the experiences of real managers struggling to find a balance between their work and private lives.-Ed.]

Larry Grant sat in his office two hours after everyone else had gone home, smoking his fortieth cigarette of the day. He was staring at a printout of next year's production goals for his division. He was deeply absorbed by the problem of what to do about the low figures for Xylac, their flagship antihypertensive drug. The patent that his company, Chemco, had held on the drug for five years had expired and several aggressive competitors had entered the field. The separate strands of three possible strategies for keeping Xylac the leader in the field were weaving together in his head when the telephone rang, shattering his concentration.

"Larry." It was Gloria, his wife. "Have you forgotten about dinner?" Tonight was the occasion for one of the major events of the Philadelphia social season, and Gloria was naturally as excited as an ingenue.

"Sorry," Larry said. "You can go without me, can't you?"

"I should have known." Gloria's voice fell. "Sweetheart, it doesn't look good for me to keep going to these things by myself."

"Sorry, honey, I've got to finish this."

Gloria retorted, "I'm sorry, too." There was a click as she hung up.

Larry put the phone down and turned back to the printout. Within minutes he was once again immersed in the intricacies of formulating a competitive strategy for Xylac.

Larry had always felt uncomfortable and shy at the social events his wife so much enjoyed, although at work his shyness vanished and he was comfortable and confident, the Larry Grant respected and admired by almost all of his coworkers. To these coworkers, Larry seemed to lead a charmed life. Only forty-one, he was Executive Vice President in charge of the Pharmaceuticals Division. His technical

---

skills, native intelligence, and easygoing demeanor impressed top management and sped his ascent ever since he joined the company as a financial analyst fresh from his MBA at Wharton.

Back in those Wharton days, Gloria had dazzled Larry. She was a Main Line debutante attending Bryn Mawr College, and her upper-crust background was so different from that of his own family, which was solidly middle class. It wasn't that Larry was ashamed of his background—his father was a self-made man who had started out washing cars and ended up owning a successful car dealership in Trenton, New Jersey—it was just that Larry wanted more for himself. Though his parents had become affluent, they were always frugal and lived modestly. They had instilled in Larry the values of hard work and integrity, and he intended to make the most of himself. Marrying Gloria had been a first step on that road, or so he had thought.

Half an hour after Gloria's call, Larry was still buried in thought about the Xylac problem. There was a knock at the door, and Ed Brentano peeked in.

Ed was a chemist in the development lab. Though he was several levels below Larry, the two were good friends. They were often the only two left working after hours. (Ed, a bachelor, was sometimes rumored to spend entire nights in the lab, napping as he waited for time to lapse on his experiments.) Many evenings Ed and Larry ran into each other in the halls or at the coffee machine and ended up talking about developments in the lab or business trends. Larry loved these discussions. He sensed a kindred spirit in Ed. It felt good to talk to someone with intelligence, who understood the complexities of Larry's job. In Ed Larry also admired a certain maverick quality, a slight contempt for the accepted rules of worklife. This was probably because Larry himself did not always act on his own rebellious impulses.

"Hey Larry!" Ed called out, coming into Larry's office with several scraps of paper in his hand. "I'm glad you're still here. Got a minute? Take a look at this."

Larry's eyes lit up. He needed a break from what he was doing. He looked at the slips of paper Ed had tossed on his desk.

"Are these on the most recent compound?"

"Exactly!"

"But the tolerance is so high!"

"Right! And you know what that means, don't you?" Ed had tutored Larry in basic research chemistry.

"Yeah. It means a broader application."

"That may be an understatement! Of course, this has to be confirmed by independent tests."

Larry shook his head in wonder. "Think of all the implications, if this is true!"

And the two of them took off with speculations about the possibilities. Before Larry knew it over an hour had passed. It was nine o'clock. Reluctantly, he told Ed he had to get home. Sometimes he wished he didn't have family obligations. Sometimes he wished he could stay up all night working when he felt like it.

In his youth, Larry had always worked hard; his achievements had always been of utmost importance to him. He enjoyed the feeling of accomplishment, as well as the praise and rewards he got from his parents and teachers for doing well. Larry's achievements were also important to his parents, who had held great expectations for him. He was the first in his family to go to college, and he felt very special because of it. So he worked even harder in college and graduate school than he ever had before. He liked the strangely thrilling, almost romantic feeling of aloneness in the darkened dorm or in the corner of the library late at night.

When Larry got home, he found his daughter Karen, age twelve, in the den watching a movie on the VCR.

"Have you done your homework?"

"Yeah," Karen replied, her eyes glued to the screen.

"Where's your brother?"

"In his room."

That kid! Larry thought to himself. Matthew, age sixteen, had recently taken to locking himself in his room and listening to music. Larry knew that kids Matthew's age were prone to rebellion, but the boy really was beginning to concern Larry. It had gotten to the point where his grades—always high before and a source of pride to Larry—had begun to slip.

Gloria had been the first to notice a problem. Larry had been working on performance appraisals in his study one Sunday (he claimed that was the only way to get them done) when Gloria came in and announced, "I'm concerned that Matthew's been hanging around with a fast crowd. Do you know what time he got in last night? Two o'clock in the morning. I can't talk to him. I think you need to."

Larry had been annoyed at the intrusion. "He's a teenage kid, Gloria. Teenagers do things like that." At the time he had assumed she was making a big deal out of nothing. But lately Larry had noticed Matthew bringing home some unsavory-looking friends, and he was becoming hostile and unresponsive to Larry's attempts to talk to him. He was always off somewhere, and he was neglecting his household duties.

Tonight, for example, was the night to take out the trash—Matthew's job—and it was still in the garage. Larry went up to Matthew's room and knocked. No answer. He tried the knob—the door was locked. He banged louder. Finally Matthew opened the door. A pair of earphones closed out the world.

"Take those things off!" Larry yelled.

"What?" Matthew replied as he pulled the headphones down around his neck.

"I though I told you not to lock your door. And didn't your mother ask you to take out the trash? You're not too old to be grounded, young man."

"Yeah, right. Just because I don't want to work all the time like you do!" And he slammed the door.

Larry stared at the closed door for a moment, then turned and walked away. The kid was getting out of hand. But this wasn't the time to do anything about it. Larry prided himself on his ability to put problems out of his mind when there was nothing he could do about them. It was a reaction that served him well at work, and he saw no reason why it couldn't work equally well at home.

Larry went to the kitchen and made himself a sandwich. He sat at the kitchen table and read the *Wall Street Journal* as he ate. Soon Matthew appeared, looking sheepish.

"I took out the trash, Dad. I'm sorry I yelled at you. I was wondering if— there's a basketball game at school tomorrow night. Could I have the car?"

Larry thought: So, the kid is willing to work a deal, is he? An apology and good behavior in return for the car. "You want the car on a week night?" he asked.

Matthew shifted his feet. "C'mon Dad, everyone is going!"

"So ride with someone else."

"Aw, you know the guys are counting on me to drive. C'mon."

"I can't have you talking to me with such disrespect, Matthew."

"I know, Dad. I said I was sorry."

Larry felt a twinge of guilt. Maybe it was wrong to hold it over the kid's head like that. But he had to get some control. "OK, but you be home by eleven," he said.

"Thanks, Dad!" Matthew ran out.

Finally feeling tired, Larry went off to bed. Gloria had not returned from the benefit. Probably still "mingling," strengthening her social contacts. He wondered if anyone at work was there? And what they thought of her being there alone? He brushed those thoughts away—he'd never cared what they thought. He did what he thought was right and he figured that those with enough sense respected him for it. Those were Larry's last thoughts as he dropped off to sleep.

Larry had always prided himself on his independent attitude. He knew he was intelligent and insightful about business, and he preferred to operate by his own lights. Yet he was also aware of organizational realities. He had been lucky to have a mentor in his early days, a vice president of finance, who had seen Larry's aptitude and motivation and advised him that the route to the most comprehensive understanding of the industry—and to the top of Chemco—was through broad exposure to all functions and aspects of the business. He convinced Larry to spend a couple of years in production, at a plant. Gloria, just getting into the swing of things as a Philadelphia wife, chafed at the prospect of moving to Oklahoma. But Larry assured her that it was only for a couple of years and then they could move back to the city and he would have a much bigger and better job. Gloria acquiesced and they moved, just after she gave birth to Matthew.

Then, to his surprise, Larry found that he was fascinated by production and by life at the plant. So, instead of moving back to Philadelphia, they embarked on a series of moves, "From one hick town to another," as Gloria would remark to others. In each new town, Gloria joined the "right" clubs and committees—the Junior Leagues, the Historical Preservation Societies, the Friends of the Hospitals, the Theatre Centers, the Arts Guilds. Though being a "big fish in a small pond," as she put it, was fun at first, the novelty soon wore off. Having grown up in a world of high culture and finishing schools, she had little in common with small-town people.

When she had first met Larry, he was like nobody she had ever known. He was such a go-getter, so ambitious and intelligent he was bound to be a success.

And he was certainly attractive in an all-American kind of way. Sure, he was a bit rough around the edges, but that would go away with time and her help. So she was shocked to discover that he actually liked the quiet small-town lifestyle. She had tried her best to initiate him into the excitement of social life, to no avail. So she bided her time and finally, a year ago, they had moved back to Philadelphia. In a wish to bring in some innovative new ideas to recharge a stagnant area, top management had chosen Larry to take over the Pharmaceuticals Division.

The next morning Larry woke up to find Gloria asleep next to him. As he got out of bed she opened her eyes.

"You missed a fabulous party. Everyone was asking about you. I told them you were sick."

Every response Larry could think of was bound to start an argument, so he said nothing except, "The new compound Ed's been working on turns out to have an amazingly high tolerance. This could really cut back on some of our development times. . . ."

"Mm-hmm," said Gloria, distractedly inspecting her manicure.

Why do I even try to talk to her about work things, thought Larry to himself. "Matthew's taking the car to a basketball game tonight," he said.

"What? With all the tricks he's been pulling lately you reward him with the car? I told you, I don't like the looks of his friends. Who knows what he's been getting into."

Any doubts or concerns Larry might have had were swept away by Gloria's reaction. "You're too protective—stop worrying. He can take care of himself. Didn't you ever do crazy things when you were in high school?" Of course, he knew she hadn't. In fact, neither had he.

As a teenager, Larry had been every mother's dream. Captain of the football team, vice-president of the Student Council, active in his church's youth group. Most of his friends were from church and Student Council, and their relationships revolved around the activities of those groups. Everyone looked up to Larry, and he enjoyed his stature among his peers.

Larry was gratified by his accomplishments in and of themselves, but he was also responding to what he knew was his parents' desire for him to accomplish great things. They didn't say this in so many words, it was just obvious in everything they did for him, in the way they made over him when he did well and were so disappointed when he would occasionally not do his best.

Though on the surface Larry's choice of Gloria as a wife flew in the face of his parents' middle-class values, the similarities ran deeper than the differences. Gloria, like Larry's mother, was a traditional wife and mother who, though she was more socially ambitious than Larry's mother, shared the value placed on family and stability. She was also like Larry's mother in her rational and pragmatic attitude toward life. Gloria had no patience with "over-blown" emotions. This was comfortable for Larry. He and his parents had never shared personal feelings. His parents had rarely expressed anger and had disapproved when Larry got angry or upset. Very occasionally as an adult Larry would lose his temper, as he had with Matthew and as he sometimes did with members of his staff, but he tried to avoid this. He saw himself as a calm and steady person and he liked for others to see him this way too.

For this reason, rather than get into an argument with Gloria that morning, Larry lit a cigarette and left the bedroom to her. He got dressed quickly and took coffee and a micro-waved pastry in the car with him. He had a meeting scheduled first thing with Sally O'Brien. Sally was a financial analyst on Larry's staff. In fact, she held the same job Larry had held when he first joined Chemco, and she was a brand new and very bright MBA just as Larry had been. Larry thought of himself as a mentor to her. Her obvious admiration and respect for him was flattering. More than that, though, he really liked her. They had good conversations about business. They seemed to share many likes, dislikes, and interests. On the few occasions they had traveled together for business, Larry had had a great time. But of course, he told himself, their relationship was strictly business. They never talked about their lives outside of work. He had once met her husband, a banker, at an office party. Gloria had met Sally there, too. After the party, Larry had asked Gloria if she'd liked Sally. "Who? The mousy one?" Oh well, Gloria didn't have to like her. He liked her, and that was all that mattered.

The purpose of the meeting was for Sally to present to Larry a financial report she had prepared at his request.

"Larry, I have to tell you. I don't know why no one has ever thought of breaking the figures down this way before. Sometimes you just amaze me."

Larry scanned the top sheet of paper and smiled. She had done a good job. "Why don't you just summarize the main points to me."

Sally went through the report, highlighting the key points.

"What would your recommendations for action be, Sally, based on this report?" This was an unorthodox question to ask of Sally in light of her inexperience and junior status. But Larry liked to challenge his sharp young people with ideas. She looked taken aback but rose to the occasion, as Larry had known she would.

Sally's answer led her and Larry into a long and enjoyable brainstorming session on possible changes in the company's financial reporting procedures. Finally she glimpsed the clock on Larry's wall.

"Oh! I wish we could keep talking but I have another meeting. I just want to say, I really appreciate how you give me the chance to be involved in these problems. Most people around here can't be bothered with my opinions. It really makes my job a whole lot more enjoyable to feel like I can contribute."

Larry was a little embarrassed. He stood up. "Good! This will get you more acquainted with the workings of the division. Why don't you put those recommendations in writing for me, and copy your boss too?"

Sally was unable to suppress the grin that appeared on her face as she left Larry's office. Larry gave himself a moment to bask in the admiration she had for him and the gratification he got being helpful to her.

That afternoon, Larry was scheduled to give a presentation to the Executive Committee. It was just a status report, but he had spent many hours preparing it.

Presentations always made him anxious, even though he had devoted a great deal of attention to honing his speaking skills. He suspected that he still took more time preparing—or overpreparing—than he needed to, but it made him feel better to do so. Today, as usual, he was armed to the hilt with charts and overheads. All the top brass were there, including his own boss. With a flush of excitement, he gave his presentation, touching on the past year of the division, new product opportunities, current development activities, problems the division was facing, and ideas for their solution. The executives were impressed.

"That was very well put together."

"Sounds like Pharmaceuticals is finally coming around."

"I like the new way of breaking down the financials."

"Larry, can you come to next month's meeting and give us an expanded picture of new products with some ideas on how you might get together with other divisions?"

Larry beamed as he left the conference room. He would never admit it to anyone, and he didn't know exactly why, but the praise and esteem he got from the Executive Committee pleased him more than it did coming from anyone else. It gave him feelings of security and warmth and happiness. God knows, he thought, I get enough positive feedback from most people around here, and from most of the things that I do, that I don't need to rely on praise from my bosses. And I certainly don't kowtow to them. When I disagree, I say so! Larry was aware, however, that when he disagreed it was with good reason, and his bosses respected him even more because of it.

As he drove home that evening, Larry thought about the presentation he had been asked to do for next month. The part about getting together with his peers in other divisions didn't excite him. He didn't think too highly of most of the other division heads and didn't like spending much time with them. Most, in Larry's opinion, had been in their jobs too long. They insisted on sticking with their outmoded ideas even though they had become a detriment to Chemco's productivity. This bothered Larry and made him more than a little angry at times.

Larry was getting home at 7:30, a reasonable hour for a change. He looked forward to a restful evening. He poured himself a drink and went to his study to watch the news. Gloria and the kids were probably somewhere in the house. No, he remembered, Matthew was going to the basketball game. They probably had eaten dinner already, without Larry. He didn't mind eating alone after the buzz of his day at work, though. A little TV, a little dinner, maybe another drink would relax him just fine.

A couple of hours later, Larry was awakened from a snooze in his easy chair by Gloria. Her face was white. "The police just called. Matthew wrecked the car and was arrested for drunk driving. And they found some kind of barbiturate in his blood in addition to the alcohol. He wasn't at the basketball game at all—he was on the other side of town. At a party in the woods."

Waiting at the police station later, Larry felt floods of emotion wash over him. Frustration and anger. Anger toward Matthew. What had happened—he had been such a good kid before! Now he'd really screwed up, and totaled the car to boot. Anger toward Gloria. Taking care of the kids was her job. She had never been able to discipline them. Plus, she was so busy with her damn society parties that the kids probably got the short end of the stick. But, he remembered, Gloria had tried to get him to help her deal with Matthew. Larry wondered, have I done anything wrong myself? No, I've tried to discipline Matthew—just last night, for example, I've been trying to be a good father, when there's time.

It turned out that part of Matthew's penalty required the family to see a counselor assigned by Juvenile Court. The counselor they got was a young man named Carl. He asked many questions about the family's lifestyle and activities, then he said, "Sometimes when a teen engages in this kind of behavior it has to do with problems in family relationships. Can any of you recall any evidence of such problems?"

"There's nothing wrong with our family life. He just got in with a bad crowd," Larry responded, feeling defensive.

"What kinds of things do you do together—any recreation, sports, or hobbies?"

"Well, I haven't had much time lately."

"Can you tell me more about that?"

"My work load has gotten heavier lately, since we came back to Philadelphia. You know, moving into a new job, trying to make some changes in the organization. . . ."

"Has it ever occurred to you that Matthew may be missing spending time with his father? Missing having a relationship with his father?"

Gloria added, "I think he's right. You're never around—the kids hardly know you, except for the once in a while when you come in and yell at them. And you know, it might not be a bad thing for all of us if you were around a little more."

Later at home, Larry asked Gloria about her statement.

"Well, the two of us haven't seen much of each other either. Remember when we used to do things together—day trips; dinners, movies?"

Larry thought about this and slowly it all began to come together. He really hadn't had much to do with his family at all lately. He'd been so caught up in his work. Even when he was at home with his family, he was usually thinking about work. He really did love all of them. It was just that he didn't seem to have much in common with any of them any more. The kids were into their kid things. Gloria was into her social things. He was into his work. Maybe it was his fault. Maybe he needed to spend more time with them. That was it! He made a vow to himself to try to balance the time and energy he spent working with more time and energy with his family. Enthusiastically, he told Gloria and the kids about it. They seemed pleased. This would be the ticket to turning things around in the family, Larry assured himself.

Larry began to make a point of coming home and having dinner with the family. It seemed strained at first. He would ask the kids, "What did you do today?" They would respond, "Nothing," or "Same old thing," or "Went to school." He would say, "How was school today?" They would say, "Fine" or "Boring." It was bound to get better, he told himself, after everyone got used to having him around.

Matthew was stuck in the house a lot since Larry had grounded him after the drunk-driving incident. Larry hadn't said much to Matthew about that incident—he didn't know what to say. He tried to draw Matthew into conversations about what he was doing in school, but the boy was sullen and Larry sensed resentment. Larry would suggest they go to a baseball game together, or fishing, but Matthew was never interested. He would try to get the boy to help with the home chores Larry was once more getting involved in—painting the shutters, cleaning out the garage—but Matthew would just stand around. Larry would inevitably end up yelling at him, and Matthew would react by retreating into angry silence. Larry was frustrated—he was trying to do what he should do, and what the family claimed they wanted him to do, spend more time with them, but the family didn't seem to appreciate his efforts.

He spent more time with Gloria in the evenings. Sometimes they ate dinner with the kids and watched TV. Other times they went out, to what Larry called "Gloria's things" —but these evenings out were a strain on Larry, who became even more convinced that her friends were shallow and pretentious. He said nothing, however. In an attempt to preserve the apparent harmony with Gloria, he tried to act as if he were having a good time, though he always breathed a secret sigh of relief when the evening was over and he could retreat to his study or his bed.

One night Larry and Gloria went to a party at a neighbor's house. Larry had taken to having a few drinks at these events—it helped to loosen him up and relieve some of the strain. He had had a few too many on this evening when he was accosted by the hostess, a woman whom he particularly disliked. She was a prominent hostess in town, but Larry thought she was loud and arrogant.

She grabbed Larry by the arm and said, "Darling, you don't have to be so stuffy! You've barely said two words to anyone all evening. Why don't you loosen up and have a good time? Gloria's told me about those dull engineers you spend all your time with. You should consider yourself lucky to have this chance to get away from all that!" And she laughed.

Larry felt fury rising up inside him. What right did this woman have to foist her warped values on him? Before he could stop himself, the words came out. "You know what I really think? Not a single person in here is fit to wipe the shoes of those engineers. They're good, hard-working people and you all are full of crap!"

The woman gasped. "Well! I never—Gloria!" she called. "Larry is not enjoying our company and would like to go home!" She walked away in a huff.

"What's this all about?" asked Gloria as she walked up to Larry.

"Never mind, let's just leave."

"But wait, I was just talking to someone. . ."

Larry guided Gloria out of the house.

As they drove home, Larry told her what had happened.

"How could you? Those are all very important, very powerful people. I'm so embarrassed! We'll never be invited anywhere again!"

"That would be most delightful," Larry replied sarcastically. "I've always thought I hated these people and now I know why."

"But I thought you were finally beginning to enjoy yourself, finally beginning to see that there is more to life than just the office."

"I have never had a good time. God knows I've tried. But I hate every minute of it and I've had enough."

"Fine," she replied. "Ruin my life while you're at it."

They finished the drive home in silence. They did not speak to each other the rest of the evening.

The next morning at breakfast, Larry announced to the whole family, "I think we all need to take a vacation together. Get away, relax, have a good time. I'll arrange my schedule at work so I can get away for a couple of weeks."

Gloria was delighted. "Great! We'll go to the Caribbean! How about St. Thomas? Great beaches, great shopping. . . ."

Larry held up his hands. "Hold on, now. I think we should do something interesting. We've always said we wanted to take the kids out West. See the Grand Canyon, Mount Rushmore, that kind of thing. While we're at it, we can visit your aunt and uncle in Chicago, and my brother Pete in Denver."

The discussion continued, both Larry and Gloria trying to stay reasonable and controlled, but both stubbornly holding onto their own ideas about the kind of vacation they wanted. Larry managed to clear up two weeks of his schedule. A couple of months later, the family went on vacation—on a car trip, to visit relatives and see the sights out West.

Six months after the vacation, Gloria asked Larry for a divorce.

What happened? Larry had been taking steps to balance his time and improve his family life—or so he thought. His view of the problem was that his investment of time and energy between work and home was out of balance, that he was too focused on his work and too inattentive to his family. When he tried to turn more time and attention to his family, somehow it fell flat.

He felt betrayed by Gloria. He had tried to correct the emerging problems in the only way he knew. When he asked her why she wanted to end the marriage, she replied, "You're not the same person I married. You weren't there for us— even when you were in the house, you weren't there."

What led her to feel this way, and what Larry didn't understand, was that underneath the patterns of his behavior, underneath his focus on work and his inattention to his family, lay deep-rooted reasons why he had structured his life in the way that he had. His focus on work satisfied his need to feel competent and to appear competent in the eyes of others. And his inattention to family helped him to avoid intimacy and emotion, a side of experience that was unfamiliar and threatening to him.

Larry's need to be competent had been evident ever since his childhood—his parents had subtly pressed him to achieve and rewarded him when he did so. His youthful lifestyle revolved around structured activities oriented toward achievement, and the esteem and stature he gained from his leadership roles in these activities served as added rewards. In his role as a competent achiever, Larry could play the part of strong, rational, unemotional—all the qualities he came to see as "good."

In contrast, Larry had never learned to be intimate—he had never shared personal feelings with his parents, never learned to understand or express his emotions. This was reflected in his personal relationships as an adult, both at work and at home. The relationships with coworkers that he enjoyed so much were focused on task accomplishment. Even with his family, all he could do was try to engage his wife and children in activities. This was partly because task-forced interaction was all that he had known. It also may have been that becoming intimate, expressing emotion and vulnerability, represented a threat to the strong and competent person that Larry wanted to be.

Thus, when Larry tried to bring balance into his life by allocating his time and energy more evenly, he missed the boat because he was still focusing on competence and goal-orientation, and still avoiding intimacy and emotional expression.

This is not just a story about Larry Grant, but about many managers and others who have become successful in their careers by focusing on work rather than family, and on achievement rather than intimacy. The question is: Do we have to choose one or the other? Can we have achievement and intimacy, work and love? Possibly. But first we must be honest with ourselves, we must face the issue squarely. Here are some suggestions for beginning to work toward a more balanced life:

1. Become aware of what you truly value. Be honest with yourself about the importance of work to your self-esteem. How does it compare with the esteem you get from being a spouse and parent?

2. If you value your relationships as parent and spouse, consider the nature of those relationships, not just the amount of time you devote to them. Do you share *yourself* as well as your time? Do you know your family as unique people with hopes and fears, dreams and desires, and not just as your wife, your son, your daughter?

3. Recognize that the rewards of intimacy and sharing are different from the rewards of work. You may get from your work a sense of achievement and competence that draws you toward it; you may seek the same sorts of rewards in other areas of your life. But relationships don't have to be goal-directed. They can provide other kinds of rewards that are just as satisfying in different ways, rewards such as love, a sense of belonging, giving and receiving support, sharing sorrow and joy.

4. Recognize that expressing emotion and vulnerability with your family does not take away from your strength and competence at work. Though expressing vulnerability may not be functional in most work situations, it is essential in developing close relationships. Similarly, though cultivating strength and competence is useful at work, these attributes are not the cornerstone of intimate relationships.

5. Look for opposites within. Perhaps the real secret to balancing work and personal life is to find within yourself the counterweight to whatever qualities you have worked so hard to make preeminent. If you have striven to take charge, be a follower; if you have worked to be strong, look for the weakling; if you have driven yourself to achieve, look for the laggard. In becoming aware of the weaknesses we have worked so hard to banish and forget, we may find a truer self who can work and who can love.

◆

Characteristics of Workaholics*

Diane Fassel

It is clear from the foregoing information that addiction to work is indeed cunning and baffling. Not only are there various types of workaholics, the characteristics of the disease may manifest differently in different people. I want to describe the characteristics of workaholism in the individual but I do this with a certain amount of trepidation.

I am suspicious of lists of characteristics. In our trickiness, we go through these lists mentally clicking off "That's me, that's not me." Then the list-makers tell us how many "that's me's" we need to be "one." Frequently, we use the list as an external referent—looking outside ourselves for information about how to act, what to say, or how to respond. It tells us; we don't check out internally whether the description fits. Ultimately, however, we have to ask ourselves if our lives are becoming unmanageable in relation to our busyness, rushing, and working. If from inside the answer is "yes," we may need to face the possibility that we have an addiction to work.

Here are the primary characteristics of workaholics:

- multiple addictions
- denial
- self-esteem problems
- external referenting
- inability to relax
- obsessiveness

These characteristics and the following stories come to me from workaholics themselves and from the material generated by the first Workaholics Anonymous groups in the United States. Whether one, two, or most of the characteristics fit is not the issue. The issue is this: is your life increasingly unmanageable in relation to work, busyness, rushing, or caring?

MULTIPLE ADDICTIONS

I have never met a person with only one addiction. Anyone who attends an Alcoholics Anonymous (AA) meeting understands this— the room is filled with smoke and the coffeepot is perking! As Anne Wilson Schaef, a well-known author on the topic of addictions, says, "Most recovering addicts find that we must face-off with the addiction that is giving us the most trouble. After we face it we find another addiction waiting to be worked."

For example, many work addicts find that their work addiction goes hand in hand with a relationship addiction. They cannot bear to disappoint others or to say "no" to excessive demands, for fear of others' disapproval. Perhaps as ACOAs (adult children of alcoholics and dysfunctional families) they constantly seek approval and affirmation, which they receive through work. Some people who are well on the way to beating their chemical addiction may now be working with the same intensity with which they abused alcohol. Or workaholics, in their pain, may find themselves "taking the edge off" a hard day by having too many alcoholic drinks.

I find that the three usual backup addictions of workaholics are money, food, and relationships. Often, people fly among these three: not taking time to carefully consider shaky business deals because they promise big bucks; over-working and then nurturing themselves by overeating; prolonging work or staying late to please a boss or colleague. In each of these instances, the backup or secondary addiction kicks in to justify or blunt the primary addiction to work.

Ultimately, we have to address the underlying addictive process. Workaholism gives us many opportunities to understand both our inner dynamics and the dynamics of the disease. If work is the common denominator in all the areas where one's life is getting crazy, that is the addiction to be faced; but we should not congratulate ourselves that we have licked the addictive process! Addictions are a progressive process and so, too, is recovery. For example, we cannot recover from our overwork and continue in our food and relationship addictions without still being in a life-threatening situation. Facing our addictive process, whatever the specific addiction, is a lifelong task.

DENIAL

Every addiction rests squarely on denial. Denial is the first defense of the addictive process. Without denial, addictions crumble. When you break through your denial and acknowledge you are a workaholic, you are on the road to recovery. Unless you confront denial, it is useless to deal with any other steps to recovery.

The workaholic's denial is one of the trickiest of all denials because there appears to be no denial. Workaholism is one of the few addictions people boast about. They boast socially, publicly, and to the media. In print we see such stories as, "Ten women under 30 who made a million. They work hard, they play hard, they're workaholics and love it." It is extremely difficult to admit your addiction—especially if you have trouble with your boundaries and identity, as work addicts do—in the face of societal pressure telling you work addiction is positive.

There are several dimensions to the work addicts' denial. Some stay in denial by the process of comparison. They say, "I know I'm a workaholic, but it's better than a lot of other things I could be. We all have to die of something. It may as well be work." Another technique is the trade-off. "Sure I'm a workaholic, but look at the benefits I've received. As a result of my working, rushing, caring I've" . . . (you fill in the blanks). The illusion in this denial is that none of these benefits would come without the workaholism. A third form of denial is that workaholics admit their addiction, but they do not see it as dangerous for them. This form is the scariest of all. One of the characteristics of the addictive disease is a progressive loss of judgment, a lowered ability to make decisions that are in our best interests. The disease progresses in us whether we are aware of it or not.

The workaholic denies, and the family supports the denial. When loved ones turn away from their awareness of the effects of the workaholic on them, they enter the addictive process with the work addict. They are also in pain in relation to the workaholic, but they refuse to acknowledge their pain to themselves or their loved one. They mimic the denial of the workaholic in their own complaints: "He's a great provider, but we never see him"; or, "I suppose she could be doing worse things than working all the time, like running around with other men"; or this line from a Glasbergen cartoon, "Do you have any perfume that smells like a desk? My husband is a workaholic."

SELF-ESTEEM PROBLEMS

Work addicts have either overinflated or underinflated perceptions of themselves. They truly have a hard time seeing themselves honestly and accepting themselves for who they are. They fluctuate between seeing themselves as the most capable people or the most incapable. Consequently, they will make promises they can't fulfill (based on illusions of capability), only to feel embarrassed and shameful later. Or they bypass projects they could easily handle (based on illusions of worthlessness) and then punish themselves for lost opportunities.

Problems with self-esteem lead to a high degree of dishonesty. Believing that people will not accept them for who they are, workaholics tend to exaggerate their achievements and rarely mention their failures.

I experienced this aspect of the disease when I was interviewing a nurse for a job in a clinic. Her CV was sterling. She had apparently been a success from the beginning. After hiring her, however, the clinic discovered she lacked some rudimentary nursing skills and her personality was horrible. She compensated by working twice as hard as everyone else, but her rushing and busyness resulted in knocked-over bottles, botched appointments, and a host of errors that had to be cleaned up behind her. Needless to say she was fired, and I feel sure the clinic that fired her does not appear on her new CV. I can only guess how many previous jobs aren't there either!

It is important to recognize that not only was the nurse dishonest in her CV, she lives in an organizational milieu that expects people to promote themselves as flawless. What job counselor ever said, "Show the way you've grown through both success and failure"? The nurse was doing exactly what she believed was acceptable in a workaholic culture. Many work addicts report that they were only praised for success, not growth.

Many people in the addictions field point to self-esteem as the central issue in the predisposition to addictions. I don't believe there is one primary cause of addictions, and I do see self-esteem as a key struggle in recovery. Workaholics, like every addict, eventually have to face the pain that work numbs. Addictions take us out of touch with our lives, and we disengage from every aspect of our knowing and feeling. The workaholic's self-esteem issue is the fear that there may be no one inside worth knowing or, worse, there may be no one at all.

Regaining a true sense of self is one of the risks of recovery from workaholism, and it is also one of its promises.

EXTERNAL REFERENTING

External referenting is looking outside yourself for clues to how to act, what to feel. People who grow up in dysfunctional families spend inordinate amounts of time focused outside themselves. This is necessary in order to survive. Sometimes your very life depends upon anticipating the actions of the addict in your family. Unfortunately, this basic training of childhood is the perfect setup for work addiction.

Years before I decided to write a book about work addiction, I noticed a curious trait in a friend, a chief executive officer (CEO) in a large company. I would meet him for lunch and ask him how he was, and he responded by telling me what he was doing! Later, I realized workaholics are the addicts who will tell you what they do in response to how they are.

Accomplishments are the workaholic's primary external means of knowing who they are. Because they judge themselves by their accomplishments, they have the illusion they must always be doing something worthwhile in order to feel good about themselves. Of course, "worthwhile" accomplishments are visible (to others). Therefore a work addict would resist thirty minutes of solitude, even if it meant being more effective at work, because solitude could not be observed. Or the workaholic will take thirty minutes of solitude and find a way, in conversation with colleagues, to justify why solitude enabled them to work harder than before. For the work addict, every activity and nonactivity must justify itself in terms of its support of work, otherwise it has no reason for being—just as the workaholic believes he or she has no reason to be without the justification of work.

Since feeling good is related to task accomplishment, workaholics are often facing depression. They usually assign themselves more work than they can hope to do, so they inevitably disappoint themselves and those who count on them. My friend Jackie says she discovered a way to avoid even the feelings of disappointment. She moved on to another task so quickly that she didn't have time to feel anything!

Work addicts are inveterate list makers. The list serves as the ultimate external referent: if it is not on the list, it doesn't exist and it doesn't get attention. Workaholics' styles of list making are truly mind-boggling.

Richard has a master list done by categories: phone calls, correspondence, projects (long-term and short-term), follow-up, new contacts, personal, personal-family, personal-friends, and so on. Everyday he constructs a daily list from the master list. New things keep getting added to the master list, and some things that don't get done on the daily list have to be carried over to the following day. (Tired yet?) When I spoke to Richard he had eight months of lists he carried in a file everywhere he went. He felt obsessed with going back over each list and never throwing one away until everything on the list was done.

"Oh, I can do one better," said Elizabeth, a book agent. "If an item does not appear on my list, it does not get done—no matter what. If it does appear, it gets done—even if I know in the moment that activity is useless or inappropriate. For example, I will not exercise or spend time with my kids unless I see '2 p.m.–4 p.m. —time for kids' on the list. The list dictates my life. Without it, I would be lost." "But what about your kids?" I asked. "What if they don't want to spend from 2 o'clock to 4 o'clock with you? What about their needs and schedules?" "Too bad," Elizabeth shrugged. "If they want time with their mom, this is when it is."

I left this encounter feeling pensive. In the era of two-career families and single parents, we've heard a lot about spending quality time with children, making every moment count, especially when there are not very many moments. Elizabeth's style seems to have abandoned quality altogether. Her kids are just another item to be checked off the list. She may not be present to them; they may not be present to her. In the end they just "did it." I began to see the power of workaholism as a generational disease. Elizabeth's children were learning a rudimentary skill of the dysfunctional family: external referenting of life by the list.

INABILITY TO RELAX

I noted earlier that workaholics run on hyper-adrenaline. The adrenaline is a major contributor to the inability to relax. Even when the work addict is ready for sleep, the system may not be able to turn off.

Work addicts have an endless array of tasks, and they always feel the need to get just a few more done. Since work is the "stash," when present tasks are done, there are a few more.

I knew a housewife who felt discomfort in face-to-face conversation. She felt others would see through her, and she felt unworthy. Still, she was social and enjoyed company. When guests came over, she busied herself in the kitchen while they talked. After dinner she was the first to jump up and clean the dishes. When her guests offered to help with the dishes, she demurred. She was comfortable visiting people in the kitchen so long as she had something to do. So she dried silverware, folded napkins, cleaned out cracks on appliances. Others protested she should quit, relax, and join them in the living room, but she set it up so that rarely happened and people eventually drifted into the kitchen when they desired her company. Of course, she made it difficult for them to confront her because she was always serving them. All she ever knew about her compulsion to work and her inability to relax was that she needed "something" between herself and other people. And she fiercely guarded that something all her life.

Procrastinators and work anorexics have difficulty relaxing, although you would never know it by looking at them. They are in constant internal turmoil. They feel resentment about having to complete tasks. They cannot concentrate on the task at hand. They punish themselves by avoiding work and then beating up on themselves for procrastinating—not a very relaxed place to be!

Many workaholics operate in a constant crisis mode (usually because they schedule themselves for more than they can handle); consequently, they feel the uproar of the crisis, but they rarely experience their true emotions. Work addicts cannot just sit and be. They say repeatedly, in almost every interview, that it is simply too terrifying to just sit and be. Some work addicts acknowledge that if they relaxed, they might feel emotions they wish to avoid. Others have a terror of the void, an emptiness too fearful to explore. Whatever it is they fear, they readily acknowledge that work keeps these feelings down and inaccessible on a daily basis.

Many workaholic businesses use the crisis orientation as an excuse for a corporate inability to relax. In these companies, people are always dropping what they are doing to respond to a seemingly more critical need. A consultant who deals with workaholic companies observed that her most difficult challenge is to show managers that they do not need to react if they have planned their business. They become so frightened about knowing what they really need to do that they would rather close their eyes and put out fires.

The inability to relax does not come from work itself but from incessant work and the way we work. When work is a fix it carries a burden it cannot sustain. Work cannot give us an identity. It cannot *make* us happy. When we expect our work to do things for us that we are not willing to do for ourselves, we become exhausted. More is not better where work is concerned.

Healthy people are enlivened and stimulated by work. They don't expect work to make them whole. They are whole and they choose to work. Sure, such people are tired at the end of a day, but not with the disabling exhaustion of the work addict.

The inability to relax is a serious symptom for the workaholic because it signals that the physical and psychological systems are running on overload. Like an out-of-control train streaking down a mountainside, the brakes are of no avail. Only a crash will stop it.

OBSESSIVENESS

To be obsessive is to be driven. Many work addicts describe themselves as being on automatic pilot. They move through a day, but they are not actually in the driver's seat. One of the symptoms indicating the disease is worsening is the sense that someone besides yourself has taken over. An accompanying signal is that you think of work constantly—in bed, in the shower, during conversations, while watching TV, and while driving.

Obsessiveness is not particular about its object. You can be obsessively perfectionistic about the form of a letter or doing good works. Carol, a nurse, directed her obsessive serving toward poor migrant workers. At the time her obsessive serving peaked, she was on four boards and was the chairperson of three of them. She now sees that her workaholism got hooked because she believed it was for a good cause. Raised as a "good Christian," Carol looked askance at those who worked hard only to accumulate wealth for themselves. But the migrant programme was not for her advancement—in fact, she took a cut in pay—but for those more needy than she was.

Carol left her quarters at 8 a.m. and returned at midnight. She would use the toilet only twice in that period—once before she left and when she returned at night. She drove from migrant camp to migrant camp and ate only candy bars and chocolate shakes. She existed on sugar. In addition, Carol was in a crazy relationship—they spent their "free" time fixing up their rental house in order to leave a better place for the next person, and also to avoid dealing with their conflict with each other.

By the time Carol quit the migrant project she was physically strung out and barely able to provide the services she had come to do. She went back to her hometown and took a job at a hospital, where she worked sixty hours a week. The sixty hours felt like a vacation after the migrant project. She thought she was doing well until one evening, after a typical day at the hospital, Carol chopped off her finger while fixing supper. This accident gave her an enforced two weeks off work, a period that turned her around.

Carol knew something was wrong with her life. During her time off, she obsessively searched for an answer. She read compulsively, looking for a cure—first New Age, then crystals and herbs, then addiction books. "I 'drank books' the way any drunk does alcohol. I had been obsessively sick, now I was going to get well; but I was doing 'well' the way I did sick," said Carol.

Carol's realization that she was trying to recover in an obsessive manner was a key point in her recovery. She has faced her obsessiveness and now is more gentle with herself.

Obsessiveness can extend to areas beyond work, as Carol's story exemplifies. I knew a man who had an excessive desire to understand everything in his life and in his family's life. He would spend hours in self-examination, asking himself, "Why did I do that? Why do I feel this way? Why are others acting as they do?" He exhausted himself and others, not to mention how disrespectful he was in his incessant poking into everyone's motivation.

Obsessiveness can endanger your life. Carol lost a finger, a daily reminder to her about her disease. Workaholics are always trading stories about missed train stops, driving past highway exits, driving into the rear ends of stopped cars due to preoccupation with thoughts about work or whatever it is they are focused on.

Some use these events to wake up to the reality of work addiction in their lives; others are too obsessed with understanding why it happened to use the event to change their lives.

OTHER CHARACTERISTICS

The foregoing six characteristics are reported to me by most work addicts. In addition, work addicts share other characteristics:

- dishonesty
- self-centeredness
- isolation
- control
- perfectionism
- piles and files
- lack of intimacy
- self-abuse
- physical and psychological problems
- spiritual bankruptcy

Dishonesty

In order to protect their supply, work addicts lie. They lie about how much they work, and how often they work. As closet workers, they hide work. They are dishonest with themselves and with others. Like denial, dishonesty is essential in keeping up the facade that says "I'm OK," when actually their lives are crumbling down around them.

Self-Centeredness

Work addicts have an exaggerated sense of the importance of their projects. Children of workaholic parents recall that nothing interfered with a parent's work. Their work came first, and all other plans gave way. Addicts will do anything to get to their fix, including running over loved ones and breaking promises. Workaholics prefer jobs with important titles or the opportunity to control others. They think of others as servants, not peers. Their self-centeredness expresses itself in acting superior, finding fault with experts, and so on.

Careaholics persist in the illusion that without them no one would be served. It is always a shock to the careaholic to see others pitch in and carry on when they leave. Of course, the self-centeredness keeps us in the disease; and while it fosters our workaholism, it prevents us from attaining true self-love in which we are at the center but not at the expense of others or ourselves.

Isolation

Workaholics tend to remove themselves from others in several ways. First, the obsession with work, with rushing, and busying is inherently isolating because others cannot keep up with the addict. Like an airplane on an aborted landing, work addicts touch down and take off again. Second, as others become concerned about the workaholic, the workaholic begins removing himself or herself from those who may accumulate enough information to confront the problem. Finally, work addicts work alone when others decide to limit their hours or say "no" to excessive demands.

Control

The illusion of control dies slowly for work addicts because control pervades so many aspects of their lives. They have the illusion that they can control the amount they work and the intensity. They believe they can control how others see them. Managers and workaholic organizations attempt to control workers, and they assume that a workaholic approach will ultimately control productivity. Time management may be the height of the control illusion, for addicts truly believe there is a way to handle time so they have more of it!

As work addiction progresses, the attempts at control become greater. The work addict's inner life is in chaos, so the efforts to hold it together must be made externally. Giving up the illusion of control is extremely difficult, but doing so is a key building block of recovery.

Perfectionism

Perfectionism is fuelled by the illusion that "I am not human." Workaholics have trouble with humanness. Humans need sleep, make mistakes, have feelings and needs. This is not a description of a workaholic. Perfectionistic bosses and colleagues are candidates for burnout because they believe their efforts and their control of themselves and other people will make things turn out the way they want it. They are frequently disappointed when things don't go perfectly.

I knew a perfectionistic manager whose perfection made him a basket case in relation to his staff. He had certain ways of doing things, and he taught those to his staff. He believed in delegating, so he gave away a lot of responsibility. Unfortunately, his staff didn't do tasks perfectly; they made mistakes. When he observed the mistakes he said, " See, if I trust them with the work, they don't do it right and I have to do it over. Therefore, why delegate to them in the first place? I only end up doing the work anyway." The result of his perfectionistic attitude was that he precipitated more mistakes on the part of his staff because they had fewer opportunities to learn by doing. Also, he did his own work and a large part of their work because it was the only way he could guarantee it would be done perfectly—that is, his way.

Perhaps perfectionists are the only ones who work themselves to death while those they hired to help stand by watching!

Piles and Files

All addicts have their stash, and workaholics are no exception. Piles and files are two common stashes for work addicts.

I once did a simple test with a workshop group. I said, "If I came into your house and cleared out your liquor cabinet, pitched all the bottles and you'd never see them again, how would you react?" Most (not the alcoholics!) replied they would be upset, but it would not be the end of their lives. "Well," I said, "If I came into your office and I went to your filing cabinet and I pitched your files and you'd never see them again, how would you feel?" The majority gasped. Several said, "I would panic and immediately begin to scheme where and how I could get copies of those files." Said others, now getting more honest, "I could not live without my files."

The files represent a continuing supply of work, projects upon projects for years to come. You never get ahead; and when you finish one, another is waiting. An organizational consultant who helps work addicts deal with their personal productivity told me, "Peace of mind is so uncomfortable." She says she deals with a client who cannot get his desk organized. Nothing seems to be working with this man. One day he did get his desk organized, and he let slip to the consultant, "Oops! Now that my desk is in order I have to face up to myself." Work addicts can stay busy for years with seemingly important pieces of paper, shuffling them around from place to place, all in the service of staying out of touch with their own internal processes.

Jeri lives among skyscrapers of piles at home and at the office. She believes that if she puts things away she won't do them, so she needs them constantly in her line of vision or they'll be forgotten. This method confounds her: "I end up with piles everywhere. Then I don't see the things on the bottom. I put the important work on my desk, but then the other stuff gets put on top. Finally, my urgent work is placed on the centre of my desk. I know to do it first, but even that pile is half-done."

We see the same pattern in Jeri's flat. For a year and a half she has lived among unpacked boxes. She realizes that her control is in her belief she can arrange her flat exactly the way she wants it. Since this goal is unattainable, she refuses to go even halfway to create a comfortable place for herself. "The boxes stand, always handy to take me away from myself. I never say, 'Today I'll unpack half a box.' It's all or nothing. It's a big, unmanageable chunk that can't be done, and it is constantly there to remind me."

Jeri's flat looks the same as it did a year and a half earlier. Friends are waiting for invitations to dinner, but Jeri is too ashamed for them to see the flat. Besides, where would they sit? A procrastinator at home, she is a binge worker at the office. When the pressure is on, she closes her door and works five hours straight to clear her desk. Jeri spends enormous energy beating herself up for not doing it right; then, exhausted mentally and emotionally, she has no energy to take the steps that would relieve her of this disease process.

Files and piles aren't the addictive process itself. They are the tools a work addict uses to stay in the addiction. Given our lifestyle in the twentieth century, we'll always have "stuff" that needs attending. When we believe we can and should control these things, we're in trouble. There's some truth to the saying, "We are what we do." When what we do is live preoccupied with our files and piles, we become just as lifeless as these objects.

Lack of Intimacy

It is easy to see how work addicts use working, rushing, and busyness to stay out of touch with themselves and with others. In the previous example, the man with the cluttered desk didn't want to clear his desk for fear he'd have to face himself. In the same way, workaholics use work as the means to avoid intimacy with self.

It is not true, however, that work addicts are loners hiding behind stacks of papers. Some work addicts are sociable; they have acquaintances, but frequently their social contacts are really work contacts. Or, as a recent article in *Fortune* put it, "All socializing by the workaholic generation is for the purpose of making future business contacts."[1] This type of socializing supports work addiction and prevents true intimacy. Workaholics use work to avoid intimacy. They stay busy with interesting projects and never meet the challenges of knowing another or being known themselves. True intimacy requires giving up the illusion of control—a difficult task for the work addict.

Work addiction affects at least three levels of intimacy. On the first level, workaholics are out of touch with self. They have no awareness of feelings, only emotional poverty. On the second level, workaholics have no genuine connection with loved ones, be they spouses, children, or friends. They may meet on the run, or have some superficial sharing, but there is not a closeness born of time to know and be known. On the third level, workaholics have no intimacy with work itself. The work—which is the thing they are losing their life in —becomes an object to satisfy the addiction, not a source of liveliness.

Self-Abuse

The workaholic lifestyle is self-abusive. It is emotionally abusive because it results in cycles of internal messages based on comparison: "I'm no good," "I'm not enough," and so on. It is physically abusive because it sets people into a pace that eventually has to result in burnout. At all levels, work addiction is destructive, and the destruction ripples out from the addict to family, organization, and eventually the world.

Physical and Psychological Problems

As the workaholic's disease progresses, it is inevitable that various physical and psychological symptoms appear. The danger, however, is that workaholics are so out of touch with their own physical processes that they require a serious disease like a heart attack to get their attention.

In this generation we have seen the rise of exotic fatigue diseases and swift killers. *Karoshi*, or "death from overwork," is a disturbing phenomenon in Japan. The disease, which is linked to too much work and not enough play, typically affects men who put in twelve-to-sixteen-hour days over many years. The victims, usually between the ages of forty and fifty, have no previous health problems. They apparently just work themselves to death. Two-thirds of the deaths are from brain hemorrhages, one-third from myocardial infarction. According to Japan's

Ministry of Health and Welfare, *karoshi* may account for 10 per cent of all deaths of working men in Japan, making it the second-largest killer of this population.[2]

Over the past ten years we have seen the rise of chronic fatigue syndrome, variously called Epstein-Barr and Yuppie flu because it tends to affect upwardly mobile professional women in their twenties and thirties. Characterized by swollen glands, fever, sore joints, and overpowering fatigue, these chronic viral syndromes can last for months, even years. Researchers are still puzzled about the causes of chronic fatigue. However, a recent research study found striking similarities between the characteristics of chronic cocaine abuse and fatigue syndrome, suggesting that addictive process disorders may result in chronic fatigue.[3] Certainly, the constant stress of workaholism suppresses the immune system, which is then ripe for viral infection.

In addition to chronic fatigue and death from overwork, work addicts also experience such stress-related ills as ulcers, gastrointestinal problems, backaches, difficulty sleeping, headaches, and high blood pressure. Even with such severe symptoms, work addicts ignore their pain. A woman confided: "We workaholics don't feel pain. I would not have told you I hurt. I was so high on my adrenaline I felt great. It was only when my body gave out that I began to feel the pain, and I ignored the symptoms for months, thinking it was just psychosomatic and I could push through the pain."

Psychologically, work addicts experience progressive deadening of their feelings. Some workaholics may have used their disease since childhood to compensate for the pain of the dysfunctional family. Thus, the separation from feelings is longstanding. Said one ACOA (Adult Children of Alcoholics) airline mechanic: "I used busyness starting at age eight as a way to avoid my crazy family. I cleaned house, joined clubs, had hobbies, pleased my parents and school authorities—anything to keep at bay the terror of living in my mixed-up family. Even now, I don't allow myself to feel satisfaction at my success. I move immediately on to something else."

Other work addicts exhibit severe mood swings, fluctuating between manic euphoria and severe depression. This moodiness is often related to work styles. Euphoric workers work hard, like binge workers, and their productivity goes in spurts. Depressed workers resemble anorexic workers. They procrastinate and can hardly get moving at all.

Most workaholics suffer from forgetfulness. Research on substance and process addiction has shown that memory loss is a characteristic of the disease. A recovering workaholic observed that if he had counted the time he spent searching for his keys, creating uproars over lost papers (which "mysteriously" reappeared on his desk), and sending secretaries on errands to buy replacements for lost items that were eventually found, he would have another lifetime to live.

Not only do work addicts lose things, they forget appointments and commitments. They forget ideas and plans. Addicts are people who make promises they cannot keep or do not intend to keep. They say "yes" when they mean "no," so they promptly forget things they agree to do. The workaholics' hectic pace is such that they cannot possibly meet all the commitments they set for themselves. They usually feel they are playing catch-up. This results in irritability, fits of temper, feelings of being misunderstood, and a tendency to suffer.

The work addict's life gradually unravels physically and emotionally. Family members may become immune to the addict. In their denial, they believe, "That's just the way Mom or Dad is." In truth, a disease process is gaining ground in the person's life. If not interrupted, it causes death.

Spiritual Bankruptcy

All addictions affect our morality: they result in spiritual bankruptcy. On a daily basis, work addicts are dishonest, controlling, self-centered, perfectionistic, and abusive to themselves and others. No wonder their morality is affected. You cannot lead such a life without losing your moorings. Your grounding in basic values is lost in the relentless pursuit of the addiction.

Spiritual bankruptcy is the final symptom of workaholism; it usually heralds a dead end. It means you have nothing left. Many workaholics have said, "I no longer knew right from wrong in any of my dealings. And I despaired there was a God out there who could help me." I believe this aspect of workaholism is the most terrifying. It is frightening to be out of touch with a power greater than yourself and to find your disease, which you know is destructive, ruling you.

Fortunately, when the workaholic downward spiral is reversed, spirituality is one of the first things recovering people regain.

Notes

1. Walter Kiechel, III, "The Workaholic Generation," *Fortune* (April 10, 1989): 51.

2. Ronald Yates, "Japanese live[. . .]and die[. . .]for their work," *Chicago Tribune* (November 13, 1988): 1.

3. Joel F. Lehrer, MD and Leila M. Hover, MLS, "Fatigue Syndrome," *Journal of the American Medical Association*, Vol. 259, No. 6: 842-843.

Chapter 9

Managing Ethically

Allmembers of a society experience pressures to behave ethically—that is, to do what is right and not what is wrong. These pressures come from at least two sources. First, one's actions are evaluated by other people who will reward and punish the individual according to how they judge the person's actions *vis-à-vis* their criteria for what is right and wrong. Second, individuals have their own internal standards of what is ethical behavior. These standards are developed through one's life experiences, which include attempts by parents and institutions to establish ethical behavior and by the numerous cases in which the judgments of others have been directed at the individual. These experiences seem to produce an internal standard of what is right and wrong. This internal standard (called by various names such as the *superego* by Freud, or the *impartial spectator* by Adam Smith, or the *conscience* in common parlance) serves to pressure a person to behave in accordance with its dictates.

We begin with the assumption that no universal agreement on the content of the standard exists. First, substantial differences between cultures exist. Second, contradictions among the standards within societies are also prevalent. One set of contradictions that is of particular interest in American business stems from tensions between the pursuit of self-interest and the achievement of some social good. Our long-standing acceptance of the invisible hand, operating through free markets to channel individual self-interests into actions that promote the common good, is a major ethical force underlying the free-enterprise system. At one extreme, this belief can serve to justify the view that "greed is enough"; other ethical principles are simply unnecessary for managers. On the other hand, many people argue that considerable constraint must be exercised on human self-interest if anything approaching ethical behavior is to be achieved. This debate, seldom far from the surface in discussions of business ethics (at least in the United States), is central to this section's articles.

Even though the content of the internal standards varies widely among social systems, the particular standards that exist within a system play an important part in helping human beings to establish and sustain cooperation. People whose actions are guided by common standards find it easier to predict what others will do. Moreover, to the degree that these standards inhibit acting on impulses to harm others and introduce more altruistic inclinations, they increase the level of trust in a social system. Knowing what to expect of other people, particularly knowing that they are unlikely to harm others, makes it easier to begin doing business with them or to cooperate in some other way. In short, ethical behavior is very important for achieving management's central task—coordination of human effort.

When organizations are superimposed on human relationships, new dimensions are added to knowing what is right and wrong and doing what is appropriate. For example, as we saw in the last section, as organizations become especially central to people, people face strong temptations to do what they perceive to be good for the organization even when it means they act inconsistently with the standards of ethical behavior.

Organizations appear to have a negative effect on ethical actions in at least five ways. First, they may operate in ways that lead people to perceive that they are rewarded for such behavior. Second, organizations provide ways to help individuals justify behavior that they may consider to be wrong in some other context. (For example, members of an organization sometimes come to believe that all of their competitors behave in unethical ways and if they fail to follow suit, their organization will fail.) Third, organizations add new variables that seem to make it difficult to do what one personally feels is right. James Gordon's discussion in "James Gordon, Manager" provides an excellent example of such complicating factors as well as showing how an organization's climate can help people to do what they think is right.

In this context, it is important to note that the ambiguous nature of the ethical issues managers face makes the organization's climate especially powerful. The ethical dilemmas that confront managers seldom have a "right answer." Given such ambiguity, some very subtle elements within organizations have major consequences on what people do. Faced with ambiguity, individuals search for cues about what to do and are extremely susceptible to social influence. Actions by key organizational members are apt to have great impact under such conditions. Such actions can not only affect what one perceives as right or wrong but can be a source of ideas for rationalizing a given course of action.

The fourth negative effect of organizations on ethical behavior stems from a discontinuity between one's intentions and the consequences of one's actions—a discontinuity that is far greater than in less complex and more personal settings. This contrast can be illustrated by comparing a small group (such as a small nuclear family) with a large organization. In the former, each person is well-known to the others and has frequent face-to-face contact with the others. As a result, each can observe and discuss the consequences of various actions on each other and can explain or alter these to achieve the intended effects. Although even in a family many times one's intentions produce unintended consequences that are very difficult to change, a person has a far better chance to adjust his or her actions to produce the intended consequences. In a large complex organization, however, any action can have so many consequences that the results one intends are difficult to monitor. So many other people and events are affected that one's intentions are often unrelated to the consequences of one's actions. In some ways, organizations are very blunt instruments.

Finally, organizations create situations that require attention to issues in ways that more personal relationships seldom do. Policies must be set that govern the behavior of people in their organizational roles. The organization comes to have special obligations that in some sense impose greater constraints on their members than do other institutions. The example of dealing with the environment in this section is but one such example. ("Business Takes on a Green Hue"). "The Case of the Mismanaged Ms." in Chapter 7 on Managing Human Resources is another. Organizations spawn dilemmas that other contexts do not. As the scope of business grows, more complications arise. Of special relevance today is the fact that the business arena is now a global one. In such a world, the cultural relativity of the personal standards one has learned and the organizational standards that organizations in any given nation have evolved become evident. Ambiguity increases dramatically.

Most of the articles in this section develop some of these and other complications. Several of them also reveal a less pessimistic side of things—organizations can help people do what they believe is right. The article "Working for Mr. Clean Jeans" describes the responses of Levis to ethical challenges and shows that managers can build an important emphasis on ethics through their policies and practices. Levis has a "core curriculum" on ethics and diversity for employees and a set of ethical guidelines for foreign contracts. Many modern organizations control massive resources that their managers could use to help make things "right." On the other hand, this sort of ethical behavior can be very expensive and what is right remains uncertain. Many conflicting points of view exist about whether this is the "right" way for managers, as agents of the stockholders, to spend corporate resources. The complexity of the matter is increased by the fact, as noted in the article, that even such a significant step can be seen as unethical from some perspectives. To repeat Toffler, the ethical dilemmas that managers face simply have no right answer.

Somewhat paradoxically, the lack of clarity can provide a second way for managers to resolve some of their ethical dilemmas as they attempt to balance competing demands. The lack of an external norm can give the manager some latitude—the manager's own personal standards are not in direct competition with any prescription. Once managers realize this, they can act on their own personal standards of right and wrong. Stated boldly, under such conditions, a manager's personal standards are all he or she has to go by. As the title of the article by Sir Adrian Cadbury puts it, "Ethical Managers Make Their Own Rules."

◆

Ethical Managers Make Their Own Rules*

Sir Adrian Cadbury

In 1900 Queen Victoria sent a decorative tin with a bar of chocolate inside to all of her soldiers who were serving in South Africa. These tins still turn up today, often complete with their contents, a tribute to the collecting instinct. At the time, the order faced my grandfather with an ethical dilemma. He owned and ran the second-largest chocolate company in Britain, so he was trying harder and the order meant additional work for the factory. Yet he was deeply and publicly opposed to the Anglo-Boer War. He resolved the dilemma by accepting the order but carrying it out at cost. He therefore made no profit out of what he saw as an unjust war, his employees benefited from the additional work, the soldiers received their royal present, and I am still sent the tins.

My grandfather was able to resolve the conflict between the decision best for his business and his personal code of ethics because he and his family owned the firm which bore their name. Certainly his dilemma would have been more acute if he had had to take into account the interests of outside shareholders, many of whom would no doubt have been in favor both of the war and of profiting from it. But even so, not all my grandfather's ethical dilemmas could be as straightforwardly resolved.

So strongly did my grandfather feel about the South African War that he acquired and financed the only British newspaper which opposed it. He was also against gambling, however, and so he tried to run the paper without any references to horse racing. The effect on the newspaper's circulation was such that he had to choose between his ethical beliefs. He decided, in the end, that it was more important that the paper's voice be heard as widely as possible than that gambling should thereby receive some mild encouragement. The decision was doubtless a relief to those working on the paper and to its readers.

The way my grandfather settled these two clashes of principle brings out some practical points about ethics and business decisions. In the first place, the possibility that ethical and commercial considerations will conflict has always faced those who run companies. It is not a new problem. The difference now is that a more widespread and critical interest is being taken in our decisions and in the ethical judgments which lie behind them.

Secondly, as the newspaper example demonstrates, ethical signposts do not always point in the same direction. My grandfather had to choose between opposing a war and condoning gambling. The rule that it is best to tell the truth often runs up against the rule that we should not hurt people's feelings unnecessarily.

There is no simple, universal formula for solving ethical problems. We have to choose from our own codes of conduct whichever rules are appropriate to the case in hand; the outcome of those choices makes us who we are.

Lastly, while it is hard enough to resolve dilemmas when our personal rules of conduct conflict, the real difficulties arise when we have to make decisions which affect the interests of others. We can work out what weighting to give to our own rules through trial and error. But business decisions require us to do the same for others by allocating weights to all the conflicting interests which may be involved. Frequently, for example, we must balance the interests of employees against those of shareholders. But even that sounds more straightforward than it really is because there may well be differing views among the shareholders, and the interests of past, present, and future employees are unlikely to be identical.

Eliminating ethical considerations from business decisions would simplify the management task, and Milton Friedman has urged something of the kind in arguing that the interaction between business and society should be left to the political process. "Few trends could so thoroughly undermine the very foundation of our free society," he writes in *Capitalism and Freedom,* "as the acceptance by corporate officials of a social responsibility other than to make as much money for their shareholders as possible."

But the simplicity of this approach is deceptive. Business is part of the social system and we cannot isolate the economic elements of major decisions from their social consequences. So there are no simple rules. Those who make business decisions have to assess the economic and social consequences of their actions as best as they can and come to their conclusions on limited information and in a limited time.

WE JUDGE COMPANIES—AND MANAGERS—BY THEIR ACTIONS, NOT THEIR PIOUS STATEMENTS OF INTENT

As will already be apparent, I use the word ethics to mean the guidelines or rules of conduct by which we aim to live. It is, of course, foolhardy to write about ethics at all because you lay yourself open to the charge of taking up a position of moral superiority, of failing to practice what you preach, or both. I am not in a position to preach nor am I promoting a specific code of conduct. I believe, however, that it is useful to all of us who are responsible for business decisions to acknowledge the part which ethics plays in those decisions and to encourage discussion of how best to combine commercial and ethical judgments. Most business decisions involve some degree of ethical judgment; few can be taken solely on the basis of arithmetic.

While we refer to a company as having a set of standards, that is a convenient shorthand. The people who make up the company are responsible for its conduct and it is their collective actions which determine the company's standards. The ethical standards of a company are judged by its actions, not by pious statements of intent put out in its name. This does not mean that those who head companies should not set down what they believe their companies stand for—hard though that is to do. The character of a company is a matter of importance to those in it, to those who do business with it, and to those who are considering joining it.

What matters most, however, is where we stand as individual managers and how we behave when faced with decisions which require us to combine ethical and commercial judgments. In approaching such decisions, I believe it is helpful to go through two steps. The first is to determine, as precisely as we can, what our personal rules of conduct are. This does not mean drawing up a list of virtuous notions, which will probably end up as a watered-down version of the Scriptures without their literary merit. It does mean looking back at decisions we have made and working out from there what our rules actually are. The aim is to avoid confusing ourselves and everyone else by declaring one set of principles and acting on another. Our ethics are expressed in our actions, which is why they are usually clearer to others than to ourselves.

Once we know where we stand personally we can move on to the second step, which is to think through who else will be affected by the decision and how we should weight their interest in it. Some interests will be represented by well-organized groups; others will have no one to put their case. If a factory manager is negotiating a wage claim with employee representatives, their remit is to look after the interests of those who are already employed. Yet the effect of the wage settlement on the factory's costs may well determine whether new employees are likely to be taken on. So the manager cannot ignore the interest of potential employees in the outcome of the negotiation, even though that interest is not represented at the bargaining table.

BLACK AND WHITE ALTERNATIVES ARE A REGRETTABLE SIGN OF THE TIMES

The rise of organized interests groups makes it doubly important that managers consider the arguments of everyone with a legitimate interest in a decision's outcome. Interest groups seek publicity to promote their causes and they have the advantage of being single-minded: they are against building an airport on a certain site, for example, but take no responsibility for finding a better alternative. This narrow focus gives pressure groups a debating advantage against management, which cannot evade the responsibility for taking decisions in the same way.

In *The Hard Problems of Management*, Mark Pastin has perceptively referred to this phenomenon as the ethical superiority of the uninvolved, and there is a good deal of it about. Pressure groups are skilled at seizing the high moral ground and arguing that our judgment as managers is at best biased and at worst influenced solely by private gain because we have a direct commercial interest in the outcome of our decisions. But as managers we are also responsible for arriving at business decisions which take account of all the interests concerned; the uninvolved are not.

At times the campaign to persuade companies to divest themselves of their South African subsidiaries has exemplified this kind of ethical high-handedness. Apartheid is abhorrent politically, socially, and morally. Those who argue that they can exert some influence on the direction of change by staying put believe this as sincerely as those who favor divestment. Yet many anti-apartheid campaigners reject the proposition that both sides have the same end in view. From their perspective it is self-evident that the only ethical course of action is for companies to wash their hands of the problems of South Africa by selling out.

Managers cannot be so self-assured. In deciding what weight to give to the arguments for and against divestment, we must consider who has what at stake in the outcome of the decision. The employees of a South African subsidiary have the most direct stake, as the decision affects their future; they are also the group whose voice is least likely to be heard outside South Africa. The shareholders have at stake any loss on divestment, against which must be balanced any gain in the value of their shares through severing the South African connection. The divestment lobby is the one group for whom the decision is costless either way.

What is clear even from this limited analysis is that there is no general answer to the question of whether companies should sell their South African subsidiaries or not. Pressure to reduce complicated issues to straightforward alternatives, one of which is right and the other wrong, is a regrettable sign of the times. But boards are rarely presented with two clearly opposed alternatives. Companies faced with the same issues will therefore properly come to different conclusions and their decisions may alter over time.

A less contentious divestment decision faced my own company when we decided to sell our foods division. Because the division was mainly a U.K. business with regional brands, it did not fit the company's strategy, which called for concentrating resources behind our confectionery and soft drinks brands internationally. But it was an attractive business in its own right and the decision to sell prompted both a management bid and external offers.

Employees working in the division strongly supported the management bid and made their views felt. In this instance, they were the best organized interest group and they had more information available to them to back their case than any of the other parties involved. What they had at stake was also very clear.

From the shareholders' point of view, the premium over asset value offered by the various bidders was a key aspect of the decision. They also had an interest in seeing the deal completed without regulatory delays and without diverting too much management attention from the ongoing business. In addition, the way in which the successful bidder would guard the brand name had to be considered, since the division would take with it products carrying the parent company's name.

In weighing the advantages and disadvantages of the various offers, the board considered all the groups, consumers among them, who would be affected by the sale. But our main task was to reconcile the interests of the employees and of the shareholders. (The more, of course, we can encourage employees to become shareholders, the closer together the interests of these two stakeholders will be brought.) The division's management upped its bid in the face of outside competition, and after due deliberation we decided to sell to the management team, believing that this choice best balanced the diverse interests at stake.

ACTIONS ARE UNETHICAL IF THEY WON'T STAND SCRUTINY

Companies whose activities are international face an additional complication in taking their decisions. They aim to work to the same standards of business conduct wherever they are and to behave as good corporate citizens of the countries in which they trade. But the two aims are not always compatible: promotion on merit may be the rule of the company and promotion by seniority the custom of the country. In addition, while the financial arithmetic on which companies base their decisions is generally accepted, what is considered ethical varies among cultures.

If what would be considered corruption in the company's home territory is an accepted business practice elsewhere, how are local managers expected to act? Companies could do business only in countries in which they feel ethically at home, provided always that their shareholders take the same view. But this approach could prove unduly restrictive, and there is also a certain arrogance in dismissing foreign codes of conduct without considering why they may be different. If companies find, for example, that they have to pay customs officers in another country just to do their job, it may be that the state is simply transferring its responsibilities to the private sector as an alternative to using taxation less efficiently to the same end.

Nevertheless, this example brings us to one of the most common ethical issues companies face—how far to go in buying business? What payments are legitimate for companies to make to win orders and the reverse side of that coin, when do gifts to employees become bribes? I use two rules of thumb to test whether a payment is acceptable from the company's point of view: Is the payment on the face of the invoice? Would it embarrass the recipient to have the gift mentioned in the company newspaper?

The first test ensures that all payments, however unusual they may seem, are recorded and go through the books. The second is aimed at distinguishing bribes from gifts, a definition which depends on the size of the gift and the influence it is likely to have on the recipient. The value of a case of whiskey to me would be limited because I only take it as medicine. We know ourselves whether a gift is acceptable or not and we know that others will know if they are aware of the nature of the gift.

As for payment on the face of the invoice, I have found it a useful general rule precisely because codes of conduct do vary round the world. It has legitimized some otherwise unlikely company payments, to the police in one country, for example, and to the official planning authorities in another, but all went through the books and were audited. Listing a payment on the face of the invoice may not be a sufficient ethical test, but it is a necessary one; payments outside the company's system are corrupt and corrupting.

The logic behind these rules of thumb is that openness and ethics go together and that actions are unethical if they will not stand scrutiny. Openness in arriving at decisions reflects the same logic. It gives those with an interest in a particular decision the chance to make their views known and opens to argument the basis on which the decision is finally taken. This in turn enables the decision makers to learn from experience and to improve their powers of judgment.

Openness is also, I believe, the best way to disarm outside suspicion of companies' motives and actions. Disclosure is not a panacea for improving the relations between business and society, but the willingness to operate an open system is the foundation of those relations. Business needs to be open to the views of society and open in return about its own activities; this is essential for the establishment of trust.

For the same reasons, as managers we need to be candid when making decisions about other people. Dr. Johnson reminds us that when it comes to lapidary inscriptions, "no man is upon oath." But what should be disclosed in references, in fairness to those looking for work and to those who are considering employing them?

The simplest rule would seem to be that we should write the kind of reference we would wish to read. Yet "do as you would be done by" says nothing about ethics. The actions which result from applying it could be ethical or unethical, depending on the standards of the initiator. The rule could be adapted to help managers determine their ethical standards, however, by reframing it as a question: If you did business with yourself, how ethical would you think you were?

Anonymous letters accusing an employee of doing something discreditable create another context in which candor is the wisest course. Such letters cannot by definition be answered, but they convey a message to those who receive them, however warped or unfair the message may be. I normally destroy these letters but tell the person concerned what has been said. This conveys the disregard I attach to nameless allegation but preserves the rule of openness. From a practical point of view, it serves as a warning if there is anything in the allegations; from an ethical point of view, the degree to which my judgment of the person may now be prejudiced is known between us.

SHELVING HARD DECISIONS IS THE LEAST ETHICAL COURSE

The last aspect of ethics in business decisions I want to discuss concerns our responsibility for the level of employment; what can or should companies do about the provision of jobs? This issue is of immediate concern to European managers because unemployment is higher in Europe than it is in the United States and the net number of new jobs created has been much lower. It comes to the fore whenever companies face decisions which require a trade-off between increasing efficiency and reducing numbers employed.

If you believe, as I do, that the primary purpose of a company is to satisfy the needs of its customers and to do so profitably, the creation of jobs cannot be the company's goal as well. Satisfying customers requires companies to compete in the marketplace, and so we cannot opt out of introducing new technology, for example, to preserve jobs. To do so would be to deny consumers the benefits of progress, to shortchange the shareholders, and in the longer run to put the jobs of everyone in the company at risk. What destroys jobs certainly and permanently is the failure to be competitive.

Experience says that the introduction of new technology creates more jobs than it eliminates in ways which cannot be forecast. It may do so, however, only after a time lag and those displaced may not, through lack of skills, be able to take advantage of the new opportunities when they arise. Nevertheless, the company's prime responsibility to everyone who has a stake in it is to retain its competitive edge, even if this means a loss of jobs in the short run.

Where companies do have a social responsibility, however, is in how we manage that situation, how we smooth the path of technological change. Companies are responsible for the timing of such changes and we are in a position to involve those who will be affected by the way in which those changes are introduced. We also have a vital resource in our capacity to provide training, so that continuing employees can take advantage of change and those who may lose their jobs can more readily find new ones.

In the United Kingdom, an organization called Business in the Community has been established to encourage the formation of new enterprises. Companies have backed it with cash and with secondments. The secondment of able managers to worthwhile institutions is a particularly effective expression of concern because the ability to manage is such a scarce resource. Through Business in the Community we can create jobs collectively even if we cannot do so individually, and it is clearly in our interest to improve the economic and social climate in this way.

Throughout, I have been writing about the responsibilities of those who head companies and my emphasis has been on taking decisions, because that is what directors and managers are appointed to do. What concerns me is that too often the public pressures which are put on companies in the name of ethics encourage their boards to put off decisions or to wash their hands of problems. There may well be commercial reasons for those choices, but there are rarely ethical ones. The ethical bases on which decisions are arrived at will vary among companies, but shelving those decisions is likely to be the least ethical course.

The company which takes drastic action in order to survive is more likely to be criticized publicly than the one which fails to grasp the nettle and gradually but inexorably declines. There is always a temptation to postpone difficult decisions, but it is not in society's interests that hard choices should be evaded because of public clamor or the possibility of legal action. Companies need to be encouraged to take the decisions which face them; the responsibility for providing that encouragement rests with society as a whole.

Society sets the ethical framework within which those who run companies have to work out their own codes of conduct. Responsibility for decisions, therefore, runs both ways. Business has to take account of its responsibilities to society in coming to its decisions, but society has to accept its responsibilities for setting the standards against which those decisions are made.

James Gordon, Manager*

Barbara Ley Toffler

I am a corporate administration manager, although I'm an engineer by background and have only been in the administrative world for three years. The responsibility of our group is to come up with a set of procedures and systems support for our function. Basically, we develop the systems to improve productivity and quality of the personnel work. We train 150 people out in our facilities who are the main interface with employees on administrative issues.

Part of the strength of this company is that it isn't really a company in a sense. It's very decentralized, very fragmented; I believe individuals can use that fragmentation to build for themselves the environment they want. So if you're really looking for a lot of structure, you can find it here. There are some organizations, a finance organization for one, that is very structured. There's no two ways to add numbers together; you do it a certain way. You can also find yourself in a complete lack of structure. I positioned myself in a place where our organization is typically unstructured, although my job has structure to it and I can use both pieces to satisfy myself. And I can be an entrepreneur. I've got a million-dollar budget here. I can run that pretty much the way I want.

The company is many things to many people, so a lot of people feel satisfied with it. I just saw the results of the survey that was done in one of the company's groups. Ninety-five percent of the people that work in that group said they would recommend this place to a friend as a good place to work. I think that pretty much wraps it up. I enjoy our success, I enjoy being part of the company. I enjoyed it even before we became well known, but I'm convinced that in 10 years we'll be as well known as the biggest in the business right now. There's an ego thing for me when I tell people I work here. I feel like I'm part of a winner.

When I joined the company, they handed me the company's philosophy. It was the first time that I said to myself, "I think they're serious." With every other company in which I've worked, they said, "Here are the golden rules for the company." Then when I would begin working for that company, I would realize it was all bullshit, that the profit motive was probably the thing that drove most people, and that individuals would get chewed up because it was best for the system. Our philosophy here says that it's not enough to tell customers the truth; it's your

---

responsibility to make sure that whomever you're talking to understands the truth. And that was written at a time when we had problems with customers because we couldn't deliver enough product; demand was so high. But it was the first time I'd ever seen that articulated in such a way. I sit on a policy committee for the company, and time and time again I've seen things that looked like they would be terrific for the company voted down because they would be bad for the individual. I have seen people being taken care of by the company, far beyond anything that was the law or that the company's policy would dictate, because of a feeling about the individual. I have seen individuals in the company who don't have any formal power change the company because they had the right ideas. I think that's all on purpose and by design.

On the other side of that coin, there are things that happen that are not on purpose and aren't by design, which are as nasty as things that go on in other organizations. But they happen for a different reason. I see them happening in other organizations because an individual decides, "I'm going to get that bastard," and the structure allows it to happen. In this company, because we're so unstructured, because we're so decentralized, and because we are typically comprised of very bright, very strong people, there are no support structures for those individuals who are hired in and need the support. If you're sensing some confusion where people are concerned, you're right. This company, because of the lack of structure, ends up chewing up a lot of people. But it is not by design. It's a function of the culture, and any attempts to try to create structure are going to be countercultural and will destroy a lot of things I like about the place.

What I am trying to do is balance the part that says "This is the best place I've ever worked for, they care about the individual and they really are committed to that," against the fact that if you went out and took some measurements, you'd find some individuals who were in pain, who don't know who the hell their boss is or how to do their jobs or what their goals are. For people who care about what they're doing, that's going to be painful. In other organizations, you see people in pain and it's controllable by one or two individuals who are causing that pain. In this company, I see people in pain, but it's a result of the fact that the system is not structured in a way to help the individual. So an employee in trouble may not have anywhere to go other than to work the system. And some people don't do that very well. We don't do a very good job of telling people that, either. We just sort of assume everybody knows.

When I think about ethics, I think there are certain things that somehow get programmed into us early on in life around what's good and bad. And goodness for me, in that context, without intellectualizing at all, is just a gut feeling. Goodness for me is helping your fellow man, and not doing anything to damage others, and spending extra time helping people that are in trouble, and so on. Bad is doing anything that would harm other people. Somewhere in the back of my mind there's a tape that plays that. Intellectually, that's different for me than what's right and wrong. A lot of what's the right thing to do and what's the wrong thing to do, I think is, for me, situational. But there's the whole piece around what's good and bad that has to do with basic values. I think of all this as a matrix that looks like this:

Situational Action	Values	
	Good	Bad
Right		
Wrong		

Let me give you some examples. The good thing to do and the organizationally right thing to do is fair and equal treatment for folks. The good thing to do but the wrong thing to do in an organizational setting is being too honest, thereby undermining organizational effectiveness. So, for example, good things say you'll always tell the truth and you're always straightforward with people, but organizationally that can get you into a whole bunch of hot water and undermine your effectiveness. So from an organizational point of view, that's often the wrong thing to do. A bad thing to do is to tell white lies; goodness says you never lie. But sometimes that is the right thing to do, for instance, to help someone save face. That's doing bad for the right reason. And bad and wrong is, say, deliberately causing personal pain. This matrix sort of puts things in perspective for me in terms of being able to articulate the constant tugging inside me. I spent eight years in a Catholic grammar school, four years in a Catholic youth organization as an officer, four years in a Catholic fraternity college. I've had that whole Judeo-Christian good-bad stuff drummed into my head. And yet I know damn well that I operate oftentimes in this matrix.

I have been in organizations where the right thing to do from the organization's perspective felt awful to me, and the reason it did is because I think I felt it was not only the wrong thing to do, but that my definition of goodness and badness was so strong around the issue that I said, "Not only is that bad, that's also wrong." And so even though I've been in some situations where I've been able to say the bad thing to do was really the right thing to do, I've also been in situations in other organizations where the bad thing to do has also been what I thought was the wrong thing to do. And then I've been faced with a dilemma around the organization telling me "You gotta do it," and I believe it was bad and it was wrong. That's when dilemmas have really felt awful to me. The interesting thing about this company is that there are very few organizational imperatives around what to do. So I feel much freer to be consistent with this matrix. Generally speaking, when I do the bad thing, it's for the right reason organizationally, and it feels good in here (points to his stomach), yeah. I have not been put into a position in the three years I've been with the company where I've ever had to do what I consider to be the bad and the wrong thing. I've had to do the bad and right, but that bad, as I said, is not an intellectual bad for me, it's a gut-feel value programmed in very early on by a bunch of nuns and a bunch of other folks, my parents and whomever, who probably didn't always live by those either.

Here is an interesting example. We've got a woman who works in our department, Mary, and she has had virtually every disaster that can happen to a person happen during the past two years: death of both parents, major physical problems, incredible personal problems with a sibling and other relatives. She got very sick. OK. The good thing to do is to take care of your fellow man. There is some question in my mind about whether the company policies would say what I did was right or wrong, from an organizational point of view. I chose to do what I think our chairman would agree was the right thing.

A little bit of background on this woman: she's a local person; she grew up in the community in which we are headquartered, went to high school there, and has always dreamed of working for this company. There's a whole piece around community relations that subtly entered my head around her and I said, "Part of me wants to treat her well because she's a local person working for us." The other thing I noticed was that she works in a place where you start at eight, you take your coffee break, you take your lunch break, and you take your coffee break in the afternoon, and the rest of the time you're just out straight; you get driven by the phones. Two women, Mary and Sue, handle on the order of 3500 phone calls a month. And they love it. When we were getting ready to move over here, Sue came in to me and she said, "Mary and I have talked, and we're not going to be able to pack those files for the move and answer the phones at the same time. Would you mind if we came in on Saturday? We don't care about the pay, but would you care if we did that?" I'm saying, "Holy . . . !" I mean, where do you find these people? Well, that's what Mary is all about, too. She is really dedicated. So I say, "The hell with the company policy. I'm going to treat her well." So, essentially, I paid her for a lot of the time she was out. I didn't want to take away all of her sick time. She was beginning to chew into her vacation time. There she was, someone whose life involves getting up in the morning, taking care of her relatives, working here, going home, taking care of her relatives, and also going to school. She was going to community college to pick up some credits. And I'm saying, "I'm not going to pile any more crap on that lady." Now, I don't know if that's the right or the wrong thing to do from the company's point of view, but I think our chairman would probably support the concept of disregarding sick time, short-term disability, and long-term disability. That, to me, was a fairly easy dilemma to work myself out of. It certainly was the good thing to do. There was a little bit of question about the right thing to do from an organizational point of view, but again, this company has convinced me that the right thing in that case was to disregard company policy and to use my own judgment around what I did with her.

Actually, the only dilemma piece was that the company policy states she should have used up her sick time, vacation time, and then gone on short-term disability. So I said, "I'm probably taking a risk here." The other nice thing was, I went in to my boss and said, "Look I've got a person in my group . . . ," and I told him her background, and I said, "I'm not asking for you to do anything other than to understand that I'm going to treat her well, because I think she deserves it. She's given loyalty and hard work and dedication to this department and to the company; she's a local person; I just think there's a whole bunch of things that we need to do for her."

Q: What was the risk?

Part of the risk was other people in the department knowing that I'd done it, and saying, "Hey, you did it for her. I want to take next week off, because I think I just need some R&R time." Another part of the risk was somebody poking around and finding out I was paying her as if she were here when she wasn't. But I really feel as if no one in the company would challenge what I did because it was the right thing to do. When I say I feel that, I feel that now. But when I was going through the decision making on it, I still had some question as to whether somebody would force the company policy on me (which in itself is fairly liberal, it treats people fairly well).

But this company, quite frankly, does treat people differently, depending on their situation, and in spite of all company policy. And I see the only risk being one of doing it in some kind of discriminatory fashion, where you're doing it just for white males, for example. Then I think you're really opening yourself up for a risk. But as I've said before, the company has really made me feel like I'm owning my own business here; I'm an entrepreneur. And if I owned my own business and could afford it, I probably would've done exactly the same thing. So there was a piece of me that said, "Look, I'm running a business here, and what I want to do is to treat that person well, because her loyalty has been such, and the amount of work she's put in is such that I don't think the policy applies to her." If it ever ended up in a one-on-one conversation between the chairman and me, which it never would, I've got a feeling he'd probably support me. I think the nice part about being here is I don't have a whole lot of dilemmas that are placed on me by the organization because I think, first of all, it is very moral and ethical in the way it positions itself, and second of all, it's so decentralized that there isn't that kind of pressure that says "The right thing for the company to do, you jerk, is this. Now you go off and do it."

So the ethical question was: here is a person who I would like to be able to help during a very trying part of her life, but I know that some of the things I'm doing are against company policy and procedure, which, by the way, I helped write. Is that really the right thing to do? Should I really be going that extra mile, or should I say to myself, "Policy was written because we know some people are going to get themselves sick and need time off. She'll get 80% of her salary for a while and then two-thirds of her salary. Sorry, that's just the way life is sometimes." So I went through that whole thought process of "Do I really want to go against company policy around how I treat people? What if everybody did that? Then the policy would be worth garbage, and the company would be spending all kinds of money." So I put all the stuff aside and I said, "Well, let me look at her as an individual. I can't justify not helping her out." Now, she is on short-term disability. There came a point when we had to say, "OK, we've done everything we know how, and now we're going to try to preserve her vacation time for her," which we did. But I probably gave her seven or eight days that should have been vacation or sick time or something. So I'm not talking about huge amounts of money. But there came a point at which I said, "OK, she is going to be out for an extended period of time. (She had an operation.) Now it's time for short-term disability to come into play."

It sent a message to the other people in the department. I've heard a little bit of feedback that said people really appreciated what I did for her. The message says (a) Jim's a humane manager, and (b) he must work for a fairly humane company to allow him to get away with that. I think most people know it wasn't something I hid, and I didn't have to get devious to make that happen. I just made a decision that that's the way it should be. So there were all kinds of payoffs to the company because there are 16 other people out there who all say this really is a neat place to work—look what they did for Mary. And they don't even try to personalize it and say, "Son of a bitch, what are they going to do for me now?" or "Why would they do that for her and not for me?" They all understand she's a unique case. In fact, we had one individual who has been out. She went through a real attitudinal thing for whatever reason, things going on at home. Then she hurt her back. She wanted to take some extra time around a funeral, and from everything I could tell, it really wasn't a close relative. And she was told "No, you've been out X number of days." I have two people between myself and that individual, and they came to me and said, "We're going to get tough with Ellen about coming in. We just want you to know we're doing it. We think it's the proper thing to do." And I supported it. And never once did she come back and say—that's where the danger was—"Well, look what you've done for Mary and you're not willing to give me. . . ." I believe she knew there was a difference between just being in a lousy mood and being in bed.

Look at the matrix. When I'm in the bad and the right box, the thought process I find myself using is sort of incremental rationalization which means that each step makes sense within the context of doing the right thing from a situational point of view. And I'm fairly comfortable about overriding the bads as long as I can incrementally justify each step as being the right thing to do. Now it feels different when I do it in the Mary case. In the case where it's good but it may be wrong, my decisions tend to be binary. They tend to be: that's what I'm going to do. I mean, I'll do some talking about it ahead of time, but there's very little rationalizing. With Mary I made a decision that I was going to do something and I didn't have to incrementally rationalize it, I just said, "BOOM. I believe that this is the right thing to do. I know I'm taking some risk personally here, but screw it. BOOM! I'm going to do it." Combined with the piece that said if she had been another employee who gives me 40 hours and goes home and does not have her dedication to the company and dedication to the job, then I could very easily say, "It's a situation defined by the policy and what I can do for you is this. Thank you very much." So there was a rightness that had to do with the quality of the person. It was an organizational rightness, I felt, that had some fringes that were kind of frayed because the policy kept nipping away at me and I had to sort of balance that stuff. But it wasn't incremental for me. It was "Consider all that stuff and then BOOM."

The hardest box in the matrix to be in is the bad-wrong. It's a bad thing to do, and I think it's the wrong thing to do organizationally, and somebody says you have to do it. And I've been in those situations a couple of times. That's a tough one for me to deal with because I generally end up folding and doing it because you can't win. I guess you do have a choice. The choice is to leave. Or to start laying the groundwork for leaving the organization. You can't do too many of those. By the way, lest you get the wrong idea, the matrix came directly as a result of your asking me to think about ethics. One of the things you should know about me is that I don't generally have a very structured way of sitting down and processing my own feelings and thoughts. The matrix came out of my attempt to sit down and take a generic question around ethical dilemmas. I started just playing around with "Well, what is ethics?" And that's how it came up. What I was trying to structure was situations where a dilemma occurs for me. I have a friend who did his divorce that way. It was mind-boggling. He did pros and cons and guess what? He had two pros and 57 cons and said, "It's time to leave." This guy's an MIT grad and very bright. The thing to know about me is I don't have the structure I probably should have around some of these questions. I tend to go with my gut more often than not.

When there are competing claims, what I think happens is that somehow I process all of those claims, give a certain weight to each, and then end up in one of these boxes, saying, "Yeah, overall, after I weigh everything together, the right thing to do is going to mean taking a couple of bad steps or whatever. Understanding that some people are going to be hurt by that, and some people are going to benefit by that, but the overall right thing to do is this." Then the question is, is the right really my new set of values? Is that my real set of values or is the good and the bad my real set of values? It's hard; I haven't thought about it a lot. And it's hard because you can probably argue that my real set of values is the right and wrong, and that the good and bad are just sort of childhood underpinnings, sort of a base which I don't subscribe to all that strongly. Sometimes it feels that a lot of things I was taught were bad, I find myself being able to rationalize in terms of what's right. I mean, if I went out and told the truth to everyone in my department, there would be very few people standing up. And I'm sure they could do the same to me. So I guess my values really are that the right thing to do is to protect that shell, and organizations tend to encourage that. This company less than others. We tend to encourage people to be honest about what they're thinking. The first couple of times I made presentations here, I said, "I'm either failing or I'm doing real good. I can't figure out which." Oh, the stuff that gets stirred up: "I don't agree with that." "That's bullshit." And I found that people are doing that because they were really wired into what you were saying, instead of sort of sitting there. It takes some time to get used to that.

There's a tremendous amount of consistency between the way I view myself as an individual and the way I feel the company views itself and wants me to act. And so I've yet to really confront an issue and have to worry about inconsistency between what I believe is right to do and what the company believes is the right thing to do. And they don't define "right" all that well. They say, "You're sitting closest to it, you do the right thing." "Right" means not doing a dumb thing just because the policy book says to do it that way, or because you've got a memo saying to do it that way. So I guess I'm very fortunate to feel that consistency, that congruency, and it's nice because it's congruent with the rest of my life. I don't have to set up one set of behaviors and values here, and silence all the ethical questions, and just go out and do what's best for the organization. And I don't have to do that at home. I don't have to make decisions at home that are in conflict with what the company wants. It's a nice balance for me.

Postscript

One year after I interviewed James Gordon, he had to make the difficult decision to fire Mary. He had continued to bend the rules for her until it came to a point where, for a number of personal reasons on her part, she was unable to fulfill the requirements of her job. He explains the decision in terms of incrementally doing the "right" thing until it gets to a point where the next step no longer is justifiable from a "good" or a "right" perspective.

COMMENTS

In Jim Gordon's matrix, we see reflected a theme relevant to most of the dilemmas discussed in these pages: How do I balance basic beliefs and values with being effective and responsible in a complex and ambiguous world? We need to recognize that for all the pain represented by his model, Jim, in his present organization, has it easier than some. The reason is that the matrix is based on the assumption that Jim—or whoever is using it—*can* act as he chooses and is not subject to a "do it" command from above. Jim mentions that when he says the "awful" situation to find yourself in is to be in the bad/wrong box on an action which your superior insists you do.

As Jim talks about his dilemma with Mary, it is clear he felt *he* could decide what to do and his decision either would be supported by the company or, if not, would not involve great personal risk for him. According to his matrix, Jim was in the good/wrong box—it is good to help a person in need, but it is wrong to compromise an organizational policy. Jim says that in a good/wrong situation he just does what he feels is right, BOOM, regardless of the risks or other circumstances. Certainly that seems to be the case in the Mary situation.

Jim believed he *could* get the job done, but there was an organizational value system in place as well. Jim felt he could adjust the disability policy because (1) the company does believe in treating people differently, in spite of policy, as long as the different treatment is not discriminatory, (2) the role of policy in the company is not clear, and (3) if he went one-on-one with the chairman, Jim believed the chairman would back him up.

The supportive corporate environment allowed Jim to resolve his dilemma with some useful devices. First, he was able to focus almost solely on a single stakeholder, Mary; so the key question became "What is best for her?" With the company behind him, he did not feel pulled in too many directions at once. Second, he did not have to hide his action or engage in other covert activities. He told his boss and allowed his decision to become public knowledge in the company, which mitigated any sense of "wrong" and reinforced for him the doing of good.

Jim's situation raises a critical concern about the role of policy in organizations. Policy is written to express corporate values in a particular area and to set the guidelines for actions relating to that area. But the general nature of a policy cannot take into account all of the possible configurations of events—the exceptions—that must occur in any organization. The question is: How do you deal with the exceptions? Rigid policy that demands absolute adherence can be dysfunctional and even ethically harmful to a company by compromising both the integrity and competence of managers within it. On the other hand, policy that can be ignored or distorted or interpreted in a variety of ways can lead to similar outcomes by creating a too anarchic environment. In Jim's and his company's case, the line between blind compliance to, and manipulation of, a policy was trod with finesse. The outcome supported Mary, the company, the other employees, and Jim. As Jim points out, however, his actions might have set a precedent which could have eroded the respect for policies, rules, and procedures in the organization.

------------◆------------

Working for Mr. Clean Jeans*

Jim Impoco

Levi's leader, Robert Haas, cares about morals as well as making money.

A few months ago, Levi Strauss chief executive Robert Haas joined dozens of his employees for a 3 1/2-day group grope in the Santa Cruz Mountains. The discussions were not about stitching jeans or marketing polos. Instead, the group

---

*Reprinted from *U.S. News and World Report,* August 2, 1993, pp. 49–50.

bandied about such wooly notions as "empowerment," "new behaviors" and "diversity." As part of the program, members of the jeans team—including Haas, the 51-year-old great-great-grandnephew of corporate founder Levi Strauss him-self—were asked to compose their own obituaries, an exercise intended to get them in touch with their values. Haas isn't revealing the contents of the obituary he wrote for himself, but he's certain it won't resemble the real one newspapers are likely to run someday. "In the end," he muses, "your tombstone isn't going to say things like, 'I sewed 137,000 jeans.'"

Haas, a former Peace Corps volunteer and medieval literature buff, no doubt has a point about the tombstone stuff. But what does all this morbid psychobabble have to do with making and selling dungarees? The loose interpretation of the human potential movement is a footnote in the self-induced upheaval now taking place at Levi Strauss, the world's largest apparel maker. The privately held San Francisco-based company is attempting to reshape its corporate culture, disman-tle parts of its hierarchy, reorganize factory floors and overhaul the way it designs, manufactures and sells clothing.

Across the shell-shocked American economic landscape, many companies are also in the throes of major-league re-engineering schemes. But 140-year-old Levi's is undertaking the changes at a time when its business has never been better. Paced by the runaway success of Dockers at home and booming jeans sales over-seas, the company generated revenues of $5.6 billion last year, up from $2 billion in 1979.

Green machine   Perhaps it's true, as the TV commercials say, that nobody does green like Dockers—green as in cash. Designed for soft-in-the-middle male boomers, Dockers may be the fastest growing brand in the history of the apparel industry. Nearly 7 in 10 American men now own at least one pair of Dockers. Since its launch in 1986, the popular line of casual cotton wear has gone from nothing to a billion-dollar-plus business, a veritable *Fortune* 500 company unto itself. To put that in perspective, consider the fact that it took Levi's as a whole a century and a quarter before it reached the billion-dollar mark.

You'd think Haas would be resting on his denim laurels. But a year and a half ago, Levi's surveyed its top retailers and discovered its own Achilles heel—poor customer service. Retailers were full of praise for the products and the marketing muscle behind them, but they had harsh words about things like Levi's ability to deliver on time. "During the bad old days, we took an order and didn't ship it out until the season was over," admits Tom Kasten, who now heads Levi's customer-service initiative.

Rapid response   Stung by the criticism, Levi's soon began mapping out everything it does, from the moment a product is conceived to its final sale. Next, the company took 125 employees out of day-to-day business and formed 20 separate "initiative" teams. Based on their findings, Levi's decided to revamp its entire operation, from consolidating corporate divisions to streamlining distribution networks. The goal is to be able to replenish a product on the store shelf within 72 hours, down from the three weeks it takes to do so today.

As part of its $400 million re-engineering effort, Levi's is converting all 37 of its North American factories to team manufacturing. In place of the traditional Henry Ford-style assembly-line process, in which one worker repeats the same task over and over again, there will be self-directed teams of cross-trained sewing operators who produce garments from start to finish.

Levi's will spend more than 40,000 hours per plant training employees in everything from conflict resolution to managing production flows. The new setup not only reduces the monotony of factory work but also seems to cut down on mistakes. Tommye Jo Davies, who manages Levi's Murphy, N.C., plant, points out that defects have dropped from more than 4 percent to around 2 percent since the team system got going a year ago.

Perhaps the most striking alterations taking place at Levi's are its attempts to build ethics into its bottom line. In the late 1980s, Haas oversaw the development of the Levi Strauss Aspirations Statement, an effort to define shared values that will guide both the work force and corporate decisions. From Haas on down, each employee is expected to take part in the so-called Core Curriculum—a series of training programs, like the one in Santa Cruz, Calif., that deal with ethical practices, empowerment and an appreciation of diversity. Part of the idea is to put more power into the hands of Levi's rank and file and encourage employees to become actively involved in corporate decision making. "We are like the leaders of China before the Tiananmen [crackdown]," says Haas. "We are releasing enormous forces."

Business ethics   And what better example than China to illustrate how Levi's moral high road has sometimes led to controversy. Today, more than half of Levi's products are manufactured overseas. So nearly three years ago, the company created a task force to come up with a set of ethical guidelines for doing business with foreign contractors. The resulting "Terms of Engagement" run the gamut from environmental, safety and health requirements to the right of free association. The jeans maker soon audited more than 600 of its overseas contractors and severed ties with 30 of them for their failure to meet the new standards.

Then, in May, Levi's startled both Washington officials and corporate America with its decision not to invest in the booming Chinese market and to phase out contracts with Chinese clothing manufacturers. The company cited what it termed "pervasive violations of basic human rights" as the reason for its partial withdrawal from China. Levi's claims that its decision was not political, even though it took place just as the Clinton administration was debating whether to renew China's most-favored-nation trading status—which it did anyway.

Haas insists that Levi's emphasis on values is "not just nice behavior" but smart business, too. Levi's jeans are often equated with the rugged individualism and free spirit of America's old West. And the company is concerned that dubious business practices, at home or abroad, could damage its image—and perhaps its commercial success. "Consumers are looking more and more to the company behind the product," says Haas. "Companies have to wake up to the fact that they are more than a product on a shelf. They're behavior as well."

It's hard to pinpoint how Levi's own changing behavior is affecting its bottom line. "It's clear that our culture is moving, and there's definitely a connection to the financial side," says Haas. "We're on our way to a fifth straight year of record earnings, and this is in the middle of a bad U.S. economy and sickly economies in Europe." It's also clear that no one will be writing an obituary for Levi's anytime soon—unless he is asked to.

The New York Times, September 2, 1990.

Business Takes on a Green Hue[*]

Deborah L. Jacobs

Alliances with environmental groups seek to reduce waste.

Several staff members of the Environmental Defense Fund recently spent a day flipping hamburgers at McDonald's to see how a restaurant works. McDonald's executives, in turn, are to get a crash course from E.D.F. experts in composting and recycling.

The fast-food chain—long criticized for its disposable packaging—and the environmental lobby established a joint task force last month to identify options for reducing and recycling waste at the McDonald's Corporation's 11,000 restaurants worldwide.

There is nothing binding about the pact; either party can bow out at any point. "The jury is out as to whether there's going to be more meat in this initiative than in their hamburgers," says James Post, who teaches environmental management at Boston University. But Shelby Yastrow, McDonald's senior vice president for environmental affairs, said the company would "explore everything that isn't silly or unworkable."

Whatever conflicts arise between McDonald's and the environmental group, their alliance is one of a growing number of management initiatives to address environmental concerns. References to ecology are turning up in annual reports, corporate newsletters and employee incentive programs. Whether they're responding to Government regulation or consumer activism, managers find environmental awareness can cut costs, and increasingly are designing strategies with help from environmental groups.

"Industry is moving from a position of reaction" to a stage where environmentalism "provides the motivation and stimulus for innovation," said Joel S. Hirschhorn, president of EnviroSearch-East, a Washington-based consulting firm.

A trend setter is Patagonia Inc., the outdoor clothing manufacturer in Ventura, Calif. It contributes 10 percent of its before-tax profits to environmental groups and engages in what Michael Harrelson, a spokesman, called "relentless" energy-saving measures:

- Employees must sort and empty their trash at office recycling depots.
- Low-flow toilets, using less than two gallons of water per flush instead of the usual five, have been installed.
- Low-energy lightbulbs cut energy use—and the annual electric bill, by $15,000.
- Copying machines use recycled paper.
- The company letterhead is printed with soy-based ink.
- The on-site daycare center uses cloth diapers.

At the Polaroid Corporation, an employee's contributions to the pollution-control program can affect compensation and promotion, said William Schwalm, senior manager of environmental programs in manufacturing. It was employees [who] suggested using a scraper device to clean a production vat at the company's Waltham, Mass., plant, and thus salvage chemicals that would otherwise be discarded.

Companies with incentive programs—including Dow Chemical and the 3M Company, as well as Polaroid—have found that savings from pollution control can be considerable. At 3M, for example, employees have developed 2,700 projects to eliminate the causes of pollution, saving the company more than $500 million in the past 14 years, according to Robert P. Bringer, staff vice president for environmental engineering.

Early on, innovations can be expensive. The International Business Machines Corporation, for example, expects to spend $100 million to eliminate ozone-depleting chlorofluorocarbons by the end of 1993, said MacKnight Jeffery, a spokesman. But, he noted, the program has helped combat negative publicity generated last summer when the Environmental Protection Agency said that I.B.M. was a major emitter of the pollutant.

Public attitudes about the environment are "requiring major rethinking about how business is organized and what its goals are," said Susan Hayward, vice president of the research firm, Yankelovich Clancy Shulman, which conducts an annual study of consumer values and attitudes.

Esprit de Corps, the San Francisco clothing manufacturer, is undergoing an audit "to become more ecologically efficient," said Susan Alexander, manager of the company's new "eco desk," which provides information to employees and consumers. Other companies—including Hallmark Cards, Keebler and J. C. Penney—sent managers to a June colloquium on environmental issues offered by the Institute for International Research, a New York conference planner. Executive Enterprises Inc., another New York management education group, sponsors approximately 250 conferences each year on environmental issues.

To train the next generation of executives, the Corporate Conservation Council of the National Wildlife Federation is developing a business school course on environmental management. The Federation's effort has drawn criticism from "friends in the environmental community," said Barbara Haas, director of the council, who say it just offers a safe harbor from environmental lawsuits. But she defends the "forum for discussion."

"It's an opportunity to educate corporations on things they can do to become environmentally sensitive," she said. "It would be a mistake to ignore that opportunity."

Chapter 10

Managing Diversity

The work force of the nineties and of the twenty-first century is dramatically more diverse than was the case in earlier eras. In addition, awareness of differences between and among people in organizations is much greater than in the past. Diversity manifests itself in ethnicity, in gender, in disability, in age, to name some of the more recognizable bases for difference. Typically, this is a phenomenon that is talked about and addressed within North American organizations. As we become more aware of the global nature of enterprise, it becomes evident that diversity is the norm facing managers. There are no regions of the world that do not require attention to the differences that constitute the organization of today.

Diversity has become big business as is pointed out in "Scrambling to Manage a Diverse Work Force." There is a rapid growth in the availability of consultants, training videos and exercises, and so forth. An important question in this context is whether all this activity is contributing to better understanding of the ways that people who are different from some "model employee" can contribute to the goals of the organization. There is always the danger when a management topic is identified as hot, that the form rather than the substance of the topic will be catered to by all the experts and those who hire them. It is too early to tell whether this is happening around diversity.

Managers need to understand how bias against those who are different from those in control in organizations prevents the progress of effective people up and across the organization hierarchy. Further, prejudice blinds managers to the contributions that a diverse work force can make to improved performance in the organization. Bias and prejudice confronting many black managers is the focus of "The Struggle for Minority Managers." Many managers are unaware that their attitudes and actions are prejudicial to those they manage. This is partly a function of awareness efforts of the past in organizations and in society. These interventions sometimes have the effect of uncovering the obvious indicators of prejudice while obscuring the more damaging and deepseated effects. True prejudice sometimes goes underground. We have learned to be "politically correct" or "politically aware" in our behaviors and actions without necessarily making any real change in our attitudes. When this condition is accompanied by assumptions that everything is "OK" in the relationships between managers or employees who are different, then nothing substantive is accomplished to remove the barriers that result from prejudice. What happens in the trenches of organizations typically will determine whether diversity will be treated as a positive or a destructive force in organizations.

Much has been written about diversity in the form of ethnicity and gender in the past several years. A much more recent arena of difference to receive attention is that of disability. Some disabilities stem from genetics. However, increasingly, many disabilities come from environmental causes such as accidents and illnesses. At the societal level, legislative interventions are making a difference to the cause of disabled workers ("The Americans with Disabilities Act of 1990: Implications for Managers"). Also, many organizations are undertaking initiatives to make themselves more attractive to workers with disabilities ("Mastering the Language of Disability"). Two specific examples mentioned in this article are a recruiting book published in English and Braille by the Bank of Montreal and a US West training package for sensitizing employment officers to people with disabilities.

Barriers to performance based on difference are not a new phenomena. All cultures and social systems have favored some members and excluded others. One cost of such discrimination is a loss of vitality, a loss of contribution to the innovativeness that nourishes a system. Ironically, such exclusion can blind those in the system to the loss, to the contributions of those who are different from those in control. For example, the relative absence of women among the writers, poets, artists, scientists and inventors in earlier eras can be attributed to barriers to entry to these professions. Women had no property rights until the turn of the century and were discounted in any activities that did not contribute to family activities. Even when women did write, paint or invent, the contributions were disguised or discounted. (See, for example, "A Lab of Her Own" by Marguerite Holloway, *Scientific American*, November, 1993, pp. 94–103.) The experience of women inventors who were refused patents or denied recognition is chronicled in "Mothers of Invention." The losses to individuals and to society become apparent in such outcomes.

Managing diversity is a focus of considerable attention in the present era. We will know we have made progress in developing a work world where difference is valued and supported when it becomes no longer necessary to isolate the topic as one for educating managers. In the meantime, there is much to be done and we are likely to see many bold and innovative interventions to make difference an asset. Companies that address diversity successfully will likely have an edge in their effectiveness in the years ahead.

The New York Times, December 15, 1992

Scrambling to Manage a Diverse Work Force[*]

Lena Williams

From the palm-fringed Burger King headquarters in Miami to the Towers Perrin offices on Park Avenue in Manhattan, corporate managers and employees are playing the diversity game, literally and figuratively. They are trying everything from board games to real-life case studies to learn how to turn diversity to advantage.

The games and case studies are the brainchildren of consultants—anthropologists and psychologists, as well as M.B.A.'s. Such consultants are increasingly being hired by employers who need help managing a diverse work force, in which members of minority groups, immigrants and women now hold more than half the jobs.

Diversity as Good Business

Managing diversity, or multiculturalism, has been defined as a desire to recognize, respect and capitalize on different strands and backgrounds in American society, like race, cultural origin and gender. Over the years the definition has been broadened to incorporate age, sexual orientation, physical disabilities, socioeconomic background and ways of living.

Only a few years ago, the idea of diversity in the work place was being dismissed by employers as an amorphous theory with little or no relevance to production and profit. Many employers believed that changing the corporate status quo would alienate their predominantly white, male work force.

Today, more and more employers view diversity as good business as well as good public relations. The executives who set aside company time—and money—to cultivate diversity hope the results will be fewer costly discrimination suits and a more tolerant, innovative work place.

What's more, dealing with diversity, one of the most popular management concepts of the 90's, is also becoming a booming multimillion-dollar business.

"In the next two to five years, diversity might very well be a billion-dollar industry," said Dr. Ron Brown, the president of Banks Brown and a San Francisco consultant, whose firm specializes in fostering and managing diversity in the work place.

Neil Pickett, director of program management at the Hudson Institute, said, "Diversity has created a new career, a new vision of service."

But Mr. Pickett, along with many others who have witnessed the rapid growth in the industry, fears that some consultants may be entering the business primarily for the money. Dr. Sondra Thiederman, a consultant from San Diego, said, "Some are in it because they want to do good, others because they see it as a lucrative business."

Dr. Thiederman said she receives three or four queries a day from people asking how to get into the business. Many of these requests, she added, come from people with little training in work-place diversity, including former Peace Corps volunteers and spouses of corporate executives who have worked overseas.

And, she went on, some of those touting themselves as experts on managing diversity are minimally qualified to advise a company on the subtleties of issues involving race and gender in the work place. Of equal concern to some industry experts is the unsettling reality that some companies are hiring diversity consultants merely as window dressing. Reducing the effort to pure public relations, they argue, subverts the whole idea of diversity.

In 1987, the Hudson Institute produced "Workforce 2000," a study on work and workers for the 21st century that is credited by advocates of work-place diversity with giving an important impetus to the turnaround in the industry.

The study, which was done for the United States Labor Department, concluded that the overall work force would increase to 150.7 million in 2005, up from 124.7 million in 1990. Of the 26 million new workers, 85 percent would be members of minority groups, women and immigrants.

As one indication of the demand for specialists in managing diversity, Diversity Consultants Inc. of Atlanta, one of the nation's leading authorities on the subject, has seen its revenues double since 1989. In February, Towers Perrin, an international consulting firm, acquired Diversity Consultants. Diversity Consultants, founded in 1984 by Dr. R. Roosevelt Thomas Jr., has already trained several dozen Towers Perrin employees in diversity planning and strategy. The revenue figures were furnished by Robert L. Lattimer, the managing director.

Problems Followed Affirmative Action

In the 1960's and 70's many corporations adopted affirmative-action programs and hired professionals in human resources to find, hire and promote blacks and women in fields that were previously closed to them. But then many companies failed to deal with the internal problems that arose after these hirings.

While programs dealing with diversity incorporate the traditional approaches, consultants also try to help a company and its employees to adjust psychologically and emotionally to the changing work force.

Consultants agree, however, that they can only do so much to overcome years of ingrained organizational behavior and established management patterns. Indeed, several conceded that they are sometimes temporary crutches for a company and that unless a company's management accepts what it has learned and applies it daily, the impact will be negligible.

Many consultants first conduct what they call a "corporate audit." They interview groups of employees about the company's corporate culture: the ways employees are selected, assigned jobs and promoted; whether extroversion is valued over introversion, and whether employees' ideas are routinely sought. Managers are asked to review the information to identify perceived or real obstacles to advancement.

Besides these audits, some consultants have managers and employees take personality tests like the Myers-Briggs Test, which helps determine how certain personality traits lead to race or gender stereotypes.

Nancy Hutchens, an anthropologist who has conducted numerous diversity workshops with Dr. Benjamin Reese, a clinical psychologist, said, "People tend to react to each other based on race and gender without realizing that what they are responding to was personality characteristics."

Diversity Programs and Individuals

Trainers can also do fine tuning with specific employee problems. In one instance, Dr. Thiederman was able to convince a white male manager that an Asian employee's reluctance to give an oral presentation was motivated by cultural differences, not caused by a professional inadequacy.

Dr. Thiederman suggested that the manager team the Asian woman with a colleague and have them present the project as a team. The manager agreed and, in Dr.

Thiederman's word, the Asian employee was "eloquent."

Diversity programs appear to be having an impact. On the advice of Dr. Thomas, Avon Products, for example, capitalized on its own diversity. It gave black and Hispanic managers substantial authority over its unprofitable inner-city markets. The result: these markets are now among Avon's strongest performers.

Meanwhile, the Burger King Corporation, a unit of Grand Metropolitan D.L.C., is using everything from "The Diversity Game," a board game, to three-day training seminars and has expanded the percentage of blacks and members of other minority groups in its work force to 28 percent last year, from 12 percent in 1986. And it has increased its business with suppliers owned by members of minority groups to $74 million this year, from $2 million in 1986, said Ray Hood-Phillips, vice president of human resources and diversity affairs for Burger King.

A Training Method: Ruffling Feathers

"Upper-level white managers in charge of large numbers of people that include minorities can be taught to lead and manage those below them in a way that gets better business results across racial, ethnic and gender lines," said Floyd Dickens Jr., who with his wife, Jacqueline, founded 21st Century Management Services, in West Chester, Ohio. "But you first have to get inside people's heads and change behavior, and you can't do that without ruffling some feathers."

Around the country, conferences on diversity are attracting hundreds of managers from government and industry. Several colleges and universities now offer courses on diversity awareness, and a body of literature, including how-to books, has blossomed.

Among the most popular new training tools are videotapes, in which actors play out work situations illustrating everything from "exclusive bad-boy networks" to racial and sexual discrimination.

According to various industry reports, 40 percent of American companies have some form of diversity training. One-fourth of some 1,400 companies polled last January by Haygroup of Philadelphia said that adapting to work force diversity "is a priority."

Of 645 national companies surveyed in 1990 by Towers Perrin, 29 percent offered programs in managing diversity. A 1991 follow-up of more than 200 of the same organizations found that work-related programs had increased since 1989, recession and economic woes notwithstanding.

Is It 'Touchy-Feely' or the Real Thing?

But more than a handful of blacks, Hispanic people and women express doubts about whether employers are sincere in their efforts to understand diversity or are merely paying lip service to it. These skeptics say that most employers have training in diversity awareness, but stop short of making extensive systemic changes.

"It's all this touchy-feely stuff— 'I'll respect you, if you respect me,'" said a black woman, an account executive at a large consumer-products company in New Jersey, who spoke on condition that she not be identified. "Once you leave the room, it's back to business as usual. Nobody wants to hear about your day-care problems or your sick parent."

Indeed, a few employers acknowledge that the change of heart in favor of diversity came more from the business imperative than from altruism.

"There is some variation in the degree of commitment to diversity," Mr. Lattimer said. "Nearly all companies report that progress is occurring. However, results are not improving as quickly as had been previously anticipated or desired."

Of 11 companies—among them Aetna Life and Casualty, A. T. & T., Gannett, Eastman Kodak and Mobil—that participated in a Towers Perrin study of diversity, every one cited bias as a primary obstacle to upward mobility.

"Bias is reported to be particularly acute among middle managers who have not bought into the vision of senior management and are ignorant of the cultural issues of concern to women and minorities," Mr. Lattimer said. "One company found that managers are perceived as not believing upward mobility was a problem, or that discrimination exists."

Nevertheless, many consultants say, most employers are gradually facing the fact that the future of America in a global economy will rest with people who can understand cultural differences and can function across racial, ethnic, cultural and linguistic lines.

Diversity Leads to Better Performance

"There is also a growing sentiment that diverse employee teams tend to outperform homogeneous teams of any composition," Mr. Lattimer said. "Managers tell us that homogeneous groups may reach consensus more quickly, but often they are not as successful in generating new ideas or solving problems, because their collective perspective is narrower."

Among the early converts was Burger King, which tells its customers, "Have it your way."

Since 1986, the 170 senior managers and 700 employees at Burger King's headquarters have gone through what is now described as their "basic training" in diversity awareness: a three-day session, including three hours playing "The Diversity Game."

The creator of the game, Dr. Alan Richter, vice president of Quality Educational Development in Manhattan, said: "The game tests players' knowledge while raising their awareness of diversity issues. Four teams of up to 20 players compete to answer multiple-choice questions in different categories, including demographics, jobs, legislation and society."

Mrs. Hood-Phillips said, "It's a wonderful way to learn, because it's interactive." After playing the game, she ordered 20

copies (retail price, $395 each) for franchise managers.

Dr. Lawrence G. Flores, designer of the Multicultural Promotional Track Game, uses a game strategy different from that of Dr. Richter. Players choose roles opposite to their own sex, racial or ethnic identity and try to reach the top of the corporate ladder, not necessarily by answering correctly, but by most closely simulating the methods, including office politics, traditionally used to advance in their own work places.

Dr. Flores, a former social worker who now works as a consultant, said, "I felt I wanted to take people to the action level to begin to see what it might feel like to be black, Hispanic or female and work your way up the promotional ladder."

Humor, and a Quest for Standards

While some consultants use games, others use humor.

"I usually start out by telling an audience to impulsively raise their hand or keep it down," said Donald Kao, an Asian-American who is a New York City youth worker. "Then I ask, 'How many racists are in the room?' and then I immediately raise my hand and people are confused."

He conducts what he calls "supportive confrontation" workshops on college campuses. "I see the confusion on their faces," he continued. "Then I say, 'For the next two hours we are not going to worry about who is or isn't racist, but who is going to do something about racism and who isn't.'"

Dr. Sylvia S. Wagonheim, director of the Center for the New American Workforce at Queens College of the City University of New York, a resource network for business, education and government, said the center hoped to cut down on the confusion by creating minimum standards and criteria for professional trainers and consultants in diversity.

"Because diversity in business is so relatively new and there are so few hard facts, you have to sell it from a standpoint that it is competitive, effective and efficient," Dr. Wagonheim said. "Everybody has gone through the sensitizing stage, where there is an awareness. Now what? How do you resolve conflict? How do you try to make sure that person is happy in his or her work, that they can move ahead to fulfill their self-actuation?"

The New York Times, March 7, 1993

The Struggle for Minority Managers[*]

Veronica Byrd

White workers are often oblivious to the racism black supervisors must face.

It can happen in unobtrusive ways: a subtle disregard by a subordinate for an assigned task, an absence of urgency in completing a chore, a neglect of comments made during a meeting. Or it can be a feeling of always having to prove oneself or of not being seen as a team player because of a lack of interest in after-hours socializing or weekend golf.

As middle- and upper-level managers, African-Americans reaching for the next rung on the corporate ladder are often confronted with these day-to-day challenges. Most often, their colleagues—usually white and male—are oblivious to these problems. But they are all too real to black managers.

"People are not aware of the difficulties that exist," said Floyd Dickens Jr., a consultant on diversity issues and co-author with Jacqueline B. Dickens, his wife, of "The Black Manager: Making It in the Corporate World" (American Management Association). Mr. Dickens became involved in diversity issues while an engineer and manager at the Procter & Gamble Company, where he worked for 21 years.

Mel E. Lyons, senior program director at the New York-based American Management Association, said he has heard complaints from black managers about their struggle to delegate authority and responsibility: "Some feel they don't get the same level of respect that their counterparts get or that assignments they give are not acted upon with the same sense of urgency."

This kind of behavior could be the result of tension or jealousy felt by white employees, who may never have been supervised before by a minority manager. What's more, at least some of the white employees might not even be aware of what they are doing.

"Unfortunately, people don't leave their prejudices or anger at home," Mr. Lyons said.

But given the increased number of minority members and women in the workplace, learning to recognize and manage ethnic, racial, gender and cultural differences is at the top of many corporate agendas.

The bottom line for most corporations: diversity is no longer a matter of choice but a matter of survival.

Organizations need to have a real commitment to hiring and promoting minority employees and "not just give lip service," Mr. Lyons added.

At the Xerox Corporation, based in Stamford, Conn., training seminars are offered not only in such standard management areas as decision-making and delegating tasks, but also in more sensitive topics like race relations, including white backlash, and sex and age discrimination.

Beatriz J. Vidal, manager of corporate work-force diversity at Xerox, said workshops on sensitivity and diversity have "had an impact on the way we treat our people and the way we manage our work force."

About 12 percent of the senior management at Xerox is black; 4 percent is Hispanic and 4 percent is Asian. Fourteen percent of middle and upper-level managers are female. Over all, 26 percent of Xerox employees are minority members or women.

Despite the increase in numbers elsewhere in corporate America, complaints abound. Having her credibility questioned, for example, is a major thorn for Alean C. Saunders, an organizational consultant for diversity programming at Kaiser Permanente Medical Care Programs in Oakland, Calif.

"I feel I'm always proving myself," said Dr. Saunders, who holds a doctorate in education. "Getting people to think that I have anything to say that is worthwhile and that I have the credentials to do what I do is a constant challenge. I don't fit the normal, traditional European male model of management."

Adds Jacqueline Dickens: "We certainly don't want to imply that everyone is consciously running around being a racist. But these attitudes are so ingrained in our society that we don't often realize we are practicing the behavior."

Some companies have tried to raise the level of awareness through seminars and workshops. The American Management Association sponsors an annual conference on cultural, communication and social challenges facing minority managers. The conference is broadcast to companies in a nationwide satellite hookup. Other seminars are offered periodically by the A.M.A.

Still, some black managers question how committed companies are to diversity and say their prospects for further advancement seem bleak.

"There aren't that many of us," said Vivyen J. Ray, the New York-based director of human resources and training for the Gannett Company. "The limitations are blatant. I can't say that I will one day become the C.E.O. of this company. I can see myself only going so far. There is definitely a glass ceiling."

Companies must "not only talk the talk, but walk the walk," said Mr. Lyons of the A.M.A. "Organizations will initially say they are willing to work with minorities and women to get them in the door. But that's often as far as they get—in the door. There's not much movement up the ladder."

◆

The Americans with Disabilities Act of 1990: Implications for Managers*

John P. Kohl and Paul S. Greenlaw

Despite advances in equal job opportunity for a number of disenfranchised groups, one group that has continued to suffer both job and economic discrimination is the disabled:

- Disabled people in the workforce have unemployment rates almost double those of nondisabled people.
- Two-thirds of disabled Americans between sixteen and sixty-four are not working, and 66 percent of those not working say they would like to work.
- Disabled workers with thirteen or more years of education earn only 71 percent of the earnings of similarly educated nondisabled workers. Those with less than twelve years of education earn less than one-third the earnings of similarly educated nondisabled workers.[1]

On 26 July 1990, the Americans with Disabilities Act (ADA) became law. The Act extends the protections afforded under the Rehabilitation Act of 1973 and will eventually affect all firms with fifteen or more full-time employees. In order to help business owners and managers understand the law and respond to its requirements, we will (1) review the background and provisions of the ADA and (2) recommend courses of action for employers.

THE LEGISLATIVE ENVIRONMENT

A series of laws have addressed employment discrimination against various groups. Title VII of the 1964 Civil Rights Act prohibits employment discrimination based on race, religion, sex, color, and national origin. The 1967 Age Discrimination in Employment Act extends protection to individuals forty years of age and older. The 1973 Rehabilitation Act was the first national law to address employment protections for disabled individuals. The act prohibits employment discrimination against otherwise qualified disabled workers by federal, state, and local governments, their agencies, and certain federal contractors.[2] However, despite this act and numerous related state and local regulations, almost fifteen million workers with disabilities in the private sector still lacked protections against employment discrimination. The ADA was enacted to fill this gap in coverage.

The ADA contains five titles or sections dealing with various business activities:

---

*Reprinted from the *Sloan Management Review* Reprint Series, Spring 1992, Vol. 33, No. 3.

- Title I provides for equal employment opportunities;
- Title II requires equal availability and accessibility to all services provided by state and local governments, including transportation;
- Title III prohibits discrimination in public accommodations and services operated by a wide range of private businesses, including hotels, recreational facilities, and retail stores;
- Title IV concerns telecommunications;
- Title V contains miscellaneous provisions such as protection for individuals invoking their rights under the ADA.

We will limit our discussion to Title I, equal employment opportunity, but employers should be aware that other sections of the law—specifically, Title III—may prove the most costly and difficult to implement.

DEFINITION OF DISABILITY

The ADA defines disability in virtually the same way as Section 504 of the Rehabilitation Act: "(A) a physical or mental impairment that substantially limits one or more of the major life activities of such individuals; (B) a record of such an impairment; or (C) being regarded as having such an impairment."[3] This definition is deliberately broad. Consequently, the law will affect most U.S. business firms.

The ADA avoids a "laundry list" of impairments that may be classified as disabilities. Some impairments may be disabling for some people but not for others, depending on, for instance, the stage of a disease, presence of other impairments, and so forth. Some impairments are specifically included or excluded. For example, HIV infection is considered a disability, whereas obesity or a concussion generally are not. The Equal Employment Opportunity Commission (EEOC) has listed a number of specific conditions excluded from ADA coverage, such as compulsive gambling, kleptomania, pyromania, transvestism, transsexualism, exhibitionism, voyeurism, and pedophilia.[4]

In the case of illegal drug use, the ADA amends the Rehabilitation Act by excluding individuals currently using drugs from protection.[5] Decisions regarding other disabilities will need to be made on a case-by-case basis.

COMPLIANCE DATES

The ADA has a phased-in set of compliance dates. Employers with more than twenty-five employees must meet the law's provisions beginning 26 July 1992. After 26 July 1994, employers with fifteen or more full-time employees will have to comply. The lead time provided for compliance with the act is unusually long. When the Civil Rights Act was enacted, firms had one year in which to comply, and when it was amended in 1978 with the passage of the Pregnancy Discrimination Act, firms were required to comply within six months. The long lead time indicates how difficult compliance is expected to be.

THE HEART OF THE LAW

Three interrelated concepts that affect employer actions under the ADA are "qualified individual," "essential function," and "reasonable accommodation." Under the ADA it is illegal to discriminate against a disabled individual who is otherwise qualified to perform the essential functions of the job with or without reasonable accommodation.

According to the Act, essential functions of the job are the primary job duties that are intrinsic to the position. Reasonable accommodation involves a change in the job or work environment that permits the disabled person to perform the job's essential functions.

An illustration provided by the EEOC clarifies the interrelationship of these terms. Assume that a law firm requires all incoming attorneys to have graduated from an accredited law school and to have passed the appropriate state bar examination. The firm would not need to provide any accommodation to an individual with a visual impairment who had not met these two criteria. However, a disabled person who has met these two criteria is "otherwise qualified" to perform the job's essential functions. Under these circumstances, the law firm would be required to provide reasonable accommodation, such as a machine to magnify print, unless the employer can prove that such accommodation would impose an undue hardship.[6]

Reasonable Accommodation

"Reasonable accommodation" is at the heart of both the Rehabilitation Act of 1973 and the ADA. It may include modifying the job process, work environment, or even the circumstances under which the job is performed. The EEOC describes how the concept applies to a job that involves moving heavy sacks on a loading dock. The job's essential function is to move the sacks, not lift them. To accommodate someone with a bad back who is otherwise qualified for the position, the firm could provide a handtruck.

Similar accommodations can be easily and readily made at minimum effort and cost. For someone in a wheelchair, a firm might place blocks under a desk to raise its height or adjust equipment to allow the employee to reach and manipulate the controls.

Process changes could include modified or part-time work schedules for employees who are physically unable to work complete or regular shifts. Such an arrangement can prove mutually beneficial to the company and employee at little or no cost to the firm.

Neither the Act nor the EEOC definitively states what employers must do to fulfill the reasonable accommodation requirements. The widely varied needs of the disabled make precise conclusions difficult to draw. The EEOC has promised more detailed guidance in its "Compliance Manual on ADA," which is currently under development. Until its release, the specific contours of the Act will no doubt be developed on a case-by-case basis. Managers will need to evaluate each job, identify the firm's unique requirements, and consider specific accommodations in order to make appropriate decisions concerning the level and degree of accommodation.

Previous Case Law

Until the EEOC completes its compliance manual, managers seeking specifics will need to look elsewhere, such as at the body of case law that has developed surrounding the Rehabilitation Act. The EEOC provides a few examples of that case law in its proposed and final rules.

For example, in one case the court agreed with a small firm that it had too few employees to be able to accommodate a disabled person by reassigning tasks, and in another case, the court agreed that a firm's peak production periods made accommodations difficult.[7] The type and cost of accommodations have also been addressed by the courts. The accommodation must enable the disabled employee to perform the job's essential functions, but it does not have to be the "best" accommodation. In the example of moving sacks on the loading dock, the employer does not need to provide state-of-the-art equipment; a dolly is sufficient.[8] Issues of reasonableness and cost will continue to be addressed by the courts.

Cost Estimates

The EEOC has estimated costs for reasonable accommodation based on studies conducted in the early 1980's concerning costs to federal contractors under the Rehabilitation Act. One study found:

- 51.3 percent of all accommodations entailed no cost;
- 18.5 percent of accommodations cost between $1 and $99; and
- 11.9 percent of accommodations cost between $100 and $499.

Thus, 80 percent of all accommodation in this study cost less than $500, and the average cost per accommodation was only $304. The EEOC has used this average along with two other averages to estimate an overall mean cost per accommodation of $261.

Costs are likely to be lower for smaller firms than for larger firms. Firms with fifteen to twenty-five employees will have two years to watch larger firms comply with the law and thus time to learn the easiest and least expensive means for compliance. The EEOC also estimates that larger firms will be thirty times more likely to need to make an accommodation than their smaller counterparts, given the number of disabled people seeking employment.

Unfortunately, these are only estimates. The EEOC's analysis of costs involved with accommodation under the Rehabilitation Act is nearly a decade old, and no effort has been made to factor in inflation or other increased costs. Medical costs, for example, have increased at a rate far in excess of the inflation rate over the past ten years, and such costs could affect expenses associated with some accommodations.

Many indirect costs have also not been included, such as making existing facilities—break areas, lunch rooms, training areas, and so on—accessible to disabled employees. Indirect costs involving job restructuring would include those associated with undertaking a thorough job analysis to determine essential functions. The sum of such indirect costs may actually exceed direct costs of reasonable accommodation.

In addition, the statistical probability of accommodations may be of little comfort; what was once considered unlikely may become extremely expensive.

RECOMMENDATIONS FOR MANAGERS

The ADA requires all employers to reevaluate their employment practices and procedures. We offer the following suggestions:

1. Employers should watch for additional information issuing from the EEOC. The EEOC plans to release several sections of its compliance manual before 26 July 1992.[9] In the interim, questions concerning the ADA can be addressed directly to the EEOC at its national or regional offices.
2. Managers should stay apprised of changes in local and state legislation affecting the disabled. It is likely that the ADA will serve as a model for future legislation at all government levels. State and local laws frequently are as strict as or stricter than their federal counterparts and generally cover organizations of all sizes, not just those with more than twenty-five employees. Even the smallest businesses must remain alert to changes in local and state employment laws.
3. Small businesses should note the special provisions for them (see Table 1). This law is unusually sensitive to smaller firms. Both Congress and the EEOC have attempted to accommodate the needs of smaller businesses by setting later compliance dates, allowing tax credits, and eliminating reporting requirements (the lack of reporting requirements applies to larger businesses as well).
4. Managers should be aware that compliance with the ADA will involve hidden and as yet unknown indirect costs. Costly activities will include job analysis and job redesign.
5. Firms should prepare by undertaking job analyses to determine the essential and marginal functions of jobs. A thorough analysis takes time and resources that may not be available when a position is suddenly open and needs immediate filling.

TABLE 1

TITLE I	**PROVISIONS OF THE AMERICANS WITH DISABILITIES ACT AFFECTING SMALLER FIRMS**

1. Phased-in compliance dates. Firms with twenty-five or more employees will need to comply after 26 July 1992, and firms with fifteen or more employees will need to comply after 26 July 1994.
2. Title I has no written reporting requirements for firms, regardless of size.
3. Tax credits are available for smaller firms with twenty-five or fewer employees (some larger firms may also qualify for this credit). Credits are equal to 50 percent of the amount between $250 and $10,250 per accommodation.
4. Title I exclusions include bona fide private clubs and religious organizations.

6. Take note of Title III. We have limited ourselves to discussion of Title I, but Title III, which governs access to all public accommodations and services, may be more costly to employers in the long run. Neither the Act nor the proposed rules address the possible costs of complying with Title III.

In the 1990's, we will see a period of increasing equal job opportunity for those with disabilities. The enactment of Title VII of the Civil Rights Act in 1964 was the beginning of the expansion of equal job opportunity for disenfranchised Americans. The ADA continues that journey.

Notes

This research was funded, in part, by a grant from First Interstate Bank of Nevada and the Center for Business and Economics, University of Nevada, Las Vegas.

1. Studies cited by the EEOC in 56 *Federal Register* at 8581.

2. The Rehabilitation Act of 1973 requires federal contractors and subcontractors with contracts exceeding $2,500 per annum to practice nondiscrimination and employ affirmative action in their hiring practices. In addition, those contractors and subcontractors with annual contracts of $50,000 and more, and more than fifty employees, must develop and maintain written affirmative action plans that satisfy requirements of the Office of Federal Contract Compliance Programs.

3. All materials, references, and direct quotations are drawn either from the Americans with Disabilities Act (Public LAW 101-336, 104 Stat. 329) or from the EEOC's Proposed Rules on the ADA in 56 *Federal Register* 8577, 28 February 1991, or Final Rules and Regulations in 56 *Federal Register* 35726, 26 July 1991.

4. 56 *Federal Register* at 35736. This section also states, "Homosexuality and bisexuality are not impairments, and so are not disabilities as defined in this part."

5. 56 *Federal Register* at 35736. The reference is to those "currently engaging in the illegal use of drugs." However, "the terms *disability* and *qualified* individual with a disability may not exclude an individual who (1) has successfully completed a supervised drug rehabilitation program and is no longer engaging in the illegal use of drugs,. . . [or] (2) is participating in a supervised rehabilitation program and is no longer engaging in such use."

6. 56 *Federal Register* at 35748.

7. 56 *Federal Register* at 35743. The EEOC cites *Treadwell v. Alexander*, 707 F. 2d 473 (11th Cir. 1983) and *Dexler v. Tisch*, 660 F. Supp. 1418 (D. Conn. 1987) in support of both possibilities.

8. 56 *Federal Register* at 35748. See *Carter v. Bennett*, 840 F. 2d 63 (D.C. Cir. 1988).

9. 56 *Federal Register* at 35726.

The New York Times, February 10, 1991

Mastering the Language of Disability[*]

Claudia H. Deutsch

Recruitment may be a matter of Braille booklets or just plain getting the word out.

There are plenty of jobs at the Bank of Montreal that people who are deaf, blind, or learning impaired could do. And since Canadian companies, like their American counterparts, face legal and demographic pressures to hire more people with disabilities, the bank wishes more of them would apply. But for years, applicants with disabilities have been few and far between.

So this year G. Stephen Cobbold, the bank's manager of recruitment and employment equity, is trying something new. He has published a recruiting booklet with a dual language cover: English and Braille. He had urged all of the bank's department managers not to exclude people with disabilities from the running for such jobs as bank teller. And he recently hired a woman who, due to a head injury a few years ago, has such mental disabilities as memory loss. The woman is writing letters, loading data bases and handling word processing tasks in Mr. Cobbold's department.

"My hope is that the Brailled brochure will show not only blind people but people with any kind of disability that the bank welcomes them to apply," Mr. Cobbold said. "And if I hire a severely impaired person myself, it becomes easier to ask the rest of the bank's departments to do so."

Building wheelchair ramps and buying special phones for the deaf are important. But more and more companies are recognizing that rolling out an emotional welcome mat for people with disabilities—and persuading nondisabled managers to keep it rolled out—means even more. Increasingly, these companies are providing their in-house recruiters with directories of organizations that can point them toward candidates with disabilities, and training them in how to best match those candidates with jobs. And they are teaching their nondisabled employees how to avoid language or gestures that colleagues with disabilities might find offensive.

"There's nothing magic about it—if word gets out to the community that you make people with disabilities comfortable, then they'll come to you for work," said Gwendolyn D. Sheard, director of equal employment opportunity for the Friendly Ice Cream Corporation, which estimates that 1,600 of its 30,000 employees have disabilities.

Many companies have found that the best spokespeople to the community are employees with disabilities themselves—particularly those who have risen to high levels.

Two years ago, Honeywell Inc.'s Council of Honeywell Employees With Disabilities—a group that despite its name, includes nondisabled people among its members—sponsored a symposium at which management level people with such disabilities as deafness or post-polio mobility problems spoke about their jobs and the hurdles they had to overcome to get them or function in them.

"The important thing was showing that their disabilities did not stop them from

ACCEPTABLE LANGUAGE

Here are substitutes for terms that disabled people often find offensive:

Term	Substitute
Afflicted with, suffering from, crippled by	Has
Defect, disease	Condition
Handicap	Disability
Normal, healthy, ablebodied	Nondisabled
Confined to a wheelchair	Uses a wheelchair

Source: US West Communications

getting ahead here," said Angela C. Johnson, an engineer with rheumatoid arthritis who is the Council's chairperson.

Now Honeywell is shifting its emphasis to sensitizing nondisabled managers. Last year it sent 60 people from its various human resource and training departments to take Windmills, a program developed by the California Governor's Committee that helps non-disabled people identify—and exorcise—stereotypes they have about people with disabilities. The managers, who went through such exercises as picking which of several disabilities they would be most willing to have and which they would hate most, will hold their own Windmills sessions throughout Honeywell this year.

"One of the biggest problems disabled people encounter is the stigmatism, the discomfort, that nondisabled people feel around them," said Ms. Johnson. "Any program that helps nondisabled people explore their own negative attitudes is going to help."

She would get no argument from Holly M. Delcambre, the nondisabled manager in charge of US West Communications Inc.'s efforts to make accommodations to people with disabilities.

Two years ago a group of deaf employees at US West's Seattle office persuaded the telecommunications company to form a disability committee comprising people with and without disabilities from offices in 14 states. The committee, which meets each month via conference call, has helped initiate Windmills training throughout US West. It is helping Friends, a group of employees with disabilities and their nondisabled colleagues that sprang up in the Omaha office, open chapters elsewhere. And, it is putting together a training package to make sure that US West's employment officers impart to applicants with disabilities the company's commitment to them.

"We want word to get out that we are willing to buy computers that print in braille, and that we hold sign language classes for hearing managers, and that we know enough not to use words like 'cripple,'" Ms. Delcambre said.

Los Angeles Times, September 23, 1992
Mothers of Invention*

Pamela Warrick

Women's inventiveness seldom has been adequately acknowledged, or rewarded.

The Telephone. The light bulb. The automobile. Quick. Name the inventors. Of course you can. How about flat-bottomed paper bags, bullet-proof vests and Scotchgard? The dishwasher, the fire escape, AZT?

Of course you can't.

Why? Because these inventors are women, says historian Anne Macdonald. That's why they're hard to find in history books. Or in any books.

"For a long time, it was thought women were only creative biologically," says Macdonald. "While we know that's not true, there is no question that when it comes to inventions, women have been horribly ignored."

Hedy Lamarr was ignored. You know, the *inventor* Hedy Lamarr. Famous for appearing nude in the 1933 movie "Ecstasy" and for saying, "Any girl can be glamorous. All you have to do is stand still and look stupid." Lamarr was also highly mechanical, one of Hollywood's best-kept secrets.

In 1940, Lamarr invented a sophisticated, and unique, antijamming device to foil Nazi radar. As Hedwig Keisler Markey, the actress patented the device with partner George Antheil, a film score composer, and offered it to the U.S. War Department.

She was stunned when her offer was declined. But she was not surprised years later when her patent expired and Sylvania adapted the invention. Today, the device speeds satellite communications around the world.

While Lamarr, now retired in Florida, has said she was happy to make a contribution, she would have been even happier with a little recognition.

"Never a letter, never a thank you, never money," Lamarr recently complained to a *Forbes* magazine reporter. "I guess they just take and forget about a person."

Not all are forgotten, of course. Dr. Gertrude Elion, for example, won a Nobel Prize in 1988 for developing drugs to fight herpes, cancer and other diseases.

Since 1937, when she was refused a laboratory job because she was "too cute" and threatened to distract the other workers, Elion has patented 45 of her discoveries. But the less cute Thomas Edison still holds the record with 1,093 patents.

That men dominate the world of invention—and most certainly of patented inventions—cannot be disputed. Among the more than five million patents issued in the U.S. since 1790, the *mothers* of invention are barely represented.

And while numbers are improving, they are not improving very much or very fast. It has taken a century and a half for women's share of patents to rise from one to six percent. And that's not good, says author Macdonald, herself a patentholder.

"I believe things should be moving along faster than they are, but after my own experience, I certainly understand why they are not," says Macdonald, who spent three years and $6,000 to patent her Argyle knitting device, which keeps yarns separate.

It was Catherine Greene, according to some 19th century accounts, who helped her farm mechanic, Eli Whitney, build the first cotton gin. And it was an early design by Ann Harned Manning that led to the creation of Cyrus McCormick's famous reaper.

Although Manning probably invented the mower on which the reaper was modelled, it was her husband who held the patent. Married women had no property rights until the turn of the century. And "ladies" were not encouraged to own up to their mechanical talents.

Rather than admit to such unladylike leanings, writes Macdonald, it was not unusual for women in the 1800s to claim to be under the influence of spirits when defending their inventiveness.

Amanda Theodosia Jones, for example, told the world that her idea for vacuum canning, the genesis of an entire food industry, came not from any personal cleverness but from her brother's ghost instructing her from the grave.

"How many women's inventions are hidden under the name of fathers, husbands, brothers and sons, we cannot of course know," lamented Charlotte Smith, founder of the National Women's Industrial League in 1890 and the first to try to tally the number of women patentholders.

Smith found that women inventors gave up patents—and profits—for many reasons. Ellen Eglin, who invented the clothes wringer and sold the patent rights for $18, told Smith's Woman Inventor newspaper why:

"You know I am black, and if it was known that a Negro woman patented the invention, white ladies would not buy the wringer." Eglin's invention made a lot of money, but not for her.

Black hairstylist Margorite Joyner was more fortunate. Her 1928 invention of a Permanent Wave Machine—which straightened black women's hair and curled white women's hair—made her wealthy, even though she gave her employer the patent.

Inventive (read: desperate) mothers have been responsible for designs to ease their child-care load from the first baby-jumper, invented by Jane Wells in 1872, to the disposable diaper, patented by Marion Donovan in 1951.

Ann Moore invented the Snugli child carrier after a West African tour with the U.S. Peace Corps—and then went on to patent a personal carrier for portable oxygen supplies.

Certainly, the stories of modern women and their inventions don't all have happy endings.

Ruth Siems, the General Foods home economist who invented Stove Top Stuffing, got a plaque and a $125 bonus. But it didn't help her keep her job of 33 years when the company was taken over by Philip Morris, according to author Macdonald.

Still, Siems had the last word. In 1984, when the one-billionth package of stuffing rolled off the assembly line and no one invited her to the celebration, Siems found her response in the message on the back of the commemorative T-shirt: "Stuff It."

Chapter 11

International Management

We have included this section in recognition of the increasing globalization of business and the increased emphasis on both increasing the volume of exports and establishing international alliances of one sort or another. For example, during the past twenty years U.S. foreign direct investment, based on historical cost, went from $59 billion to over $370 billion—6.4 times the amount in 1967.

In their efforts to deal with global competition, U.S. companies have moved significant portions of their manufacturing activities abroad. The overseas activities may take several forms. They may be wholly owned subsidiaries, joint ventures with a company in the foreign country, licensing agreements where the foreign organization is licensed to use parts of the domestic organization's technology, or turnkey plants where the domestic company builds a plant in the host country, trains indigenous employees in its operations and then turns the operation over to an organization in the host country. The location of the these activities increasingly is in one or more of the developing or underdeveloped countries.

Likewise, banks, accounting firms, insurance companies and other service-type activities have established foreign operations in markets where their principal accounts are, to prevent competitors from gaining access to those accounts. Recent advances in communication also have made it possible in some instances to utilize lower cost but effective employees.

This trend has literally brought about a revolution in the doing of business and the processes of managing. Matters are much more complicated for an international company than for a one-country operation. Each of the traditional functions of management has become more complex, in most instances calling for adaptation to foreign laws, languages, customs, attitudes, and cultures. For example, the host country may have laws that seriously limit the domestic company's discretion in the hiring or firing of employees. These and other problems affecting human resource management are discussed at length in the opening selection, "Human Resource Systems in an International Alliance: The Undoing of a Done Deal?"

The globalization of business has proven to be a bonanza for skilled linguists because it has become necessary to translate more and more material from English into foreign languages. Belatedly, corporations have recognized that they must make accommodations to the families of people they wish to relocate abroad. The accommodations often include language and culture training for the family members and reluctance to send family members to some of the less developed countries. The increasing number of two-career families also limits the willingness of some employees to accept overseas assignments. These developments are discussed in "Companies Use Cross-Cultural Training to Help Their Employees Adjust Abroad."

Continuing globalization of business has been accompanied by the development of trading blocs. We have been accustomed to the aggressiveness of Japan, but the slowly emerging European Community poses still further barriers to U.S. trade abroad. The adoption of the North American Trade Agreement linking Canada, the United States, and Mexico promises to further encourage trade among the three countries. "Asia's Wealth" relates the massive shift taking place in the global economic balance of power as the economies of East Asia catch up with Japan and the West. The dominant force behind this shift is the wealth accumulated and being invested in industrialization by the network of ethnic Chinese and the economic planners of the East Asian countries. As yet, some of these countries do not have open capital markets. However, Asia has become a major player in world trade and is expected to continue growth. China's premier is working hard to reform the banking system and encourage the stock exchanges and bond markets. Similar moves are underway in Taiwan and South Korea. The challenge for these countries is seen as continuing the development of such institutions and channeling accumulated wealth into development.

As noted earlier, many U.S. businesses have moved significant elements of their operation overseas. So have many Japanese and Western European firms. Many people think of these firms' foreign employees as unskilled or at best semi-skilled and requiring extensive training. "Your New Global Work Force" points out the fallacy of such a generalization. The article also illustrates how increasingly sophisticated technology raises the productivity of employees, which in turn requires fewer people to produce more goods and services. The author raises the specter of more people than jobs worldwide. He also offers convincing support for the argument that employment opportunities in the developed countries will decline. While this thesis is contrary to the forecasts of many economists, it gives us food for thought. Another selection relates how the traditional work ethic in Japan is changing to include more emphasis on family life. Just as American managers who have survived the massive corporate restructuring have abandoned loyalty to the job, so have many Japanese. The trend is receiving support from a number of Japanese firms. It will be interesting to see whether this new trend survives Japan's emergence from recession several years from now.

◆

Human Resources in an International Alliance: The Undoing of a Done Deal?*

Wayne F. Cascio and Manuel G. Serapio, Jr.

In a global alliance, people with different cultures, career goals, compensation systems, and other HR baggage often have to hit the ground working together. Unless the ground has been smoothed, this "people factor" can halt the alliance's progress, sometimes permanently.

Two years ago Dresser Industries, Inc. and Komatsu, Ltd. formed an alliance in the United States to compete more effectively against industry leader Caterpillar Inc. Komatsu took over Dresser's U.S. construction equipment plants and the production of selected lines of Dresser tractors; the alliance also let Komatsu use Dresser's distribution network to sell its tractors in the United States. The advantage for Dresser was that it gained access to Komatsu's sophisticated tractor manufacturing processes. Both companies are counting on the alliance to boost their market share against Caterpillar in the fiercely competitive U.S. construction equipment market.

This partnership reflects an important trend in international business. Over the past decade, we have seen more and more international collaboration between companies—collaboration designed to give them a better position in the world economy. International cooperative ventures among companies in telecommunications, computers, electronics, transportation equipment, aerospace, financial services, and many other industries are rapidly increasing. The types of international collaboration involved are many and varied—marketing and distribution partnerships, research consortia, licensing arrangements, and joint ventures, to name just a few.

This collaboration among companies on an international scale poses new and complex challenges for those involved. Managers of international alliances know how important it is to effectively link their financial, technological, production, or marketing resources with those of their collaborators.

However, international collaboration often requires partners to share more than money, technology, or products; a partnership of people is also frequently involved. In international partnerships where managers and workers from two or more companies work closely together, like the alliance between Komatsu and Dresser, managers from both firms must ensure that people-oriented issues receive adequate attention.

We have spent more than three years studying the organizational functioning of four international alliances in the United States and monitoring several others.

*Reprinted from *Organizational Dynamics*, Winter 1991, Vol. 19, no. 3, pp. 63–74.

These international alliances include two joint ventures between a U.S. partner and a Japanese partner, an R&D-based minority participation by a Japanese company in a U.S. high technology company, and a production-and-marketing alliance between a Japanese firm and a U.S. company. Because the firms involved in these four international alliances asked that their identities remain confidential, we have left them anonymous.

Our focus is on selected human resources management issues in international alliances, and our discussion relies heavily on the lessons learned from studying the sample companies mentioned above. To put the subject matter of this article in perspective, we first look at the growth of international collaboration and define the various types of international alliances involved.

THE BOOM IN INTERNATIONAL COLLABORATION

According to *Fortune* magazine, U.S. companies entered into some 2,000 alliances with European companies alone in the 1980s. A 1989 report by the United Nations Center on transnational corporations identified more than 850 interfirm technology arrangements formed by companies from France, West Germany, Italy, Japan, the U.S., the U.K., and the Benelux countries between 1984 and 1986.

Most major U.S. multinational companies maintain numerous international cooperative arrangements. Over the past few years, General Electric has formed eight alliances with companies in Europe, Japan, and South Korea in such fields as fluorescent lamps and factory automation. Corning, Inc. maintains more than a dozen cooperative ventures with major multinational companies in Europe, Australia, China, Japan, and South Korea. General Motors has entered into separate partnerships with Toyota, Isuzu, Suzuki, and Daewoo. American Telephone and Telegraph (AT&T), one of several U.S. companies with extensive networks of international collaborative arrangements, had about 20 such major alliances in 1987.

Companies collaborate for several reasons. As noted earlier, Komatsu and Dresser joined forces in the United States to compete against Caterpillar. Texas Instruments and Hitachi teamed up to develop a 16-megabit dynamic RAM chip. AT&T linked up with N.V. Philips to enhance its market access to buyers of switching equipment in Europe. International collaboration makes it possible for companies to share the costs and the risks of doing business. It enables companies to share financial resources, technology, production facilities, marketing know-how, and human resources.

The major driving forces behind the trend toward an increase in international collaborative arrangements are the rapid development of technology and the globalization of markets and products. Not even the largest multinational companies can any longer acquire from their own laboratories all of the technology they need. Many of these companies have to ally themselves with other companies to secure access to new technologies or to share the risks associated with the huge capital investments that some technologies require (e.g., 16-megabit DRAM microchips).

In addition, markets and products are becoming more global. Europe 1992 has led even the largest regional companies in Europe to join forces with other organizations. For example, Ahold (the large Dutch retailer) is forging new ties with other retailers in Europe. Clearly, as Kenichi Ohmae observed, international collaboration has become a competitive necessity for any firm that aspires to be a player in global markets.

A TYPOLOGY OF INTERNATIONAL ALLIANCES

The term *international alliance* means different things to different people. For the purposes of this study, we define international alliance as a collaboration between two or more multinational companies that is developed to let them jointly pursue a common goal. The alliance may be between multinational companies from the same home country (e.g., Digital Equipment Corporation and Apple) or between companies of different home-country origins (e.g., Mitsubishi and Daimler-Benz). In this article, we discuss international alliances between companies from different home countries—and therefore different national cultures.

An important attribute of an international alliance is that it covers only some of the activities of the collaborating partners. The partners therefore maintain their individual identities and engage in other activities, separate from those of the alliance. Thus, in the highly publicized alliance between Mitsubishi Heavy Industries, Kawasaki Heavy Industries, Fuji Heavy Industries, and Boeing, the partners agreed to cooperate on the 757 project, but they remained active competitors in other businesses. This attribute distinguishes an international alliance from an international merger or acquisition, in which the identities and activities of the partners are fully merged.

During the past decade, we have seen different types of international alliances. Some examples are:

- *International joint ventures.* In 1987 Mitsubishi and Chrysler formed a joint venture called Diamond Star Corporation in Normal, Illinois. The plant, managed by Mitsubishi, produces the Plymouth Laser and the Eagle Talon for Chrysler Motors, and the Eclipse for Mitsubishi.
- *Marketing and distribution agreements.* AT&T and Olivetti entered into a marketing and distribution agreement in 1984. Under the agreement, AT&T sells Olivetti UNIX-based personal computers in the United States. Olivetti sells AT&T UNIX-based minicomputers in Europe and AT&T office automation products in Asia.
- *Research and development partnerships.* In 1989 Texas Instruments and Hitachi formed an R&D alliance to develop the next generation of memory chips.
- *International consortia.* In 1984 the European Community and European private industry launched an international consortium called European Strategic Program for Research and Development in Information Technologies (ESPRIT). The stated purpose of ESPRIT is "to provide the European information technology industry with the technological base it needs to become and stay competitive worldwide in the next ten years."

- *Licensing arrangements.* In 1990 AT&T struck a licensing agreement with Nippon Electric Corporation (NEC) that would exchange some of AT&T's computer-aided design technology for NEC's advanced logic chips.

International alliances may be classified on the basis of their goals: production, marketing, research and development, technology transfer, or a combination of these. From the perspective of human resources management (HRM), we may classify international alliances according to the extent to which the collaboration requires interaction among people (managers, workers, or both) from the collaborating companies. Thus we may view international alliances in terms of a spectrum of collaborative interfirm dealings. One end of the spectrum represents a minimum amount of interaction among each partner's people; the other, a maximum amount. These ideas are represented in Exhibit 1.

As Exhibit 1 shows, some types of international alliances involve more interaction among people from the two partners than others do. In general, a joint venture involves more interaction than does a marketing or distribution partnership or a licensing arrangement.

There are, however, some exceptions to the typology presented in the exhibit. For one, the degree or nature of interaction among the employees in an international alliance may also be influenced by other factors, such as the relative importance of the alliance to each partner or the types of resources the partners share or exchange. Thus, it is not uncommon to have a significant amount of

EXHIBIT 1 SPECTRUM OF INTERFIRM DEALINGS INVOLVING PEOPLE INTERACTION

	DEGREE OF INTERACTION AMONG EACH PARTNER'S PEOPLE		
	Minimum Amount	Moderate Amount	Maximum Amount
Examples of International Alliances in Each Category	Licensing arrangements Supplier-buyer agreements	Marketing distribution agreements Research and development agreements	Manufacturing joint ventures International production consortium

	DIMENSIONS OF PEOPLE/UNIT INTERACTION BETWEEN PARTNERS		
	Minimum Amount	Moderate Amount	Maximum Amount
Level of Interaction Between Each Partner	Functional departments Functional specialists	Product/functional departments Functional specialists Product managers Technical specialists	Whole organization General management Functional/product managers Technical specialists Significant and sustained
Frequency of Interaction	Low	Moderate	
Number of People Interacting	Limited	Limited	Many

partner-to-partner interaction among people in multimillion-dollar research partnerships or in alliances featuring an exchange of high-technology products
between partners.

HR ISSUES IN INTERNATIONAL ALLIANCES

Each type of international alliance shown in Exhibit 1 carries with it a different set
of implications for human resources management. The HR issues involved vary
with the degree of interaction among each firm's people. Thus, international manufacturing joint ventures suggest the largest number of HR issues, while licensing
arrangements suggest the fewest. Let us begin our treatment of this issue by
describing some of the major issues that arise when there is significant, sustained
interaction among the employees of collaborating firms.

Blending of Cultures and Management Styles

AT&T's alliance with Olivetti, mentioned above, illustrates how an alliance's failure to blend its partners' divergent cultures and management styles can impede
the partnership's success. Robert Kravner, an AT&T senior executive, blames
most of the problems in the alliance on differences in culture and management
style. According to an article in *The Wall Street Journal* (March 26, 1990), he said,
"I don't think we or Olivetti spent enough time understanding behavior patterns.
We knew that culture was different but we never really penetrated. We would get
angry and they would get upset."

This kind of international alliance, which requires people from different organizational and national cultures to work together, inevitably triggers problems that
can be traced to cultural differences. To overcome such problems, both parties
must be willing to invest considerable time and effort in understanding each other's culture, on teambuilding efforts, and on continually improving two-way communication. The approaches used by two international alliances, GMF Robotics
Corporation and one of our sample companies, show how to achieve this.

When General Motors (GM) and the Fanuc Company of Japan formed the
joint venture GMF Robotics Corporation, their management styles were quite
different from each other. In contrast to the managers in bureaucratic GM,
Fanuc's managers were used to having more autonomy. Yet despite this and other
differences, GM and Fanuc were able to arrange a workable alliance. During the
negotiation stage and the early years of the venture, both parent companies
focused their efforts on building trust and on understanding each other's operations. To build trust, both avoided conflict and acceded to each other's demands
during the formative stage of the joint venture. Today, GMF Robotics Corporation holds the dominant share of the heavy robotics market in the U.S.

Managers in one of our sample companies, a manufacturing joint venture
between a U.S. company and a Japanese company, attribute the excellent relationship among their people in the alliance to the two years the partners spent "dating." Before forming the joint venture, both partners agreed to work together for
two years on smaller projects: a buyer-supplier arrangement and a licensing agreement. "We wanted to learn more about their operations and their way of doing

business before entering into a joint venture with them. We wanted to give our people a chance to know their people," said a senior executive of the Japanese partner in the joint venture.

Job Design

As a strategy to increase quality and productivity, an international partner may sometimes want to redesign the way jobs are done. Such was the case at the General Motors–Toyota NUMMI joint venture in Fremont, California, and in one of the sample companies in this study.

Before the NUMMI joint venture, General Motors' Fremont plant had one of the worst records in the company for poor labor relations and defective production. It was a typical assembly-line plant in which workers and supervisors were encouraged to push as many parts as possible down the line—and to let quality control inspectors ferret out defects at the other end.

Four years after the joint venture commenced, its productivity and quality levels rivaled Japan's best and exceeded anything in the American auto industry. What changed? Not the workers; they are still members of the United Auto Workers (UAW), and they are paid union-scale wages and benefits. Nor did the change spring from the introduction of advanced robotics. Instead, it occurred because of a revolutionary team-production system run by the workers themselves. Each worker is responsible for quality control—for ensuring that no car moves on to the next station unless every job already done on it has been done perfectly. That system was worked out jointly with the plant's Japanese and American managers by the third partner in the joint venture: the UAW rank-and-file on the assembly line.

Obviously, not all attempts at job redesign will be as successful as NUMMI's. In a company in this study, the partners disagreed on how to redesign the jobs in the alliance. Each partner, believing that it had superior technology and a better production method, pushed for its own approach to job design. The result: several months of delay in implementing the joint venture.

This type of conflict is common in international alliances, especially in partnerships between high-technology companies filled with big egos. NUMMI's lessons for these alliances are simple ones: Involve all parties in the effort to redesign jobs. Be willing to listen, and be receptive to new ideas. Learn from each other's strengths and weaknesses.

Recruiting and Staffing Strategies

A host of important issues arise in this context. For example, how will the number of employees required and their skills mix be determined for the international alliance? Who is responsible for forecasting net human resources demands for the venture at different future time periods? Will all the recruitment be done individually by the partners, or will they do at least some joint recruiting? What labor markets will new employees be recruited from? What percentage of the international alliance's employees will come from home, host, or third countries? For whom do the new employees work—for one partner or the other or for the alliance itself as a separate entity? Who has authority to make decisions regarding new hires? Will such authority be vested in a single person or position (e.g., a plant manager), or must there be concurrence among representatives of all partners in the alliance? How will conflict among the various parties be resolved when they disagree over the appropriate qualifications of personnel?

These kinds of issues are important: They should be incorporated into the broad strategic planning process for the alliance, not left to chance or to "ad hoc" decision making by the respective parties. Unfortunately, we found the opposite case in our study. Partners in international alliances tend to establish their alliance first and work out the recruiting and staffing details later.

According to Oded Shenkar and Yoram Zeira, some partners in international joint ventures require that staffing policy be specified in the contract and documents of incorporation. Their research indicated that when staffing policies are not detailed in a written contract, severe friction is likely to develop between the partners.

In lieu of a contract, the partners in an international alliance can formulate written "house rules" on recruitment and staffing. House rules, which offer many of the advantages of a contract, give the alliance important guidelines on staffing policy and a basis for settling disputes. And they give the alliance's managers even more flexibility in recruiting and staffing than a contract does.

Orienting and Training the Alliance's New Hires and Current Employees

Orientation for employees in the alliance is critical, since it must incorporate an introduction to the organizational (and perhaps national) cultures of all parties to the alliance. Such an introduction should include an overview of the history, traditions, and corporate values of the partners. Then it should include a description of the new venture, its organization, and its management structure, followed by an introduction of the employee to the manager, department, and co-workers.

Orientation has to be more than a sketchy overview of the basics. It should be an in-depth process that has been thoroughly planned in advance, takes a long-term approach, and includes provisions for follow-up and evaluation. Two years after developing such a system, Corning, Inc. showed a 69 percent reduction in voluntary turnover among new hires, a 8:1 benefit/cost ratio in the first year, and a 14:1 ratio annually thereafter.

Orienting and training their employees constituted one of the first priorities of both the General Motors–Toyota NUMMI joint venture and the Chrysler–Mitsubishi Diamond Star alliance. Each joint venture spent millions of dollars on orientation and training long before they formally started their manufacturing operations in the U.S.

The success of these companies suggests that international alliances should be at least as concerned with preparing new employees to deal with the social context of their jobs and to cope with the insecurities and frustrations of a new learning situation as they are with developing the technical skills that employees need to perform their jobs effectively.

Performance Appraisal

The major issue here is "What (or whose) performance standards will be used?" To illustrate the nuances that emerge in this context, let us describe some differences in performance appraisal preferences and practices between the U.S. and Japanese partners in our study. In evaluating employee performance, U.S. partners tended to focus more on objective measures while Japanese companies stressed the importance of both objective and subjective measures. The Japanese partners also tended to take a longer time horizon than did their American counterparts in judging both organizational and employee performance. A case example that illustrates these differences comes from an alliance formed several years ago between Kyocera Corporation, one of Japan's largest ceramics companies, and LaPine Technology Corporation, a U.S. computer disk-drive manufacturer.

LaPine gave Kyocera the rights to manufacture its computer disk drives in exchange for rights to market them in Asia. But just after Kyocera invested $6 million in the alliance, an unexpected shift in market demand made LaPine's technology obsolete. According to an article in *Business Week* (July 21, 1986), one of LaPine's top executives said, "We expected to have our heads handed to us with a Samurai sword." Instead, Kyocera gave LaPine time to work on a new design.

In terms of style in communicating with employees and giving them feedback, the U.S. managers in our study tended to criticize their subordinates directly and in writing. By contrast, the Japanese managers tended to be more subtle and indirect in relaying criticism. Furthermore, U.S. managers tended to commend workers individually; Japanese managers tended to praise them as a group.

As these few differences illustrate, performance appraisal practices and preferences between partners in an international alliance can vary considerably. An alliance that fails to consider such differences before appraisals are done may create a great deal of misunderstanding and personal offense. Those who want to avoid such problems should consider taking the following actions:

1. Determine the purpose of the appraisal (e.g., administrative decision making versus personal development of the employee).
2. Whenever possible, develop performance objectives for job assignments or tasks (i.e., know what you want to accomplish).
3. Allow more time to achieve results in the new alliance than is customary in your own domestic market.
4. Keep the objectives of the appraisal system flexible and responsive to potential market and environmental contingencies.

Compensation and Benefits

Will the compensation systems of the partners be linked or will they be synthesized into a common one? Will compensation rates be pegged to benchmark jobs in local labor markets, or will they be tied to pay rates for similar jobs in each partner's home country? Often, each partner has an established pay policy, but those policies differ.

At the very least, the partners should reach agreement on the broad objectives of the compensation program for employees of the alliance. With respect to the current employees of each partner in the alliance, such objectives might include the following:

1. Attract and retain employees who are qualified for assignment to international cooperative ventures.
2. Facilitate transfers between international alliances and between home-country and foreign locations.
3. Establish and maintain a consistent relationship between the compensation of employees in all international alliances.
4. Maintain compensation that is reasonable in relation to the practices of leading competitors.

Employee benefits may vary drastically from country to country or from industry to industry. In Europe, for example, it is common for employees to receive added compensation in proportion to the number of their family members or the extent of their unpleasant working conditions. In Japan, a supervisor whose weekly salary is only $500 may also receive benefits that include family income allowances, housing or housing loans, subsidized vacations, year-end bonuses that can equal three months' pay, and profit sharing.

To deal with these differences, international alliances sometimes provide benefits according to a "best of both worlds" model, especially for their expatriate personnel. That is, the expatriate is given home-country benefits coverage wherever possible—but in areas where there may be no home-country plan, such as disability insurance coverage, the employee may join the host-country plan.

Some international alliances offer their managers a choice of different compensation systems. This approach was adopted in the American operation of Nomura Securities, the world's largest financial institution. In an article in the *Harvard Business Review* (July–August 1989), Yoshihasa Tabuchi (president and CEO of Nomura Securities and a partner in several international alliances with American companies) said, "We actually have two or three different employment [compensation] systems. For example, the American employment system at Nomura is by contract; under that system, we are prepared to pay the best possible price now. The Japanese employment system, in contrast, is very traditional—step by step. . . If our American employees would accept the Japanese system, we would be glad to offer it. But as of today, no American has signed up for it."

Failure to establish a uniform compensation policy in an international alliance that requires high interaction among employees from different partners can lead to predictably adverse effects. Differences in compensation systems, especially for employees doing the same jobs, often lead to feelings of inequity among those receiving lower compensation and benefits. Morale and motivation therefore suffer among group members.

Research by Shenkar and Zeira on international joint ventures has shown that some members of the lower-paid group may make special efforts to establish contact with and show loyalty to the partner(s) in the alliance that pay better. Further, they may disassociate themselves from the organization that recruited them or defect to other organizations that offer better pay. These employees were not lured away; they initiated their own transfers. Compensation and benefits are emotional issues for employees. To keep them from becoming major obstacles to the effective day-to-day management of the international alliance, a consistent set of compensation objectives and policies must be established at the outset—not hurriedly cobbled together after people problems escalate.

Career Issues
Major issues here involve employee promotions. Can new employees of the international alliance really be promoted, or are promotional paths blocked by home-country employees of the respective partners? To illustrate, consider the case of two sample companies in this study, both of them manufacturing joint ventures between a U.S. and a Japanese partner. Each of them employed many Japanese nationals in management—in fact, Japanese expatriate managers in both companies held an average of 70 percent of the top-management positions (e.g., president, senior vice-president) and 45 percent of the middle-management positions (e.g., vice-president, division manager) at the time that they started their operations in the U.S.

This concentration of management in the hands of Japanese expatriate managers limited opportunities for local managers to advance in their careers. Fearing that this would demoralize the local managers, both companies redesigned their organizational structures. The companies reassigned over half of their Japanese expatriate line managers to newly created positions of advisors. The new structure opened up more management positions for local managers and increased the local managers' opportunities for career advancement.

A further issue is job security, or lack thereof. If the venture fails, which company do the employees work for? If they were hired specifically as employees of the alliance itself, then their jobs are only as secure as the alliance is. However, if they were hired as employees of the respective partners, then their job security may be subject to the employment policies of the respective partners. Whatever the case, to avoid future misunderstanding, employees need to be told in advance where the partners stand on this issue.

Labor–Management Relations
Before entering into an international alliance, it is important to understand the characteristics of each partner's industrial relations system. For example, contrast the following two situations: In the first, a German firm (where roughly 40 percent of the workforce is represented by unions domestically) forms an alliance with a Swedish firm (where roughly 93 percent of the workforce is represented by a union domestically). Both partners are quite sympathetic to the desires of the workers to be represented collectively and for their workers to be associated with national or international unions.

In a second situation, a Japanese firm (whose U.S. plant is non-unionized) forms an alliance with a U.S. company whose unionized workers are members of a federation of trade unions. This was the case in two of the sample companies in this study. When asked for their most important concern about their partnership, the plant managers involved cited the fact that their alliance called for two companies with different industrial relations systems to work together.

Obviously, the industrial relations issues that managers must address in these two situations (e.g., the relative amount of influence of the host-country government on relations between managers of the alliance and trade unions, the tenor of relations between management and labor in the alliance, and the degree of voluntary or mandatory employee participation in the management of the company) are quite different. Understanding the implications of, and agreeing to abide by, a particular type of industrial relations system before consummating an international alliance is critically important.

Some other industrial relations issues that need to be addressed in advance, regardless of union or non-union status, include the handling of employee grievances, the development of consistent policies for administering discipline, and policies regarding the disclosure of trade secrets.

Lessons Learned

The fact that international cooperative ventures represent an "alliance of people" is often overlooked or ignored. Unfortunately, HRM or people-related issues in international cooperative ventures are all too often addressed only after the venture had already been formed. Financial issues are addressed early on, but HRM issues tend to be postponed—perhaps because of management's belief that these can be worked out later, or perhaps in an effort to maintain secrecy in negotiating and planning such ventures. (The fewer people that have to be included on both sides, the better.)

As the examples in this paper illustrate, addressing HRM issues later on is a mistake. In fact, company experiences suggest the following checklist of lessons learned.

1. *Blending of cultures and management styles.* The GMF Robotics alliance showed that such a fusion is possible if both partners are willing to spend time building trust, trying to understand each other's operations, and accommodating each other's demands during a venture's formative stages. Alternatively, prospective partners may spend time "dating"—that is, working together on small projects before formalizing an alliance.

2. *Job Design.* It is understandable for each partner in an international alliance to believe that its own technology, production, or service delivery methods are superior to its counterpart's, and therefore to emphasize its own approach to job design. However, the experience of NUMMI indicates that success can be achieved more rapidly if both partners are willing to listen to each other's ideas first, thereby capitalizing on each other's strengths and proving once again that the whole is greater than the sum of its parts.

3. *Recruitment and staffing policies.* Instead of establishing such policies before forming an alliance, we found that partners in international alliances seem to expect that such policies will evolve after the alliance is

established. This often leads to misunderstandings and conflict among the partners. To avoid such problems, staffing policies might be specified either by contract or by "house rules" that give managers of the alliance broad guidelines and increased flexibility.

4. *Orientation and training of new hires and current employees of international alliances.* Study after study confirms the fact that these issues are critically important to long-term success. That is, managers in international alliances should be at least as concerned with preparing new employees to deal with the social context of their jobs and to cope with the insecurities of a new learning situation as with developing the technical skills employees need to work effectively.

5. *Performance appraisal.* As the LaPine-Kyocera alliance showed, performance appraisal problems are less likely to occur to the extent that the partners clarify issues of purpose and objectives, allow a liberal time frame in which to achieve results, and maintain flexibility in the appraisal system as market and environmental demands change.

6. *Compensation and benefits.* In alliances that require considerable interaction among employees from different partners, it is important to establish a uniform policy with respect to compensation and benefits. Choice is still possible—as Nomura's "contract" versus "non-contract" systems showed. A major objective is to avoid feelings of inequity by one partner's lower-paid employees who are doing the same jobs as the other partner's higher-paid employees.

7. *Careers.* Managers of international alliances need to take steps to avoid "dead ending" employees and to open up more management positions for local managers. Further, they need to clarify employees' expectations regarding job security in the event that the alliance fails.

8. *Labor–management relations.* Often partners in international alliances come from different industrial relations systems. At the outset of an international alliance it is important to understand and agree to meet the terms and conditions of the industrial relations systems in question.

The Wall Street Journal, August 4, 1992

Companies Use Cross-Cultural Training to Help Their Employees Adjust Abroad*

Joann S. Lublin

Dale Pilger, General Motors Corp.'s new managing director for Kenya, wonders if he can keep his Kenyan employees from interrupting his paper work by raising his index finger.

"The finger itself will offend," warns Noah Midamba, a Kenyan. He urges that Mr. Pilger instead greet a worker with an effusive welcome, offer a chair and request that he wait. It can be even trickier to fire a Kenyan, Mr. Midamba says. The government asked one German auto executive to leave Kenya after he dismissed a man— whose brother was the East African country's vice president.

Mr. Pilger, his adventurous wife and their two teenagers, miserable about moving, have come to a Rocky Mountain college town for three days of cross-cultural training. The Cortland, Ohio family learns to cope with being strangers in a strange land as consultants Moran, Stahl & Boyer International give them a crash immersion in African political history, business practices, social customs and nonverbal gestures. The training enables managers to grasp cultural differences and handle culture-shock symptoms such as self-pity.

Cross-cultural training is on the rise everywhere because more global-minded corporations moving fast-track executives overseas want to curb the cost of failed expatriate stints. "Probably between $2 billion and $2.5 billion a year is lost from failed assignments," says J. Stewart Black, an associate professor of business administration at Dartmouth's Tuck School. Nearly half of major U.S. companies now give executives cross-cultural training before foreign transfers, compared with about 10% a decade ago, consultants estimate.

The number of cultural-training providers also is growing. Berlitz International Inc. will set up a cross-cultural division this year, officials say, because a recent survey of 200 corporate clients found they needed cultural orientation more than its foreign-language training.

American businesses "are dumb if they don't use cross-cultural training," says Richard B. Jackson, personnel vice president of Reynolds Metals Co.'s overseas arm. The big aluminum maker's high rate of expatriate burnout fell "to almost zero," Mr. Jackson notes, after the company began using cross-cultural training in the late 1970s. Other concerns train U.S.-based executives as well because their global duties often take them abroad.

Growing Criticism

But as cross-cultural training gains popularity, it attracts growing criticism. A lot of the training is garbage, argues Robert Bontempo, assistant professor of international business at Columbia University. Even customized family training offered by companies like Prudential Insurance Co. of America's Moran Stahl—which typically costs $6,000 for three days—hasn't been scientifically tested. "They charge a huge amount of money, and there's no evidence that these firms do any good" in lowering foreign-transfer flops, Prof. Bontempo contends.

"You don't need research" to prove that cross-cultural training works because so much money has been wasted on failed overseas assignments, counters Gary Wederspahn, director of design and development at Moran Stahl.

General Motors agrees. Despite massive cost cutting lately, the auto giant still spends nearly $500,000 a year on cross-cultural training for about 150 Americans and their families headed abroad. "We think this substantially contributes to the low [premature] return rate" of less than 1% among GM expatriates, says Richard Rachner, GM general director of international personnel. That compares with a 25% rate at concerns that don't properly select and coach expatriates, he adds.

The Pilgers' experience reveals the benefits and drawbacks of such training. Mr. Pilger, a 38-year-old engineer employed by GM for 20 years, sought an overseas post but never lived abroad before. He finds the sessions "worthwhile" in readying him to run a vehicle-assembly plant that is 51% owned by Kenya's government. But he finds the training "horribly empty. . . in helping us prepare for the personal side of the move."

Scant Knowledge

Dale and Nancy Pilger have just spent a week in Nairobi. But the executive's scant knowledge of Africa becomes clear when trainer Jackson Wolfe, a former Peace Corps official, mentions Nigeria. "Is that where Idi Amin was from?" Mr. Pilger asks. The dictator ruled Uganda. With a sheepish smile, Mr. Pilger admits: "We don't know a lot about the world."

The couple's instructors don't always know everything about preparing expatriates for Kenyan culture, either. Mr. Midamba, an adjunct international-relations professor at Kent State University and son of a Kenyan political leader, concedes that he neglected to caution Mr. Pilger's predecessor against holding business dinners at Nairobi restaurants.

As a result, the American manager "got his key people to the restaurant and expected their wives to be there," Mr. Midamba recalls. But "the wives didn't show up." Married women in Kenya view restaurants "as places where you find prostitutes and loose morals," notes Mungai Kimani, another Kenyan trainer.

The blunder partly explains why Mr. Midamba goes to great lengths to teach the Pilgers the art of entertaining at home. Among his tips: Don't be surprised if guests arrive an hour early, an hour late or announce their departure four times.

The Moran Stahl program also zeros in on the family's adjustment (though not to Mr. Pilger's satisfaction). A family's poor adjustment causes more foreign-transfer failures than a manager's work performance. That is the Pilgers' greatest fear because 14-year-old Christy and 16-year-old Eric bitterly oppose the move. The lanky, boyish-looking Mr. Pilger remembers Eric's tearful reaction as: "You'll have to arrest me if you think you're going to take me to Africa."

While distressed by his children's hostility, Mr. Pilger still believes living abroad will be a great growth experience for them. But he says he promised Eric that if "he's miserable" in Kenya, he can return to Ohio for his last year of high school next year.

To ease their adjustment, Christy and Eric receive separate training from their parents. The teens' activities include sampling Indian food (popular in Kenya) as well as learning how to ride Nairobi public buses, speak a little Swahili and juggle, of all things.

By the training's last day, both youngsters grudgingly accept being uprooted from friends, her swim team and his brand-new car. Going to Kenya, "no longer seems like a death sentence," Christy says. Eric mumbles that he may volunteer at a wild-game reserve.

But their usually upbeat mother has become increasingly upset as she hears more about a country troubled by drought, poverty and political unrest—where foreigners live behind walled fortresses. Now, at an international parenting session, she clashes with youth trainer Amy Kaplan over whether her offspring can safely ride Nairobi's public buses, even with Mrs. Pilger initially accompanying them.

"All the advice we've gotten is that it's deadly" to ride buses there, Mrs. Pilger frets. Ms. Kaplan retorts: "It's going to be hard" to let teenagers do their own thing in Kenya, but then they'll be less likely to rebel. The remark fails to quell Mrs. Pilger's fears that she can't handle life abroad.

"I'm going to let a lot of people down if I blow this," she adds, her voice quavering with emotion.

The Pilgers' experience suggests that U.S. managers and their families may need extra training overseas. At Procter & Gamble Co., for instance, cultural familiarization doesn't even begin until expatriates reach a foreign country. "For deep-rooted, subtle concepts, it's more effective" to train people that way, says Dartmouth's Prof. Black. "But it's more effective to do it before" expatriates leave home "than not at all."

The London Observer

More Men Switching Loyalties from Firms to Their Families[*]

Jennifer Veale

Not so long ago they were corporate warriors with little of their beloved company's time to spare on their families.

Now many of Japan's fathers want a change of image. They have fallen out of love with the company as the mutual obligations that guaranteed job security for decades erode. The recession has forced companies to cut overheads, even firing loyal employees.

Japanese men are coming to feel that they owe their employers less and their families more. "I worked at the same company for 20 years," say Tateo Morikawa, a 49-year-old Yokohama resident. "Recently it became clear that I would not rise any further. I asked myself, 'Why should I spend so much time in the office?'"

His predicament reflects a growing feeling among men his age. Once reviled as "deadwood" by wives who despaired of their sloppy domestic habits, many men want to become more than a mere family figurehead.

The renowned Japanese work ethic is as healthy as ever. Workers, especially young men, are still expected to spend most of the day in the office, and diligence and discipline remain the most valuable qualities an employee can demonstrate. In fact, company restructuring caused by the recession has meant even longer hours for many employees. But the Japan emerging from this sobering slump wants to be a "lifestyle superpower" as well as an economic one.

Symptoms of a community discontent—such as "karoshi" or death from overwork, and growing homelessness—have convinced the authorities that a booming economy fraught with social tensions is destined to be short-lived.

---

[*]Reprinted from the *London Observer* as it appeared in *The Vancouver Sun*, July 17, 1993, p. A9.

A couple of hours spent watching Japanese television illustrates the gradual attitude change. In the '80s, advertisements lauded the go-ahead worker, chained to his office and setting his face like flint on the road to success. Work was his religion and the company his god.

That species still exists, but the focus is shifting to soft and cuddly images of family life. See dad play Scrabble with daughter, mah jong with son. See dad do the unthinkable—cook for wife!

Many companies are catching on to the trend. Fuji Photo Film, House Food International and Sanyo Electric have aired commercials depicting caring fathers who are not afraid to make mistakes—a very un-Japanese trait. The airwaves are replete with sensitive new-age guys.

Flip through comic books (a national obsession) or radio stations and the message is the same. Father figures in newer comics are "Cosby Show" prototypes, lovable bumblers with names like My Home Papa and Trendy Papa.

Two tragic deaths have underscored for many Japanese the importance of the devoted family man. The grief of Takehito Nakata, whose United Nations volunteer son was killed in Cambodia this year, moved the nation. Rather than launching bitter recriminations, he quit his job to devote himself to international volunteer work.

"Nakata showed masculine love for his son," media commentator Itsuo Kohama says. "He is a good example of the saying that knowing what is right without doing it betrays your cowardice."

Masaichi Hattori's son Yoshihiro, an exchange student, was shot dead by a Louisiana man when he entered the wrong house in search of a Halloween party. Masaichi's grief was compounded by the acquittal of his son's killer. A stunned Masaichi accepted the verdict and launched a gun-control program in the United States. He recently set up a fund to bring American students to study in gun-free Japan.

◆

Asia's Wealth

Peter Engardio, with Joyce Barnathan and William Glasgall

To fathom the magnitude of the changes sweeping East Asia, drop by the antique-filled suite Nanoo G. Pamnani occupies on the 24th floor of a Singapore skyscraper. In the late 1960s, Pamnani began his carer with Citibank in a region rocked by turmoil. War raged across Indochina. Destitute China was paralyzed by the mass terror of the Cultural Revolution. Malaysia and Indonesia were torn by ethnic bloodshed.

Twenty-five years later, the urbane, Pakistan-born art connoisseur directs Citi's booming Asian private-banking business, which won't handle accounts smaller than $1 million. His list of clients illustrates just how many fortunes are being made: There are ethnic Chinese tycoons from Southeast Asia who control multibillion-dollar real estate empires, Hong Kong small factory owners who have made fortunes exporting, and even Taiwanese taxi drivers who hit it big in the stock market. In the past four years, the number of Pamnani's Asian clients has quadrupled, to 8,000. "The market of millionaires is growing incredibly fast," Pamnani marvels.

Wealth. To most Asians just one generation ago, it meant moving to the U.S.—or selling natural resources to Japan. But now, East Asia is generating its own wealth on a speed and scale that probably is without historical precedent. The number of non-Japanese Asian multimillionaires is expected to double to 800,000 by 1996. Years of export surpluses, combined with high savings rates and prudent fiscal policies, have left East Asian governments with foreign reserves of $250 billion, triple those of Japan. An additional $600 billion in cash reserves is on the balance sheets of the region's corporations. And many of these companies are still growing exponentially. "In 10 years," says Hong-Kong Bank corporate-lending executive Clinton Marshall, "you will be looking at some truly gigantic companies."

Under way is nothing less than a massive shift in the global economic balance of power, as the economies of East Asia catch up with Japan and the West. The emerging powerhouse combines Hong Kong, Taiwan, and China with the blossoming economies of Southeast Asia—whose business classes are dominated by ethnic Chinese. Throw in South Korea, and gross domestic product totals $2 trillion. East Asia will surpass Japan in purchasing power within a decade. And with savings increasing $550 billion annually, it is becoming the world's biggest source of liquid capital. "In Asia," says Olarn Chaipravat, chief executive of Siam Commercial Bank, "money is everywhere."

Sudden Impact   East Asia's rise presents both opportunities and challenges to the West. There are new markets for everything from Mercedes-Benz cars to Motorola mobile phones to Fidelity mutual funds. But the days when Asians depended almost exclusively on Western capital are over. Business leaders who have finally figured out Japan's *keiretsu* now need to understand a distinctively Chinese model, where tycoons cut megadeals in a flash and heads of state wheel and deal like CEOs. Western politicians must learn to respond to the changes, too. President Bill Clinton has taken an important step with the summit of Asia-Pacific leaders that took place in Seattle on Nov. 20. [1993]

The political ramifications within Asia are likely to be just as profound. Authoritarian rulers from Beijing to Jakarta believe that an increasingly wealthy population will gladly forgo personal liberties, but the new middle classes have already helped oust autocrats in Taiwan, Thailand, and South Korea. The tycoons' penchant for insider dealing in secretive networks also will be challenged as middle classes and modern capital markets demand greater transparency.

What makes East Asia's financial scene so remarkable is that the leap from rags to riches came so suddenly. To find the nearest precedent, you need to rewind U.S. history 100 years to the days before strong unions, securities watchdogs, and antitrust laws. The analogy isn't lost on Hong Kong's Gordon Y.S. Wu, the chief of property and infrastructure for giant Hopewell Holdings Ltd. The Princeton University-educated Wu likens Asia's leading tycoons to the "robber barons" who built America's first railroad, banking, and steel empires.

The daunting challenge for Asians is to learn to manage this money. Many of Asia's streets aren't even paved with concrete yet, much less gold. The slums of Jakarta and Bangkok make some U.S. inner cities appear middle-class. For all of Asia's immediate riches, its future capital needs will be enormous. Over the next decade the region must mobilize more than $1 trillion for highways, telephone lines, and power plants. Billions more are needed to build capital-intensive industries such as microelectronics, steel, and petrochemicals.

All of this is required if Asia is to complete the progression from cheap-labor sweatshops to advanced industrialized status. China's capital needs alone are so vast, says National Taiwan University economist Chi Schive, "that it could become a black hole" sucking in the region's wealth. So East Asia must create financial and capital markets that allow it to funnel its wealth into building a brighter future.

"Silent Revolution" Wall Street is now elbowing its way in on Asia's opportunities. U.S. insurance, pension, and mutual funds are eager for the rich returns offered by investing in Asian power plants, telephone systems, and property developments. Morgan Stanley, Goldman Sachs, and GE Capital, among others, are amassing direct-investment war chests and underwriting foreign bond offerings, stealing a march on their plodding Japanese rivals.

But foreigners are hardly critical to Asia's success. That's because Asians are fast accumulating enough wealth to finance most of their development needs internally. While governments control some of this wealth, far more is in private hands. Most passes through a type of financial structure outsiders have yet to comprehend fully. The system revolves around ethnic Chinese power brokers, who depend on their dealmaking acumen and extensive personal ties to regional leaders. As a result, their business groups are "like giant LBO funds," says John S. Wadsworth Jr., managing director of Morgan Stanley Asia Ltd. While extraordinarily powerful, the network has no formal structure. "It has no head, no organization, no politics, no boundaries," says Peter Kwong-ching Woo, chairman of Hong Kong-based Wharf (Holdings) Ltd.

Billionaires are just part of the picture. Indeed, wealth is being created across a large base. At the lowest rung, in what the World Bank calls a "silent revolution," the percentage of people living below the poverty line has decreased from 33% to 10%, even though the region's population has ballooned by 40% since 1970. Moreover, the ranks of the middle class are soaring. The number of non-Japanese Asian households earning $18,000 annually is expected to increase fourfold to 75 million by the year 2000.

One danger is that much of this wealth will be frittered away on real estate boondoggles or lost to capital flight. Governments with long histories of corruption also may mismanage their riches. While "red capitalists" in South China cruise in Lexuses and impress each other by smashing $200 bottles of cognac at the banquet table, millions of peasants still live in poverty. Acute problems persist even in the richest capitals, as the monstrous traffic snarls of Taipei and Bangkok testify. And though regional banks are among the world's most solid, entrepreneurs have difficulty getting loans.

Yet Asians are moving forward. To channel savings, economic planners are building securities exchanges, bond markets, banking systems, and pension systems. "The development of capital markets will be as important as physical infrastructure," says Howard Pollack, managing director of Lehman Brothers Asia Ltd's Hong Kong office, which has pioneered the region's "dragon bond" market of dollar-based corporate bonds.

Making the great leap into high finance is now a top priority of Beijing's reformers. China's banks, which have some $2.3 trillion in deposits, still have loan policies dictated by the government, which makes them redirect savings into unprofitable state industries. With few legal financial instruments to park cash other than low-yielding savings deposits and bonds, local governments and state companies have stashed their loot in real estate or siphoned it offshore into shadowy Hong Kong companies.

Object Lessons   Fearing economic problems that could spark social unrest, the Communist Party in mid-November approved dramatic reforms. Last summer, economic czar Zhu Rongji launched measures to stop wasteful lending. Now, the banking system is undergoing an overhaul that will enable banks to lend based on commercial rather than political criteria. The fledgling stock exchanges, where market capitalization has grown from nothing to $32 billion in two years, are getting a Western-style regulatory system and hundreds of new listings. China also is introducing a secondary bond market and mutual funds. As it dumps central planning, Beijing can pick ideas from the many successful economic models in the region. From Korea, it is learning how to form giant heavy industrial combines. From Hong Kong, it is learning the art of the deal. But for managing wealth, it is looking at Singapore.

That's not a bad idea. With it's sleek subway, dazzling telecommunications networks, and manicured boulevards, the city-state of 2.3 million is a technocrat's dream world. It has foreign reserves of at least $46 billion and many more billions in the balance sheets of state-controlled blue chips such as Singapore Airlines Ltd. and Singapore Telecom. The state finances lavish technology parks and even a $330 million silicon-wafer fabrication joint venture with Texas Instruments Inc. And rather than China's "Iron Rice Bowl" of cradle-to-grave care for workers, Singapore has a $31 billion compulsory savings program that helps Singaporeans buy their own homes and collect big benefits when they reach 55.

No Chewing Gum   Singapore is hardly a paradise. Its technocratic elite limits freedom of speech and intrudes heavily into the lives of citizens, banning everything from' chewing gum to *Cosmopolitan* magazine. Still, the biggest dilemma for Singapore is how to invest its riches. The government can't release too much of its stash into Singapore's economy without causing massive inflation. So it is looking at its neighbors. Together with Indonesia's Salim Group, the government is pouring $3 billion into industrial parks and tourism complexes in Indonesia. Singapore is also charging into China. Led by big government-linked companies such as Temasek Holdings and Keppel Corp., it has formed a $200 million consortium to develop a 27-square-mile site in Suzhou, 50 miles from Shanghai, into an industrial zone. If Suzhou succeeds, says Finance Minister Richard Hu, "we could replicate it elsewhere in China and even Vietnam."

Malaysia, an ethnic hodge-podge of Muslims, Chinese, and Indians, is also proving what can be done through wise management of its wealth. To conquer its jungles and tie together a far-flung nation, Malaysia requires massive capital for power plants, expressways, and airports. But it has minimal foreign debt, a balanced budget, and is cutting taxes. The key: an aggressive but orderly privatization drive, some of the most modern bond and equity markets in the region, and a prudently managed $22 billion fund that channels workers' savings into infrastructure.

Such success makes other Tigers envious. Taiwan, for example, is in danger of bungling the management of its considerable wealth. The country has seen its savings rate, which peaked at 40% of GDP in the mid-1980s, fall to 27%. The government has also fallen short of its ambitious goal of spending some $200 billion on everything from subways to nuclear plants over the next decade. Central Bank Governor Samuel Shieh flares up at suggestions that he tap into Taiwan's $80 billion in foreign reserves, fearing the excess liquidity would fuel inflation. "We have enough savings to finance the entire plan," he snaps. "The question is how you get at it."

Taiwan's authoritarian legacy also hinders the management of its wealth. While the government has been a regional leader in allowing more democracy, it controls the biggest banks, which it uses to reward political allies. That means banks have no incentive to lend to a promising computer maker over a well-connected property developer. "If we privatized the government banks, this problem would disappear," admits Chen Chi-Chu, senior vice-president of state-owned International Commercial Bank of China.

Hong Kong's wide-open financial markets are the extreme opposite of those in Singapore or Taiwan, and that has made it a thriving center of Chinese capitalism. Hong Kong is where red capitalists, property barons, and Chinese big wheels from Southeast Asia intermingle to form Asia's greatest concentration of wealth. The enclave of 6 million has 1,200 Rolls Royces and property prices fast approaching Tokyo levels. Counting government and corporate reserves, investment property, savings, and consumers' stock holdings, Citibank figures that $1 trillion in investable capital is sitting in the tiny British colony.

Hong Kong may look dangerously like Japan's "bubble economy" of the late 1980s. But unless severe political upheaval erupts in China, Hong Kong's corporate sector probably won't suffer a major downturn. Its banks have some of the most solid capital ratios in the world, averaging 6% to 9%. And its developers, airlines, and utilities have remarkably little debt, typically no more than 20% of equity. "Almost to a fault, they have become debt-adverse," says John M. Mulcahy, Hong Kong-based managing director of UBS Securities Ltd.

There is, of course, the fear that China will become a Waterloo for Asia's dealmakers, deflating East Asian growth. Since Beijing opened China's property and retail sectors to foreigners last year, city after cash-starved city has been giving overseas Chinese the first crack. So tycoons from Hong Kong, Taiwan, and elsewhere are staking claims to factories, infrastructure projects, and choice real estate.

High Stakes   Chinese officials are so eager for cash that they offer sweeteners—such as tax holidays and easy bank loans. Overall, Hong Kong-based investors have signed letters of intent for more than $100 billion in mainland projects in the past three years.

But what makes this mad dash less dangerous than it might seem is that very few investors are committing more than 10% of their fortunes in China. Take Wharf Holdings' master plan for the sooty industrial city of Wuhan in central China. Wharf wants to develop a container-shipping terminal, turn 10 square miles of countryside into an industrial park, and liven up the drab downtown with an office tower. But Wharf's actual outlay has only been about $1.5 million. It plans to build just 2 of the 36 berths that Wuhan wants. The rest, including the industrial parks, will have to wait until there is proven demand. Wuhan officials want Wharf to move faster, but Wharf Chairman Peter Woo is determined not to get in over his head. "Our resources aren't unlimited," he says.

On the upside, pioneers such as Wharf could hit a bonanza if even a fraction of their plans pan out. There is an acute shortage of office and residential space in China's biggest cities, which are growing at a 20% annual clip and are attracting the world's biggest multinationals. Merrill Lynch, GE Capital, and others are courting the big dealmakers to get a piece of the action.

When it comes to bringing in partners, however, the most lucrative stakes will stay within the ethnic Chinese network. Tycoons such as Salim Group's Liem Sioe Liong, Kerry's Robert Kuok, and Henderson Land's Lee Shau-kee have long been moving funds around the region. And they prefer to dive in and out of properties and corporate takeover targets.

A $7 Billion Player   Nobody plays the game much better than Li Ka-shing, who is estimated by bankers to be worth up to $7 billion. Five years ago, his main vehicles, the $2.7 billion Hutchison Whampoa Ltd and property giant Cheung Kong Holdings Ltd., were diversifying in the West. After losing big on British telecoms and Canada's Husky Oil Ltd., Li expanded his network to include powerful allies in the mainland, teaming up with Beijing-controlled Citic Pacific, Guangzhou International Trust & Investment Corp., state-run steelmaker Shougang Corp., and even Deng Zhifang, the son of China's senior leader Deng Xiaoping. Recently, Li has helped Shougang take over Hong Kong's Tung Wing Steel, Santai Manufacturing, and Kader International.

The concentration of so much financial firepower in so few hands may seem threatening, especially given the tycoons' reliance on secrecy and back-channel dealings. "But the networks also serve an important function," says University of Hong Kong management professor S. Gordon Redding, a leading authority on the overseas Chinese. In a region where capital markets are primitive, financial disclosure is thin, and the rule of law is often weak, interpersonal networks are critical for moving information and capital quickly.

To get into the loop, insiders spend years cultivating politicians and building trust. When they learn of an opportunity, they give friends first crack. Financing for a $100 million property deal can be arranged in days, with personal trust taking precedence over due diligence. One needn't be Chinese to be a player. "But to be a part of it," says Wharf's Woo, "you have to bring something to the table and understand how deals are done here."

The ultimate manifestation of this Chinese network is New China Hongkong Group, founded earlier this year with $65 million in capital. Its partners are the biggest names in China investments, including, among others, Li, Riady, the Singapore government, Taiwan International Securities, and 20 mainland companies and ministries.

Lining up the investors was easy, says founder T.T. Tsui, who sports a diamond-studded gold watch as he relaxes amid the rare Chinese porcelains and 8th-century terra-cotta figurines lining his office. "Nobody minds having a little more *guanxi*"—connections, that is. Tsui's *guanxi* already has brought a flurry of deals, including a military jeep factory, an $800 million highway project, and a joint venture with the city of Beijing to refurbish and market 20 pre-Communist estates.

While New China Hongkong does include token foreigners such as Goldman Sachs, such organizations suggest to some outsiders that the loosely knit Chinese business bloc will start to take institutional form and lock out foreigners. Yet most analysts think that's unlikely. For one thing, Chinese tycoons may tie up when particular deals are in their interests. But unlike the Japanese, they are generally too headstrong and individualistic for serious collective efforts. Some observers argue that in a decade or two, mainland officials won't need the overseas Chinese middlemen. "The [mainland] Chinese are going to say: 'Why did we give away half our city to them?'" says Francis Yeoh Sock Ping, chairman of Malaysian construction company YTL Corp.

Raw Power   Indeed, that is a question much of Asia may ask once the giddiness of sudden riches fades into the sober realities of building advanced industrial societies. To the future middle-class residents of Guangzhou and Shanghai, the tycoons who built fabulous fortunes through political favors and inside dealing will look more and more like robber barons from another era. Men like Li Ka-shing are not the patient capitalists who made the heavy investments in R&D that produced Sony, Motorola, or Siemens. The secretive old-boy networks won't propel Asia on to the next economic level.

The great hope is that the younger generation of cosmopolitan, Western-trained executives will come to the fore to build world-class manufacturing conglomerates. In keeping with Asia's postwar economic model, governments will be involved in kick-starting strategic industries that could grow into East Asia's General Motors Corp. or Intel Corp. But government alone won't be enough. Asia needs maverick visionaries—and financial institutions that think long term—to make it globally competitive. It may not be easy. Witness Taiwan's humiliating failure in the past two years to get its corporate elite to make the island a world player in aerospace by agreeing to mergers with McDonnell Douglas Corp. or British Aerospace PLC.

Thus, the most critical question facing the region is how it manages its raw financial power. Sticking to some of the models that got them this far, technocrats will continue to deploy their war chests of reserves into R&D consortiums, seed capital for industries, and even strategic alliances with Western high-tech giants. They will continue with prudent financial management techniques. But they will also have to make sure that their financial systems mature sufficiently to allow Asia's wealth to move out beyond a narrow network of Chinese tycoons and their friends in government. Success is by no means assured for all Asians. A corrupt oligarchy reduced the Philippines from one of the region's richest nations 30 years ago to one of the poorest today. Now China, in particular, is at a crossroads. Many Communist Party officials prefer to enrich themselves in secret by dealing with the overseas Chinese networks. Beijing's reformers, on the other hand, want the wealth to be in the hands of modern capital markets.

Asia's winners will be those countries that harness the billions generated by shopkeepers, small manufacturers, and white-collar workers, making them the driving force of development. That will require more efficient and transparent capital markets that funnel wealth to projects and ideas that build a future. The Asians who master the challenge of managing their wealth will "have embarked on a permanent path for development," says Kwok Kwok-Chuen, chief economist at Standard Chartered Bank in Hong Kong. "And development tends to feed on itself." That will change the face of Asia and the world.

◆

Your New Global Work Force*

Brian O'Reilly

Jobs are fast moving abroad, propelled by companies seeking to tap a vast new supply of skilled labor around the world. The big question: Are there too many workers?

A fundamental shift is under way in how and where the world's work gets done— with potentially ominous consequences for wealthy, industrialized nations. The key to this change: the emergence of a truly global labor force, talented and capable of accomplishing just about anything, anywhere. Says Larry Irving, an executive of Daniel Industries who moved from Houston to run a factory that his company bought in eastern Germany: "The average American doesn't realize that there is a truly competitive work force out there that is vying for [his or her] job. The rest of the world is catching up."

Just what is driving U.S. companies—and some from Europe and Japan—to locate that new plant not in Waltham, Massachusetts, or Tucson, Arizona, but instead in Bangalore, India, where 3M makes tapes, chemicals, and electrical parts, or Guadalajara, Mexico, where Hewlett-Packard assembles computers and designs computer memory boards? It isn't only the search for cheap labor. Corporations also want to establish sophisticated manufacturing and service operations in markets that promise the most growth, often emerging nations. The migration of jobs to new lands isn't a straightforward one-for-one proposition either, one job gained there for every one lost to an industrialized country. New technology and the continuing drive for higher productivity push companies to build in undeveloped countries plants and offices that require only a fraction of the manpower that used to be needed in factories back home. In part because of this, the statistics on the number of foreign workers employed by multinational companies don't adequately reflect the shift of work abroad.

It is far from clear what form the new world of work will ultimately take. But there's already plenty to be concerned about, and excited by, in the transition taking place.

What happens when the corporate drive for greater efficiency collides with the expansion of the supply of labor available around the globe? Will there be enough jobs to go around? Some experts aren't so sure. Says Percy Barnevik, CEO of ABB Asea Brown Boveri, the $29-billion-a-year Swiss-Swedish builder of transporation and electric generation systems: "It is a fallacy to think that industry will increase employment overall in the Western world, at least in our industry."

Barnevik forsees "a massive move from the Western world. We already have 25,000 employees in former communist countries. They will do the job that was done in Western Europe before." More jobs will shift to Asia, he says. ABB, which employed only 100 workers in Thailand in 1980, has 2,000 there now, and will have more than 7,000 by the end of the century. Put it all together, and Barnevik's forecast borders on the apocalyptic: "Western European and American employment will just shrink and shrink in an orderly way. Like farming at the turn of the century."

A. Gary Shilling, an economist in Springfield, New Jersey, predicts the overhang of workers will hold down wages all over the developed world. "Four years ago people were talking about a shortage of labor" in the U.S., he says. "But with the push for productivity in the West and Japan, and the rise of the newly industrialized countries and Mexico and Indonesia, we will have a surplus." Technology and capital move easily around the world, he observes, and the only things likely to stay put are locally produced services, like haircutting. "Unless you have labor that is uniquely suited to what you're doing, there is no assurance the entire process won't move to another place."

The trend unfolding is likely to be more complex, uneven, and subtle than Shilling and Barnevik paint it. Interviews with executives around the globe reveal that increasingly sophisticated work is indeed being parceled out to faraway nations, whose labor forces are exceedingly capable. Says a top executive at

Siemens, the giant German industrial and electronics company: "Thirty years ago they could barely spell 'steam turbine' in India. Now we are building the biggest ones in the world there."

The move toward a global work force takes many forms and consists of far more than a stampede to backward low-wage countries. For example, American direct foreign investment still appears to be creating jobs at factories and operations in high-wage countries, primarily Canada and Europe. In 1990, the latest year for which U.S. Commerce Department data are available, American companies employed 2.8 million people in Western Europe, up 4% from the previous year. That was a bigger jump than the 2% rise, to 1.5 million, in Asian workers they employed, or a similar 2% increase in Latin American employees, to 1.3 million. The explanation, in part, is that up until now most direct foreign investment has been aimed at expanding a company's presence in relatively affluent markets.

When work does move to less developed lands, it's by no means automatic that the shift will bring Western levels of employment and prosperity to new host countries. Martin Anderson, a vice president specializing in global manufacturing for the Gemini Consulting firm in Morristown, New Jersey, notes that new factories abroad, even in low-wage countries, tend to be far more labor efficient than their counterparts in the company's home country. That's one reason why counting noses is not a good guide to the value of goods and services produced offshore. "Some of the most Japanese-looking American plants are going up in Brazil," he observes. Not only is the number of blue-collar workers reduced, says Anderson, but staff and managerial employees are as well. Says David Hewitt, another consultant at Gemini: "If companies reduce one million jobs at home through reengineering their work, they may add 100,000 overseas."

The other reason figures on foreign employment don't fully reflect the dispersal of work abroad: Unlike 10 or 15 years ago when companies were more vertically integrated, factories abroad [today] owned by Americans, Europeans, and Japanese are increasingly likely to outsource—to contract for parts and labor from independent local suppliers. Outsourcing requires no bricks-and-motar investment, nor does it add to the employment tallies of the corporation buying the goods or services. Subramanian Rangan, a doctoral student in political economy at Harvard who has studied the phenomenon, says outsourcing is difficult to measure but already large enough to amount to "new channels of trade." Anderson calculates that at least half of the value of goods shipped from American-owned electronics factories abroad was actually added at independently owned plants.

How difficult is it to find so-called sourcers abroad? No trouble at all in some industries. Charles Komar, president of a big clothing company in New York that bears his name, says agents for foreign factories prowl through department stores studying the labels in clothing. "I get calls all the time from people saying they know of a factory in Turkey that can sew the clothes for less than I'm paying now."

Janet Palmer, a professor at New York City's Lehman College specializing in the movement of office work abroad, was called by a consultant from California looking for a cheap place to have text and numbers typed into a computer. She told him of typing mills in the Philippines that would do it for 50 cents per 10,000 characters—approximately five pages, double spaced. A few days later the man called back and announced he had found an outfit in China charging only 20 cents.

Those foreign sourcers are becoming increasingly capable. An example: For years, Ron Ahlers was an industrial designer for J.C. Penney. His job included designing the control panels on the private-label microwave ovens that Penney bought from Samsung Group in Korea to make them easy to use and consistent across several models. One year a while back, when Samsung engineers came to New York to see Ahler's work, they were embarrassed by how much better his designs were than the ones they created for their own brand-name appliances. Ahlers and his colleagues were astonished when one of them said, "The designer will be punished." The proposal from Korea in the next model year was much better. Penney, in fact, soon began shifting microwave design to Samsung. Eventually the U.S. company shut down its entire in-house design office.

Visits to the global labor force in places like Eastern Europe, India, and Jamaica reveal just how ready these folks are to handle complex work, but they also suggest the looming oversupply of workers. Says Anderson of Gemini Consulting: "Sit in any boardroom and it is absolutely clear that those countries are the kinds of places in competition for capital. Smart companies see they have to keep technology and capital fluid, and move them to where they can make best use of the advances countries achieve."

"Look out the window from any tall building here, and what do you see?" asks Larry Irving, a Texan, in his not-so-tall office in Potsdam, a town a few miles south of Berlin in what used to be East Germany. "Smokestacks!" That's good news for Irving's company, Daniel Industries, which makes meters that measure the flow of natural gas through pipelines. The smokestacks exist because most of Eastern Europe relied on coal for heating and electricity, and Irving figures there will soon be rapid construction of new pipelines throughout the region—and a market for his meters. That new market looks all the more attractive in light of a slowdown in the company's business back home.

Daniel Industries debated setting up a factory in West Germany, but the cost of land, labor, and buildings was too high. Instead, early this year the company bought the assets of Messtechnik Babelsberg, a measuring-instrument firm that was formerly part of a huge state-run conglomerate in East Germany. Irving is dazzled by the skills and training of the East German workers he inherited. They underwent years of demanding apprenticeship, much like West German workers, before entering the work force. Though not up to speed on the use of computerized technology in the factory or the final product, they are so well grounded in engineering that they are easily trained. Not least, they cost about half as much as West German workers.

But foreign investment can't repair all the problems of the former East Germany fast enough to avoid painful dislocations. Three years ago the plant Daniel Industries acquired employed 600 workers. Bringing in better technology, Daniel needed only a fraction of them to make the meters it expects to sell next year. So despite their impressive skills, the company kept only 60 of the 600. Their low wages have not eliminated the need for large and continuing capital improvements to stay competitive. The company is installing a million-dollar computerized machining tool that will do the work of many workers. Across eastern Germany the actual unemployment rate is approaching 40%. "If you include workers who were forced into early retirement or who will be unable to get work when current training programs end, it is that high," says Hermann Wagner, an executive at Treuhandanstalt, the German agency that is privatizing East German factories.

In Hungary, General Electric saw an opportunity to acquire a recognized brand name and existing lines of distribution to west and east European markets when in 1990 it bought Tungsram, a big Budapest light bulb maker. What GE also got in the bargain turned out to be a work force that was one of the best in the world at designing and making advanced lighting fixtures. Hungarian engineers are excellent, says Peter Harper, acting finance director at the Tungsram plant. "Give them a concept and they will go out and develop it." The Budapest plant makes automotive lamps used in cars built in Japan and Europe. A Tungsram factory in Nagykanizsa, Hungary, has become GE's leading center for making advanced compact fluorescent bulbs, with many of the bulbs now going to the United States. Tungsram managers are understandably weak in marketing and financial management, but GE has replicated there the executive training programs it offers in the U.S. "With their analytical background as engineers, they handle it very well," concludes Harper.

But Hungary too is suffering an insufficency of jobs for skilled workers. The official unemployment rate, less than 1% three years ago, is now at 12% and will probably go higher. Tungsram employed 18,600 workers when it was acquired, but a third have been let go.

If you thought your job was immune from globalization because you were in a service business, don't go back to sleep. Recent advances in telecommunications technology and agressive efforts by out-of-the-way nations to boost their educational systems have put wings on everything from insurance work to engineering and computer programming.

In Jamaica, 3,500 people work at office parks connected to the U.S. by satellite dishes. There they make airline reservations and process tickets, handle calls to toll-free numbers, and do data entry. More than 25,000 documents a day, including credit card applications, are scanned electronically in the U.S. and copies transmitted to Montego Bay and Kingston for handling.

More sophisticated service work travels even farther. A New Yorker calling Quarterdeck Office Systems, a California-based software company, with a question about how to work a particular program will often detect a brogue on the answerer's voice. Beginning at four in the morning, New York time, before Californians are at work, the calls are routed to Dublin, where Quarterdeck has its second phone-answering operation. At the same place, scores of multilingual workers take calls from all over Europe. That would have been almost impossible a few years ago, until the Irish government spent billions to upgrade the country's phone system. It did so expressly to turn the island into a telecommunications-based service center.

Quarterdeck originally used Ireland as a center for translating instruction manuals and software for use in Europe. It gradually came to realize the Irish schools were turning out impressive numbers of technically trained graduates.

Increasingly complex software chores were assigned there, and Irish nationals were sent to California to develop original programs. Quarterdeck eventually leased special high-quality telephone lines to link offices in Dublin and Santa Monica, California. Once that connection was in place, it was a small step and little added cost to use the line to reroute customer calls from the U.S.

All across Ireland are dozens of offices devoted to handling complex service work from the U.S. In the village of Fermoy, in County Cork, 150 Metropolitan Life workers analyze medical insurance claims to determine if they are eligible for reimbursement. This is not grunt work. It demands considerable knowledge of medicine, the American medical system, and the insurance business. Met Life's Irish workers also review new policies sold by salesmen in the U.S. for gaps and errors.

Near Limerick, workers at another U.S. insurance company monitor the movement of money in and out of American corporate clients' employee pension accounts to make sure they comply with American laws. The job is far more complex, insists the office manager—who doesn't want to be identified—than mere medical claims processing.

Why do companies relocate work to Ireland? In part because it is cheaper. Operating costs are about 30% to 35% less than in the U.S., says Frank Verminski, head of the Met Life office. And the Irish Development Authority provides generous tax and other incentives worth about a year's pay for each new job created.

Even more important, there appears to be a strong work ethic intensified by a serious shortage of jobs in Ireland. In a nation with only 1.1 million jobs for a population of 3.5 million, Irish men and women consider themselves very fortunate to get a "permanent and pensionable position." The Met Life job requires 18 weeks of training. What is the annual turnover rate in Ireland? "About 1%," says Verminski. "We've lost three people in three years." The manager of the insurance office handling pensions says the work was sent to Ireland in part because workers in Hartford goofed off so much that managers gave up trying to improve productivity there. Now, she says, "we think all the time of what other work could be handled here."

Ireland is one of those countries that belie the notion that educating your work force will solve all your economic problems. It sends over a quarter of its 18-year-olds off to college—far more than most European countries. But as in India and the Philippines, there are political, cultural, and unfathomable reasons why some nations simply fail to create or attract a lot of industry. In such places, college grads too often end up twiddling their thumbs. Smart managers recognize the opportunity such underemployed grads represent: a big and growing supply of hypereducated workers they can tap into. Some workers may even be willing, or eager, to relocate for a job.

Recently a recuiter for Phillips, the Dutch electronics company, marched into Trinity College in Dublin and guaranteed a job in Holland to every computer science graduate of the class.

Don't scoff just because you never heard of the University of Limerick or the Indian Institute of Science in Bangalore. Corporate recruiters have, and they are often impressed. Says Stuart Reeves, senior vice president for Dallas-based EDS, the information technology management company: "If you're hiring college types, there isn't a lot of difference in quality across nations. The difference among college graduates by countries is a lot less than the difference among day laborers and high-schoolers. And there's a lot of pent-up talent out there."

In the mid-eighties, Texas Instruments started setting up an impressive software programming operation in Bangalore, a city of four million in southern India. "We came because of the amount of talent that was available here," says Richard Gall, managing director of TI in India. "We couldn't hire enough software designers in Europe to meet demand, and India was producing more than it could use." And even though TI had to install its own electrical generators and satellite dishes to operate efficiently, wages are low enough that work still gets done for half what it costs in the U.S.

Since TI's arrival, 30 more companies, including Motorola and IBM have set up software programming offices in the area, on a cool plateau west of Madras. The 3M company created a software writing operation in Bangalore several years ago. Based in part on the managerial and technical talent it found, 3M began expanding its manufacturing operations, which are pictured on *Fortune's* cover. Its new plant employs 120 people and makes electrical connectors, chemicals, and pressure-sensitive tapes.

Indian-owned software companies like Infosys, with up to 350 programmers, have sprung up, too, and are performing work for General Electric, among others. Are Indian programmers any good? "They are less expensive, but that's not why we went there," says Albert Hoser, President of Sieman's U.S. subsidiary, whose parent company uses them. "They do some of the best work in the world."

The potential for a further shift of programming to offshore sites is considerable. Software programming accounts for a third or more of the R&D budgets at many high-tech companies. Says Gall: "As designs and software get more complex, the cost advantage of India becomes greater. We've only scratched the surface of what could happen here."

In the face of what some see as a worldwide glut of skilled workers, a few nations actually experience a shortage of labor. But their drive to boost their own prosperity by keeping good jobs at home and shipping lower-wage work to neighbors has the effect of expanding the world labor supply. Japan, for example, uses neighboring countries as a place to offload messy and unpleasant work, such as painting and building construction, that it can afford to disdain.

Singapore is helping to make Asian labor markets more accessible to Western companies. That small country (pop. 2.7 million) has done such a good job of attracting foreign investment that it began running out of semiskilled workers. AT&T decided to make telephones there in 1985. "The operation was successful beyond our wildest dreams," says Jeff Inselmann, vice president for AT&T's manufacturing in Singapore. Hundreds of other companies similarly set up plants in Singapore. The result: Managerial and technical skills flowed rapidly to the city-state, hastened by special tax breaks to companies that establish regional headquarters there.

But foreigners wouldn't keep expanding operations and assigning more complex and high-wage work to Singapore if the place ran out of factory workers. So the government recently persuaded Indonesia to turn a chain of that nation's islands 12 miles across the Strait of Malacca from Singapore into industrial parks. With a population of 181 million underemployed people crammed mostly on the island of Java, Indonesia was happy to cooperate. In less than two years, more than 40 companies, including AT&T, Thomson, and Sumitomo Electric Industries, have established factories in the new parks, chiefly on Batam Island, two-thirds the size of Singapore.

Batam is still mostly raw jungle, criss-crossed by roads carved out of the bright red earth and dotted with factories, dormitories, and radio towers. Labor shortage? AT&T set up its factories and recruited 700 workers from Java and Sumatra in eight months. Their pay is a third the cost of comparable labor in Singapore. Batam's population is expected to grow sixfold, to 700,000, by the end of the decade.

Which leaves Singapore free to do what it does very well: design and manage, often for American and European corporations, and help them make efficient use of local labor and talent. Hewlett-Packard's new portable inkjet printer business is run from Singapore—design, manufacture, and profit responsibility. Singaporeans designed and manufacture two popular pagers for Motorola—one accepts voice messages, the other is the size of a credit card. Originally meant for Asian markets, they have proved so popular that Motorola is beginning to ship them to the U.S.

Though the bulk of Motorola's research is still done in the U.S., the company is expanding the amount of R&D work performed in Southeast Asia. AT&T Bell Laboratories already has researchers there. Should American engineers be panicked that their jobs could go abroad? Says William Terry, executive vice president at Hewlett-Packard: "Panicked? No. America will always be an attractive market. People will want to buy things designed and made in the U.S. But worried? Yes."

What happens when these deep, heretofore inaccessible pools of labor and talent are plumbed by the rest of the industrialized world? That will depend in part on the pace of change. Will wealthy nations and companies have the time and the wits to adapt their skills and organizations to take advantage of the change, perhaps moving on to some new, higher form of economic activity? Will prosperity come fast enough to countries long denied it that workers won't riot in a revolution of rising expectations?

It's clear that there is something almost incomprehensibly vast going on—a realignment perhaps, as Percy Barnevik suggests, on the order of the end of the agricultural era in Western nations, when people moved off the land and into cities for factory work. Says Gemini's Anderson: "It's some sort of shift from the industrial age to an information age. But it's not that simple. People will still need cars and refrigerators, and people will have to make them. I'm not sure I know exactly what it is."

In the face of such change, whatever form it eventually takes, one should keep in mind a few emerging verities: More than ever before, work will flow to the places best equipped to perform it most economically and efficiently. For one thing, the speed and thoroughness of information delivery in the nineties guarantee that managers will now *know* where work can best be done.

To try to restrict the flow of work in the name of saving jobs in this country or that is futile, certainly in the long run. Some nations may succeed at it for a short time, but the cost will be punishing dislocations. It would, for example, be ridiculous and dangerous for the U.S. to try to "stanch the flow of jobs to Mexico," as protectionists might describe it. True, open trade with Mexico will mean that some jobs in the U.S. may disappear, but they wouldn't have lasted long anyway, given the pressures of foreign competition. And with U.S. exports likely to go up substantially, many more jobs will be created—on both sides of the border.

As in the past, countries will do well economically if they concentrate on doing what they do best, pursuing policies that will enhance those industries and services in which they can add the most value. Their particular competence may change over time; consider the example of Singapore. But the prize will consistently go to those countries eager to embrace the new.

Chapter 12

Futures

B usiness organizations are powerful entities in our society and the world beyond. Organizations are major centers of power in all industrialized societies and are thoroughly interwoven with other aspects of human endeavor. Their influence is so strong that they can be said to *make* history. Their agendas shape our personalities, the forms of technologies that develop, the content of dominant ideologies, and the nature of government.[1] The influence of organizations seems likely to expand as the nature of economic activity becomes more global. In fact, one writer has predicted that the modern corporation will rival the nation state in the global affairs of the future.[2] Consequently, the role of managers appears likely to become both more important and more complex as we approach the next century.

Of course, predicting the future is difficult and even an intuitively obvious prediction such as the one made in the previous sentence can be quite erroneous. In thinking about the future, most people find it difficult to do much more than project trends of the present forward in time. At certain points in history, such projections may have been good guides for approaching decades, centuries, and even millennia. In view of the rapid changes in the contemporary world, it seems highly unlikely that such an approach will yield successful predictions beyond a very few years. In fact, things are changing so fundamentally and rapidly that we considered not having a chapter on futures fearing it would become dated too quickly. On the other hand, we thought it important to raise the issues that the following selections raise.

Nevertheless, please keep the following thought in mind when reading them. For the most part, the articles in this section could very easily refer to little more than current trends and concerns projected forward. Looking at the future is a lot like looking at history. Both are always viewed from the current point in time.[3] It is difficult to look either at the past or the future without the nature of today's world having a major impact. Nevertheless, the themes that run through these articles are widely believed to be important for the future. This perceived importance and the strong pressures that seem to be driving these trends make it difficult to imagine many scenarios (with the exception of great political and/or economic upheaval) where these matters would not be of central concern to managers—at least for the next decade.

All of the selections, in one way or another, point to developments that will require organizations to be more flexible. Of course, as organizations become more flexible, people who work in them will have to be more flexible. Further, personal dislocations are likely as organizations merge to form networks and redivide to meet the new contingencies they face. Undoubtedly, the effects of these dislocations will spill over into the character of individuals and human institutions. (The first article, "Building a Learning Organization," describes what the demand for learning by organizations may mean for how managers think and act.) Moreover, as organizations attempt to become more flexible, the rigid, mechanistic structures of the past will increasingly be replaced by those that build on committed people to achieve coordination.

Yet another trend that seems almost certain to continue is the use of technology to manage information and control organizations. It is possible that these systems may allow information to be managed so effectively that a central staff or person (recall the selection on the control system at Mrs. Fields) can combine sophisticated decisions and centralized control with the flexibility of a small, entrepreneurial firm of the distant past. In fact, if the nature of work changes in ways suggested in the final selection, organizations may come to look much like they did a century ago when prior to the industrial revolution, many people worked at home in what has come to be known as cottage industry. Modern information systems present the possibility that many people can once again work at home—telecommuting from their electronic cottages. If this happened on even a moderately large scale, consider some of the implications for our society. Begin by thinking about how many features of the way we live and the systems that have grown to serve us have developed around people working in settings some distance from their homes. (The effects of changes in real estate values alone could constitute a major social revolution.) In such a world, the nature of organizations and what managers do would undoubtedly differ markedly from today's patterns.

It also seems almost certain that business will become increasingly global. Thurow's piece in Chapter 1, highlighted some changes along this line, but exactly what demands this will place on managers is very difficult to know. However, various forms of joint ventures are currently being attempted, and it seems very likely that as business becomes increasingly global, managers will be required to coordinate the efforts of people from diverse cultures within the bounds of an organization. For an excellent book on this subject see Bartlett and Ghoshal.[4] Clearly, at first, these requirements will create significant challenges. Over time, however, one would expect that not only will effective forms for doing this be developed but that homogeneity among people from various countries will increase.

Of course, new types of challenges can be expected to emerge. As we have tried to show throughout, the major constant in managerial reality is the dialectical process created by the tensions produced as organizations attempt to coordinate human efforts by superimposing themselves on individuals. As human societies evolve, so will management. This we know from history. In the future, we expect the reverse direction will take on even greater importance—as the organizations and management evolve, so will human society.

The first of the selections in this chapter, "Building a Learning Organization," treats some general skills/orientations that might be helpful in dealing with what appears to be a major focus for current and future organizations. The second selection, "You Don't Necessarily Have To Be Charismatic. . ." focuses on Anita Roddick's frame-breaking approach to leadership. Her orientation to establish harmony within her organization and between it and its environment may well be an important leadership strategy for the future. The final selection, an interview with Peter Drucker, is much more concrete in trying to predict the exact nature of work and management in the near future.

Among other things, the ways that we have long conceptualized what organizations are and what is involved in managing them appear to be changing. If Peter Drucker is correct, much of our traditional understanding of management will act more as a barrier than an aid to success and understanding in the future. To get a good picture of how rapidly things appear to be changing, we suggest you compare what Peter Drucker says in his interview with George Harris with the first selection in this book on the emergence of management, which was reprinted from a book that Drucker wrote as recently as the early 1970s.

Notes

1. C.E. Lindblom, *Politics and Markets* (New York: Basic Books, 1977).

2. A. Madsen, *Private Power* (New York: Quill, 1982).

3. Donald P. Spence, "Saying Good-Bye to Historical Truth," *Philosophy of the Social Sciences*, Sage Publications.

4. Christopher A. Bartlett and Sumantra Ghoshal, *Managing Across Borders: The Transnational Solution*, HBS Press, 1989.

◆

Building a Learning Organization[*]

David A. Garvin

Continuous improvement programs are sprouting up all over as organizations strive to better themselves and gain an edge. The topic list is long and varied, and sometimes it seems as though a program a month is needed just to keep up. Unfortunately, failed programs far outnumber successes, and improvement rates remain distressingly low. Why? Because most companies have failed to grasp a basic truth. Continuous improvement requires a commitment to learning.

How, after all, can an organization improve without first learning something new? Solving a problem, introducing a product, and reengineering a process all require seeing the world in a new light and acting accordingly. In the absence of learning, companies—and individuals—simply repeat old practices. Change remains cosmetic, and improvements are either fortuitous or short-lived.

A few farsighted executives—Ray Stata of Analog Devices, Gordon Forward of Chaparral Steel, Paul Allaire of Xerox—have recognized the link between learning and continuous improvement and have begun to refocus their companies around it. Scholars too have jumped on the bandwagon, beating the drum for "learning organizations" and "knowledge-creating companies." In rapidly changing businesses like semiconductors and consumer electronics, these ideas are fast taking hold. Yet despite the encouraging signs, the topic in large part remains murky, confused, and difficult to penetrate.

MEANING, MANAGEMENT, AND MEASUREMENT

Scholars are partly to blame. Their discussions of learning organizations have often been reverential and utopian, filled with near mystical terminology. Paradise, they would have you believe, is just around the corner. Peter Senge, who popularized learning organizations in his book *The Fifth Discipline*, described them as places "where people continually expand their capacity to create the results they truly desire, where new and expansive patterns of thinking are nurtured, where collective aspiration is set free, and where people are continually learning how to learn together."[1] To achieve these ends, Senge suggested the use of five "component technologies": systems thinking, personal mastery, mental models, shared vision, and team learning. In a similar spirit, Ikujiro Nonaka characterized knowledge-creating companies as places where "inventing new knowledge is not a specialized activity. . . it is a way of behaving, indeed, a way of being, in which everyone is a knowledge worker."[2] Nonaka suggested that companies use metaphors and organizational redundancy to focus thinking, encourage dialogue, and make tacit, instinctively understood ideas explicit.

---

[*]Reprinted from the *Harvard Business Review,* Jul.–Aug. 1993. Reprinted by permission of the President and Fellows of Harvard College.

Sound idyllic? Absolutely. Desirable? Without question. But does it provide a framework for action? Hardly. The recommendations are far too abstract, and too many questions remain unanswered. How, for example, will managers know when their companies have become learning organizations? What concrete changes in behavior are required? What policies and programs must be in place? How do you get from here to there?

Most discussions of learning organizations finesse these issues. Their focus is high philosophy and grand themes, sweeping metaphors rather than the gritty details of practice. Three critical issues are left unresolved; yet each is essential for effective implementation. First is the question of *meaning*. We need a plausible, well-grounded definition of learning organizations; it must be actionable and easy to apply. Second is the question of *management*. We need clearer guidelines for practice, filled with operational advice rather than high aspirations. And third is the question of *measurement*. We need better tools for assessing an organization's rate and level of learning to ensure that gains have in fact been made.

Once these "three Ms" are addressed, managers will have a firmer foundation for launching learning organizations. Without this groundwork, progress is unlikely, and for the simplest of reasons. For learning to become a meaningful corporate goal, it must first be understood.

WHAT IS A LEARNING ORGANIZATION?

Surprisingly, a clear definition of learning has proved to be elusive over the years. Organizational theorists have studied learning for a long time; the accompanying quotations suggest that there is still considerable disagreement. Most scholars view organizational learning as a process that unfolds over time and link it with knowledge acquisition and improved performance. But they differ on other important matters.

Some, for example, believe that behavioral change is required for learning; others insist that new ways of thinking are enough. Some cite information processing as the mechanism through which learning takes place; others propose shared insights, organizational routines, even memory. And some think that organizational learning is common, while others believe that flawed, self-serving interpretations are the norm.

How can we discern among this cacophony of voices, yet build on earlier insights? As a first step, consider the following definition:

> *A learning organization is an organization skilled at creating, acquiring, and transferring knowledge, and at modifying its behavior to reflect new knowledge and insights.*

This definition begins with a simple truth: new ideas are essential if learning is to take place. Sometimes they are created de novo, through flashes of insight or creativity; at other times they arrive from outside the organization or are communicated by knowledgeable insiders. Whatever their source, these ideas are the trigger for organizational improvement. But they cannot by themselves create a learning organization. *Without accompanying changes in the way that work gets done, only the potential for improvement exists.*

This is a surprisingly stringent test for it rules out a number of obvious candidates for learning organizations. Many universities fail to qualify, as do many consulting firms. Even General Motors, despite its recent efforts to improve performance, is found wanting. All of these organizations have been effective at creating or acquiring new knowledge but notably less successful in applying that knowledge to their own activities. Total quality management, for example, is now taught at many business schools, yet the number using it to guide their own decision making is very small. Organizational consultants advise clients on social dynamics and small-group behavior but are notorious for their own infighting and factionalism. And GM, with a few exceptions (like Saturn and NUMMI), has had little success in revamping its manufacturing practices, even though its managers are experts on lean manufacturing, JIT production, and the requirements for improved quality of work life.

Organizations that do pass the definitional test—Honda, Corning, and General Electric come quickly to mind—have, by contrast, become adept at translating new knowledge into new ways of behaving. These companies actively manage the learning process to ensure that it occurs by design rather than by chance. Distinctive policies and practices are responsible for their success; they form the building blocks of learning organizations.

BUILDING BLOCKS

Learning organizations are skilled at five main activities: systematic problem solving, experimentation with new approaches, learning from their own experience and past history, learning from the experiences and best practices of others, and transferring knowledge quickly and efficiently throughout the organization. Each is accompanied by a distinctive mind-set, tool kit, and pattern of behavior. Many companies practice these activities to some degree. But few are consistently successful because they rely largely on happenstance and isolated examples. By creating systems and processes that support these activities and integrate them into the fabric of daily operations, companies can manage their learning more effectively.

1. Systematic problem solving. This first activity rests heavily on the philosophy and methods of the quality movement. Its underlying ideas, now widely accepted, include:

- Relying on the scientific method, rather than guesswork, for diagnosing problems (what Deming calls the "Plan, Do, Check, Act" cycle, and others refer to as "hypothesis-generating, hypothesis-testing" techniques).
- Insisting on data, rather than assumptions, as background for decision making (what quality practitioners call "fact-based management").
- Using simple statistical tools (histograms, Pareto charts, correlations, cause-and-effect diagrams) to organize data and draw inferences.

Most training programs focus primarily on problem-solving techniques, using exercises and practical examples. These tools are relatively straightforward and easily communicated; the necessary mind-set, however, is more difficult to establish. Accuracy and precision are essential for learning. Employees must therefore become more disciplined in their thinking and more attentive to details. They must continually ask, "How do we know that's true?", recognizing that close enough is not good enough if real learning is to take place. They must push beyond obvious symptoms to assess underlying causes, often collecting evidence when conventional wisdom says it is unnecessary. Otherwise, the organization will remain a prisoner of "gut facts" and sloppy reasoning, and learning will be stifled.

Xerox has mastered this approach on a company-wide scale. In 1983, senior managers launched the company's Leadership Through Quality initiative; since then, all employees have been trained in small-group activities and problem-solving techniques. Today, a six-step process is used for virtually all decisions. Employees are provided with tools in four areas: generating ideas and collecting information (brainstorming, interviewing, surveying); reaching consensus (list reduction, rating forms, weighted voting); analyzing and displaying data (cause-and-effect diagrams, force-field analysis); and planning actions (flow charts, Gantt charts). They then practice these tools during training sessions that last several days. Training is presented in "family groups," members of the same department or business-unit team, and the tools are applied to real problems facing the group. The result of this process has been a common vocabulary and a consistent, companywide approach to problem solving. Once employees have been trained, they are expected to use the techniques at all meetings, and no topic is off-limits. When a high-level group was formed to review Xerox's organizational structure and suggest alternatives, it employed the very same process and tools.[3]

2. Experimentation. This activity involves the systematic searching for and testing of new knowledge. Using the scientific method is essential, and there are obvious parallels to systematic problem solving. But unlike problem solving, experimentation is usually motivated by opportunity and expanding horizons, not by current difficulties. It takes two main forms: ongoing programs and one-of-a-kind demonstration projects.

Ongoing programs normally involve a continuing series of small experiments, designed to produce incremental gains in knowledge. They are the mainstay of most continuous improvement programs and are especially common on the shop floor. Corning, for example, experiments continually with diverse raw materials and new formulations to increase yields and provide better grades of glass. Allegheny Ludlum, a specialty steelmaker, regularly examines new rolling methods and improved technologies to raise productivity and reduce costs.

Successful ongoing programs share several characteristics. First, they work hard to ensure a steady flow of new ideas, even if they must be imported from outside the organization. Chaparral Steel sends its first-line supervisors on sabbaticals around the globe, where they visit academic and industry leaders, develop an understanding of new work practices and technologies, then bring what they've learned back to the company and apply it to daily operations. In large part as a result of these initiatives, Chaparral is one of the five lowest cost steel plants in the world. GE's Impact Program originally sent manufacturing managers to Japan to study factory innovations, such as quality circles and kanban cards, and then apply them in their own organizations; today Europe is the destination, and productivity improvement practices the target. The program is one reason GE has recorded productivity gains averaging nearly 5% over the last four years.

Successful ongoing programs also require an incentive system that favors risk taking. Employees must feel that the benefits of experimentation exceed the costs; otherwise, they will not participate. This creates a difficult challenge for managers, who are trapped between two perilous extremes. They must maintain accountability and control over experiments without stifling creativity by unduly penalizing employees for failures. Allegheny Ludlum has perfected this juggling act: it keeps expensive, high-impact experiments off the scorecard used to evaluate managers but requires prior approvals from four senior vice presidents. The result has been a history of productivity improvements annually averaging 7% to 8%.

Finally, ongoing programs need managers and employees who are trained in the skills required to perform and evaluate experiments. These skills are seldom intuitive and must usually be learned. They cover a broad sweep: statistical methods, like design of experiments, that efficiently compare a large number of alternatives; graphical techniques, like process analysis, that are essential for redesigning work flows; and creativity techniques, like storyboarding and role playing, that keep novel ideas flowing. The most effective training programs are tightly focused and feature a small set of techniques tailored to employees' needs. Training in design of experiments, for example, is useful for manufacturing engineers, while creativity techniques are well suited to development groups.

Demonstration projects are usually larger and more complex than ongoing experiments. They involve holistic, systemwide changes, introduced at a single site, and are often undertaken with the goal of developing new organizational capabilities. Because these projects represent a sharp break from the past, they are usually designed from scratch, using a "clean slate" approach. General Foods' Topeka plant, one of the first high-commitment work systems in this country, was a pioneering demonstration project initiated to introduce the idea of self-managing teams and high levels of worker autonomy; a more recent example, designed to rethink small-car development, manufacturing, and sales, is GM's Saturn Division.

Demonstration projects share a number of distinctive characteristics:

- They are usually the first projects to embody principles and approaches that the organization hopes to adopt later on a larger scale. For this reason, they are more transitional efforts than endpoints and involve considerable "learning by doing." Mid-course corrections are common.
- They implicitly establish policy guidelines and decision rules for later projects. Managers must therefore be sensitive to the precedents they are setting and must send strong signals if they expect to establish new norms.
- They often encounter severe tests of commitment from employees, who wish to see whether the rules have, in fact, changed.
- They are normally developed by strong multifunctional teams reporting directly to senior management. (For projects targeting employee involvement or quality of work life, teams should be multilevel as well.)
- They tend to have only limited impact on the rest of the organization if they are not accompanied by explicit strategies for transferring learning.

All of these characteristics appeared in a demonstration project launched by Copeland Corporation, a highly successful compressor manufacturer, in the mid-

1970s. Matt Diggs, then the new CEO, wanted to transform the company's approach to manufacturing. Previously, Copeland had machined and assembled all products in a single facility. Costs were high, and quality was marginal. The problem, Diggs felt, was too much complexity.

At the outset, Diggs assigned a small, multifunctional team the task of designing a "focused factory" dedicated to a narrow, newly developed product line. The team reported directly to Diggs and took three years to complete its work. Initially, the project budget was $10 million to $12 million; that figure was repeatedly revised as the team found, through experience and with Diggs's prodding, that it could achieve dramatic improvements. The final investment, a total of $30 million, yielded unanticipated breakthroughs in reliability testing, automatic tool adjustment, and programmable control. All were achieved through learning by doing.

The team set additional precedents during the plant's start-up and early operations. To dramatize the importance of quality, for example, the quality manager was appointed second-in-command, a significant move upward. The same reporting relationship was used at all subsequent plants. In addition, Diggs urged the plant manager to ramp up slowly to full production and resist all efforts to proliferate products. These instructions were unusual at Copeland, where the marketing department normally ruled. Both directives were quickly tested: management held firm, and the implications were felt throughout the organization. Manufacturing's stature improved, and the company as a whole recognized its competitive contribution. One observer commented, "Marketing had always run the company, so they couldn't believe it. The change was visible at the highest levels, and it went down hard."

Once the first focused factory was running smoothly—it seized 25% of the market in two years and held its edge in reliability for over a decade—Copeland built four more factories in quick succession. Diggs assigned members of the initial project to each factory's design team to ensure that early learnings were not lost; these people later rotated into operating assignments. Today, focused factories remain the cornerstone of Copeland's manufacturing strategy and a continuing source of its cost and quality advantages.

Whether they are demonstration projects like Copeland's or ongoing programs like Allegheny Ludlum's, all forms of experimentation seek the same end: moving from superficial knowledge to deep understanding. At its simplest, the distinction is between knowing how things are done and knowing why they occur. Knowing how is partial knowledge; it is rooted in norms of behavior, standards of practice, and settings of equipment. Knowing why is more fundamental: it captures underlying cause-and-effect relationships and accommodates exceptions, adaptations, and unforeseen events. The ability to control temperatures and pressures to align grains of silicon and form silicon steel is an example of knowing how; understanding the chemical and physical process that produces the alignment is knowing why.

Further distinctions are possible. Operating knowledge can be arrayed in a hierarchy, moving from limited understanding and the ability to make few distinctions to more complete understanding in which all contingencies are anticipated and controlled. In this context, experimentation and problem solving foster learning by pushing organizations up the hierarchy, from lower to higher stages of knowledge.

3. Learning from past experience. Companies must review their successes and failures, assess them systematically, and record the lessons in a form that employees find open and accessible. One expert has called this process the "Santayana Review," citing the famous philosopher George Santayana, who coined the phrase "Those who cannot remember the past are condemned to repeat it." Unfortunately, too many managers today are indifferent, even hostile, to the past, and by failing to reflect on it, they let valuable knowledge escape.

A study of more than 150 new products concluded that "the knowledge gained from failures [is] often instrumental in achieving subsequent successes. . . . In the simplest terms, failure is the ultimate teacher."[4] IBM's 360 computer series, for example, one of the most popular and profitable ever built, was based on the technology of the failed Stretch computer that preceded it. In this case, as in many others, learning occurred by chance rather than by careful planning. A few companies, however, have established processes that require their managers to periodically think about the past and learn from their mistakes.

Boeing did so immediately after its difficulties with the 737 and 747 plane programs. Both planes were introduced with much fanfare and also with serious problems. To ensure that the problems were not repeated, senior managers commissioned a high-level employee group, called Project Homework, to compare the development processes of the 737 and 747 with those of the 707 and 727, two of the company's most profitable planes. The group was asked to develop a set of "lessons learned" that could be used on future projects. After working for three years, they produced hundreds of recommendations and an inch-thick booklet. Several members of the team were then transferred to the 757 and 767 start-ups, and guided by experience, they produced the most successful, error-free launches in Boeing's history.

Other companies have used a similar retrospective approach. Like Boeing, Xerox studied its product development process, examining three troubled products in an effort to understand why the company's new business initiatives failed so often. Arthur D. Little, the consulting company, focused on its past successes. Senior management invited ADL consultants from around the world to a two-day "jamboree," featuring booths and presentations documenting a wide range of the company's most successful practices, publications, and techniques. British Petroleum went even further and established the post-project appraisal unit to review major investment projects, write up case studies, and derive lessons for planners that were then incorporated into revisions of the company's planning guidelines. A five-person unit reported to the board of directors and reviewed six projects annually. The bulk of the time was spent in the field interviewing managers.[5] This type of review is now conducted regularly at the project level.

At the heart of this approach, one expert has observed, "is a mind-set that. . . . enables companies to recognize the value of productive failure as contrasted with unproductive success. A productive failure is one that leads to insight, understanding, and thus an addition to the commonly held wisdom of the organization.

An unproductive success occurs when something goes well, but nobody knows how or why."[6] IBM's legendary founder, Thomas Watson, Sr., apparently understood the distinction well. Company lore has it that a young manager, after losing $10 million in a risky venture, was called into Watson's office. The young man, thoroughly intimidated, began by saying, "I guess you want my resignation." Watson replied, "You can't be serious. We just spent $10 million educating you."

Fortunately, the learning process need not be so expensive. Case studies and post-project reviews like those of Xerox and British Petroleum can be performed with little cost other than managers' time. Companies can also enlist the help of faculty and students at local colleges or universities; they bring fresh perspectives and view internships and case studies as opportunities to gain experience and increase their own learning. A few companies have established computerized data banks to speed up the learning process. At Paul Revere Life Insurance, management requires all problem-solving teams to complete short registration forms describing their proposed projects if they hope to qualify for the company's award program. The company then enters the forms into its computer system and can immediately retrieve a listing of other groups of people who have worked or are working on the topic, along with a contact person. Relevant experience is then just a telephone call away.

4. Learning from others. Of course, not all learning comes from reflection and self-analysis. Sometimes the most powerful insights come from looking outside one's immediate environment to gain a new perspective. Enlightened managers know that even companies in completely different businesses can be fertile sources of ideas and catalysts for creative thinking. At these organizations, enthusiastic borrowing is replacing the "not invented here" syndrome. Milliken calls the process SIS, for "Steal Ideas Shamelessly"; the broader term for it is benchmarking.

According to one expert, "benchmarking is an ongoing investigation and learning experience that ensures the best industry practices are uncovered, analyzed, adopted and implemented."[7] The greatest benefits come from studying *practices*, the way that work gets done, rather than results, and from involving line managers in the process. Almost anything can be benchmarked. Xerox, the concept's creator, has applied it to billing, warehousing, and automated manufacturing. Milliken has been even more creative: in an inspired moment, it benchmarked Xerox's approach to benchmarking.

Unfortunately, there is still considerable confusion about the requirements for successful benchmarking. Benchmarking is not "industrial tourism," a series of ad hoc visits to companies that have received favorable publicity or won quality awards. Rather, it is a disciplined process that begins with a thorough search to identify best-practice organizations, continues with careful study of one's own practices and performance, progresses through systematic site visits and interviews, and concludes with an analysis of results, development of recommendations, and implementation. While time-consuming, the process need not be terribly expensive. AT&T's Benchmarking Group estimates that a moderate-sized project takes four to six months and incurs out-of-pocket costs of $20,000 (when personnel costs are included, the figure is three to four times higher).

Benchmarking is one way of gaining an outside perspective; another, equally fertile source of ideas is customers. Conversations with customers invariably stimulate learning; they are, after all, experts in what they do. Customers can provide up-to-date product information, competitive comparisons, insights into changing preferences, and immediate feedback about service and patterns of use. And companies need these insights at all levels, from the executive suite to the shop floor. At Motorola, members of the Operating and Policy Committee, including the CEO, meet personally and on a regular basis with customers. At Worthington Steel, all machine operators make periodic, unescorted trips to customers' factories to discuss their needs.

Sometimes customers can't articulate their needs or remember even the most recent problems they have had with a product or service. If that's the case, managers must observe them in action. Xerox employs a number of anthropologists at its Palo Alto Research Center to observe users of new document products in their offices. Digital Equipment has developed an interactive process called "contextual inquiry" that is used by software engineers to observe users of new technologies as they go about their work. Milliken has created "first-delivery teams" that accompany the first shipment of all products; team members follow the product through the customer's production process to see how it is used and then develop ideas for further improvement.

Whatever the source of outside ideas, learning will only occur in a receptive environment. Managers can't be defensive and must be open to criticism or bad news. This is a difficult challenge, but it is essential for success. Companies that approach customers assuming that "we must be right, they have to be wrong" or visit other organizations certain that "they can't teach us anything" seldom learn very much. Learning organizations, by contrast, cultivate the art of open, attentive listening.

5. Transferring knowledge. For learning to be more than a local affair, knowledge must spread quickly and efficiently throughout the organization. Ideas carry maximum impact when they are shared broadly rather than held in a few hands. A variety of mechanisms spur this process, including written, oral, and visual reports, site visits and tours, personnel rotation programs, education and training programs, and standardization programs. Each has distinctive strengths and weaknesses.

Reports and tours are by far the most popular mediums. Reports serve many purposes: they summarize findings, provide checklists of dos and don'ts, and describe important processes and events. They cover a multitude of topics, from benchmarking studies to accounting conventions to newly discovered marketing techniques. Today, written reports are often supplemented by videotapes, which offer greater immediacy and fidelity.

Tours are an equally popular means of transferring knowledge, especially for large multidivisional organizations with multiple sites. The most effective tours are tailored to different audiences and needs. To introduce its managers to the distinctive manufacturing practices of New United Motor Manufacturing Inc. (NUMMI), its joint venture with Toyota, General Motors developed a series of specialized tours. Some were geared to upper and middle managers, while others were aimed at lower ranks. Each tour described the policies, practices, and systems that were most relevant to that level of management.

Despite their popularity, reports and tours are relatively cumbersome ways of transferring knowledge. The gritty details that lie behind complex management concepts are difficult to communicate secondhand. Absorbing facts by reading them or seeing them demonstrated is one thing; experiencing them personally is quite another. As a leading cognitive scientist has observed, "It is very difficult to become knowledgeable in a passive way. Actively experiencing something is considerably more valuable than having it described."[8] For this reason, personnel rotation programs are one of the most powerful methods of transferring knowledge.

In many organizations, expertise is held locally: in a particularly skilled computer technician, perhaps, a savvy global brand manager, or a division head with a track record of successful joint ventures. Those in daily contact with these experts benefit enormously from their skills, but their field of influence is relatively narrow. Transferring them to different parts of the organization helps share the wealth. Transfers may be done from division to division, department to department, or facility to facility; they may involve senior, middle, or first-level managers. A supervisor experienced in just-in-time production, for example, might move to another factory to apply the methods there, or a successful division manager might transfer to a lagging division to invigorate it with already proven ideas. The CEO of Time Life used the latter approach when he shifted the president of the company's music division, who had orchestrated several years of rapid growth and high profits through innovative marketing, to the presidency of the book division, where profits were flat because of continued reliance on traditional marketing concepts.

Line to staff transfers are another option. These are most effective when they allow experienced managers to distill what they have learned and diffuse it across the company in the form of new standards, policies, or training programs. Consider how PPG used just such a transfer to advance its human resource practices around the concept of high-commitment work systems. In 1986, PPG constructed a new float-glass plant in Chehalis, Washington; it employed a radically new technology as well as innovations in human resource management that were developed by the plant manager and his staff. All workers were organized into small, self-managing teams with responsibility for work assignments, scheduling, problem solving and improvement, and peer review. After several years running the factory, the plant manager was promoted to director of human resources for the entire glass group. Drawing on his experiences at Chehalis, he developed a training program geared toward first-level supervisors that taught the behaviors needed to manage employees in a participative, self-managing environment.

As the PPG example suggests, education and training programs are powerful tools for transferring knowledge. But for maximum effectiveness, they must be linked explicitly to implementation. All too often, trainers assume that new knowledge will be applied without taking concrete steps to ensure that trainees actually follow through. Seldom do trainers provide opportunities for practice, and few programs consciously promote the application of their teachings after employees have returned to their jobs.

Xerox and GTE are exceptions. As noted earlier, when Xerox introduced problem-solving techniques to its employees in the 1980s, everyone, from the top to the bottom of the organization, was taught in small departmental or divisional groups led by their immediate superior. After an introduction to concepts and techniques, each group applied what they had learned to a real-life work problem. In a similar spirit, GTE's Quality: The Competitive Edge program was offered to teams of business-unit presidents and the managers reporting to them. At the beginning of the 3-day course, each team received a request from a company officer to prepare a complete quality plan for their unit, based on the course concepts, within 60 days. Discussion periods of two to three hours were set aside during the program so that teams could begin working on their plans. After the teams submitted their reports, the company officers studied them, and then the teams implemented them. This GTE program produced dramatic improvements in quality, including a recent semifinalist spot in the Baldrige Awards.

The GTE example suggests another important guideline: knowledge is more likely to be transferred effectively when the right incentives are in place. If employees know that their plans will be evaluated and implemented—in other words, that their learning will be applied—progress is far more likely. At most companies, the status quo is well entrenched; only if managers and employees see new ideas as being in their own best interest will they accept them gracefully. AT&T has developed a creative approach that combines strong incentives with information sharing. Called the Chairman's Quality Award (CQA), it is an internal quality competition modeled on the Baldrige prize but with an important twist: awards are given not only for absolute performance (using the same 1,000-point scoring system as Baldrige) but also for improvements in scoring from the previous year. Gold, silver, and bronze Improvement Awards are given to units that have improved their scores 200, 150, and 100 points, respectively. These awards provide the incentive for change. An accompanying Pockets of Excellence program simplifies knowledge transfer. Every year, it identifies every unit within the company that has scored at least 60% of the possible points in each award category, and then publicizes the names of these units using written reports and electronic mail.

MEASURING LEARNING

Managers have long known that "if you can't measure it, you can't manage it." This maxim is as true of learning as it is of any other corporate objective. Traditionally, the solution has been "learning curves" and "manufacturing progress functions." Both concepts date back to the discovery, during the 1920s and 1930s, that the costs of airframe manufacturing fell predictably with increases in cumulative volume. These increases were viewed as proxies for greater manufacturing knowledge, and most early studies examined their impact on the costs of direct labor. Later studies expanded the focus, looking at total manufacturing costs and the impact of experience in other industries, including shipbuilding, oil refining, and consumer electronics. Typically, learning rates were in the 80% to 85% range (meaning that with a doubling of cumulative production, costs fell to 80% to 85% of their previous level), although there was wide variation.

Firms like the Boston Consulting Group raised these ideas to a higher level in the 1970s. Drawing on the logic of learning curves, they argued that industries as a whole faced "experience curves," costs and prices that fell by predictable amounts as industries grew and their total production increased. With this observation, consultants suggested, came an iron law of competition. To enjoy the benefits of experience, companies would have to rapidly increase their production ahead of competitors to lower prices and gain market share.

Both learning and experience curves are still widely used, especially in the aerospace, defense, and electronics industries. Boeing, for instance, has established learning curves for every work station in its assembly plant; they assist in monitoring productivity, determining work flows and staffing levels, and setting prices and profit margins on new airplanes. Experience curves are common in semiconductors and consumer electronics, where they are used to forecast industry costs and prices.

For companies hoping to become learning organizations, however, these measures are incomplete. They focus on only a single measure of output (cost or price) and ignore learning that affects other competitive variables, like quality, delivery, or new product introductions. They suggest only one possible learning driver (total production volumes) and ignore both the possibility of learning in mature industries, where output is flat, and the possibility that learning might be driven by other sources, such as new technology or the challenge posed by competing products. Perhaps most important, they tell us little about the sources of learning or the levers of change.

Another measure has emerged in response to these concerns. Called the "half-life" curve, it was originally developed by Analog Devices, a leading semiconductor manufacturer, as a way of comparing internal improvement rates. A half-life curve measures the time it takes to achieve a 50% improvement in a specified performance measure. When represented graphically, the performance measure (defect rates, on-time delivery, time to market) is plotted on the vertical axis, using a logarithmic scale, and the time scale (days, months, years) is plotted horizontally. Steeper slopes then represent faster learning.

The logic is straightforward. Companies, divisions, or departments that take less time to improve must be learning faster than their peers. In the long run, their short learning cycles will translate into superior performance. The 50% target is a measure of convenience; it was derived empirically from studies of successful improvement processes at a wide range of companies. Half-life curves are also flexible. Unlike learning and experience curves, they work on any output measure, and they are not confined to costs or prices. In addition, they are easy to operationalize, they provide a simple measuring stick, and they allow for ready comparison among groups.

Yet, even half-life curves have an important weakness: they focus solely on results. Some types of knowledge take years to digest, with few visible changes in performance for long periods. Creating a total quality culture, for instance, or developing new approaches to product development are difficult systemic changes. Because of their long gestation periods, half-life curves or any other measures focused solely on results are unlikely to capture any short-run learning that has occurred. A more comprehensive framework is needed to track progress.

Organizational learning can usually be traced through three overlapping stages. The first step is cognitive. Members of the organization are exposed to new ideas, expand their knowledge, and begin to think differently. The second step is behavioral. Employees begin to internalize new insights and alter their behavior. And the third step is performance improvement, with changes in behavior leading to measurable improvements in results: superior quality, better delivery, increased market share, or other tangible gains. Because cognitive and behavioral changes typically precede improvements in performance, a complete learning audit must include all three.

Surveys, questionnaires, and interviews are useful for this purpose. At the cognitive level, they would focus on attitudes and depth of understanding. Have employees truly understood the meaning of self-direction and teamwork, or are the terms still unclear? At PPG, a team of human resource experts periodically audits every manufacturing plant, including extensive interviews with shopfloor employees, to ensure that the concepts are well understood. Have new approaches to customer service been fully accepted? At its 1989 Worldwide Marketing Managers' Meeting, Ford presented participants with a series of hypothetical situations in which customer complaints were in conflict with short-term dealer or company profit goals and asked how they would respond. Surveys like these are the first step toward identifying changed attitudes and new ways of thinking.

To assess behavioral changes, surveys and questionnaires must be supplemented by direct observation. Here the proof is in the doing, and there is no substitute for seeing employees in action. Domino's Pizza uses "mystery shoppers" to assess managers' commitment to customer service at its individual stores; L.L. Bean places telephone orders with its own operators to assess service levels. Other companies invite outside consultants to visit, attend meetings, observe employees in action, and then report what they have learned. In many ways, this approach mirrors that of examiners for the Baldrige Award, who make several-day site visits to semifinalists to see whether the companies' deeds match the words on their applications.

Finally, a comprehensive learning audit also measures performance. Half-life curves or other performance measures are essential for ensuring that cognitive and behavioral changes have actually produced results. Without them, companies would lack a rationale for investing in learning and the assurance that learning was serving the organization's ends.

FIRST STEPS

Learning organizations are not built overnight. Most successful examples are the products of carefully cultivated attitudes, commitments, and management processes that have accrued slowly and steadily over time. Still, some changes can be made immediately. Any company that wishes to become a learning organization can begin by taking a few simple steps.

The first step is to foster an environment that is conducive to learning. There must be time for reflection and analysis, to think about strategic plans, dissect customer needs, assess current work systems, and invent new products. Learning is difficult when employees are harried or rushed; it tends to be driven out by the pressures of the moment. Only if top management explicitly frees up employees' time for the purpose does learning occur with any frequency. That time will be doubly productive if employees possess the skills to use it wisely. Training in brainstorming, problem solving, evaluating experiments, and other core learning skills is therefore essential.

Another powerful lever is to open up boundaries and stimulate the exchange of ideas. Boundaries inhibit the flow of information; they keep individuals and groups isolated and reinforce preconceptions. Opening up boundaries, with conferences, meetings, and project teams, which either cross organizational levels or link the company and its customers and suppliers, ensures a fresh flow of ideas and the chance to consider competing perspectives. General Electric CEO Jack Welch considers this to be such a powerful stimulant of change that he has made "boundarylessness" a cornerstone of the company's strategy for the 1990s.

Once managers have established a more supportive, open environment, they can create learning forums. These are programs or events designed with explicit learning goals in mind, and they can take a variety of forms: strategic reviews, which examine the changing competitive environment and the company's product portfolio, technology, and market positioning; systems audits, which review the health of large, cross-functional processes and delivery systems; internal benchmarking reports, which identify and compare best-in-class activities within the organization; study missions, which are dispatched to leading organizations around the world to better understand their performance and distinctive skills; and jamborees or symposiums, which bring together customers, suppliers, outside experts, or internal groups to share ideas and learn from one another. Each of these activities fosters learning by requiring employees to wrestle with new knowledge and consider its implications. Each can also be tailored to business needs. A consumer goods company, for example, might sponsor a study mission to Europe to learn more about distribution methods within the newly unified Common Market, while a high-technology company might launch a systems audit to review its new product development process.

Together these efforts help to eliminate barriers that impede learning and begin to move learning higher on the organizational agenda. They also suggest a subtle shift in focus, away from continuous improvement and toward a commitment to learning. Coupled with a better understanding of the "three Ms," the meaning, management, and measurement of learning, this shift provides a solid foundation for building learning organizations.

Notes

1. Peter M. Senge, *The Fifth Discipline* (New York: Doubleday, 1990), p. 1.

2. Ikujiro Nonaka, "The Knowledge-Creating Company," *Harvard Business Review*, November-December 1991, p. 97.

3. Robert Howard, "The CEO as Organizational Architect: An Interview with Xerox's Paul Allaire," *Harvard Business Review*, September-October 1992, p. 106.

4. Modesto A. Maidique and Billie Jo Zirger, "The New Product Learning Cycle," *Research Policy*, Vol. 14, No. 6 (1985), pp. 299, 309.

5. Frank R. Gulliver, "Post-Project Appraisals Pay," *Harvard Business Review*, March-April 1987, p. 128.

6. David Nadler, "Even Failures Can Be Productive," *New York Times*, April 23, 1989, Sec. 3, p. 3.

7. Robert C. Camp, *Benchmarking: The Search for Industry Best Practices that Lead to Superior Performance* (Milwaukee: ASQC Quality Press, 1989), p. 12.

8. Roger Schank, with Peter Childers, *The Creative Attitude* (New York: Macmillan, 1988), p. 9.

◆

"You Don't Necessarily Have to Be Charismatic. . . :" An Interview with Anita Roddick and Reflections on Charismatic Processes in the Body Shop International[*]

Jeannie Gaines
UNIVERSITY OF SOUTH FLORIDA—ST. PETERSBURG

In 1976, Anita Roddick opened a small shop in Brighton, England to sell 15 naturally based skin and hair products. These products grew out of previous travels where she observed how women in other cultures cared for their bodies without buying a single cosmetic. The Body Shop was conceived out of pragmatism and irritation. Gordon Roddick, Anita's husband, was leaving for two years to travel by horseback from Buenos Aires to New York; Anita needed enough income to take care of herself and two small daughters during his absence. The irritation grew out of her inability to buy cosmetics in small amounts without excessive packaging and false claims of dramatic tranformation. Gordon made it as far as Bolivia, but returned to England in 1977 when one of his horses died. There he found two Body Shops operating successfully, and a niche for himself bottling, labeling, and delivering supplies to both shops as well as managing the operational side of the business. In 1978, Gordon put together the first franchise agreements, which turned out to be the key to The Body Shop's rapid expansion.

   In 1984, Anita and Gordon launched The Body Shop as a public company on the London Stock Exchange, where it was valued at 8 million pounds. It was at

[*]Reprinted from *Leadership Quarterly*, Vol. 4, no. 3. Copyright © 1993 by JAI Press Inc. Reprinted with permission of the publisher.

this point of financial security that Anita and Gordon made a decision that The Body Shop International could and would proactively champion for social change. They have sponsored campaigns as diverse as "AGAINST ANIMAL TESTING," "REUSE, REFILL & RECYCLE," and "ALL HUMAN BEINGS ARE BORN FREE," an international plea for human rights. All Body Shop flat surfaces (including store windows, free pamphlets, T-shirts, bags, truck sides, etc.) are used to educate and raise the consciousness of consumers and passers-by. They contain provocative messages concerning issues such as the environment; human, civil and animal rights; preservation of indigenous tribes; Romanian Relief, and AIDS awareness.

Today, there are almost 1000 shops trading in 43 countries and 19 languages, and market value stands at approximately 365 million pounds—all without one penny of paid advertising. The Body Shop now offers over 400 products in both company-owned and franchised shops, is a vigilant steward of the environment, pursues an aggressive TRADE NOT AID program with Third World producers, actively engages in community-based projects (on company time), and underwrites numerous other humanitarian campaigns and projects.

The phenomenal success of The Body Shop is typically credited to Anita Roddick, a woman who exudes intelligence, energy, humor, spontaneity, and impatience, and who relies a great deal on her intuition. But most of all, she is passionate and uncompromising when it comes to her core values as they relate to the mission of the organization. Anita is indeed the public face of The Body Shop. She is a person with strong opinions, many of which are controversial. She thoroughly enjoys sharing those opinions with the media as well as information regarding The Body Shop philosophy, policies, and products. Consequently, Roddick has become an extremely high-profile leader, as evidenced by the plethora of articles about her and/or The Body Shop found in popular press publications such as *The Wall Street Journal, People Magazine, Money Magazine, Time, Forbes, Fortune, Business Week*, and *INC*. However, to date, none of these articles or interviews has focused on Anita's style of leadership, or on any other leadership patterns or practices in The Body Shop.

Although Anita avoids referring to herself as a charismatic leader, most of those who know her, or have experienced her through audio-visuals, would fervently disagree. According to Bryman's list of characteristics that differentiate charismatic from noncharismatic leaders (1993), Roddick clearly "is deemed to be exceptional by . . . her followers," has "a mission or vision" that is central to attracting followers, and inspires "resolute commitment" because of her exceptional characteristics and mission (pp. 291–292).

The questions that follow are variations on three themes: Anita Roddick's leadership style and how it fits into Weber's definitions of charismatic leadership; routinization of charisma at The Body Shop; and maintenance of charismatic leadership at The Body Shop. In addition to Anita's answers (found in **bold type**) to the questions posed, I have attempted to integrate other pertinent information, such as previously published articles, personal observations, and interviews conducted at The Body Shop Headquarters in Littlehampton, England during July, 1993. Through this combination of data sources, I hope to provide a glimpse of charismatic processes in one of the world's most remarkable organizations.

CHARISMATIC LEADERSHIP QUALITIES

How would you characterize your leadership style?

I want work to be a fulfilling experience so my aim has always been to make staff feel empowered and involved. The tools I use are passion, optimism, quirkiness, imagination, education and accountability.

How would your employees depict your leadership style?

Strong, blunt, persuasive, pro-active, ideas-driven. I'm naturally impatient so I'm sure staff would also say I'm impetuous and idiosyncratic bordering on erratic.

According to Bryman (1992, 1993), one of the defining characteristics of charismatic leadership (CLS), from a Weberian point of view, is the social nature of the relationship between leader and followers. In other words, CLS is not a personal trait of the leader; rather, it is the attribution of exceptional qualities to the leader by the followers. It is clear that Roddick sees herself in a mutual relationship with her employees. When asked about leadership style, the first thing she refers to is the involvement and empowerment of her staff.

As she states above, a combination of extraordinary facets, such as passion, optimism, quirkiness, and imagination, are manifest in her leadership style. These exceptional qualities were evident when Anita was described as "creative," "energetic," "passionate," "determined," "driven," "dynamic," "inspirational," and "charismatic" by different staff I interviewed at The Body Shop Headquarters. One employee shared a story that, in days gone by, one could actually feel Anita's presence as her plane approached the runway at Gatwick Airport!

However, as most strong personalities who tend to operate at the extremes, Roddick was also described as "demanding," "inconsistent," and "irritant," and as one who had been known to have "Italian temper fits." In a recent *People* magazine article (Brock, 1993), Gordon described Anita as "mercurial and marginally eccentric, and usually right, which drives everybody mad" (p. 105). In the same article, Gus Colquhoun, who shoots in-house videos for The Body Shop, explained, "[T]here aren't many in the organization who find it easy to disagree with her" (p. 106). He also made it clear that he is a big fan of Roddick.

It seems apparent that Roddick meets the first CLS criterion; she is involved in a social exchange relationship with her staff, who consider her to have extraordinary characteristics. My own sense is that Anita is very much aware of how she is perceived by her employees. Certainly, this was affirmed by her answers to the above questions. I fully expect that she will continue to say and do outrageous things, to evoke strong emotions in staff (both positive and negative), and to be cherished by the people who choose to work with her.

What is your personal vision for The Body Shop?

I have always seen the company as a force for social change and a model for other businesses. And now our social awareness has inevitably carried us into the political arena, especially in the U.S. That's a development I'm really looking forward to pursuing.

To what degree and in what ways is the vision shared by The Body Shop employees and franchises?

Whether they're aware of it or not, everyone connected with the company acts on our corporate vision. Take our suppliers—the declaration we insist they sign puts them in the vanguard of the campaign against animal testing in the cosmetics industry. Our staff are activists by nature of our in-store campaigns, educational activities, and community projects. The same with franchisees—every store is a focus of community activities. Again, our U.S. franchisees were very active in voter registration during the American presidential campaign.

The second criterion of CLS is that the leader have a mission or a vision (Bryman, 1993). It is difficult to imagine a leader, especially a business leader, who is more committed to a vision than Anita Roddick. She articulates her vision for The Body Shop as "a force for social change." However, unlike many corporate mission statements, this goal is actively pursued through numerous avenues. Examples of specific objectives for achieving social change in The Body Shop include:

- To trade ethically with suppliers, employees, franchisees, and consumers.
- To empower employees and consumers through education.
- To raise the consciousness of staff and consumers by stirring their passions.
- To campaign for human, animal, and environmental rights.
- To give something back to the community where they are located.
- To assist development in Third World countries while preserving indigenous cultures.
- To conduct business with love and to behave in a caring manner to staff.
- To make work fun.

Roddick not only sees vision as prerequisite to leadership, she calls for authority to be grounded in *moral* vision: "I don't understand how anybody can be a leader without a clearly defined moral vision. If your ambitions and interests do not extend beyond the role of making money or expanding your business, as far as I am concerned you are morally bankrupt" (Roddick, 1991, p. 226). Although she is well aware that profits make it possible for The Body Shop to enact her vision of broad social change, Anita views the accumulation of wealth per se as immoral. In other words, a portion of all successful organizations' profits can and should be used as a means to achieve endstates such as the objectives stated above. Anita believes that by adopting a moral vision, the book on business can be written, and a new and better business paradigm created (Burlingham, 1990).

Describe the relationship between you and your employees.

I challenge them, they challenge me. I feel a pressure in living up to expectations. The best way round that is to encourage a tit-for-tat dialogue based on a delicate balance of respect and irreverence.

Is great personal loyalty important in choosing an employee or a franchisee?

No. That smacks of a cult of personality, which makes my flesh creep. Loyalty to values is much more important.

Do you feel you have a sort of "spiritual" link with your employees and franchisees?

If shared values can create a "spiritual" link, then the answer is "yes." We also share a faith that we can make a difference. When you contemplate the enormous scale of the problems facing the world, you have to accept that such a faith is based on something more than pragmatism.

The third criterion of CLS involves the devotion and loyalty leaders enjoy from their followers (Bryman, 1993). In fact, Bryman (1992) stated that "the charismatic leader is regarded by his or her followers with a mixture of reverence, unflinching dedication and awe" (p. 41). This seems to be a point of partial divergence between the Weberian perspective on CLS and the leadership of Anita Roddick. She described her leadership with employees as one of "respect and irreverence" rather than reverence. My sense, after spending time in The Body Shop Headquarters, is that there is more reverence felt by staff than Roddick would want or admit.

Her responses about "loyalty to values" and a "faith that we can make a difference" were affirmed by the staff I interviewed. One employee described "an underlying spiritual link between Anita and employees based on a similarity in values." In The Body Shop, the shared mission and values seem to engender the kind of commitment typically found in a religious organization or political movement (cf. Bryman, 1993). One of the intriguing questions is whether the vision and the resulting loyalty now belong to The Body Shop rather than just to Anita.

In summarizing the relationship between CLS, as examined by Weber (1968) and Bryman (1992; 1993), and the leadership style of Anita Roddick, we find a great deal of overlap. However, Greenleaf's (1970) model of servant-leadership, discussed by Graham (1991), may be a more precise description of Roddick. The servant-leader is certainly a visionary, but his or her followers are encouraged to develop their own "moral reasoning capacity" (Graham, 1991, p. 116) as well as their knowledge and skills. A servant-leader's goal is to create intelligent, autonomous beings who question the leader's vision for the organization and ultimately cultivate their own moral codes. In addition, servant-leaders attempt to serve and protect the "least privileged in society" (Graham, 1991, p. 117) as well as the more traditional organizational stakeholders. This seems to be a fairly accurate description of the type of charisma that exists between Roddick and her employees.

ROUTINIZATION OF CHARISMA

What qualities do you look for when selecting an employee and/or franchisee?

The simplest answer is I look for people like me because then I know how to keep them motivated and entertained and get the best from them. Obviously, I like people who share our values, people who are bright enough to question authority and never settle for less, strong individuals who love what we do.

What roles do rules, procedures, and policies play in The Body Shop?

A staff charter defines corporate attitudes and clarifies for everyone just where they stand in the company—and where the company stands for them. We practice humanistic management rather than management by the stopwatch but as a service oriented business, we obviously hold fast to clear guidelines: cleanliness, customer care and so on. In addition, as a global company with nearly 1000 stores in 43 countries, we have to have guidelines to guarantee consistency in presentation.

Is it possible to keep a family atmosphere in an organization that is growing as rapidly as The Body Shop?

Our growth has made the family feeling of yore a thing of the past, but I hope it's still possible to give everyone the sense of intimacy and individualized concern that created that feeling. We'll never again be a company where I know everyone I pass in the hallway, but we're endeavoring to create a network of family-style divisions under The Body Shop's umbrella.

What kind of person do you envision your successor to be?

I don't want a duplicate, I want someone who will take my breath away with his or her ability to push what I've done much further.

As Bryman (1993) points out, Weber's discussion of routinization has been omitted in the majority of contemporary investigations of CLS. This is perhaps due, in part, to the stark contrast between our perceptions of charisma as exciting and routinization as dull or boring. Apparently, Weber also saw them as opposite in nature, but he was convinced that routinization was inevitable if the charismatic force was to endure (Bryman, 1992). Two dimensions of routinization, development of structure and establishment of a successor, were explored in this interview.

The *development of structure* includes a codified set of beliefs, roles, positions, policies, and procedures that reflect the charismatic leader's vision (Bryman, 1993). Although The Body Shop remains one of the least bureaucratic organizations today, given its size and scope, there is definitely a structure emerging. It may not be in written form yet, but Anita's vision is in the process of becoming routinized.

Selection, as a mechanism for routinization, plays an important role in perpet-uating a leader's vision or charisma. Anita was quite up front in her answer to the selection question—"I look for people like me. . . who share our values." A great deal has been written about the questions that job candidates and potential fran-chisees are asked: "If you were a car, what car would you be and why?" and "How would you like to die?" (Brock, 1993). In fact, applicants are asked about a wide range of personal issues in order to ensure a good match between their values and The Body Shop values. *Business Week* (Zinn, 1991) reported that, at one point, Anita was in the process of hiring a new retail director when she discovered he enjoyed hunting. He ended up hunting—for a different job!

What appears to be happening now is more formalization in the way staff are selected. At The Body Shop Headquarters, job candidates (internal and external) are interviewed by three different panels comprised of a cross-section of employ-ees. Each member of the panel chooses the questions they want to ask and each has an equal vote (although a decision by consensus is encouraged). As one man-ager put it during a recent interview in Littlehampton, "selection is critical in maintaining the values of The Body Shop."

Another aspect of structure is the appearance of *formal statements regarding ideology, roles, tasks, rules, procedures, and policies*. In spite of the fact that they laughed at me in Littlehampton when I asked for an organization chart (by the time one is put in writing and distributed, it is outdated), there is evidence that "the way things are done" at The Body Shop is making its way into writing. Anita mentioned the Staff Charter (see Appendix 1), which is a statement of the organi-zation's philosophy. The principles that guide the Trade Not Aid program have also been put in writing (see Appendix 2). I was able to locate performance appraisal forms and written objectives in some departments, but could not find job descriptions. Several departments, such as R&D, were in the process of putting procedures in writing. At the individual shop level, all storefronts and dis-plays must follow a prescribed format, and each shop contains a thick manual of product information available for staff and customers alike (Jacob, 1992). In addi-tion, each poster, pamphlet on products, and public awareness brochure is designed and written at headquarters to ensure consistency (Wallace, 1990). Clearly, formalization is knocking on The Body Shop's door, but it is not yet receiv-ing a whole-hearted welcome.

The Body Shop's rapid growth has presented an additional structural dilem-ma—how to retain the sense of intimacy and informality that contributed so heav-ily to the success of the organization. One of the managers I interviewed made the following observation on structure: "Management [at The Body Shop] is very *decentralized*, but product lines are very centralized." This seems to summarize the situation well. The managing directors are fiercely protective of the products that are sold in the shops, but are much more relaxed about the management styles of staff and franchisees.

Growth mandates change, but The Body Shop Directors are adamant that it will not diversify, not dilute its core vision (a force for social change), and not lose its sense of family. There is evidence, in fact, that the family metaphor is still alive and well. While I was in Littlehampton, a new division was formed—ostensibly to increase efficiency. But rumor had it that Gordon discovered he did not know everyone's name, so it was time to reorganize again! It is probably unreasonable to think that Gordon and Anita will continue to have personal relationships with all employees. However, it appears that they are both committed to retaining the family atmosphere through decentralization of the parent organization into smaller companies, where top management will to able to establish relationships with each employee.

Successorship is the second dimension of routinization that Weber (1968) addressed. As with the emergence of structure, who is to follow the charismatic leader is critically important if the vision is to endure. Although Anita did not mention specific individuals when asked about a successor, she did discuss the possibility of daughters Justine and Samantha joining the business in *Body and Soul* (Roddick, 1991). Sam accompanied Anita to the Forest People's Gathering in Brazil during 1988 and made an impassioned plea for donations at the international franchise meeting that netted over 200,000 pounds. Both Justine, age 24, and Sam, age 22, were heavily involved in The Body Shop Romania Relief Project that began in 1990 to renovate orphanages, send supplies, and provide volunteers to care for and play with the children. The Romania project has since become quite successful apart from The Body Shop. Sam is currently publishing a newspaper in Vancouver, Canada, that deals with environmental issues; Justine is doing public relations for The Body Shop (Brock, 1993).

At this point, Justine and Sam appear to be uninterested in joining Gordon and Anita in the business on a permanent basis. Clearly, Anita has a vision of something different: "I am not worried that it will all disappear after Gordon and I have gone. We have our Charter and we have a whole lot of young people who live and breathe The Body Shop who will provide our moral backbone in the future and who will be able to take over for me. Maybe Sam will be the one—she will certainly never let our ideals be diminished" (Roddick, 1991, pp. 176-177). "Sam thinks on a grand scale. She wants to save the planet and the cosmos. Justine has a real sense of local care. . . for the family unit and the community spirit. Justine has a great sense of design, while Sam has a great sense of fun. Together they could do great things in the company" (pp. 254-255).

It seems obvious that Roddick prefers succession through bloodlines or heredity, one of the forms of succession discussed by Bryman (1993). But Anita has been careful not to pressure Justine and Sam into any large-scale commitments at this point in their lives. She has also left the door open for succession by designation, referring to "a whole lot of young people who live and breathe The Body Shop." Whatever life choices Justine and Sam make, they will not merely inherit their parents' financial interest in The Body Shop. As Anita so delicately puts it: "We believe it would be obscene to die rich. . . to stack up a pile of accumulated wealth which goes on and on. . . for generation after generation" (Roddick, 1991, p. 255). Gordon and Anita intend for their personal wealth to be distributed by a foundation after their deaths. Consequently, Justine and Sam may be forced to make deliberate decisions about their future involvement with The Body Shop, as opposed to waiting passively to inherit titles, roles or stock shares.

MAINTAINING CHARISMA

How do you motivate or influence your employees?

There aren't many motivational forces more potent than giving staff an opportunity to exercise and express their idealism. The company is driven by an ongoing dialogue between company and staff, shops and customers, business and community. I also find blunt honesty and bawdy humor are good motivational bedfellows.

How do you handle problems or conflict within the organization?

Again, the key is wide-open channels of communication. Everyone is encouraged to speak their minds. For particularly touchy problems, we have a direct line of communication to the company directors via a red-letter system.

What are the hallmarks of The Body Shop's culture as you see it?

Genuinely global, responsible, accountable, pro-active, concerned, lateral, enthusiastic, ethical, honest, open and committed to education.

Where do you see The Body Shop in the year 2000?

We're a cosmetic company with a communications arm. That will only get bigger—I used to joke that by the year 2000, we'd be a communications company with a cosmetics arm. But now I realize that the integration of profits and principles is the shaping factor in our corporate culture. Only by becoming a bigger, better retailer can we be a bigger, better force for change.

Do you see your role changing in the coming years? If so, in what ways?

What rivets me now is the transformational thinking that has emerged in the U.S. After years of being a retailer who was aggressive in the pursuit of her vision, I can feel a kinder, gentler—if you'll pardon the phrase—side of my personality emerging. I will stay absolutely committed to the values and educational aspects of The Body Shop's business, but I can see my role becoming less hands-on in areas such as product development, where I've always been very active in the past.

What have been the key factors in your success with The Body Shop?

Energy, passion, commitment, curiosity, and the undying sense that nothing is impossible.

I have chosen to title this section "Maintaining Charisma," rather than "Loss of Charisma," as Bryman (1993) does. The choice of words came from my analysis that Anita Roddick has gradually increased the scope of her vision through charisma, as opposed to experiencing a decrease such as Bryman (1993) contends happened with Iacocca, Burr, and Jobs. The real question is: how has Roddick successfully sustained charismatic leadership in The Body Shop over a span of 17 years? Weber (1968) was very clear about two things: (1) charisma cannot be maintained without adequate routinization; and (2) charisma is fragile and in constant need of validation for followers. This suggests that charisma is difficult to sustain, especially since routinization and the effervescent quality of charisma could be considered mutually exclusive (Bryman, 1993).

Evidence has been presented that routinization is in process at The Body Shop. This corporation provides a prototype of a highly organic structure that operates in a continuous state of flux. The Body Shop truly embraces change, which means by the time something is written, it is probably outdated. Consequently, codifying rules, procedures, policies, and so forth may well be a never-ending task.

But there are other, more subtle, signs of routinization. One of Anita's bandwagons has been her resistance to hire anyone from a business school—most especially Harvard Business School[1] (Distelheim, 1998). I did not hear of any Harvard graduates employed at The Body Shop, but I did interview at least one upper-level manager at Littlehampton with a business school degree. In addition, during the past three years, several senior-level managers have been hired from the managerial ranks of other large organizations. These trends seem to indicate a softening of some of Anita's earlier hardline stances in response to the larger, more complex group of organizations that form The Body Shop International. And, in fact, she admitted in the interview to feeling "a kinder, gentler" side of her personality emerging.

With the shadow of routinization hovering over The Body Shop, how does Anita continue to reveal her exceptional qualities to her staff? Some of the answer seems to lie in the nontraditional way she and the management team interface with employees. For instance, Anita motivates staff by linking social causes to selling skin and hair products. Educating is the focus rather than the selling; passion is favored over predictability; and principles are emphasized more than profits. Problems or conflicts within the organization are handled by straightforward, honest dialogue. One of the most striking aspects of interviewing staff in Littlehampton was their openness in sharing thoughts and feelings—both positive and negative. Unlike field research experiences I have had in many other organizations, The Body Shop employees seemed to feel no apprehension of reprisal from management concerning their comments.

These atypical business practices are only a partial answer to the enigmatic CLS that Anita Roddick demonstrates. Bryman (1992) suggested that the key is for charismatic leaders to minimize their involvement in the emerging organizational structure, to distance themselves from day-to-day administrative matters. This is difficult, if not impossible, in most business settings because accountability for the "mundane matters of management" (Bryman, 1992, p. 170) ultimately rests with the charismatic leader. However, this is not the case with The Body Shop. Gordon Roddick has had responsibility for the operations side of the organization since he returned from South America in 1977 (Burlingham, 1990). In fact, the analysts in London consider him to be "the financial wizard behind Anita's success" (Elmer-Dewitt, 1993, p. 54).

Gordon is the driving force behind routinization in The Body Shop, especially the development of structure. Anita is then free to burst into meetings unexpectedly to share her latest adventure, to encourage staff to break the rules, and to denigrate hierarchy, profit-and-loss statements, and the entire banking establishment. They are an ideal team—Gordon checking Anita's ideas to be sure they make sound business sense and Anita keeping the company energized, visible, and visionary.

This approach has allowed Anita to remain aloof from the ensuing structure but at the heart of every creative and ethical decision. In fact, she alluded to this phenomenon when I asked about her changing role: "I will stay absolutely committed to the values and educational aspects of The Body Shop's business, but I can see my role becoming less hands-on in areas such as product development, where I've always been very active in the past." Research and Development is becoming increasingly formalized, technical, and regulated by outside groups (European Community restrictions, and so forth). To distance herself from the activities of this department seems a shrewd business decision, but one that Anita probably made by instinct or intuition, as opposed to calculation. To maximize the strengths that are primarily responsible for her success—"energy, passion, commitment, curiosity and the undying sense that nothing is impossible"—is to ensure her charismatic impact will continue through rather than be diluted by the routinization process.

It would seem, at least in this example, that it is the way routinization of charisma is implemented that determines whether it will be maintained or lost. Not all charismatic leaders have a partner who can manage rountinization, allowing them to be a free spirit infusing excitement and vision into the organization. However, it may be that charismatic leaders would do well to each team up with another person who has the ability to positively rountinize the spirit of their charisma.

CONCLUSION

In the past 15 years, there has been a resurgence of interest in and research on CLS (see House, 1977; Zaleznik, 1977, 1990; Peters & Waterman, 1982; Bass, 1985; Bennis & Nanus, 1985; Peters & Austin, 1985; Conger & Kanungo, 1987, 1988; Sashkin, 1988; Bennis, 1989; Conger, 1989; Nadler & Tushman, 1989, 1990; Westley & Mintzberg, 1989; Hickman, 1990; Kotter, 1990; Tichy & Devanna, 1990). However, various writers have used different terminology, such as tranformational, visionary, and magical leadership, to refer to what may be generically called CLS. Bryman (1992) made an effort to integrate these themes using a concept called the "new leadership" (p. 111). The major dimensions of the new leadership include: a vision or mission; motivating and inspiring others; creating change and innovation; empowerment of others; creating commitment; stimulating extra effort; use of intuition; and a proactive approach to the environment. It is difficult to read the above interview with Anita Roddick without seeing the parallels between this conceptualization and her style of leadership. The charismatic processes that currently permeate The Body Shop reflect Roddick's core beliefs, sustained through her personal willfulness and an emerging set of routinizing mechanisms. There will, no doubt, continue to be distinctions drawn by scholars among the various forms of CLS. However, it appears that Roddick embodies much of the core meaning of CLS—in spite of her disclaimer, quoted in the title of this article: "You don't necessarily have to be charismatic, you just have to believe in what you are doing so strongly that it becomes a reality" (Roddick, 1991, p. 225).

Appendix 1
The Body Shop Charter as an Example of Routinization
The following six principles are found in an in-house publication, This is The Body Shop (Summer, 1993, p. 1).

1. The success of The Body Shop proves that profits and principles can go hand in hand, and that business can be a force for social change.
2. We address the concerns and needs of our customers. Our products look to the traditions of the past for inspiration, with ingredients that are backed by centuries of safe human usage.
3. We want to put back more than we take out. This is only possible if we respect the planet and the life it supports.
4. Our products express our ideals; we won't test on animals and we ethically source our ingredients to reward primary producers in the majority world.
5. We try to make work a meaningful, pleasurable challenge for staff.
6. Our business is a celebration of life; we will never take anything about it for granted. We must always challenge our success.

Appendix 2
The Body Shop's *Trade Not Aid* Principles as an Example of Routinization
This list is excerpted from Roddick (1991, p. 165).

1. We respect all environments, culture and religions.
2. We utilize traditional skills and materials.
3. We create trade links that are not only successful but sustainable.
4. We trade in replenishable natural materials.
5. We encourage small-scale projects that could be easily duplicated.
6. We provide a long-term commitment to all projects.

Acknowledgments

The author is extremely grateful to those who facilitated her visit to The Body Shop Headquarters in Littlehampton—Mark and Judy Kuhn, Justine Roddick, Diane Lyndon-Smith, Nicole Thomas, Carole Greiner, and Russ Ciokiewicz. She is also indebted to Anita Roddick and the Body Shop staff who graciously agreed to be interviewed, and to Ken Roberts for his assistance with this project. Finally, she is appreciative of John Jermier's encouragement to pursue research at The Body Shop, and for his comments on earlier drafts of this article.

Note

1. Several weeks before the first U.S. Body Shop was to open in New York, *The Wall Street Journal* quoted a Harvard Business School professor as saying that success in the U.S. market would require "at minimum" a major advertising campaign (Roddick, 1991, p. 137). Not being all that enamored with business types anyway, Anita was incensed and responded that The Body Shop "would never hire anybody from Harvard Business School" (p. 137).

References

Bass, B. M. (1985). *Leadership and performance beyond expectations*. New York: Free Press.

Bennis, W. G. (1989). *On becoming a leader.* Reading. MA: Addison-Wesley.

Bennis, W. G., & Nanus, B. (1985). *Leaders: The strategies for taking charge.* New York: Harper & Row.

Brock, P. (1993). Anita Roddick, *People*, May 10, 101-106.

Bryman, A. (1992). *Charisma and leadership in organizations*. London: Sage.

Bryman A. (1993). Charismatic leadership in business organizations: Some neglected issues. *Leadership Quarterly*, 4, 289-304.

Burlingham, B. (1990). This woman has changed business forever. *INC*, June, 34-46.

Conger, J. A., & Kanungo, R. N. (1987). Towards a behavioral theory of charismatic leadership in organizational settings. *Academy of Management Review*, 12, 637-647.

Conger, J. A., & Kanungo, R. N. (1988). Behavioral dimensions of charismatic leadership. In J. A. Conger & R. N. Kanungo (Eds.), *Charismatic leadership: The elusive factor in organizational effectiveness*. San Francisco: Jossey-Bass.

Distelheim, L. (1988). The entrepreneur. *Life*, November, 21-23.

Elmer-Dewitt, P. (1993). Anita the agitator. *Time*, January 25, 52-54.

Graham, J. W. (1991). Servant-leadership in organizations: Inspirational and moral. *Leadership Quarterly*, 2, 105-119.

Greenleaf, R. K. (1970). *The servant as leader*. Newton Centre, MA: The Robert K. Greenleaf Center.

Hickman, C. R. (1990). *Mind of a manager, soul of a leader*. New York: Wiley.

House, R. J. (1977). A 1976 theory of charismatic leadership. In J. G. Hunt & L. L. Larson (Eds.), *Leadership: The cutting edge* (pp. 189-207). Carbondale, IL: Southern Illinois University Press.

Jacob, R. (1992) What selling will be like in the '90's. *Fortune*, January 13, 63-64.

Kotter, J. P. (1990). *A force for change: How leadership differs from management*. New York: Free Press.

Nadler, D. A., & Tushman, M. L. (1989). What makes for magic leadership? In W. E. Rosenbach & R. L. Taylor (Eds.), *Contemporary issues in leadership* (pp. 135-148). Boulder; Westview.

Nadler, D. A., & Tushman, M. L. (1990). Beyond the charismatic leader: Leadership and organizational change. *California Management Review*, 32, 77-97.

Peters, T., & Austin, N. (1985). *A passion for excellence*, New York: Random House.

Peters, T., & Waterman, R. H. (1982). *In search of excellence: Lessons from America's best-run companies*. New York: Harper & Row.

Roddick, A. (1991). *Body and soul*. New York: Crown.

Sashkin, M. (1988). The visionary leader. In J. A. Conger & R. N. Kanungo (Eds.), *Charismatic leadership: The elusive factor in organizational effectiveness*. San Francisco: Jossey-Bass.

Tichy, N. M. & Devanna, M. A. (1990). *The transformational leader,* 2nd ed., pp. 122-160. New York: Wiley.

Wallace, C. (1990). Lessons in marketing—from a maverick. *Working Woman*, October, 81-84.

Weber, M. (1968 [1925]), *Economy and society*, edited by G. Roth & C. Wittich. 3 vols. New York: Bedminster.

Westley, F. R., & Mintzberg, H. (1989). Visionary leadership and strategic management. *Strategic Management Journal*, 10, 17-32.

Zaleznik, A. (1977). Managers and leaders: Are they different? *Harvard Business Review*, 55, 67-78.

Zaleznik, A. (1990). The leadership gap. *The Executive*, 4, 7-22.

Zinn, L. (1991). Whales, human rights, rain forests—and the heady smell of profits. *Business Week*, July 15, 114-115.

◆

The Post-Capitalist Executive: An Interview with Peter F. Drucker*

T. George Harris

For half a century, Peter F. Drucker, 83, has been teacher and adviser to senior managers in business, human service organizations, and government. Sometimes called the godfather of modern management, he combines an acute understanding of socioeconomic forces with practical insights into how leaders can turn turbulence into opportunity. With a rare gift for synthesis, Drucker nourishes his insatiable mind on a full range of intellectual disciplines, from Japanese art to network theory in higher mathematics. Yet, he learns most from in-depth conversations with clients and students; a global network of men and women who draw their ideas from action and act on ideas.

Since 1946, when his book, *Concept of the Corporation*, redefined employees as a resource rather than a cost, Drucker's works have become an ever-growing resource for leaders in every major culture, particularly among Japan's top decision makers in the critical stages of their rise to world business leadership. A goodly share of productive organizations worldwide are led by men and women who consider Drucker their intellectual guide, if not their personal mentor.

Drucker's most productive insights have often appeared first in the *Harvard Business Review*. He has written 30 HBR articles, more than any other contributor. In the September–October 1992 issue, he published core concepts from his major new work, *Post-Capitalist Society* (HarperCollins, 1993). HBR editors sent T George Harris, a Drucker collaborator for 24 years, to the Drucker Management Center at the Claremont Graduate School in California for two days of intensive conversation about the book's practical implications for today's executives.

HBR: *Peter, you always bring ideas down to the gut level where people work and live. Now we need to know how managers can operate in the post-capitalist society.*

Peter F. Drucker: You have to learn to manage in situations where you don't have command authority, where you are neither controlled nor controlling. That is the fundamental change. Management textbooks still talk mainly about managing subordinates. But you no longer evaluate an executive in terms of how many people report to him or her. That standard doesn't mean as much as the complexity of the job, the information it uses and generates, and the different kinds of relationships needed to do the work.

---

*Reprinted from the Harvard Business Review, May–June 1993, Vol. 71, no. 3., pp. 115–122.

Similarly, business news still refers to managing subsidiaries. But this is the control approach of the 1950s or 1960s. The reality is that the multinational corporation is rapidly becoming an endangered species. Businesses used to grow in one of two ways: from grassroots up or by acquisition. In both cases, the manager had control. Today businesses grow through alliances, all kinds of dangerous liaisons and joint ventures, which, by the way, very few people understand. This new type of growth upsets the traditional manager who believes he or she must own or control sources and markets.

How will the manager operate in a work environment free of the old hierarchies?

Would you believe that you're going to work permanently with people who work for you but are not your employees? Increasingly, for instance, you outsource when possible. It is predictable, then, that ten years from now a company will outsource all work that does not have a career ladder up to senior management. To get productivity, you have to outsource activities that have their own senior management. Believe me, the trend toward outsourcing has very little to do with economizing and a great deal to do with quality.

Can you give an example?

Take a hospital. Everybody there knows how important cleanliness is, but doctors and nurses are never going to be very concerned with how you sweep in corners. That's not part of their value system. They need a hospital maintenance company. One company I got to know in Southern California had a cleaning woman who came in as an illiterate Latino immigrant. She is brilliant. She figured out how to split a bed sheet so that the bed of a very sick patient, no matter how heavy, could be changed. Using her method, you have to move the patient about only six inches, and she cut the bed-making time from 12 minutes to 2. Now she's in charge of the cleaning operations, but she is not an employee of the hospital. The hospital can't give her one single order. It can only say, "We don't like this; we'll work it out."

The point is, managers still talk about the people who "report" to them, but that word should be stricken from management vocabulary. Information is replacing authority. A company treasurer with outsourced information technology, IT, may have only two assistants and a receptionist, but his decisions in foreign exchange can lose—or make—more money in a day than the rest of the company makes all year. A scientist decides which research *not* to do in a big company lab. He doesn't even have a secretary or a title, but his track record means that he is not apt to be overruled. He may have more effect than the CEO. In the military, a lieutenant colonel used to command a battalion, but today he may have only a receptionist and be in charge of liaisons with a major foreign country.

Amidst these new circumstances, everybody is trying to build the ideal organization, generally flat with few layers of bosses and driven directly by consumer satisfaction. But how do managers gear up their lives for this new world?

More than anything else, the individual has to take more responsibility for himself or herself, rather than depend on the company. In this country, and beginning in Europe and even Japan, you can't expect that if you've worked for a company for 5 years you'll be there when you retire 40 years from now. Nor can you expect that you will be able to do what you want to do at the company in 40 years time. In fact, if you make a wager on any big company, the chances of it being split within the next 10 years are better than the chances of it remaining the way it is.

This is a new trend. Big corporations became stable factors before World War I and in the 1920s were almost frozen. Many survived the Depression without change. Then there were 30 or 40 years when additional stories were built onto skyscrapers or more wings added onto corporate centers. But now they're not going to build corporate skyscrapers. In fact, within the past ten years, the proportion of the work force employed by *Fortune* 500 companies has fallen from 30% to 13%.

Corporations once built to last like pyramids are now more like tents. Tomorrow they're gone or in turmoil. And this is true not only of companies in the headlines like Sears or GM or IBM. Technology is changing very quickly, as are markets and structures. You can't design your life around a temporary organization.

Let me give you a simple example of the way assumptions are changing. Most men and women in the executive program I teach are about 45 years old and just below senior management in a big organization or running a midsize one. When we began 15 or 20 years ago, people at this stage were asking, "How can we prepare ourselves for the next promotion?" Now they say, "What do I need to learn so that I can decide where to go next?"

If a young man in a gray flannel suit represented the lifelong corporate type, what's today's image?

Taking individual responsibility and not depending on any particular company. Equally important is managing your own career. The stepladder is gone, and there's not even the implied structure of an industry's rope ladder. It's more like vines, and you bring your own machete. You don't know what you'll be doing next, or whether you'll work in a private office or one big amphitheater or even out of your home. You have to take responsibility for knowing yourself so you can find the right jobs as you develop and as your family becomes a factor in your values and choices.

That's a significant departure from what managers could expect in the past.

Well, the changes in the manager's work are appearing everywhere, though on different timetables. For instance, I see more career confusion among the many Japanese students I've had over the years. They're totally bewildered. Though they are more structured than we ever were, suddenly the Japanese are halfway between being totally managed and having to take responsibility for themselves. What frightens them is that titles don't mean what they used to mean. Whether you were in India or France, if you were an Assistant Director of Market Research, everybody used to know what you were doing. That's not true any more, as we found in one multinational. A woman who had just completed a management course told me not long ago that in five years she would be an assistant vice president of her bank. I'm afraid I had to tell her that she might indeed get the title, but it would no longer have the meaning she thought it did.

Another rung in the ladder?

Yes. The big-company mentality. Most people expect the personnel department to be Papa- or Ma-Bell. When the AT&T personnel department was at its high point 30 years ago, it was the power behind the scenes. With all their testing and career planning, they'd know that a particular 27-year-old would be, by age 45, an Assistant Operating Manager and no more. They didn't know whether he'd be in Nebraska or Florida. But unless he did something quite extraordinary, his career path until retirement was set.

Times have certainly changed. And, in fact, the Bell people have done better than most, because they could see that change coming in the antitrust decision. They couldn't ignore it. But most people still have a big-company mentality buried in their assumptions. If they lost a job with Sears, they hunt for one with K mart, unaware that small companies create most of the new jobs and are about as secure as big companies.

Even today, remarkably few Americans are prepared to select jobs for themselves. When you ask, "Do you know what you are good at? Do you know your limitations?" they look at you with a blank stare. Or they often respond in terms of subject knowledge, which is the wrong answer. When they prepare their resumes, they still try to list positions like steps up a ladder. It is time to give up thinking of jobs or career paths as we once did and think in terms of taking on assignments one after the other.

How does one prepare for this new kind of managerial career?

Being an educated person is no longer adequate, not even educated in management. One hears that the government is doing research on new job descriptions based on subject knowledge. But I think that we probably have to leap right over the search for objective criteria and get into the subjective—what I call *competencies*. Do you really like pressure? Can you be steady when things are rough and confused? Do you absorb information better by reading, talking, or looking at graphs and numbers? I asked one executive the other day, "When you sit down with a person, a subordinate, do you know what to say?" Empathy is a practical competence. I have been urging this kind of self-knowledge for years, but now it is essential for survival.

People, especially the young, think that they want all the freedom they can get, but it is very demanding, very difficult to think through who you are and what you do best. In helping people learn how to be responsible, our educational system is more and more counterproductive. The longer you stay in school, the fewer decisions whether to take French II or Art History is really based on whether one likes to get up early in the morning. And graduate school is much worse.

Do you know why most people start with big companies? Because most graduates have not figured out where to place themselves, and companies send in the recruiters. But as soon as the recruits get through training and into a job, they have to start making decisions about the future. Nobody's going to do it for them.

And once they start making decisions, many of the best move to midsize companies in three to five years, because there they can break through to top management. With less emphasis on seniority, a person can go upstairs and say, "I've been in accounting for three years, and I'm ready to go into marketing." Each year I phone a list of my old students to see what's happening with them. The second job used to be with another big company, often because people were beginning to have families and wanted security. But with two-career families, a different problem emerges. At a smaller organization, you can often work out arrangements for both the man and the woman to move to new jobs in the same city.

Some of the psychological tests being developed now are getting better at helping people figure out their competencies. But if the world economy is shifting from a command model to a knowledge model, why shouldn't education determine who gets each job?

Because of the enormous danger that we would not value the person in terms of performance but in terms of credentials. Strange as it may seem, a knowledge economy's greatest pitfall is in becoming a Mandarin meritocracy. You see creeping credentialism all around. Why should people find it necessary to tell me so-and-so is really a good researcher even though he or she doesn't have a Ph.D.? It's easy to fall into the trap because degrees are black-and-white. But it takes judgment to weigh a person's contribution.

The problem is becoming more serious in information-based organizations. As Michael Hammer pointed out three years ago in HBR, when an organization reengineers itself around information, the majority of management layers become redundant. Most turn out to have been just information relays. Now, each layer has much more information responsibility. Most large companies have cut the number of layers by 50%, even in Japan. Toyota came down from 20-odd to 11. GM has streamlined from 28 to maybe 19, and even that number is decreasing rapidly. Organizations will become flatter and flatter.

As a result, there's real panic in Japan, because it's a vertical society based on subtle layers of status. Everybody wants to become a *kachō* a supervisor or section manager. Still, the United States doesn't have the answer either. We don't know how to use rewards and recognition to move the competent people into the management positions that remain. I don't care for the popular theory that a generation of entrepreneurs can solve our problems. Entrepreneurs are monomaniacs. Managers are synthesizers who bring resources together and have that ability to "smell" opportunity and timing. Today, perception is more important than analysis. In the new society of organizations, you need to be able to recognize patterns to see what is there rather than what you expect to see. You need the invaluable listener who says, "I hear us all trying to kill the new product to protect the old one."

How do you find these people?

One way is to use small companies as farm clubs, as in baseball. One of my ablest friends is buying minority stakes in small companies within his industry. When I said it didn't make sense, he said, "I'm buying farm teams. I'm putting my bright young people in these companies so they have their own commands. They have to do everything a CEO does in a big company."

And do you know the biggest thing these young executives have to learn in their new positions? My friend continued, "We have more Ph.D.'s in biology and chemistry than we have janitors, and they have to learn that their customers aren't Ph.D.'s, and the people who do the work aren't." In other words, they must learn to speak English instead of putting formulas on the blackboard. They must learn to listen to somebody who does not know what a regression analysis is. Basically, they have to learn the meaning and importance of respect.

A difficult thing to learn, let alone teach.

You have to focus on a person's performance. The individual must shoulder the burden of defining what his or her own contribution will be. We have to demand—and "demand" is the word, nothing permissive—that people think through what constitutes the greatest contribution that they can make to the company in the next 18 months or 2 years. Then they have to make sure that contribution is accepted and understood by the people they work with and for.

Most people don't ask themselves this question, however obvious and essential it seems. When I ask people what they contribute to an organization, they blossom and love to answer. And when I follow with, "Have you told other people about it?" the answer often is "No, that would be silly because they know." But of course "they" don't. We are 100 years past the simple economy in which most people knew what others did at work. Farmers knew what most farmers did, and industrial workers knew what other factory workers did. Domestic servants understood each other's work, as did the fourth major group in that economy: small tradesmen. No one needed to explain. But now nobody knows what others do, even within the same organization. Everybody you work with needs to know your priorities. If you don't ask and don't tell, your peers and subordinates will guess incorrectly.

What's the result of this lack of communication?

When you don't communicate, you don't get to do the things you are good at. Let me give an example. The engineers in my class, without exception, say they spend more than half their time editing and polishing reports—in other words, what they are least qualified to do. They don't even know that you have to write and rewrite and rewrite again. But there are any number of English majors around for that assignment. People seldom pay attention to their strengths. For example, after thinking for a long time, an engineer told me he's really good at the first design, at the basic idea, but not at filling in the details for the final product. Until then, he'd never told anybody, not even himself.

You're not advocating self-analysis alone, are you?

No. You not only have to understand your own competencies, but you also have to learn the strengths of the men and women to whom you assign duties, as well as those of your peers and boss. Too many managers still go by averages. They still talk about "our engineers." And I say, "Brother, you don't have engineers. You have Joe and Mary and Jim and Bob, and each is different." You can no longer manage a work force. You manage individuals. You have to know them so well you can go and say, "Mary, you think you ought to move up to this next job. Well, then you have to learn not to have that chip on your shoulder. Forget you are a woman; you are an engineer. And you have to be a little considerate. Do not come in at 10 minutes to 5 on Friday and tell people they have to work overtime when you knew it at 9 A.M."

The key to the productivity of knowledge workers is to make them concentrate on the real assignment. Do you know why most promotions now fail? One-third are outright disasters, in my experience, while another third are a nagging backache. Not more than one in three works out. No fit. The standard case, of course, is the star salesman promoted to sales manager. That job can be any one of four things—a manager of salespeople, a market manager, a brand manager, or a super salesman who opens up an entire new area. But nobody figures out what it is, so the man or woman who got the promotion just tries to do more of whatever led to the promotion. That's the surest way to be wrong.

Expand on your idea of information responsibility and how it fits into post-capitalist society.

Far too many managers think computer specialists know what information they need to do their job and what information tends to focus too much on inside information, not the outside sources and customers that count. In today's organization, you have to take responsibility for information because it is your main tool. But most don't know how to use it. Few are information literate. They can play "Mary Had a Little Lamb" but not Beethoven.

I heard today about a brand manager in a major OTC drug company who tried to get the scientific papers on the product he markets. But the corporate librarian complained to his superior. Under her rules, she gives hard science only to the company's scientists and lawyers. He had to get a consultant to go outside and use a computer database to pull up about 20 journal articles on his product so he'd know how to develop honest advertising copy. The point of the story is that this brand manager is way ahead of the parade: 99 out of 100 brand managers don't know they need that kind of information for today's consumers and haven't a clue how to get it. The first step is to say, "I need it."

And many people don't recognize the importance of this step. I work with an information manager at a large financial institution that has invested $1.5 billion in information. He and I talked all morning with his department's eight women and ten men. Very intelligent, but not one began to think seriously about what information they need to serve their customers. When I pointed this out, they said, "Isn't the boss going to tell us?" We finally had to agree to meet a month later so that they could go through the hard work of figuring out what information they need and—more important—what they do not need.

So a manager begins the road to information responsibility first by identifying gaps in knowledge.

Exactly. To be information literate, you begin with learning what it is you need to know. Too much talk focuses on the technology, even worse on the speed of the gadget, always faster, faster. This kind of "techie" fixation causes us to lose track of the fundamental nature of information in today's organization. To organize the way work is done, you have to begin with the specific job, then the information input, and finally the human relationships needed to get the job done.

The current emphasis on reengineering essentially means changing an organization from the flow of things to the flow of information. The computer is merely a tool in the process. If you go to the hardware store to buy a hammer, you do not ask if you should do upholstery or fix the door. To put it in editorial terms, knowing how a typewriter works does not make you a writer. Now that knowledge is taking the place of capital as the driving force in organizations worldwide, it is all too easy to confuse data with knowledge and information technology with information.

What's the worst problem in managing knowledge specialists?

One of the most degenerative tendencies of the least 40 years is the belief that if you are understandable, you are vulgar. When I was growing up, it was taken for granted that economists, physicists, psychologists—leaders in any discipline—would make themselves understood. Einstein spent years with three different collaborators to make his theory of relativity accessible to the layman. Even John Maynard Keynes tried hard to make his economics accessible. But just the other day, I heard a senior scholar seriously reject a younger colleague's work because more than five people could understand what he's doing. Literally.

We cannot afford such arrogance. Knowledge is power, which is why people who had it in the past often tried to make a secret of it. In post-capitalism, power comes from transmitting information to make it productive, not from hiding it.

That means you have to be intolerant of intellectual arrogance. And I mean intolerant. At whatever level, knowledge people must make themselves under-stood, and whatever field the manager comes from, he or she must be eager to understand others. This may be the main job of the manager of technical people. He or she must not only be an interpreter but also work out a balance between specialization and exposure.

Exposure is an important technique. For an exotic example, look at weather forecasting, where meteorologists and mathematicians and other specialists now work with teams of experts on satellite data. Europeans, on the one hand, have tried to connect these different disciplines entirely through information man-agers. On the other hand, Americans rotate people at an early stage. Suppose you put a Ph.D. in meteorology on a team that is to work on the new mathematical model of hurricanes for three years. He isn't a mathematician, but he gets exposed to what mathematicians assume, what they eliminate, what their limitations are. With the combination of exposure and translation, the American approach yields forecasts that are about three times more accurate than the European, I'm told. And the exposure concept is useful in managing any group of specialists.

Is the fact that some teams provide exposure as well as interpreters a reason why the team has become such a hot topic?

There's a lot of nonsense in team talk, as if teams were something new. We have always worked in teams, and while sports give us hundreds of team styles there are only a few basic models to choose from. The critical decision is to select the right kind for the job. You can't mix soccer and doubles tennis. It's predictable that in a few years, the most traditional team will come back in fashion, the one that does research first, then passes the idea to engineering to develop, and then on to manufacturing to make. It's like a baseball team, and you may know I have done a little work with baseball-team management.

The great strength of baseball teams is that you can concentrate. You take Joe, who is a batter, and you work on batting. There is almost no interaction, nothing at all like the soccer team or the jazz combo, the implicit model of many teams today. The soccer team moves in unison but everyone holds the same relative position. The jazz combo has incredible flexibility because everyone knows each other so well that they all sense when the trumpet is about to solo. The combo model takes great discipline and may eventually fall out of favor, especially in Japanese car manufacturing, because we do not need to create new models as fast as we have been.

I know several German companies that follow the baseball-team model, whether they know it or not. Their strength is clear: they are fantastic at exploiting and developing old knowledge, and Germany's midsize companies may be better than their big ones simply because they concentrate better. On the other hand, when it comes to the new, from electronics to biotech, German scientists may do fine work, but their famous apprenticeship system discourages innovation.

So, beyond all the hype, teams can help the executive navigate a post-capitalist society?

Thinking about teams helps us highlight the more general problem of how to manage knowledge. In the production of fundamental new knowledge, the British groups I run into are way ahead of anybody. But they have never done much with their expertise, in part because many British companies don't value the technically oriented person enough. I don't know of a single engineer in top management there. My Japanese friends are just the opposite. While they still do not specialize in scientific advances, they take knowledge and make it productive very fast. In this country, on the other hand, we have not improved that much in existing industries. The automobile business, until recently, was perfectly satisfied doing what it did in 1939. But, as we are discovering in computers and in biotech, we may be at our very best when it comes to groundbreaking technology.

Where is the lesson in all this for the manager?

The lesson is that the productivity of knowledge has both a qualitative and a quantitative dimension. Though we know very little about it, we do realize executives must be both managers of specialists and synthesizers of different fields of knowledge—really of knowledges, plural. This situation is as threatening to the traditional manager, who worries about high-falutin' highbrows, as it is to the intellectual, who worries about being too commercial to earn respect in his or her discipline. But in the post-capitalist world, the highbrow and the lowbrow have to play on the same team.

That sounds pretty democratic. Does a post-capitalist society based more on knowledge than capital become egalitarian?

No. Both of these words miss the point. *Democratic* bespeaks a narrow political and legal organization. Nor do I use the buzzword *participative*. Worse yet is the *empowerment* concept. It is not a great step forward to take power out at the top and put it in at the bottom. It's still power. To build achieving organizations, you must replace power with responsibility.

And, while we're on the subject of words, I'm not comfortable with the word *manager* any more, because it implies subordinates. I find myself using *executive* more, because it implies responsibility for an area, not necessarily dominion over people. The word *boss*, which emerged in World War II, is helpful in that it can be used to suggest a mentor's role, someone who can back you up on a decision. The new organizations need to go beyond senior/junior polarities to a blend with sponsor and mentor relations. In the traditional organization—the organization of the last 100 years—the skeleton, or internal structure, was a combination of rank and power. In the emerging organization, it has to be mutual understanding and responsibility.

Conclusion

We intend this conclusion to be a transition—a few words that will bring some central themes into focus so that they may be transported by students into the future and into their management careers. Some of these themes have been explicit throughout and will be restated here. A few themes have been more implicit; in fact, they only became clear to us after we had put the various pieces of this volume together.

Taken together, the contributors to this volume make it very clear that the realities of management are interwoven with a broad spectrum of other human endeavors. At a very general level, organizations as we know them depend on certain biological characteristics (for example, language, abilities to write, potential for cooperation) as well as social and technological developments. At a more specific level, the characteristics of organizations at a particular point in time are influenced by a host of past, present, and anticipated future events. The demands on organizations, the resources they have available, how they are viewed by members of society, and the characteristics of managers themselves and the people they manage are all influenced by these events. Finally, we have seen that organizations themselves have come to make history. In short, organizations, management, and human society evolve together.

It goes without saying that what people who write about management have to say is part and parcel of the same evolution. The contents of this book are no exception. With this in mind, it is instructive to examine the major framework of the book critically. Let us reconsider Figure 1 (the triangle) in the Introduction and our assumption that management is above all else a complex balancing act.

THE TRIANGLE AND BALANCING RECONSIDERED

At an abstract level, the issues of technique, practice, and values that define the triangle seem likely to have rather enduring significance. The content and the emphasis given to each issue will vary over time. For example, had we put this collection together even a year or two earlier, it is doubtful that we would have given nearly as much attention to ethics as we did.

In addition, throughout the book, along with our contributors, we emphasized that management is a balancing act. It is worth noting that many recent books have used the same or a very similar metaphor. For example, Robert Lamb refers to management as a "balancing game,"[1] Gareth Morgan discusses the need for managers to "hook everything together,"[2] and Harold Leavitt writes of "keeping the whole act together."[3] It would be extremely inconsistent with the theme of relativity that we have seen throughout this book if we did not urge the reader to recognize that our metaphor, too, is a product of its time.

One other observation on the managerial balancing act is necessary. It is very unlikely that the three elements will be equally important to all managers at a given time or to the same manager at different times. Perhaps, for instance, matters of technique simply dominate one's attention either because they are so important or because the issues of practice and values seem so clearly defined that they simply are ignored. Moreover, while to some degree every individual needs to come to terms with the three issues in one way or another, it is possible to view the balance as something that must be achieved by the organization as a whole and not necessarily a problem for very many individuals most of the time. For example, it is possible to envision an organization assigning responsibility for each of the issues to different people and achieving balance by integrating the efforts of the "specialists." In other words, it is possible that the balancing act we have attributed to managers is something that is primarily achieved by organizations, not by each manager.

Regardless of how the attention to the three issues is divided, somehow managers must recognize their importance and see to it that their organizations address them. What implications does this fact have for preparing people to manage?

PREPARING MANAGERS

Our thoughts about preparing managers and the need for organizations to balance technique, practice, and values are linked to two sets of assumptions. One set concerns the nature of organizations in the future and the second involves our beliefs about how managers are currently being trained.

First, let us review the assumptions about modern organizations. As we have said, we see modern organizations as superimposed on other human activities. We also see organizations as playing increasingly important roles within nations and in the global political economy. Given the rapid change in technology and in the social, political, and economic relationships within and among nations, organizations will need to become increasingly more flexible and able to deal with complexity.

Second, it is our impression that managers are not being prepared to respond to these demands. As we have noted, managers have not been encouraged to see the tight relationships between organizations and other aspects of human endeavor. We believe that, more recently, there has been a strong inclination to prepare managers in matters of technique. Less attention has been given to practice and even less to values. Moreover, there has been a tendency for business education to be ethnocentric. Although there are some notable exceptions, business schools have given little attention to an in depth understanding of other nations and cultures.

The contrast between these sets of assumptions is clear. Unfortunately, ways to close the gap are less so. We believe, however, that the contents of this book point towards a useful orientation. They suggest that managers must be prepared to deal with the full range of human beings and their institutions. This preparation cannot be achieved through the study of science and technique alone. While this study is essential, it must be embedded in an understanding and appreciation of other aspects of human experience.

How can this understanding and appreciation be attained? Again, no simple answers, but two thoughts. First, the gap we have noted needs to be observed and taken seriously. Second, managers and those who attempt to develop them must draw on resources that help develop the breadth of knowledge that understanding and appreciating the complexity of human experience and social organization require. We suggest these resources include the arts, language, anthropology, the humanities, philosophy, and spirituality to name a few.

If organizations are the fully human systems we have described, their managers must have the capacity to relate to the full range of human experiences. There is much to draw on. The starting point is recognition that these seemingly tangential bodies of knowledge and experience are in fact part of the essence of management.

Notes

1. R.B. Lamb, *Running American business* (New York: Basic Books, 1987), p. 302.

2. G. Morgan, *Riding the waves of change* (San Francisco: Jossey-Bass, 1988), p. 154.

3. H.J. Leavitt, *Corporate pathfinders* (Homewood, Ill,: Dow Jones-Irwin, 1986), p. 209.